THE COMPLETE BOOK OF

SPORTS

NICKNAMES

Louis Phillips & Burnham Holmes

RENAISSANCE BOOKS

Los Angeles

Louis Phillips: For Bobby, Lynn, and Ryan Hoffman and all our friends in CYO Little League who, even though they don't have nicknames, are all good sports and have a great love for the game.

Burnham Holmes: For the love of my life, Vicki Reid (1947–1998).

Copyright © 1994, 1998 by Louis Phillips and Burnham Holmes

All rights reserved. This book may not be reproduced, in whole or in part, in any form, without written permission. Inquiries should be addressed to: Permissions Department, Renaissance Books, 5858 Wilshire Boulevard, Suite 200, Los Angeles, California, 90036.

Library of Congress Cataloging-in-Publication Data

Phillips, Louis.
    The complete book of sports nicknames / Louis Phillips & Burnham Holmes.
        p. cm.
    Rev. ed. of: Yogi, Babe, and Magic. 1st ed. 1994.
    Includes index.
    ISBN 1-58063-037-5 (trade paper : alk. paper)
    1. Athletes—Nicknames. 2. Athletic clubs—Names. I. Holmes,
Burnham. II. Phillips, Louis. Yogi, Babe, and Magic.
III. Title.
GV706.8.P47 1998
796—dc21   98-38168
                                                                     CIP

10 9 8 7 6 5 4 3 2 1

Design by Susan Shankin
Distributed by St. Martin's Press, New York
Manufactured in the United States of America
Second Edition

CONTENTS

ACKNOWLEDGMENTS

A work of this nature could never have seen the light of day without the generous assistance of many persons in and out of libraries. The authors would especially like to extend acknowledgments to Mr. George Hobart, Reference Specialist at the Library of Congress in Washington, D.C.; Ms. Mary Ternes of the Martin Luther King Library of the Washington (D.C.) Public Library system; Jean Boyce, librarian of the Rutland (Vermont) Free Library; Ms. Ivy Fischer Stone, who found the publisher; the School of Visual Arts and its president, David Rhodes; the SVA Writing Center, with particular thanks to Hugo Jimenez and Neil Friedland; Ian and Matthew Phillips, who came up with numerous suggestions, most notably in the areas of baseball, basketball, and wrestling; copy editor Christina Schlank; and, last but not least, our editor, Jim Parish, who did not lose his patience nor his sense of humor when confronted with our mountain of material.

INTRODUCTION

To make a name for one's self is a worthy goal of men and women in and out of the sports world. Many times, however, sports personalities end up with more of a nickname than they bargained for. The world of sports is clearly marked by the signposts of colorful monikers. In those woods there are Babes aplenty (along with Bucks and Docs). There is also a Vulture (baseball's Phil Regan) and Rabbits (baseball's Walter Maranville, basketball's John Barnhill, boxing's Floyd Patterson, football's Louis Weller, and hockey's Charles McVeigh), not to mention Moose (baseball's Bill Skowron, basketball's Ed Krause, football's Carl Eller, golf's Julius Boros, hockey's Andre DuPont, and track and field's Wilbur Thompson), as well as a Mouse (boxing's Bruce Strauss, football's Pat Fischer, and hockey's Stan Mikita). There is even a nursery rhyme sounding Little Miss Poker Face (tennis' Helen Wills Moody).

But where do nicknames come from? The process is mysterious: it can involve ancestry, family history, birthplace, initials, inheritance, physical characteristics, what the individual does during competition or off the field, a favorite expression, opposites, popular culture, sobriquets bestowed by sportswriters, free association, word play, and rhyming names. Very few persons, however, get to choose their own sobriquets. (One who did was pitcher Walter Mails, who immodestly called himself "The Great," years before Muhammad Ali declared that he was "The Greatest.")

In Denny McLain's autobiography, *Nobody's Perfect* (written with Dave Diles), Mr. McLain credits Detroit pitcher Pat Dobson for his penchant to hand out nicknames to teammates. McLain claims that Dobson invented nicknames for everybody. One day the second string catcher Jim Price announced he wanted be called "The Big Guy," but Dobson said he didn't qualify for that nickname and told him, "Your nickname is Thunderthighs and you're stuck with it." Indeed he was.

McLain's anecdote points out an important though sad truth. A person may not want to be called Thunderthighs or Catfish (Bill Klem) or Mugsy (John McGraw), but such eponymic fate is usually beyond the individual's control. Back in 1983, Boston Red Sox pitcher Mike Brown was quoted as saying (in response to the high expectations that team officials and fans had for him): "I'm a rookie, not a savior." One can imagine the nickname Savior being hung around that guy's neck right then and there. Mike Brown may not have wanted it, but it could have been his. Like writers, baseball players learn early on in their careers that their own words have a way of coming back to haunt them. Sometimes, "Thou art thine own worse enemy."

For ease of discussion, the world of nicknames can be broken down into numerous, frequently overlapping, categories.

ANCESTRY

Sports fans have rarely allowed ethnic sensitivity to get in the way of handing out nicknames. Chances are that any person called Chief was a Native American, though, of course, this is not always the case. Charles Zimmer, a Cleveland catcher who caught 125 consecutive games in 1890 to set a National League mark, received his nickname when he was the captain/manager at Poughkeepsie. "Since we were fleet of foot, we were called the Indians," he once explained. "As I was the head man of the Indians, someone began to call me 'Chief.' It stuck." Zimmer, however, appears to be the exception to the rule. Find a player called Chief and you'll almost always discover someone with Native American blood flowing through the veins.

Persons of German or Dutch descent are often nicknamed—you guessed it—Dutch. Cornelius Warmerdan, who in 1940 became the first pole-vaulter to clear fifteen feet, was known in the sports pages as Dutch. Henry Dehnert, who is often credited with developing the first pivot play in basketball, was also known as Dutch. The same nickname was slapped on Frank Nighbor, the first National Hockey League player to receive the Hart Trophy, awarded to hockey's Most Valuable Player. Most baseball fans know that Hall of Fame shortstop Honus Wagner was called The Flying Dutchman—an epithet borrowed from the opera by Richard Wagner. And Norm Van Brocklin, the football quarterback, was simply The Dutchman.

The Greek community has always been proud whenever one of their countrymen makes it into the big time. New York Yankee catcher Gus Iahros was known simply as Greek; Boston Red Sox first baseman Harry Agannis was dubbed The Golden Greek. But after succumbing to leukemia at the age of twenty-five in the middle of the 1955 season while hitting a lofty .313, Agannis turned out to be one of baseball's most tragic stories.

Barney Pelty, who pitched for the St. Louis Browns from 1903 to 1912, was Jewish. Without any pangs of guilt, the fans often called him The Yiddish Curver. Baseball's Stanley George Bordagaray, basketball's John DeMoisey, boxing's Albert Belanger, and football's John Fuqua were all known as Frenchy. Baseball's Leo Cardenas (whose family was Cuban), basketball's Charles Vaughn, and hockey's Glenn Resch (by way of Moose Jaw, Saskatchewan) were Chicos (Spanish for kid). For those with foreign heritages who in the heat of battle seemed to be possessed, they were on occasion nicknamed Mad. Baseball's Al Hrabosky was The Mad Hungarian and auto racing's Bill Vukovich was The Mad Russian.

FAMILY HISTORY

Many nicknames are foisted upon athletes while they are still children. Football's Ward Lambert was Piggy because he wore pigtails as a kid. Baseball's Harold Reese was Peewee because as a youngster back in Louisville he had been a marbles champion using a peewee for a shooter. Some are barely out of the maternity ward before they're loaded down with an "eke name" (Old English for *nickname*). After one look at Harry Lee Lowrey, his grandfather exclaimed, "He's no bigger than a peanut." From then on, even when he was roaming the outfield for the Chicago Cubs, Lowrey was called Peanuts. The origin of quarterback Norman "Boomer" Esiason's nickname went back even further. When he was in his mother's womb, his father said, "He must be a boomer, because he kicks so much."

PLACE OF ORIGIN

Rocky Marciano was called The Brockton Bomber or The Brockton Blockbuster because he was born in Brockton, Massachusetts. Jake Lamotta was affectionately known as The Bronx Bull. (Lamotta won the world's middleweight title by knocking out Marcel Cerdan on June 16, 1949—a date not quite as famous as June 16, 1904, Bloomsday in James Joyce's *Ulysses*.) Tommy Kelly was The Harlem Spider. Lou Ambers, who was voted into boxing's Hall of Fame because he lost only six times in 102 bouts, was hailed as The Herkimer Hurricane. Joe Shugrue, who fought his first professional fight at age sixteen and came from Jersey City, was quickly tagged The Jersey Bobcat. To the south was The Pittsburgh Kid in the person of Billy Conn.

Even though boxing seems to have a lock on the city nickname, other sports figures have also been dubbed with their places of origin. Mickey Mantle was given the sobriquet, The Commerce Comet, because this speedster came from Commerce, Oklahoma; his Yankee manager was called Casey because he came out of Kansas City (K.C.) Wahoo Sam Crawford was from Wahoo Nebraska, where the chief activity on Saturday nights might have been watching his father give haircuts; Vinegar Bend Mizell was from a wide spot in the road next to a curve in the river called Vinegar Bend, Arkansas. Ron Bonham, who once set a high-school record by pouring in fifty-three points during a basketball game for Muncie Central High School, was known as The Muncie Mortar.

INITIALS

Baseball players Tod Davis, Sam Mele, and Cap Peterson all received their nicknames from the initials of their full names. (TOD—Thomas Oscar Davis; SAM—Sabath Anthony Mele; CAP—Charles Andrew Peterson.) Gee Gee stood for the initials of Gus Getz. (A variation on a theme is horse racing's Gilbert Patrick. His nickname was Gilpatrick.)

For some reason, the single initial nickname is favored by more basketball players than any other sport. For example, there is Double D—Dwight Davis, Dr. J—Julius Erving, Big O—Oscar Robertson, and Big Z—Zelmo Beaty. Just one initial will do the trick for cagers to get the crowd standing and cheering at courtside.

INHERITANCE

A player who bears the same name as a previous player will sometimes inherit the earlier player's nickname. Former Cincinnati Reds infielder Samuel Meeks was called Buttermilk simply because an old-time ballplayer named Sam Meeks had been given that nickname.

In a variation of this principle, an athlete who shows great promise will be nicknamed after the original legend. Arnold Malcolm Owen reminded many observers of the great catcher Mickey Cochrane, so Owen became Mickey, too. Golf's Babe Zaharias received her nickname as a teenager because she was as terrific an athlete in track and field and women's baseball as Babe Ruth was in the major leagues.

PHYSICAL CHARACTERISTICS

Joe Garagiola in *Baseball Is a Funny Game* points out that baseball players show no hesitation in making fun of a fellow player's physical appearance: "If you're bald, you're Skinhead, Onion Head, Knob Head." But of course, name-calling is not the same thing as passing out nicknames, though name-calling certainly must have inspired certain epithets. "Players wearing glasses," Mr. Garagiola continues, "get it good. Lee Walls is Captain Midnight. Bill Virdon answers to Cyclops. Clint Courtney is called The Sealed Beam Catcher." George Glamack of basketball fame had bad eyesight and he wore wire glasses. Thus, he was cursed with the nickname, The Blind Bomber. On a more flattering note, quarterback Bobby Layne had blond good looks and a strong arm, so he became The Blond Bomber. John Gagnon, the hockey player, had jet black hair and a swarthy complexion, so he was labeled The Black Cat. And on the subject of animals, golf's Jack Nicklaus was big and blond, so he was known as The Golden Bear. Football's Lance Alworth was small and fast, so this wide receiver went by the nickname of Bambi. Basketball's Reese Tatum was Goose. Boxing's William Jones was Gorilla. Because he had a squeaky voice, George Tebbetts was better known to baseball fans as Birdie Tebbetts. And because he was only 5' 3", goaltender Roy Worters was known as Shrimp.

The record books are filled with Reds, including the Ol' Redhead in the announcer's booth, Red Barber. Other common nicknames are Whitey, Lefty, and Slim (for, among others, Herzog, Grove, and Salee).

Mordecia Peter Centennial Brown is always referred to as Three Finger Brown. (Interestingly, part of his name was Centennial because he was born in 1876, Uncle Sam's birthday.) Even though he had lost two fingers on his pitching hand in a farming accident, he managed to compile a career earned run average of 2.06, plenty good for any pitcher with any number of fingers. And while on the subject of hands, Johnny Bench was called Hands because he could hold seven baseballs at a time in only one. American League pitcher Harry Ables, who was known as Hans because he had large hands and he was of German heritage.

Nervous tics can also be the source of permanent nicknames. Luke Hamlin was known as Hot Potato because he shifted the baseball back and forth in his hand before pitching. Outfielder Harry Walker was called The Hat because he adjusted his cap so frequently that he went through twenty new caps a season. Gordie Howe was called Blinkie because he had suffered a serious hockey accident that caused him to blink uncontrollably when under pressure. Playing during five different decades, Mr. Howe later matured into Old Blinky.

Not all physical characteristics have to be permanent to warrant a nickname, however. Consider the case of Milton John Byrnes of the 1943 St. Louis Browns. He turned up at the ballpark one day with a stiff neck, and the manager started calling him Stiffy. That name stuck, long after the kinks had been worked out.

WHAT THE PERSON DOES DURING COMPETITION

Hockey star Bernard Geoffrion earned the nickname Boom Boom because when his hockey stick hit the puck there would be one boom, and when the puck hit the endboards there would be a second boom. Baseball's Walter Beck was also called Boom Boom, but this pitcher earned his nickname because he gave up so many booming hits. Football's L. G. Dupree was fleet of foot, so this halfback's initials led to his being called Long Gone. Miss Chop and Drop described Elizabeth Ryan's tricky forehand that seemed to die just over the tennis net. Quarterback Ken Stabler was called Snake because in high school he had snaked down the field for a long touchdown. Another Snake was hockey's Jacques Plante. Jake the Snake would snake away from the crease to grab an errant shot and pass it off to a teammate.

Ted Radcliffe, a star catcher in the Negro Leagues was called Double Duty because he frequently caught the first game of a double header and pitched the second game. Golf's James Barnes was Long Jim for he was not only tall but drove the ball long off the tee.

WHAT THE PERSON DOES OFF THE FIELD

A person who is active in church work is often tagged Deacon. Pirate pitcher Vernon Law received this nickname for his work in the Mormon Church. Bill McKechnie, Claude Passau, and Charles Phillippe—all of professional baseball—were also dubbed Deacon. Joe Namath was, of course, Broadway Joe—an allusion to his active social life far from the madding crowd at Shea Stadium.

Harold Joseph Traynor was such a fan of his mom's baked pies that this third baseman was called Pie. Few even knew his real name. Virgil Lawrence Davis was nicknamed Spud because this catcher ate potatoes no less than three times a day. The second baseman, Oscar Melillo, was called Spinach because he ate a lot of the green stuff since it was thought to be a cure for his Bright's disease. And pitcher Reggie Cleveland was Snacks, which naturally led to his other nickname, Double Cheeseburger.

A PERSON'S FAVORITE EXPRESSION

Shortstop David Bancroft was called Beauty, because whenever a teammate would make a good play, he would cry out "Beauty!" Sports announcer Mel Allen invariably cried out "How about that?" over a stellar play, and got tagged with Mr. How About That. So, did Willie Mays say "Hey"?

In addition to their peculiar expressions, some athletes simply talk a lot. Gabby Street kept a steady stream of chatter flowing behind the plate. Leo Durocher was known as Leo the Lip, Leo Lippy, Lippy, or simply The Lip for his combative talkativeness. ("I never questioned the integrity of an umpire," he once said. "Their eyesight, yes.") And before Muhammad Ali settled into his elder statesman role as The Greatest, he had been known as Cassius the Brashest and The Louisville Lip.

OPPOSITES

Speaking of athletes who talked a lot, catcher Gabby Hartnett was quiet, so his nickname was ironic. Other opposite nicknames were Tiny for a 6' 2" 215-pound pitcher named Ernest Bonham, Wee Willie for football's 6' 6", 280-pound tackle Wilbur Wilkin, and Happy for Burt Hooton, a pitcher who always looked like he had just lost his best last friend.

POPULAR CULTURE

Cartoon characters dot the landscape of sports nicknames. Baseball's Joe Gordon was known as Flash Gordon, basketball's Cliff Hagen was nicknamed Li'l Abner, football's Richard Wood was called Batman, hockey's Clint Smith was Snuffy Smith.

Similarly, in a culture dominated by movie and television characters and larger-than-life personalities, it is only natural that a huge inventory of nicknames should fall into this category. For instance, here are just a few. (They are presented in the same format as the entries in this book.)

HOOT—Walter Arthur Evers [1921–   ] Baseball. This outfielder for the Detroit Tigers in the 1940s was called Hoot because when he was a child, his favorite cowboy movie star was Hoot Gibson.

HONDO—John Havlicek (1940–   ) Basketball. H/F When this forward who led the Boston Celtics to eight NBA championships played for Ohio State, his roommate thought that he resembled the John Wayne character in the movie *Hondo*.

TARZAN—Don Bragg (1935–   ) Track and field. H/F In 1960, this muscular pole vaulter used brute strength to set a world record of 15' 9¼" with an aluminum pole. Don Bragg had also once hoped to play Tarzan in the movies when he hung up his track spikes.

SOBRIQUETS BESTOWED BY SPORTSWRITERS

In addition to reporting the sports news, many sportswriters create colorful nicknames for the people they are glorifying. Reporter Eddie Murphy wrote an article in the *New York Sun* about the section of Philadelphia where Eddie Stanky had been raised, calling him "The Brat from Kensington." Shortened to The Brat, this label followed Stankey wherever he went and follows him to this day.

Damon Runyon, who made many contributions to the English language, also knighted many a boxing character. When James J. Johnston was a promoter and a manager with four world champion boxers of the 1920s and 1930s under contract, it was Runyon who branded the peerless Mr. Johnston as The Boy Bandit. A nickname like that speaks reams. Needless to say, it did not help his reputation for doing reputable business.

Another influential sportswriter, Jimmy Cannon, had a long-running column "Nobody asked me, but . . ." read by sports fans and such literary masters as Ernest Hemingway. Cannon is the one who called Luke Hamlin Hot Potato and he once wrote that Joe Louis was a credit to his race—the human race.

Today, sportscaster Chris Berman has come up with a long list of clever nicknames for players, names such as Bert "Be Home" Blyleven (by eleven) or Luis "Say It Isn't" Sojo. (There was even a website where these nicknames could be accessed—http://www.splintersweb.com) but, for some reason, these nicknames —as funny and imaginative as they are— have not become part of the permanent vocabulary. Sports nicknames really don't take hold unless they appear in print.

FREE ASSOCIATION

Creating nicknames is an activity that is only a few steps removed from writing poetry. The imagination blooms and blossoms when it rises to the task of looking at the world in a fresh way.

In New York City there was once a famous fire engine called the Big 6. The New York Giants also had a pitcher who was good at putting out rallies before they blazed up. It was only a matter of time before some knight of the keyboard would connect these two facts to create a metaphor. Before long, Christy Mathewson had become the Big Six.

When William G. Werle was studying entomology at the University of California, teammates started referring to their pitcher with the 25–2 record as Bugs. The nickname followed him all the way across the continent when Werle began hurling for the Pittsburgh Pirates.

In 1955, Howard Cassady won the Heisman Trophy. That year the Ohio State halfback rushed for 958 yards and scored fifteen touchdowns, but it was his last name that triggered his nickname

Hopalong. Cassady even had publicity photos taken with William Boyd, the actor who played Hopalong Cassidy on the silver screen.

WORD PLAY

Sometimes the word play is a manipulation of the person's last name. The Oakland Raider's John Matuszak was simply Tooz. Walt Bellamy, who was the NBA Rookie of the Year in 1962, was called Bells. Although he did not have any, Philadelphia Phillies catcher Clayton Dalrymple was nicknamed Dimples. Tennis player Ile Nastase became Nasty. Doubled with his last name was his all too frequent on-court behavior to match.

The name play is sometimes associative. Football's John L. Cain becomes Sugar, for sugar cane, and a player named Rhodes will invariably be called Dusty.

RHYMING NAMES

This popular type of nickname, a subdivision of word play, deserves its own category. Stan The Man, who earned his moniker in 1946 when he hit thirteen for fifteen against the Brooklyn Dodgers comes to mind. As Musial was not so easy to say, the Ebbets Field faithful just referred to the St. Louis Cardinal outfielder as The Man, as in, "Oh, no, here comes The Man again!"

Basketball's Clyde Drexler is Clyde the Glide for the way he smoothly glided into the basket for another layup. Football's Cunningham was Sam Bam for the way the fullback slammed into the defensive linemen. Hockey's Wayne Gretzky has a near rhyme with The Great One. Lesser lights would be boxing's The Marlin Starlin' and wrestling's "Classy" Frederick Blassey.

It almost goes without saying that sports fans can come up with thousands of other examples of nicknames. (The authors would love to hear about the nicknames that you feel should go in subsequent editions.)

William Shakespeare, another old sport, once asked, "What's in a name?" Well, we ask? "What's in a nickname?" Walt Williams, an outfielder known as No-Neck, has one possible answer: "Nicknames stay with you longer than regular names." And of course, even The Bard of Avon didn't escape scot-free.

HOW TO USE THIS BOOK

To help you find your way through the hundreds of nicknames included here, this volume is separated into four sections:

- Part 1 features the roster of colorful nicknames, providing the stories behind the nicknames given to some of our best-known sports figures.

- Part 2 contains team names. Here you will find the histories of the names of teams in the National Hockey League, the National Basketball Association, baseball's American League and National League, and the National Football League, along with the names of all the major college teams and their conferences.

- Part 3 includes some of the names given to special plays, teams, and events.

- Part 4 is a more comprehensive list of sports nicknames. Although the entries are shorter here than in Part One, many also contain colorful sketches that will both illuminate and delight.

- Finally, an index of players' real names at the end of the book can lead you to the nicknames included in this volume.

Words that appear in small caps are cross-referenced in the other parts of the book. H/F references a member of the Hall of Fame.

PART 1

THE ROSTER OF COLORFUL NICKNAMES

ACE OF THE THIRTIES—John Kundla [1916–   ] Basketball. George Mikan, Jim Pollard, Herm Schaffer, Vern Mikkelsen, and Slater Martin are just a few basketball stars who rose to greatness under the coaching of Johnny "Ace of the Thirties" Kundla. In the 1930s he was a star player for the University of Minnesota (where he also played first base for the Gophers baseball team). From 1947 to 1959, Kundla was the coach of the Minneapolis Lakers, leading them to six Western Division Championships and five world titles. His Lakers compiled a record of 423 wins against 302 losses. After the Lakers moved to Los Angeles, Kundla returned to the University of Minnesota to be their head basketball coach.

A. D.—Adrian Dantly [1956–   ] Basketball. Dantley, who was the NBA Rookie of the Year in 1977, used his initials for his nickname. (In high school, the 6' 2", 220-pound Dantley had been called Baby Fats.) In 1980-1981, he led the league with a 30.7 point average; in 1983-1984, he scored more than 800 points from the free-throw line.

AIR JORDAN—Michael Jordan [1963–   ] Basketball. Jordan was given this nickname because of his incredible hang time as he maneuvers to score against hapless defenders. Jordan became not only one of the best players in the history of the game (some might claim he is the best athlete of the twentieth century), but one of the most popular. His beaming smile is immediately recognizable around the world and sells everything from cornflakes to sneakers to clothing. To show how dramatic his presence is in a game, take for example the game on November 11, 1992. In overtime between the Chicago Bulls and the Detroit Pistons, the lead had changed hands five times in the last thirty-seven seconds. The basket that clinched the Bulls' 98-96 victory came when Scotty Pippin inbounded the ball to Bill Cartwright, who passed to Air Jordan, who swished a three-pointer from seven feet behind the three-point line. In typical fashion, Jordan had finished strong down the stretch, scoring five of his thirty-seven points in the last few seconds. (For this finishing flourish, you can also look back to the 1982 NCAA final, when he sank the winning basket for North Carolina at the buzzer).

ALABAMA ANTELOPE [THE]—Don Hutson [1913–1997] Football. H/F Hutson ran the 100-yard dash in 9.7 seconds, the 220 in 21.3, and played end on the University of Alabama football team. In the 1934 Rose Bowl game, Hutson caught seven passes, two for touchdowns, as Alabama upset Stanford 29-13. In 1935, on his very first play as a pro, Hutson caught a pass and ran 80-yards for a touchdown, then kicked the extra point to lead the Green Bay Packers over the Chicago Bears, 7-0. Curly Lambeau, the coach of the Green Bay Packers, assessed Hutson's skills this way: "He would glide downfield, leaning forward as if to steady himself close to the ground. Then, as suddenly as you gulp or blink an eye, he'd feint one way and go to the other, reach up like a dancer, gracefully squeeze the ball, and leave the scene of the accident—the accident being the defensive backs who tangled their feet up and fell trying to cover him." Once Hutson even swung around a goalpost with one hand to change direction, then snared a pass for a touchdown. Sportswriters who watched him in action bestowed the nickname The Alabama Antelope on the speedy Hutson. One of his most impressive performances came on October 7, 1945, when he caught four TD passes and kicked five extra points— all in the first quarter. During his eleven-year career, Hutson caught 488 passes for 7,991 yards and 105 touchdowns. All-Pro nine times, The Alabama Antelope was also called the first Super End.

AMAZIN' AMAZON—Margaret Smith Court (1942–   ) Tennis. H/F Standing 5' 8¾" and weighing 150 pounds (hence the reason for her rhyming or near-rhyming nickname), Margaret Smith Court from Australia became in 1970 only the second woman to win Tennis' Grand Slam. (Maureen Connolly, in 1953, was the first.) The Amazin' Amazon was a tennis prodigy, who had won sixty trophies by age fifteen. By the time she retired from competition, she had won twenty-six Grand Slam titles. She once said (perhaps in reference to her nickname), "My femininity is something I have always tried to preserve in this dog-eat-dog world."

AMBLING ALP (THE)—Primo Carnera (1906–1967) Boxing. The world heavyweight champion of 1933 received his nickname because he was so big and awkward (6' 6" and 300 pounds). Legend has it that he was discovered touring with a circus in Europe as the strong man. Budd Schulberg based his character in *The Harder They Fall* on Carnera. Carnera was also called The Preem, Ponderous Primo, and The Vast Venetian.

AMERICAN GIANT (THE)—Charles Freeman (d. 1845) Bareknuckles boxing. Freeman was from Michigan and stood 6' 10" and weighed in at 300 pounds. When "Big Ben" Caunt who was scheduled to fight him laid eyes on him, he chose to become his promoter instead. The two went on to give boxing exhibitions all over the British Isles. The American Giant's only official fight was against Bill Perry; after seventy rounds it was called because of darkness. After thirty-seven rounds the next day, the referee disqualified Perry for lying down on the ground every time Freeman was going to hit him.

AMERICAN SKATING KING (THE)—Jackson Haines (1840–1876) Figure skating. Jackson Haines, who had been trained as a ballet master in the United States, practically invented the art of figure skating. Early skating routines were stiff and unimaginative working out of "figures," but Jackson Haines put on colorful costumes, skated to music, and expanded on the kinds of routines presented on the ice. When he traveled to Vienna, he electrified the city with his waltzes on ice and founded the Vienna School of Skating. The American Skating King was the first ice-skating star to achieve worldwide fame. In 1876, Haines died while taking a sled trip from St. Petersburg, Russia, to Stockholm. He was also called American Ice Master.

A.M.-P.M.—Mitchell Aaron (1956–   ) Football. He received his nickname from Dallas Cowboys' teammate Charlie Walters, who said of Aaron's opponents, "They're wide awake when he hits 'em and their lights are out when he walks away." That explains the nickname as well as it can be explained.

ANIMAL— Dick Butkus (1942–   ) Football "With the highest respect," commented Mike Ditka, a teammate and later the head coach of the Chicago Bears, "I've got to say Dick is an animal. He works himself up to such a competitive pitch that the day of the game he won't answer a direct question. He'll grunt." Butkus was also called The ENFORCER and PADDLES.

ANIMAL (THE)—George Steele (active 1970s–1980s) Wrestling. Al Vass, a wrestling referee, once said of Steele: "He's the worst. I've been in the ring with that man many times, and

I've never seen a crazier wrestler. I never know if he even understands me when I tell him to break a hold. He just looks at you with those rolling eyes and starts grunting and groaning like a rhinoceros in heat. Refereeing a George Steele match is like being in a cage with a rabid St. Bernard." A rhinoceros or a St. Bernard? Either way you look at it, sporting a shaved head and massive hairy body, and using any tactic he could to win, Steele truly earned his nickname.

ANTELOPE (THE)—Emil Verban (1915–1989) Baseball. This second baseman received his nickname because of the graceful way he turned the double play with shortstop Marty "The Octopus" Marion for the St. Louis Cardinals. In the 1944 World Series, Verban batted .412 for the victorious Cardinals. Verban was also sometimes called Dutch because of his heritage.

APOLLO OF THE BOX (THE)—Tony Mullane (1854–1944) Baseball. Mullane, who could pitch with either arm, put up some phenomenal numbers. He won thirty or more games five straight times and 285 games in all during his thirteen-year career. The switch-hitting Mullane also had a .247 batting average and could play both infield and outfield. Mullane's efforts did not go unnoticed by the ladies either. His good looks led the management of the Cincinnati Reds to start their first Lady's Day—free admission for every woman accompanied by a man. Mullane's other nickname was The Count for the fine way he dressed and conducted himself.

APPLE (THE)—Constance Applebee (1873–1980) Field hockey. In 1901, Constance Applebee brought field hockey to the United States from her native England. Promoting her favorite sport as developing both "physical and mental strength," she coached thousands of girls in junior and senior high schools, as well as thousands of women in colleges, clubs, and organizations. With no time-outs during two thirty-minute periods, it certainly was a demanding sport. While a coach at Bryn Mawr, Ms. Applebee also edited and published *The Sportswoman*. In addition to field hockey, this first sports magazine for women also featured articles on archery, fencing, lacrosse, skating, and swimming. Even after passing her one-hundredth birthday, Constance Applebee remained vigorous. The Apple certainly was a fitting nickname for this woman with such a zesty personality.

ARKANSAS TRAVELER (THE)—Ernest Joseph Harrison (1910–   ) Golf. H/F Harrison was known as the Arkansas Traveler because he had been born in Conway, Arkansas, and he played all over the continent. In 1939 and again in 1951, he won the Texas Open; in 1951, he won the Canadian Open; and in 1953, the Western Open. Also known as Dutch for his heritage, Harrison played on the American Ryder Cup team three times.

ARKY—Joseph Floyd Vaughan (1912–1952) Baseball. H/F Given his nickname because of his birthplace of Clifty, Arkansas, Vaughan played for the Pittsburgh Pirates from 1932 to 1941, and then was with the Dodgers until the end of his playing career in 1948. His best year in the majors was 1935, when he led the league with a .385 batting average and a .607 slugging average. He also led the league in walks that year, receiving ninety-seven bases on balls. Arky ended his career with a .318 lifetime batting average—2,103 hits in 6,622 at-bats.

ARRIBA—Roberto Clemente [1934–1972] Baseball. H/F "Arriba!" ("Let's go!") is what the many Latin fans would shout to Clemente. During his tenure at Pittsburgh, this right fielder took four batting titles and rapped 3,000 base hits en route to a career .317 batting average. In 1972, he was killed in a plane crash while on a goodwill mission to deliver supplies to victims of an earthquake in Nicaragua. Clemente was also called The Great One.

ARTFUL DODGER [THE]—Roger Staubach [1942–   ] Football. H/F Beginning in high school, continuing for Navy and then the Dallas Cowboys, quarterback Staubach's ability to dodge incoming defensive linemen gave his receivers the time to break free. In high school, it was once said of him, "Tackling Staubach is like trying to tackle the wind." Things were no different years later in the pros. Staubach was probably most effective in the last two minutes of the game. In the 1972 playoffs, for instance, Staubach replaced Craig Morton in the final two minutes and led the Cowboys to two touchdowns to beat San Francisco. Perhaps his most famous moment was his "HAIL MARY" pass with only seconds left in the 1975 play-off game with Minnesota. Staubach threw a long pass into a crowd in the end zone, and Drew Pearson caught it. The Artful Dodger is both a rhyme with Roger as well as an allusion to the character in Charles Dickens' *Oliver Twist.* He was also called Captain America and The Dodger.

AUTOMATIC OTTO—Otto Graham [1921–   ] Football. H/F Otto Graham once wrote, "Football is a game, the most wonderful game in the world. I've played football, thought football, and lived football all my life. Football has taught me how to work hard and play hard with my fellow men in the true spirit of sportsmanship." And when he said he played football, he meant it. He remains one of the greatest quarterbacks the T-formation has ever known. He was the very first quarterback for the Cleveland Browns and first in the All-American Football Conference (AAFC), leading the Browns to four consecutive division and league championships. Later, in the National Football League (NFL), he again put the Browns on the map. In 1950, the first year that the Browns were part of the NFL, Automatic Otto (so named because when he got the ball, his passes seemed to guarantee an automatic gain) tossed four touchdown passes in the championship game as the Browns defeated the Los Angeles Rams. Graham had announced his retirement before the 1955 season, but Coach Paul Brown coaxed him back. Graham then quarterbacked the Browns to yet another championship and was the NFL's passing leader. In the championship game, Automatic Otto threw for two touchdowns and ran for two more as the Browns beat Los Angeles 38–14. After the game, Graham hung up his cleats for good, leaving at the peak of his career. His career totals include 1,464 completed passes for a total of 23,584 yards and 174 touchdowns. He completed 55 percent of his passes and threw only ninety-four interceptions.

AWFUL NAME—Ed Abbatticchio [1877–1957] Football. This nickname was understandably bequeathed by the sportswriters who wrote about this first professional kicker who played football around 1900. The fans of the team from Latrobe, Pennsylvania also called him Mr. Punt and Abby. Abbatticchio later played infield for Philadelphia, Boston, and Pittsburgh from 1897 to 1910. In 1905, he had a league-leading 601 at-bats and hit .279.

AZIE—Avon Foreman [1914–   ] Flagpole sitting. In 1929, the fifteen-year-old Foreman sat on an ironing board atop a pole in his backyard as the flagpole-sitting craze reached the juvenile set. Crowds of up to 4,000 watched the youngster for ten days, ten minutes, and ten seconds, as he became "the champion juvenile flagpole sitter of the world."

BABE—Charles Benjamin Adams [1883–1968] Baseball. Adams was the first ballplayer with the nickname Babe. It was due to his handsome features. In 1909, Adams pitched three winning games for Pittsburgh in the World Series, including a seventh-game shutout. By the time he retired in 1926, after nineteen seasons in the big leagues, he had won 194 games and lost 140, with an ERA of 2.76.

BABE—Donald G. Chandler [1934–   ] Football. As a kicker Babe Chandler played for the 1956-1964 New York Giants and the 1965-1967 Green Bay Packers. In 1957, he led the NFL in punting, and in 1963, he was the number one scorer.

BABE—George Herman Ruth [1895–1948] Baseball. H/F When Baltimore Oriole manager Jack Dunn introduced George Herman Ruth for the first time to his teammates in 1914, Coach Steinman said, "Boys, here's Jack's new Babe." The nickname stuck. Perhaps Ruth's greatness is shown by the number of nicknames he sported. To his opponents he was known as Monk or Monkey; to his teammates Jidge (a mispronunciation of George). Ruth was also called Bambino or the Mighty Bambino (the diminutive form of bambo, Italian for child or baby), The Sultan of Swat (for hitting home runs), and The Idol of the American Boy (the nickname Ruth chose for himself). Before Ruth became a hard-hitting outfielder, he was a fine pitcher. In fact, he pitched the longest World Series game that ended in victory. Ruth was once asked if he had any superstitions. "Just one," was his reply. "Whenever I hit a home run, I make certain I touch all four bases."

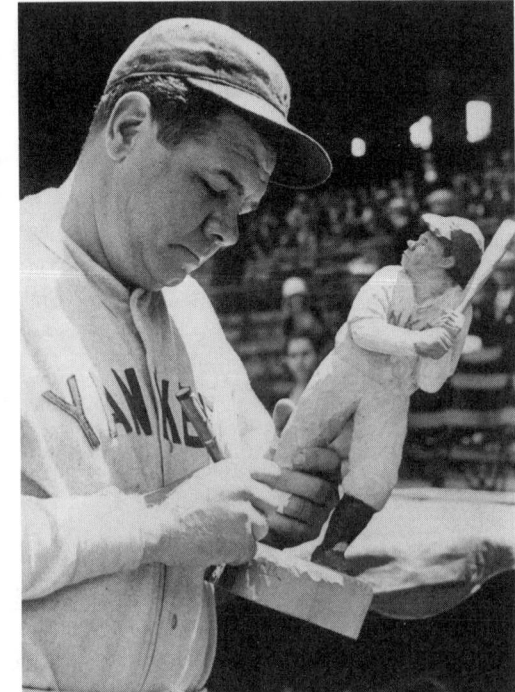

BABE—George Herman Ruth
(1895-1948) Baseball.
The Sultan of Swat signs
the Idol of the American Boy.

BABE—Albert Siebert [1904–1939] Hockey. H/F Siebert played for the Maroons in the early 1930s and was a member of their famed S Line with Nels Stewart and Hooley Smith. He also played for the Rangers, the Bruins, and the Canadiens. He won the Hart trophy as the league's most valuable player for the 1935–1936 season. In his career he scored 140 goals and was credited with 140 assists. Siebert drowned in August 1939, shortly before he was to start coaching the Canadiens.

BABE—Mildred Didrikson Zaharias [1914–1956] Track and field, golf. H/F This all-around athlete was called Baby as a toddler. Later, her nickname was changed to Babe. When as a seventeen year old, she won seven track and field events in the American Athletic Championships of 1931, she became to women's sport what "Babe Ruth" was to baseball. After starring in high-school basketball in Texas, the 5', 105-pound Didrikson won gold medals in the javelin (143' 4") and the eighty-meter hurdles (11.7 seconds) as well as a silver medal in the high jump (5' 5") at the 1932 Olympic Games. Next, Babe took up golf. Soon she was driving balls over 300 yards. (She also once threw a baseball 296 feet.) Didrikson's goal in life was straightforward: "to be the greatest athlete that ever lived." "In all my years at the sports desk," wrote Paul Gallico, "I never encountered any man who could play as many games as well as the Babe." (Babe sometimes said that she was good at every game except dolls.) Playing at the Los Angeles Open in 1938, Babe met and later married George "The Crying Greek from Cripple Creek" Zaharias, a professional wrestler. Babe Zaharias went on to win seventeen straight golf tournaments from 1946-1947, including the U.S. Women's Amateur and the British Women's Amateur. In 1948, 1950, and 1954, Babe won the U.S. Women's Open (by twelve strokes the last time, even though she was stricken with the cancer that would take her life the next year). Voted Woman Athlete of the Year five times, the word woman might have been dropped from these titles. She was also the Associated Press' top woman athlete of the twentieth century.

BABE RUTH OF CUBA [THE]—Christobel Torriente [1895–1938] Baseball [Cuban Leagues, Negro Leagues]. This was a nickname given to Torriente by the *Los Angeles Times* in 1920. In an exhibition game, Torriente hit three home runs whereas Ruth didn't hit any. He was also called The Cuban Strong Boy for his powerful build and long home runs. Torriente was a right fielder and a .352 hitter in Cuba, a .339 hitter in the Negro Leagues, and a .311 hitter against major-league pitching.

BABE RUTH OF THE NEGRO LEAGUES [THE]—Josh Gibson [1912–1947] Baseball. H/F "Josh hit seventy to seventy-two home runs one year," said Buck Leonard, a teammate. "In 1939 he hit more home runs in Griffith Stadium than all the right-handed hitters in the American League combined." Because of his achievements in the Negro Leagues, Josh Gibson was elected to Baseball's Hall of Fame in 1972.

BABY BULL [THE]—Orlando Cepeda [1937–   ] Baseball. Cepeda's father was known as the Babe Ruth of Puerto Rico and was also called The Bull. Thus, it came to be Orlando Cepeda's lot to be known as The Baby Bull. He was a great hitter for the San Francisco Giants and was the National League's Rookie of the Year in 1958. By the time he retired, he had played seventeen seasons, compiling a lifetime .297 average and banging out 2,351 hits, including 417 doubles, 27 triples, and 379 homers. Cepeda was also called Cha-cha.

BABY DOLL—William Chester Jacobson [1890–1977] Baseball. Some nicknames are difficult to live down and "Baby Doll" is one of them. When Jacobsen played outfield for Mobile in 1912, the female fans thought he looked so handsome that they hung the nickname "Baby Doll" on him. Bench jockeys no doubt had a field day with that one! Jacobson is not well remembered now, but his lifetime hitting records are more than respectable: he compiled a .311 batting average in 1,472 games, and knocked out 328 doubles, 94 triples, and 84 homers, playing for such teams as the St. Louis Browns, the Boston Red Sox, the Cleveland Indians, and the Philadelphia Athletics. In 1920, he hit .355 and had 122 RBIs (second only to Babe Ruth that year). He retired in 1930.

BABYFACE—Jimmy McLarnin [1906–   ] Boxing. Babyface was not only the title of a world famous gangster film of the 1930s, but it is also the nickname given to World Welterweight Champion Jimmy McLarnin. This very talented boxer, trained by "Pop" Foster, won the Championship in 1933 and reigned for two years. His most famous fights were the title bouts with Barney Ross. By the time Babyface McLarnin retired he was very wealthy. He had won sixty-three fights, lost eleven, and drew three.

BABY FACED ASSASSIN [THE]—William Corbus [1911–   ] Football. The Baby Faced Assassin is the kind of nickname that seems best applied to a member of Al Capone's gang and not to a football player. The moniker, however, was applied to Bill Corbus when he played at Stanford University under Glenn "Pop" Warner. Ranked among the nation's top collegiate football players, the youthful-looking Corbus was a tough blocker.

BAD GIRL—Red Badgro [1902–1998] Baseball, football. H/F Born Morris Hiram Badgro, he played only two seasons of major-league baseball (1929 and 1930 with the St. Louis Browns). As an outfielder, he managed only a .257 batting average in 143 games. Still he is memorable for at least three reasons: (1) He was an impressive two-sport athlete. In addition to playing baseball, he also played professional football. From 1927 to 1936, he played for all three New York City football (yes, football!) teams—the Yankees, Dodgers, and Giants. (2) His strange nickname can perhaps best be explained as a sardonic variation on his last name, *Badgro,* which sounds like *bad girl.* (3) In 1981, he became the oldest player ever elected to the Professional Football Hall of Fame. He was seventy-nine years old.

BAD JOE—Joseph Henry Hall [1882–1919] Hockey. H/F A newspaperman gave this sobriquet to Joe Hall, but it did not seem to be an apt nickname. Joe Hall's teammate Joe Malone was once quoted as saying, "As far as I'm concerned he should have been known as *Plain* Joe Hall and not *Bad* Joe Hall. That always was a bum rap."

BAD NEWS—Jim Galloway [1887–1950] Baseball. Working as a telegraph operator while playing semipro ball, Galloway arranged to receive bad news before games so that he would be excused from work and be able to play. Although he only hit .185 in twenty-one games with the St.

Louis National League club in 1912, Bad News Galloway did compile a more respectable lifetime average of .317 in the minor leagues.

BALD EAGLE—Charles Whittingham [1913–   ] Horse racing. H/F Although he wanted to be a jockey, he ended up as one of the greatest horse trainers of all time. He earned his trainer's license in 1931, and in 1939, he joined Horatio Luro as his assistant trainer. When World War II broke out, Whittingham joined the Marines and served in the Pacific. He contracted a disease in the tropics which caused him to lose all of his hair. Hence, he became known as Bald Eagle. After WW II, the Bald Eagle returned to work for Luro and then eventually went on to start his own stable. From 1970 to 1974, Whittingham-trained thoroughbreds topped $1,000,000 in earnings. Among the horses he trained were Kentucky Derby winner Ferdinand, 1971 Horse of the Year Ack Ack, and Eclipse Award Winner Turkish Trousers. Whittingham has, in fact, trained more stakes winners than any other trainer.

BAMBI—Lance Alworth [1940–   ] Football. H/F Alworth's nickname came from the deer-like way he ran. He was fleet of foot like Walt Disney's animated film character (from Felix Salten's book). He could scamper into the midst of a forest of defenders, leap high to catch the ball, and then bound into the end zone. Although he had been an All-American halfback at Alabama, it was thought he was too small for that position in the pros. Coach Sid Glickman of the San Diego Chargers switched him to wide receiver, and it proved to be a good move. "He had the greatest hands I have ever seen," said Glickman. "Nobody could jump and catch a ball as Lance did." In 1964, Alworth caught thirteen passes for touchdowns. He played for the Chargers from 1962 to 1970 and the Cowboys from 1971 to 1972.

BANTAM BEN—William Benjamin Hogan [1912–1997] Golf. H/F Bantam suggests lightweight, but there was nothing lightweight about the way Bantam Ben played golf. He played with determination and grace and is frequently mentioned among the greatest golfers of all time. In 1953, he won the U.S. Open (for the fourth time), the Masters (for the second time), and the British Open. When he returned to the United States that year, he was greeted with a tremendous ticker-tape parade in New York City. The Golf Writers Association of America in 1973 named Hogan one of the five all-time great golfers. In the 1950s a film of Bantam Ben's life was made starring Glenn Ford. Hogan was also called Golfdom's Mighty Mite. See THE HAWK and THE ICEMAN.

BARBADOS DEMON [THE]—Joe Walcott [1873–1935] Boxing. H/F This Joe Walcott, born in Barbados, West Indies, is not to be confused with Jersey Joe Walcott who was the World Heavyweight Champion, 1951-1952. The Barbados Demon was the World Welterweight Champion from 1901 to 1906. He earned his nickname because of his devil-like ability to give and withstand punishment; he became the champion in 1901 when he knocked out Rube Ferns in five rounds at Fort Erie. When he retired in 1911, he had fought 150 bouts, winning 81 of them, drawing 30, and losing 24, with 15 no decisions.

BARBER [THE]—Salvatore Anthony Maglie [1917–1992] Baseball. A New York Giants pitcher who always seemed to be in need of a shave, Maglie also gave close shaves to the batters he faced. About his nickname Maglie once said, "It beats being called the Shoeshine Boy." In 1950, Maglie was 18–4; in 1951, he was 23–6. During his ten-year career, Maglie was 119–62 and appeared in three World Series.

BARON (THE)—Adolph Rupp (1901–1977) Basketball. H/F This long-time coach at Kentucky had a lordly manner and a habit of winning. "I'd rather be the most hated winning coach in the country than the most popular losing one." He had a point. Rupp could boast of an 874-190 record at Kentucky and twenty-five All-American Wildcats during his forty-two-year career. He guided Kentucky to four NCAA titles (1948, 1949, 1951, and 1958). He is the all-time college wins leader. He was also called the Man in the Brown Suit for his habit of wearing brown suits during games.

BATTLING SIKI—Louis Phal (1897–1925) Boxing. In 1922, Siki was boxing Georges Carpentier in Paris for the light heavyweight crown. Suddenly, Siki stepped up his barrage of blows and sent Carpentier sprawling for the count. When Siki was disqualified for tripping, the spectators went wild until the verdict was reversed: Carpentier's corner threw in the towel. Siki lost to Mike McTigue in 1923. In 1925, he was murdered in New York City. Phal was also called The Singular Senegalese.

BEAR—Paul William Bryant (1913–1983) Football. This famous coach of Alabama University's football team led the Crimson Tide to 6 National Championship (1961, 1964, 1965, 1973, 1978, 1979) and compiled a record of 232 wins, 46 losses, and 9 ties. In Murray Herskowitz's 1987 biography *The Legend of Bear Bryant* (McGraw Hill) Bryant told the author how he received, at age fourteen, the nickname Bear:

> A carnival came through town and they had this little ole scraggly bear. A man was offering anybody a dollar a minute to wrestle it. Somebody dared me to do it. I said I would. . . . I got the bear pinned, holdin' on real tight. The man kept whispering, 'Let him up. Let him up.' He wanted action. Hell, for a dollar a minute I wanted to hold him till he died. The bear finally shook loose and the next thing I knew his muzzle had come off. I felt a burning sensation behind my ear and when I touched it I got a handful of blood. The damned bear bit me. I jumped from the stage and fell into the empty chairs in the front row. Still have the marks on my shins. Then I ran up the aisle and out the theater. When I came around later the man from the circus was gone. I never did get my money. All I got were some scars and a name.

Bryant was also called The Man.

BEAUTY—David Bancroft (1891–1972) Baseball. H/F When he played shortstop in the National League from 1915 to 1930, compiling a lifetime average of .279 in 1,913 games, he often called out "beauty" when one of his teammates made a particularly good play. He appeared in four World Series (for the Philadelphia Phillies in 1915 and for the New York Giants in 1921, 1922, and 1923).

BEEZER—John Vanbiesbrouck (1963–) Hockey. The nickname for this one-time New York Ranger goalie is a play on the second syllable of his last name. "At the end of the game," reported the *Daily News* (December 22, 1992), "the crowd rose and chanted, 'Beezer, Beezer, Beeezer,' for Vanbiesbrouck's fourteenth career shutout and his twenty-first victory over the Devils."

BENDIGO—William Thompson [1811-1880] Boxing. H/F Thompson wore a fur cap called a Bendigo. Some say he received his nickname from the Biblical character Abednego. He also fought under the name Abed-Nego of Nottingham. From 1839 to 1940, Bendigo was the British bareknuckles heavyweight champion. After his boxing career was over, Thompson retired to become an evangelist. Hence, he was given the sobriquet—The Reformed Pugilist.

BENICIA BOY [THE]—John Camel Heenan [1835-1873] Boxing. Heenan lived in Benicia (near San Francisco), the former capital city of California. Fighting John "OLD SMOKE" Morrissey for the championship in 1858, Heehan broke his hand against a ring post in the ninth round. After two more rounds he was unable to continue.

BEVO—Clarence Francis [1932-   ] Basketball. Bevo was actually nicknamed Beeve after a soft drink by his father. But over time the fizz went out and it became Bevo. Newt Oliver, Bevo's high school coach moved to tiny Rio Grande College in Ohio along with his 6' 9" center. His first year was nothing short of sensational. In one game he scored 116 points and his average for the year was over 50 points. Unfortunately, most of these games were not played against accredited institutions so were wiped off the record book. During the 1953-1954 season lots of four-year schools wanted to play against Rio and Bevo. That season Bevo Francis netted the most points in a game (113), the highest average per game 46.5, the most field goals made in a game (38), and the most free throws made in a game (37). With two years of eligibility still remaining, Bevo dropped out of college to play for the team that toured with the Harlem Globetrotters.

BIG A—Eddie Arcaro [1916-1997] Horse racing. H/F He may have been only 5' 2" and 114 pounds, but Arcaro was big in the racing world for thirty years. Riding in 24,092 horse races, Arcaro came in first 4,779 times, second 3,807 times, and third 3,302 times. Big A was sometimes called Banana Nose because those along the rail could see Arcaro in profile, and what a banana nose of a profile it was. Ironically, Arcaro's racing motto was "Don't get beat by no noses." He was also called King of Little Men, King of the Stakes Riders, and THE MASTER.

BIG BEAR—George Musso [1910-   ] Football. H/F When Big Bear Musso came to play tackle for the Chicago Bears in 1933, he played for the magnificent sum of $90 per game. George Halas even threw in five dollars for expenses, three dollars for train fare, and two dollars for expenses. He was the first player in NFL history to win all-league honors, first as a tackle in 1935, then as a guard in 1937. The fact that he was big and played for the Bears gave him his intimidating nickname.

BIG BEN—Benjamin Brain [1753-1794] Boxing. H/F The English Boxing Champion from 1791 to 1794, he outweighed most of his opponents and most of the boxers of the day. He was nick-named after the famous clock tower in London. On August 30, 1790, he was defeated by William Hopper in a bout that lasted 180 rounds.

BIG BILL—Bill Tilden [1893–1953] Tennis. H/F At 6' 2", Big Bill dominated tennis in the Twenties. With a booming serve that he called on only when he got into trouble, a backhand that was as good as his forehand, and a head for strategy, in 1920 Big Bill was the first American to capture the Wimbledon Singles Championship. In addition to winning Wimbledon that year, he won the singles championship there two more times and the Wimbledon doubles once. Tilden also won the U.S. Singles Championship seven times, the National Doubles Championship five times, the National Mixed Doubles Championship four times, the U.S. Clay Championship seven times, the Indoor Doubles Championship four times, and the Indoor Singles once. In 1930, Big Bill was the winner of the Australian Singles, Doubles, and Mixed Doubles Championships. Tilden was also called Court Jouster.

BIG CAL—Robert Cal Hubbard [1900–1973] Football, baseball. H/F Hubbard was a 265-pound tackle who helped the Green Bay Packers win championships in 1929, 1930, and 1931. After his playing days were over, he went on to become an umpire in the American League, something that came as no surprise to his college coach. "I never met anyone who knows the rules better behind the plate." One day when Yogi Berra was second-guessing Hubbard, Big Cal leaned over and said to the Yankee catcher: "Yogi, my boy, there's just no point in both of us umpiring this game at the same time. I think one of us should leave. Since I'm being paid to stay here, I'm afraid it will have to be you." Yogi kept his mouth shut for the rest of the game. Hubbard went on to become umpire-in-chief for his league and is the only person inducted into both the pro football and the pro baseball Halls of Fame. He was also called HIS MAJESTY.

BIG D—Don Drysdale [1936–1993] Baseball. H/F Drysdale was a big pitcher in more ways than one, winning 209 games and losing 166 for the Dodgers over a fourteen-year span. The "D" stands for his name, but could just as well stand for Dodgers. Big D stood 6' 5" and weighed 200 pounds. He was also called DOUBLE D and The Sidewinder because of his pitching motion.

BIG DADDY—Don Garlits [1933–   ] Drag racing. H/F This nickname refers not to size but accomplishments. Garlits dominated the drag-racing scene from the early 1960s to the mid-1970s. Not only did he have the most wins, but he also set the speed records. On July 12, 1964, Big Daddy Garlits was the first drag racer to exceed 200 mph—drag racing's equivalent of the four-minute mile. And in 1972, this Floridian broke the next tough barrier of 240 mph, powering his Swamp Rat to a speed of 243 MPH.

BIG DADDY—Gene Lipscomb [1931–1963] Football, wrestling. When Eugene Lipscomb played for the Los Angeles Rams, he had the habit of calling everyone Little Daddy. As Lipscomb himself was 6' 6" and weighed 285 pounds, he naturally became Big Daddy. In 1956, Big Daddy Lipscomb started playing for the Baltimore Colts. The Cleveland Browns would sometimes have to assign four players to block this defensive tackle. Lipscomb himself once said he sometimes had to tackle four people before he found the ball carrier. Big Daddy Lipscomb's Herculean strength and speed helped the Colts win the NFL championship in 1958 and 1959. He was also called Fifteen-Yard Daddy because of his many unnecessary-roughness penalties.

BIG DIPPER [THE]—Wilt Chamberlain [1936–] Basketball. H/F When Wilt was ten years old, he banged his head going through the doorway of a deserted house. Someone mentioned that he had to dip to get under it. That day his friends started calling him Dip and Dippy. Later this nickname was changed to The Dipper, and finally to The Big Dipper (a humorous reference to the constellation over our heads). Another nickname was Hook and Ladder; and a sportswriter started calling him Wilt the Stilt, a nickname Chamberlain never liked. The Big Dipper went on to become one of the greatest offensive players with his Dipper Dunk in the history of basketball, setting NBA records in almost every category. But 1962 was a particularly outstanding year. He averaged 50.4 points a game that year for the Philadelphia Warriors; and on March 2, 1962, against the New York Knicks, Wilt Chamberlain scored 100 points in a single game. The Big Dipper was 28–32 at the free-throw line and 36–63 from the field as the Warriors won 169–147. Ten years later, Chamberlain was still at the top of his game and the key to the Lakers' success as they rolled to thirty-three straight victories and sixty-nine wins during the season. On March 25, 1973, he played his last game. During his NBA career, Chamberlain had 23,924 rebounds and never fouled out of a game.

THE BIG DIPPER—
Wilt Chamberlain
(b. August 21.1936)
Basketball.
On March 2, 1962,
The Big Dipper proved
more than worthy of his
nickname when he scored
100 points against the
New York Knicks.

BIG DOG—Ernie Nevers [1903–1976] Football. H/F Nevers was the Big Dog during his playing era. "We blocked below the hips," said Nevers. "Show me a good blocker, a man who doesn't flinch, who loves the game for itself and not only the money in it, and I'll show you a real football player who won't get hurt." Even when Nevers got hurt, he still played. Though he broke his ankle during the last game of the season, he ran for 114 yards in the Rose Bowl. He outgained the Four Horsemen of Notre Dame in Stanford's 27–10 loss. As a pro, Nevers (also called the Blond Bull) usually played all sixty minutes. Most of his games during his five pro seasons were for the Duluth Eskimos—a team Grantland Rice dubbed "The Iron Men from the North." But finishing out his career for the Chicago Cardinals, Nevers scored six touchdowns and four extra points against the Chicago Bears on Thanksgiving Day in 1929. His forty points in a game was a NFL record.

BIG DOGGIE—Tony Perez [1942–   ] Baseball. When Tony Perez was named to manage the Cincinnati Reds for the 1993 season, sportswriters had a field day over the fact that the new manager (born in Cuba) had long borne the nickname Big Doggie for his ability to knock in runs. The reason for the amusement was that Marge Schott, owner of the Reds, had a St. Bernard named Schottzie 02, and candidates for the job of manager were asked how they felt about the owner's dog running onto the field during practice. Tony Perez, who was one of the more popular players in the 1970s and part of the BIG RED MACHINE, told the press: "A lot of people think I'll be a sleeping dog. But I'm not a sleeping dog. I can do the job." He certainly did the job on the field, where as a player he slugged 371 home runs in twenty-one years, compiling a .279 batting average with 1,652 RBIs.

BIG E [THE]—Elvin Hayes [1945–   ] Basketball. H/F The Big E was truly big. He stood 6' 9" and weighed 235 pounds. The Big E's biggest night in college basketball was when he hit thirty-nine points and pulled down fifteen rebounds to help Houston stop Lew Alcindor and UCLA's forty-seven-game winning streak. Hayes was the San Diego Rockets' top draft pick in 1968. Although he never lived up to his clippings, his tenure on the Washington Bullets with Wesley Unseld produced some of his best basketball. In ten years of professional play, Hayes scored 2,194 points, averaging 22.9 points per game.

BIG ED—Edward Delahanty [1867–1903] Baseball. H/F At 6' and 170 pounds, playing outfield for the Philadelphia Phillies in 1899, Big Ed hit .408. During his sixteen-year career his average was .346 with 2,597 hits, including 521 doubles. In fact, he led the league in doubles five times. Also called The Only Del, Delahanty was the only one of his four pro football-playing brothers—Joe, Jim, Frank, and Tom—to be inducted into the Hall of Fame.

BIGHOUSE—Clarence Gaines [1923–   ] Basketball. H/F The first basketball Hall of Fame coach to spend his entire career at a Black college, Bighouse coached the Winston-Salem State University basketball team to seventeen twenty-victory seasons. Perhaps his most famous player was Earl "THE PEARL" Monroe who, in 1967, led the team to a NCAA postseason tournament title.

BIG JACK—Inman Jackson [active 1930s] Basketball. One of the original Harlem Globetrotters, Big Jack was 6' 4" and an accomplished ball handler. One day in Michigan the Trotters were playing a team that was outdoing them in fancy play. In desperation, Big Jack dropkicked the basketball right through the hoop. It was to become one of the Globetrotters' standard routines.

BIG JAKE—John Albert Kramer (1921–   ) Tennis. H/F Jack Kramer was not only one of the great tennis players of his time, but he was also one of the game's great promoters. During the 1950s most of the world's top tennis players were playing under his auspices. At age fourteen he was a tall, blond Californian who won the National Boys Singles and Doubles Championships. He liked to refer to himself as Big Jake and the nickname stuck. He won the Wimbledon title in 1947, and, in October of that year, he turned professional. *Time* magazine wrote that Kramer "plays tennis the way Joe Louis stalks an opponent in the ring."

BIG M (THE)—Frank Mahovlich (1938–   ) Hockey. H/F Mahovlich earned his nickname because of his last name, his long skating strides, and his long reach with the hockey stick. When he played for Detroit, he was on THE PRODUCTION LINE with Howe and Delvecchio. Mahovlich was only the fourth person to score over 500 goals. He had also scored fifty goals in playoffs and he had been on six Stanley Cup winning teams. But the pressure of playing hockey in the NFL had often been a problem for him. "I have the body of an athlete and the mind of a librarian," Frank Mahovlich once said. "I don't mean smart—I mean maybe I was meant to live a quiet life."

BIG MAC—Kevin McReynolds (1959–   ) Baseball. McReynolds (his nickname is an ironic reference to McDonald's world-famous hamburger) was the minor league Player of the Year in 1982 and 1983. He became the Padres' regular centerfielder in their 1984 NL pennant-winning season and in his first full season he hit twenty homers and batted .278. In 1986, Big Mac was dealt to the Mets, but he never seemed to catch fire.

BIG MO—Maurice Stokes (1933–1970) Basketball. Six foot and 240 pounds, Big Mo played for the Cincinnati Royals and was Rookie of the Year. In 1958, he fell victim to a crippling brain injury, and teammate Jack Twyman became his legal guardian. Mo battled for twelve years until he died of a heart attack. His life was made into the 1973 film *Maurie* with Bernie Casey.

BIG MOMMA—JoAnne Carner (1939–   ) Golf. H/F Before her marriage, JoAnne Gunderson was the Great Gundy for her golfing ability; afterwards, she was Big Momma. It wasn't her size as much as it was her heart. Everyone liked Big Momma. Carner was an amateur for twelve years—winning the U.S. Women's Amateur five times and playing on four straight Curtis Cup teams. She was the last amateur to win an LPGA event, winning the 1969 Burdine's Invitational. In 1970, she turned pro and was Rookie of the Year. She won the U.S. Women's Open in 1971 and 1976, and in 1985 won five tournaments (and topped $300,000). In 1986, Big Momma's winnings went over the $2 million mark.

BIG NUMBER 99—George Mikan (1924–   ) Basketball. H/F The 6' 10", 245-pound George Mikan, his thick glasses held on by an elastic band, wore number ninety-nine. With the help of coach Russ Meyer, the once awkward Mikan became a three-time All American at De Paul. Turning pro, Mikan spent a year with the Chicago Bears, before joining the Minneapolis Lakers. In his first year, Mikan led the Lakers to the championship and was voted the MVP. In 1951, Because of Mikan, the NBA widened the lane from six to twelve feet and put in a three-second rule. In his NBA career from 1947 to 1956, Mikan scored 11,376 points and was the first big attraction. (The marquee outside Madison Square Garden would read: "Geo. Mikan vs. Knicks.") Mikan helped make basketball the popular sport it is today. Later, Mikan became a lawyer and the first commissioner of the ABA. Mikan was also the one to come up with the idea for the red-white-and-blue basketball that lurked in many a kid's closet.

BIG O [THE]—Oscar Robertson [1938–   ] Basketball. H/F Oscar Robertson was the big player for the University of Cincinnati and led the nation in scoring three years in a row during the early 1960s. At that time James Thurber's *The Wonderful "O"* was popular, so Robertson became known as the Big O. Oscar Robertson had always played big. He had led his Indianapolis high school to two state championships; he was the Player of the Year and an All-American at the University of Cincinnati; he was co-captain of the U.S. team that won the gold medal at the 1960 Olympics. Robertson's career in the pros was just as impressive. In ten years for the Cincinnati Royals and four years for the Milwaukee Bucks, the Big O had 2,931 assists (he led the league seven different years), as well as 9,887 rebounds and 26,710 points. Oscar Robertson was Rookie of the Year in 1961, the MVP in 1964, and a member of the All-Star team from 1961 to1969.

BIG POISON—Paul Waner [1903–1965] Baseball. H/F Although Paul was slightly smaller than his brother Lloyd he was called "Big" because he was the older brother. "Poison" may have been a Brooklyn mispronunciation of *person.* In 1926, Paul hit .336 as a rookie; his career average was .333. During his twenty-year career, Big Poison played in 2,549 games, had 9,459 at-bats, 3,152 hits (including 603 doubles and 190 triples). His statistics were bigger than Lloyd's, too. Lloyd was known as LITTLE POISON.

BIG SIX—Christy Mathewson [1880–1925] Baseball. H/F Sam Crane, a New York City sportswriter, once wrote in his column, "Mathewson is certainly the 'Big Six' of pitchers." Though Mathewson wore the number six, Crane was alluding to Big Six, the fastest fire engine in New York City that covered many large fires around Manhattan. Christy Mathewson was just as effective in putting out the fire of opposing batsmen with his famous fade-away pitch (a screwball). Ten seasons he won twenty or more games; and in 1904, 1905, and 1908, Big Six won 34, 32, and 35 games. He was also called Husk and Matty the Great.

BIG SMOKE—Jack Johnson [1878–1946] Boxing. H/F Johnson was a 6' 1", 221-pound heavyweight. Smoke was slang at the time for an African American. Johnson won seventy-eight fights during his career; forty-five were knockouts. He was the champion from December 26, 1908 to April 5, 1915. In his eleven title fights, he won five, lost one with four no decisions and one draw. Johnson is credited with throwing one of the hardest punches ever. In a 1909 title fight with Stanley Ketchel, Johnson was angered by being floored by Ketchel in the twelfth round. Johnson got up and knocked out the challenger. Later, it was discovered that two of Ketchel's teeth were lodged in the leather of the champ's glove. Johnson was also called The Galveston Giant and Li'l Arthur.

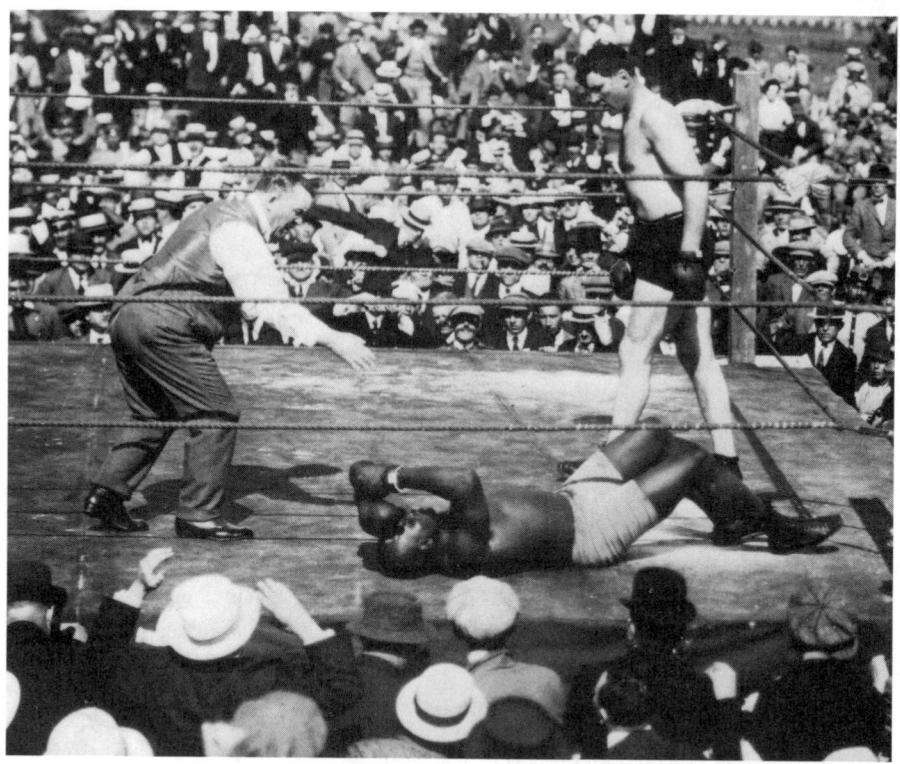

BIG JESS—Jess Willard (1883-1968) Boxing. The Great White Hope (Willard) is shown standing over BIG SMOKE—Jack Johnson (1878-1946) Boxing.

BIG TRAIN—Walter Johnson [1887-1946] Baseball. H/F Sportswriter Grantland Rice conferred the title "Big Train" upon Walter Johnson when he wrote in his column: "The Big Train comes to town today." Although Johnson may have boarded a train for the trip from Utah to Washington and fame, his nickname instead refers to the mechanical precision of his pitching motion and the speed of his fastball. Cliff Blankenship's scouting report testified to the latter: "He throws a ball so fast nobody can see it, and he strikes out everybody. His control is so good that the catcher just holds up his glove, shuts his eyes, then picks the ball, which comes to him looking like a little white bullet, out of the pocket." Coupled with a weak curve, his fastball was the only real pitch in his arsenal. "The great thing about Walter Johnson," said Ty Cobb, "was that even though you knew a fastball was coming, it didn't help." (The only way Cobb and Eddie Collins could get a hit off Johnson was to get two strikes; then Johnson would often serve up his curve.) Playing twenty-one years for the traditionally weak Washington Senators, Johnson racked up some amazing statistics. He had twelve twenty-win seasons and 3,508 strikeouts. He started 666 games and finished 531 of them. He won 416 games and 110 were shutouts. (He also pitched seven opening day shutouts.) Johnson was also called Grand Veteran, Best Pitcher in Baseball, Swede (after his heritage), and Barney (after the racecar driver Barney Oldfield).

BIRD—George Yardley (1928–   ) Basketball. H/F Surprisingly, Yardley's nickname did not come from his ability to soar with a basketball. Going through fraternity hazing, he was forced to do the menial-type tasks one associates with the "Yardbirds" in the army. The name stuck and was shortened to Bird. Playing for the Detroit Pistons during the 1957-1958 season, Bird was the first to score over 2,000 points in a season. During the seven years that George Yardley played in the NBA, he led his team to the playoffs seven times.

BIRD (THE)—Mark Fidrych (1954–   ) Baseball. In 1976, the Detroit Tigers unveiled one of the most exciting rookie pitchers in the history of the game. His name was Mark Fidrych, and in his first year he won nineteen games and lost nine, with a league-leading 2.34 ERA. The fans roared when they saw The Bird talking to himself on the mound. Some thought he was talking to the base-ball, but The Bird said, "I never did talk to the ball. I'm talking to myself. I ain't sayin', 'hey c'mon ball, c'mon ball. I'm saying, c'mon, Mark, you gotta throw a strike." Paul Richards, then, managing the Chicago White Sox, watching the crowd responding to Fidrych's animated antics said, "Babe Ruth didn't cause that much excitement in his brightest day." Unfortunately, he never lived up to his promise and five years later he was out of baseball, having won twenty-nine games, losing nine-teen, and striking out 170 batters. His lifetime ERA was 3.10. Mark Fidrych and Tom Clark (J.B. Lippincott Co., 1977) recount how he got his nickname in *No Big Deal.* A coach at Bristol, Jeff Hogan, conferred the name upon him:

> I just run out in the field and he goes, "Bird." And I just turn around. And he goes, "That's your nickname I gave you." And you know, he told me—he goes, "If you stick in baseball, that name's gonna stick with you. And you watch that name's gonna be." And it was weird, and I said, "What did you call me that for?" And he said, "You look like that goofy bird in *Sesame Street*," and I said, "Whatdaya mean?" He gives, "Hey you just look like the bird on Sesame Street. So that's your nickname. I can't—Fidrych is too hard to, y' know, *say.*"

BLACK BABE RUTH (THE)—Josh Gibson (1912–1947) Baseball (Negro Leagues). H/F Although Gibson played for the best teams in the Negro Leagues, the Pittsburgh Homestead Greys and the Pittsford Crawfords, the record keeping was sadly lacking. Nevertheless, Josh Gibson topped Ruth's record by hitting seventy-five home runs in 1931, and Gibson's batting average was over .350 for his seventeen-year career. Gibson swatted 278 home runs during one four-year period and once socked a ball 580 feet in THE HOUSE THAT RUTH BUILT. He was also called The Black Bomber.

BLACK CAT (THE)—Dobie Moore (1893-1926) Baseball. Playing for Kansas City in the old Negro Leagues, The Black Cat compiled a lifetime .359 batting average. Casey Stengel said of him: "That Moore was one of the best shortstops that will ever live! That fellow could stand up to the plate and hit right-handed. He could hit line drives out there just as far as you want to see." Moore received his nickname because he was so graceful and quick at making plays at short.

BLACK DIAMOND (THE)—Jose Mendez (1888–1928) Baseball (Negro Leagues). Mendez was also called El Diemente Negro. He frequently outpitched major leaguers. In 1908, he barely missed a no-hitter, beating the Cincinnati Reds 1-0. John McGraw said of him, "Jose Mendez is better than any pitcher except Mordecai Brown and Christy Mathewson—and sometimes I think he's better than Matty."

BLACK HONUS WAGNER—John Henry "Pop" Lloyd (1884–1965) Baseball. H/F Lloyd and Wagner were both playing at the same time with the same style in the field and at the plate. "They called him the Black Honus Wagner and I was anxious to see him play," said the real Honus Wagner. "Well, one day I had the opportunity to see him play, and after I saw him I felt honored that they would name such a great player after me." During his playing days from 1908 to 1931, Lloyd batted .342 in the Negro Leagues. He also hit .321 against major-league pitching in exhibition games.

BLACK TERROR (THE)—Bill Richmond (1763–1829) Bareknuckles boxing. Earl Percy, a British general of the occupying force on Staten Island, had this former slave as his valet. Claimed as one of the spoils of war, Percy took Richmond to England where the young man went on to become a boxing sensation. When Richmond retired from the ring, he opened the Horse and Dolphin, a tavern popular with Lord Byron and other followers of THE FANCY.

BLACK TY COBB—Oscar Charleston (1896–1954) Baseball (Negro Leagues). H/F Charleston had a lifetime average of .353 in the Negro Leagues, but he was an all-round player who could also win games with his outstanding fielding in the outfield. Some say he was the best player ever to play the game, and a few writers have suggested that Ty Cobb should be known as the White Oscar Charleston. He was also called The Hoosier Comet.

BLAZE—Carol Ann Blazejowski (1956–   ) Basketball. H/F During her junior and senior years at Montclair State College in New Jersey, Blaze was one of *the* best, if not the best, known players in women's basketball, In 1977, she averaged 33.5 points per game, leading the nation in that department. She also led the nation in scoring in 1978, when she averaged 38.6 points per game. Blaze was not only a shortened form of her last name, it was an appropriate nickname as well, for her ability to blaze through opponents' defenses. She finished her college basketball career with a record high 3,199 points.

BLINKY—Gordon Howe (1928–   ) Hockey. H/F During Howe's thirty-five-year career with the Detroit Red Wings, he played in 1,841 games and scored 786 goals. He received his nickname because in a 1950 Stanley Cup play-off game with the Toronto Maple Leafs, Howe collided with Ted Kennedy of Toronto. Howe's skull was fractured and he suffered a lacerated right eye. The accident left him with a tick that caused compulsive eye blinking. At the end of his career, when he played with the Hartford Whalers, he was already a grandfather, and two of his sons—Marty and Mark— were playing alongside him. When he retired at age fifty-two, he had set records for the most games played (2,421), most assists (1,519), and most goals scored (1,071). He was the NHL's most valuable player six times. The Whalers retired his number nine jersey.

*BLINKY—Gordie Howe (b. March 31, 1928) Hockey. The above photo gives some insight
into the appropriateness of his nickname. He ranks second only to Wayne Gretzky
on the all-time NHL list in goals (801) and points (1,850).*

BLOND BOMBER (The)—Terry Bradshaw (1948–   ) Football. H/F The Blond Bomber
was Bradshaw's nickname in college. As his hair thinned, he was called this less and less. The MVP
in two Super Bowls, Bradshaw quarterbacked the Pittsburgh Steelers to four Super Bowl victories
(1975, 1976, 1979, 1980). He was also called The Rifleman for his bullet passes and OZARK IKE.

BLOND BOMBER [THE]—Robert Dale Fenimore [1925—   ] Football. Some consider Fenimore the greatest football player ever to play for the Oklahoma State University Cowboys. During his four years at Oklahoma, he played tailback for O.S.U., and he set numerous rushing and passing records. He was so accurate at passing the football for long passes and was so fast at crashing through the opposition's defenses, he was called The Blond Bomber. In 1945 and 1946, he led his team to twenty-one consecutive victories, taking them to the 1945 Cotton Bowl and the 1946 Sugar Bowl. While in college, he also was a track and field star, setting an Oklahoma State freshman record of 9.7 seconds in the 100-yard dash.

BLOND BOMBER [THE]—Bobby Layne [1926–1986] Football. H/F Layne's nickname came from his blond good looks and his strong arm. His fifteen-year career statistics of 1,814 completions and 194 touchdowns were secondary to his burning desire to win. In 1952 and 1953, the Blond Bomber led the Detroit Lions to two successive NFL championships. Although surpassing SLINGIN' SAMMY Baugh by compiling 26,721 yards, Layne once said, "I'm not interested in records. They're just a reminder I'm getting old." "Bobby never lost a game in his life," said Doak Walker of his teammate who could score by passing, punting, and running the ball, kicking extra points and field goals. "Time just ran out on him."

BLOOD—Johnny McNally [1903–1985] Football. H/F A good way to pass a rainy afternoon would be to draw up a list of famous persons who took their names or nicknames from motion picture titles. Blood would be near the top of the list. When he was playing college ball, McNally wanted to play for a professional team. In order to do that without losing his eligibility, he needed an alias. He and a friend walked past a movie theater and the title *Blood and Sand* was featured on the marquee. "That's it!" McNally exclaimed. "I'll be Blood and you be Sand." And so it was. He played as Johnny Blood for fifteen years in the NFL for such teams as the Duluth Eskimos, The Green Bay Packers, and the Pittsburgh Pirates (1937-1939). He was also a poet. He was elected to the Pro Football Hall of Fame in 1963. McNally was also called the Vagabond Halfback (he had an adventurous life travelling about the world).

BO—Vincent Edward Jackson [1962—   ] Baseball, football. Mrs. Jackson named her eighth child after her favorite TV actor, Vince Edwards who played Ben Casey. But this wasn't the name that stuck. As a youngster, Jackson was nicknamed Boar. His cousin was referring to Jackson's toughness: he "was as tough as a boar." This was eventually shortened to Bo. Bo was a standout in track, football, and baseball in high school and college. Pursued by both pro football and baseball teams, Bo turned down a $3 million offer from the Tampa Bay Buccaneers to sign with the Kansas City Royals for $200,000. "In life, you take chances," he reasoned. "My goal is to be the best baseball player Bo Jackson can be." In 1987, Bo Jackson began playing football during his off-season for the Los Angeles Raiders. In a game that season he gained 221 yards, highlighted by a ninety-one-yard sprint for a touchdown. But it was still in baseball that Jackson generated the most excitement. Even baseball players stopped to watch Jackson's towering home runs in batting practice. Unfortunately for Jackson's future health and the game of baseball, Bo did not stick to his earlier decision to play only baseball.

BOBBY HOCKEY—Bobby Orr (1948–) Hockey. H/F Although Orr was never really saddled with a nickname that stuck this one fit as well as any that were given him. For during his playing days, the name Bobby Orr was synonymous with hockey. Bobby Orr revolutionized the position of defenseman. He was an offensive defenseman. No defenseman had ever scored 100 points in a season; Orr did it five years in a row. Orr scored more goals (211) and had more assists (522) in his eight seasons than any defenseman had during a long career. (Orr's career was shortened by knee injuries.) Yes, Bobby Orr revolutionized the position. Orr also had the Revolutionary city of Boston up in his arms. As Mrs. Weston Adams, the widow of the former owner, said at his induction ceremony to the Hall of Fame in 1979: "I give you Bobby Orr, number four in your program, number one in our hearts."

BOBBY HOCKEY—Bobby Orr (b. March 20, 1948) Hockey. He was an eight-time Norris Trophy winner as the best defenseman in the NHL.

BOBO—Norman Newsom [1907–1962] Baseball. Newsom's first nickname was Buck; however, when he said Buck, it would come out Bo. Compounding the error, Newsom started calling himself, as well as everyone else, Bobo. Bobo bounced back and forth from one team to another and back to the same team for twenty years—twenty-one uniform changes in all—to register a record of 211–222. On September 18, 1934, Newsom had a heartbreaker: a no-hit game until he lost on one hit to the Red Sox in the tenth. That year Bobo was playing for the St. Louis Browns. (*Bobo* is sometimes used to mean the pet of the manager.)

BOBO—Carl Olson [1945–   ] Boxing. Bobo was Olson's little sister's way of saying brother, and soon all boxing fans knew the strong, unrelenting fighter as Bobo Olson. Beginning his professional boxing career in 1945, Olson was the World Middleweight Champion from 1953 to 1955. He fought SUGAR Ray Robinson three times in his career, but lost each time. Olson retired in 1966.

BOILERMAKER [THE]—James J. Jeffries [1875–1953] Boxing. H/F As the heavyweight champ from 1899 to 1903, Jeffries had a couple of tough fights. It took him twenty-three rounds to knock out Jim Corbett in 1900. Jeffries was suffering cuts to the face and a broken nose when he knocked out Bob Fitzsimmons in the eighth. A boilermaker is a good strong punch to the jaw. Jeffries was also called The California Hercules and The Beast.

BOMBARDIER—Billy Wells [1888–1967] Boxing. Wells had been a boxing champion in the British army in India with a reputation for hitting hard. From 1911 to 1919, he was the British heavyweight champion. He was also the European heavyweight champion from 1911 to 1913, when he lost his title to Georges Carpentier in four rounds. In their rematch, Wells was knocked out in only seventy-three seconds. In his 1924 book *Physical Energy: Showing How Physical and Mental Energy May Be Developed By Means of the Practice of Boxing,* Bombardier Billy Wells (that's how his name appears on the title page) tells his readers:

> We are all born to a vocation, but many of us fail to discover what it is until it is too late. Without desiring for a moment to compare my own modest career with that of the great names I mention here, I would like to point out that my youthful talent for boxing was determined to find expression in the same way as the boy Mozart's genius for music or young Murillo's for painting. These two prodigies of artistic genius were enthusiasts each in his own way and thereby accomplished great things. I...following on a much lower plane of youthful activity, brought no less enthusiasm to bear in the accomplishment of my humbler ambition, and in due course attained the goal at which I aimed. Enthusiasm is the great dynamo of human endeavor.

Wells was also called Battling Billy.

BONEHEAD—Fred Merkle [1888–1956] Baseball. Although Merkle played for sixteen years, he is best remembered for one play during the 1908 season. With two outs in the bottom of the ninth, Merkle was on first base for the Giants with a teammate on third. The next batter hit a single and the man on third scored for the win over the Cubs. Merkle saw the fans running onto the field, so he ran to the dugout. Johnny Evers called for the ball and tagged second for the out. The game did not count, and by the end of the season, the Giants and Cubs were tied with identical 98–55 records. The game was replayed: Three-Finger Brown defeated Christy Mathewson 4–2. Merkle's bonehead play had cost the Giants the pennant.

BONES—Hugh Taylor [1923–1992] Football. In the mid-1960s, Hugh Taylor was the head coach for the Houston Oilers. During his playing days, he had been a wide receiver for the Washington Redskins. Before he landed the head coaching job for the Oilers (1964–1965), Bones Taylor served as an assistant coach with the New York Titans (forerunners of the Jets), the San Diego Chargers, and the Pittsburgh Steelers. He most likely received his nickname for his thin frame.

BOOB—Eric McNair [1909–1949] Baseball [Negro Leagues]. McNair received his nickname because of the similarity of his name to a Rube Goldberg comic strip character called Boob McNutt. A shortstop with the As, White Sox, and Tigers, McNair led the American League in doubles with forty-seven in 1932. He was also called Prez and Rabbit.

BOOJUM—Jud Wilson [1899–1963] Baseball [Negro Leagues]. In Cuba, he was known as Jorocon—The Bull, but in the United States, playing for the black leagues, Wilson was called Boojum because of the sound his line drives made ricocheting off the outfield walls. No less a baseball player than the great Josh Gibson said that Boojum Wilson was the best hitter he ever saw. His lifetime average was a whopping .370.

BOOM-BOOM—Walter William Beck [1904–1987] Baseball. Beck began his baseball career as a pitcher for the St. Louis Browns in 1924, when he pitched all of one inning. Then, three years later, he returned to the major leagues, and pitched eleven more innings for the Browns. He ended his career in 1945 with the Detroit Tigers. All in all, he won thirty-eight games and lost sixty-nine, with a 4.30 ERA. So why was he called Boom-Boom? In 1934, when he was pitching for the Brooklyn Dodgers, Brooklyn's manager Casey Stengel came out to the mound to take Beck out of the game. Beck, who was nursing a lead against the Phillies, became so infuriated at Stengel, that he took the baseball and tossed it into right field. The ball hit the tin-plated wall of the Baker Bowl, went "boom-boom" and rebounded into center field. The center fielder, Hack Wilson, thinking the ball was in play, chased the ball down and tossed it back to the infield. By then, Beck was out of the game, but was given a colorful nickname. See ELMER THE GREAT.

BOOM BOOM—Bernie Geoffrion [1931–   ] Hockey. H/F In his first game of the 1951–1952 season, Bernie Geoffrion scored two goals for the Montreal Canadiens. But what really impressed fans was the sound of Geoffrion shooting the puck. When Geoffrion slapped the hockey stick against the puck, that was one boom; when the puck smashed into the end boards, there was the sound of another. Although Boom Boom Geoffrion was a mainstay over many winning years for Montreal, he was not always popular with the hometown fans because of the popularity of another player, Maurice "POCKET" Richard. Toward the end of the 1954–1955 season, Richard, the scoring leader, was suspended. After Boom Boom surged ahead of his teammate to win the scoring title, Geoffrion was booed in the Forum. However, by the time Boom Boom won his second scoring title and the Hart Trophy in 1961, he was fully appreciated. Over all, Boom Boom scored a total of 393 goals.

BOOMER—Norman Esiason [1961–   ] Football. Before Norman's birth, his father said to his mother: "He must be a boomer (a football term for kicker) because he kicks so much." Instead, Boomer became a quarterback.

BOOMER—George Charles Scott [1944–   ] Baseball. Movie fans have one George C. Scott, but Boston Red Sox fans, especially those who lived through the 1967 season of the Impossible Dream, have Boomer. Scott boomed out nineteen homers that year and hit .303. By the time he retired at the conclusion of the 1979 season, he had compiled a .268 lifetime average, with 1,992 hits and 271 home runs in 7,433 at-bats.

BOSS [THE]—Mike Bossy [1957–   ] Hockey. H/F Mike Bossy played for the New York Islanders from 1977–1987. During his ten years with the team, the Islanders won the Stanley Cup four times (1980–1984). In his rookie season Bossy scored fifty-three goals; nine times he scored fifty-or-more goals. In Stanley Cup play the Boss scored eighty-five goals. In 1980, Bossy declared he would match Maurice "THE ROCKET" Richard's record of fifty goals in fifty games. Amazingly, the Boss scored his fiftieth goal with five minutes remaining in the fiftieth game. Bossy made good on his claim early in his career that he would not fight. "Each time you knock me down," he had said, "I will get back up and score more goals." The Boss scored a total of 537 goals.

THE BOSTON STRONG BOY—John L. Sullivan (1858-1918) Boxing. Also known as The Great John L. In 1945, a film about the women in this boxer's life was released under the title The Great John L.

BOSTON STRONG BOY (THE)—John L. Sullivan (1858–1918) Boxing. H/F Born in Roxbury, Massachusetts, John L. Sullivan was intimidating in both size and boxing skills. He began his professional bareknuckles-boxing career in 1878; by 1882 he had become the heavyweight champion with a knockout of Paddy Ryan. His last defense of his bareknuckle title was in 1889 in Richburg, Mississippi with a KO of Jake Kilrain in the seventy-third round. The first modern-day boxing match (padded gloves and Queensberry Rules) was on September 7, 1892, in New Orleans. James J. Corbett knocked out the Boston Strong Boy in the twenty-first round. After his defeat, Sullivan toured the country giving boxing exhibitions. He was also called The Great John L.

BOW-WOW—Hank Arft (1922–   ) Baseball. Anyone who has read the comic strip "Little Orphan Annie" is no doubt well aware that Annie's dog Sandy goes "Arf." Thus, Hank's last name gave birth to a most (and, perhaps, unwanted) nickname. Arft played five years for the St. Louis Browns and compiled a lifetime .253 batting average in 906 at-bats, with thirteen home runs. Bow-Wow, however, did lead the American League in fielding first base from 1948–1950.

BOXING BELL HOP (THE)—Fred Apostoli (1913–1973) Boxing. Fred Apostoli, the World Middleweight Champion from 1937–1939, was known as The Boxing Bell Hop because he was once a hotel page boy before turning to professional boxing. He won the World Middleweight crown in 1937, when he defeated Marcel Thil of France, but his title was in dispute in the State of New York. New York recognized Freddie Steele as the Champion. Apostli, however, bypassed the New York ruling and defended his crown twice. He lost his title on October 2, 1939, when Ceferino Garcia of the Philippines defeated him. The war intervened and made it impossible for him to regain his championship. He officially retired from the ring in 1948. In 72 fights, The Boxing Bell Hop won sixty-one, drew one, lost ten.

THE BROCKTON BOMBER—Rocky Marciano. Boxing. (left)
THE MANASSA MAULER—Jack Dempsey. Boxing. (center)
THE BROWN BOMBER—Joe Louis. Boxing. (right)

BOY WONDER [THE]—Stanley Harris [1896–1977] Baseball. H/F Harris was only twenty-eight when as a player-manager he led the Washington Senators to victory in the 1924 World Series and second place in the 1925 Series. After playing a steady second base for twelve years, he turned to managing full time. Harris was also called Bucky.

BRAT [THE]—John McEnroe [1959–   ] Tennis. McEnroe often subjected linesmen, umpires, and even fans to his bouts of temper. He may not have been the most gracious and popular player, but for many years he was one of the best. His deft touch carried him to victory in the 1979, 1980, 1981, and 1984 U.S. Opens. He also won Wimbledon in 1981, 1983, and 1984. One of his most memorable matches was the Wimbledon final he lost to Bjorn Borg on July 5, 1980. It was a five set-ter (1–6, 7–5, 6–3, 6–7, 7–6) that took four hours and fifty-three minutes. In the fourth set McEnroe and Borg extended each other in a thirty-four-point tiebreaker. He was also called Junior.

BROADWAY JOE—Joe Willie Namath [1943–   ] Football. H/F Bear Bryant called him "the greatest athlete I ever coached." And although at first he had his critics, Namath silenced them all in 1969 when, after a night of partying in Miami, he led the New York Jets to a 16–7 victory over the Baltimore Colts in Super Bowl III. It was the game that truly put the American Football League on the map, although the AFC hasn't won that many Super Bowls since. Joe Willie Namath got his nickname after posing in Times Square for the cover of a 1965 *Sports Illustrated.* Namath may have played miles from the bright lights of Broadway, but he lit up the city with his football playing and partying. During his career, he compiled many impressive statistics. He had passed for 27,663 yards in 3,762 attempts, for an average of 7.35 yards per pass. His autobiography is titled *I Can't Wait Until Tomorrow Cause I Get Better Looking Every Day.*

BROCKTON BOMBER [THE]—Rocky Marciano [1923–1969] Boxing. H/F *The Encyclopedia Brittanica* says Marciano was known as the Brockton Blockbuster, but he was probably better known to his many fans as The Brockton Bomber (Brockton, in homage to the Massachusetts town where he was born). Although The Brockton Bomber retired early, at age thirty-two, after defending his heavyweight championship only six times, the fight (September 23, 1952) in which he won his heavyweight title—against Jersey Joe Walcott—is considered one of the great fights of all time. Marciano had been knocked down by Walcott in the first round and he was behind on pounds into the thirteenth round, when Marciano landed one of his famous knockout punches. Marciano said: "I started to holler and I wanted to whoop it up because I was so thrilled at winning. But when I looked at him, all I could think of was how awful he must have felt." Marciano called his KO punch Suzy Q. He was also known as The Brockton Bull and The Brockton Buster.

BRONKO—Bronislau Nagurski [1908–1990] Football, wrestling. H/F When Nagurski's mother took her son to registration at the school in International Falls, Minnesota, the teacher couldn't understand his mother's Polish accent, recounts Nagurski, "So finally the teacher said, 'Do you mean Bronko?' and my mother decided she'd had enough so she just nodded in agreement." At 6' 2" and 230 pounds, Bronko starred at footback for the University of Minnesota. "Back then, the linemen were often called tackle backs," he once explained. "We'd play on the line for a while, then go back and carry the ball for a while." Some newspapers listed him as All-American at both tackle and fullback. What kind of a fullback was he? "Tackling Bronko," said teammate Ernie Nevers, "was like trying to tackle a freight train going downhill." Bronko went on to play nine years for the Chicago Bears. Although statistics were somewhat haphazard in those days, Bronko carried the ball 872 times for 4,031 yards. The Bronk finished his sports careers as a wrestler. "Wrestling wasn't fixed on the scale it is now," reported Nagurski, "but I wish I hadn't done it. I wasted a lot of time." He was also called The Big Ukrainian, The Bronk, and Indomitable Bronk.

THE BROWN BOMBER—
Joe Louis (1914–1981) Boxing.
When someone stated that Joe
Louis was a credit to his race,
a sportswriter replied, "Yes, the
human race." A class act in
boxing and beyond.

BROWN BOMBER [THE]—Joe Louis [1914–1981] Boxing. H/F Joe Louis (whose real name was Joseph Louis Barrow) was an African American with paralyzing punching power. This led to many nicknames, though The Brown Bomber stated it best and was the one most often used. In 1934 Louis won the AAU light heavyweight championship. Turning pro, The Brown Bomber ran up a winning streak of twenty-three fights (including former heavyweight champion Primo Carnera) before being knocked out by Max Schmelling in the twelfth round. Louis went on to become the heavyweight champion by knocking out Jim Braddock in the eighth round of their title fight on June 22, 1937. In their return bout the next year, The Brown Bomber KO'd Max Schmelling in the very first round. For Louis, this victory was "bigger almost than getting to be the champ." Louis scored twenty-five consecutive victories (twenty-two KOs), including two difficult fights with Billy Conn. "He can run, but he can't hide," said Louis upon hearing that Conn was predicting victory in their second bout. True, some of Louis' opponents had been weak—what some wags had termed the Bum of the Month Club—however, Louis had remained champion for a record eleven years and eight months. After knocking out Jersey Joe Walcott in 1948, Louis retired undefeated. Unfortunately, Louis' financial troubles with the IRS forced a comeback. ("I took to having a good time with my winnings," he once said, "and I had plenty of people to help me.") In 1950, he lost a decision to Ezzard Charles in a fifteen-round fight; in 1951 he was knocked out by Rocky Marciano in the eighth round. ("I feel bad about beating Joe," said Marciano. "He was my idol.") Nevertheless, The Brown Bomber with his record of 68–3 (and fifty-four knockouts) remains one of the most popular and respected fighters in boxing history. Upon his death in 1981, Muhammad Ali said of Joe Louis: "I idolized him. I just give lip service to being the greatest. He was the greatest." Louis was also known as Alabam' Assassin, Black Beauty, The Brown Bludgeon, The Brown (Bronx) Behemoth, The Brown Embalmer, Dark Destroyer, Detroit's Dun Demon, The Licorice Lasher, Michigan Mauler, Ring Robot, Sable Sphinx, Sepia Sniper, The Tan Thunderbolt, Wildcat Warrior.

BUCK—Charles Williams [1960–   ] Basketball. As a boy, Williams had the nickname Hucklebuck. In high school this was shortened to Buck. This 1981–1982 NBA Rookie of the Year has been a stalwart rebounder in the NBA for years. In 1992, he was a steady presence for the Portland Trailblazers when they finished second to the Chicago Bulls in the NBA finals.

BUCKEYE BULLET—Jesse Owens [1913–1980] Track and field. H/F Jesse Owens, the track athlete from Cleveland and Ohio State, won four gold medals at the 1936 Olympic Games: 100 meters, 200 meters (20.7), long jump (26' 5⅜"), and 440-meter relay. (This performance outshone Paavo "The Flying Finn" Nurmi's three gold medals in the 1924 Olympics.) About the Olympic 100-meters race, Owens once said: "It was a million thrills packed into one. Ralph Metcalfe of Marquette University still was ahead of me at seventy meters, and one hundred twenty thousand people were roaring. Between seventy and ninety meters, Ralph and I were streaking neck-and-neck. Then I was in front at the finish." Owens was also called The Brown Bombshell and The Black Antelope.

BUCKY—Russell Earl Dent [1951–   ] Baseball. Dent's grandmother gave him this nickname which means "small Indian boy." Boston Red Sox fans probably wish he had played for the Indians instead of the Yankees in 1978, for when the Red Sox and the Yankees ended the season in a tie for first place, the pennant was decided by a one game playoff at Fenway Park. Shortstop Dent hit a home run to lead the Yankees to victory and broke the hearts of every Red Sox fan. He went on to become the MVP in the World Series.

BUFF— Aldo T. Donelli [1907–1994] Football. Donelli attained a rare distinction in 1941, when he became the only person ever to coach both a college football team (Duquesne) and a professional football team (Pittsburgh Steelers) in the same season.

BULLDOG—Clyde Turner [1919–] Football. H/F After graduation from high school in Sweetwater, Texas, Turner worked a year as a cattle trader. He not only dressed like a cowboy, he could also bulldog steers. After earning enough money in a year to enter Hardin-Simmons in Abilene, Turner tried out for center. Although he could play any position except quarterback, Turner had found the position that would later make him Mr. Center in a thirteen-year career with the Chicago Bears. One of his specialties was intercepting passes. (Players played both ways in those days.) His most memorable interception came in 1947 when he ran back a Sammy Baugh pass for a ninety-six-yard touchdown. He was also called The Dog and The Kid from Sweetwater.

BULLET BILL—William McGarvey Dudley [1921–] Football. H/F Although some colleges considered the 5' 10", 152-pound halfback too small for football, Dudley eventually played for the University of Virginia. In 1941, he was elected the youngest U.S. college team captain. That year Dudley led the nation in scoring with 134 points (eighteen touchdowns, twenty-three conversions, and one field goal). From scrimmage he was as fast as a bullet. When he passed the football he was fast and accurate. In 1946, Bullet Bill, playing for the Pittsburgh Steelers, won the Joe F. Carr MVP trophy. In his pro career (he played for the Steelers, the Lions, and the Redskins) he finished with 3,057 yards gained rushing for a 4.0 yard per carry, and he caught 123 passes for 1,383 yards (11.2 yard average). He also tossed six touchdown passes, completing eighty-one of 222 passes for 985 yards.

BULLET BOB—Bob Hayes [1942–] Football, track and field. In the 1964 summer Olympic Games at Tokyo, Bob Hayes was billed as The World's Fastest Human Being. He certainly lived up to his reputation, bringing home two gold medals for the U.S. Winning the 100 yard dash in ten seconds flat, he set a new world's record for that distance. After the Olympics, Bullet Bob was signed to play professional football with the Dallas Cowboys. He played ten seasons for them and was one of the outstanding runners in the game. He was selected All-Pro in 1966. See THE FULLBACK.

BULLET JOE—Joe Rogan [1889–1967] Baseball [Negro Leagues]. H/F Satchel Paige said of Bullet Joe Rogan: "Rogan was one of the world's greatest pitchers." He was simply a great all-round player. Not only did he compile a .341 lifetime batting average in the black leagues, but as pitcher he won 109 games and lost 43. He was inducted into baseball's Hall of Fame in 1998.

BULLET JOE—Joe Simpson [1893–1973] Hockey. H/F Simpson's nickname came from his speed on the ice as well as wounds received during World War I. Once called "the greatest living hockey player," this defenseman helped the Edmunton Eskimos win the Western Canada Hockey

League championship twice. He also played for the New York Americans in the NHL from 1925-1931, then managed them from 1932-35 before moving on to New Haven and Minneapolis. Simpson was also Blue Streak from Saskatoon.

BUN—Fred Cook [1903–   ] Hockey. Cook's nickname Bun or Bunny stemmed from his being as fast as a rabbit. Cook is also credited as being one of the first to use the slap shot and the drop pass. Cook and his brother Bill played on a line with Newsy Lalone for the Saskatoon Crescents in the 1924–1925 season. Later he was on the Cook-Boucher-Cook line for the New York Rangers.

BUS [THE]—Jerome Bettis [active 1990s] Football. This running back for the Pittsburgh Steelers earned his nickname at Notre Dame because of the way he was able to maneuver around tackles. In 1996, for instance, he scored eleven touchdowns and rushed for 1,431 yards.

BUS—Emil Mosbacher, Jr. [1922–   ] Yachting. Before "Bus" Mosbascher became Chief of Protocol in the State Department, he proved himself to be an excellent yachtsman. The New York Yacht Club's 1962 and 1967 entries in the American Cup races were under Bus' command. In 1962, he skippered the *Weatherly* and defeated the Australian entry *Gretel.* In 1967 his yacht was the *Intrepid.*

BUSHER—Harvey Jackson [1911–1966] Hockey. H/F Jackson was called "a fresh busher" (bush leaguer) when as a rookie he would not carry something for the Maple Leafs' trainer. Even when Jackson went on to become one of the top scorers in the NHL as a member of the famed KID LINE for Toronto (not to mention becoming a member of the Hall of Fame), he was still known as Busher.

BUZZ—Russell Arlett [1899–1964] Baseball. In 1965, the Society of American Baseball Researchers named him the "Greatest Minor Leaguer of All Time." In seventeen years of minor league play, he had a lifetime average of .341 and drove in 100 or more runs for eight straight seasons, and yet, in spite of his accomplishments, he played only one year in the major leagues. In 1931, in 121 games with the Philadelphia Phillies, he hit .313.

BYE-BYE—Steve Balboni [1957–   ] Baseball. This first baseman's nickname was for the many baseballs he hit over the fence. His best year was with Kansas City in 1985 when he socked thirty-six home runs. Unfortunately, he also struck out a league-leading 166 times. Balboni was also called Bones.

CALIFORNIA COMET [THE]—John Donald Budge [1915–   ] Tennis. H/F Don Budge was not the only tennis star to bear the sobriquet of The California Comet, but he was the most appropriate to be given that title. He was the first amateur tennis player to win the Grand Slam—that is, to win in a single calendar year the four major singles championships of the United States, Great Britain, France, and Australia. In 1937, The California Comet (he was born in Oakland, California)

became the first tennis player to be awarded the James E. Sullivan Trophy as the outstanding U.S. amateur athlete of the year.

CAMILLE THE EEL—Camille Henry [1933–1997] Hockey. Henry earned his nickname The Eel because of all the slippery moves he performed as a member of the New York Rangers, the Chicago Blackhawks, and the St. Louis Blues. He played in 727 games over fourteen seasons for the National Hockey League, and scored 279 goals, and had 249 assists. In all that time he amassed only eighty-eight penalty minutes. After the 1953–1954 season Camille the Eel was awarded the Calder Memorial Trophy as the N.H.L.'s Rookie of the Year. He was also called Cammy.

CANDY—William Cummings [1848–1924] Baseball. H/F To watch this pitcher, who wore a leather glove on his pitching hand to improve his grip, throw his newfangled curve ball that he began experimenting with in 1964 was a treat. Once the pleasure of watching this sweet pitcher was increased when he hurled two complete games on the same day. Cummings was also called The Father of the Curveball.

CANNONBALL—Erwin George Baker [1881–1960] Motorcycle racing. E. G. Baker cannonballed his motorcycle across the United States over 100 times to set and reset record after record. In 1941 at the age of sixty, he completed his last transcontinental run in six days, six hours, and twenty-five minutes.

CANNONBALL—Eddie Martin [1903–   ] Boxing. Eddie Martin (he Americanized his name from Edwardo Vittorio Martin) was given the nickname Cannonball because of his strong KO punch. Winning his crown when he outpointed Abe Goldstein in New York City, Cannonball Eddie was the World Bantamweight champion from 1924 to 1925. Martin later gained weight and lost a fight with Ted Morgan for the junior-lightweight title. Cannonball Eddie retired in 1932, after fighting ninety bouts (seventy-two wins, eleven losses, three draws, and four no-decisions).

CANNONBALL [THE]—Dick Redding [1891–1940] Baseball [Negro Leagues]. "Dick Redding was like Walter Johnson, nothing but speed," according to Frank Forbes, a player on the Lincoln Giants. "That's the reason they called him Cannonball. He just blew that ball by you. I've seen Redding knock a bat out of a man's hand." Redding had a total of twelve no-hitters in the Negro Leagues and once struck out Babe Ruth three times on nine pitches.

CAP—Adrian Anson [1852–1922] Baseball. H/F Anson was called Cap (short for Captain) after becoming the player-manager of the Chicago White Stockings in 1879, a post he held for twenty years. Anson led the National League in batting in 1881 and 1888 with .399 and .344 averages. The first baseman's batting average over twenty-two years was .334. Anson was also called The Marshalltown Infant (for his youth when starting out) and Pop (for his age toward the end of his career when he was a player-manager).

CAR PARK GOLFER [THE]—Severiano Ballestros [1957–   ] Golf. When this Spanish golfer (he was born in Pedrana, Spain) won the 1979 British Open, his drives were a bit erratic, to say the least. His wild booming drives (which looked as if they were headed for the parking lot) gave rise to the humorous sobriquet The Car Park Golfer. In fact, Jack Nicklaus quipped, "Severiano hits his first and then sees whether he can play his second." Ballestros went on to win the U.S Masters in 1981. He was also called The Matador.

CASEY—Charles Dillon Stengel [1890–1975] Baseball. H/F Stengel's nickname Casey originated because he was from Kansas City (K.C.), Missouri. This fourteen-year veteran outfielder, who hit the first homer in Yankee Stadium (an inside-the-park homerun in 1923) and batted .393 in three World Series, later became famous as the manager of the Yankees and Mets. (He managed the BRONX BOMBERS to ten first place finishes and the hapless Mets—"Can't anybody here play this game"—to four tenth place finishes.) One of the most quotable characters who ever donned a uniform, Casey once said of the Yankees: "It isn't sex that wrecks these guys. It's staying up all night looking for it." Another time Casey revealed that "the secret of managing is to keep the guys who hate you away from the guys who are undecided." He was also called The Old Professor.

CASH AND CARRY—Charles C. Pyle [1882–1939] Sports Promoter. Pyle promoted bike races, dance contests, tennis exhibitions—whatever came his way—but the money had to be up front. A *Chicago Tribune* sportswriter converted the Charles C. to Cash and Carry. One of his biggest coups was getting Red Grange $3,000 per game to play for the Chicago Bears. Pyle and Grange helped to put football on the map. Pyle also arranged a motion picture contract for Grange, THE GALLOPING GHOST, to appear in two silent films produced by Joseph Kennedy—*One Minute to Play* and *The [Auto] Racing Romeo.* Because of Pyle's entrepreneurial skills, Grange also endorsed ginger ale, dolls, shoes, and caps. For a time, Charles Pyle also owned half interest in the New York Yankees of the American Football League.

CAT [THE]—Harry Breechen [1914–   ] Baseball. Breechen came off the mound to pounce on the ball like a cat. The Cat was 133–92 from 1940 to 1953 and 4–1 in World Series play. He played for the Cards his whole career except for the last year when he went over to the Browns.

CAT [THE]—Emile Francis [1926–   ] Hockey. H/F Francis received his nickname because he tended goals with catlike quickness and grace. In a game in 1948, he used a glove that looked like a first baseman's and was good for trapping the puck. Referee King Clancy said it was all right, and by year's end it had become standard equipment for NHL goalies. As a coach for New York, Emile Francis won more games than any other coach in Ranger history.

CATFISH—Jim Hunter [1946–   ] Baseball. H/F When Jim Hunter ran away from home as a child, he returned with two catfish. That's one version. Another version is told by Catfish himself in his autobiography *Catfish: My Life in Baseball* (co-written with Armen Keteyian in 1988). In that book, Catfish says that Charles O. Finley, the Oakland A's owner, gave it to him and made up the story about catching catfish as a young boy. Finley began using the nickname to jazz up Hunter's name. His pitching game, however, didn't need any jazzing up. He was also called Cat and The Cat.

CATHERINE THE GREAT—Catherine Lacoste [1945—   ] Golf. Lacoste received her nickname from one who knew about greatness, JoAnne Gunderson Carner. (Carner had once been called The Great Gundy.) In the late 1960s, Catherine the Great (the daughter of Rene "The Crocodile" Lacoste) won the U.S. Women's Amateur, the British Amateur, the Western Amateur and the U.S. Women's Open.

CAVE MAN—Thomas Bryan Barlow [1896–1983] Basketball. H/F Conjuring up images of brute force and dumb, muscle-bound, unshaven masculinity, Cave Man is a nickname that seems more fitting to a wrestler than to a professional basketball player. But the 6' 1", 200-pound Barlow was a tough, physical player who engaged in numerous fights. After leading the Philadelphia Warriors to the 1926 championship series with the Boston Celtics, the marquee at Boston Garden billed the contest as "Tommy (Cave Man) Barlow of Philadelphia vs. the Celtics." All in all, not a complimentary nickname. From 1926 to 1932, Cave Man Barlow was the highest paid professional basketball player. And how much did he receive? Only forty-five dollars a game.

CHAIRMAN OF THE BOARD [THE]—Whitey Ford [1928—   ] Baseball. H/F Whitey (Edward Charles) Ford pitched the big games for the New York Yankees. He was a Harry Truman ("the buck stops here") type. During his sixteen-year career, his record was 236–106. He was also called SLICK.

CHAIRMAN OF THE BOARDS [THE]—Eamonn Coghlan [1952—   ] Track and field. Eamonn Coghlan received this nickname for his string of seven consecutive Wanamaker Mile wins at the Millrose Games, run on the small eleven laps-to-the-mile boards of the indoor track of Madison Square Garden. In 1983, Coghlan set an indoor mile record of 3 minutes 49.78 seconds at the Meadowlands Arena in New Jersey. Ten years later, Coghlan was aiming at becoming the first masters runner (over forty) to break the four-minute barrier in the mile.

CHAMP [THE]—Guy Chamberlain [1894–1967] Football. H/F To know why Chamberlain was nicknamed the Champ one need only look at his career. During his two years at the University of Nebraska, the team won every game. Playing end in the pros for Chicago, Canton, and Cleveland, Chamberlain helped his team win the championship five out of six years. As Coach Earl RED Blaik said at Chamberlain's induction into the Hall of Fame: "Chamberlain never learned how to lose."

CHAMPION OF CHAMPIONS—Bob Mathias [1930—   ] Track and field. H/F At seventeen and the youngest member of the Olympic team, Bob Mathias won the gold medal in the decathlon at the 1948 Olympic Games in London, even though he was inexperienced in four of the events. Four years later in Helsinki, Mathias became the first person ever to repeat the feat, this time setting an Olympic and world record of 7,887 points. Mathias later served four terms in the House of Representatives.

CHAPO—Edwin Rosario [1963-1997] Boxing. Chapo was a three-time world champion in the Lightweight division. In 1983, he defeated Jose Luis Ramirez in a twelve-round decision to win his first lightweight championship for the World Boxing Council. Rosario later lost his championship in a controversial bout with Hector Comacho. In 1986, he won the World Boxing Association lightweight title in Miami Beach, Florida, when he knocked out Livingstone Bramble. He received his nickname Chapo when he was growing up in Ingenio, a barrio of Toa Baja. Chapo is short for *chappito,* meaning "little man."

CHARGER [THE]—Arnold Palmer [1929–   ] Golf. H/F Palmer was known for his purposeful manner and charging around the golf course in his patented come-from-behind victories. In the 1960 Masters, for example, Palmer birdied the last two holes, including a twenty-five-foot putt on the seventeenth, to defeat Ken Venturi by one stroke. That same year he was the PGA Player of the Year, an honor he also received in 1962. In 1968, The Charger became the first golfer to win over $1 million. During a career that has shown him to be as popular as he is prolific, Palmer has recorded victories in four Masters, two British Opens, and one U.S. Open.

THE CHARGER—Arnold Palmer (b. September 10, 1929) Golf. The Charger, in 1968, became the first golfer to win more than $1,000,000 in his career.

CHARLIE HUSTLE—Pete Rose [1941–   ] Baseball. In the spring of 1963, a brash young kid was trying out for the Cincinnati Reds. Watching him run down to first base after drawing a walk, the Yankee's Mickey Mantle dubbed him "Charlie Hustle." Growing up, Pete Rose had been called "Pee-Wee" for his size and "Gimp" for his manner of running; but Charlie Hustle was the nickname that stuck. Although Pete Rose had an illustrious career, he will most likely be remembered for two things. The first was that he broke Ty Cobb's record of 4,191 career hits. The second was that because of his out-of-control betting habits Pete Rose was banned from baseball.

CHEESY—Gerry Cheevers [1941–   ] Hockey. H/F "I became a goalie," said Cheevers, "because I wasn't good enough to be anything else." That may have been true in the beginning, but when he turned pro he was in demand by many teams. "For a while there, I had to look down at my uniform to see what team I was playing for that night. I never knew where I was. After a while, all the towns and arenas looked the same. The human yo-yo was at home anywhere." And when the World Hockey Association began, Cheevers went from the established Boston Bruins (winners of the Stanley Cup in 1970 and 1972) to the fledgling Cleveland Crusaders for a long-term contract at $200,000 a year—three times his previous salary.

CHI CHI—Juan Rodriguez [1935–   ] Golf. Rodriguez was called Chi Chi because his favorite baseball player back in Puerto Rico had sported that nickname. At seventeen Rodriguez was second in the Puerto Rican Open. On the tour, he won eight tournaments and was a favorite with the gallery for covering the hole with his hat after sinking birdies and for his jokes. "I asked my caddie for a sand wedge," he once said, "and ten minutes later he came back with a ham on rye." One of the things he is most proud of is the Chi Chi Rodriguez Youth Foundation. Each year 600 kids from low- income families are introduced to the game of golf.

CHICOUTIMI CUCUMBER—Georges Vezina [1887–1926] Hockey. H/F Montreal goalie Georges Vezina, born in Chicoutimi, Quebec, Canada, played as "cool as a cucumber." He also played in every game—328 in all—from December 31, 1910 to November 28, 1925. "Cripes, Georges probably figured that playing goal in an NHL game was the quietest spot in his life," said King Clancy. "After all, he was the father of twenty-two children." The Vezina Trophy given each year to the outstanding goaltender is named for Georges Vezina.

CHIEF—George Edward Armstrong [1930–   ] Hockey. H/F Armstrong had a Cree (American Indian) mother and a Scottish father. For twenty years he played for the Toronto Maple Leafs and was their captain for thirteen. Armstrong scored 296 goals during the regular season and 20 goals in 45 playoff games. The Leafs won four Stanley Cups during his playing days.

CHIEF—Louis Socalexis [1871–1913] Baseball. Socalexis was called Chief because he was a member of the Penobscots. When he started playing outfield for the Cleveland Spiders of the National League in 1897, he was sensational. By the middle of the summer, he had sixteen stolen bases, thirty-nine RBIs, forty runs scored, and a batting average of .328. But then his career went downhill due to injuries and alcohol. His last year in baseball was 1899. In 1915, a contest was held by a Cleveland newspaper to name the new ball club in the American League. The winning entry was in honor of Socalexis.

CHIEF—Jay Strongbow [active 1970s—1980s] Wrestling. Born in Pawhuska, Oklahoma, Chief Strongbow dressed in authentic Indian regalia and performed a thrilling war dance before each of his bouts. In 1972, he held the World Wrestling Federation tag-team championship (with his partner Sonny King), and he won that title again in 1977, with Chief Billy White Wolf.

CHIEF—Charles L. Zimmer [1860—1949] Baseball. Zimmer got his nickname in 1886 when he was a playing manager at Poughkeepsie. He later told reporters, "Since we were fleet of foot, we were called the Indians. As I was the head man of the Indians someone began to call me 'Chief.' It stuck." This catcher for Cleveland in 1888 was baseball's original iron man. He caught 125 consecutive complete games in 1890 to establish a new record for catchers. In 1890, Zimmer was also elected President of the Player's Protective Organization.

CHINA WALL [THE]—Johnny Bower [1924—   ] Hockey. H/F Goalie Bower guarded the net with such great success that he was compared to one of the world's great walls. In 1967, at the age of forty-two (he had begun his second career in the NHL when he was thirty-three), Bower alternated in goal with Terry Sawchuck to help defeat first the Chicago Black Hawks and then the Montreal Canadiens to win the Stanley Cup. Johnny Bower continued in goal until he was forty-five. Bower was also aptly called Ageless and The Great Wall of China.

CHOO CHOO—Irene May Hickson [active 1943—1951] Baseball [All-American Girls Baseball League]. Hickson got her nickname because she was from Chattanooga, Tennessee, and the *Chattanooga Choo Choo* was a popular song of the time. An All-Star in 1943, Hickson was the league's oldest player.

CHUCK—Kevin Connors [1921—1992] Basketball, baseball. Chuck Connors was a center on the Boston Celtics in 1946 and a pinch hitter for the Chicago Cubs in 1951 before turning to acting. A little known fact is that Connors was the first player ever to shatter a glass backboard. It happened on November 5, 1946, before the very first NBA game in Boston. Trying a set shot before the game between the Celtics and the Chicago Stags, the glass shattered because it had not been properly installed. One of Chuck Connor's most memorable acting roles was in *The Rifleman,* a 1958-63 western television series.

CINDERELLA MAN [THE]—James J. Braddock [1905—1974] Boxing. H/F This former world heavyweight champion received his nickname because his life was a true rags-to-riches (or Cinderella) tale. The nickname was given to him by writer Damon Runyon. Braddock worked his way up from being a dockworker to becoming the heavyweight champion of the world from 1935—1937. He won the world title in June of 1935, by outpointing Max Baer, even though, the year before, Braddock was so poor that he had been forced to apply for public relief because he was unemployed. When he defeated Max Baer, the odds were 10—1 against his winning the title, and it was after that bout that Braddock received his nickname. On June 1937, Braddock lost his heavyweight crown to Joe Louis, when Louis knocked him out in the eighth round. During his twelve years of boxing, The Cinderella Man fought eighty-four bouts. He lost seventeen of them.

CLOWN PRINCE OF BASEBALL [THE]—Max Patkin [1920–   ] Baseball. Patkin got his start during World War II when many major leaguers were playing baseball in the Hawaiian Army-Navy League. One night when Patkin was pitching, Joe DiMaggio hit a towering home run. Immediately, Patkin turned his cap sideways and copied JOLTIN' JOE's trot around the bases. In 1946, Bill Veeck hired Max Patkin to be the first-base coach for Cleveland. But Patkin had the clown in him to such an extent that by 1947 he began his career of entertaining crowds at minor-league baseball stadiums. "Clowns are not the happiest people in the world," confides a melancholic Patkin. "They get into the business because they crave attention. They want people to like them. They want to be loved." Patkin wants to keep going as long as possible. "When I die, I want some of my ashes spread on home plate and the rest put in the rosin bag—so I can stay in baseball forever."

CLOWN PRINCE OF BASKETBALL [THE]—Meadow George Lemon [1933–   ] Basketball. MEADOWLARK (he was as cheerful as a lark in the meadow) Lemon was long the player-comedian center with the Harlem Globetrotters. He took over many of Goose Tatum's stunts, such as shooting a free throw with a ball that had a strong rubber cord attached to it. As the basketball flew back into his hands, the other players jumped for a non-existent rebound.

CLOWN PRINCE OF BASKETBALL [THE]—Reece Tatum [1921–1967] Basketball. In the beginning, Tatum was a baseball player, first a left fielder for DOUBLE DUTY Radcliffe's team and then a first baseman for the Indianapolis Clowns. Stretching off first base, stomping on the bag, Tatum was funny; however, his huge hands and eighty-four-inch arm span made basketball an even better opportunity for his special brand of comedy. Playing center for the Harlem Globetrotters, Tatum stuffed the ball under his shirt to fake out the opposition, wheeled left and right to passing teammates before shooting it himself, used an elastic on a ball to snap it back to him when shooting a free throw, and squawked and carried on to the delight of fans around the world. In 1956, Tatum started his own group called the Harlem Road Kings. He was also called GOOSE.

CLYDE—Walt Frazier [1945–   ] Basketball. H/F Frazier seemed similar to the Warren Beatty character in *Bonnie and Clyde,* a popular 1967 movie. Fazier's flashy clothes and car, and stylish and cool ways seemed to be basketball's version of Clyde Barrows. One day on a road trip Frazier bought a Borsalino hat. When he walked into the dressing room, trainer Danny Whelan called him Clyde. The name stuck. Walt Frazier not only set the mark in fashion but also in Knick career statistics. He had the most total games (759) and the most minutes (28,995). He made the most field goals (5,736) and had the most attempts (11,669). He made the most free throws (3,145) and had the most attempts (4,017). Clyde also led in total points with 14,617.

COLOSSUS OF RHODES [THE]—James Lamar Rhodes [1927–   ] Baseball. In appreciation of Rhodes's two pinch-hit home runs and seven RBIs in the 1954 World Series, he was nicknamed after one of the Seven Wonders of the World, the colossal bronze statue of the sun god Helios guarding the harbor on the Island of Rhodes. As with many another Rhodes, he was also called Dusty.

COMMERCE COMET—Mickey Mantle [1931–1995] Baseball. H/F Mantle was a speedy ballplayer who went from high school in Commerce, Oklahoma, to Yankee Stadium, where he was to carry on in the great tradition of center fielders, replacing the YANKEE CLIPPER. Mantle was the all-time leader among switch hitters with fifty-four homers in one season (1961) and 536 home runs during his eighteen-year career. "I hated to look at the opposing pitcher when I hit a home run because I knew how he felt," said Mantle. "He didn't tip his hat and jump around when he struck me out, so I didn't do it when I hit one out." Mantle was also called The Mick.

CONDOR [THE]—Matt Hoffman [active 1990s] Freestyle cyclist. The Condor received his nickname at age fifteen because of the way he appears to soar like a bird when doing high-flying stunts upon his bicycle. He was the World Champion Freestyle Cyclist from 1987 to 1990. Hoffman has said of his nickname, "At first I thought it was a cool nickname. Then I saw the big, ugly bird. I thought, 'Oh, man, my buddies are dissin' me.'"

COOL PAPA—James Bell [1903–1991] Baseball [Negro Leagues]. H/F Bell, who began his career as a pitcher and outfielder with the St. Louis Stars, received his nickname during his early days because he didn't get nervous before big games. Bell was also known as THE BLACK TY COBB because of his speed. He once scored all the way from first on a sacrifice bunt; at the age of forty-two he was the leader in stolen bases in the Negro Leagues. "He was so fast," once remarked a bemused SATCHEL Paige, "he could turn out the light and be in bed before the room got dark."

COON—Harry Rosen [1908–   ] Softball. It is estimated that Rosen won 3,000 softball games as a pitcher. He pitched at least 300 no-hitters. One afternoon he pitched a double-header and struck out thirty-seven batters, yet still lost both games 1–0 because of fielding errors. It was a feat that qualified him for a place in Ripley's *Believe It or Not.*

COOZ—Bob Cousy [1928–   ] Basketball. H/F After being an All-American at Holy Cross College, the Cooz (his nickname oozed with the sound of his last name) knocked around with a couple of teams before he made it to the Celtics—And then it was only by chance. He had been playing for a team that folded and the players were picked by the other NBA teams. "We got stuck with the greatest player in the league when we drew his name out of a hat," said Celtics' coach Red Auerbach. What Cousy meant to the Celtics as a clutch player and as a player down the stretch is best exemplified in a 1953 semifinal playoff game with the Syracuse Nats for the Eastern Division. Cousy scored fifty points, seventeen of the Celtics' last twenty-one points in their four overtime victory. Led by the ball handling of Bob Cousy and the rebounding of Bill Russell, the Celtics won NBA championships from 1959 to 1963. See THE HOUDINI OF THE HARDWOOD.

CORDUROY KILLER—Bobby Fischer [1943–   ] Chess. Fischer, who favored corduroy pants, beat Boris Spassky for the world championship in chess in 1972. Refusing to play again,

Fischer was stripped of his title in 1975. He didn't play an international chess match again until 1992, when he once again defeated Spassky. Fischer was also called Boy Robot and Sweatshirt Kid.

CORKSCREW KID [THE]—Charles McCoy [1873–1940] Boxing. Some credit McCoy with originating the expression "The Real McCoy" when he once knocked out a man who was impersonating him. Actually, McCoy's real name was Norman Selby. He was also a movie actor who appeared in several boxing movies. He was also called Kid McCoy.

CORNS—Hugh Bradley [1885–1949] Baseball. Corns Bradley (he received his nickname for the painful corns on his toes) played first base for the Boston Red Sox (1910–1912) and for Pittsburgh (1914–1915) in the old Federal League, compiling a lifetime .261 average. He frequently had to soak his feet before being able to put on his spikes to play the game. In 913 at-bats, he slugged all of two home runs.

COUNT [THE]—John Montefusco [1950–   ] Baseball. The Count of Montefusco (his nickname was an allusion to a character in Alexander Dumas' *The Count of Monte Cristo*) had a terrific year in 1975. In his first at-bat for the Giants Montefusco hit a home run; later, he predicted and delivered a shutout over the Dodgers. By year's end his 15-9 record won him Rookie of the Year.

CRAB [THE]— Johnny Evers [1881–1942] Baseball. H/F He was a crotchety, finicky, crabby man to play with. When he covered second base his sideways motion was crablike. Playing for the Chicago Cubs from 1902 to 1913, he was the keystone to one of baseball's greatest double-play combinations—Tinkers to Evers to Chance. It was The Crab, in a crucial game with the Giants in 1908, who noticed that Fred Merkle after making what should have been the game-winning hit did not touch second. (If it hadn't been for his sharp eyesight, Fred Merkle might well have escaped the ignominy of being called BONEHEAD.) The Cubs in the replay of the game went on to defeat the Giants and win the pennant. Evers co-authored the book, *Touching Second*. He was also called The Trojan (because of his endurance) and THE FIGHTING IRISHMAN FROM TROY.

CRAZY—Frederick Schmidt [1868–1940] Baseball. In their book, *Low and Inside,* Ira L. Smith and H. Allen Smith write, "Crazy Schmidt was a pitcher with a poor memory. Whenever he was at work on the mound he always had a little notebook in his hip pocket. As each batter came to the plate, Schmidt got out the book, riffled through it, and checked his private record of the man's potential weakness. One day in 1894, Cap Anson, four time batting champion of the National League, stepped to the plate and faced Crazy Schmidt. The pitcher got out his notebook and studied it for a few moments. Then in a loud voice he read from it: 'Base on Balls.' Anson walked."

CRAZYLEGS—Elroy Hirsch [1923–   ] Football. H/F Elroy Hirsch suffered a near career-ending skull fracture in 1948 while playing for the Chicago Rockets. Hirsch surprised doctors by returning to the game—this time as an end for the Los Angeles Rams—even though his legs seemed to be crazily out of control when he ran. As Rams quarterback Norm van Brocklin said: "You've heard about the fellow who zigged when he should have zagged. Well, Roy also has a 'zog' and a couple of varieties of 'zug.'" (A movie called *Crazy Legs: All American* was made of this near tragedy.) Hirsch's best season was 1950–1951, the year the Rams won the championship. Crazylegs caught 66 passes for 1,495 yards and 17 touchdowns.

CRIME DOG—Fred McGriff (1963–) Baseball. Crime Dog at first seems like a strange nickname to hang upon San Diego Padre star Fred McGriff, but the sobriquet is a playful reminder of the comic strip character McGruff. A crime-fighting dog in a trench coat, McGruff has appeared widely in numerous advertisements. McGriff came to the Padres in a major trade involving Tony Fernandez, Joe Carter, and Roberto Alomar. While playing for the Toronto Blue Jays in 1989, McGriff led the American League in home runs.

CROAT COMET (THE)—Fritzie Zivic (1913–1984) Boxing. Zivic hailed from Pittsburgh and was one of five boxing brothers. He fought a total of 232 bouts, winning 159, losing sixty-four, drawing nine. Although he has a reputation for being a "dirty" fighter—he sometimes threw low punches and frequently ground the laces of his gloves into his opponent's cuts—he was a very popular boxer with the fans. The Croat Comet held the Welterweight Championship of the World from 1940–1941. After his retirement, he enjoyed renewed popularity as an after-dinner speaker.

CURLY—Earl Lambeau (1898–1965) Football. H/F Lambeau got his nickname for his wavy hair, and the Green Bay Packers got its start because of him. In 1919, Curly asked his employer at the Indian Packing Company to help him start a football team. Frank Peck contributed $500 and the rest, as they say, is history. Lambeau (sometimes called the Bellicose Belgian by sportswriters) spent thirty-one years as both a player and a coach at Green Bay. The first years were rough; in 1919, each player received only $16.75 from contributions from the crowd. But after the Green Bay Football Corporation was founded in 1923, the team's fortunes improved. During Curly Lambeau's time at Green Bay, the Packers won six National League championships and seven divisional championships with an overall record of 236 wins, 111 losses, and 23 ties.

CY—Denton True Young (1867–1955) Baseball. H/F Young's nickname came about because his pitches once damaged a cyclone fence, as well as for the more obvious reason that his pitches seemed to have the velocity of a cyclone. In his first complete season, Young notched twenty-seven wins. The next year, 1892, he gained thirty-six victories. Indeed, for fourteen straight seasons, Young won twenty or more games, capping it off with the first perfect game in 1904. During the course of his twenty-two years, Young won 511 games—tops in the history of the majors. The Cy Young Award, presented annually to the outstanding pitcher in the American and the National leagues, is named in his honor.

CZAR OF BASEBALL—Kenesaw Mountain Landis (1866–1944) Baseball. H/F Named for a Civil War battle in Georgia (Landis' father was wounded in that battle), this man had a real name more colorful than most people's nicknames. Taking over the office of the Commissioner of Baseball after the Black Sox scandal of 1920, Landis set about to make baseball respectable again. He wielded absolute power—hence his sobriquet. When the Baseball Hall of Fame opened in Cooperstown, New York, on June 12, 1939, it was Landis who delivered the dedicatory address.

DAFFY— Paul Dean (1913–1981) Baseball. As DIZZY Dean's brother, Paul went along for the zany ride and was nicknamed Daffy. The brothers were notorious for their practical jokes. One day at the team's hotel, the two brothers set up ladders and hauled out buckets of paint and brushes as if to redecorate the lobby. They pushed guests out of the way and caused general havoc until their prank was discovered. Paul Dean's stellar years were in 1934 and 1935 when he was 19–11 and 19–12. In 1934, he also threw a no-hitter for the Cards against the Dodgers and he was 2–0 in the World Series. See GASHOUSE GANG.

DIZZY AND DAFFY DEAN—Jay Hanna Dean (1911-1974) Baseball (left) and Paul Dean (1913-1981) Baseball (right). Perhaps the most colorful brothers ever to pitch together in the big leagues.

DARLING—Carling Bassett (1968–   ) Tennis. Darling is a rhyming nickname for this cute blonde from Canada. "How would *you* like to be fifteen, pretty, have made a movie, and be a tennis champion?" her wealthy father once asked. In 1983, she almost beat Chris Evert in the finals of the WTA Championships. Without winning a major tournament, Darling Carling made lots of money in endorsements ($500,000 from 1984 to 1986), married tennis player Robert Seguso, and disappeared from the tennis tour.

DAUNTLESS DOAK—Ewell Doak Walker (1927–   ) Football. H/F As a college football player, Walker starred for Southern Methodist University, where "Dauntless Doak" (or "Dynamic Doak" as he was sometimes called) rushed for slightly over 1,950 yards, averaging 4.2 yards per carry. He passed for 1,638 yards, and returned 50 punts for 750 yards. He also punted 80 times for an average of 39.5 yards per kick. In all, Walker was the all-round player, who could pass, run, block, punt, kick field goals and extra points, as well as call signals and play superb defense. He won the Maxwell Award in 1947, and the Heisman Trophy in 1948. After SMU, Walker joined the Detroit Lions and played for them for five seasons. He led the NFL in scoring in 1950. He helped the Lions win two NFL titles (1952, 1953), and by the time he retired, at age twenty-eight, he had gained 1,520 yards rushing (with twelve touchdowns), and had passed for 2,539 yards (twenty-one touchdowns). Walker was also called The Doaker, All-American Mustang, and Little Man in Pro Football.

DAZZY—Clarence Vance (1891–1961) Baseball. H/F Vance picked up the expression "daisy" from a neighbor back in Hastings, Nebraska, who used it for everything he thought was awfully good. The pronunciation was "dazzy." Vance, a pitcher for the Brooklyn Dodgers most of his career, had a dazzling fast ball. In 1924, he was 28–6, with 262 strikeouts and a 2.16 ERA. For seven straight years he was the strikeout leader in the National League. Although Vance didn't win his first major-league game until he was thirty-one, he won twenty-two games at the age of thirty-seven. Vance was also called The Dazzler. See GASHOUSE GANG.

DEACON—David Jones (1938–   ) Football. H/F Jones got his nickname for once leading his teammates at South Carolina State College in a prayer meeting. Later, he was a stalwart member of the defensive line of the Los Angeles Rams, known as the FEARSOME FOURSOME. A 6', 250-pound defensive left end, Deacon was quick for his size. Bart Starr once said he had thought Jones was one of his own backs because he got into the Packer backfield so quickly. In 1967 and 1968, Deacon Jones was named the outstanding defensive player in the NFL.

DEERFOOT—Louis Bennett (1830–1896) Running. A promoter of distance running named George Martin nicknamed Bennett after this member of the Seneca nation raced against a horse and won. After a successful running career in the United States (his twelve-mile time of 1:02:2.5 is still a professional record), Deerfoot went over to England in 1861 where for the next two years he won races at distances anywhere from four miles to twelve miles. His four-mile time was 20:15.5; his ten-mile time was 51:26 seconds. Bennett was also called Red Jacket.

DESTROYER (THE)—George Arthur Foster (1948–) Baseball. Nicknamed The Destroyer because of his ability to destroy a pitcher with his towering home runs, George Foster slugged 348 homers in his career. His most memorable season was probably 1977 when he became only the tenth player in major league history to hit fifty or more home runs in a season. That year The Destroyer hit fifty-two roundtrippers, knocked in 149 RBIs, and was named the National League's Most Valuable Player. In 1982, the outfielder signed a multi-million-dollar contract with the New York Mets, giving him a salary that made him the highest paid player in baseball at that time. Unfortunately, his years with the Mets when he averaged only twenty homers a year were a great disappointment to his team, his fans, and to himself. In 1986, he ended his playing days batting .216 for the Chicago White Sox. Foster finished his career with 1,925 hits, 1,239 RBIs, and a .274 average.

DIESEL—John Riggins (b. 1949–) Football.
He ran over and by and through opponents like a diesel engine.

DEVIL [THE]—Willie Wells [1909–1989] Baseball. H/F The best shortstop in Negro League history must have seemed like the devil himself to his opponents. Not only was he a splendid fielder for the St. Louis Stars and the Newark Eagles, but he was a great hitter as well. No one in the Negro Leagues pounded out more doubles, and in 1993, Wells led the NNL with a .403 batting average. He hit home runs as well—for example, in the 1929 season, Wells hit twenty-seven home runs in an eighty-eight-game season. Wells was part of the Eagles' so-called million dollar infield with Mule Suttles at first, Dick Seay at second, and Ray Dandridge at third. In 1946, Wells managed the Eagles to a pennant. On that team were such great players as Ernie Banks, Monte Irvin, and Larry Doby.

DIDDIE—Julie Vlasto [active 1920s] Tennis. In an exhibition at Cannes on February 16, 1926, Julie Vlasto teamed up with Suzanne Langlen to defeat Helen Wills and Helene Contostavlos. Vlasto was instrumental in their doubles win, because Langlen was exhausted from her earlier exhibition victory over Wills. This was the only day that Langlen and Wills, the two tennis greats of that era, were on the court together.

DIESEL—John Riggins [1949–   ] Football. H/F Fullback Riggins earned his nickname, because at 6' 2" and 240 pounds, he ran like a diesel engine. After breaking Gayle Sayers' rushing record at the University of Kansas, Riggins spent fourteen years as one of the premier running backs in the NFL with the Jets and the Redskins. Riggins rushed for 100 or more yards in thirty-five games; he gained over 1,000 yards five different seasons and scored 104 touchdowns (third behind Jimmy Brown and Walter Payton). Riggins also received the MVP in Super Bowl XVII as he ground out 166 yards and scored the winning touchdown in Washington's victory over Miami. He was also called Riggo.

DIPSY DOODLE DANDY FROM DELISLE—Max Bentley [1920–1984] Hockey. H/F Max Bentley was one of the best centers ever, a real dipsy doodle dandy who hailed from Delisle, Canada. Playing for Chicago in 1946 and 1947, he scored the most goals in the NHL. After being traded to Toronto, Bentley led the Maple Leafs to three straight Stanley Cup championships. Two years later, the Dipsy Doodle Dandy from Delisle helped Toronto win another Stanley Cup.

DIXIE KID [THE]—Aaron Brown [1883–1935] Boxing. This was not only a nickname (Brown was born in Fulton, Missouri), but also the principal name he fought under. In 1904, The Dixie Kid defeated Joe Walcott (when Walcott fouled out in the twentieth round) for the World Welterweight Championship. Defending his crown all over the world, Aaron Brown's career record was seventy-eight wins, eighteen losses, and six draws.

DIZZY—Jay Hanna Dean [1911–1974] Baseball. H/F Jay Hanna Dean (he also went by the name of Jerome Herman Dean) was born in Lucas, Arkansas, the son of Albert Dean, an itinerant sharecropper. Dean's mother died when he was very young. The greatest pitcher of his era, Dean pitched in the majors for the St. Louis Cardinals from 1930–1937 and for the Chicago Cubs from 1938–1948 (and one sad attempt at a belated comeback in 1947 with the St. Louis Browns when he appeared in only one game). Dizzy won 150 games, lost eighty-three, and finished with 1,115 strikeouts and an earned-run-average of 3.03. During that span, Dizzy turned in some amazing seasons. At the beginning of the 1934 season, for example, Dizzy predicted, "Me and Paul are going to win forty-five games." He was almost right. In 1934, Dizzy and Daffy won forty-nine games between them—of course, Dizzy won thirty of them, leading the league with most victories, while he lost only seven, compiling a league-leading won-lost percentage of .811. That year he also led his league with twenty-four complete games. On September 24, 1934, in the first game of a doubleheader, Dizzy pitched a one-hitter against the Dodgers. In the second game, however, his brother Paul pitched a no-hitter. When reporters talked to Dizzy after the game about the no-hitter, Ol' Diz told them, "If I had known what Paul was going to do, I would have pitched one too." It was because of his crazy clubhouse antics and his effervescent good humor that he received the nickname Dizzy. Brother Paul, naturally, became DAFFY. They were perhaps the most colorful brothers ever to pitch in the major leagues. Dean was also called Ol' Diz and The Great Man. See GASHOUSE GANG.

DOC—Roland Lombard (active 1960s–1970s) Sled dog racing. Lombard, a veterinarian from Massachusetts, won seven out of ten World Championship Sled Dog races from 1963 to 1973. (This is a seventy-five-mile race held at Anchorage each year.) Lombard said of his fascination with the sport: "I'm always looking for that perfect day when the weather is just right, the snow is fast, the dogs are running in unison, and you move through the woods effortlessly, with only the rhythmic panting and the jangling of harnesses to hear."

DOCTOR J—Julius Erving (1950–   ) Basketball. H/F "Doctor" referred to Julius Erving's skill at handling a basketball; "J" was for his first name. Erving could dunk the ball when he was in the seventh grade. By the time he reached high school, he had cultivated various types of stuff shots. One of his favorites was to go airborne by the free-throw line, to rotate his body and come in for the dunk. In his two years at the University of Massachusetts Erving scored 1,370 points and grabbed 1,049 rebounds. Then he signed with the Virginia Squires in the ABA. His first year he averaged 27.2 points and 15.7 rebounds and became the Rookie of the Year. Later on he was also sometimes called the Doughnut (because like the bakery item, he was made to dunk).

DOCTOR K—Dwight Gooden (1964–   ) Baseball. This nickname was given to Gooden because his overpowering fastball scored 276 strikeouts during his rookie season. (K is the symbol for a strikeout in official baseball scoring.) In 1985, his best year, Gooden had a record of 24–4, an ERA of 1.53 (second only to Bob Gibson since 1950), 268 strikeouts, and 8 shutouts. Since then he has become a mere mortal and is now simply called Doc.

DODO—Dorothy May Bundy Cheney (1916–   ) Tennis. As the daughter of two very successful tennis players, Dorothy Cheney seemed to be born to the tennis court. (Dodo was a childhood nickname, a repetition of the first two letters of her first name.) Cheney started playing tennis at the age of eight; at the age of 25 she won her first national title—the 1941 U.S. indoor doubles with her partner, Pauline Addire. By the end of 1983, Dorothy Cheney had won a record 131 national tennis titles.

DOGGIE—Tony Perez [1942—] Baseball. When Tony Perez was named to manage the Cincinnati Reds for the 1993 season, sportswriters had a field day over the fact that the new manager (born in Cuba) had long borne the nickname Doggie. The reason for the amusement was the irony that Marge Schott, owner of the Reds, had a St. Bernard named Schottzie 02, and that candidates for the managerial job were reportedly asked how they felt about the owner's dog running onto the field during practice. Tony Perez, who was one of the more popular Reds players in the 1970s told the press, "A lot of people think I'll be a sleeping dog. But I'm not a sleeping dog. I can do the job." He certainly did the job on the field, where as a player he slugged 371 home runs in twenty-one years, compiling a .279 batting average with 1,590 RBIs.

DOGGIE—Thomas Gawthrop Trenchard [1874–1943] Football. Trenchard, who excelled at football and baseball at the Lawrenceville Preparatory School in New Jersey, received his unflattering nickname because he had long, shaggy hair, and he had the tenacity of a bulldog. In college he led Princeton to a 6–0 victory over Yale in 1893, clinching the National Championship, and ending Yale's thirty-seven-game winning streak. Richard Harding Davis, the colorful journalist, stated in *Harper's Weekly* that Princeton's victory over Yale that year was "the greatest sports spectacle New York or America has ever witnessed." Doggie Trenchard went on to play pro football briefly in Latrobe, Pennsylvania in 1897, and then later he coached football at numerous universities, including the University of North Carolina and West Virginia. During World War I, he was, at age forty-three, a physical education instructor with the YMCA in France.

DOLLAR BILL—Bill Bradley [1943—] Basketball. H/F Although Bill Bardley was one of the highest paid basketball players of his day ($500,000 for four years), his nickname was in reference to his frugality. His New York Knick teammates knew him as a man who had shirts with paper clips for missing buttons and an apartment that "looked like a Holiday Inn room before the maid shows up." A standing joke was that he still had the first dollar bill he ever made. At Princeton, Bradley was known as Mr. President and The Secretary of State. As it turns out, these are more prophetic nicknames than Dollar Bill because Bradley, a former U.S. Senator from New Jersey, is sometimes mentioned as a future presidential candidate. He was also called Mr. Knickerbocker.

DOLLAR BILL—Bill Bradley (b. July 28, 1943) Basketball. Bradley (on the left) was the captain of the gold-medal winning 1964 U.S. Olympic Basketball Team. After a great career in professional basketball, Dollar Bill Bradley began a successful career in politics.

DOMINICAN DANDY [THE]—Juan Marichal [1937–   ] Baseball. H/F Born in Laguna Verde in the Dominican Republic, Marichal took pains with how he dressed and looked; he took the same care on the mound. "It is his consistency that awes you," said fellow pitching great Sandy Koufax. "He pitches every fourth day and he pitches nine innings every game. He's as great as any I ever faced." Marichal won over twenty games per season in six seasons. Most of these were also complete games. In 1964, he was 21–8 and completed twenty-two games; in 1968, he was 26–9 and finished thirty. For his nine-year career he was 170–77.

DOUBLE D—Don Drysdale [1936–1993] Baseball. H/F Double D was a power pitcher for the Brooklyn Dodgers and then the Los Angeles Dodgers. In 1962, he was 25–9; and in 1965, Drysdale teamed with Sandy Koufax to register a combined record of 49–20. Drysdale was also a terrific hitter, often pinch-hitting. In 1965, he won 20 games and batted .300. During his fourteen-year career, Drysdale whiffed 2,486 batters and tossed 49 shutouts. Double D also consistently used a brushback pitch, setting a modern-day record for hitting batters with 154. "If one of our guys went down," Drysdale once explained, "I just doubled it." He was also called Big D.

DOUBLE DUTY—Ted Radcliffe [1902–   ] Baseball [Negro Leagues]. One of the stars of the Homestead Grays and the Pittsburgh Crawfords, as well as twelve other teams over a period from 1928 to 1950, Ted Radcliffe got his nickname in 1932 during the Pittsburgh Crawfords' exhibition doubleheader at Yankee Stadium. Radcliffe caught Satchel Paige's 5–1 victory in the first game; Radcliffe pitched the second game and won 4–0. In the stands was none other than Damon Runyon. It was worth the admission price of two to see Double Duty out there in action, wrote Damon Runyon in the paper the next day. Double Duty Radcliffe not only loved pitching and catching, but he also loved doubleheaders. One day he even played a game in the morning, a doubleheader in the afternoon, and a game at night. The next morning when he woke up, Radcliffe was still wearing his uniform.

DOUBLE X—Jimmy Foxx [1907–1967] Baseball. H/F A catcher who played first base and later third, Jimmy Foxx had as many nicknames as World Series he played in: three. Double X, the most popular, was for the way he spelled his last name. The Maryland Strong Boy was for the way this man from Sudlersville, Maryland was built. And The Beast was for the way Foxx smacked hard line drives. In Double X's first season he batted .328. That kind of consistency (his career average was .325) carried over to his home run hitting, too. Foxx hit thirty or more homers twelve different seasons. And speaking of home runs, Old Double X smashed fifty-eight in 1932—tying him for fourth with Hank Greenberg for most home runs in a season. Who was third? Babe Ruth had fifty-nine in 1921. Oh yes, on occasion there was a fourth nickname: The Right-Handed Babe Ruth.

DUCKY—Joe Medwick [1911–1975] Baseball. H/F Some said he swam or walked like a duck. However, this nickname probably came from sportscasters who heard that a fan had said he had made a "ducky wucky play." Medwick preferred the nickname of Mickey, although many of his teammates called him Muscles for his physique and fans often called him Ducky Wucky. In 1937, Medwick was the Triple Crown and MVP winner with a .374 average and set the National League record of fifty-six doubles. During his seventeen-year career he hit 540 doubles and compiled a .324 average.

DUKE—Edwin Donald Snider [1926–] Baseball. H/F Although Snider ruled his position in center field for the Dodgers from 1947 to 1957 like a member of royalty, that was not how he got his nickname. His father called him Duke one day when Edwin returned home from kindergarten bursting with self-confidence. The 1950s was a golden age for center fielders in New York: Willie Mays was holding court at the Polo Grounds, Joe DiMaggio and then Mickey Mantle at Yankee Stadium, and the Duke at Ebbett's Field. Snider was also called The Duke of Brooklyn, The Duke of Flatbush, and The Silver Fox (for his gray hair).

DUKE OF TRALEE [THE]—Roger Bresnahan [1879–1944] Baseball. H/F This catcher told his Giant fans that he had been born in Tralee, Ireland; but actually he had been born in Toledo, Ohio. There was no fooling about his speed, though. Four times he batted over .300, his personal best coming in 1903 when he hit .350. He also stole 212 bases during his seventeen-year career. Bresnahan contributed to the Tools of Ignorance by inventing shin guards, something that quickly became standard equipment for catchers.

DUMMY—William Ellsworth Hoy [1862–1961] Baseball. A deaf-mute, Hoy's nickname of Dummy was not offensive to him; in fact, he even liked it. Umpires began using the hand signals for balls and strikes that are standard today, so that Hoy would know the call and the count. Over his fourteen-year career, Hoy had a resounding 2,044 hits and a batting average of .287. To show their appreciation, the fans waved handkerchiefs instead of applauding.

DUSTY—Johnnie Baker [1949–] Baseball. This was a nickname from childhood and referred to how Baker looked when he returned home with his dog named Dusty. Baker spent seventeen years in the majors, batting .280 as an outfielder with Atlanta, Los Angeles, and San Francisco. One noteworthy day was on September 20, 1972, when Dusty Baker came to bat three times in a single inning for the L.A. Dodgers. Another was on December 16, 1992, when the forty-three-year-old Baker was appointed the manager of the San Francisco Giants. "This is the greatest day of my life, so far," said Baker. He was also called Doctor Scold.

DUTCH—Earl Harry Clark [1906–1978] Football. H/F Clark's nickname was for his German heritage. (This is true of almost everyone with the nickname of Dutch.) Clark's Hall of Fame status was for his passing, running, and drop-kicking. From 1932 to 1938, he gained 2,757 yards and scored twenty-three touchdowns. As Potsy Clark once said of Dutch: "He is like a rabbit in the brush heap when he gets in the secondary; he has no plan but only instinct and the ability to cut, pivot, slant, and run in any direction equally well."

DUTCH—Cornelius Warmerdam [1915–] Track and field. H/F Warmerdam had two nicknames: Dutch for his heritage and Corny for a shortened form of his first name. On April 13, 1940, Warmerdam became the first pole-vaulter to vault fifteen feet. In 1942, he cleared his best vault ever—15' 7¾". Dutch held the world's pole-vault record from 1940 to 1957.

EASY ED—Ed Macauley [1928–   ] Basketball. H/F At 6' 8" and 190 pounds, Macauley was not a physically dominating center. To make up for this lack of bulk, he concentrated on his playmaking and shooting abilities. Thus, Macauley's nickname served a double function. Not only was he an easy-going person, but also, his driving lay-ups and graceful hook shots looked so easy that they seemed almost automatic. For six seasons Easy Ed played for the Boston Celtics and averaged over seventeen points a game. Then he returned to his hometown of St. Louis to play for the Hawks. In 1957–1958, Macauley, Cliff Hagen, and Bob Petit led the Hawks to the NBA championship. Easy Ed Macauley was the MVP in the very first All-Star Game in 1951, and he went on to make the All-Star team seven times.

ECK [THE]—Dennis Eckersley [1955–   ] Baseball. Eckersley was a starting pitcher before becoming a reliever. As a starter he had 367 starts and 100 complete games. Since becoming a closer, he has over 220 saves. He chalked up three seasons of forty-plus saves and registered 185 saves from 1987 to 1991. In 1992, he won the Cy Young Award by serving up his Yakkers (curves) and Cheese (fastballs) to gain fifty-one saves in fifty-four chances. His strikeout-walk ratio is third behind Juan Marichal and Ferguson Jenkins. "The highs on this job are not as great as the lows," says Eckersley. "You can be dazzling for a month. Then, one bad outing and you forget about the whole month. The memories go blank. The good ones are gone."

EE-YAH—Hugh Ambrose Jennings [1869–1928] Baseball. H/F He's there, all right, on a plaque in the Hall of Fame in Cooperstown: "Ee-Yah" Jennings. He earned his colorful nickname by shouting "Ee-yah" from the coaching box when he was a player-manager for the Detroit Tigers from 1907 to 1920. It paid off plenty because he led the Tigers to three straight pennants. As a player, Jennings was one of the great hitting shortstops, compiling a lifetime .314 average with 1,520 hits in 4,840 at-bats, 227 doubles, 88 triples, and 19 round trippers. Jennings was a fiery competitor with the Baltimore Orioles—a National League team in the 1890s—always crowding the plate and daring the pitchers to throw at him. Many did; Ee-Yah suffered three skull fractures.

EL DYNAMITERO—Bernabe Ferreyra [1909–1972] Soccer. This Argentine soccer star was extremely popular with the fans. By the time he retired from competition, he had appeared in 195 games and scored 204 goals. He received his nickname because his shots at the goal seemed to come at the goalie as if they were explosive.

EL MAESTRO—Martin Dihigo [1905–1971] Baseball [Negro Leagues]. H/F Buck Leonard (who can be seen in Ken Burns' TV documentary on baseball) once said of El Maestro: "I say he was the best ball player of all-time, black or white. He could do it all." As a hitter, Dihigo compiled a .304 lifetime average, and in a career that spanned twenty-five years, he won 256 games as a pitcher. In Cuba, fans called him "El Immortal."

EL PURS—Ruben Olivares [1947–   ] Boxing. H/F Olivares was the bantamweight champion (1969–1970, 1971–72), the WBA Featherweight Champion (1974), and the WBC Featherweight Champion in 1975. His nickname means loosely "the fox."

EL TERRIER—Pascual Perez [1926–1977] Boxing. H/F In his professional career The Terrier won eighty-four, lost seven, and drew one. He was the 1948 Olympics Flyweight Gold Medalist for Argentina. (His boyhood hero was the Argentinian heavyweight champion Luis Firpo.) He won the flyweight championship in 1954, and did not relinquish his crown until six years later when, on April 16, 1960, he lost the title match to Pone Kingpetch in Bangkok.

$11,000 LEMON—Rube Marquad [1889–1980] Baseball. H/F In 1908, John McGraw bought Rube Marquard for this amount; the most that had ever been paid for a minor-league contract. For the first three years, this future Hall of Famer was 9–16. Hence, the $11,000 lemon. But in 1911, he was 24–7. The following year he was 26–11. Rube Marquard had become the $11,000 Wonder.

ELMO THE DANCER—Elmo Wright [1949–   ] Football. Today, football fans are quite familiar, and sometimes appalled, by the antics of players in the end zone after scoring a touchdown. Elmo Wright is one such player; he received his nickname because of the way he danced in both college and as a pro in and around the end zone after scoring a TD. He played college ball for the University of Houston Cougars, and in his first varsity game against Tulane, he caught three passes for two touchdowns and a total of 162 yards. He set many records for the Cougars, and became the first Houston player to be drafted in the first round by the NFL. Elmo the Dancer signed with the Kansas City Chiefs, and as a rookie in 1971, he won the Mack Lee Hill Award as the team's top rookie. After playing with the Houston Oilers and the New England Patriots, Wright retired right before the 1976 season. He had caught the ball seventy times for 1,116 yards and six touchdowns.

ENFORCER [THE]—Dick Butkus [1942–   ] Football. H/F During his high-school years in Chicago, Butkus was named All-State fullback as well as defensive lineman. As a two-time All-America linebacker, Butkus turned the losing University of Illinois football team into a winning one. In his junior year, the "Illini" went to the Rose Bowl. The Chicago Bears drafted him as their first draft pick, and the faith of owner-coach George Halas was rewarded. Runners said that when linebacker Butkus tackled them, it was like being hit by a truck. He enforced the rules and the plays. Butkus played his entire professional career with the Bears (1965–1973). See ANIMAL and PADDLES.

ERNIE D—Ernie DeGregorio [1951–   ] Basketball. Through dedication and hard work, DeGregorio turned himself into a basketball player. All-State in high school, he took his Providence team his senior year to the semifinals of the NCAA tournament. After signing with the Buffalo Braves for $2 million, he averaged fifteen points and led the league in assists and free-throw percentage to become the Rookie of the Year in 1973–74. But by his second year, he hurt his knee and his play faltered. He then began to be called Ernie No D. In this case, the D stood not for his last name but for Defense.

ESPEN THE EAGLE—Espen Bredesen [19__–   ] Skiing. Winner of the Gold medal in the ninety-meter ski-jump in the 1994 Winter Olympics in Lillehammer, Norway. In 1992, Bredesen finished in last place and that dismal effort had earned him the derisive nickname Espen the Eagle, after the British jumper Eddie Edwards, the original Eagle whose fame was based on comical ineptness.

ESPO—Phil Esposito (1942–   ) Hockey. H/F Nicknamed Espo because it's easier to say, Espo had a workman-like attitude toward the game. In 1971, he scored 60 goals to go with his 67 assists for 127 points. This eclipsed his earlier NHL record of 126 points set in 1969. Still, Esposito remained evenhanded in his assessment of himself. "Orr has the magnetism. Hull is explosive. I'm a workman. I'm just Esposito, never a crowd-pleaser. Hey, I've watched myself on videotape and I wouldn't cheer for me either." He was also called Trader Phil. See BOBBY AND PHIL AND THEM.

E.T.—Christy Henrich (1972–1994) Gymnastics. She missed gaining a berth on the 1988 U.S. Olympic Team by 0.118 of a point. She suffered from anorexia nervosa, and at the time of her death this superb gymnast weighed only sixty pounds and was too weak to compete in gymnastic events. She earned her nickname E.T. (an allusion to the immensely popular Steven Spielberg film) because the initials stood for "Extra Tough."

EVANGELIST (THE)—William Frederick Dahlen (1870–1950) Baseball. Bill Dahlen played twenty-one years in the National League for Chicago, Brooklyn, and Boston, compiling a .274 lifetime batting average with 2,482 hits in 9,046 at-bats. In 1894, playing for the Cubs, Dahlen hit safely in forty-two straight games. He played with the Brooklyn Superbas at the turn of the century and managed the Dodgers for four years. He was the Brooklyn manager in 1913 when the Dodgers moved from old Washington Park into Ebbets Field. Dahlen was nicknamed The Evangelist when a religious leader came to Brooklyn and nearly persuaded Dahlen to go forth in search of converts. But if you asked a dyed-in-the-wool old-timer, he would tell you that Bill Dahlen was better known as Bad Bill, a nickname earned for his feisty fighting spirit. In 1912, for example, when the Giants beat the Superbas 4–3, Dahlen and umpire Cy Rigler got into a fistfight. Bad Bill was later fined $100 by league president Tom J. Lynch.

EVANGELIST (THE)—William Ashley Sunday (1862–1935) Baseball. Billy Sunday won this nickname after his days of playing in the outfield were over. Word has it that he was a hard liver and drinker when he was with Chicago and Philadelphia. But one day after hearing a street preacher, he left the game to devote himself to becoming an evangelist. He became so famous at his new profession that he rated a line in the popular song: "Chicago, Chicago, the town that Billy Sunday could not shut down."

FANCY PANTS—Anthony Joseph "A. J." Foyt, Jr. (1935–   ) Auto racing. H/F The son of a midget car driver, A. J. Foyt, Jr., received his nickname Fancy Pants because he would wear freshly laundered and starched white pants on the midget and stock car circuits where he started racing at age eighteen. (*Fancy Pants* was also the name of a popular Bob Hope film of the day.) In 1958, Foyt Jr., driving for Dean Van Lines, qualified for the Indianapolis 500 and finished sixteenth. Since that time he has scored an impressive number of victories in major races. He was, for example, the first driver to capture both the Indianapolis 500 and LeMans. His autobiography, written with the help of William Neely, and published in 1983, is immodestly titled *A.J: My Life As America's Greatest Race Car Driver.*

FATHER OF AMERICAN BASEBALL—Alexander Joy Cartwright [1820–1892] Baseball. H/F Cartwright (not Abner Doubleday) developed the rules for the modern-day game of baseball. Some of Cartwright's rules that are still in play are three outs per side, nine players on a side, nine innings per game, ninety feet between bases, and no throwing at the runner to get him out. The first actual game was played on June 19, 1846, at the Elysian Fields in Hoboken, NJ. The New York Nine defeated Cartwright's New York Knickerbockers, 23–1.

FATHER OF AMERICAN FOOTBALL [THE]—Walter Camp [1859–1892] Football. H/F Walter Camp coached at Yale beginning in 1888, but his biggest influence was on the college football rules committee. A few of his new rules were the scrimmage line (instead of the rugby scrum), eleven players on a side (instead of fifteen), and a series of downs to gain yards. Not only did he begin the election of All-American teams, but he also wrote over thirty books on football and fitness.

FATHER OF AMERICAN GOLF [THE]—John Reid [1840–1916] Golf. In 1888, Reid and some friends laid out six holes in Yonkers, NY— the first golf course in the United States. Four years later, they laid out another six holes and used an apple tree to hang their coats on. So, they became known as the APPLE TREE GANG. In 1894, Reid and his friends laid out a nine-hole golf course; and in 1897, they began what would become the first eighteen-hole golf course in America, located in Mt. Hope, NY.

FATHER OF BASKETBALL—Dr. James Naismith [1861–1939] Basketball. H/F Naismith invented the game of basketball in December of 1891 in Springfield, Massachusetts. "I thought of the different games ... football had a goal line and goalposts ... soccer, lacrosse and hockey had goals into which the ball might be driven," reasoned Naismith. "Tennis and badminton had marks on the court inside which the ball must be kept. Thinking of all these, I mentally placed goals at the end of the floor." But what would the game be called? One of the student-players suggested Naismith ball. But as the janitor had nailed peach baskets up for goals, another student suggested basketball.

FATHER OF THE ENGLISH SCHOOL OF BOXING [THE]—Jack Broughton [1704–1789] Boxing. H/F Broughton, the third heavyweight champion of England, developed a set of rules for boxing. He was also called The Father of Boxing.

FATTY—Bob Fothergill [1897–1938] Baseball. Fothergill was 5' 10" and weighed 230 pounds when he joined Detroit, and he put on more weight during his career. This outfielder also had a hefty batting average of .326 for his twelve years in the majors.

FEMININE TED WILLIAMS [THE]—Helen Callaghan [1923–1993] Baseball. Callaghan was one of the stars of the All-American Girls Professional Baseball League. "I was very feminine," said Callaghan, "but when I got on the ballfield, I was all business." Not only was she outstanding at third base, but what really was striking about her playing was when she stepped up to the plate. "She had that smooth, sweeping swing," said Dottie Wiltse Collins, an opposing pitcher. Callaghan also has a son, Casey Candaele, who plays for the Houston Astros. Casey uses a thirty-four-ounce bat. His mother's bat weighed thirty-six ounces. Callaghan was called "Calhoun" by her teammates because, it seems, a fan had once mistakenly thought that was her name. See ALL-AMERICAN GIRLS PROFESSIONAL BASEBALL LEAGUE. (The movie *A League of Their Own* tells the story of the All-American Girls Professional Baseball League.)

FIGHTING MARINE [THE]—Gene Tunney [1898–1978] Boxing. Tunney beat Jack Dempsey in 1926 in a ten-round decision. On September 27, 1927, Tunney survived a long count in the seventh round to defend his title against Dempsey. See THE MANASSA MAULER and THE BATTLE OF THE LONG COUNT.

FIRPO—Fred Marberry [1898–1976] Baseball. An early specialist in relief pitching, Marberry played mostly for the Detroit Tigers, but ended his career with the New York Giants and Washington Senators. He compiled a lifetime record of 147 victories, 89 losses, and a 3.63 ERA. Because Marberry stood 6' 2" and weighed 210 pounds, he was given the nickname Firpo as a nod to the towering heavyweight boxing champion Luis Firpo.

FIRST LADY OF FIGURE SKATING [THE]—Theresa Blanchard [1893–1978] Figure skating. H/F As the First Lady of Figure Skating, Theresa Blanchard recorded many firsts. In 1914, she won the first U.S. Women's National Championship and the first U.S. Waltz Championship; in 1920, she was the first American woman skater in the Winter Olympics, winning a bronze medal. She won the U.S. national championship four more times and the U.S. Pairs Championships nine times with her partner Nathaniel Niles. She also started *Skating* magazine with Niles. When Blanchard hung up her skates, she became a judge for skating competitions around the world.

FISHIE—Donna de Varona [1947–   ] Swimming. H/F This was a nickname she received at the age of nine because she was spending so much time in the swimming pool. In 1960, she was the youngest member of the Olympic team. At the 1964 Olympics de Varona won two gold medals—one in the 400-meter medley and the other on the 400-meter freestyle relay team.

FLIP—Melvin "Tony" E. Bettenhauser [1916–1961] Auto racing. H/F If you race automobiles for a living, Flip is most likely not a nickname you would like to be given; but Flip was applied to Bettenhauser because that's what his midget cars did more than a few times. As a young man he was such a good fighter that he was nicknamed "Tunney" —in honor of Gene Tunney, the heavyweight champion. Eventually his nickname evolved (or devolved, depending upon how one considers these things) into Tong. In 1961, Flip Bettenhauser was killed while testing a car for his friend Paul Russo. He was also a member of the Indianapolis Hall of Fame.

FLO-JO—Florence Griffith Joyner [1959–   ] Track and field. H/F Track athletes try to peak during Olympic years; Flo-Jo certainly accomplished that in the summer of 1988. (That was the year that sportswriters bestowed her nickname on her for her scintillating speed and stunning track suits; she was also called Fluorescent Flo.) At the Olympic trials Flo-Jo set a world record of 10.49 in the 100 meters. At the Olympic Games in Seoul she won a silver medal in the 4/400-meter relay and gold medals in the 4/400-meter relay, the 100-meter dash, and the 200-meter dash—establishing a world record of 21.34 in the 200.

FLOWER [THE]—Guy Lafleur [1951–   ] Hockey. H/F Lafleur's nickname was based on the sound and meaning of his last name. Playing right wing for the Montreal Canadiens in the late 1970s, Lafleur had six consecutive fifty-goal seasons as the Canadiens won four Stanley Cups. A six-time All-Star, this right-winger won the scoring title three times, the Hart Trophy (the NHL's MVP award) twice, and the Conn Smythe Trophy (the MVP for the playoffs) once. After being voted a member of the Hall of Fame, Lafleur came out of a four-year retirement to play briefly for the Rangers and the Nordiques.

FLUFF—Mike Cowan [19__–   ] Golf. Fluff is perhaps the most famous caddie of the twentieth century, achieving prominence carrying the clubs for Tiger Woods. "I didn't think a caddie would ever become so important," Cowan once told the press. "I caddied for twenty years without any of that." Tiger Woods said of Mike "Fluff" Cowan: "Fluff us not just a caddie for me. He's a best friend. We're very close."

FLYING DUTCHMAN [THE]—John Peter "Honus" Wagner [1874–1955] Baseball. H/F Wagner received his nickname The Flying Dutchman because he was fast and his family was Dutch. During his twenty-one-year career with the Pittsburgh Pirates, Wagner had a lifetime average of .327—the highest ever for a shortstop. His speed helped him collect 3,415 hits, including 640 doubles and 252 triples, as well as leading the league five times in stolen bases and achieving a career total of 722. Wagner was also called Honus and Hans because they are similar to John in German.

FLYING FINN [The]—Paavo Nurmi [1897–1973] Track and field. From Abo, Finland, Nurmi was the first scientific runner. He kept detailed notes on his training and could be seen running with a stopwatch in his hand. Nurmi paced himself throughout a race rather than jogging before a mad dash to the finish line. Nurmi won twelve gold medals in the Olympic Games and held world records from 1,500 to the 20,000 meters. In the 1924 Olympics, the 1,500 and the 5,000 meter-races were held less than an hour apart. He not only won both but set world records. Nurmi was also called Peerless Pavo and THE PHANTOM FINN.

FLYING HOUSEWIFE [THE]—Fanny Blankers-Koen [1920–   ] Track and field. At the age of sixteen Fanny Blankers placed sixth in the high jump for Holland at the 1936 Olympic Games in Berlin. The next time the Olympic Games were held was after World War II. Now married and the mother of two small children, Fanny Blankers-Koen was ready. Affectionately known all over Europe as The Flying Housewife (she was also sometimes called The Marvelous Mama of Holland), Fanny Blankers-Koen entered five events in the Olympics at London in 1948. As if that weren't grueling enough, she won gold medals in four of them: the eighty-meter hurdles, the 100- and 200-meter dashes, and the 400-meter relay.

FOGHORN—George Miller (1853–1929) Baseball. Miller only played two seasons of major-league ball. His first season was in 1877, when he caught for Cincinnati. Then he was sent down to the minors and didn't return to the majors until 1884, where he appeared in all of six games—once again for Cincinnati, but this time in the American Association. All in all "Foghorn" Miller, known for his deep booming voice, came to bat only fifty-seven times and hit an anemic .193. Thus, like many other athletes, he is better known for his colorful nickname. Also called Doggie and Calliope.

FOOTHILLS—Bob Kurland (1924–) Basketball. H/F Kurland got his nickname as a seven-foot freshman at Oklahoma State. He also was the reason for a change in the rulebook on blocking shots. After his first year the rule was changed to prohibit goaltending—the ball could no longer be blocked when it was on its downward path toward the basket. Kurland helped the Aggies win two straight NCAA championships. One of his most memorable games came in 1946. With EASY ED Macauley of St. Louis University guarding him, Kurland scored fifty-eight points.

FORDHAM FLASH (THE)—Frankie Frisch (1898–1973) Baseball. H/F Frankie Frisch earned his nickname for his speed on the bases. The second baseman led the league in stolen bases in 1921 (with forty-nine), 1927 (with forty-eight), and 1931 (with twenty-eight). The Fordham Flash's total was 419 stolen bases in his nineteen-year career. See GASHOUSE GANG.

FRANCHISE (THE)—Lou Brock (1936–) Baseball. H/F Thousands of fans turned out to watch Brock in his successful attempts to break Ty Cobb's long-standing base-stealing record of 892. They were rewarded many times over as Brock eventually wound up with 938. (He stole seven bases in two different World Series.) Brock did more than just steal bases. The outfielder collected a total of 3,032 hits and batted over .300 eight times. He was also called The Base Burglar.

FRANCHISE (THE)—Tom Seaver (1944–) Baseball. H/F Seaver, also known by the alliterative nickname of Tom Terrific, was simply that for an otherwise lackluster New York Mets. The best pitcher in baseball for a second division team, he was The Franchise. In 1967, Seaver was 16–13 and Rookie of the Year for the last-place Mets. Two years later, the miserable Mets had become "the Miracle Mets of 1969" by capturing the World Series. In their banner year, Tom Terrific was 25–7 (2.21 ERA) and winner of the Cy Young Award. Tom Seaver won twenty or more games in 1971, 1972, 1975, and 1977 and two more Cy Youngs (1973 and 1975). He also led the league in ERA three more times and strikeouts five times. When striking out batters Seaver created the most excitement. "Pitching, to me, is throwing strikes" he once remarked, "and throwing strikes down low." Toward the end of his twenty-one-year career, The Franchise also played for the Reds, the White Sox, and the Red Sox. He finished with a 311–205 record and 3,640 strikeouts.

FRANCHISE (THE)—David Thompson (1954–) Basketball. Thompson was the youngest All-American at eighteen, the year he led North Carolina State to a record 27–0. His first year as a forward with the Denver Nuggets he averaged twenty-six points per game. Although he is only 6' 4", Thompson is able to jump forty-two inches off the floor.

FRENCHY—John Fuqua [active 1969–1977] Football. Although Fuqua was born in Detroit, Michigan, he was of French extraction; thus, the nickname. In 1972, a pass from Terry Bradshaw to halfback John Fuqua bounced off safety Jack Tatum, who was covering Fuqua, and into the hands of Franco Harris who scored a touchdown for a 13–7 Steeler win over the Raiders. This pass has come to be called the Immaculate Reception.

FULLBACK [THE]—Bob Hayes [1942–   ] Track and field, football. H/F The barrel-chested and thick-legged Hayes looked more like a football player than he did a track star. But track star he was. In 1962, he set a world record of 9.1 in the 100-yard dash. And in 1964, he won the gold medal at the Olympic Games in Tokyo with a world-record tying 10.0 in the 100-meter dash. For this feat (as is true for all winners of the 100-meters at the Olympics), he would be called "The World's Fastest Human." About his running, Hayes once said: "I had an unusual style. I was larger than most of the sprinters at my age. I broke the world's record at 192 pounds. But it set a trend. Now most of the sprinters are large and there are plenty of winning runners with styles as unusual as mine. What it boils down to, in part, is that you can't teach a person how to run. You can teach him the techniques of running. But the important thing is you must be born with talent." When Hayes returned to Florida A & M, he turned his attention to football. He earned spots as a flanker on post-season teams in the North-South game and the Senior Bowl. He also caught a fifty-three-yard pass from Joe Namath in the Senior Bowl for a 7–7 tie. The Dallas Cowboys drafted him, and five years later, Hayes had forty-nine touchdowns and an average per catch of just less than twenty yards. See BULLET BOB.

FUZZY—Frank Urban Zoeller [1951–   ] Golf. The nickname Fuzzy is based on the initials of Frank Urban Zoeller. Zoeller is noted for winning the Masters in 1979 on his very first attempt. Only two other players have ever done this: Horton Smith in 1934 and Gene Sarazen in 1935.

GABBY—Charles Leo Hartnett [1900–1972] Baseball. H/F Sometimes nicknames reveal salient traits possessed by their owners, but in Hartnett's case, the nickname started out as strictly ironic. When he reported for spring training in 1921 with the Chicago Cubs, he barely said a word to the sportswriters, and so they dubbed him "Gabby." Eventually, he lost his shyness and became quite talkative. Thus, his sobriquet turned out to be prophetic. So popular was the tag that few base-ball fans today are aware that he had a real first name. Gabby was the kind of player who allowed his accomplishments to speak for him. In twenty seasons with the Cubs, the 6' 2", 190-pound catcher handled pitchers superbly, leading the Cubs to four pennants (1929, 1932, 1935, and 1938), and leading National League catchers in fielding percentage and assists six times. Gabby holds the major-league record for catchers for most games played with 1,790 and most putouts with 7,292, as well as the National League record for double plays with 173. He was no slouch at the plate either. In 1935, he batted .344; in 1937, he hit .354. In 6,432 at-bats Hartnett collected 1,912 hits and 236 homers, compil-ing a lifetime average of .297. He was also called Man in the Iron Mask and Old Tomato Face.

GALLOPING GHOST (THE)—Red Grange (1901-1991) Football. In the photo above,
Grange shows the evasive running style that won his nickname.

GABBY—Charles Evard Street (1882-1951) Baseball. Street talked a blue streak behind the plate. This .208 hitter had nineteen years between his next-to-last and his last appearance as a catcher. (He filled in during one game in 1931 after he had become a manager.) When he was a manager, he was called Old Sarge, the rank he had held in WW I. As a manager of the Cardinals for six years, his record was 368–339, and 13–6 in two World Series. See GASHOUSE GANG.

GALLOPING GHOST (THE)—Harold "RED" Grange (1903-1991) Football. H/F On October 18, 1924, Grange of Illinois ran back the opening kickoff ninety-five yards for a touchdown. Before twelve minutes had elapsed, Grange had three more touchdowns from 67, 56, and 44 yards against mighty Michigan. (Coach Fielding "HURRY UP" Yost's team had not lost a single game in three years.) Grange was then taken out of the game until the fourth quarter. But by game's end, Grange had five touchdowns and a total of 402 yards. Grantland "GRANNY" Rice gave Grange his nickname for his ability to evade and speed away from would-be tacklers:

He runs as Nurmi runs and Dempsey moves, with almost no effort, as a shadow flits and drifts and darts ... upon effortless legs with a body that can detach itself from the hips, with a change of pace that can come to a dead stop and pick up instant speed, so perfect is the coordination of brain and sinew.

One night during his senior year Grange went to the theater and met a Charles C. "CASH AND CARRY" Pyle, the owner of the theater, who told Grange how to make $100,000. Grange dropped out of school after the last football game and went on a barnstorming tour of the country with the Chicago Bears. Playing ten games in seventeen days, Grange was only so-so (in San Francisco he was called a "broken idol"), but he did help to promote pro football around the country. In 1926, Red Grange appeared in the film *One Minute to Play*. Mordaunt Hall, the *New York Times* film critic, wrote: "In his first screen touchdown 'Red' Grange demonstrated his ability to tackle the role of a college hero and portray it far more convincingly than most of the handsome young men who are thoroughly accustomed to greasepaint and facing the camera." (Music for the film included the "Red Grange Collegiate Gambol" played by the Red Grange Quartet.) This gives a clue as to just how popular The Galloping Ghost was at the height of his fame. In his second year in the pros, however, Grange was injured. Although he didn't retire until 1934, he displayed none of his former brilliance. Even though The Galloping Ghost holds no records now, football historians agree that he was the player most responsible for professional football's popular success in the 1920s. Grange was also called The Wheaton Iceman.

GALLOPING GHOST [THE]—Bill Wheatley (1909–) Basketball. Wheatley got his nickname because he was quick to bring the ball upcourt. He never played college basketball, but he had a sterling career as an amateur. He was the one chosen to stand on the victory stand at the 1936 Berlin Olympics to receive the gold medal for the team.

GASMAN [THE]—Tom Hickman (1800s) Bareknuckles boxing. William Hazlitt, the English critic, was also a boxing fan. This is part of his account of the bout between Tom "The Gasman" Hickman and Bill "The Bristol Bull" Neate in 1822:

About the twelfth it seemed as if it must have been over: Hickman generally stood with his back to me; but in the scuffle he had changed position, and Neate just then made a tremendous lunge at him, and hit him full in the face. It was doubtful whether he would fall backwards or forwards; he hung suspended for a second or two, and then fell back, throwing his hands in the air, and with his face lifted up to the sky. I never saw anything more terrific than his aspect just before he fell. All traces of life, of natural expression were gone from him. His face was like a human skull, a death's head, spouting blood. The eyes were filled with blood, the nose streamed with blood, the mouth gaped blood. He was not like an actual man, but like a preternatural, spectral appearance, or like one of the figures in Dante's *Inferno*.

GENE THE MACHINE—Gene Littler (1930–) Golf. H/F Littler received his nickname for his smooth, seemingly effortless swing. Gene the Machine won tournaments from 1954 to 1977.

(Only Nicklaus and Snead had tournament wins over a greater number of years.) Although Littler was one of the top money winners, he only won one major, the U.S. Open in 1961. In 1980, he joined the Senior PGA Tour.

GENTLE BEN—Benjamin Crenshaw (1952–   ) Golf. Crenshaw is called Gentle Ben because he speaks softly and is always unfailingly polite. He was also without fail a great golfer in college, winning the NCAA championship from 1971 to 1973. On the pro tour, he was often in the money but never quite seemed to put it all together to take a major tournament. It was not until 1984 that Gentle Ben edged out Tom Watson to win The Masters by two strokes.

GENTLE JEEMS—James Galvin (1856–1902) Baseball. H/F Galvin's nickname refers to his gentle disposition and a popular pronunciation of his first name. This pitcher was also called Pud for making pudding out of the other team and THE LITTLE ENGINE THAT COULD for his tirelessness. Twice Galvin had forty-six-win seasons and he posted 639 complete games during his career.

GENTLEMAN JACKSON—John Jackson (1769–1845) Boxing. H/F Jackson defeated Daniel Mendoza for the heavyweight championship in 1795. This was the beginning of the Golden Era of Boxing, a period when Jackson's boxing academy on Bond Street in London had the likes of Lord Byron dropping by to spar. Jackson was later elected to a seat in Parliament.

GENTLEMAN JIM—James J. Corbett (1866–1933) Boxing. H/F Corbett's nickname Gentleman Jim came from his pleasant manners and personality, as well as his style of dress. He cut a striking contrast with some of the rougher characters in boxing. A former bank teller, Gentleman Jim won the heavyweight title on September 7, 1892, in New Orleans by knocking out John L. Sullivan in the twenty-first round. This was the first modern-day bout: padded gloves were used instead of bare knuckles and the Queensberry Rules were used instead of no holds barred. Gentleman Jim was also regarded as the first scientific boxer. He feinted and counterpunched instead of just walking in with a straight-ahead style. (This was why he was sometimes called The Dancing Master.) Corbett lost the heavyweight title in 1896 to Robert P. Fitzsimmons. In attempted comebacks in 1900 and 1903, Corbett lost to Jim Jeffries. He was also called Pompadour Jim for his hairstyle.

GEORGIA PEACH (THE)—Ty Cobb (1886–1961) Baseball. H/F Cobb was born in Narrows, Georgia, and Georgia is the Peach State. He was also one peach of a player. Only one year out of twenty-four (his rookie season) did he hit less than .320. Along the way he won twelve batting average titles and eight most hits titles. In 1911 and 1912, Cobb batted .420 and .410. When he was thirty-five, his record was .401; his last year in the game, he had a .323. Although his record of 4,191 hits was broken by Pete Rose, his career average of .367 has not been topped. His runs total of 2,245 also ranks first. Cobb stole 892 bases (a record broken by Lou Brock and Rickey Henderson), including thirty-five of home plate. Mention is often made of his difficult temperament toward others. Cobb had this to say about that: "If any one of them learned I could be scared, I would have lasted two years in the major leagues and not twenty-four." Cobb did more than survive. Of his 123 records, fifteen still remain. Cobb is arguably the finest player ever to play the game. He was also called The Idol of Baseball Fandom.

THE GEORGIA PEACH—Ty Cobb (1886-1961) Baseball. He was born in Georgia,
the Peach State, but the nickname was not entirely appropriate, because he definitely was no "peach"
to play with, to play against, nor to live with.

GHOST WITH A HAMMER IN HIS HAND—Jimmy Wilde [1892-1969] Boxing. H/F Wilde barely weighed more than a hundred pounds, but he hit with authority because he had developed precision timing. Wilde knocked out hundreds of men, while only losing four times in eleven years. Once at a fair, this Welshman KO'd fifteen in a row who were attempting to remain in the ring for three rounds. He was also called The Tylerstown Terror and The Mighty Atom.

GIPPER [THE]—George Gipp [1895-1921] Football. When Gipp who had quarterbacked Notre Dame to two perfect seasons (4,833 total yards), was dying of pneumonia, he told Coach Knute "THE ROCK" Rockne: "Sometime, Rock, when things are wrong and the breaks are beating the boys, tell them to go in there with all they've got and win one just for the Gipper. I don't know where I'll be then, Rock, but I'll know about it. And I'll be happy." In a 1928 half-time pep talk to spirit Notre Dame to a 12–6 victory over Army, legend has it that coach Knute Rockne begged his Notre Dame team to "win one for The Gipper."

GLADIATOR [THE]—Louis Rogers Browning [1858-1905] Baseball. This outfielder battled against pitchers with a ferocity. Browning must have received a lot of thumbs down from the fans of the opposing teams, as he knocked out 1,654 hits and a .343 batting average during his thirteen years in the arena. Browning had his bats made to order. As they were fashioned in Louisville, Kentucky, his bats became known as Louisville Sluggers. Louisville Sluggers are still made today.

GLOOMY GIL—Gilmour Dobie [1879-1948] Football. H/F Although the common epithet is Gloomy Gus, Gilmour Dobie was dubbed Gloomy Gil because of his pessimistic outlook on life. "Just because you win this game," he would tell his teams, "it doesn't mean you are going to win the next one." From 1899 to 1902, he played quarterback for the University of Minnesota, but he did not go on to pro ball. Instead, after assisting his college coach, Dobie was named in 1906 to be the head football coach at North Dakota State University. In 1908, he was named head coach at the University of Washington. He later coached at the U.S. Naval Academy and at Cornell, where he received an unprecedented ten-year contract. During his thirty-three-year coaching career, Gilmour Dobie compiled a 180–45–15 record, a .781 winning percentage. Also The Magnificent Skeptic.

GLUE-FINGERS—Dante B. J. Lavelli [1923—   ] Football. H/F In 1946, Lavelli led the AAFC in receptions (when he caught forty) and in total reception yardage (843). It was a great comfort to quarterbacks to know that when they threw the ball to Lavelli, Glue-fingers was going to catch it and hold on to it. In the 1950 NFL championship game between the Cleveland Browns and the Los Angeles Rams, Glue-fingers caught eleven passes for Cleveland, two of them for touchdowns.

GOLDEN BEAR [THE]—Jack Nicklaus [1940—   ] Golf. H/F Nicklaus earned his nickname because of a thatch of blond hair, a sturdy build, a tendency to put on weight, and an extraordinary career. After playing golf at Ohio State University and winning the U.S. Amateur Championship for the second time, Nicklaus turned pro at twenty-one. The next year he won the 1962 U.S. Open, outdueling Arnold Palmer in a playoff to become the youngest golfer ever to capture that title. Probably the best golfer since Bobby Jones, Jack Nicklaus has earned the respect of golfers everywhere by winning the big ones. "My goal is to win more major championships than any other man," Nicklaus once said. The Golden Bear has certainly accomplished his goal, winning twenty major titles: Six Masters (1963, 1965, 1966, 1972, 1975, 1986), five PGA Championships (1963, 1971, 1973, 1975, 1980), four U.S. Opens (1962, 1967, 1972, 1980), three British Opens (1966, 1970, 1978), and two U.S. Amateur Championships. (Bobby Jones only won thirteen.) Nicklaus is also the only golfer in U.S. history to win all four major tournaments—the Masters, the U.S. Open, the British Open, and the PGA championship—at least three times. And his last Masters victory at the age of forty-six makes him the oldest player to do so. In recent years, he has turned to designing golf courses. When the twentieth century winds down and sportswriters start working on their lists, The Golden Bear may be voted the greatest golfer ever. He was also (once) called Ohio Fats.

GOLDEN BOY [THE]—Paul Hornung [1935–   ] Football. H/F Halfback Paul Hornung received this nickname because of his blond good looks and the fact that his career seemed so golden. At Notre Dame, Hornung was an All-American in 1955 and a Heisman Trophy winner in 1956. Playing for Vince Lombardi's Green Bay Packers, the Golden Boy helped the Packers win the NFL championship in 1960, 1961, and 1962. (Surprisingly, some of his Packer teammates called him Goat because of the way his shoulders sloped without shoulder pads.) In 1960, Hornung scored fifteen touchdowns, fifteen field goals, and forty-one points after touchdown for a total of 176 points. In 1961, he was the Most Valuable Player. In 1962, Paul Hornung and Alex Karras of the Detroit Lions were suspended for almost a year for betting on football. This tarnished the reputation of the Golden Boy somewhat, but in 1965 he won it back when he scored five touchdowns in one game.

GOLDEN BRETT—Brett Hull [1964–   ] Hockey. Like his father, Bobby Hull, Brett Hull shot the puck at speeds approaching 100 mph. Brett Hull's nickname was also fashioned after his father's. Bobby Hull was the Golden Jet; therefore, Brett Hull was the Golden Brett. The younger Hull started his career slowly, but in the 1989–1990 season, the Golden Brett scored seventy-two goals. In the following season he did even better, cashing in with eighty-six goals. When asked about the secret to his success, the Golden Brett answered simply: "It must be in the genes."

GOLDEN GIRL [The]—Sonja Henie [1912–1969] Figure skating. Sonja Henie was one of the best athletes ever to come out of Norway. At the age of twelve she was called "the Wonder Child" and "the Norwegian Doll" even when she finished last at the 1924 Olympics. But she went on to win over 1,500 prizes, as well as Olympic gold medals in 1928, 1932, and 1936. After her career as an athlete, blonde Henie turned to show business. Billed as the "golden girl," she starred on skates in eleven movies for Darryl F. Zanuck and Twentieth Century-Fox. Before dying of leukemia at the age of fifty-seven, Sonja Henie had earned $47 million. SEE THE PAVLOVA OF THE SILVER SKATES.

GOLDEN JET [THE]—Bobby Hull [1939–   ] Hockey. H/F Hull's nickname flowed from his blond hair (later a hair piece), his torso chiseled like a statue from the Golden Age of Greece, as well as his speed on skates and his power with a hockey stick. The puck from Hull's curved stick was once clocked at 140 miles per hour. Goalie Jacques Plante once told what it was like to be in goal against Hull: "His shot once paralyzed my arm for five minutes." He played for the Chicago

Black Hawks and then the Winnipeg Jets. (The latter was even named for him.) Needless to say, Hull gave the new league needed name recognition to draw the fans. But as Hull was later to say: "The World Hockey Association was great to me and I hope that I did something good for the game, and good for the players. But, let's face it, I had that Black Hawks' Indian head tattooed on my chest. Every time I put on the jersey for fifteen years, it was a trip. Those were the greatest years in my life." The Golden Jet led the NHL in scoring seven times, scoring 610 goals and 560 assists in 16 NHL seasons. In Stanley Cup play he scored sixty-two goals and had sixty-seven assists. Bobby Hull was also the first player to score more than fifty goals in a single season. It came on March 14, 1966. At 5:34 of the third period, Hull flashed toward the net and sent the puck screaming under the stick of goalie Cesare Maniago for number fifty-one, breaking the record held by Maurice "ROCKETT" Richard, Bernie "BOOM BOOM" Geoffrion, and the Golden Jet himself.

GOOFY—Vernon "Lefty" Gomez [1909–1989] Baseball. H/F Gomez was 6–0 in five World Series and 189–102 during his fourteen-year career. His best year was 1934 when he was 26–5, and his three All-Star wins established the record. Gomez was called Goofy because of his whimsical sense of humor. Because he loved a good time and was Spanish, he was also called The Gay Castilian.

GOOSE—Leon Allen Goslin [1900–1971] Baseball. H/F This player got his nickname because of his last name and his beak-like nose. In 1928, Goslin hit .379, and during his eighteen-year career, he batted .316. Goose Goslin holds several American League records for left fielders: 2,007 games played, 4,395 putouts, 4,791 chances, and 195 errors.

GOOSE—Reece Tatum [1921–1967] Baseball, basketball. During a high school basketball game, Reece Tatum jumped up for a pass. A shout rang out: "Look at the ol' Goose fly!" From then on, it was Goose Tatum. Tatum started out as a left fielder on DOUBLE DUTY Radcliffe's baseball team. After an argument with Radcliff, Goose went to play for the Indianapolis Clowns. Goose was a serious enough baseball player; he went so far as to wear his uniform at his wedding. Goose was also a funny enough first baseman, but with his big hands and eighty-four inch arm span he was to become an even funnier basketball player and center for Abe Saperstein's Harlem Globetrotters. Tatum was also called THE CLOWN PRINCE OF BASKETBALL.

GORGEOUS GUSSIE—Gertrude Moran [1923–   ] Tennis. Moran was the glamour girl of tennis in the post-World War II years. "It used to bother me a bit that they didn't write up the tennis," complained one competitor. "All they wrote about was Gussy's panties." Moran's best streak of tennis came at the National Indoor Championships in 1949 where she won at singles, doubles, and mixed doubles.

GORGO—Richard Alonzo Gonzales [1928–1995] Tennis. H/F Better known as Pancho Gonzales, he won the U.S. professional championship in men's singles eight times, accomplishing the feat seven years in a row (1953–59). The sobriquet Gorgo was attached to him, referring to Gorgonzola, because he was for a time "the greatest cheese champion in American tennis."

Coming from a decidedly unprosperous Mexican-American family, without formal tennis lessons, without access to rich tennis clubs, Pancho became a consistent crowd-pleaser with his 112-mph serve. Gorgo was the big cheese. When Pancho undertook to instruct Arthur Ashe, Ashe said, "It was the greatest break of my life. Pancho not only was the best tennis player in the world but most people agree he had the sharpest tennis mind. He could look at you once and diagnose all your mistakes." See PANCHO.

GORILLA—William Jones [1910–1982] Boxing. Jones was a lefty, and appeared like King Kong or at least a gorilla to his opponents. In 1932, Gorilla Jones knocked out Oddone Piazza in six rounds to win the world middleweight crown. He successfully defended this crown until 1937 when he lost it to Freddie Steele. In 1940, Gorilla Jones retired, having won ninety-eight fights, drawing thirteen, and losing twenty-one.

GRÄFIN—Steffi Graf [1969–] Tennis. During her early years, the German sportswriters gave her this nickname, which means Duchess in German, for her courtly demeanor. From the time she was four Graf played tennis. First under the eye of her father, then other coaches, she drove herself to be the best. "My dream is to be as perfect a tennis player as I can be. It is for myself; it is not for being number one or anything." In 1987, she beat Martina Navratilova in the finals of the French Open, and in 1988, she won three Grand Slam tournaments.

GRAND OLD MAN OF AMERICAN FOOTBALL [THE]—Amos Alonzo Stagg [1862–1965] Football. "Winning isn't worthwhile unless one has something finer and nobler behind it," wrote Amos Alonzo Stagg in 1927 in his book *Touchdown.* "When I reach the soul of one of my boys with an idea or an ideal or a vision, then I think I have done my job as a coach." And what a coach he was! He had the longest coaching career—seventy-one years—in the history of football. He coached the University of Chicago for forty-one years, and he remained a coach until he was ninety-eight years old. Stagg was a member of the first All-American team; he also is the only person selected as both a player and a coach for the National Football Hall of Fame in New Brunswick, New Jersey. Amos Alonzo Stagg made so many innovations to the sport that Knute Rockne claimed: "All football comes from Stagg."

GRANNY—Dawn Fraser [1937–] Swimming. H/F This Australian swimmer won three gold medals—the last at the age of twenty-seven at the 1964 Tokyo Olympics. In the world of championship swimming, twenty-seven is ancient, which is why she was called Granny. In 1985, she was elected to the International Women's Sports Hall of Fame in East Meadow, NY.

GRANNY—Grantland Rice [1880–1954] Sportswriter. Grantland Rice was a much-loved sports scribe during the GOLDEN AGE OF SPORTS in the 1920s. Even today he is often quoted, particularly for his description of THE FOUR HORSEMEN and for the following excerpt from his poem titled "Alumnus Football." "When the last great scorer comes/To mark against your name,/He'll write not 'won' or 'lost'/But how you played the game." Rice was also called The Dean of American Sportswriters.

GRAY EAGLE [THE]—Tristram Speaker [1888–1958] Baseball. H/F Speaker played a very shallow center field for the Boston Red Sox and later the Cleveland Indians. When a ball was hit, the gray-haired Speaker swooped back like an eagle in flight to snare the ball. Not only could he field, he could also hit; from 1907 to 1927 Speaker had an average of .344. He was also called Tris and Spoke.

THE GRAY EAGLE—Tris Speaker (1888-1958) Baseball. This Boston Red Sox and Cleveland Indians Hall-of-Famer soared in his gray uniform like an eagle in center field. Some rank him as the greatest center-fielder of them all.

GREASY—Earle Neale [1891–1973] Football, baseball. H/F Neale was so elusive as a ball carrier that his college coach gave him the nickname Greasy. After playing baseball eight years for Cincinnati (his high point was batting .357 in the 1919 World Series), Neale coached the Philadelphia Eagles for many years.

GREASY VEST—Al Weill [1894–1969] Boxing. Weill was a matchmaker and a manager, but he dressed so sloppily and spilled so much food on his clothing that sportswriters called him Greasy Vest. Sportswriter Dan Parker said, "He took his meals on the fly and the fly retaliated by taking his meals on Al."

GREAT ONE [THE]—Wayne Gretzky [1961–   ] Hockey. As accomplished in his field as Jackie Gleason was in his, Gretzky has certainly earned this verbal play on the sound of his name. His rookie year in the NHL, The Great One tied Marcel Dionne for the scoring lead with 137 points. In 1980-1981, Gretzky scored 164 points to top Esposito's record and had 109 assists to outdistance Orr's mark. In 1981-1982, he scored 92 goals and 137 points, and set a NHL record of 215 points (52 goals; 163 assists) in 1985-1986. The Great One took the scoring title every season from 1980 to 1987. Along the way, he led the Edmonton Oilers to four Stanley Cups and won four straight Art Ross trophies and five consecutive Hart trophies. Since the Great Trade to the Los Angeles Kings in 1988, The Great One has eclipsed the legendary Gordie Howe's record of total points scored (1,850). And on October 26, 1990, The Great One surpassed 2,000 points. By the end of the 1991-1992 season Gretzky had 2,263 points, 1,514 assists, and 749 goals (Gordie Howe scored 801). Gretzky also holds the all-time Stanley Cup record for points (306), assists (211), and goals (95).

THE GREAT ONE—Wayne Gretzky (b. January 26, 1961) Hockey. When it comes time to vote on the greatest hockey player of this century, Gretzky's name will be at the top of many ballots. His nickname also alludes indirectly to his last name.

GREATEST [THE]—Muhammad Ali [1942–] Boxing. H/F This was the nickname that Ali chose for himself. Earlier, as the Louisville Lip, Cassius Clay, as he was then called, won a gold metal for light heavyweights at the 1960 Olympic Games. (Before he changed his name after he converted to Islam, he was also known as Cassius the Brashest and Gaseous Cassius.) On February 25, 1964, Clay fought for the heavyweight championship. Although he acted hysterical at the weigh-in (he was in super shape at 6'3" and 210 pounds), he was relaxed and confident in the ring. With his cornermen shouting, "Float like a butterfly, sting like a bee," Ali did just that, and a weary Sonny Liston did not come out for round seven. His next bout with Liston on May 25, 1965 was won again not by a TKO, but by a PHANTOM PUNCH in the first round by the boxer now known as Muhammad Ali. Ali then went on to defeat Floyd Patterson, George Chuvalo, Henry Cooper, Brian London, Carl Mildenberger, Cleveland Williams, Ernie Terrell, and Zora Folley. Muhammad Ali refused to be inducted into the armed forces because of his religious beliefs and was stripped of his title in 1967. When the Supreme Court overturned his draft conviction in 1970, Ali returned to boxing. On March 8, 1971, Ali and Frazier fought for the heavyweight title in THE FIGHT OF THE CENTURY. Although Ali lost in a fifteen-round decision, he was back. In their next bout that took place on January 28, 1974, Ali defeated Frazier in the twelfth round. On October 30, 1974, Ali regained the heavyweight title with an eighth-round knockout of George Foreman. Ali referred to the fight in Zaire as THE RUMBLE IN THE JUNGLE. And on October 1, 1975, Ali scored a fourteenth round KO of Frazier in THE THRILLA IN MANILLA. The three fights between Muhammad Ali and Joe Frazier are often considered to be the greatest fights in the history of boxing. On February 15, 1978, Ali lost to Leon Spinks in fifteen rounds; on September 15, Ali defeated Spinks to win the heavyweight title for the third time. But time was running out. In 1980, Ali attempted a comeback but was defeated by Larry Holmes. And in a loss to Trevor Berbick in December of 1981, Ali had fought his last fight in the ring. In recent years, Ali has been in ill health—the victim of too many blows to the head.

GREAT WHITE HOPE [THE]—James J. Jeffries [1875–1953] Boxing. H/F After Jack Johnson became the first black heavyweight champion in 1910, pressure built for Jim Jeffries to come out of his five-year retirement to gain it back. As Jack London wrote: "Jim Jeffries must now emerge from his alfalfa farm and remove that golden smile from Johnson's face. Jeff, it's up to you. The White Man must be rescued." The fight was held in Reno in 1910. Jeffries was a 10–7 betting favorite. In the fifteenth round, Johnson knocked Jeffries down for the third time. Tex Richard, the referee (who also had promoted the fight) wouldn't stop it until Jeffries' corner finally threw in the towel. This nickname has now entered the language. Jeffries was also called The Beast, Big Jeff, THE BOILERMAKER, The California Hercules, and the California Grizzly Bear.

GREAT WHITE HOPE [THE]—Jess Willard [1883–1968] Boxing. Although the term "white hope" was applied to any boxers who hoped to defeat Jack Johnson, the first black man to become Heavyweight Champion of the World, it was due to the play *The Great White Hope* by Howard Sackler that the nickname has now come to rest on the broad shoulders of Jess Willard. (In Sackler's play, however, the fighters are given different names.) In his autobiography, Jack Johnson claims to have deliberately thrown the fight with Willard:

The fight was originally intended to end in the tenth round, but when the round arrived the money had not been paid. It was nearing the twenty-sixth round when the money was turned over to Mrs. Johnson. I had specified that it would be in $500 bills in order that the package should be small and the amount quickly counted. After examining it she gave me the signal. I replied that everything was O.K. by a pre-arranged sign and she departed. In the twenty-sixth round I let the fight end as I did.

Most boxing experts, however, including Nat Fleischer, who had seen the fight, and who had purchased Johnson's confession in 1916 for $250 (the confession was not published until 1968) felt that Johnson did not throw the fight and was merely trying to save face, because he had not trained properly. In any case, Jess Willard did become the world heavyweight champion, and the champions remained white until the great Joe "THE BROWN BOMBER" Louis came along. Willard was also called Cowboy Jess, Kansas Giant, Pottawatomie Giant, Tall Pine of the Pottawatomie.

GREAT WHITE SHARK [THE]—Greg Norman [1955—   ] Golf. Norman received his nickname for his shock of whitish blond hair and because of his love of deep-sea fishing. And once while fishing back home in Australia, he had opened fire on some sharks circling the boat. Starting golf at the age of sixteen, Norman taught himself to play with the help of Jack Nicklaus books. After he turned pro in 1974, Greg Norman won his fourth tournament. After winning twenty-nine tournaments, he joined the pro tour in 1984. In 1986, he won the British Open but came in second to Fuzzy Zoeller in the U.S. Open, after losing their eighteen-hole playoff. In 1993, Norman shot a record 267 in the British Open (thirteen under par for the seventy-two holes). "That was the best golf I've ever played in my life," said a happy Norman afterward. He was also called the Awesome Aussie.

GUMBALL KID [THE]—Ralph Mulford [1884–1973] Auto racing. H/F Mulford, who liked to chew on gumballs during races, would have won the very first Indianapolis 500 in 1911 if it had not been for an error in the timing. In all he took part in ten Indy 500s, finishing second in 1911 and third in 1916. He was also the AAA national driving champion in 1911 and 1918.

GUMP—Lorne Worsley [1929—   ] Hockey. H/F Worsley received this nickname as a child because he reminded people of the cartoon character Andy Gump. Worsley did not use a facemask until 1974—the last holdout among NHL goalies. (Before he donned the mask as an adult, he still bore a striking facial resemblance to the unflappable Andy.) "Being a goaltender is not a job that would attract any normal, straight-thinking human," Worsley once said. "People don't even know who we are. The rule book only says that each team is allowed to dress seventeen men—plus two goalies."

GUS—Charles E. Dorais [1891–1954] Football. On November 1, 1913, Notre Dame upset Army 35–13. (The previous summer: Quarterback Dorais and Knute Rockne had spent weeks practicing their secret weapon, the forward pass.) That fall afternoon Dorais completed seven passes to Rockne and fourteen passes altogether for 243 yards and three touchdowns. A new era in football had begun.

HACK—Lewis Robert Wilson (1900–1948) Baseball. H/F In the days when Wilson played outfield, there was a strong wrestler named Hackenschmidt. So, Wilson who was also very strong was given the nickname Hack. Hack could also have been known for his hitting ability. In 1930, Wilson hit fifty-six home runs (the National League record) and knocked in 190 runs (the major-league record) on the way to a .356 batting average. Playing for a total of four National League teams (New York, Chicago, Brooklyn, and Philadelphia) during a twelve-year career, Hack wound up with a batting average of .307. He was also called The Million Dollar Baby from the 5 & 10 Cent Store.

HAIG (THE)—Walter Hagen (1892-1969) Golf.
Dressed to a T (or in this case, a tee), the Haig shows off his proze-winning style.

HAIG [THE]—Walter Hagen [1892–1969] Golf. H/F Based on his last name, Hagen's nickname almost sounds as solid as an institution. To be The Haig was to be the cat's pajamas, to be the tops, to be as smooth as silk, and that was what Walter Charles Hagen was to the game of golf during the 1920s all the way to 1937, when he was selected as the non-playing captain of America's Ryder Cup team. (Ogden Nash's poem "A Definition of Marriage" opens: "Just as I know that there are two Hagens, Walter and Copen") Dressed to a *t* (he threw out the traditional golfers' tweeds to outfit himself in silk shirts, flannel pants, and white bucks), The Haig would lean against a club on the first tee to wonder out loud who was going to come in second. Through his colorful play and flamboyant personality, he popularized the saying, "I never wanted to be a millionaire, I just wanted to live like one." He lived in high style, earning a million dollars and spending it on parties, good clothes, chauffeurs, and extravagant tips. The Haig also did for golf what BABE RUTH did for baseball. He not only increased the sport's popularity but also the social standing of its players. It may seem odd in this day of sports superstars, but Hagen wrangled permission for golfers to change in the clubhouse rather than in the more humble caddieshack. During his career The Haig won eleven national golf championships: U.S. Opens in 1914 and 1919; British Opens in 1922, 1924, 1928, and 1929; and five PGA Championships, including four in a row. A poll of sportswriters in 1950 ranked The Haig as the third-best golfer of the first half-century (behind Bobby Jones and Ben Hogan). In 1956, Walter Hagen published his autobiography, *The Walter Hagen Story.*

HAMMER [THE]—Dave Schultz [1950–   ] Hockey. Schultz earned his nickname for his tactics of intimidation. From 1972 to 1975 this forward for the Philadelphia Flyers drew more minutes in the penalty box than anyone else on the ice. Nevertheless, his brutish style of play helped the Flyers win the Stanley Cup. In fact, if The Hammer's total number of penalty minutes were piled up after eight seasons of "play," the Hammer would have spent more than fifty-seven entire games in the penalty box. In spite of the Flyers' solid performance leading to a Stanley Cup in the early 1970s, it was Schultz's brutish style of play that helped the team become known as the BROAD STREET BULLIES.

HAMMERIN' HANK—Henry "Hank" Aaron [1934–   ] Baseball. H/F "Getting a ball past his bat," complained a pitcher in 1973, "is like trying to sneak the sun past a rooster." One of Aaron's strong points was his consistency. This outfielder never really had a bad year and he had no theories about his success. "The secret of hitting is to keep swinging," said Aaron. But he did study pitchers, and sometimes seemed to miss a pitch in order to get it again. Ron Perranoski of the Dodgers said, "He not only knows what the pitch will be but where it will be." Aaron's nickname was given to him early in his career and he lived up to it. He hit 755 home runs to shatter one of the all-time records of sport—Babe Ruth's career home run record of 714. Hammering' Hank also has the RBI record of 2,297. He was also called Bad Henry, The Hammer, and The New Sultan of Swat.

HAMMERIN' HANK—Henry Greenberg [1911–1986] Baseball. H/F This first baseman led the league in home runs and RBIs four times. In 1938, he hammered fifty-eight home runs, which ties Jimmy Foxx for the most homers in a season by a right-handed hitter. But for Greenberg his best year was in 1937. That was the year he batted .337, hit 40 home runs, and knocked in 183 RBIs. "I just loved to hit," confessed Hank. "For me, there were few satisfactions in life equal to stepping into a baseball and really driving it." See GREENBERG GARDENS.

HANK—Angelo Luisetti [1916–   ] Basketball. H/F Hank pioneered the revolutionary outside one-hand push shot. (Until then, the two-handed set shot had been used exclusively.) He had first practiced it while he was in high school. "I don't know how I came to think of it," Hank later said. "It just seemed to be the natural way to get the ball in the air." Luisetti led the Stanford Indians—today they are known by the more politically correct nickname of Cardinals—to three straight titles from 1936 to 1938. In one game he pushed in 50 points; during his career he scored a total of 1,596 points.

HAPPY HUSTLER [THE]—Bobby Riggs [1918–1998] Tennis. H/F In 1939, Riggs won the Wimbledon singles, doubles, and mixed doubles. (He even had laid down bets on himself that he would pull this off.) Although he also won the 1939 and 1941 U.S. men's singles and the 1940 mixed doubles, it was as a hustler that Bobby Riggs made his name and his nickname. His most publicized hustles came in 1973 when he challenged two of the biggest names in women's tennis to play him. Riggs defeated Margaret Court (6–2, 6–1) but lost to savvy Billie Jean King (4–6, 3–6, 3–6) in the mega-media event known as the Battle of the Sexes.

HARD-NOSED DEMON OF THE OVALS—Anthony Joseph "A. J." Foyt [1935–] Auto racing. H/F This four-time winner of the Indianapolis 500 used to have such a thirst for driving that he would sometimes show up unannounced at small tracks. If he didn't make the qualifying run, he would buy someone's last place car so that he could drive. Foyt was also called The Houston Hurricane and Super Tex. See FANCY PANTS.

HARDROCK—Clyde Mitchell Shoun [1915–1968] Baseball. Shoun's nickname came from his high-school days in Tennessee when he was a rock-'em, sock-'em football player. In 1943, Shoun had the leading won-loss percentage of .813 (13–3) in the National League. The next year he pitched a no-hitter as the Cubs set down the Boston Braves.

HARPO—John Howard Vaught [1909–   ] Football. Anybody who has seen films featuring the Marx Brothers is well aware of the wild head of hair worn by the mischievous Harpo. Vaught, a leading college football player and later a coach for the University of Mississippi, had thick, curly hair that led to his teammates calling him "Harpo." Coaching the Mississippi Rebels for twenty-four seasons, Vaught led his teams to six SouthEast Conference Championships, four undefeated seasons, and ten bowl game wins (out of a total of eighteen bowl appearances).

HARVARD EDDIE—Edward Leslie Grant [1883–1918] Baseball. Grant went to Harvard before playing ten years at third base in the majors. He was one of the countless soldiers killed in the Argonne Forest during WW I.

HAWK [THE]—Tony Dorsett [1954–   ] Football. H/F Dorsett is one of the greatest running backs in NFL history. As a college player, he was the 1976 Heisman Trophy winner and the first player in NCAA history to have four straight 1,000-yard seasons. He ranks third on the all-time NFL list with 12,739 yards gained. He was the NFC player of the year in 1981. In 1988, The Hawk published his autobiography, *Running Tough*. He was also known as TD, which is most appropriate since his initials correspond to the abbreviation for touchdown.

HAWK—Ken Harrelson [1941–   ] Baseball. Harrelson's profile won him his epithet. But he also was a high flyer. "The major contribution of Harrelson," sportswriter Leonard Koppett once noted, "was that he proved a player didn't have to conform." Hawk was the first player to wear batting gloves, sweatbands, lampblack under the eyes, and high stirrups (showing the white socks underneath)—things that are now standard equipment. But it was in another area that Hawk really blazed a trail. Harrelson was the first free agent. After Charles Finley, the owner of the Athletics, released him in the middle of the 1967 season, Harrelson chose an offer from the Boston Red Sox. Hawk had flown from a salary of $19,000 to a $75,000 signing bonus and a $100,000 contract for two years. Ever the realist, Harrelson set the record straight about his nine-year career as an outfielder and first baseman with "I was the highest paid .240 hitter in all of baseball."

HAWK—Connie Hawkins [1942–   ] Basketball. H/F Though the Hawk was banned in 1961 for his alleged participation in college betting scandals, he played in the American Basketball League (MVP in 1962), the American Basketball Association (MVP in 1968), and for the Harlem Globetrotters. After an out-of-court settlement, Hawkins joined the Phoenix Suns in 1969 and was later named a forward to the NBA All-Star team. His nickname is simply a short form of his last name.

HAWK [THE]—Ben Hogan [1912–1997] Golf. H/F Hogan avoided publicity and refused to give autographs. One of the reasons for this aloofness was that Hogan believed in practice, practice, practice, and in total preparation. Once a tournament began, he was all business and concentration. In the United States, this dedication and concentration gained him the nickname The Hawk; in Britain, he was known as The Iceman. Although he had a wicked hook, Hogan straightened it out and developed the fade to perfection. In 1946, his hard work paid off with a total of thirteen tournament wins, including a major. The Hawk/Iceman went on to win nine major championships—six of them coming after a life-threatening automobile accident in 1949. He was also called BANTAM BEN and Golfdom's Mighty Might.

HAWK [The]—Aaron Pryor [1955–   ] Boxing. Pryor won thirty-nine fights and lost only one. He was the WBA Junior Welterweight Champion from 1980 to 1983, and the IBF Junior Welterweight Champion 1984–1985.

HEC—Clarence Edmundson [1886–1964] Track and field, basketball. Hec Edmundson received his nickname because of his habit of yelling "ah, heck" when he became dissatisfied with his own athletic efforts. He was an excellent runner, and in the 1912 Olympics in Stockholm, Sweden, he finished seventh in the 800-meter race. From there he went on to become the basketball and track and field coach at the University of Idaho from 1913 to 1917. He later moved to the University of Washington where he coached for thirty-five years, and became one of the first college basketball coaches to achieve 500 career victories.

HERSHEY HURRICANE—Henry B. Picard [1927–   ] Golf. H/F Picard's nickname is a curious one. It might lead you to think that he was born in Hershey, Pennsylvania (he was actually born in Plymouth, Massachusetts), or that he was black (he was not). The only golfer to defeat

Walter Hagen in a playoff, Picard received his nickname because he made his professional debut at the Hershey Pennsylvania Country Club. Hence, he was also called Chocolate Soldier. During his twenty-year career, he won thirty tournaments. He was also called Homey Boy Henry.

HIGH POCKETS—George Lange Kelly [1895–1984] Baseball. H/F After leaving Polytechnic High School in his senior year to play baseball with Victoria in the Pacific National League, Kelly was quickly acquired by the New York Giants and started his big-league career in 1915. However, it took him five more years before he found himself in the lineup on a regular basis. Because he was such a tall first baseman for his day (6' 4"), Damon Runyan called him High Pockets. Seven times High Pockets batted over .300, and he compiled a lifetime batting average of .297 with 1,778 hits, 1,020 RBIs, 337 doubles, and 148 home runs. He also led the National League in homers in 1921 with twenty-three, and in 1924, he slugged seven in six games. In the field, this Hall of Famer set an all-time record in 1920 for most total chances at first base (1,873) and most putouts (1,759). After his career as a player, Kelly worked as a coach for the Cincinnati Reds (1935–1937, 1947–1948) and for the Boston Braves (1938–1943).

HIS MAJESTY—Cal Hubbard [1900–1973] Baseball. H/F Hubbard projected an imperial manner as an umpire on baseball diamonds in the American League. He has the distinction of being the only person ever selected for the Baseball Hall of Fame, the College Football Hall of Fame, and the Pro Football Hall of Fame. See BIG CAL.

HIT 'EM WHERE THEY AIN'T—William Henry Keeler [1872–1923] Baseball. H/F In 1898, Keeler batted .379, a National League record. His batting average over nineteen years was .345—the fifth highest ever. Keeler rapped out a total of 2,962 hits, and out of that total 2,536 of them were singles. To illustrate what a great contact hitter he was, he only struck out thirty-six times during his career. His 201 singles in 1898 is the National League record. Keeler was also called Wee Willie.

HOBEY—Hobart Baker [1892–1918] Hockey. H/F Hobie won Hall of Fame honors on the basis of a spectacular hockey career at Princeton University. To give some idea of his fame, F. Scott Fitzgerald once wrote of Hobey: "An ideal worthy of everything in my enthusiastic admiration, yet consummated and expressed in a human being who stood within ten feet of me."

HOLLER GUY [THE]—Jacob Nelson Fox [1927–1975] Baseball. H/F If you can locate a copy of the September 5, 1955 issue of *Life* magazine, you will find therein a poem by Ogden Nash. The poem, a tribute to the great Chicago White Sox second baseman, is titled "The Holler Guy" and one line asks, "What does he holler when he's hollering?" What he was hollering, of course, is "Come here baby," referring to the baseball. If there was a chance of fielding the ball, Fox wanted it. He was the American League's MVP in 1959. He played for nineteen seasons in the major leagues and compiled a lifetime .288 batting average. Fox was also called NELLIE.

HOME RUN—John Franklin Baker [1886–1963] Baseball. H/F Before Babe Ruth arrived on the scene, the home-run king of the American League was Frank "Home Run" Baker. In 1911, for example, Baker playing third base for the Philadelphia Athletics led the American League with eleven (count them, eleven) round-trippers. Although Baker was first in the league in home runs from 1911 to 1914 (11, 10, 12, and 9) and finished his thirteen-year career with ninety-six homers and a .307 batting average, it was his hitting in a World Series that provided Baker with his nickname. In the 1911 World Series, Frank Baker hit a home run against Rube Marquard of the New York Giants (who had twenty-four wins that year on his way to the Hall of Fame) in the sixth inning of the second game for a 3–1 victory for Connie Mack's Philadelphia A's. The next day Baker hit a Christy Mathewson pitch (twenty-six wins and another Hall of Famer) over the fence to tie the game in the ninth inning. The A's went on to win the game and the series. Home Run Baker enjoyed hitting against the best pitchers in baseball (in six World Series he batted .363, one of the highest averages in post-season play). Moreover, he just enjoyed playing the game. In 1915 and 1920, he chose to play semipro baseball and stay on his farm rather than play for the Athletics and the Yankees. He did not feel playing for less than the best to be a letdown. "The game of baseball itself is what interests me," said Baker. "Baseball is baseball anywhere—and I love it."

HOME RUN—John Franklin Baker (1886-1963) Baseball.
He was the home run king before Babe Ruth arrived upon the scene.

HOME RUN—Willard Brown [1913–   ] Baseball. Given his nickname by Josh Gibson, Brown was not only a heavy hitter in the Negro Leagues, but also in Puerto Rico where he was known as El Hombre ("The Man"). In addition, Brown was the first African American to hit a home run in the American League, putting it over the fence for the St. Louis Browns in 1948.

HONDO—John Havlicek [1940–   ] Basketball. H/F Mel Nowell, a teammate at Ohio State began this nickname because Havlicek liked reading western novels, plus he bore a resemblance to John Wayne, the star of the movie *Hondo.* Hondo could have played wide receiver for the Cleveland Browns, but instead he joined the Boston Celtics. During his sixteen-year career as a Celtic forward, Havlicek scored 26,395 points for an average of over twenty points per game. He also pulled down 8,007 rebounds and made 6,114 assists. When Hondo was a Celt, Boston won eight NBA championships (1963, 1964, 1965, 1966, 1968, 1969, 1974, and 1976).

HOPALONG—Howard Cassady [1934–   ] Football. In the 1950s when television came of age, the most popular western hero was an actor named William Boyd who played Hopalong Cassidy. Hopalong Cassidy wore black and rode a white horse named Topper. So, when this football player came along with the last name Cassady he was naturally called Hopalong. Cassady's nickname was also appropriate because of his explosive speed. After much success in football and baseball in high school, Cassady went on to play those two sports at Ohio State University, where his coach Woody Hayes said: "the greatest player I ever had playing for me was Hop Cassady." In his senior year for the Buckeyes, Hopalong rushed for 958 yards and scored fifteen touchdowns. That year, 1955, he was the winner of the Heisman Trophy and was named the Associated Press Player of the Year. His career in pro football was less stellar. Playing for the Detroit Lions, the Cleveland Browns, and the Philadelphia Eagles—Hopalong rushed for 1,229 yards and 6 touchdowns, and caught 111 passes for 1,601 yards and 18 touchdowns. After his retirement from football, Cassady took a job as physical fitness director for the New York Yankees baseball team.

HORSE [THE]—Alan Ameche [1933–   ] Football. Ameche received his nickname because he was such a workhorse. Drafted first by the Baltimore Colts, this Heisman Trophy winner rambled seventy-nine yards for a touchdown in his very first NFL game in 1955. By game's end, Ameche had 194 yards against the Bears' defense. He led the NFL that year with 961 yards. In the 1958 NFL championship game, Ameche scored the winning touchdown in sudden death. The Colts won the championship again in 1959. Ameche's football career came to an end in 1961 when his Achilles tendon snapped as he set up a block for Johnny Unitas.

HOUDINI OF THE HARDWOOD—Bob Cousy [1928–   ] Basketball. H/F Cousy got this nickname at Holy Cross College for his slick ball handling. His large hands and peripheral vision were keys to his success. But Cousy had begun the long hours of practice back when he was twelve years old. "I didn't have full control," he said later, "but that year I got so I could move the ball back and forth from one hand to the other without breaking the cadence of my dribble. I wasn't dribbling behind my back or setting up any trick stuff, but I was laying the groundwork for it." Cousy was also called COOZ.

HUMAN BUZZSAW (THE)—Henry Armstrong (1912–1988) Boxing. H/F Henry Armstrong (his real name was Henry Jackson) was called The Human Buzzsaw for his frenetic boxing style and Homicide Hank for his lethal punching. Over a ten-month period in 1937–1938, the hyperactive Armstrong won the featherweight crown from Petey Sarron, the welterweight championship from Barney Ross, and the lightweight championship from Lou Ambers. Armstrong was also called Hurricane Henry.

HUMAN GRASSHOPPER (THE)—Ed Delahanty (1867–1903) Baseball. H/F Known also by the nickname BIG ED, 6' 1" Ed Delahanty was dubbed The Human Grasshopper by the *Washington Post.* He received that less-than-complimentary sobriquet because, beset by gambling and drinking problems, Big Ed jumped from team to team to team. At the time of his death, he had even accepted a $4,000 advance to play for the New York Giants, even though he was still under contract to the Washington Senators. One of baseball's biggest mysteries is Delahanty's death. It seems that in the summer of 1903, Big Ed disappeared from his Detroit hotel room. Several days later, his mangled body was found at the base of Niagara Falls. (A recent book about that strange case is *July 2, 1903: The Mysterious Death of Hall-of-Famer Big Ed Delahanty* by Mike Sowell.) Big Ed finished his career in the big leagues with one of the highest lifetime batting averages—.346 in 7,493 at bats— and was the only player ever to win the batting crown in both the American and National leagues.

HUMAN HAIRPIN (THE)—Harry Harris (1880–1959) Boxing. He was the World Bantam Weight Champion from 1901 to 1902. He received his nickname because of his incredibly lean appearance. He stood 5' 8" yet weighed only 105 pounds.

HUMAN WINDMILL (THE)—Harry Greb (1894–1926) Boxing. H/F Harry Greb, who was the World Middleweight Champion from 1923 to 1926, came at his opponents with such a constant flurry of punches, punch after punch thrown without letup, that he was dubbed The Human Windmill. The only fighter ever to defeat the great Gene Tunney, Greb fought nearly two-dozen bouts a year. In 1919, he fought forty-four times. When The Human Windmill finally stopped fighting, he had had 294 bouts, winning 112 of them, losing only 8, drawing 3, and 170 no decisions. Greb was also called The Pittsburgh Windmill.

HURRY UP—Fielding Harris Yost (1871–1946) Football. H/F Yost, a college football coach, came by his nickname because he was always exhorting his athletes to "hurry up." In his first four seasons at the University of Michigan, Yost's teams won fifty-five games while losing only once, including a 49–0 defeat of Stanford in the very first Rose Bowl game (1902). From 1901–1927, Hurry Up Yost was the head football coach at Michigan, compiling a record of 164–20–10. (In 1905, he even found time to write a book, *Football for Player and Spectator.*) When he retired from coaching, he assumed the post of athletic director. In fact, Yost was Michigan's coach or athletic director for forty-one years. As fellow coach Bob Zuppke declared, "His greatest career at mighty Michigan extended from Heston to Harmon and back again. Try and erase that!" When he finally retired, Yost held until his death the title of Professor Emeritus of the Theory and Practice of Athletics. He was also called Point-a-Minute.

ICE MAIDEN (THE)—Chris Evert (1954–   ) Tennis. H/F Virginia Wade and Jean Rafferty had this to say about Chris Evert in the book, *Ladies of the Court:* "She was unnervingly cool, a robot disguised in a pretty dress but foregoing any pretence at emotion. Tennis as computer games. Audiences, especially in Britain, were cool to her." As the years went by, this image of Evert softened; however, at one time it was the common perception of her style of tennis. Hence, the nickname. She was also called Little Miss Cool.

THE ICE MAIDEN—Chris Evert (b. December 21, 1954) Tennis.
Chrissie was always calm, cool, and collected on the court.

ICEMAN [THE]—George Gervin [1952—   ] Basketball. Fatty Taylor of the Virginia Squires gave Gervin this nickname for being cool on the court. He showed little emotion even when his shooting turned hot as it often did. After being traded to San Antonio, Gervin led the Spurs to the playoffs in 1974, 1975, and 1976. In the late 1970s, Gervin was the first guard to win the NBA scoring title three straight times. Gervin was also called Ice.

INDIA RUBBER MAN [THE]—John Wooden [1910—   ] Basketball. H/F Wooden was nicknamed the India Rubber Man because as a three-time All-American at Purdue from 1930 to 1932 he always seemed to be bouncing up off the floor. As a pro he made 138 straight free throws. As the coach at UCLA he led the Bruins to seven straight NCAA titles (1967–1973) and nine championships in ten years. His teams won seventy-five straight games and used a full-court zone press to perfection. John Wooden has the distinction of being elected to the Hall of Fame both as a player and a coach.

INDIAN JOE—Joseph Guyon [1892–1971] Football. H/F Guyon was a Chippewa with a Native American name of O-Gee-Chidaha. "The government only gave us a sixth-grade education and as a result it was hard trying to make anything out of yourself," he once said. "Sports were one of the few ways a youngster could pull himself up." Guyon was an All-American halfback and a teammate of Jim Thorpe's at Carlisle; Guyon was also on the 1917 Georgia Tech team that didn't lose a game. He joined Jim Thorpe at Canton the next year and the Bulldogs went undefeated for three years. All told Guyon played for seven pro teams; the last was on the championship 1927 New York Giants.

INVINCIBLE ONE [THE]—Warren Spahn [1921—   ] Baseball. H/F There was good reason for the Boston Braves fan to chant: "Spahn and Sain and pray for rain." (Johnny Sain was the team's only other good pitcher.) Over a twenty-three-year career, Spahn threw 382 complete games—the most in recent times and the highest ever for a lefthander. He threw sixty-three shutouts and won twenty or more games thirteen times. Spahn was also called Hook and Spahnny.

IRON DUKE—Hank Iba [1904–1993] Basketball. H/F Coach Iba taught deliberate, defensive ball-control basketball at Oklahoma State. He believed that "airtight defense will get you a win more often than a high-geared offense." Iron Duke ruled his practices and teams the way his players slowed down and controlled the tempo of the games. (Rivals would sometimes call them the Slowpokes from Stallwater, instead of the Cowpokes form Stillwater.) But his thorough preparation of his players paid off; and this extended to his Olympic teams, which won two gold metals in 1964 and 1968 and one silver metal in 1972. (In 1968, he molded an Olympic team of relative unknowns into winners.) His college record was a sterling 767–338.

IRON HORSE [THE]—Lou Gehrig [1903–1941] Baseball. H/F Gehrig played in 2,130 consecutive games as if he were as unstoppable as a locomotive made of iron. His highest batting average for a season was .379 in 1930; and over a seventeen-year career, this first baseman batted .340. His one-season total for RBIs is 184 (1931), a record that has never been broken. In fact, THE PRIDE OF THE YANKEES, as he was also called, is third in career RBIs (behind Ruth and Aaron). Gehrig won MVP in 1927 and 1936; but he really scored as MVP in the hearts of fans with his tearful farewell in

1939. "I am the happiest man on the face of the earth," said Gehrig. At the time he was sick with a disease of the muscles (amyotrophic lateral sclerosis), now known as Lou Gehrig's disease, that would later kill him. He was also known as The Iron Man of Baseball, Columbia Lou (he attended Columbia University), Larrupin' Lou (he rapped the ball soundly), and Old Biscuit Pants (he filled out the seat of his uniform). Early in his career, he was sometimes referred to as Tanglefoot Lou.

IRON MAN [THE]—Joe McGinnity [1871–1929] Baseball. H/F Joe McGinnity could pitch practically every day. In 1903, he pitched and won a doubleheader three times. Five different seasons he pitched a total of over 400 innings. The Iron Man started 381 games and finished 314. In 1899, his rookie season, McGinnity won twenty-eight games. His best year was 1904 when he won thirty-five games and lost only eight. But over his entire ten-year career he averaged twenty-five wins a season.

IRON MAN—Emil Zatopek [1922–   ] Track and field. This distance runner had terrific stamina. At the 1952 Olympic Games, Zatopek won gold metals in the 5,000 meters (an Olympic record of 14:06:6), the 10,000 meters (an Olympic record of 29:17), and the marathon (a world record of 2:23:03:2).

IRON MIKE—August [Mike] Michalske [1903–1983] Football. H/F Michalske's family nickname was Mike; his football nickname was Iron Mike. Not only did he play on both offense and defense (as players did in those days), but he stayed free of injury through it all. "The players used to kid me," Michalske said. "They used to say I must have been getting paid by the minute." Iron Mike played for the Green Bay Packers with Johnny "BLOOD" McNally and Robert "BIG CAL" Hubbard on the championship teams from 1929 to 1931. He was one of the first linemen to use the BLITZ, also called RED-DOG. Iron Mike also liked to switch positions with another defensive lineman before the ball was snapped—a technique now called stunting. After his nine-year playing career was over, he coached in college and the pros until he retired in 1957.

IRON MIKE—Mike Tyson [1965–   ] Boxing. Tyson was as tough as iron and hit as if his gloves were filled with it. At nineteen, he became the youngest heavyweight champion and held the undisputed championship from 1987 to 1991, when he was upset by an overweight longshot, Buster Douglas. Before beginning a six-year jail sentence in 1991 for rape, Tyson had compiled a record of 41–1 with thirty-six KOs. Since his release, he has not regained his earlier prowess.

JACKIE ROBINSON OF GOLF [THE]—Charlie Sifford [1923–   ] Golf. Sifford began as a caddie back in North Carolina and later was the golfing instructor for singer Billy Eckstine. When Sifford first began playing on the tour in the 1960s (the PGA was all white until 1960), this African American was unable to stay in some of the hotels and even to play in some of the tournaments. But he persevered and in 1967 won the Hartford Open and in 1969 the Los Angeles Open. As a member of the Senior PGA Tour, Sifford won the 1980 Suntree Classic. Charlie Sifford gained his nickname by breaking the color barrier in golf as Jackie Robinson had for baseball in 1947.

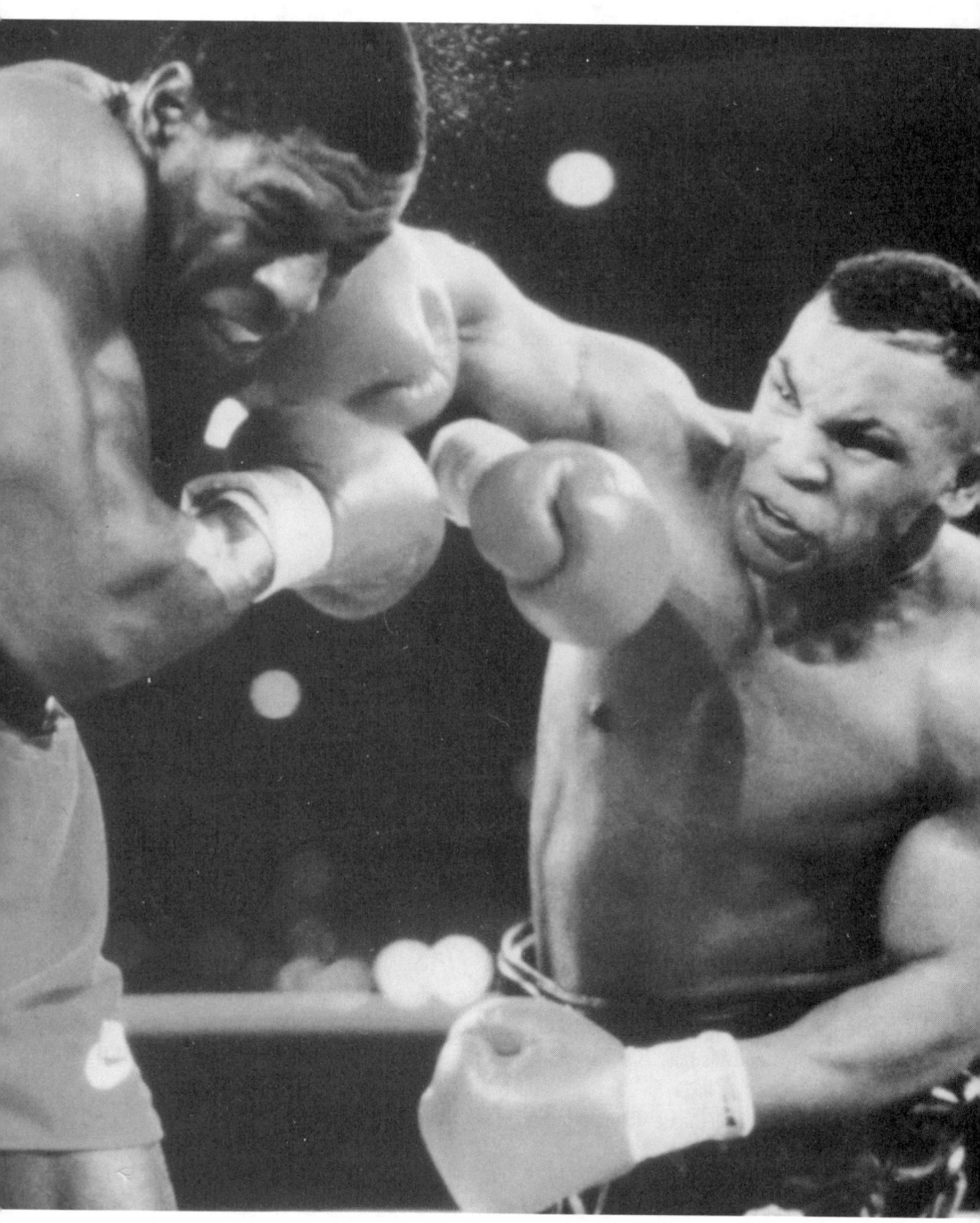

IRON MIKE—Mike Tyson (b. June 30, 1966) Boxing.
He might have been a great heavyweight boxer,
had not legal and personal problems overshadowed his accomplishments in the ring.

JAKE THE SNAKE—Jacques Plante [1929–1986] Hockey. H/F Plante brought two innovations to goaltending. The first was to wear a facemask on a regular basis. The second was to snake away from the crease to grab a shot wide of the mark and pass it off to a teammate. This new method of net minding, of roaming away from the net, along with spearing the puck with his glove, brought him the nickname of Jake the Snake. "Goaltending a normal job?" Plante once remarked. "Sure! How would you like it in your job if every time you made a mistake, a red light went on over your desk and fifteen thousand people stood up and yelled at you?" Plante shared the Vezina Trophy in 1969 with MR. GOALIE, Glenn Hall.

J.C.—Jean Claude Tremblay [1939–   ] Hockey. This defenseman for the Montreal Canadiens scored 57 goals and had 306 assists in 794 regular season games. In 108 playoff games, he scored 14 goals and had 51 assists.

JEPTHA—Eppa Rixey [1891–1963] Baseball. H/F Eppa Jeptha was a rhyming nickname. Four times Rixey won twenty or more games; his best year was 25–13 in 1922. At the end of his twenty-one-year career he had 266 wins. Because this pitcher was 6' 6" and from Culpepper, Virginia, he was also called The Eiffel Tower of Culpepper.

JET [THE]—Joe Perry [1927–   ] Football. H/F Perry received his nickname from San Francisco quarterback Frankie Albert: "When that guy comes by you to take a handoff, his slipstream darn near knocks you over. He's jet-propelled." Perry's first handoff in his first game in the NFL resulted in a fifty-eight-yard touchdown. Durable, Perry played fullback for sixteen years. He was only the fourth back to have carried the ball over 1,000 yards in a season and the first to gain 1,000 yards in two consecutive seasons. By career's end he had rushed for 9,723 total yards for a five-yards-per-carry average and seventy-one touchdowns. As a pass receiver, he had caught 260 passes for 2,021 yards and twelve touchdowns.

JH—John Henry Taylor [1871-1963] Golf. Taylor (his nickname, of course, was for his initials) won the British Open five times (1894, 1895, 1900, 1909, and 1913); five times he was the runner-up. Along with Harry Vardon and James Braid, JH was a part of the GREAT TRIUMVIRATE.

JIMBO—Jimmy Connors [1952–   ] Tennis. H/F Connors, one of the true greats of modern tennis, grew up in Belleville, Illinois, and attended college at UCLA, where he was named All-American. He turned professional in 1972. In 1974 he won the men's singles titles in England, the United States, and Australia. He went on to win Wimbledon in 1982 and the U.S. Open again in 1976, 1978, 1982, and 1983. In 1991, at the age of thirty-nine Connors captured middle-aged hearts everywhere by making it all the way to the semifinal round at the U.S. Open.

JIM THORPE OF HASKELL [THE]—John Levi [1896–1946] Football, baseball, basketball, track and field. Levi was the all-round athlete at Haskell Institute that Jim Thorpe had been at Carlisle. Once during a baseball game, he won the shot put, discuss, and high jump between innings. When he wasn't engaged in baseball and track, he was in spring football practice. Levi was also called Big Skee. (His younger brother was called Little Skee.)

JIMBO—Jimmy Connors (b. September 2, 1952) Tennis. In contrast to "Sweet Pete" Sampras, Connors had a bad temper and frequently exhibited bad behavior on the tennis court. But what a player! Jimbo won 109 pro single titles in his career.

JOCKO—John Bertrand Conlan (1898–1988) Baseball. H/F Conlan was nicknamed after a second baseman named Arthur Joseph Conlan who had the nickname Jocko (for bench jockey). One day in July of 1935, Jocko Conlan was injured—and having a lackluster career with the White Sox anyway—when he volunteered to take over for a sick umpire for the second game of a double-header between Chicago and the St. Louis Browns. He liked the experience so much that the next year he was umpiring in the minors. Four years later he was an umpire in the National League. Jocko was known for using his left hand to make all signals and his quickness for ejecting players. He was also the first umpire in the National League to wear an outside chest protector. Conlan was selected to be an umpire in six All-Star Games and six World Series.

JOHNNY-WON'T-HIT-TODAY—John William Henry Tyler Douglas (1882–1930) Cricket. This ironic nickname came from Douglas's initials and his defensive batting in cricket during the early 1900s. It was somewhat undeserved as he hit close to 25,000 runs and took slightly less than 2,000 wickets.

JOLLY CHOLLY—Charlie Grimm [1896–1983] Baseball. This first baseman was anything but grim; as his nickname attests, he loved to have a good time. After a long career playing for the Cubs, he had another long career managing them. Grimm left his heart in Wrigley Field, along with his ashes after his death. He was also called The Young Pretender.

JOLTIN' JOE—Joe DiMaggio [1914–] Baseball. H/F This onomatopoeic nickname was first used in 1938 when Joe jolted the American League with a .381 average. And it was cinched in 1941 by his as-yet-unbroken record of hitting safely in fifty-six straight games. Not only was the country following the box scores for a month and a half, but also this center fielder's exploits were captured in the song "Joltin' Joe DiMaggio" by the Les Brown Band. Years later DiMag's effect is still being felt. He has been called baseball's greatest living player; and even Simon and Garfunkel have referred to him in the lyric of one of their popular songs. DiMaggio was also called Big Guy, DiMag, Joe D, and YANKEE CLIPPER.

JUDGE [THE]—Jeff Torborg [1941–] Baseball. Jeff Torborg earned this nickname because he could usually be found sitting on the *bench* during his playing days from 1964 to 1973 with the Los Angeles Dodgers and the California Angels. Although The Judge backed up two All-Star catchers for the Dodgers—first John Roseboro and then Tom Haller—Torborg still managed to catch two no-hitters (Sandy Koufax in 1965 and Bill Singer in 1970). Catching a third no-hitter (Nolan Ryan of the Angels in 1973) left him only one shy of the record of four no-hitters caught by Ray Schalk. When his playing days were over in 1974, Torborg launched a second career. He returned to Rutgers, his alma mater, as a coach before moving up to the Cleveland Indians. And in 1977, Torborg became the manager of the Indians. Fired from that position, Torborg spent the next ten years as a coach for the New York Yankees. This prepared him for his second go-round at managing. Hired by the Chicago White Sox in 1988, Torborg finished his second year as the manager of the year with a 94–68 record. Then he struggled with the so-so New York Mets before being replaced by Dallas Green in 1993.

JUDY—William J. Johnson [1899–1989] Baseball [Negro Leagues]. H/F Johnson was one of the great black baseball stars for the Homestead Grays and the Pittsburgh Crawfords. As Connie Mack once remarked: "If Judy were only white, he could name his price." In 1926–1927, Judy Johnson batted a superb .374 and played a masterly third base. In 1930, he was player-manager for the Homestead Grays. With the Crawfords in 1935, he batted .367, leading that legendary team to a National Negro League Championship over the New York Cubans. Although records were often incomplete, his lifetime batting average is considered to be .344. In 1975, major-league baseball recognized his greatness by inducting him into the Baseball Hall of Fame at Cooperstown. Johnson also called The Black Pie Traynor and Jing.

JUICE [THE]—O. J. Simpson [1947–] Football. H/F O. J. Simpson's real name is Orenthal James, but it was believed in some quarters that the initials stood for orange juice. After all, he was from California. This nickname must have seemed formal, as it was shortened to The Juice. And when Simpson played for the Buffalo Bills, the offensive line was known as The Electric

Company—for "springing loose the juice.") As a running back for the University of Southern California, The Juice helped the Trojans to their number one ranking in 1966 and to a 14–3 victory over Indiana in the 1968 Rose Bowl. For his record-setting 1,309 yards rushing in 1968, O. J. Simpson won the Heisman Trophy. (Simpson also helped break a record in another sport; he was a member of the 440-yard relay team that set a world record in 1967.) The records didn't stop when he joined the Buffalo Bills (then of the American Football League) as pro football's number one draft pick. In the very first game of the 1973 season, O. J. broke the all-time single game rushing mark by galloping 250 yards against the New England Patriots. That season The Juice also set a single-season rushing record of 2,003 yards. (In 1984, Eric Dickerson playing for the Los Angeles Rams broke this record with 2,105 yards.) In 1975, The Juice scored twenty-three touchdowns—a record that still stands. During his eleven-year career, O. J. Simpson rushed for 11,236 yards or 4.7 yards per carry. His popularity increased when he appeared in television commercials with golfing-great Arnold Palmer and in the Naked Gun films. Nowadays, he is best known for being brought to trial for the alleged murder of his ex-wife.

JUMBO—James F. Elliot [1915–1981] Track and field. H/F Jumbo Elliot, who helped develop so many runners over the years, was the head track coach at Villanova. His athletes set fourteen world records and thirty-one American indoor records; twenty-two of his athletes were in the Olympics.

JUMPIN' JOE—Joe Fulks [1921–   ] Basketball. H/F Fulks' leaping ability and his pivot shots made him the first big scorer in the NBA with a 23.2 point average in 1947, the year Philadelphia won the championship. This forward's high during his career was sixty-three points against Indianapolis in 1949. In 489 games from 1947 to 1954, Jumpin' Joe scored 8,591 points.

JUMPIN' JOHNNY—John Green [1933–   ] Basketball. The 6' 6" Green was one of the game's best jumpers. At Michigan State he pulled down 1,036 rebounds. During a long career with many teams in the pros, he was extremely accurate from the floor; however, he never could seem to sink free throws.

JUNIOR—Jim Gilliam [1928–1978] Baseball. Gilliam was called junior because at twenty he was the youngest player on the Baltimore Elite Giants in the Negro National League. In 1953, as a member of the Brooklyn Dodgers, Gilliam was Rookie of the Year. After his playing days were over, he was a coach for the BUMS until his untimely death. The L.A. Dodgers retired this infielder/outfielder's number—19.

JUNK MAN [THE]—Eddie Lopat [1918–1992] Baseball. In the 1940s and 1950s, Eddie Lopat threw a wide assortment of off-speed pitches for the Yankees. Ben Epstein, a writer for the New York *Daily Mirror,* wrote an article about Lopat titled, "The Junkman Cometh," an ironic take-off on the title of Eugene O'Neill's play. Lopat was also called Steady Eddie.

KAISER [THE]—Franz Beckenbauer [1945—] Soccer. In the late 1960s and early 1970s, Beckenbauer played sweeper for Bayern Munchen and West Germany, where he brought great changes to the tactics of defending the goal. He was in every sense an attacking sweeper, and he was the leader of his teams—hence the nickname. Beckenbauer was the European Player of the Year in 1972 and 1976. Kaiser Franz ended his European playing career with a total of 103 goals, a record in Germany. He also played for the New York Cosmos in the North American Soccer League.

KAMIKAZE—Alan Mayer [1952—] Soccer. Although soccer is the most popular sport in the world and one of the most popular in the United States for children and teenagers to play, it has never really caught on in the U.S. at the professional level. Consequently, many of the best soccer players here fail to become as well known as their counterparts in baseball, football, and basketball. Kamikaze Mayer is one such player. Playing in the Major International Soccer League (MISL) for the New Jersey Rockets and the San Diego Sockers, Mayer was an exciting goalkeeper whose daring and spectacular style of play earned him the nickname Kamikaze. (In WW II, the Kamikaze— a word meaning "Divine Wind"— was the Japanese air corps that flew suicide missions against U.S. targets, especially ships.) Mayer was voted the North American Player of the Year in 1978, was twice the winning goalie in the MISL's All-Star Game, was the MISL's Most Valuable Player in 1983, and played for the U.S. national soccer team eighteen times.

KANGAROO KID [THE]—Jim Pollard [1922–deceased] Basketball. H/F Although he stood 6' 3", Pollard received his nickname for his ability to leap high off the floor and drop the ball through the hoop. This forward had a thirteen-point average for the Minneapolis Lakers from 1948 to 1955 and was on four All-Star teams. Good at all phases of the game, and possessing a superb jump shot, the Kangaroo Kid was once selected as the best player in the history of the NBA, even ahead of Big George Mikan! (This was long before Michael Jordan appeared on the scene.) During his career he made 1,417 assists and collected 2,487 rebounds. He later coached four different pro teams and had a 130–165 record.

KANSAS IRONMAN [THE]—Glenn Cunningham [1909–1988] Track and field. H/F Badly burned in a childhood accident, the young Cunningham was not expected to walk again. However, he battled back to become a runner in high school and at the University of Kansas, where he ran both the half-mile and the mile. Cunningham did not have a strong finishing kick, so he often had to make his move to the front of the pack at the halfway point or earlier. In 1913, Glenn Cunningham, broke the world record for the mile (4:06.8) and the indoor record for the 1500 meters (3:52.2). He was also called The Kansas Flyer and The Kansas Flash.

KENTUCKY COLONEL [THE]—Earle Combs [1899–1976] Baseball. H/F Combs, who played outfield and was a member of the New York Yankees' MURDERER'S ROW, hailed from Pebworth, Kentucky. Three times Combs led the American League in triples and he boasted a twelve-year career batting average of .325. As a leadoff hitter, he was also known as Waiter; he would get on base and wait for others to get him home. From 1948 to 1952, he managed the archival Red Sox. Combs was also called The Mail Carrier and The Southwestern Gentleman.

KENTUCKY COLONEL [THE]—Frank Vernon Ramsey [1931–   ] Basketball. H/F Born in Madisonville, Kentucky, Ramsey was a 1948 High School All-American. He went on to play for the University of Kentucky, and from there became the first-round draft pick for Red Auerbach's Boston Celtics. The highlight of this forward's fine career occurred in the double-overtime of game seven of the championship series between the Celtics and the St. Louis Hawks. Throwing off-balance, The Kentucky Colonel sunk a twenty-foot basket that gave the Celtics their first NBA title. When he retired, he had scored 81,378 points, averaging 13.4 points a game.

KI—Charles C. Aldrich [1916–1983] Football. Member of the College Football Hall of Fame, Aldrich played most of his career with the Washington Redskins. He received his nickname from a slightly older brother who called Charles a "ki" baby because he cried a lot as a baby.

KID [THE]—Steve Cauthen [1960–   ] Horse racing. As a seventeen-year-old, The Kid took America by storm as a jockey with victories in 487 races in 1977 and by winning the Triple Crown atop Affirmed in 1978. There was even a biography by Pete Axthelm about this eighteen-year-old. But after losing 110 in a row the winter of 1978–1979 at Santa Anita, Cauthen went off to race in England. Nowadays he races in England, on the Continent, in Australia, and Hong Kong. "When I started riding as a kid in Ohio," said Cauthen in 1992, "I honestly thought that if I could be the leading jockey at River Downs, that would be great. Now I travel all over the world riding good horses. That is what I want to do. I'm just delighted with my life."

KID—Charles Keinath [1886–1966] Basketball. Keinath was such a good ball handler that the rule against using both hands to dribble was put into effect. Keinath's ability to control a game can be seen in Penn's 16–15 win over Columbia in 1908—a game in which he scored all of Penn's sixteen points and his ball control kept the game so low scoring. Keinath did not care for the modern style of basketball. (Imagine what he would think of the high-flying, slam-dunking, high-scoring basketball played today!)

KID—Charles Augustus Nichols [1869–1953] Baseball. H/F Nichols began his major-league pitching career at twenty-one. Before his fifteen-year career was over, Kid Nichols had started 562 games and completed 533 of them. He had won thirty or more games seven times and thrown forty-eight shutouts. His record was 360–202 with an ERA of 2.94.

KID [THE]—Ted Williams [1918–   ] Baseball. H/F Ted Williams received his first nickname from Johnny Orlando, the equipment manager of the Boston Red Sox. When Williams arrived for training camp in 1938 two weeks late, Orlando asked him who he was. After being told, the crusty manager replied, "So, the kid has finally arrived." Williams' teammates on the Boston Red Sox were soon calling him The Kid. Sometimes they called him The Malted Milk Kid; since at the time he was seventeen and weighed only 148, Williams had developed the habit of drinking four or five of them a day. He was also called The Big Guy, THE SPLENDID SPLINTER, and Teddy Ballgame.

KILLER—Harmon Killebrew [1936–   ] Baseball. H/F Killebrew's name and his slugging earned him his nickname. He was the home-run leader six times and had forty-nine homers in 1969—the same year he won the MVP. During his twenty-two-year major-league career Killer hit 573 home runs. He was also called The Fat Kid because of his less than perfect physique.

KING—Francis M. Clancy [1903-1986] Hockey. H/F The nickname of this 135-pound defenseman was handed down from his father who had been a star football player. In 1957, Clancy said that the *M* in his name stood for Moses (actually it was Michael), and like Moses he was going to lead his team out of the wilderness. King Clancy persevered through a seventy-year career in the NHL as a player, coach, umpire, and general manager.

KING—Carl Hubbell [1903-1988] Baseball. H/F In the 1933 World Series, King Carl had a shutout going for eleven innings. And in the 1934 All-Star Game, Hubbell struck out Babe Ruth, Lou Gehrig, Jimmie Foxx, Al Simmons, and Joe Cronin in a row (and all were later to become Hall of Famers). For five straight seasons Carl Hubbell used his screwball to win twenty or more games. He was also called THE MEAL TICKET and Money.

KING—Michael Joseph Kelley [1857-1894] Baseball. H/F Kelley led the National League in 1886 with a batting average of .388; and his lifetime average was .307. When he ran around the bases, people in the stands would holler, "Slide, Kelly, slide!" King obliged with his new-fangled hook slide or even a slide on his belly. He was also called THE $10,000 BEAUTY.

KING [THE]—Hugh McElhenny [1928-   ] Football. H/F McElhenny was called King because of the way he performed on the field. For instance, in the closing minutes of a game in 1953 with Los Angeles, San Francisco called a screen pass to McElhenny. Even though the Rams were expecting the play and half the team had a shot at him, they couldn't stop McElhenny as he galloped seventy-one yards. At the nine-yard line he was pushed out of bounds, thus setting up the game-winning field goal. In his thirteen-years as a running back—McElhenny was one of the first players not to be on the field for both offense and defense—The King averaged 4.8 yards per carry for a total of 5,281 yards.

KING KONG—Dave Kingman [1948-   ] Baseball. Kingman's nickname was for the great fictional ape of page and screen King Kong. He was 6' 6" and crunched 442 home runs. Another nickname for Kingman was Sky King, referring to the old radio show to describe his towering homers.

KING OF AMATEUR SWIMMING—Mark Spitz [1950-   ] Swimming. Spitz, who won a record seven gold medals at the 1972 Summer Olympics, had this to say about winning the last medal. "Mentally, this last race was the hardest one for me to get up for.... I concerned myself with winning this as if it was the first race of the Games."

KING OF THE DAREDEVILS—Evel Knievel [1939-   ] Motorcyclist. "Jumping, I stand or lean forward on the balls of my feet," explained Knievel about the art of jumping over cars or canyons or whatever. "The motorcycle's tendency is to buck and come down over backwards on me.

So I try and lean forward to hold it down. I want to go off the ramp right at the top of the power curve. If I do, it'll go straight through the air. If I don't, this motorcycle has a tendency to drift sideways and cross up."

KING OF THE LINKS—Bobby Jones [1902–1971] Golf. H/F Jones won thirteen of the twenty-seven major tournaments he entered (and second in many of those he didn't win). In 1930, Jones set himself the goal of winning the Grand Slam (the British Open, the British Amateur, the U.S. Amateur, and the U.S. Open Championship). When he succeeded (the only one who ever did), he turned to his law career and other interests. In all, Jones won three British Opens, four U.S. Opens, and five U.S. Amateurs. In 1934, Jones founded the Masters tournament. See THE LILY PAD SHOT.

KING OF SOFTBALL [THE]—Eddie Feigner [1925–] Softball. Eddie Feigner, the last of the true barnstorming softball players, was determined to be the greatest softball pitcher of all time. Creating a four-man softball team called The King and His Court (since 1965, his son Eddie Feigner, Jr., has played shortstop), Feigner and three others have played nine-member teams all over the United States. During one incredible stretch with the King of Softball throwing a 104-mile-per-hour pitch, Feigner's team won all fifty-seven games played in forty-one days. The King and His Court have performed for millions of sports fans and have been instrumental in increasing the popularity of the game.

KING OF THE SPORTS PROMOTERS—Tex Rickard [1870–1929] Promoter. H/F For the bout between Jack Dempsey and Georges Carpentier on July 2, 1921, Rickard was the first promoter of a million-dollar gate. Eighty thousand people shelled out close to $1.8 million to see Dempsey's fourth round knockout of the Frenchman.

KING RICHARD—Richard Petty [1937–] Auto racing. H/F Petty is the all-time career leader for NASCAR with 200 victories. In the words of the Roger Miller song he is the "King of the Road." During his thirty-four years on the racing circuit, King Richard started from the pole position 127 times and won the Daytona 500 seven times and the Pepsi 400 three times. He was also called King of the Stockers.

KITTEN [THE]—Harvey Haddix [1925–] Baseball. There was a similarity between the way pitchers Harvey Haddix and Harry Breechen bounded off the mound to field. Because Breechen was known as THE CAT, Haddix became known as The Kitten. Harvey Haddix was 136-113 with twenty shutouts. On May 26, 1959, he pitched a perfect game for twelve innings; but in the thirteenth he allowed a hit, and the Pirates lost to Milwaukee 1–0.

KLU—Ted Kluszewski [1924–1988] Baseball. Klu wore short sleeves to show his bulging biceps. He displayed this power with a league-leading 49 home runs in 1954 and 192 hits in 1955. For a big man, though, he was a graceful fielder at first base.

KNIGHT OF KENNETT SQUARE [THE]—Herb Pennock [1894–1948] Baseball. H/F Pennock was 5–0 in four World Series. On the great Yankees' teams between 1923–1933, Pennock's record was 164–90. The Knight of Kennett Square (he was born in Kennett Square, Pennsylvania, and pitched as if he were in the service of King Arthur) was 240–162 during his twenty-two-year career.

KOKOMO KID [THE]—Don Johnson [1940–] Bowling. H/F Nicknamed the Kokomo Kid because he was born in Kokomo, Indiana, Don Johnson achieved considerable fame in bowling during the 1960s and 1970s. In 1971 and 1972, the Bowling Writers Association of America named him the Bowler of the Year. During his career, The Kokomo Kid bowled sixteen American Bowling Congress sanctioned 300 games; and Johnson compiled a .190 average over a twenty-year career.

LADY LINDY—Amelia Earhart [1898–1937] Aviation. After completing a Trans-Atlantic flight with two others (she had held the controls for only a minute), Earhart was given this nickname by publisher G. P. Putnam for whom she was writing her autobiography. Lady Lindy seemed especially appropriate for this aviatrix because not only was she the first woman to fly across the Atlantic (Charles Lindburgh, THE LONE EAGLE, had made the journey only the year before), but she also bore a striking resemblance to "Lucky Lindy." Later on, Lady Lindy was the first woman to fly the Atlantic alone, the first to fly nonstop across the United States, and the first woman to fly from Hawaii to the United States. Attempting to fly around the world, Earhart and her navigator, Fred Noonan, disappeared with their aircraft, the *Flying Laboratory,* on July 2, 1937. She was also called A.E.

LADY LINDY—Amelia Earhart (1898-193_). Flying. Perhaps in a different world, Charles A. Lindbergh would have been known as GENTLEMAN EARHART?

LADY MAGIC—Nancy Lieberman-Cline [1958–   ] Basketball. Also known as Fire (because of the intensity of her play), Nancy Lieberman-Cline was one of the outstanding women basketball players, whose uniform jersey, no. 10, is on display at the Basketball Hall of Fame in Springfield, Massachusetts. In 1980, Lieberman-Cline was named the Jewish Athlete of the Year, and when the Woman's American Basketball Association (WABA) was formed in 1984, Lady Magic signed a three-year contract for $250,000 with the Dallas franchise. Unfortunately, the WABA folded before Lady Magic could complete her first full season. In 1986, when she signed to play with the Springfield Flames, Lieberman-Cline became the first woman to play in a men's professional basketball league.

LAUGHING LARRY—Lawrence Joseph Doyle [1886–1974] Baseball. The spirited enthusiasm embedded in his nickname can be grasped in his often-quoted cry; "It's great to be young and a Giant." Laughing Larry played shortstop primarily for the New York Giants from 1907 to 1923.

LAWNMOWER—Larry Csonka [1946–   ] Football. H/F This nickname refers to this 6' 3", 230-pound fullback's habit of lowering his head and mowing down the would-be tackler rather than running around him. This running style also caused Csonka pain—two concussions and many broken noses. He was also called ZONK.

LE GROS BILL—Jean Beliveau [1931–   ] Hockey. H/F Big Bill stood 6' 3", weighed 205 pounds, and was arguably the best center who ever played in the NHL. Le Gros Bill (Big Bill in French) played for the Montreal Canadiens from 1951 to 1971 and led them to ten Stanley Cups. In the 1955–1956 season he won the Art Ross Trophy for scoring the most points in a single season when he scored forty-seven goals and had forty-one assists for eighty-eight points. Twice he won the Hart Trophy (given to the NHL player judged to be the most valuable to his team). By the time he retired, Le Gros Bill had played in 1,055 games, and scored 482 goals with 661 assists. He was also called Big Jean.

LEFTY—Robert Moses Grove [1900–1975] Baseball. H/F Only certain lefthanders are known better as Lefty than by their real first names. Lefty Grove was one of these pitchers. From 1925 to 1933, Grove pitched for Connie Mack's Athletics; and from 1934 to 1941, he pitched for the Red Sox. Nine times he was the ERA leader and five times he had the best winning percentage (both major-league records). Lefty Grove's career record was 300-141. He was also called Old Mose.

LIGHT-HORSE—Harry Cooper [1904–   ] Golf. H/F Cooper was called Light-Horse because he played so quickly on the golf course. In 1926, he won the first Los Angeles Open; in 1932 and 1937 he won the Canadian Open. Also in 1937, Cooper won the first Vardon Trophy, given for the lowest average scores.

LIGHT OF ISRAEL [THE]—Daniel Mendoza [1764–1836] Boxing. H/F Mendoza was smaller (5' 7", 160 pounds) than his bigger heavyweight opponents, but he fought smarter. Even so, he was called a coward by many for his hit-and-run style. Mendoza was champion until 1795 when GENTLEMAN JACKSON dethroned him by grabbing his hair and hitting him repeatedly.

LI'L ABNER—Cliff Hagan [1931–   ] Basketball. H/F Hagan got his nickname because he was strong (6' 4" and 215 pounds) and from Kentucky. This two-time All-American could play center at Kentucky because of his aggressive play and hook shot. On the St. Louis Hawks, he was one of the stalwarts, averaging eighteen points a game for ten years, and helping them to win the NBA championship in 1958. Hagan closed out his career on the ABA Dallas Chapparals as a player-coach with a fifteen-point average and a 109–90 record. See UNMATCHABLES.

LINK—Roy Lyman [1898–1972] Football. H/F Lyman played tackle for a 1921 University of Nebraska team that scored 283 points to its opponents' seventeen points, a 1922 and 1923 Canton Bulldogs pro team that won two NFL titles in a row, a 1924 Cleveland team that won the league championship, and on the Chicago Bears when they won the NFL championship in 1933. Lyman made good things happen. As Steve Owen, the New York Giants head coach once said, "Link was the first defensive lineman to ever move from his position before the ball was centered. His movements kept you guessing all the time, and most of the time you guessed wrong."

LIP [THE]—Leo Durocher [1905–1991] Baseball. H/F In 1927, Yankee players on the famed MURDERERS' ROW called their teammate Lippy for his brash talk and cocky manner. His name was later shortened to The Lip. Durocher went on to become the captain of the 1934 St. Louis Cardinals (see GASHOUSE GANG) and was the epitome of the good fielding, no-hit shortstop. But it was for his mouth that The Lip made his mark as a player and a manager (his confrontations with umpires were legion) and as a baseball commentator ("Goodbye Dolly Grey," he'd say whenever a homer was hit). He was married to movie star Loraine Day. This one-time manager of the Dodgers is also remembered for having said during the 1947 pennant race of rival Giants' manager Mel Ott: "Nice guys finish last." He was also called Lippy, Leo Lippy, and Little Shepherd of Coogan's Bluff.

LITTLE BILL—William M. Johnston [1895–1946] Tennis. H/F At 5' 8" and 120 pounds, Johnston was one of the smallest men ever to win the National Championship, defeating Maurice McLoughlin in 1915 and BIG BILL Tilden in 1919. Johnston's major weapon was a wicked Western topspin forehand and a knack for volleying. In 1920 and 1922–1925, Little Bill was second to Big Bill.

LITTLE CAESAR—Abe Saperstein [1901–1966] Basketball. H/F Saperstein, who began the Harlem Globetrotters, was given this nickname by his players, who often found the 5-foot-tall Saperstein dictatorial. Little Caesar was involved in every aspect of the team. At one time he was even the only substitute. He was also called The Barnum of Basketball.

LITTLE CHOCOLATE—George Dixon [1870–1909] Boxing. H/F Born in Nova Scotia, Dixon's first nickname referred to his skin color; his second (The Fighter Without a Flaw) to how good he was. (Speaking of firsts, Dixon was the first nonwhite to hold a world championship and the first boxer to use shadowboxing in his training.) Over a twenty-year period, Dixon fought an amazing 800 fights. In 1890, he became the featherweight champion by defeating Nunc Wallace of England in the eighteenth round. In 1891, he became the featherweight champion by beating Abe Willis of Australia in the fifth. Little Chocolate held that title until 1900.

LITTLE DUTCHMAN [THE]—Bob Zuppke [1879–1957] Football. Zuppke moved from Germany as a child and was too small to play football. However, he did become the head coach at Illinois and talked RED Grange into going out for football. Later, Zuppke developed the flea flicker and the screen pass. His overall record was 131–81–12.

LITTLE EVA—William Alexander Lange [1871–1950] Baseball. This nickname that sounds like the stage name of a burlesque dancer signifies that Lange liked ballroom dancing. He received his unflattering nickname because of his mincing walk. But there was no doubt that this outfielder could grind it out at the plate. His seven-year career batting average was a sizzling .330. He was also called Twinkletoes and (a contradictory) Big Bill.

LITTLE JOE—Joe Morgan [1943–   ] Baseball. H/F Morgan may have been only 5' 7" and 150 pounds, but he is the only second baseman to win two MVPs in a row. And in the seventh game of the 1975 World Series, he knocked in a run in the ninth inning to give the Reds the victory. "I will never be able to compare myself to Stan Musial or Willie Mays or Mickey Mantle," said Morgan. "They left big footprints and I left small ones. But I'm in the Hall of Fame, too."

LITTLE MARY—Mary Decker [1959–   ] Track and Field. Decker first came to the attention of the track world in her early teens. When she was fourteen years old she stood only five feet tall and weighed eighty pounds (hence, her nickname). The following year, 1974, she set an indoor record in the 880, lowering it a week later to 2:02.3. Since then she has set world indoor records from 800 meters to two miles and the United States outdoor records from 800 meters to 10,000 meters. Unfortunately, in the 1984 Olympic Games, she fell down, after being entangled with Zola Budd of Germany, and was out of the race that she had been favored to win.

LITTLE MISS ALMOST—Sarah Palfrey [1913–   ] Tennis. H/F Only 5' 3", Palfrey had been in the finals of the United States National Singles Tournament twice before she finally won it in 1941 at the age of twenty-eight. She won again in 1945, defeating Pauline Betz, 3–6, 8–6, 6–4. Palfrey retired immediately afterwards.

LITTLE MISS GRUNT—Monica Seles [1973–   ] Tennis. When Monica Seles stepped onto Center Court for her first Wimbledon final in 1992, fans in the stands carried tabloids that called her Public Enemy No. 1, and Little Miss Grunt. It seems that many fans and officials were displeased with Seles' habit of making grunts and high-pitched braying U-n-n-h-H-E-E-E sounds on almost every shot. One paper in Britain stated, "We must trust that she learns to curb the sound effects before the women's game begins to go the way of all-in wrestling." She stopped grunting in her Wimbledon finals match and lost 6–2, 6–1 to Steffi Graf. Still, one wonders why everyone is making such a big fuss over some honest athletic sounds. Few could say that Seles, after winning three legs of the Grand Slam—the French Open, the U.S. Open, and the Australian Open—in 1991 and 1992, did not deserve her Number 1 ranking. One who did was an unemployed thirty-eight-year-old man from East Germany. In a scene that could have been right out of an Alfred Hitchcock movie, Seles was resting during a changeover in a match with Magdalena Maleeva in Hamburg, Germany, when this deranged spectator rushed forward and stabbed Seles with a nine-inch boning knife.

LITTLE MISS PIGTAILS—Dorothy Augusta Schroeder (1928–   ) Baseball (All-American Girls Baseball League). Schroeder started playing shortstop at fifteen and wore her hair in pigtails. She played all eleven years the league was in existence, making the change from underhanded softball in 1943 to side-arm baseball in 1946 to overhanded baseball in 1948.

LITTLE MISS POKER FACE—Helen Wills (1906–1998) Tennis. H/F It was Grantland Rice who dubbed Wills Little Miss Poker Face for not showing any emotion on the tennis court. She neither acknowledged her opponent nor paid attention to the crowd. Wearing the green-lined white eyeshade that was her trademark, she was all business. As Helen Wills Moody wrote in her auto-biography *Fifteen-Thirty:* "I had one thought and that was to put the ball across the net. I was simply myself, too deeply concentrated on the game for any extraneous thought." In 1926, Wills met Suzanne Lenglen, the premier player of that day, at Cannes. "I never had such a thrill in my life," said the twenty-one-year-old Phi Beta Kappa student who had taken the semester off from U.S.C. "It was our only meeting and the greatest match I ever played. Suzanne was just as good as I thought she was." Langlen won 6–3, 8–6. From 1927 to 1938, Little Miss Poker Face won nineteen Grand Slam tournaments (eight Wimbledon singles, seven U.S. championships, and four French singles titles). She was also called The Princess and Queen Helen.

LITTLE MISS POKER FACE—
Helen Wills (1906-1998) Tennis. She rarely showed emotion on the courts.

LITTLE MISS SURE SHOT—Annie Oakley (1860–1926) Sharpshooter. From thirty paces, Annie Oakley (her real name was Phoebe Anne Oakley Moses) could hit a playing card on edge, a dime tossed into the air, a cigarette from someone's mouth. She could also break six glass balls thrown into the air, firing three double-barrelled shotguns. Even after her retirement as a star attraction with Buffalo Bill Cody's Wild West Show, Oakley could still at the age of sixty-two score 100 in a row trapshooting. She was also called Little Missy.

LITTLE MISS SURE SHOT—Annie Oakley (1860-1926) Sharpshooter.
Free passes to sporting events were once called Annie Oakleys because of the holes punched.

LITTLE MO—Maureen Catherine Connolly (1934–1969) Tennis. H/F Guided by the great tennis coach, Eleanor "TEACH" Tennant, Maureen Connolly developed into a great baseline player and the first sixteen year old to win the U. S. women's singles championship. From 1951 to 1954, Connolly won three Wimbledon tournaments, three U. S. championships, two French championships, and one Australian championship. In 1953 she was the first woman ever to win a Grand Slam—the four major championships in a calendar year. Maureen's nickname Little Mo was given to her by Nelson Fisher, a sportswriter for *The San Diego Union.* It referred to the *Missouri,* a World War II battleship. The 5' 3" Maureen Connolly's arsenal of tennis weapons could seem as powerful as the guns of this battleship. At the age of nineteen, Little Mo's tennis career was cut short by a horseback-riding accident.

LITTLE NAPOLEON—John J. McGraw (1873–1934) Baseball. H/F Like Napoleon, John J. McGraw was a small man who drove himself and his men. This third baseman became the manager of the New York Giants in 1902. Maintaining that position until 1938, he and his Giants won championship after championship in the National League and victories in all nine of their World Series. Little Napoleon once proudly proclaimed, "With my team, I'm absolute Czar." He was also called Muggsy, a nickname he hated.

LITTLE POISON—Paul Runyon (1908–   ) Golf. H/F Runyon was nicknamed Little Poison because he was small at 5' 7" but played tough on and around the greens. In 1934, Runyon won seven tournaments and repeated his record the next year. In all, he won fifty tournaments before turning to teaching full time. See BIG POISON.

LITTLE PROFESSOR (THE)—Dom DiMaggio (1917–   ) Baseball. A center fielder for the Boston Red Sox and Joe's brother, The Little Professor looked scholarly in his wire-rim glasses.

LITTLE RASCAL (THE)—Doug Flutie (1962–   ) Football. This is what Flutie's teammates at Boston College called their 5' 9", 175-pound quarterback. The Boston sportswriters often referred to Flutie who specialized in last-minute touchdowns to win games as Little Big Man. He was also called The Magic Flutie.

LITTLE STEAM ENGINE (THE)—James Francis "Pud" Galvin (1856–1902) Baseball. H/F Born on Christmas day before the Civil War, St. Louis Red Stocking pitcher "Pud" Galvin was no gift to batters. In 675 games, he won 361, lost 309, and hurled 57 shutouts, striking out 1,786. Because of his energetic windup and delivery, the 5' 8" Galvin earned the nickname The Little Steam Engine (Daniel Webster, a noted orator of the day was called a Steam Engine in Pants), but he is better known to baseball fans as Pud because he could reduce most batters to pudding. He was elected to the Baseball Hall of Fame in 1965. Galvin was also called GENTLE JEEMS, a variation of Jim and a comment on his pleasant and soft-spoken personality.

LON—Laurence Myers (1858–1899) Track and field. H/F Myers was the greatest track athlete of his time, holding all the American records from fifty yards to a mile, and the world records in the 440 and 880. His best times were as follows: 10.0 in the 100-yard dash, 22.6 in the 220, 48.6 in the 440, 1:55.4 in the 880, and 4:27.6 in the mile.

LONE EAGLE [THE]—Charles Augustus Lindbergh [1902-1974] Aviation. When American heroes of the twentieth century are recorded, the name Lindbergh will be high up on most lists. He showed the world the power, courage, and daring of one man alone against the elements. On May 20-21, 1927, he electrified the world when at the age of twenty-five, he became the first person to fly nonstop across the Atlantic. By the time he landed his plane (named *The Spirit of St. Louis*) at Le Bourget Field, near Paris, his name was on its way to becoming a household word. He had flown solo for 3,600 miles in thirty-three and a half hours. There were songs written in his honor, a dance (The Lindy) named for him, and President Coolidge presented him with the Congressional Medal of Honor and the very first Distinguished Flying Cross. In the 1950s James Stewart portrayed the aviator in the film *The Spirit of St. Louis.* Lindbergh was also called Lucky Lindy.

LORD BYRON—Byron Nelson [1912-   ] Golf. H/F Nelson was nicknamed Lord Byron because he played as if he had been knighted on the links. From 1937 to 1946 he played with supreme authority, winning fifty-four tournaments. Nelson started out as a caddy in Fort Worth, Texas. After turning pro in 1932, he didn't win a tournament until 1937. But when he did, it was the Masters. In 1939, he won the U.S. Open; in 1940, he beat out Snead for the PGA Championship. He outlasted Hogan in a playoff for the 1942 Masters. And in 1945, Lord Byron won eleven tournaments in a row; from 1945 to 1946, he won a total of twenty-six tournaments. Nelson went out at the top of his game and retired to his ranch. He returned for an occasional tournament and later was a color analyst for golf on television. He was also called The Mechanical Man for his smooth and flawless golf game.

LOTTIE—Charlotte Dod [1872-1960] Tennis. H/F Lottie was a family nickname, something Charlotte called herself as a small child. But it was a name she latter grew to dislike. "Pray do not call me Lottie," she once told an interviewer. "My name is Charlotte and I hate to be called Lottie in public." Charlotte Dod learned to play tennis in her own backyard in Bebington, Cheshire, England. (Although she had a strong volley and overhead smash, she served underhanded as was the custom for women of her day.) By fifteen she was in the Wimbledon finals in women's singles, defeating Blanche Bingley Hillyard, 6–1, 6–0. She went on to win five Wimbledon championships, three in a row. In Wimbledon play she lost only one set; during her entire career she lost only five matches. At the age of twenty-one she retired from tennis to take up other sports. She played field hockey for England against Ireland; in 1904, Dod won the British National Golf championship for women; in 1908, she won the silver medal in archery at the Olympic Games in London. "The great joys of games," said Charlotte Dod, "is the hard work entailed in learning them."

LOUISIANA LIGHTNING—Ron Guidry [1950-   ] Baseball. White lightning is good old moonshine and packs a wallop, but it would take strong lightning to match the speed and wallop of a Ron Guidry fastball. Nicknamed Louisiana Lightning because he was born in Lafayette, Louisiana, Guidry is one of the greatest of New York Yankee pitchers. Few Yankee fans will forget the 1978 season, when the lefthander compiled a 25-3 season, an .893 winning percentage (the highest won-lost percentage in major-league history for any twenty-game winner.) Nine of his wins were shutouts. His ERA was 1.74 and he struck out 248 batters. In the World Series against the Dodgers, Louisiana Lightning won three games for the Bronx Bombers. Some season! He was also called Gator.

LT—Lawrence Taylor (1959–   ) Football. This ten-time All-Pro linebacker for the New York Giants, and 1986 Player of the Year (the first defensive player so designated) who helped the Giants win Super Bowls XXI and XXV, is a sure bet for the Pro Football Hall of Fame.

MACHINE (THE)—Travis Grant (1950–   ) Basketball. This three-time All-American forward racked up points like a scoring machine. He had games of sixty-eight and seventy-five points; and his senior year he scored sixty-five percent from the field and seventy-seven percent from the free throw line for a thirty-nine point average. With 4,045 career points, Grant was the first player to go over the 4,000-point mark. He was also called Machine Gun.

MAD DOG—Greg Maddux (1966–   ) Baseball. Maddux is a pitcher for the Atlanta Braves. He is the first pitcher in the major leagues to win the Cy Young Award for three years in a row. He narrowly missed a fourth. When he led his league in 1994 with an ERA of 1.56 and then again in 1995 with an ERA of 1.63, he became the first pitcher since Walter Johnson to post back-to-back ERAs below 1.70. His nickname is a bit of a word play upon his last name.

MAD HUNGARIAN (THE)—Al Hrabosky (1949–   ) Baseball. This relief specialist of Hungarian descent had a unique approach for the St. Louis Cardinals in the 1970s. Hrabosky muttered to himself, stalked toward second base, pounded his glove, then spun around and sprinted to the pitcher's mound to peer through his Fu Manchu for the sign from the catcher. His antics on the mound were sometimes as effective as his pitching. The Mad Hungarian didn't seem so mad toward the end of his career when he signed a contract with the Atlanta Braves that would pay him either $2.2 million for five years or $5.9 million over thirty-five years.

MAD MONK (THE)—Russ Meyer (1923–1997) Baseball. As a pitcher for the Brooklyn Dodgers and the Philadelphia Phillies, Meyer posted a lifetime record of ninety-four wins and seventy-three losses. He received part of his nickname because of his fiery outbursts of temper. The Monk part of the sobriquet came about because of the football player Monk Meyer. Russ Meyer was once quoted as saying: "There was a great football player named Monk Meyer. I was a halfway decent football player in high school, so they called me Monk. It just stuck with me during the baseball." In 1949, The Mad Monk went 17–8 for the Phillies and compiled a 3.08 ERA. Also called Rowdy.

MAD RUSSIAN (THE)—Lou Novikoff (1915–1970) Baseball. Given the epithet "Russian" because of his surname, the "Mad" part was in reference to his erratic behavior. For instance, he didn't want to play outfield in Wrigley Field because he feared contracting poison ivy from the ivy-covered walls. Nevertheless, Novikoff hit a rock-steady .282 during his five years in the majors.

MAD RUSSIAN [THE]—Bill Vukovich [1918–1955] Auto racing. H/F The Mad Russian (a nickname conferred upon him because of his fearless recklessness) was one of the truly great speed drivers of all time. He was the West Coast Midget Champion in 1946 and 1947, but his most impressive feat was winning the Indianapolis 500 in 1953 and 1954—his last victory setting a new speed record of 130.84 mph. He might well have won his third consecutive Indianapolis 500 in 1955, because he was far out in front of the pack when tragedy struck. On his fifty-seventh lap, at 150 mph, Vuckovich ran into a multi-car pileup. His car was hurled over the fence, landed upside down and burst into flames. The Mad Russian was instantly killed. He was also called Vukie.

MAGIC—Earvin Johnson, Jr. [1959–   ] Basketball. In 1974, playing for Everett High School in Lansing, Michigan, Earvin Johnson scored thirty-six points, pulled down eighteen rebounds, made sixteen assists, and stole the ball twenty times. Fred Stanley, a newspaper reporter, was searching for a way to describe this high school student. His first instinct was to call him "The Big E," but Elvin Hayes already had that nickname sewn up. Then he realized that Johnson's play that day had been like magic. After checking it out with Earvin, Magic became the nickname that would eclipse the player's real name. Playing guard for the Los Angeles Lakers in the NBA, Magic Johnson became one of the players who would boost basketball to become one of the most popular sports in the country, not to mention, the world. (As Julius "DOCTOR J" Erving assessed Johnson's impact on basketball: "Magic is the only player who can take only three shots and still dominate a game.") Among Magic Johnson's achievements are the NBA's all-time assist leader and the MVP in 1987, 1989, and 1990. Magic was the catalyst of "show time" and the Lakers' NBA championships in 1980, 1982, 1985, 1987, and 1988. After Magic announced his retirement in 1991 because he had tested HIV-positive for AIDS, he came back to play in the 1992 NBA All-Star Game. It was show time once again and Johnson was the MVP for the game. Johnson then joined the gold medal-winning U. S. Olympic basketball team for the 1992 Olympic Games in Barcelona. Buoyed by the experience, Magic attempted a comeback for the 1992–1993 NBA season; however, he retired a second time after playing in exhibition games because some players were concerned about the possibility of contracting the HIV virus on the basketball court. See DREAM TEAM.

MAGIC—Gayle Sayers [1943–   ] Football. H/F Sayers' nickname had to do with the grace, fluidity, and explosive speed with which he ran the football. An All-American at Kansas in 1963 and 1964, this halfback averaged 6.5 yards per carry over his varsity season as a Jayhawker. In his rookie season with the Chicago Bears, Sayers scored four touchdowns against the Vikings and six touchdowns against the 49ers. After the San Francisco game, George Halas told reporters that the best runners he had ever seen were "Red Grange, George McAfee, and Gayle Sayers, and not necessarily in that order." In his seven-year career for the Chicago Bears, Sayers rushed for 4,957 yards and thirty-nine touchdowns. He was also called The Kansas Comet.

MAGIC DRAGON [THE]—Dragan Dzajic [1946–   ] Soccer. Dzajic was an outstanding left winger for Yugoslavia. His nickname is a punning reference to a popular Peter, Paul, and Mary song of the 1960s—"Puff, the Magic Dragon." A master at dribbling the ball past his opponents, Dzajic was named Yugoslav Football Player of the Year in 1963, 1966, 1968, 1969, 1970, and 1972. He scored twenty-five goals in international competition and led the Yugoslav league in goals three times.

MAHATMA [THE]—Branch Rickey [1881–1965] Baseball. H/F This baseball executive broke the color barrier by inserting Jackie Robinson into the line-up for the 1947 Brooklyn Dodgers. Tom Meany, a sportswriter, gave Rickey his nickname, getting the idea from John Gunther's description of Mohandas K. Gandhi ("a combination of God, your own father, and Tammany Hall.") In 1965, Rickey was felled at a sports banquet in Columbia, Missouri by a heart attack. In a twist of fate, an African American named Harold Robinson came to the aid of Mr. Rickey at his death scene. Rickey was also called The Brain.

MAN IN THE IRON MASK [THE]—John Jacob Berwanger [1914–   ] Football. In 1935, Berwanger, as an All-American halfback at the University of Chicago, became the first person to win the coveted Heisman Trophy. His nickname, an allusion to the famous novel by Alexander Dumas, was given to him because during his freshman year at the University of Chicago, he broke his nose and so, from then on, he wore a specially designed facemask. After winning the Heisman Trophy, he could have been drafted into pro ball by the Chicago Bears, but John Berwanger opted for a career in business instead.

MAN OF A THOUSAND MOVES [THE]—Elgin Baylor [1934–   ] Basketball. H/F This two-time All-American from Seattle was a difficult player to guard. Starring for the Lakers from 1958 to 1978, this forward scored seventy-one points in a game in 1960 and averaged 38.3 points a game during 1962. He was selected to ten All-Star teams and led the Lakers to eight NBA finals. During his career Elgin Baylor scored a total of 23,149 points. In film history, Lon Chaney was known as "The Man of a Thousand Faces." Baylor's sobriquet is a variation on that theme.

MAN OF STEEL [THE]—Tony Zale [1913–1997] Boxing. H/F A comic book or movie fan may tell you that Superman was the man of steel, but a boxing fan can point to Anthony Florian Zaleski who earned the nickname on two counts. First, he was born in the steel town of Gary, Indiana, and for a time he worked in the steel mills there. Second, he possessed a steel-like ability to withstand physical punishment from his opponents. In 1941, he defeated Georgia Abrams in his first big fight, but it was his three bouts with Rocky Graziano that captured worldwide attention. Although hurt, Zale won their first fight in 1946 with a KO in the sixth round. In 1947, Graziano was barely able to see out of one eye but was still able to unleash an onslaught of punches that caused the referee to stop their second fight in the sixth round. In 1948, Zale knocked out Graziano in their final fight to regain the middleweight title. Zale was the World Middleweight Champion from 1940 to 1948 (he served in the U.S. Navy for four years during WW II). In his ninety fights, The Man of Steel won seventy of them, drew two and lost eighteen.

MANASSA MAULER [THE]—Jack Dempsey [1895–1983] Boxing. H/F Hailing from Manassa, Colorado (Grantland Rice bestowed the nickname on him), Jack Dempsey was notorious for brawling in bar rooms and dance halls. The Manassa Mauler began fighting professionally at nineteen; and in 1919 he became the heavyweight champion by defeating Jess Willard. In 1921, Dempsey beat Georges Carpentier; in 1923, Dempsey knocked out Luis Angel Firpo. The bout with Firpo, the WILD BULL OF THE PAMPAS, was held before 90,000 at the Polo Grounds. Dempsey knocked down Firpo seven times in the first round. Then suddenly, Firpo sent Dempsey through the ropes.

Observers at ringside helped the fighter back into the ring. "I remember that when I came out for the second round, ammonia stinging my nostrils," said Dempsey, "I saw twenty Firpos. They were everywhere. Every time I saw one, I let him have it. They tell me Firpo went down like a poled steer in the second." After this bout, Dempsey did not defend his title for three years. In 1926, he finally stepped in the ring with Gene Tunney and lost a ten-round decision. When his wife asked him how he had been defeated, Dempsey replied, "Honey, I just forgot to duck." Their second bout, also won by Tunney, has been called THE BATTLE OF THE LONG COUNT. Dempsey was also called The Champ, Jack the Giant Killer, Kid Blacky, Mighty Jack, and The Thor of the Ring.

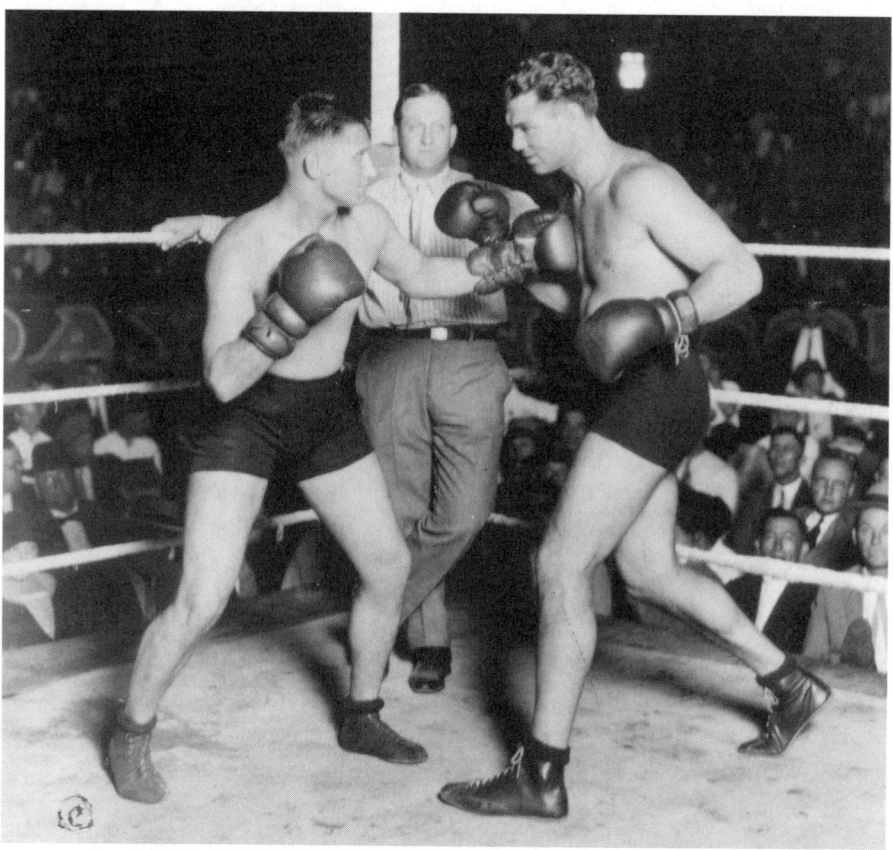

THE MANASSA MAULER—(right) Jack Dempsey (1895-1983) Boxing. The noted sportswriter Grantland Rice bestowed this nickname upon the great heavyweight boxer.

MARSE JOE—Joseph McCarthy (1887–1978) Baseball. H/F McCarthy was manager of the Cubs, the Yankees, and the Red Sox. In the Thirties, he won a record six consecutive World Series (with Yankee teams of Ruth, Gehrig, and DiMaggio). Over his twenty-four years, McCarthy has the highest winning career percentage (.614) of any manager before or since. McCarthy was the master (the meaning of *marse*).

MASTER [THE]—Eddie Arcaro [1916–] Horse racing. H/F In 1955, when the Jockey's Hall of Fame opened in Pimlico, Maryland, the first three jockeys to be inducted were Earl Sande, George Woolf, and Eddie Arcaro. Arcaro was so admired by his fellow jockeys that he had been dubbed "The Master" at his craft. He was The Master because he went on to win a total of seventeen Triple Crown races (the Kentucky Derby, the Preakness, and the Belmont). This was Arcaro's assessment of racing: "Every top rider has strong back and shoulder muscles. Even a really little guy like Shoemaker is built like a lightweight fighter from the waist up. You develop those muscles by pushing with the horse on every stride, by showing him you're boss and making him keep his mind on his job." He was also called King of Little Men, King of the Stakes Riders, and Big A.

MASTER MELVIN—Mel Ott [1909–1958] Baseball. H/F Master because he was only sixteen years old when he started in pro ball, and Master because he had mastered the arts of hitting and fielding. One sports writer in Ott's heyday waxed eloquent about Ott in right field, pointing out that Ott is "particularly famous for two tricks. On a long fly ball, he can take one look at the ball, turn his back and run to the exact spot where the ball will drop! He owns a buggy whip for an arm and can run a country mile for a fly. The other uncanny gift is playing rebounds off the Polo Grounds fences. He judges angles like an Einstein. Where other fielders go crazy playing caroms, Ott picks the hardest smashes off the wall on one or two bounces." And that was just Master Melvin's fielding. It was as a hitter that he truly excelled. He was the first National Leaguer to hit 500 home runs, and he finished his twenty-two years with the New York Giants with 511 homers and 1,860 RBIs. His lifetime batting average was .304. And his great feats were accomplished with one of the more unorthodox batting stances in the game. He stood very close to the plate, would lift his right leg high, and with his bat held low and nearly parallel to his upper arm, he would step forward into the pitch. Even so, Giants' manager John J. McGraw called him "the most natural hitter I ever saw." Because he stood only 5' 7" and weighed 160 pounds, Ott was sometimes called the Mighty Mite, but Master Melvin explains it best.

MASTER OF THE MOUTH—Don Cherry [1934–] Hockey. As the coach of the Boston Bruins for five years in the 1970s, Don Cherry was very outspoken. As they say in the news business, he was good copy. One time after Russian submarines had entered the Stockholm harbor, Cherry used it to knock Swedish players in the NHL: "It was easy for the Commies to hide. They just put the subs in the corner of the harbor because everyone knows Swedes don't go in the corners."

MAW—Mrs. Joseph Bogash [active 1940s–1950s] Roller skating. Mrs. Bogash was a forty-something mother and housewife in Chicago when a doctor recommended that she take up roller-skating for her health. She took it up with a vengeance, for the 160-pound Bogash became a driving force and one of the stars of the Roller Derby from the early 1940s until the mid-1950s.

MAYOR OF RUSH STREET [THE]—Harry Caray [1918–1998] Baseball. There are great sports announcers, there are good ones, and there are mediocre ones, but Harry Caray was in a league all by himself. He was far and away the most popular radio broadcaster ever to cover baseball games. Most recently he broadcast for the Cubs, but previously he announced for the White Sox, and for twenty-five years before that he was the voice of the St. Louis Cardinals on radio station KMOX. He was a legend in Chicago, where he could frequently be seen visiting the restaurants, bars, and saloons that dot colorful Rush Street. His home-run call ("It might be . . . it could . . . it is!") was his trademark, along with "Holy Cow." (Yankee announcer Phil Rizutto also uses this exclamation.) As Harry's son Harry "Skip" Caray broadcasts for Atlanta, it was a father-son matchup when the Cubs played the Braves.

MEADOWLARK—Meadow George Lemon [1933—   ] Basketball. Lemon received his nickname from his Globetrotter teammates. Perhaps it was because his name begged to be finished—he was as happy-go-lucky as a bird, Meadow was on a lark. Following in the tennis shoe prints of the first Clown Prince of Basketball, Reece "Goose" Tatum, Meadowlark Lemon took over in 1956 as the new CLOWN PRINCE OF BASKETBALL.

MEAL TICKET [THE]—Carl Owen Hubbell [1903–1988] Baseball. H/F Hubbell was a steady performer and a big-game winner on the staff of the New York Giants. He threw a screwball at different speeds that simply baffled batters. From 1933 to 1937, he won 115 games; from 1928–1943, he won 253 games and lost 154, while posting a 2.97 ERA. Hubbell was also 4–2 in three World Series. He was also called KING.

THE MEAL TICKET—Carl Owen Hubbell (b. 1903–1988) Baseball. King Carl astonished the baseball world in the 1934 All-Star game when he fanned in succession Ruth, Gehrig, Foxx, Simmons, and Cronin. This photo shows his exceptionally high kick.

MEAN JOE GREEN—Joe Green (1946–) Football. H/F Green received his nickname because when he played at North Texas State, the defense was called the Mean Green. As a Pittsburgh Steeler, Mean Joe Green played defensive tackle on THE STEEL CURTAIN with Ernie Holmes, Dwight White, and L. C. Greenwood. Green was not only All-Pro five times, but he also played on four Super Bowl winners. Joe Green's "mean" melted into kindness on a popular television commercial some years back.

MECHANICAL MAN (THE)—Charley Gehringer (1903–1993) Baseball. H/F Gehringer was a manager's dream. You wound up this second baseman and away he went. As skipper Mickey Cochrane once put it: "He says hello on opening day, and goodbye on closing day, and in between he hits .350." As a matter of fact, Gehringer hit .356 in 1934, .354 in 1936, and a league-leading .371 in 1937. During his nineteen years with the Detroit Tigers, The Mechanical Man collected 2,839 hits, 1,185 walks, and only 372 strikeouts. His batting average leveled out at .320. Gehringer was no less consistent in the field. On the all-time list for second basemen his 7,068 assists are second and his 1,444 double plays are fifth.

MERRY MADCAP (THE)—Max Baer (1909–1959) Boxing. Max Baer was not only a fine boxer (World Heavyweight Champion from 1934 to 1935), he also possessed the ability to entertain his fans as well. His comic antics in the ring earned him the title of The Merry Madcap. Baer won the world heavyweight title by defeating Primo Camera, knocking down The Ambling Alp eleven times in eleven rounds. The Merry Madcap clowned and joked around throughout most of the fight. After being defeated by Lou Nova in 1941, Baer retired from the ring with a record of seventy wins and thirty losses. Later, he appeared in a number of movies.

MICHIGAN ASSASSIN (THE)—Stanley Ketchel (1887–1910) Boxing. H/F His real name was Stanislaus Kiecal, but his nickname described the one-minded determination in which this farm boy from Michigan stalked after an opponent. Ketchel held the welterweight title on two different occasions from 1908 to 1910 and also won the middleweight and light heavyweight titles during this period. When he moved up to fight the heavyweight champion Jack Johnson, he knocked the champion down, a feat no one else had been capable of doing. Johnson, however, got up from the mat and immediately decked Ketchel for a twelfth-round knockout. Ketchel fought sixty-six bouts—winning fifty-five, drawing four, losing five, and having four end in no decision. His nickname turned out to be ironic, for Ketchel was assassinated at the age of twenty-four. As he sat down for breakfast while vacationing at a ranch in Conway, Montana, Stanley Ketchel was shot in the back with both barrels of a shotgun. He was also called The Midnight Assassin.

MICKEY—Gordon Stanley Cochrane (1903–1962) Baseball. H/F This catcher received his nickname from a minor-league manager because he was Scotch-Irish. He was also sometimes called Black Mike because he was dark; and as a football player at Boston University he had been known as Kid. Cochrane, however, simply wanted to be called Gordon. Playing for the Athletics from 1925 to 1933 and the Tigers from 1934 to 1937, Cochrane was twice the American League MVP and boasted a career batting average of .320. He played a key role in five World Series; and in the 1934 and 1935 Series, he also served as manager. Mickey Mantle received his first name because his father was a great fan of Cochrane.

MICKEY—Mary Kathryn Wright [1935–] Golf. H/F Wright's father was expecting a boy and had already chosen the name Michael. So, the little girl was called Mickey. Mickey started playing golf at age eleven, and in 1952, she won the U.S. Girls' Junior and the World and All-American Amateurs in 1954. She won her first pro tournament at the age of 21. In 1961, Mickey won ten tournaments. In 1963, she won thirteen of the thirty-one tournaments. In all, she won eighty-two tournaments, including thirteen major titles—four U.S. Opens and four LPGA titles.

MIDNIGHT EXPRESS—Edward Tolan [1909–1967] Track and field. H/F Eddie Tolan won gold medals at the 1932 Olympic Games in Los Angeles in the 100 meters (setting an Olympic record of 10.4 seconds in the preliminaries) and the 200 (with an Olympic record of 21.2). In 1929, Tolan was the first to run the 100-yard dash in 9.5.

MILKSHAKE MAN [THE]—Bill Virdon [1931–] Baseball. "We used to call him The Milkshake Man, or Mr. Milkshake, because everybody thought he was a health nut," said SPARKY Lyle. "It wasn't that. The Yankees threw a party one night, and I went, and I got to talking with him. He was standing there with a drink in his hand. He said, 'Ya know, everybody thinks I drink milkshakes all the time because I like them. The truth is, I hate them. I'll tell you why I drink milkshakes. My stomach is so damn bad, I can't drink" (from *The Bronx Zoo* by Sparky Lyle and Peter Golenbock). When he wasn't sipping through a straw, Virdon was a twelve-year .267-hitting outfielder, mainly for the Pittsburgh Pirates. As a manager from 1972 to 1984, his teams were 995–921.

MINNESOTA FATS—RUDOLF WALTER WANDERONE, JR. [1913–1996] Pool. H/F Minnesota Fats was an American legend long before the movie *The Hustler* burst upon the scene, but the nickname came to Wanderone by way of the film. As he told readers in his 1966 autobiography— *The Bank Shot and Other Great Robberies* (written with Tom Fox, and published by The World Publishing Co. in 1966): "Now right after the movie hit the theaters all over the country, every living human being started calling me Minnesota Fats. I got a kick out of it on account of it was just another nickname, only this one looks like it's going to be around a long, long time." Before the movie, Wanderone (because of his size) was known by a great many other names. He was also called Triple Fat Smarts, New York Fats, Chicago Fats, Kansas City Fats, Omaha Fats, and Johnson City Fats.

MIRACLE WORKER [THE]—Gil Hodges [1924–1972] Baseball. Although *The Miracle Worker* is the title of a famous play about Helen Keller and her miraculous teacher Annie Sullivan, Gil Hodges was also called The Miracle Worker by Brooklyn Dodgers' fans. Hodges earned his nickname because of his timely hitting and fielding. In a career that spanned eighteen seasons, Hodges clubbed 370 home runs and amassed a lifetime batting average of .273. He was a winner of three golden gloves—in 1957, 1958, and 1959.

MR. BASKETBALL—Nat Holman [1896–deceased] Basketball. H/F Holman starred for the original Celtics from 1921 to 1928. During that period they won 720 out of 795 games. Holman, a 5' 11" guard, was a great ballhandler and playmaker. Later he coached at C.C.N.Y. for thirty-six seasons and compiled a 421–188 record. His biggest thrill came during the 1949–1950 season, when the Beavers won both the NIT and the NCAA tournaments.

MR. CUB—Ernie Banks [1931–   ] Baseball. H/F Always an enthusiastic and superb ballplayer, Banks received his nickname from a sportswriter for embodying the best characteristics of what a player for the Chicago Cubs should be like. In short, this shortstop/first baseman was a quintessential Cub. Although he never played for a winner, Bank's eager attitude is displayed by his familiar expression "Let's play two." Not only did Banks win back-to-back MVPs in 1959 and 1960, but his career home run total was also a lofty 512. Bank's sunny disposition led to his other nickname Mr. Sunshine.

MR. GOALIE—Glenn Hall [1931–   ] Hockey. H/F As a goalie for the Chicago Black Hawks, Hall played in 552 consecutive games. He was not only the mainstay of the defense, he was Mr. Goalie and he invented the "butterfly" style stance (the knees forming an inverted V). Although he made eleven All-Star teams, he was always a hold out for the next season. Hall just didn't find it easy to return: "There's no such thing as an easy night for the goalie, not even if he never gets a shot on goal during the whole game." As a matter of fact, playing hockey made him sick. "I hate every minute I play," he said. "I'm sick to my stomach before the game, between periods, and from the start of the season to the end. I sometimes ask myself, 'What the hell am I doing out here?' But it's the only way I can support my family. If I could do it some other way, I wouldn't be playing goal." At the close of his career, Glenn Hall was paired with Jacques Plante on the St. Louis Blues. Mr. Goalie and JAKE THE SNAKE were in the finals three straight years and the two goalies shared the Vezina Trophy in 1969.

MR. INSIDE—Felix "Doc" Blanchard [1924–   ] Football. Blanchard had two nicknames. He was known as Doc because his father was a doctor; he was also called Mr. Inside because as a fullback he ran the ball up the middle. Doc Blanchard played on the same mid-1940s Army teams as Glenn Davis, known as MR. OUTSIDE. During Army's three unbeaten seasons, Blanchard scored thirty-eight touchdowns. (Mr. Inside and Mr. Outside scored a combined total of 536 points.) In 1945, Doc Blanchard won the Heisman Trophy.

MR. OCTOBER—Reggie Jackson [1946–   ] Baseball. H/F This right fielder always performed well in World Series play, but 1977 was exceptional. With the Yankees ahead of the Dodgers 3–2, Reggie hit three home runs, each on the first pitch, to cinch the series. He was, in his own words, "the straw that stirred the drink"—a remark that caused considerable consternation among some of his Yankee teammates. But he did hit 563 homers, and he is one of the few baseball players to have a candy bar named in his honor. Reggie was a winner. He played on teams that won eleven divisions and six pennants and he once said, "I don't mind getting beat, but I hate to lose." Reggie also has the dubious distinction of holding the major-league record for the most strikeouts by a player—2,247. But it was his heroics in World Series play (ten homers in five series, and a .357 average) that earned him his colorful nickname. And on the eve of his induction into the Hall of Fame in 1993, Reggie, as usual, had the last word. This time it was about nicknames:

> Mr. October. It's the best, better than "Say Hey Kid" or "The Mick." The Yankee Clipper—what's that? I'm not talking about them as ballplayers—they were great—but this is nicknames. You know which one I liked a lot? "The Galloping Ghost"—Red Grange. You can just picture that. Like you can Mr. October.

Jackson was also called The Straw That Stirs the Drink.

MR. OUTSIDE—Glenn Davis (1924–   ) Football.
Davis received his nickname while playing halfback for Army during the mid-1940s. He was famous for running the ball to the outside and sweeping beyond the reach of his opponents. (Doc Blanchard, MR. INSIDE, was on the same team.) Glenn Davis was also nicknamed Junior because he was born nine minutes after his twin brother Ralph. Columbia University coach Lou Little called Glenn Davis "The best running back in football history." Davis had many tremendous years playing for Army, but 1946 was certainly a year to remember when he scored eighteen touchdowns and averaged 11.5 yards per carry (breaking his own national record). For these feats he won the Heisman Trophy and was named the Male Athlete of the Year by the Associated Press. In thirty-five games for Army, Mr. Outside scored fifty-one touchdowns. During his three seasons, Army never lost a game. The Brooklyn Dodgers were so impressed by his all-around athletic ability they offered him a $75,000 contract, but Davis opted for pro football instead. A knee injury forced Mr. Outside into an early retirement from the Los Angeles Rams in 1951.

MR. UNEMOTIONAL—Paul Warfield (1942–   ) Football. H/F
The exceptionally calm Warfield excelled as a long jumper (26' 2") and as a wide receiver. In his first season with the Cleveland Browns, he caught fifty-two passes for 920 yards and made All-Pro. In 1972, Warfield had a 20.9-yard average per catch in the Miami Dolphins' unbeaten season.

MR. ZERO—Frank Brimsek (1915–   ) Hockey. H/F
Brimsek was the goalie for the Boston Bruins from 1938 to 1943 and 1945 to 1949 and for the Chicago Black Hawks from 1949-1950. During his rookie season he held the opposition scoreless in six of seven games, thus earning the nickname Kid Zero. Later he became Mr. Zero. This Hall of Fame goalie posted 40 career shutouts and had a 2.73 goals-against average.

MO—Maurice Stokes (1933–1970) Basketball.
Stokes was a 6' 7", 240-pound star for St. Francis from 1952 to 1955. He averaged twenty-two points per game and was an All-American. He joined the Cincinnati Royals and became the Rookie of the Year. Mo was a top rebounder, grabbing thirty-eight in one game, and was on the All-Star team three times. Then disaster struck. In 1958, he suffered a brain injury and was barely able to function and restricted to a wheelchair. Teammate Jack Twyman, who became his legal guardian, helped raise money with benefits, but after twelve years, Maurice Stokes died.

MONGOOSE [The]—Archie Moore [1916—   ] Boxing. H/F Archie Moore called himself The Mongoose. Obviously, he knew that the mongoose, a small animal that is a natural enemy of the cobra, is sharp-eyed, quick, and utterly fearless. In 1952, Moore beat Joey Maxim for the light-heavyweight championship. And he fought for the heavyweight championship twice, first Rocky Marciano in 1955 and then Floyd Patterson in 1956. The Mongoose kept fighting until he was almost fifty. He was also called THE OLD MONGOOSE.

MOOR—Tom Molino [1784–1818] Boxing. Molyneaux, an African American, was the best boxer in England for a time, until Tom Cribb beat him in 1810. Cribb had been knocked unconscious in the twenty-third round but recovered during a very long delay while Molyneaux's hands were checked to see if they held bullets (they didn't). Cribb came back to win in the fortieth round.

MOOSE [THE]—Julius Boros [1920–1994] Golf. H/F At six feet and 220 pounds, a slow but steady swing, and a loping gait around the golf course, Boros earned his nickname, The Moose. He was also slow in getting started in his golfing career; he didn't quit his accounting job until the age of thirty. Two years later, The Moose rocked the golf world by winning the U.S. Open and going on to become the year's biggest money winner and the PGA Player of the Year. In 1963, he won his second U.S. Open. In 1968, Boros won the PGA Championship to become the oldest player ever to win a major tournament; he was forty-eight years old.

MOOSE—Ed Krause [1913–1992] Football, basketball. H/F Krause, a 6' 3", 230-pound All-American tackle in football, played in the first college All-Star game versus the Chicago Bears in 1934. Moose (his nickname was for his size) was also a three-time All-American forward at Notre Dame on a team that had a 54–12 record. Moose was such a dominant force under the basket that the three-second rule was developed because of him. Krause coached at his alma mater, posting a 92-48 record, and also was the athletic director at Notre Dame for thirty-one years. "They talk about Gipper, Rockne, the Four Horsemen," said former Notre Dame coach Gerry Faust, "but I think [Ed Krause] was the true legend."

MOUSE—Stan Mikita [1940—   ] Hockey. H/F The Chicago Black Hawks fans would often chant, "M-I-K...I-T-A...M-O-U-S-E" when this forward would make some noteworthy play on the ice. For fifteen years, Mikita averaged seventy-six points a season (twenty-eight goals and forty-eight assists). By 1974, Mikita had 1,154 points, topping Bobby Hull's record with the Black Hawks. He was also called Stash and Stosh.

MUNCIE MORTAR—Ron Bonham [1942—   ] Basketball. Bonham, a 6' 5" forward from Muncie, Indiana, was known for his high-arching jump shot. Once he scored fifty-three points for Muncie Central High School to set a one-game record. He continued his shooting and became an All-American at the University of Cincinnati in 1963. He went on to play for the Boston Celtics from 1965 to 1966.

NAILS—Lenny Dykstra [1963–   ] Baseball. This center fielder is as hard as nails and is proud of it. His Philadelphia manager Jim Fregosi has called him "the best leadoff hitter in baseball," and that was saying a lot, considering the likes of Wade Boggs and Rickey Henderson. In 1990, Dykstra hit .325, scored 106 runs, batted in 60, and stole 33 bases. But the following year turned sour when on May sixth he drove his $91,000 Mercedes into a tree and was eventually charged with driving under the influence of alcohol. Nails was also placed on probation for a year by commissioner Fay Vincent after Dykstra testified that he had lost $78,000 gambling at poker.

NAP—Napoleon Lajoie [1875–1959] Baseball. H/F In 1901, this popular second baseman hit .422—an American League record that will probably never be broken. (His lifetime average was a lofty .339.) Unbelievably, he only struck out eighty-five times in 9,589 at-bats. Reggie Jackson, eat your heart out! Nap was also called Larry, The King of Ballplayers, and King Larry.

NASTY—Ilie Nastase [1946–   ] Tennis. H/F Nastase won his nickname for his on-court behavior. Although some players seem to find disagreements a way to pump themselves up emotionally, Nasty's disputes, sometimes ending in temper tantrums, seemed to interfere with his natural ability as a finesse player. However, when Nastase was on his game, he could be magnificent. He won the Wimbledon mixed doubles in 1970 and 1972, and the men's doubles in 1973. He won the U.S Open men's singles in 1972, the French men's singles in 1973 and the French doubles in 1970.

NELLIE—Jacob Nelson Fox [1927–1975] Baseball. Fox, who was originally called Little Nel, was not such a diminutive man at 5' 10" and 160 pounds. Perhaps that's why Nellie stuck. It was more a term of endearment, and he did endear himself to his Chicago White Sox teammates by his ability to get on base. Four times this second baseman led the American League in base hits. Out of a total of 2,663 hits and 9,232 at-bats during his nineteen-year career, Fox rapped out 2,161 singles.

NEWK—John Newcombe [1946–   ] Tennis. H/F Though this nickname was based on his last name, it sounded like the ball coming off the racket on his big and powerful serves. In 1967, Newk was the last amateur to win the Wimbledon men's singles. He won there as a pro in 1970 and 1971. Newcombe also won the U.S. Open singles in 1967 and 1973, as well as the Australian singles in 1973. Newk's quickness, agility and sense of teamwork made him particularly effective as a doubles player. He won the Wimbledon men's doubles in 1965, 1966, 1968, and 1969, the French men's doubles in 1967, 1969, and 1973, the U.S. Open men's doubles in 1973, and the Australian men's doubles in 1965, 1967, 1971, and 1973.

NEWSBOY—Abraham Hollandersky [active 1900s] Boxing. Abe the Newsboy once was noted by Robert Ripley in his *Believe It or Not* for having fought 1,043 bouts. When Abe was a young boy, his father, who had gone blind, left his family in Manchester, England, and had gone on to America to raise money. Abe, at age five, went to work selling newspapers to help raise enough money so that the family could see their father again. In his autobiography, he writes, "We made our way to Manchester, England, I was then almost five years old, and there is where I went into the newspaper business, selling the *Manchester Guardian* and other English newspapers. So, when the

English in Jamaica lost the championship to Abe, the Newsboy, I told them they had lost it to a former Englishman, and it made a hit with those sports."

NEWSY—Edouard Lalonde (1887–1971) Hockey. H/F This nickname came from Lalonde's early days of laboring in a newsprint plant. Associated with many teams during his thirty-year career, Newsy was known for both his physical play and offensive skills. Lalonde scored 441 goals in 356 games in the NHA (National Hockey Association), PCHA (Pacific Coast Hockey Association), and NHL. In1926–1927, he was the New York American's coach.

NIGHT TRAIN—Dick Lane (1928–   ) Football. H/F This cornerback for the Detroit Lions (and later the Los Angeles Rams and the Chicago Cardinals) could hit ball carriers like a locomotive. Another thing that contributed to his nickname was that Lane especially liked Buddy Morrow's song "Night Train." Lane worked hard on and off the field. For instance, after lights-out during his rookie season, he got together with one of the coaches to study the playbook. His Hall of Fame career showed that he learned his lessons well.

NINETY-SIX—Bill Voiselle (1919–   ) Baseball. Hailing from Ninety-Six, South Carolina, this pitcher's roots went so deep that he wore the same number on the back of his shirt. In 1944, Voiselle fanned 161 batters to lead the National League. His nine-year record was 74–84.

NOISY—Johnny Kling (1875–1947) Baseball. Undoubtedly Kling, one of the greatest catchers of the early 1900s, made a lot of noise in rooting his teams to success. He started his major-league career with the Chicago Cubs in 1900 and played for them through 1911 (although he sat out the 1909 season because he and the Cubs could not agree on a contract). At the end of the 1911 season, Noisy Kling was traded to the Boston Braves, and in 1912, became their player-manager. At the end of his career, he had set numerous World Series fielding records. In regular season play, he compiled a .272 batting average, collecting 1,152 hits in 4,241 at-bats. He slugged 181 doubles, sixty-one triples, and twenty homers. From 1934–1937, he owned the Kansas City American Association baseball team, which he then sold to the New York Yankees.

NONPAREIL—Jack Dempsey (1862–1895) Boxing. H/F It is easy for a non-boxing aficionado to confuse the two great fighters bearing the name of Jack Dempsey. The Jack Dempsey who was the world heavyweight champion from 1919 to 1926 took his name from the Nonpareil, the world middleweight champion from 1884 to 1891. The first Jack Dempsey (actually his name was John Kelley) so dominated the boxing of his day that no one could be found to beat him—hence, the nickname Nonpareil, meaning someone unbeatable or unrivalled. However, he finally lost his crown in 1891 to Bob Fitzsimmons. Before his defeat in the fifteenth round, Dempsey had been staggering around the ring and Fitzsimmons asked him to quit. "I'm the champion," Dempsey said. "You've got to knock me out first." Fitzsimmons did just that. During his career, Nonpareil won forty-eight bouts, drew seven, and lost three.

NOODLES—Frank George Hahn (1879–1960) Baseball. As a boy, Hahn used to carry his father's noodle soup to him at work. When the boy grew up, he threw baseballs for the powerful Cincinnati club. In 1901, he registered 239 strikeouts. During his eight-year career, he had twenty-five shutouts.

NO. 1—Bill McGowen (1896–1954) Baseball. H/F McGowen received his nickname based on his performance. From 1925 to 1954, McGowen umpired every inning of 2,500 games. "He was the greatest umpire I've ever seen," hailed Clark Griffith. He was chosen to umpire four All-Star games and eight World Series.

NUMBER SIX—Bill Russell (1934–) Basketball. H/F This 6' 10" player wore number six and revolutionized the game with his tenacious defense and his pinpoint shot blocking. He fit in exactly with Red Auerbach's idea of success for a team: "Nobody can win in this league without a big, rugged man who can grab rebounds and keep the other team from scoring." His matchups with

Wilt Chamberlain were the stuff of legends. As Jerry West, a teammate of Chamberlain's on the Lakers said: "I think Wilt is the better all-around basketball player. But for one game, I'd rather have Russell." Russell's all-time high was fifty-one rebounds in a game; 4,104 during his career. Big Number Six helped the Celtics win eight championships in a row and eleven all together.

*NUMBER SIX—Bill Russell
(b. February 12, 1934) Basketball.
Before there was "Air" there was Bill.
From 1957-1969, Number Six led the
Boston Celtics to eleven NBA titles.*

OFF-SIDE KID [THE]—Bill Hewitt [1909–1947] Football. H/F Although he was seldom, if ever, off-side, Bill Hewitt was so quick off the line that the newspapers of the 1930s dubbed him The Off-Side Kid. Not only was he quick, but he was one of the last professional players to play without a helmet. An end on both offense and defense, he played for the Chicago Bears and later the Eagles, and for one season the merged Philadelphia-Pittsburgh club. After he retired in 1939, he tried to make a comeback in 1943, even though the new rules made it mandatory for him to wear a helmet.

OHIO FATS—Jack Nicklaus [1940–   ] Golf. H/F Before 1969, Nicklaus was overweight. Then he shed twenty pounds along with his nickname. "Nobody likes to be called fat or a slob," said Nicklaus later. "I never liked reading such things about myself and now it's nice to see what adjectives writers can think up for me. The words leave a much more pleasant taste, as I'm certain anyone can understand. Especially anyone who has been overweight and called all the names that go with it." Nicklaus was also called THE GOLDEN BEAR.

OISK—Carl Erskine [1926–   ] Baseball. In game three of the 1953 World Series, the Dodgers facing the Yankees, "Oisk" (a Brooklynese shortening of his last name) set a new series record (since broken) when he struck out fourteen batters. That year 1953 had been a banner one for Oisk. He finished the season at 20–6—a league-leading won-loss percentage of .769, with 187 strikeouts and four shutouts. During his twelve-year career, Erskine was 122-78 and 2–2 in eleven appearances in five World Series.

OLD ACHES AND PAINS—Lucius Appling [1909–1992] Baseball. H/F Luke often complained about his many injuries. He created hardship for others with his bat, though. In 1936, he smashed a league-leading .388; and in 1943, he beat out others with a .328. During his twenty-year stint in the majors, he batted .310, pretty respectable for a shortstop. He was no slouch with his glove either. During his day he set records in twenty different categories. Today, his 1,424 double plays are second only to Luis Aparicio.

OLD ARBITRATOR [THE]—Bill Klem [1874–1951] Baseball. H/F United States history has its Great Compromiser, and baseball has the Old Arbitrator, probably the greatest umpire the game has ever produced. He was, in fact, the first umpire to sign a three-year umpiring contract, and in 1917 and 1918, he received $650, then $1,000 to umpire World Series games. Thus, he was important in improving working conditions for the game's most put-upon and invisible workers. When he retired in 1945 (he had started his umpiring career in 1905), he was honored with a special ceremony at the New York Giants' Polo Grounds (where he had had so many run-ins with Leo "THE LIP" Durocher). Klem told the crowd: "Baseball is more than a game to me. It's a religion."

OLD BONES—Harrison Dillard [1923–   ] Track and field. H/F While attending junior high school in Cleveland, Ohio, during the Depression, a classmate looked at Dillard's tall, lean, and underfed frame and mocked him, calling him a "sack of bones." The phrase struck, for throughout his career, he was referred to as Bones, and finally as Old Bones. But, oh how those bones could run! During an Army track exhibition during World War II, General George S. Patton called him "the best goddamn athlete" he had ever seen. Dillard was the first Olympian to win gold medals in both a sprint and the hurdles. At the Olympics in London in 1948, he tied Jesse Owens' Olympic record of 10.3 in winning the 100 meters; at the 1952 Olympics in Helsinki, Dillard clocked 13.7 in the 110-meter hurdles. He also ran on the winning 400-meter relay teams at both Olympics to bring his gold medal count to four.

OLD FOX [THE]—Clark Griffith [1869–1955] Baseball. H/F Why Griffith was called the Old Fox is illustrated by something this baseball executive did in 1914. When Walter Johnson, his star player, was thinking about jumping from the Washington Senators to the Chicago Cubs for a $10,000 bonus, Griffith went to Charles Comiskey, the owner of the rival Chicago White Sox and asked how he'd like to have Johnson drawing fans away from his club. Comiskey immediately wrote out a check for $10,000 and handed it to Griffith.

OLD HOSS—Charles Radbourn [1854–1897] Baseball. H/F Radbourn was as dependable as a workhorse. And he wasn't any colt either; he was all of 27 his rookie year. In 1883, Old Hoss won a total of forty-nine games, but that was merely a warm-up for the next year. In 1884, Radbourn was a thoroughbred. He won sixty games for the Providence Grays and lost only twelve. He completed all 73 games he started, pitched 678 innings, struck out 441 batters, and posted an ERA of 1.38. And in the season-ending series with the New York Metropolitans, Old Hoss tossed three wins in three days as the Grays took the championship of the American Association. Overall, Radbourn's won-loss record was 308–191, and his ERA was 2.67. In 1939, Old Hoss was elected to the Hall of Fame.

OLD LADY—Billie Jean King [1943–   ] Tennis. H/F King won the women's singles at Wimbledon six times and the singles at the U.S. Open four times. Altogether she won seventy-one tournaments. In addition to playing great tennis, King had a mission to put women's tennis on an equal footing with men's. After breaking away to start a women's tour (see Original Nine), King took up the challenge to play Bobby Riggs in 1973 in a match that was billed as "The Battle of the Sexes." Riggs had recently demolished Margaret Court, but King was a different story. She moved him from side to side and kept the ball in play, forcing Riggs to provide the pace. A tired Riggs lost to King, 6–4, 6–3, 6–3. She was also called King of the Courts and Tennis Tycoon.

OLD LAMPLIGHTER—Hector Blake [1912–1995] Hockey. H/F Blake played three years with the Montreal Maroons, then the rest of his career with the Montreal Canadiens. Blake was also part of the famous Punch Line with Elmer Lach and Rocket Richard. He received the sobriquet Old Lamplighter because of his ability to light up the scoreboard. He was also called Toe.

OLD MAN—Connie Mack [1862–1956] Baseball. H/F The source of Connie Mack's nickname can be found in this excerpt about the manager from *You Can't Steal First Base* by Jimmie Dykes and Charles O. Dexter:

I continued to pop off. Mr. Mack came toward me. 'Will you shut your g.d. mouth, Dykes,' he quietly ordered. I nearly fell off the bench. It was as close to profanity as I'd ever heard him go. I was so stunned that I lost my voice. As a peacemaking gesture I joined Al [Simmons] as the inning ended and we went on the field together. 'We sure got the Old Man mad,' said Al with a laugh. 'Did you hear that g.d.?' I chortled. Another player told me later that, as we went on the field, Mr. Mack had chuckled. 'Know what those two are saying? They're gloating over getting the Old Man mad!'

He was also called THE TALL TACTICIAN.

OLD MAN [THE]—Walter J. Travis [1862–1927] Golf. H/F Travis began playing golf at the ripe age of thirty-five and three years later won the U.S. Amateur in 1900. He repeated it in 1901 and in 1903, and won the British Amateur in 1904. Travis was most effective with his short game, especially his putting. He continued playing tournament golf in his fifties (hence his nickname).

OLD MASTER—Joseph Gans [1874–1910] Boxing. H/F Joe Gans received his nickname because he was as skillful a boxer as he was a hard puncher. In 1906, Gans fought Battling Nelson for a purse of $35,000 put up by sports promoter Tex Rickard. In the forty-second round of that match, Gans won because of a low blow thrown by Nelson.

OLD MONGOOSE [THE]—Archie Moore [1916–   ] Boxing. H/F Born in 1916 (although his mother said it was 1913) in Benoit, Mississippi, Archibald Lee Wright began his professional fighting career in 1935, and became one of the most colorful and longest lasting boxers. The light heavyweight champion from 1952 to 1960, he fought Rocky Marciano in 1955 for the heavyweight championship of the world, and even knocked the BROCKTON BOMBER down in the second round, although Moore was defeated in round nine. Moore didn't retire from the ring until 1963 (although in 1960, the National Boxing Association took away the Old Mongoose's title because he had been inactive so long). "I don't worry about growing old," Archie Moore once said, "because worrying is a disease." He was also called Old Man River and THE MONGOOSE.

OLD PETE—Grover Cleveland Alexander [1887–1950] Baseball. H/F To his teammates on the Phillies he was Old Pete (because of his reliability, and perhaps, because liquor during the Prohibition was known as Sneaky Pete). However, to his opponents he was known as Alexander the Great. In Alexander's rookie season in 1911, he won twenty-eight games. Over the next six years he established a remarkable win-loss record: 19–17, 22–8, 27–15, 31–10 (with an ERA of 1.22), 33–12 (including sixteen shutouts), and 30–13. One of baseball's legends came in the 1926 World Series. It was the seventh inning of the seventh game between the Cardinals and Yankees. The Yankees were batting, two outs, bases loaded, the score 3–2 in favor of the Cardinals. Having already won two games for the Cards, Old Pete was called to the mound in relief to face the Yankees' most feared batter, Tony Lazzeri. Alexander struck him out and went on to retire the side in order over the next two innings. Upon retiring in 1930, Old Pete had won 373 games. Incredibly, ninety of them had been shutouts. He was also called Old Low-and-Away.

OLD POISON—Nels Stewart [1902–1957] Hockey. H/F The goalies of the NHL gave Stewart his nickname because he was such a deadly shot from his center position on the S-Line. In 1940, Old Poison set the career-scoring record of 324 goals. This mark was later shattered by Maurice "THE ROCKET" Richard.

OLD SMOKE—John Morrissey [1831–deceased] Bareknuckles boxing. In a fight with John O'Rourke in a saloon, Morrissey was tripped and fell into the coals from an overturned stove, burning his back. That was how he won his nickname. How he won the American championship was by defeating Yankee Sullivan (who wore an American flag around his waist) in 1853.

ORATOR JIM—James O'Rourke [1852–1919] Baseball. H/F When O'Rourke spoke, his vocabulary made it sound as if he were a windy politician rather than a ballplayer in a clubhouse. For example, upon hearing that the contract of Cleveland's Louis "CHIEF" Sockalexis had a clause about not drinking, Orator Jim said, "I see that Sockalexis must forego frescoing his tonsils with Cardinal brush; it is so nominated in the contract of the aborigine" (from Lee Allen's HOT STOVE LEAGUE). Though Jim O'Rourke played most of his 1,774 games in center field and left field, he actually played all nine positions. He had the following major-league records: the most home runs in 1880 with six; the most hits in 1884 with 162; and the most triples in 1885 with sixteen. (This was during the dead ball era.) In his nineteen years in the majors, O'Rourke hit .310. As a manager for five years, his record was 246–258.

ORCHID MAN [THE]—Georges Carpentier [1894–1975] Boxing. H/F Young and handsome, Georges Carpentier was the toast of Paris and London, as at home on airy boulevards as in smoky boxing dens. He was friends with Maurice Chevalier and had tea with the Prince of Wales at St. James Palace. During WW I he was a flying ace, winning the Croix de Guerre and the Legion d'Honneur. Carpentier's first fight was in 1908 when he weighed only 100 pounds. Eventually, he went on to hold a record four titles—as a welterweight, middleweight, light heavyweight, and heavyweight—as the French champion, three titles as the European champion, and the light-heavyweight championship of the world from 1920–1922. Carpentier reigned for nine-year spans both as the light-heavyweight champion and as the heavyweight champion. One of his better known fights was a fourth-round loss to George Dempsey in 1921— the first $1 million gate in boxing history. Once when Carpentier was reminded of his nickname, he said: "Others call me by the name of a flower—not me. I was not so sweet."

OZARK IKE—Terry Bradshaw [1948–   ] Football. H/F Through the middle of 1974, Bradshaw was often disappointing and was often benched. But then he caught fire and quarterbacked the Pittsburgh Steelers to a 16–6 Super Bowl win over the Minnesota Vikings. He repeated his fine performance in 1975, leading the Steelers to a 21–17 Super Bowl victory over the Dallas Cowboys. In 1979, the Steelers again battled to the Super Bowl, beating Dallas 35–31. Bradshaw was named Player of the Year. He set Super Bowl records for most TD passes thrown (four) and most yards gained (318). Ozark Ike was born in Shreveport, Louisiana—hence the nickname.

PADDLEFOOT—Wilson Paige [dates unknown] Baseball. Wilson, the brother of "Satchel" Paige, did not make it to the big leagues. "Actually, Wilson could throw about as hard as I could," said Satchel of his pitching brother, "and we would have made one of the best two-man staffs you ever saw if he'd stuck with baseball."

PADDLES—Dick Butkus [1942–   ] Football. H/F Butkus was nicknamed Paddles during training camp his rookie year in the NFL by his Chicago Bear teammates when they saw that this linebacker wore a size 11½ EEE shoe. During an agility exercise, one of them said that Butkus "looked like an elephant on roller skates." He was also called Animal and The Enforcer.

PADDY—John Driscoll [1896–1968] Football. H/F Paddy (the nickname was a bow to his Irish heritage) was a kicker extraordinaire. His reputation began at Northwestern when he drop-kicked a forty-three-yard field goal for the team's first win over the University of Chicago in fifteen years. In 1922, playing for the Chicago Cardinals, Driscoll dropkicked two field goals in their 6–0 win over the Chicago Bears and three field goals in their 9–0 win over the Bears. In 1925, he dropkicked goals of 23, 18, 50, and 35 yards in one game. Also in 1925, Paddy Driscoll spoiled Red Grange's debut by kicking twenty out of twenty-three punts away from him. Driscoll was a Bears assistant coach from his retirement in 1929 until he became their head coach in 1956.

PANAMA—Laffit Pincay, Jr. [1946–   ] Horse racing. H/F Born in Panama, Pincay led all jockeys in earnings in the years 1970, 1971, 1972, 1974, and 1979. A five-time winner of the Eclipse Award, he has won the Kentucky Derby once and the Belmont Stakes three times. Pincay is second only to Bill Shoemaker (Shoe) in the number of wins during his career.

PANCHO—Richard Alonzo Gonzales [1928–   ] Tennis. H/F The nickname of this oldest child in a family of seven born in Los Angeles to a Mexican immigrant family is a common one among Chicanos. But there was nothing common about his tennis playing. From the time he played with a fifty-one-cent racket at the public playgrounds, he was seen as having talent. Because he turned professional at twenty-one, his name doesn't appear in the record books as often as it might. (Until 1968, pros couldn't play in the major tournaments.) Still, with his cannonball serve, delicate touch, and court intelligence, Pancho Gonzales (who was the World Professional Tennis Champion eight times) is remembered as one of the greatest players of all time. After the rules changed allowing amateurs and professionals to play each other, Pancho was in the Wimbledon finals at the age of forty-one. In a memorable match that stretched over two days, Pancho outlasted the twenty-five-year-old Charlie Pasarell to win a match that lasted 112 games—the Wimbledon record for singles. He was also called Gorgo.

PANCHO—Francisco Segura [1921–   ] Tennis. H/F Segura had a powerful two-handed forehand that helped him reach the Wimbledon men's doubles semifinals in 1946, the U.S. men's singles quarterfinals in 1946 and 1947, the U.S. men's doubles semis in 1947, and the finals of the

French men's doubles. Pancho was the coach who helped make Jimmy Connors (JIMBO) into a great player.

PAPA BEAR—George Halas [1895–1983] Football. H/F George Halas was present at the birth of the Bears and remained with them for his lifetime. After buying the Decatur Staleys, Halas in 1922 relocated the franchise to Chicago and renamed the team the Bears. Starting out as a player-coach-general manager, Papa Bear worked his way out of positions one by one. During his playing days, he ran back a fumble ninety-eight yards; during his thirty-year coaching career, he had 321 wins, 147 losses and 31 ties; after 1968, Halas kicked himself upstairs. George Halas was not only Papa to the Bears, he was also the father of pro football and one of the charter members of the Pro Football Hall of Fame.

PAT—Matthew Kennedy [1908–1957] Basketball. H/F Kennedy was a referee whose colorful actions on the court were often as entertaining as the game itself. (After calling a foul, he ran toward the player shouting, "You, you, you.") From 1950 to 1957, he refereed the games of the Harlem Globetrotters.

PATSY—Patrick Joseph Donovan [1865–1953] Baseball. Most likely an entire baseball team can be composed of baseball players, who for one reason or another, bore women's names or feminine nicknames. Patsy is a childhood name that Donovan carried with him his entire major-league career—starting with Boston in the National League in 1890 and ending with Boston in the American League. Patsy is an unfortunate nickname because of its negative connotations—to be a patsy is to be a victim of practical jokes—but Donovan had an above average career, hitting .300 with 2,249 hits and 1,318 RBIs. He also was a superb base-stealer (in 1900, playing for the St. Louis Cardinals, he led the NL with forty-five) who stole 518 bases in his lifetime. In addition, he managed the Pittsburgh Pirates in 1897 and 1899, and the St. Louis Cardinals from 1901 to 1903. But if Patsy has a claim to fame in the hearts of baseball fans, it is most likely because he is given credit for having "discovered" BABE Ruth. Patsy scouted Ruth when the Babe was playing in Baltimore and he recommended that the Red Sox buy his contract.

PAVLOVA OF THE SILVER SKATES [THE]—Sonja Henie [1912–1969] Ice skating. By the time she was twenty-four years old, Sonja Henie (or, as she was known in the newspapers, "*The Norwegian Doll*") had won ten consecutive world championships and gold medals in three consecutive Olympics (1928, 1932, and 1936). The 5' 2" blond was so graceful on the ice that when she turned professional (after the 1936 Olympics), she was billed at Madison Square Garden as "*The Pavlova of the Silver Skates*." Not only was she a successful athlete, she became a motion-picture star as well, and movie buffs are privileged to see this great skater performing in such films as *It's a Pleasure!* and *One in a Million*. She was also called THE GOLDEN GIRL.

PAYSE—Edward Payson Weston [1839–1929] Long-distance walking. In 1861, because he had lost a wager about who would win the presidential election of 1860, Payse (as he was called) walked from Boston to Washington, D.C., in ten days. Attempting to arrive in time to see

Lincoln inaugurated, Payse unfortunately arrived a few hours late, though he did get to dance at the inaugural ball that evening.

PEARL [THE]—Earl Monroe [1944–   ] Basketball. H/F Monroe earned his rhyming nickname for his smooth, flawless moves on the court; in short he was a pearl of a player. As a teenager, he honed his skills by playing "ten to eleven hours a day in the hot summer with maybe just a break for lunch." Playing guard for Winston-Salem State, he averaged over forty-one points his senior year. In 1968, he was Rookie of the Year for the Baltimore Bullets, and averaged 21.8 points a game from 1967 to 1972. Traded to the New York Knicks, The Pearl helped the Knicks win the NBA championship in 1973. He was also called Slick and Batman.

PEARL OF THE PAMPAS—Gabriela Sabatini [1970–   ] Tennis. Sabatini is from Buenos Aires, a hot bed of tennis. There are over 1,000 tennis clubs in the area, and a junior tennis program that puts on 45,000 matches a year. She is the best player from the area since Guillermo Vilas. Sabatini was also called GABY.

PECK—Clarence J. Griffin [1888–1973] Tennis. H/F In 1914, Griffin won the U.S. clay court championship as well as the doubles championship with John Strachan. Teamed with "LITTLE BILL" Johnson, Peck also won the U.S. doubles championship in 1915, 1916, and 1920.

PEERLESS JIM—Jim Driscoll [1880–1925] Boxing. Driscoll's nickname came from none other than Bat Masterson, marshal turned sportswriter, when he was describing the fight between Driscoll and Abe Attell in 1909. During his career, Peerless Jim held Welsh, British, and European featherweight titles.

PEERLESS LEADER [THE]—Frank LeRoy Chance [1877–1924] Baseball. H/F The first base side of the equation of Tinkers-to-Evers-to-Chance, this player-manager led the Cubs to four pennants from 1906 to 1911. The Cub's record of 116 wins in 1906 is a major-league record. Overall, the Peerless Leader's record was 932–640 and 2–2 in the World Series. As a player, Chance stole a record five bases in a five-game World Series and 405 during his career. He batted .296 during his seventeen-year career. He was also called Husk.

PELE—Edson Arantes de Nascimento [1940–   ] Soccer. H/F Pele received his nickname at the age of eight when his friends in Tres Coracors (Three Hearts), Brazil, began calling him by that name. No one knows what it means or where it came from. What is certain is that during his playing days Pele had the best known nickname in all of sports. Pele joined the Santos team of Brazil at sixteen and played for them until he was thirty-four. He helped Brazil win the world championship in 1958, 1962, and 1970. Pele ended his career playing for the New York Cosmos from 1975 to 1977. During his twenty-two-year playing career at forward, Pele scored three goals in a game ninety-three times, four goals in a game thirty-one times, five goals six times; and once he scored eight times. This ambassador of good will—starting out with a sock for a soccer ball and winding up with one that was four pounds of solid gold—scored a total of 1,281 goals.

PEPI—Josef Bican [1913–　　] Soccer. Pepi played for the national teams of both Czechoslovakia and Austria. He led the Czech league in scoring for eight consecutive seasons, and twice he scored fifty goals in a season.

PETE—Wilbur Henry [1897–1952] Football. H/F Henry was 6 feet and 250 pounds. That's why they called him Fats but he was solid not flabby. At Washington and Jefferson College, Walter Camp placed Henry on the All-American team calling him "one of the most remarkable performers I ever saw on the gridiron." George Halas agreed. Once he confessed that after facing this Canton Bulldog tackle in the pros hundreds of times, he had been able to block him effectively only once. Henry also became a great kicker. He practiced punting with Jim Thorpe, each man standing on the opposite goal line. In games, Henry set two records: a record ninety-four-yard punt on October 28, 1923, and a dropkicked field goal fifty yards on November 13, 1922.

PHANTOM FINN [THE]—Paavo Nurmi [1897–1973] Track and field. Nurmi, the Finnish long-distance runner who dominated the 1920, 1924, and 1928 Olympic Games and established twenty-two world records between 1920–1931, was often so far out in front of the pack that to the other runners he often seemed to have disappeared. Nurmi was also called Peerless Paavo and THE FLYING FINN.

PHOG—Forrest Claire Allen [1886–1974] Basketball, baseball. H/F Allen was nicknamed Foghorn for his booming voice when he was a baseball umpire in the early 1900s. One day a sportswriter wanted to spruce up his nickname so he shortened it and altered the spelling to Phog. Although he had a degree in osteopathy, Dr. Allen did not practice full time. He had wanted to know more about anatomy so he would be a better coach. It was one reason he stressed the defensive crouch of his players so much. Two of the innovations he brought to the game were fan-shaped backboards and having the basket raised to twelve feet. He hadn't wanted the "goons" to dominate the game, yet he was the one who had recruited Clyde Lovellette and Wilt "BIG DIPPER" Chamberlain to Kansas University. He was also instrumental in getting basketball accepted as an Olympic sport—and in 1952, Phog coached the Olympic team to victory. In forty-eight years as a coach, Phog Allen's teams compiled a record of 771–233. He was also called Dr. Foghorn and Foghorn.

PIE—Harold Joseph Traynor [1899–1972] Baseball. H/F Traynor was called Pie because he was such a big fan of his mother's baked pies. As is the case with Yogi Berra and Babe Ruth, Traynor's nickname was such a part of his identity that fans usually knew his statistics but not his real name. Although he made a lot of errors, Pie Traynor was one of the dominant third basemen of the Twenties and Thirties. A regular for the Pittsburgh Pirates for fifteen years, he was a lifetime .320 hitter and seven times knocked in over 100 RBIs.

PIGGY—Ward Lambert [1888–1958] Basketball. H/F As anyone who has read *Lord of the Flies* knows, Piggy is not exactly a nickname to be cherished. It got hung on Ward Lambert in spite of his 5' 6", 114-pound frame because as a youth he wore his hair in pigtails that hung down from his sock cap. Piggy coached at Purdue University, where his 1932 team won the national collegiate championship. This pioneer of the fast break authored an important textbook called *Practical Basketball* and compiled a thirty-year record of 371–152 at Purdue.

PIPELINE—Harry Cooper [1904–   ] Golf. H/F Cooper was born in Leatherhead, England, where he started (under the tutelage of his father, Sydney John Cooper, who was a professional golfer) to play golf at age three. Cooper, however, achieved his greatest fame in the United States. He turned pro at eighteen and won his first professional tournament one year later. Throughout his career he won thirty-nine championships, and was the leading money-winner in golf during the 1930s. He was nicknamed Pipeline because he hit so straight and true; on the greens he was so accurate it was as if he had a pipeline leading from his club to the hole. He was also called LIGHT-HORSE.

PISTOL PETE—Pete Maravich [1949–1988] Basketball. H/F Press Maravich, his father and college coach, bestowed this nickname on his son for his quick shooting and his uncanny ability to score. (He also gave him the ball at every opportunity when Pete was a child.) While at Louisiana State University from 1967 to 1970, Pistol Pete Maravich averaged forty-five points a game and scored almost 4,000 points. It was not only his scoring, but also his passing that electrified crowds. "If I can get the ball to a man by passing it behind my back, what's the difference?" asked Maravich. "That's my way. And the crowd loves it. Man, you can just feel them. When I hear the crowd roar, I swear I go wild, crazy! That's what I love most." In the NBA, Maravich played guard for the Atlanta Hawks, the New Orleans (and Utah) Jazz, and the Boston Celtics. In 1976–1977, Pistol Pete was the NBA's highest scorer with a 31.1 average. He scored a total of 15,948 points for a 24.2 career average. Pete Maravich, a four-time All-Star, died at the age of forty after suffering a heart attack while playing basketball on a school playground.

PITCHIN' PAUL—Paul Arizin [1928–   ] Basketball. H/F Pitchin' Paul played college basketball at Villanova University, where in his junior year, he scored eighty-five points in a game, setting a new single game scoring mark. In 1950, during his senior year, Arizin was selected the college player of the year. Nicknamed Pitchin' Paul because he was always in there pitchin', Arizin was drafted by the Philadelphia Warriors of the NBA. During his rookie year, he averaged seventeen points per game. By the time he retired, Arizin had pulled down 6,546 rebounds and ranked third in all-time scoring: 16,266 points for an average of 22.8 points per game.

POCKET ROCKET [THE]—Henri Richard [1936-   ] Hockey. H/F Henri Richard was the younger brother of Montreal Canadiens hockey great Maurice "THE ROCKET" Richard. At forward, Henri was the "pocket" version. Henri Richard said it best in explaining how he differed from his older brother, Maurice. "My brother's biggest thrills came when he scored many goals," said the Pocket Rocket. "I am most satisfied when I play in a close game and do not have any goals scored against me." Henri Richard helped the Montreal Canadiens win five Stanley Cup championships.

POOSH 'EM UP—Tony Lazzeri [1903–1946] Baseball. H/F Whereas on the Yankees it was left to Babe Ruth to clear the bases, it was up to Lazzeri to advance the runners. During his fourteen-year career, this second baseman had 1,840 hits and a .292 batting average.

POP—Glenn Scobey Warner [1871–1954] Football. H/F Warner coached Georgia to an unbeaten season, coached Jim Thorpe, and coached Pittsburgh to three unbeaten seasons and Stanford to three Rose Bowls. During his forty-six year career in coaching, Warner developed such innovations as the three-point stance, as well as the single wing and double-wing formations. He was elected to the College Football Hall of Fame in 1951.

POPEYE—Don Zimmer [1931—   ] Baseball. This longtime coach and manager gained his nickname as an infielder because of his strength (though he seemed to ingest chewing tobacco instead of spinach). In addition, his jowly, bug-eyed appearance reminded some of the cartoon character. After twelve years of playing third, second, and shortstop, Zimmer managed San Diego, Boston, and Texas. Popeye and the pitcher Bill Lee didn't get along, and SPACEMAN Lee referred to Zimmer as The Gerbil.

POPS—Wilver "Willie" Stargell [1940—   ] Baseball. H/F In twenty-one-years for Pittsburgh, Stargell hit 475 home runs while striking out 1,936 times (second highest in history). Playing outfield and later first base, Pops was not only a leader but also a father figure, forming the team into a family and then in 1979 leading the Pirates to the top in the World Series.

PRE—Steve Prefontaine [1951–1977] Track and field. H/F Prefontaine was his own person, a fact that made him as popular as the 13:22.8 in the 5,000 meter he ran in the Olympic trials. Although he was fourth in the 5,000 at the 1972 Olympic Games, he wasn't disappointed and looked forward to a bright future in running, until he was killed in a crash in his sports car. Two movies have been made about his life.

PRIDE OF THE YANKEES [THE]—Lou Gehrig [1903–1941] Baseball. H/F Lou Gehrig went out with class, the way he had always played. During his farewell speech on July 4, 1939, the first baseman told the fans at Yankee Stadium: "Today I consider myself the luckiest man on the face of the earth." Two years later he was dead of the disease that now bears his name. Gehrig was also called Biscuit Pants, Iron Man of Baseball, IRON HORSE, Larrupin' Lou, and Twinkle Toes.

PRINCE OF BUSTED BONES [THE]—Ralph Neves [1918—   ] Horse racing. H/F There are not many jockeys who have won races after being declared dead. Ralph Neves, in fact, may be the only one accorded this honor. In 1936, while racing at Bay Meadows Park, Neves was riding a thoroughbred named Flanders. Flanders tripped and Neves was thrown against the railing. He hit the fence so hard that he bounced into the center of the track, where four other horses galloped across his body. When the track doctor and two other doctors who happened to be in the stands reached the jockey, Neves was not breathing. The jockey was taken off the field, placed in cold storage and sent to the morgue. The track announcer asked the crowd to observe a moment of silence in memory of the dead jockey. Neves awoke in the morgue and called for help. When no one responded to his cries, he left the morgue, still wrapped in a sheet. Hailing a taxi, he went back to the track. The next day he resumed racing. If you wish to know how he earned his nickname The Prince of the Busted Bones, consider this: during his career, he broke both arms, his hip, his back, his ribcage, and fractured his skull. But he always came back. Neves was also called Portuguese Pepperpot.

PRINCE OF PESSIMISM–Chuck Daly [1930–] Basketball. H/F Even when the long-time coach of the Detroit Pistons was heading up the Dream Team in the 1992 Olympic Games, he would not let his team grow too optimistic. On the eve of the champion-ship blowout, he showed the U.S. team's last-second loss to the Soviet Union. In spite of his nickname, Daly feels he is lucky to be doing what he wants to do—coach.

PUCK GOESINSKI [THE]–Steve Buzinski [1917–] Hockey. Hurt by the war effort, the 1942 New York Rangers were desperate for a goalie. After a brief search, they located one in an intermediate league in Swift Current, Saskatchewan, named Steve Buzinski. Brought to New York, Buzinski was letting go through and around him over six goals per game. In fact, one time The Puck Goesinski snared a puck shot on goal and threw it back into his own net for yet another goal. After only nine games, Buzinski disappeared from the Rangers and the NHL.

PUDGE–Carlton Fisk [1947–] Baseball. Fisk may have had baby fat when in eighth grade (he weighed 155 before a growth spurt); however, Pudge went on to become the oldest (and one of the fittest) catchers in baseball. After failing to renew his contract—perhaps the Boston manage-ment thought his career was over—Pudge went over to the White Sox in 1980. Indeed, he has had what amounted to another career after his thirteen years with the Red Sox. Although he had injuries to his knee, his shoulder, and arm trouble that might have ended his career, Fisk has bat-tled back with rigorous training programs. At forty-four, Pudge was not only the oldest catcher to play the game but also better conditioned than when he was younger. He has compiled many of the all-time records for catchers, including most games caught and home runs. (Fisk has also hit more home runs after the age of forty than any other ballplayer ever.) Once cast off like an old shoe, Carlton Fisk is now a shoo-in for the Hall of Fame.

PUDGE–William Heffelfinger [1867–1954] Football. Here is a good trivia question to try on your friends: Who has the distinction of being the first professional football player? The answer is Pudge Heffelfinger. Pudge was not big by today's standards, but it was enough to win the six-foot, 190-pound guard his nickname. In any case, Heffelfinger was probably the best college player in the nineteenth century. He was All-American at Yale in 1889, 1990, and 1991. (One year Yale scored 698 points against opponents who all failed to score a single point.) On defense, Pudge could single-handedly disassemble the now illegal FLYING WEDGE; on offense, he originated the pulling guard to provide interference for the ball carrier. It was not hard to see why Heffelfinger was the player every team wanted. The Allegheny Athletic Association and Pittsburgh Athletic Club were two such teams involved in an intense rivalry, both with identical 6–6 records. To beat its rival, Allegheny offered to pay Pudge $500, plus $25 in expenses. Heffelfinger proved to be a good investment. On November 12, 1892, at Recreation Park in Pittsburgh, Heffelfinger playing guard forced a fumble and returned it for the only touchdown of the game.

PUMPSIE–Elijah Green [1933–] Baseball. Green once said: "Some day I'll write a book and call it *How I Got the Nickname Pumpsie* and sell it for a dollar and if everybody who ever asked me that question buys the book, I'll be a millionaire." To save everyone a buck, it was his mother who started it. It was her loving way of pronouncing his nickname Pumpkin. From 1959 to 1962, this first African American to play for Boston turned the double play at second base and shortstop for the Red Sox.

PUNCH—Harry Broadbent [1892–1971] Hockey. H/F Harry Broadbent earned his nickname for his punching ability with his fists as well as for his ability to punch the puck past his opponents. Indeed, one year he led the league in both categories: goals scored and minutes in the penalty box. Punch played on several teams between stints in the Canadian armed forces. One of his long-standing records is from the 1921–1922 season when playing for the Ottawa Senators he scored one or more goals in sixteen consecutive games.

PUNCH—George Imlach [1918–   ] Hockey. H/F Imlach was the general manager of the Toronto Maple Leafs in the late 1950s and early 1960s and later the coach of the Buffalo Sabres. As a coach—or general manager for that matter—you must always remember that when you're on your way in, you're on your way out," said Imlach. "It all depends on how fast your old wheel is turning because your only end is the boot into the street."

PUTT-PUTT—Richie Ashburn [1927–1997] Baseball. H/F Once when Richie Ashburn of the Philadelphia Phillies was mired in a bad batting slump, he decided to take his bat to bed with him. "I wanted to know my bat a little better and it me," he said. Fortunately for him and for the Phillies fans, batting slumps for Ashburn were few and far between. Three years he had over 200 hits; he batted .338 one year and .350 another; and Ashburn's fifteen-year career total was 2,574 hits with a batting average of .308. Putt-Putt was a nickname given to him by Red Sox slugger Ted Williams. One day in spring training, Williams observed Richie running the base paths and said that Ashburn ran as if there were two outboard motors stuffed inside the seat of his pants. He was also called Whitey.

QUEEN HELEN—Helen Wills Moody [1906–1998] Tennis. H/F Moody always conducted herself with an air of reserve and stateliness on the tennis court. In 1933, she was facing Helen Jacobs in the finals at Forest Hills. The match stood at a set apiece with Moody down 3–0 in the third set. Suddenly, Queen Helen walked over to the umpire, told him she was leaving, gathered her things and left the arena. No one knew it until years later, but Moody had injured her back some months earlier. As she wrote in her autobiography: "My choice was instinctive rather than premeditated. Had I been able to think clearly, I might have chosen to remain. Animals and often humans, however, prefer to suffer in a quiet, dark place." She was also called LITTLE MISS POKER FACE and The Princess.

QUEEN OF NEGRO WOMEN'S GOLF [THE]—Ann Gregory [1912–   ] Golf. Some newspapers with predominantly black readerships called Gregory by this name after she won the Chicago Women's Golf Association Tournament in the 1940s. In 1956, Mrs. Gregory was the first African American to play in the Women's Amateur tournament. As reported by the Associated Press: "A starting field of 105 players, including the first Negro in its history, was paired Saturday for match play in the fifty-sixth USGA Women's Amateur."

QUIZ—Dan Quisenbury [1953—   ] Baseball. On the mound, this premier relief pitcher was good, frequently great. Off the mound, he was frequently witty: "Even when the sinker doesn't sink I get a grounder. It's just, in that case, that the first bounce is 360 feet away," he once said. Teammate John Wathan once called him "baseball's Woody Allen." Quiz's nickname is a play upon his last name, but he is also referred to as The Australian, because his submarine style pitch comes from down under.

RABBIT—John Barnhill [1938—   ] Basketball. Barnhill received his nickname (like most athletes named Rabbit) because of his quickness and speed. He was a member of three Tennessee State NAIA championship teams and averaged over eight points in 589 games in the pros. Later he had a stint as an assistant coach of the Los Angeles Lakers.

RABBIT—Walter James Vincent Maranville [1891–1954] Baseball. H/F Slightly built (5' 5", 155 pounds), Maranville was quick as a bunny—stealing 291 bases and scoring over 1,200 runs. In his twenty-one-year career, he set records that have never been broken for the most games played by a National League shortstop (2,154) and most putouts made by a major-league shortstop (5,139).

RABBIT—Louis Weller [1904–1979] Football. Playing for Haskell Institute, Weller was known for his speed. He ran back a kickoff ninety yards and a punt ninety-five yards against Oklahoma A&M. Later he played professional football with the Boston Redskins and the Tulsa Oilers.

RAFFLES—Frank Boucher [1901–1977] Hockey. H/F When he was a seventeen-year-old, Boucher spent a year raising the money to buy his release from the Canadian Mounted Police. But that wasn't the origin of his nickname. Boucher stole the puck so frequently and in such a gentlemanly manner (he was awarded the Lady Byng Trophy for sportsmanship eight times) that he was nicknamed after the gentle burglar in the stories by E. W. Hornung.

RAGING BULL—Jake LaMotta [1921—   ] Boxing. H/F In 1947, in order to get a shot at the middleweight title, LaMotta had to take a dive for Billy Fox. Also, in order to get to fight the middleweight champion Marcel Cerdan, LaMotta had to pay $20,000 under the table to the persons handling the champion. On June 16, 1949, he fought Cerdan and stopped his opponent in the tenth round. LaMotta was such a fierce fighter that he earned the nickname Raging Bull. This was also the title of the motion picture about his life, starring Robert DiNiro. It is curious to note in these days of high-moneyed boxing bouts that the most LaMotta ever earned for a fight was $75,000, a fee he received for fighting Sugar Ray Robinson. He was also called the Bronx Bull.

RAJAH [THE]—Rogers Hornsby [1896–1963] Baseball. H/F Rogers Hornsby displayed not only a cantankerous personality but also an insistence that others pronounce the sibilant in his first name. The name rajah is an offbeat pronunciation for Roger. Though The Rajah may have been a difficult personality, he was simply a wonderful hitter. (So concerned was he about his eyesight, he refrained from reading and attending movies.) Three times Rogers Hornsby hit .400 or more, and his lifetime batting average is a lofty .358. He was also called Rajah of Swat.

RAPID ROBERT—Robert Feller [1918–   ] Baseball H/F. Feller's fastball helped him make one of the most awesome debuts ever. On August 23, 1936, the seventeen-year-old struck out the first eight batters he faced, and fifteen in the game. His hopping fastball quickly led to his nicknames. Feller went on to pitch three no-hitters, ten one-hitters, forty-six shutouts, and to strike out 2,581 batters. During his eighteen-year career for the Cleveland Indians, Feller won 266 games and lost 162. Long after his career was over, Bob Feller remained popular with fans, appearing in exhibitions and at autograph signings. He was also called Bullet Bob.

RED—Walter Lanier Barber [1908–1992] Sportscaster. H/F "The Ol' Redhead" did the play-by-play for the Cincinnati Reds from 1934 to 1938, the Brooklyn Dodgers from 1939 to 1953, and the New York Yankees from 1954 to 1967. Red Barber, the voice of the Brooklyn Dodgers, and Mel Allen (voice of the New York Yankees) were the first broadcasters to be inducted into Baseballs' Hall of Fame at Cooperstown. "Back, back, back, back, back, back," was the redheaded Barber's familiar call whenever a home run was hit, and the baseball diamond was referred to as "the pea patch." He broadcast baseball's first night game in Cincinnati (May 24, 1935) and he was on hand to broadcast the first televised baseball game (August 26, 1939). All in all, his career as the first regular baseball announcer in New York spanned thirty-three years. The novelist Philip Roth once said of Red Barber: "Henry James might himself have admired the implicit cultural ironies and the splendid possibilities for oblique moral and social commentary." Barber was the most admired broadcaster of his generation.

RED—William Holzman [1920–   ] Basketball. H/F Holzman's pro playing career was from 1946 to 1954, mostly with the Rochester Royals. His coaching career was with the New York Knicks. Holzman had at first been reluctant to become the head coach of the Knicks. He was satisfied with his job as chief scout. However, when he started in the middle of 1969, he brought two contradictory elements to the Knicks. He got them to relax and he built up their intensity. He took the pressure off CLYDE Frazier and DOLLAR BILL Bradley and had the whole team play a swarming, attacking defense. They practiced every day during the season and everyone was expected to give 100 percent. The results were spectacular. In 1970, Red Holzman was the Coach of the Year as he led the Knicks to the NBA championship. They repeated as champions in 1973.

RED—Charles Ruffing [1904–1986] Baseball. H/F After a miserable start for the Red Sox (39–96), Ruffing went on to lead the Yankees to four pennants in a row from 1936 to 1939 with seasons of 20–12, 20–7, 21–7, and 21–7. In World Series play, Red was 7–2. Ruffing was also an outstanding hitter and frequently would pinch-hit. Eight times he batted over .300; in 1930, his average was .364.

REFRIGERATOR (THE)—William Perry [active 1985–   ] Football. This defensive tackle loves to eat. The upside of this is that his weight (sometimes listed at 326) has made him a difficult target to bring down when he plays fullback. For instance, in the third quarter of Super Bowl

XX, Coach Mike Ditka opened the door for the Refrigerator to play long enough to take the ball in from the one-yard-line. It was just extra gravy as the Bears defrosted the Patriots, 46–10.

RENO ROCKET (THE)—Greg LeMonde (1961–   ) Bicycling. LeMonde, a native of Nevada, surprised the world (and Bernard Hinault) by winning the Tour de France in 1986. Not only is he the only American ever to win this legendary bike race, LeMonde fought back from a hunting accident to repeat the tour de force in 1989 and 1990.

RIFLE—Robert S. Waterfield (1920–1983) Football. H/F "Games such as the Rams and the Rifle played on Sunday are the kind that set pro football apart," began a newspaper article of the day, "give it that extra touch of quality which makes it the finest game in the land." Waterfield was called Rifle because of his powerful arm. He was one of the first quarterbacks to use the long pass as a standard part of the offense. During his rookie season he led the Cleveland team to the NFL championship. Along the way he threw an unbelievable fifty-five touchdowns and won the MVP. After the Cleveland team moved to Los Angeles, Waterfield led the Rams to the Western Conference titles in 1949 and 1950, and another NFL championship in 1951. But not only was Waterfield a great field general and passer (over 50 percent completion rate and ninety-nine touchdowns), he was also a sensational punter. His eight-year punting average was 42.48 yards. After his playing days were over, Waterfield was the Rams coach for three unsuccessful years. He was nicknamed The Great Stone Coach for his retiring personality.

ROADRUNNER (THE)—Yvan Cournoyer (1943–   ) Hockey. H/F Cournoyer, who had a talent for appearing suddenly, sneaking in a goal, and just as suddenly vanishing, was nicknamed for the cartoon character the Roadrunner. When the 5' 7", 165-pound right ring scored the winning goal (fifteen for the playoffs, a record) to give the Montreal Canadiens the Stanley Cup in 1973. Tony Esposito, the goaltender for the losing Black Hawks said, "He seemed to appear from nowhere." As his teammate, Jean Beliveau, once put it: "The key to Yvan's skating is his start. He gets a quicker jump than anyone. He also can shift speeds and put on bursts which leave his defenders standing still."

ROBBY—Frank Robinson (1935–   ) Baseball. H/F Robinson split his twenty-one year playing career between the American and National Leagues and is the only person to win MVP in both leagues. His 586 home runs ranks fourth. He also hit eight home runs in five World Series. Robinson then went on to become the first African American to become a major-league manager.

ROCK (THE)—Knute Rockne (1888–1931) Football. Rockne passed his fire and drive on to the teams he coached. It obviously worked as his teams had five undefeated seasons and six seasons when the Irish lost only one game. Rockne is also famous for having delivered one of the most impassioned halftime speeches ever, telling his footballers to, "win just one for the Gipper." He was also called The Rock of Notre Dame and The Great Man. See THE GIPPER.

ROCKET (The)—Rod Laver (1938–   ) Tennis. H/F Harry Hopman, the Australian Davis Cup coach, gave this nickname to the sixteen-year-old Laver for the way he moved around the court.

In 1962, Laver won his first Grand Slam, defeating Roy Emerson at Wimbledon, Forest Hills, and Roland Garres and Marty Mulligan at Melbourne. In 1963, Laver turned pro so he was not able to play in the major tournaments until they were opened to professionals in 1968. That year, the Rocket defeated Andres Gimeno of Spain in the Australian Open, Kenny Rosewall in the French Open, John Newcombe at Wimbledon, and Tony Roche for the U.S. Open.

ROCKET (THE)—Maurice Richard (1921–) Hockey. H/F Maurice Richard played right wing on the Montreal Canadiens' Punch Line (with center Elmer Lach and left wing Toe Blake). One day as Richard swooped down the ice in practice, one of his teammates yelled, "Look out, here comes the rocket." Glenn Hall, the Boston Bruins' goalie, provided a description of what it was like to face him: "What I remember most of all about the Rocket was his eyes. When he came flying toward you with the puck on his stick, his eyes were all lit up, flashing and gleaming like a pinball machine. It was terrifying." Maurice Richard was the first hockey player to score fifty goals in a season (in 1944–1945). What is even more remarkable is that unlike today, the season back then was only fifty games long. (One of the keys to his success was his attitude, calling hockey "the most urgent thing in my life.") As good as he was, however, he never won the scoring title. (One season when he was leading, he was suspended for hitting an official.) Teammate BOOM BOOM Geoffrin overtook him on the last weekend of the season. (See THE RICHARD RIOT.) During his eighteen-year career, Richard netted 544 regular-season goals. He was also called THE BABE RUTH OF HOCKEY.

ROCKY GRAZIANO—Rocco Barbella (1922–1990) Boxing. H/F Graziano was the middleweight champion from 1946 to 1947. During a twenty-one-month period he lost the middleweight crown to Tony Zale two out of three times. The movie *Somebody Up There Likes Me*, starring Paul Newman, was based on Graziano's life. (Although baseball may be the American pastime, more movies have been made about boxing.) He was also called Atomic Puncher. See MAN OF STEEL.

RUBE—Andrew Foster (1879–1930) Baseball (Negro Leagues). H/F Foster was the organizer of the Chicago American Giants in the old Negro leagues. He was greatly responsible for helping to create and hold together the Negro leagues through all kinds of troubles. Hence, he is sometimes called "The Father of Black Baseball." He received the nickname Rube after he beat Connie Mack's pitching star Rube Waddell in an exhibition game in 1902. In the early years of the twentieth century, Rube Foster might well have been the best pitcher—black or white—in America. Some historians of the game credit him with inventing the hit and run bunt. When he died in 1930 he was certainly the most famous black man in Chicago.

RUBY ROBERT—Robert Prometheus Fitzsimmons (1864–1917) Boxing. H/F This nickname was for the reddish tinge of his body, freckles, and hair. Fitz was both the heavyweight champion of the world (1897–1899) and the light-heavyweight champion (1903–1905). One of his most famous fights was on March 17, 1897 with Jim Corbett. After being outboxed for seven rounds, Fitz hit Corbett with the famous "solar plexus punch." Corbett went down and couldn't regain the control of his lower body in time to get up in time. In addition, to Ruby Robert, he was also called Bald-Headed Kangaroo, Knock-Kneed Crane, and A Flying Machine on Stilts.

RYAN EXPRESS [THE]—Nolan Ryan [1947–   ] Baseball. Who has won over 300 games, thrown seven no-hitters, struck out over 5,000 batters, and is the oldest pitcher to have won an All-Star Game? One doesn't have to dip very far back into history to find the pitcher; it's Nolan Ryan, also known as Nolie, Big Tex, or The Ryan Express. Hank Aaron, the man who broke Babe Ruth's home-run record, once said that he never faced a pitcher who threw any harder. What Nolie threw was a rising fastball that was once clocked at over 100 mph, a curve ball that seemed to fall off a table, and in recent years a change-up that at 89 mph was faster than some pitchers fast ball. Red Murph, a scout for the Mets, discovered Ryan in high school. At that level Ryan was overpowering. Throwing under the poor lights of local stadiums, the batters were more concerned about not getting hit than getting base hits. Things were much the same in the minors, as he later skipped from Class D to the International League. As a twenty-year-old for the New York Mets, Ryan came in and saved the third game of the World Series for the Amazin' Mets. He was later traded to the Angels for Jim Fregosi in one of the worst deals ever made, for the Ryan Express has been a dominating pitcher over the last four decades. In 1973, Ryan registered seventeen strikeouts in his second no-hitter of that year. In one at bat, Norman Cash even lugged a piano leg to the plate in tribute to Nolie. That year was a banner year: Ryan was 21–16 with 383 strikeouts. After eight seasons with the Angels, Ryan went back to Texas as a free agent with the Houston Astros where he pitched his fifth no-hitter to break Sandy Koufax's major-league record. At the age of forty-two Ryan went to the Texas Rangers. In 1989 his 5,000th strikeout victim was none other than Ricky Henderson. On a 3–2 count, Ryan smoked his money pitch, a fast ball low and away. At forty-two he threw his sixth no-hitter. And on May 1, 1991, Ryan threw his seventh no-hitter, striking out sixteen Expos enroute. Now that The Ryan Express has hung up his spikes, you can bet the ranch that he will become a member of the Hall of Fame.

SAD SAM—Samuel Pond Jones [1892–   ] Baseball. Sad Sam Jones, was given his nickname by Bill McGeehan, a sportswriter for the *New York Herald Tribune,* who called him "Sad Sam the Sorrowful from Woodsfield, Ohio." Jones started playing professional baseball in the minor leagues in 1913 in Zanesville, Ohio. He joined the Cleveland Indians in 1914 when he appeared in only one game as a reliever. After his 1915 season with the Indians, he and infielder Fred Thomas were traded to the Boston Red Sox for Tris Speaker, along with $50,000 cash (quite a sum in 1916). After years of relieving, Jones started as a regular in 1918 and compiled a record of sixteen wins and five losses. In 1922, he was traded to the New York Yankees, but by that time he had established himself (after winning twenty-three games in 1921) as a top pitcher. Jones was 229–217 during his twenty-two-year career and 0–2 in four World Series. He was also called Horsewhip because of the wicked break of his curveball.

SAILOR BOB—Bob Sharkey [1890–1981] Baseball. Sailor Bob Sharkey is the answer to a great New York Yankee Trivia Question—Who is the only player ever to pitch a baseball at the first game at the old Yankee Stadium and at the new Yankee Stadium? Sailor Bob Sharkey pitched the first game ever at Yankee Stadium in 1923 and, in 1976, he threw out the first ball at the renovated stadium. He pitched for the New York Yankees for twelve years and had four seasons of twenty or more wins. By the time he retired, he had chalked up 196 wins against 150 defeats, and compiled a lifetime ERA of 3.09. He received his colorful nickname because he spent most of 1918 aboard the battleship Arkansas. He was also called Bob the Gog.

SAM—Edgar Charles Rice (1890–1974) Baseball. H/F In 1915, Clark Griffith told reporters that his Washington Senators had a new player named Rice. When asked his first name, Griffith automatically responded "Sam." From then on Rice was known as Sam. Rice batted over .300 fifteen times, won the fielding award eight times, and had more than 200 hits in six different seasons. And in 1923, he won the Triple Crown. In his twenty seasons, Rice's batting average was .322; it was .302 for three World Series.

SATCHEL—Leroy Robert Paige (1906–1982) Baseball. H/F What can be said about Ol' Satch that has not already been said? He could have been the greatest, but because of the color of his skin, he was not allowed to pitch in the major leagues until 1948, when he was forty-two years old. Imagine being a forty-two-year-old rookie. (To put that in some perspective, consider the career of Baltimore Oriole catcher Rick Dempsey. On June 26, 1992, when Dempsey entered the game in the eighth inning, he became at age forty-two years and nine months, the oldest player ever to play for Baltimore!) In his six-year career in the majors he won twenty-eight games, lost thirty-one, but compiled a 3.29 ERA. In the Negro leagues, however, he might well have pitched 2,000 victories in 2,500 games, with 250 shutouts and 100 no-hitters. (The record keeping was haphazard.) Sometimes he even called in the outfielders while he struck out the side. Paige describes how he got his wonderful nickname in his autobiography *Maybe I'll Pitch Forever* (Doubleday and Co., 1962). At age seven he got a job at the Mobile, Alabama, train station toting bags, valises, and satchels. Satchel writes:

> We weren't going to be eating much better if I made only a dime at a time so I got me a pole and some ropes. That let me sling two, three, or four satchels together and carry them at one time. You always got to be thinking to make money. My invention wasn't a smart looking thing, but it upped my income. The other kids laughed. 'You look like a walking satchel tree,' one of them yelled. They all started yelling it. Soon everybody was calling me that, you know how it is with kids and nicknames. That's when LeRoy Paige became no more and Satchel Paige took over. Nobody ever called me LeRoy, nobody except my mom and the government.

Satchel once disclosed his six rules for success:

> Avoid fried meats which angry up the blood. If your stomach disputes you, lie down and pacify it with cool thoughts. Keep your juices flowing by jangling around gently as you move. Go very gently on the vices, such as carrying on in society—the social ramble ain't restful. Avoid running at all times. Don't look back. Something might be gaining on you.

(Film fans can see Satchel Paige in the western movie *The Wonderful Country*, with Robert Mitchum and Julie London.) See PADDLEFOOT.

SATCHEL—Leroy Robert Paige (l906-l982) Baseball. He received his colorful nickname at age seven when he was toting satchels at the local train station in Mobile, Alabama.

SAY HEY—Willie Howard Mays (1931—   ) Baseball. H/F "You don't have to say something many times to get a nickname," said Willie Mays. The year was 1951. "If I couldn't think of a fellow's name, I'd say, uh, 'Say Hey.' That was the year Mays was Rookie of the Year. Leo Durocher's assessment of Mays in his rookie year was on the money. "Willie Mays can do the five things you look for in a player—run, catch, throw, hit for distance, hit for average—better than anybody I ever saw." In 1954, Willie Mays made his famous over the shoulder catch of Vic Wertz's 450-foot drive. Then he spun around and fired it back into the infield, preventing Larry Doby from scoring. "The catch broke our backs," said Cleveland manager Al Lopez. The New York Giants went on to win the World Series in four games. In 1955, Mays hit fifty-one home runs. In 1958, he batted .347. In 1961, he hit four homers in one game. In 1963, Mays hit a home run in the sixteenth inning to give the Giants a 1–0 victory over the Milwaukee Braves. In 1964, manager Alvin Dark appointed Mays captain, the first African American to be given that distinction. By the time Mays retired in 1973, he had 666 home runs and scored 2,062 runs. And he held major-league records for center fielders of 2,843 games played, 7,431 total chances, and 7,095 putouts. In All-Star Games he set eleven records that have never been broken. Mays was in a league all by himself. He was also called Amazing Mays, Buckduck, and Willie the Wallop.

SCHOOLBOY—Waite Charles Hoyt (1899–1984) Baseball. H/F Hoyt picked up his nickname by pitching batting practice for the Dodgers while he was still a student at Erasmus High School in Brooklyn. When he graduated to the bigs, Hoyt appeared in six World Series (five for the Yankees and one for the Athletics). In the 1921 fall classic, he pitched twenty-seven scoreless innings for an ERA of 0.00, a record that may never be touched.

SCISSORS—David Luther Foutz (1856–1897) Baseball. When he played minor league ball in Colorado, Foutz was so good-looking that he was known as the "Hunkidori Boy." Later, when he was called up to pitch for St. Louis, Brooklyn (AA), and Brooklyn (NL), he was known as Scissors. In 1886, his record of forty-one wins and sixteen losses was the best in the American Association. In addition to pitching, he also played first base and the outfield. Scissors knocked out 1,254 hits, including 186 doubles, 91 triples, and 32 homers. He also stole 263 bases.

SCRAMBLER (THE)—Fran Tarkenton (1940—   ) Football. H/F Tarkenton wasn't big for a quarterback (six feet, 190 pounds), but he made up for it with an ability to get out of harm's way. Instead of staying in the pocket and waiting to be tackled, Tarkenton would scramble around the big defenders pursuing him in order to find an open receiver or even to run the ball on his own. (Of course, he sometimes lost lots of yardage; one time it was forty-five yards.) But more often than not, his playing style paid off. In 1978, Tarkenton set a record with 345 completions in 572 pass attempts. See SIR.

SHANTY—Frank Hogan (1906–1967) Baseball. Many of the Irish immigrants to the Boston area first lived in shanties upon their arrival; and Hogan was Irish and from Boston. During thirteen years split among the Braves, Giants, and Senators, Shanty played catcher and batted a not-too-shabby .295.

SHAQ [THE]—Shaquille O'Neal [1972–   ] Basketball. This 7' 1", 295-pound star for Louisville State led the NCAA in rebounds and was the winner of the Adolph Rupp Trophy and the John Wooden Award as the 1991 College Basketball Player of the Year. Becoming the center with the Orlando Magic for an estimated $40 million over seven seasons, he caused quite a stir in his first year in the NBA, even drawing Wilt Chamberlain to a rare game to see what all the fuss was about. And what he saw is someone who scores as well as rebounds, blocks shots and runs down the court like a guard leading a fast break. The University of Texas coach Tom Penders once assessed The Shaq in these words: "He's as big as Jabbar, if not bigger; stronger than Chamberlain, and runs like Magic Johnson." In other words, O'Neal is giving Mickey Mouse a run for the money as the most popular figure in Los Angeles. His stellar performance on the floor is often described as a "Shaq Attack."

SHERIFF—John Frederick Blake [1899–1982] Baseball. In *Hot Stove League,* Lee Allen explained how Blake received his nickname at the start of his career:

> One day in 1924, a young pitcher with the Cubs, John Fred Blake, was sitting around a Chicago hotel room talking with his cronies. As easily as it might have happened in such a place and at such a time, the talk turned to Prohibition, bootleggers, and revenue officers. In the course of the fanning bee, one of the men began to refer to Blake as Sheriff, though for no observable reason. The name stuck.

SHOE—Willie Shoemaker [1931–   ] Horse racing. H/F This jockey's nickname obviously comes from the beginning of his last name. Because of his quiet demeanor he has also on occasion been called the Silent Shoe. He also started life in a shoebox. Only two-and-a-half pounds at birth, he was placed in a shoebox near the stove. When he started riding as a jockey, Shoemaker was 4' 11" and weighed 103 pounds. The Shoe rode winners in the Kentucky Derby in 1955, 1959, 1965, and 1986 (at the age of fifty-four); the Belmont States in 1957, 1959, 1962, 1967, and 1975; the Preakness Stakes in 1963 and 1967. Though he may never have won the Triple Crown, the Shoe won over 8,500 races and was the biggest moneymaker ten different years. Shoemaker was paralyzed in an automobile accident in 1991, but continued to train horses.

SHOELESS JOE—Joe Jackson [1887–1951] Baseball. Before coming to the major leagues, Joseph Jefferson Jackson played without shoes. Shoeless Joe had a .356 average over thirteen years. After Jackson had been implicated in the Black Sox scandal of 1919, a young fan came up to Shoeless Joe and said, "Say it ain't so, Joe!" In 1998, Ted Williams and Bob Feller began spearheading a movement to get Shoeless Joe into the Hall of Fame.

SHORTY—Hugh Ray [1884–1956] Football. H/F Ray's nickname was for his 5' 6" height. His Hall of Fame induction was for the many ways he helped improve officiating and the game of football. Two of his innovations were to relocate the goal posts at the goal line and to streamline the ball so it could be passed more easily.

SHOE—Willie Shoemaker (b. August 9, 1931) Horse racing.
Shoe booted home 8,833 winners in a spectacular riding career.

SHOELESS JOE—Joe Jackson (1887-1951) Baseball. The photo shows that "Shoeless Joe" often wore shoes. But sometimes in the outfield he didn't. There's a movement led by Ted Williams and Bob Feller to get Shoeless Joe into the Hall of Fame where he certainly belongs.

SHUCKS—Hub Pruett [1900–1982] Baseball. This pitcher, who went from the University of Missouri campus to the St. Louis Browns, never said anything stronger than "shucks." The first time he faced Babe Ruth, Pruett struck him out on three pitches. Shucks always had the Bambino's number, striking him out fifteen out of thirty times.

SHUFFLIN' PHIL—Philip Brooks Douglas [1890–1952] Baseball. Douglas had a problem with alcohol. That accounted for his walk and also led to a letter he wrote offering to help his team lose the pennant. The letter was used against him in Judge Landis' decision to ban Douglas from baseball. Douglas may not have had equilibrium in his life, but he did have it in his career as a pitcher. His career marks were 93–93 and 2–2 in two World Series.

SILENT MIKE—Michael Joseph Tiernan [1867–1918] Baseball. In thirteen seasons in the National League, from 1887 through 1899, Silent Mike Tiernan, a nickname he no doubt earned because of his quiet manner and his disinclination to speak at length, batted for a .311 average. He played mostly outfield for the New York Giants and, in 1891, he led the National League in homers with seventeen, which was excellent in those days of the dead ball.

SILVER FOX [THE]—Tommy Armour [1895–1968] Golf. H/F Silver-haired Tommy Armour moved to the U.S. from Scotland in 1922. In 1927, he won the U.S. Open in a playoff with LIGHT-HORSE Cooper. In 1930, he won the PGA Championship; and in 1931, he returned to his native Scotland to win the British Open. Later, Armour and a designer named Penna helped make MacGregor—with Silver Scot irons, Eye-O-Matic woods, and Ironmaster putters—the golf clubs in everyone's garage. Armour also became a golf teacher and the writer of two of the most widely read books about golf: *A Round of Golf with Tommy Armour* and *How to Play Your Best Golf All the Time*. One of the things he explained to the novice was what happens to a person about to putt. He or she gets the "yips." That's that "ghastly time when with the first movement of the putter, the golfer blacks out." He was also called The Silver Scot.

SILVER FOX [THE]—Lester Patrick [1883–1960] Hockey. H/F Patrick was dubbed "The Silver Fox" because of his silver hair and sly ways. Ed Daley, the sports editor of the *New York Herald-Tribune,* gave Lester his nickname when he wrote: "Yesterday, I spent a fascinating half hour in the lair of the Silver Fox." This coach and manager of the New York Rangers in the early days was as knowledgeable about hockey as he was in how to market it. (The NFL's Patrick Division is named after him.) During the 1928 Stanley Cup championship, when regular goalie Lorne Chabot was injured in the second game, Patrick put himself into the game. Winning in overtime on a goal by Boucher, the Rangers were so inspired by their victory and the performance of their forty-two-year-old coach that they went on to win the series 3–2.

SINGING UMPIRE—William J. Byron [1872–1954] Baseball. Byron earned his nickname for the way he yodeled out "Strike Three!" And whenever a batter would complain about a call, Byron would dust off the plate and sing: "You'll have to get a little bolder / And get the bat off yer shoulder."

SIR CHARLES—Charles Barkley (1963–) Basketball. This basketball star, one of only twelve players in NBA history to score over 19,000 points, received his nickname because of his flamboyant manner on and off court. In his book, *Outrageous,* co-authored with Roy S. Johnson, Sir Charles says, "I'm no dummy. I know a lot of people I meet treat me well because I make a lot of money and play basketball for a living." Barkley is also known as Boy George (after England's famous singing star), The Round Mound of Rebound, and The Leaning Tower of Pizza (because he stands 6' 5" and weighs over 250 pounds).

SKEETER—Wilma Rudolph (1940–1994) Track and field. H/F When Wilma Rudolph was thirteen, her basketball coach referred to her as a "skeeter." Coach Clinton Gray went on to say that she zoomed "around like a regular mosquito—fast, little, and always in my way." After watching Wilma, the track coach at Tennessee A & I State University suggested that Gray start a track team at Clarksville High School. With only one year of competitive running, Wilma Rudolph made the U.S. Olympic team at sixteen and won a bronze medal in the 400-meter relay at the Melbourne Olympic Games in 1956. Next, Skeeter ran for Ed Temple at Tennessee A & I. The foursome of Rudolph, Barbara Jones, Lucinda Williams, and Martha Hudson, became the fastest women runners in the country. At the Olympic Games in Rome, these four women won six gold medals. Wilma Rudolph alone won three gold medals—the most gold medals ever by an American in a single Olympics. She won the 100-meter dash and set an Olympic record in the 200. In the 400-meter relay she anchored the U.S. team to an Olympic and world record of 44.4 seconds. The Italians called Rudolph *La Gazelle Nera* (The Black Gazelle); the French referred to her as *La Perle Noire* (The Black Pearl). But back home in Tennessee, this winner of the Sullivan Trophy was known simply as Skeeter.

SKEETS—Renaldo Nehemiah (1959–) Track and field, football. Renaldo was named Skeets by his father for crawling fast as an infant. Nehemiah held the 110-meter high hurdles record of thirteen seconds. What was especially noteworthy about this hurdler was that he combined blazing speed (the 100 meters in 10.38 seconds) with flawless technique. Needing other challenges, he became a receiver for the San Francisco 49ers (even though he had never played football before), before returning to track.

SKUZ—Ross Grimsley (1950–) Baseball. Grimsley was a pitcher for various major league teams from 1971 to 1980. He received his nickname because of his unkempt appearance. (When he was on a winning streak, he would not wash, or comb his hair, or use deodorant.) A teammate described him as the "most nauseating thing you've ever seen on two legs." He is the son of Ross "Lefty" Grimsley.

SLAMMER—Marques Johnson (1956–) Basketball. While Johnson was at UCLA, the college ban against dunking was lifted. (This was the so-called LEW ALCINDOR RULE.) At 6' 6", Marques Johnson was one of the best dunkers and rebounders in college, and then in the NBA when he played for the Milwaukee Bucks.

SLAMMIN' SAMMY—Sam Snead (1912–) Golf. H/F Sam Snead learned to play by swinging an old five-iron. It helped him later to slam many a long straight drive on the golf course. (However, his good drives were sometimes frittered away with weak putting on the greens.) Slammin' Sammy won 135 tournaments—eighty-four on the PGA Tour. He won PGA Championships in 1942, 1949, and 1951; the British Open in 1946; and the Masters in 1949, 1952, and 1954. He won four Vardon Trophies (for lowest average score) and was the highest money winner three times. Snead also played a high caliber of golf in his later years. When he was sixty, he was fourth in the 1972 PGA Championship; he was third in the 1974 PGA Championship. At the age of sixty-seven in the 1979 Quad Cities, he became the first golfer to shoot his age (67–66) in a tournament on the tour. He once told his good friend Ted Williams that golf is a much more difficult game than baseball because in golf, if a player hits the ball foul, he has to play it.

SLAPSIE MAXIE—Maxie Rosenbloom (1904–1976) Boxing. H/F Slapsie Maxie (an epithet hung on him because he did not always keep his gloves closed when he punched) learned step-dancing from film-actor George Raft, and he was a true dancer in the ring, keeping away from his opponents and fighting them at a distance. He was the World Light-Heavyweight Champion from 1930–1934, and, when he retired in 1939, he had won 210 fights, lost 35, with 23 draws, and 19 no decisions.

SLATS—Max Zaslofsky (1925–1985) Basketball. Although he played basketball in both high school (Thomas Jefferson High School in Brooklyn, New York) and college (St. John's University), he didn't really distinguish himself as a player until he turned pro in 1946 with the old Chicago Stags of the old BAA (Basketball of America Association). Slats (a common enough nickname, applied to many athletes who are tall and thin, resembling a slat of wood) led the BAA in scoring in 1947–1948, averaging twenty-one points per game. He later played for the New York Knickerbockers in the NBA and then Baltimore, Milwaukee, and Fort Wayne. He ended his professional career in 1968–1969, when he coached the New York Nets.

SLEEPY—Jim Crowley (1903–1996) Football. H/F Crowley became a legend as a member of The Four Horsemen. Notre Dame's great football coach Knute Rockne gave him the nickname Sleepy. In 1921, when Crowley appeared as a freshman on the college football team, Rockne saw a drowsy-eyed youth from Green Bay, Wisconsin, and he joked, "You look like a tester in an alarm clock factory." Crowly was called Sleepy ever after. He was, however, anything but sleepy on the football field. When he finished his career at Notre Dame, he had carried the football 294 times for 1,841 yards, a 6.3-yard average.

SLICK—Edward Charles "Whitey" Ford (1928–   ) Baseball. H/F This great New York Yankee hurler (1950–1967) appeared in twenty-two World Series games (more than any other pitcher, winning ten and losing eight). In his sixteen-year career, he won 236 games, lost 106, which comes to a winning percentage of .690, among the highest in major-league history. In the preface to *Slick* by Whitey Ford (with Phil Pepe), Mickey Mantle relates how Whitey received the nickname "Slick." According to Mantle, Casey Stengel had a favorite expression – "whiskey slick"—that he applied to some players who were getting a little too arrogant. After a while, Billy Martin and Mickey Mantle started to call Whitey "Slick." He was also known as THE CHAIRMAN OF THE BOARD, a title given to him by Yankee catcher Elston Howard.

SLEEPY—Jim Crowly (third from left) with Harry Stuhldreher, Don Miller, and Elmer Layden. Grantland Rice nicknamed them The Four Horsemen.

SLINGING SAMMY—Samuel Baugh [1914—] Football. H/F Sammy Baugh received his nickname back in high school in Sweetwater, Texas, for baseball not football. He was a third baseman with a good throw to first. But it would be in football that Slinging Sammy's fame spread. First for Texas Christian University (TCU) and then for the Washington Redskins, Baugh was famous for his far-flung passes. After quarterbacking at TCU, Slinging Sammy joined the Redskins in 1937 and led them to a league championship. Baugh was also the punter. (In fact, Baugh was also one of the league's finest punters; one season he averaged more than fifty yards a punt.) In the championship game with the Bears, Baugh stood in punt formation in his own end zone and threw a pass for a forty-two-yard gain. The Redskins went on to score in a 28–21 victory. During his sixteen-year career, Slinging Sammy passed over 3,000 times and completed over 56 percent of them. His passes had gained over 22,000 yards and scored 187 touchdowns. Slinging Sammy led the league in passing six times and he helped the Redskins to five division titles and two championships. He was also called Texas Cowboy.

SLUG—Harry Edwin Heilmann [1894–1951] Baseball. H/F Slug is one of the truly great hitters of all time. Playing right field for the Detroit Tigers, he compiled a .342 lifetime average, with 2,660 hits in 7,787 at-bats, with 542 doubles, 151 triples, and 183 home runs. In 1921, Slug Heilmann's bat set the American League on fire, when he led the league with 237 hits and a .394 batting average. His nickname, at first glance, appears to be double-edged: Is it slug for his abilities as a slugger, or for his slowness? Unfortunately, it was for the latter; he very rarely beat out infield hits. Radio fans of the Tigers know Heilmann because, after his retirement, he worked the radio booth for Detroit games from 1933 to 1951 and became very popular.

SLUG—Otis Taylor [1942–] Football. Taylor received his nickname at Prairie View A & M for slugging an opponent. Later playing wide receiver for the Kansas City Chiefs, Taylor caught sixty-seven passes for 1,100 yards. When Otis Taylor met THE ALABAMA ANTELOPE, he said, "I've read all about you, Mr. Hutson, and you were the greatest." "I've seen you play," said Don Hutson, "and you are the greatest."

SMASHING, BASHING, CRASHING, DASHING KID [THE]—Ted "KID" Lewis [active 1899–1919] Boxing. H/F This English boxer's real name was Gershon Mendeloff, and he was nicknamed for his hell-bent-for-leather boxing style. Lewis progressed from the British championship at nineteen, the European championship at twenty, and the world welterweight championship at twenty-one. In 1915, he defeated American Jack Britton for the welterweight championship; in 1916, Lewis lost it to Britton; in 1917, Lewis won it back again from Britton; in 1919, Lewis lost it again to Britton. In all the two fighters met twenty times.

SMOKEY—Walter Emmons Alston [1911–1984] Baseball. H/F Alston got his nickname from his fastball on the sandlots. But he achieved his fame not as a player (he had only one at-bat in the majors) but as a manager of the Dodgers. Over his twenty-three-year career, his teams won the pennant seven times and the World Series four times.

SMOKIN' JOE—Joe Frazier [1944–] Boxing. H/F Frazier won the gold medal at the 1964 Olympics and was fighting at the top of the pro heavyweight division from 1968 to 1975. On March 8, 1971, Frazier met Muhammad Ali in the first of their three memorable fights. Frazier won the decision, sending Ali to the hospital; Frazier spent a week in the hospital. "Frazier is not a great boxer," said Ali. "Frazier is a great street fighter." Frazier's nickname came from his hard-hitting, straight-ahead, relentless style of fighting. Frazier's three fights with Ali are considered by many to be three of the best bouts in ring history. Frazier ended his career with a record of 32–4–1, with 27 KOs.

SNAKE [THE]—Jake Roberts [active 1980s–1990s] Wrestling. Jake the Snake has earned his wrestling nickname in more ways than one. He himself has said, "I was losing, and I needed to turn my program around. In the world of today a wrestler's got to do anything it takes for a victory."

SNAKE [THE]—Ken Stabler [1945–] Football. Stabler was given his nickname in high school after he zigzagged down the football field while running back a punt. Bear Bryant called

Stabler the best quarterback he had ever coached (even better than Namath). Stabler led the University of Alabama to the national championship in 1966 and was the Most Valuable Player in the 1967 Sugar Bowl. In 1973, quarterbacking the Raiders, the Snake led the league in passing. In 1974, he was the league's Most Valuable Player. In 1976–1977, Stabler was the player of the year, leading the Raiders to a 16–1 record, including a 32–14 win over Minnesota in Super Bowl XI.

SON OF GOD [THE] [IL FIGLIO DI DIO]—Renzo De Vacchi [1894–1967] Soccer. Italy's famous soccer player was (obviously) popular with the fans.

SON OF THE WIND [THE]—Carl Lewis [1961–   ] Track and field. A truly international track star, this is Lewis' nickname in Europe. In 1984, Lewis tied Jesse Owens' record of four Olympic gold medals in track and field. Lewis also holds the world record in the 100 meters at 9.86 seconds, and for years he was the man to beat in the long jump. During his career Lewis held surpassed the twenty-eight-foot-mark in his specialty over sixty times.

SOULMAN—Rocky Johnson [active 1970s–1980s] Wrestling. When his family moved to Canada, Johnson age thirteen, made up his mind to become a professional wrestler. Another wrestler, Rockie Bollie, trained him, and when Bollie suffered a paralyzing back injury, Johnson took the first name Rocky as a tribute to his teacher. He became the Soulman of wrestling after he demonstrated his skills as a dancer on a Los Angeles television show called *Soul Brothers*.

SPACEMAN—Bill Lee [1946–   ] Baseball. Lee was given this nickname because he was unpredictable and spacey. He pitched for the Red Sox and the Expos. Lee was the one who gave his manager Don Zimmer the nickname The Gerbil.

SPACESHIP—Riddick Bowe [1967–   ] Boxing. During the 1988 Summer Olympics, a reporter labeled Bowe Spaceship because he felt that the boxer displayed "no mental stability whatsoever." Fortunately, Bowe—who went on to become World Heavyweight Champion, matured and the nickname never caught on. Bowe went on to earn over $50,000,000 as a prizefighter.

SPAHNNY [or SPAHNNIE]—Warren Edward Spahn [1921–   ] Baseball. H/F Spahn was one of the dominant pitchers of his time, chalking up a record thirteen seasons of twenty or more wins and posting a twenty-one-year mark of 363–245. At the start of his career he relied on a fastball and curve, but as the years rolled by he developed a screwball and a slider as well as a pitching intelligence that was second to none. His repertoire of pitches and his smarts helped him age like fine wine. In 1960, at the age of thirty-nine, Spain hurled his first no-hitter. The following year he threw another no-hitter. And at the age of forty-two, he repeated his 1953 personal best of 23–7. He was also called Hook and THE INVISIBLE ONE.

SPARKY—George Lee Anderson [1934–   ] Baseball. As a high-school basketball player, Anderson's temper (hurling basketballs at referees and one time at an opponent through a glass door) earned him the nickname of Sparky. In his autobiography, however (appropriately named

Sparky), Anderson says his nickname started as a joke in 1965 when he was playing at Fort Worth. He argued so much with umpires, that the announcer calling the game started saying, "And here comes Sparky racing toward the umpire again." And his name caught on. He was also called Captain Hook.

SPEEDY—Leon Gonzalez [1963—   ] Football. This wide receiver ended his career with the Atlanta Falcons. Speedy Gonzalez is one of those slang phrases that entered the English language via a popular cartoon character. In Warner Bros.' cartoons, Speedy Gonzalez was a Mexican Mouse—"the fastest mouse in all of Mexico." Mel Blanc supplied the voice. Pat Boone, in 1962, had a hit record called "Speedy Gonzalez," so any Gonzalez who shows any signs of quickness is likely to be labeled "Speedy."

SPIDER—Althea Gibson [1927—   ] Tennis. H/F With her long arms and long legs, the 5' 10" Althea Gibson pounced on the ball like a spider. Althea was the first African American tennis player to play in and win major tournaments. ("I didn't think about the racial issue or anything," admitted Gibson later. "All I thought about was how am I going to play this game and win?") She was also called Big Al.

SPIDER—Jim Kelley [1912—   ] Boxing. There have been a number of fighters with the name of Kelly who have been given the nickname Spider, including Tommy Kelly (who was the World Bantamweight Champion, 1887–1892) and Jim Kelly's son Billy Kelly (British and Commonwealth Featherweight Champion 1954–1956). Jim Kelly, like the others, received his nickname because of his long arms. He won the Irish title on September 2, 1935, when he stopped Dan Mc'Allister in three rounds.

SPIDERMAN—Nomar Garciaparra [1973—   ] Baseball. Finishing the 1997 season with a .306 batting average, thirty homers, forty-four doubles, and 209 hits, Garciaparra was unanimously voted American League Rookie of the Year. (He was the sixth unanimous winner of the AL Rookie of the Year Award.) He set major-league records for the most RBIs (ninety-eight) by a leadoff hitter and the most home runs by a rookie shortstop. He became only the ninth rookie to lead his league in hits. His nickname Spiderman (after the Marvel comic book hero) was given to him by Boston first baseman Mo Vaughn. Garciaparra was also called Super Rook.

SPLENDID SPLINTER [THE]—Theodore Samuel Williams [1918—   ] Baseball. H/F When Williams broke into the Boston Red Sox lineup, he was 6' 4" and weighed 175 pounds. He was also a splendid batsman, the last to hit over .400 for a season (.406 in 1941). His second highest average was .388 in 1957; his batting average over nineteen years was .344. Williams believed it was that little extra that made the difference between a good hitter and a so-so batsman. Not only did he not swing at any bad balls (he led the league in bases on balls eight times), but also, he swung according to the count, the score, what he had done on previous at-bats, even what the pitcher had done in previous years. Anything less he considered to be "dumb hitting." The most exciting hit of his long career came in 1941. Trailing the National League 5–4 in the All-Star Game, Williams came up with two out in the bottom of the ninth. He hit a home run. One thing that puzzled fans for years was why he did not seem more gracious. Williams once explained why he never tipped his cap or acknowledged the fans. "I realized that a lot of those guys cheering on a home run or a good catch were the same ones who led the boos at other times. . . . I hate front runners, people who are with you when you're up and against you when you're down." And another time he simply said, "You don't do things because you want to be liked." He was also called THE KID, Teddy Ballgame, and The Thumper.

SPORTSHIRT—Bill Veeck [1914–1986] Baseball. H/F Veeck (a promoter) was as colorful as his sportshirts. Many of his innovations, such as putting the names on the backs of uniforms, are standard today. He was also the first to sign an African American in the American League (Larry Doby in 1947) and to put Leroy "SATCHEL" Paige in a major-league uniform (the Cleveland Indians in 1948).

SQUARE EARL—Earl R. Anthony [1938–] Bowling. Anthony was the first professional bowler to win more than $100,000 in a single season. He accomplished that feat in 1975, when he earned $107,585. Anthony received his not too laudatory nickname because he wore glasses, sported a crewcut, and just looked (using a 1950s slang term) "square." But what a bowler he was! He won forty-one PBA victories and was elected to the PBA Hall of Fame and the ABC Hall of Fame.

SQUINT—Dorothy Hamill [1956–] Figure skating. H/F The 5' 3" skater was nicknamed Squint because she is extremely nearsighted. Hamill chose soundtracks from Errol Flynn movies to accompany her four-minute free-style routine (for which she won the gold medal) in the 1976 Olympic Figure Skating Championships, held in Innsbruck, Austria. After her Olympic victory, she gave up amateur skating to perform with the Ice Capades.

STAN THE MAN—Stan Musial [1920–] Baseball. H/F Stan Musial had an enormous series against the Dodgers at Ebbets Field in 1946 when he went 13–15. Many Brooklyn fans had trouble pronouncing the name *Musial,* so whenever he came to the plate, they simply said, "Here comes the Man again." Musial began his career as a pitcher, but became a full-time outfielder when he hurt his shoulder. After a few years in the minor leagues, Branch Rickey brought him up to the St. Louis Cardinals, making sure that no one tampered with his corkscrew batting style (coiled up at the back of the batter's box with a closed stance). Musial played in one of the great outfields with Terry Moore and Enos Slaughter. Although Musial did not like playing first base, he played it for ten years, starting at the position in each All-Star Game. In the 1954 classic, Musial hit a home run in the twelfth to win the game, 6–5, for the National League. (Musial has the record for most home runs in All-Star Games at six.) For his twenty-two-year career, Musial had a batting average of .331. (He ranks fourth for number of seasons over .300 with eighteen.) He has the major-league record for most doubles (725) and the most titles for triples (5). With 177 triples he is second to Sam Crawford's all-time record of 312. Musial was the MVP in 1943, 1946, and 1948. After his retirement in 1963, Stan the Man became the general manager of St. Louis the next year. The Cards won the pennant by ten games as well as the 1964 World Series. In addition to the records, Stan the Man remains one of the most well liked and respected players ever to play baseball.

SQUINT—Dorothy Hamill (b. July 26, 1956) Skating. She may, at times, have squinted to see, but her elegance and vitality on ice captured the heart of ice-skating fans.

STEADY EDDIE—Eddie Lopat [1918–1992] Baseball. Lopat was one of the lynchpins of the Yankee dynasty from 1949 to 1953. Even at the age of thirty-five, Steady Eddie was 16–4 and led the American League with a 2.42 ERA. Yankee announcer Mel Allen first used this nickname. It highlighted Eddie Lopat's consistency. He was also called JUNKMAN.

STEAMBOAT—Harry S. Johnson. [?–1951] Baseball. Johnson was a colorful minor-league umpire who toiled for twenty-seven years in the Southern Association. In 1919, he was the umpire for the twenty-three inning game between Atlanta and Chattanooga that ended in a 2–2 tie. At first, Johnson was known as "Bulldog" because whenever a shipment of new baseballs arrived, he would bite into the boxes and tear the boxes open with his teeth. One day, however, when he was umpiring in Atlanta, his booming voice could be heard all over the ballpark. The next day a sportswriter noted that "His voice resembles the blast of a Mississippi River sidewheeler so much that, from here on, it's Steamboat Johnson."

STONEWALL—Travis Calvin Jackson [1903–1987] Baseball. H/F Say Stonewall Jackson to a Civil War buff, and one person leaps to mind, but speak the nickname to an old-time New York Giants' fan and he or she will immediately conjure up the image of one baseball's greatest fielding shortstops. Hitting a ball to Travis Jackson was like hitting into a stone wall. He played for the Giants for his entire fifteen-season career, compiling a lifetime .291 average, with 1,768 hits, 291 doubles, 135 home runs, and 929 RBIs. Arnold Hano wrote of him: "On a team always known for its ability to bunt and squeeze out runs one at a time, Jackson was a master. He could sacrifice with deadly skill; better, he was one of the finest drag-bunters for base hits, the game ever saw."

STORK IN SHORTS—Jim Ryun [1947–   ] Track and field. H/F One of the great runners in U.S. track and field history, Ryun was tall and thin, with toothpick legs that gave him the appearance of being a stork in shorts. Stork in Shorts, in fact, was the first high school runner to break the four-minute mile, running the distance in June of 1954 in 3:59:0. One year later, competing at San Diego, California, he ran the mile in 3:55:3, defeating his main competitor Peter Snell, who had won the Olympic gold medal in Tokyo in 1964. In 1966, Stork in Shorts established a new world record for the half-mile, completing that distance in 1:44:49 in Terre Haute, Indiana, and finishing the mile at 3:53:7. Although Ryun dreamed of winning a gold medal at the 1968 Olympic Games in Mexico City, age and high altitude took their toll. He managed a silver medal, though, finishing second in the 1,500 meters with a time of 3:37:8, some five seconds slower than his own world record. Stork in Shorts was elected to the National Track and Field Hall of Fame in 1980.

STORMIN' NORMAN—Norman Van Brocklin [1926–1983] Football. H/F Say the nickname Stormin' Norman to members of today's generations and they most likely will think of General Norman Schwartzkopf, who led the American troops in Operation Desert Storm against Iraq in the Persian Gulf. Repeat that same nickname to a long-time football fan, however, and the fan will recall the glory days of the Los Angeles Rams, when Stormin' Norman Van Brocklin shared quarterbacking duties with Bob Waterfield. In 1951, Van Brocklin (who was also known as The Dutchman) led the Rams to their first NFL title. In that NFL championship game against the

Cleveland Browns, Van Brocklin tossed a seventy-three-yard touchdown pass to Tom Fears, giving the Rams a 27–24 victory.

STRAIGHT ARROW—Bob Griese (1945–   ) Football. H/F This is what the veterans on the Dolphins called their new quarterback because he seemed introspective and quiet. "I think I am more of an introvert than an extrovert," Griese has said. "And I'd still just as soon be off by myself as be with a group. But if there are a bunch of football players ready to play football, somebody has to be in command." And in charge he was, leading Miami to a 17–0 season in 1972 and two straight Super Bowls in 1972 and 1973.

STRANGLER—Ed Lewis (1890–1966) Wrestling. Robert H. Friedrich took on the name of Ed "Strangler" Lewis to spare his family the embarrassment of having a son who was a wrestler. In a career stretching from 1916 to 1937, the 260-pound Strangler Lewis captured the heavyweight freestyle championship five times. He is noted for once having wrestled in a five-and-a-half-hour match and for using a headlock that was so deadly that it was banned in Illinois. When Strangler Lewis started, wrestling was still "legitimate"; but by the end of his career, wrestlers were beginning to turn to some of the theatrics that so mark the sport today.

STRATFORD STREAK (THE)—Howie Morenz (1902–1937) Hockey. H/F Morenz was hockey's first superstar. He had played his amateur hockey in Stratford, Ontario, Canada. In 1931, Morenz netted forty goals in forty-four games. But in 1937 tragedy struck this star forward. Morenz caught his ankle on the boards and suffered a multiple fracture. Six weeks later he died of a coronary embolism. Morenz was also called the Mitchell Meteor (for he had been born in Mitchell, Ontario), the Canadien Comet, the Babe Ruth of Hockey, and Hurtling Habitant (See The Habs).

STRETCH—Willie Lee McCovey (1938–   ) Baseball. H/F The 6' 4" McCovey was able to field most errant throws to first base. He was also terrific at bat. He was home-run leader three times and finished his career with 521 homers. In 1959, he established a slugging percentage of .656—the major-league record.

STRETCH—Charles Murphy (1907–   ) Basketball. H/F Stretch would seem to be the perfect generic nickname for any basketball player of significant height, but it is surprising how few players bear the name. Charles "Stretch" Murphy, standing at 6' 6", is one. An All-American at Purdue from 1926 to 1930, Murphy played with John "India Rubber Man" Wooden on the 1930 team that was 10–0.

STYLE DOG—Rickey Henderson (1957–   ) Baseball. This outfielder's nickname is for the stylish way he plays the game; for instance, the way he routinely steals not only second base but also third base, and the way he swipes at fly balls with his glove. In 1982, Henderson stole 130 bases to eclipse Lou Brock's one-season record. In 1991, Henderson also broke Brock's career mark of 938. By the end of 1997, Rickey had 1,231 steals, and is a sure bet to steal his way into the Hall of Fame. He is also called The Man of Steal.

SUB—Carl Mays [1891–1971] Baseball. This submarine pitcher had his best year in 1921. His record was 27–9 and he batted .343. (His lifetime record was 208–126.) His worst experience occurred in 1920 when one of his pitches hit Ray Chapman in the head. The Cleveland shortstop died the next day—the only fatality in modern-day baseball.

SUDDEN DEATH—Mel Hill [1914–   ] Hockey. This right wing's nickname was bestowed on him because of his play during the 1939 Stanley Cup series between the Boston Bruins and the New York Rangers. In the first game Hill scored the game-winning goal in the third overtime period for a 2–1 victory.

SUGAR—Ray Leonard [1956–   ] Boxing. Howard Cosell gave Ray Leonard the name Sugar. Perhaps this winner of the 1976 light-welterweight medal at the Olympics reminded the sportscaster of SUGAR Ray Robinson. This fighter went on to hold five world titles. The world welterweight title he lost to Roberto Duran in fifteen rounds on June 20, 1980; he won it back on November 25 when Duran, repeating "No mas," didn't come out for the eighth.

SUGAR—Ray Robinson [1921–1989] Boxing. H/F In 1938, Walker Smith, Jr. needed an AAU card so he could fight. Because he was too young, he used one made out to Ray Robinson. He later had his name legally changed. And in 1939, a sportswriter observed to his manager, "That's a sweet boy you have." His manager agreed that he was as "sweet as sugar." Sugar Ray Robinson won every one of his eighty-nine amateur bouts as a featherweight. After turning professional, he won 122 bouts before beating RAGING BULL (Jake La Motta), to become the middleweight champion. It was a title he won and lost five times. During his career, Sugar Ray Robinson was victorious in 175 of 202 fights—109 by knockouts.

SULTAN OF SWAT—George Herman Ruth [1895–1948] Baseball. H/F Nicknames stuck to BABE Ruth like kids seeking autographs after a game. He was a player who fired the imagination. Light-verse writer Franklin P. Adams used one of these nicknames to pen a verse that went:

> Babe Ruth and Old Jack Dempsey
> Both Sultans of Swat,
> One hits where other people are —
> The other where they're not.

SUPERFINGERS—Dorothy Fothergill [1945–   ] Bowling. H/F After working as a cook in a local bowling alley in North Attleboro, Massachusetts, and practicing at night, Ms. Fothergill bowled (as an amateur) for a 207 average, which was the second highest in the nation. Because of the smooth way she released the ball, she soon became known as Superfingers. She became a professional bowler in 1967, and, as a rookie, won the BBAA All-Star tournament. She was also the first left-handed bowler to accomplish that feat. In 1968, she was named Woman Bowler of the Year. In 1970, after defeating many of the top male bowlers, Superfingers became the first woman to apply for membership in the all-male Professional Bowlers Association. Much to the shame of the PBA, her application was denied. Superfingers ranks as one of the greatest bowlers of all-time, winning some eighteen titles in her career. She is a member of the Women's International Bowling Congress Hall of Fame.

SUPERMEX—Lee Trevino [1939–   ] Golf. H/F Trevino, who started out as an assistant on a driving range in Dallas, was given his nickname because of his ethnic background. One year after joining the pro tour, Trevino won the 1968 U.S. Open. From 1968 to 1975 he was never lower than ninth in the standings. His best golf was during a four-week period in 1971 when he won the U.S., Canadian, and British Opens. In 1975, he was struck by lightning at the Western Open. Almost four years later at the age of forty-four he made a comeback to win his second PGA Championship.

SWAFFHAM GYPSY [THE]—Jem Mace [1831–1910] Bareknuckles boxing. H/F Sometimes called the Father of Scientific Boxing, Mace started out as a fiddler from Swaffham (which accounts for his nickname). When some rowdies broke his fiddle, he beat them up. A spectator, impressed with Mace's prowess, suggested he get into the fighting game. In 1861, Mace defeated Sam Hurst to win the bareknuckles heavyweight title and held it until 1873. He was also called The Gypsy.

SWEET D—Walter Davis [1954–   ] Track and field, basketball. Davis played for North Carolina, Phoenix, Denver, and Portland. He was called Mr. Greyhound for his speed and quickness and Sweet D for his playing ability. In 1978, he averaged 24.2 points and was Rookie of the Year in the NBA. Davis was also called Buddy.

SWEETWATER—Nathaniel Clifton [1922–   ] Basketball. Clifton was nicknamed Sweetwater because he liked soda so much in high school. He was the captain of the Harlem Globetrotters before joining the New York Knicks in 1951. Sweetwater was the first African American to play in the NBA.

SWINGING SAM—Samuel Jackson Snead [1912–   ] Golf. H/F Sam Snead developed what Grantland Rice called "the finest swing golf has ever known." During Swinging Sam's early days in the game he played for money, sometimes without a cent in his pocket. Snead swung slowly and carefully in order to make sure he hit the ball well. During his career, Sam Snead won over 100 tournaments, including the PGA in 1942, 1949, and 1951; the British Open in 1946; and the Masters in 1949, 1952, and 1954. He also won the Vardon Trophy four times. Snead's swing allowed him to play in top form well into his sixties. In 1974, at the age of sixty-two, he placed third in the PGA, only three strokes behind the champion.

TAFFY—Clarence John Abel [1900–   ] Hockey. From Sault Ste. Marie, Michigan, Abel was the first NHL player born in the United States. He was one of the original members of the New York Rangers, playing defense along with Ching Johnson. Frank Boucher, and Bill and Bunny Cook were on offense.

TARZAN—Don Bragg (b. 1935–) Track and field. He had a Tarzan like build, but unlike some other great athletes, he never did get to play that part in the movies.

TALL TACTICIAN [THE]—Connie Mack [1862–1956] Baseball. H/F At 6' 1" Mack was on the tall side for his day, and his long career with the Philadelphia Athletics (1901–1950) left him a lot of time for tactics. Mack cut an odd figure in the dugout. He never wore a uniform, preferring a suit, bowtie, and a straw hat, and in his hand he clenched a scorecard. See OLD MAN.

TARK THE SHARK—Jerry Tarkanian [1930–   ] Basketball. Tark the Shark is a good example of a nickname produced by rhyming slang. Tarkanian was born into a poor Armenian family. After earning a Master's Degree in Educational Management from Redlands University, he went on to coach basketball at several California high schools. He moved up to college basketball, when he became head coach of Riverside City College (1962–1966). His greatest years, however, came at the University of Nevada-Las Vegas, where he started in 1973, and where he led his teams to numerous championships. He was the UPI Coach of the Year in 1984. In recent years, his reputation has been tarnished by his ouster at UNLV and his short stint as a coach of the San Antonio Spurs.

TARZAN—Don Bragg [1935–   ] Track and field. Bragg received his nickname because of his large stature for a pole vaulter; he was 6' 3" and 197 pounds. (This was in the days when metal poles rather than fiberglass poles were used; the emphasis was on strength instead of speed and gymnastic ability.) At the 1960 Olympic tryouts, Bragg set a world record in the pole vault of 15' 19¼".

TASMANIAN DEVIL [THE]—Debbie Black [active 1990s] Basketball. Black plays guard for the Colorado Explosion and is the shortest player in the American Women's Basketball League. In 1996, The Tasmanian Devil led her league in steals with 177 and was named the ABLs Defensive Player of the Year. Her nickname is an allusion to a popular cartoon character that has a repertoire of sneaky, whirling moves.

TEACH—Eleanor Tennant [active 1920s] Tennis. Tennant was the third-ranked player in the 1920s, but it was as a teacher that she really shined. Called "Hollywood's best-known coach," she worked with a wide range of tennis students, from Clark Gable to Maureen Connolly. But perhaps her best student was Alice Marble. Tennant trained Marble hard. Playing five sets in practice was standard, so that when she arrived at a tournament she often powered her way through it. Marble zipped through one quarterfinal match in only sixteen minutes. But promoters slated her to play too much tennis in tournaments. She finally collapsed from exhaustion in 1934 at Paris's Roland Garros. Teach helped bring Marble back, paying for her medical expenses and nurturing her back into playing condition through a long recuperation. At Wimbledon in 1939, Alice Marble thrashed Hilde Krawinkel Sperling in the semifinals, 6–0, 6–0 and Kay Stammers in the finals, 6–2, 6–0.

TEE—Theresa Blanchard [Weld] [1893–1978] Figure skating. Although she is a member of the International Woman's Sports Hall of Fame because of her skating ability (she was a member of three Olympic teams and took home a bronze medal in 1920), she received the nickname Tee when she was a young girl because of her interest in golf.

TERMINATOR [THE]—Jeffrey James Reardon [1955—   ] Baseball. While the movies have their *The Terminator*, baseball has its own Terminators, relief pitchers who close out a game. Reardon once held the all-time major league record for saves.

TERRIBLE TED—Ted Lindsay [1925—   ] Hockey. H/F Lindsay played with reckless abandon and a terrible temper during his seventeen-year career. Both his willingness to fight and the results gave him his other nickname, Scarface. Lindsay scored 379 goals and was an All-Star left wing eight times. Also called Greenie the Meanie.

TEXAS TORNADO [THE]—Sheryl Swoopes [1971—   ] Basketball. Swoopes was born in Brownsville, Texas and went to Texas Tech, hence her nickname. In 1993, Swoopes scored forty-two points to lead her Texas Tech team to victory over Ohio State in the final game of the NCAA Championship. She is a member of the USA Basketball Women's National Team.

THREE FINGER BROWN—Mordecai Peter Centennial Brown [1876–1948] Baseball. H/F On a visit to an uncle's farm at the age of seven, Brown's right hand was caught in a corn shredder. This accident severed off most of his index finger and severely injured his thumb and pinkie. The effect this would have on his future baseball career was a wicked curveball. (A less-used nickname was Miner: Brown had been a miner as a teenager back home in Indiana.) Note one of his middle names—Centennial—was given to him to celebrate 1776, since he was born one hundred years later. Brown won 239 games, lost 129, and had a 2.06 ERA.

THUNDERTHIGHS—Jim Price [1941—   ] Baseball. Pat Dobson, a pitcher on the Detroit Tigers, gave Price, the second-string catcher, this nickname. Though Price had wanted to be called something more glamorous, such as The Big Guy, Price told him, "You don't qualify.... Your nickname is Thunderthighs and you're stuck with it." Price played for five seasons in Detroit, and ended with a .214 batting average in 602 career at-bats.

TIGER—Eldridge Woods [1976—   ] Golf. One of today's most talented young golfers is Tiger Woods. Woods started playing golf not long after he learned to walk, and he has been called Tiger (for his tenacious attitude) for so long that he has to stop to think what his real name is. At the age of sixteen, Tiger was one of the most publicized players at the 1992 Los Angeles Open. He is constantly being held up as a role model. "It's a pretty big burden if you think about it," Tiger says, "but I don't think about it." His recent wins in major tournaments have been directly responsible for enhancing the popularity of golf and for attracting more African American players to the sport.

TINY—Nate Archibald [1948—   ] Basketball. H/F Born in New York City, Archibald was the eldest of seven children. He received his nickname from his father, who, after Nate was born, was called Big Tiny (a glorious oxymoron that is), and Nate was Little Tiny. Archibald learned to play basketball on the playgrounds and school grounds of the Bronx, and eventually Little Tiny grew to become 6' 1"—which, of course, is not tall for a basketball player. After college, Archibald played on the Kansas City Omaha team in 1972–1973, where under the coaching of Bob Cousy, he averaged

34.9 points and 11.4 assists per game, and led the league in those categories. He eventually went on to a very successful career with the New York Nets and then the Boston Celtics. He led the Celtics into the 1979–1980 playoffs and to the 1980–1981 championship. Tiny was named MVP for the 1981 NBA All-Star game.

TOE (THE)—Lou Groza (1924–   ) Football. H/F Cleveland Browns football star Lou Groza received his nickname because of his ability to kick field goals. In fact, when the game was on the line, he was the kicker you wanted to have on the field. Take, for example, the NFL Championship game of 1950. The Browns were trailing the Rams 28–27, and there were only twenty seconds left to play. Lou "The Toe" Groza kicked a field goal to give his team the victory and the championship. He played his entire career in Cleveland (first with the AAFC League) and then with the Browns. By the time he retired he had scored 1,349 points.

TONY O—Tony Esposito (1943–   ) Hockey. H/F In his first full season (1969–1970), Tony Esposito posted fifteen shutouts, and thus became Tony O. That same year he had a goals-against average of 2.17 for the Vezina Trophy and won the Calder Trophy for Rookie of the Year. Like his older brother Phil (ESPO), Tony had a workman-like attitude. He did not defend the goal gracefully but would flop down on the ice and do whatever else was necessary to stop the puck. Tony once said: "People wonder why I don't laugh more, like Phil. Well, Phil's not a goaltender."

TOOZ—John Matuszak (active 1973–1982) Football. Tooz was a behemoth and a free liver who seemed to fit in with the Oakland Raiders. "The Raiders aren't a team where you always have to straighten up your tie and wear your hair a certain length," he said. "As long as you put out at practice and on Sundays, they don't care. As long as you stay out of jail."

TOPPER—Jerry Toppazzini (1931–   ) Hockey. Topper (it was easier to say) was the last non-goalie (he usually played right wing) to fill in at goal during a NHL game. It came during the last minute of a losing effort, Red Wings 4–1 over the Bruins. Usually a defensive forward, Topper scored 163 goals over his twelve-year career.

TORNADO (THE)—Hideo Nomo (1968–   ) Baseball. As a pitcher for the Los Angeles Dodgers, Nomo earned his nickname because of his unique pitching delivery in which his body twists and turns like a miniature tornado. Mets first baseman, Rico Brogna said of Nomo: "It's hard to pick up the ball out of his delivery. His motion makes him seem that much quicker." Nomo achieved 500 major-league strikeouts earlier in his career than any previous major-league pitcher.

TOY BULLDOG (THE)—Edward "Mickey" Walker (1901–1981) Boxing. H/F Walker was a small, pug-nosed, feisty fighter. In 1926, he defeated Tiger Flowers for the middleweight champion-ship and held it until 1931. The nickname Bulldog is usually applied to someone who is tenacious and aggressive, and this is no exception—Mickey Walker is often cited as the hardest-hitting middleweight boxer of all time. He was also extremely popular with the fans. After he retired with ninety-four wins in 163 fights, he became a successful painter. His autobiography is called *The Will to Conquer.*

TRICKY DICK—Dick McGuire (1926–   ) Basketball. H/F Long before the sobriquet "Tricky Dick" was applied to Richard M. Nixon, the title had been give to Dick McGuire, who played for the New York Knicks and the Detroit Pistons (in 1992 the Knicks officially retired his number fifteen). As a rookie for the Knicks in 1949–1950, McGuire set a NBA record with 386 assists, an average of 5.8 assists per game. His career total of 2,950 assists over eight seasons is second to Walt Frazier's club record of 4,791 assists over a ten-year span. Because he would often pass the ball when he had an open shot, and because opponents could not expect him to do the obvious, he received the nickname Tricky Dick. His teammate Carl Braun has said (as reported by Dave Anderson in the *New York Times*), "Dick was the best at passing the ball moving toward the basket. Others were great dropping the ball to the trailer, but Dick's eyes picked up colors. He'd bounce pass it between two blue shirts to a white shirt."

TUFFY—Alphonse Leemans (1912–1979) Football. H/F Playing both halfback and fullback for the New York Giants, it is no wonder that Leemans preferred to be called Tuffy (a homophone for "toughy") instead of the more formal Alphonse. In his 1936 rookie year, when Tuffy Leemans played for all of $3,500 for the season, he led the NFL in rushing with 830 yards in 206 attempts. That same year he also completed 13 passes for 258 yards and 3 TDs. By the time he retired at the end of the 1943 season, Tuffy had rushed for 3,142 yards for seventeen TDs. He was elected to the Pro Football Hall of Fame in 1978.

TURK—Walter Broda (1914–1972) Hockey. H/F As a school kid in Manitoba, Broda was dubbed "turkey egg" by his classmates after they learned that an English king had been given this nickname because of the huge freckles covering his face. Since Broda's face was also freckled, he was also saddled with the nickname; later it was shortened to Turk. As a goaltender, Broda was once involved in a well-publicized Battle of the Bulge. Fans from all over sent in suggestions on how he could lose weight.

TURK—Albert Glen Edwards (1907–1973) Football. H/F Edwards received his nickname from Washington State University football coach, Babe Hollinberry. One day Edwards was late for practice and Hollinberry asked aloud, "I wonder where that big Turk is." Since Edwards had been born in Kirkland, Washington and was not from Turkey, Turk was probably a shortened form of turkey. Turk Edwards was one of the best linemen in the game. He was a member of the All-NFL teams for 1932, 1933, 1936, and 1937. After retirement, he became head coach of the Redskins from 1946 to 1948.

TURKEY—Norman Stearnes (1901–1979) Baseball [Negro Leagues]. Turkey Stearnes hit more home runs in the Negro leagues than any other player (and he was up against some great pitchers.) Some people claim that he received his colorful nickname because of the way he flapped his elbows when he ran. He himself claimed that when he was young he looked like a butterball. His lifetime batting average in the black leagues was .352.

TURKEY MIKE—Michael Joseph Donlin (1878–1933) Baseball. Donlin started out as a pitcher, but he switched to the outfield, and occasionally played first base and shortstop for such teams as the St. Louis Cardinals and the New York Giants. He was one of the more colorful personalities of his era, and was closely associated with vaudeville, both as a performer (he toured the circuits in 1909, 1910, and 1913) and as the husband of vaudeville stars Mabel Hite and Rita Ross. Whenever the pugnacious Donlin would get involved in a heated argument or fight upon the field, Giants fans would shout, "Oh, you Mabel's Mike!" During his career he compiled a .333 lifetime average. Turkey Mike received his colorful nickname because of the peculiar strutting walk he had affected.

TWINKLE TOES BOSCO—Ron LeFlore (1948—   ) Baseball. LeFlore earned this sobriquet while playing for the Jackson State Prison baseball team. LeFlore had been sentenced to prison for armed robbery. He played nine seasons in the big leagues, mostly for the Detroit Tigers. He compiled a lifetime batting average of .288, and in 1978 he led the American League in runs scored, with 126. He received his nickname Twinkle Toes because of his great speed, and Bosco because he loved drinking chocolate-flavored milk—preferably Bosco.

TWO-TON TONY—Tony Galento (1910–1979) Boxing, wrestling. Galento received his several nicknames because he was hefty, a bartender, and his punches packed a wallop. In his heavyweight title fight with Joe Louis on June 23, 1939, he knocked Louis down in the first round; but Louis came back to win by a KO in the fourth. He was also called Battling Barkeep and Beer Barrel Palooka.

TY COBB OF THE FEDS—Benny Kauff (1890–1961) Baseball. When the rival Federal League folded after the 1915 season, their players were sold back to the American and National leagues. One of the best players was Benny Kauff who, like Cobb, played in the outfield and commanded a high salary. To acquire Kauff, the New York Giants had to pay $35,000.

UKEY—Terry Sawchuck (1930–1970) Hockey. H/F This nickname refers to Sawchuck's rather strange behavior. "Ukey's a strange bird," said a Detroit teammate. "You can be joking with him one minute in the dressing room and you'll see him on the street later and he'll just walk right by you." The pressures of goaltending took a harsh toll on Sawchuck. His demons caused him to push away friends, teammates, his wife and family, and finally to wind up in the hospital after a fight with his roommate. He was dead at the age of forty. As a player, however, he was outstanding. He won the Vezina Trophy four times, and he was also the winner of the Calder Trophy as the outstanding rookie in the 1950–1951 season. In addition to his many NHL honors, he also earned Rookie of the Year honors in the United States Hockey League (1947–1948) and for the American Hockey League (1947–1948). He is the only hockey player to be named Rookie of the Year in three different leagues!

ULCERS—Frank McCool (1918—   ) Hockey. The irony of his last name versus his more appropriate nickname was that Frank McCool sometimes had to gulp down a glass of milk during a game in order to calm his fiery stomach. In his rookie season for the Toronto Maple Leafs, Ulcers won the Calder Trophy. He then helped the Leafs beat Montreal in the semifinals in six games. In the finals against Detroit, McCool stopped the Red Wings cold: three games, three shutouts (a Stanley Cup record): 1–0, 2–0, 1–0. Detroit went on to win the next three games. During the seventh game, the pain became so intense for McCool that he escaped to the dressing room. Hap Day went after him to tell him he was the only one who could do it. Ulcers again established himself in net for a 2–1 victory and the 1944–1945 Stanley Cup.

UNCLE ROBBIE—Wilbert Robinson [1863–1934] Baseball. H/F After a seventeen-year career as a catcher—his best year was 1894 when he hit .353—Robinson turned to managing. Robinson was more in the mold of a favorite uncle than a stern manager. But he helped many future Hall of Famers during his nineteen years of managing from 1914 to 1931: Dave Bancroft, Max Carey, Burleigh Grimes, Ernie Lombardie, Al Lopez, RABBIT Maranville, Rube Marquard, CASEY Stengel, DAZZY Vance, and Zack Wheat. He was also called Grapefruit .

UNIVERSAL FEMALE ATHLETE—Eleonara R. Sears [1881–1968] Swimming, golf, tennis, squash. Sears won 240 trophies during her varied career, including three doubles championships and two singles championships in tennis. At the age of forty-six she won her final national squash championship.

VACUUM CLEANER—Brooks Robinson [1937–] Baseball. H/F Robinson received his nickname for scooping up practically every ball hit in his direction. Twelve times he won the Golden Glove Award for third basemen, and he ranks first in lifetime fielding average (.971) for all third basemen. Robinson also holds the lifetime mark for double plays (618) by a third baseman. In addition, he was MVP of the American League in 1964—a year he batted .317. And who can forget the amazing stops he made at third in the 1970 World Series? His remarkable fielding along with his sterling .429 batting average won him the series MVP that year. Robinson was also called B. Robby, The Hoover, Mr. Impossible, and Mr. Third Base.

VAULTING VICAR [THE]—Bob Richards [1926–] Track and field. In 1946, when he was twenty, Bob Richards became an ordained minister of the Church of Brethren. Two years later, The Vaulting Vicar placed third in the pole vault at the 1948 Olympic Games. In 1952 and 1956, Richards won the Olympic pole vault. At the 1956 Olympics, The Vaulting Vicar not only set an Olympic record of 14' 11½", but also preached a few sermons in Melbourne. (Richards was also an all-round athlete, winning the decathlon at the U.S. championships in 1951, 1954, and 1955.) The Vaulting Vicar's highest height—this was in an era before the fiberglass pole—was in 1957: 15' 6". By the time he had retired, Richards had surpassed fifteen feet 126 times.

VENUS—June Emerson [active 1948–1949] Baseball (All-American Girls Baseball League). Emerson's nickname referred to the armless Venus de Milo statue in the Louvre. One day in the field, the ball bounced off Emerson's head and right into the hands of a teammate who turned it into a double play. Emerson had assisted without even using her hands.

VOODOO VETERINARIAN—Hirsch Jacobs (1904–1970) Horse racing. Jacobs was a great breeder of horses and a great trainer. He, in fact, was the best horse trainer of his generation, saddling 3,569 winners. He received his sobriquet because of his uncanny ability to take losing horses and turn them into winners.

VULTURE [THE]—Phil Regan (1937–   ) Baseball. Regan was called The Vulture because he often came in to relieve a starting pitcher; like a vulture, he was finishing off what someone else had started. In 1966, Regan was 14–1 in relief with twenty-one saves; in 1968, he was 12–5 in relief with twenty-five saves—both years tops in the National League. (Who would have dreamed in those days that being a reliever would become such a respected specialty that Dennis Eckersley would win the 1992 Cy Young Award as a reliever?)

WAHOO SAM—Samuel Earl Crawford (1880–1968) Baseball. H/F Wahoo Sam was born in—where else?—Wahoo, Nebraska. Playing for Cincinnati and then Detroit, this hard-hitting right fielder is the only person to have hit the most home runs in both leagues (sixteen in the National League in 1901; seven in the American League in 1908). Crawford was also part of one of the great outfields in the history of baseball: Bobby Veach in left, Ty Cobb in center, and Crawford in right. But it was in hitting triples that Wahoo Sam's name lives on in the record books. In 1914, he hit twenty-six (a record matched only by Shoeless Joe Jackson). And his total of 312 triples will most likely remain a record for as long as baseball is played. (The highest total in recent years is Stan Musial's 177.) Even after his major-league career was over, Wahoo Sam rapped twenty-one three-baggers in 1920 playing for Los Angeles in the Pacific Coast League.

WALLSMACKER—Peter De Paolo (1898–1980) Auto racing. H/F Peter De Paolo, nephew to another auto-racing great Ralph De Palma, didn't start out to be a wallsmacker (who does?), but when he hit the wall three times during his rookie race in 1922, the name stuck. Wallsmacker, in spite of his inauspicious beginning, became one of the great racing drivers of his generation, winning the Indianapolis 500 in 1925 (that same year he also won the AAA national driving championship). All in all he raced in the Indianapolis 500 seven times, but never won that race again. In 1934, he suffered a serious accident, and his racing days ended. His autobiography is called *Wallsmacker*. He is a member of the Automobile Racing Hall of Fame.

WASHINGTON MONUMENT [THE]—Frank Howard (1936–   ) Baseball. When Howard first began playing in the majors, he was nicknamed Hondo after the movie of the same name starring John Wayne. In Spanish hondo means big, and Howard fit the description. He was 6' 7" and weighed 270 pounds. In 1965, Hondo was traded from Los Angeles to the Washington Senators and he picked up a new nickname, The Washington Monument, after the capital's famous obelisk. As Howard's home-run hitting moved into high gear (he socked forty-four in 1968, forty-eight in 1969, and forty-four in 1970), his towering homers earned him his final nickname, The Capital Punisher.

WEEB—Wilbur Charles Ewbank [1907—   ] Football, basketball. H/F Weeb Ewbank, who earned a national reputation for his ability to coach winning college and professional teams at both the college and professional levels, received his unusual nickname because he had a younger brother who, as a very young child, would mispronounce *Wilbur* as *Weeb*. The nickname stuck. Weeb Ewbank started his professional coaching career in 1949, when he became line coach for the AAFC-NFL Cleveland Browns. He became head coach of the Baltimore Colts in 1954, and stayed in that capacity until 1962, leading the Colts to NFL championships in 1958 and 1959. After leaving the Colts, Ewbank became the first coach for the New York Jets, and he capped his career when "BROADWAY JOE" Namath led the Jets to a Super Bowl victory over the Colts in 1969. With that victory, Weeb Ewbank became the first AFL coach to defeat the NFL. Among his books are: *Weeb Ewbank's Pro Football Way to Physical Fitness* (1967) and *The Greatest Football Games I Have Coached* (1972).

WHIZZER—Byron Raymond White [1917—   ] Football. Byron Raymond White was a whiz all right. How many professional football players ever become Supreme Court Justices? Whizzer, in fact, is the only one. President John F. Kennedy named him to the U.S. Supreme Court in 1962 and he remained on the bench until he retired in 1993. Born in Fort Collins, Colorado, Byron Raymond White became an all-around high school and college student. President John F. Kennedy later said that White "excelled in everything he has attempted." In college, Whizzer excelled at baseball, basketball, and football, and, in 1937, during his senior year at the University of Colorado, Whizzer White led the undefeated Colorado team to the Cotton Bowl against Rice. After he graduated, his skills were so highly sought after that when he signed with the Pittsburgh Pirates (which was the name of Pittsburgh's NFL team before they became the Steelers), for the 1938 season, he received the NFL's highest salary—all of $15,800. He spent 1939 at Oxford, then returned to the U.S. and to the NFL to play for the Detroit Lions. During World War II, White served in the Pacific as a naval intelligence officer and won two Bronze Stars. White had met John F. Kennedy while in England and had renewed his acquaintance with the future president during WW II. White supported Kennedy's nomination. On April 16, 1962, Whizzer White was sworn in to be a Supreme Court Justice. He was elected to the College Football Hall of Fame in 1954.

WILD BILL—William Hallahan [1902–1981] Baseball. Hallahan earned his nickname for leading the National League in issuing bases on balls in 1930 (126), 1931 (112), and 1933 (98). On the plus side, Wild Bill had two shutouts and an ERA of 1.34 in four World Series with the St. Louis Cardinals. See GASHOUSE GANG.

WILD BULL OF THE PAMPAS—Luis Angel Firpo [1896–1960] Boxing. Firpo was born near Buenos Aires, Argentina on October 11, 1896. He grew to be 6' 3" and 220 pounds, and once knocked out an ox. Damon Runyon gave Firpo his nickname. (His more common nickname was the far more sedate Angel.) On September 14, 1923, Firpo fought Jack Dempsey in one of boxing's greatest fights. After being knocked down seven times, Firpo knocked Jack Dempsey out of the ring. Dempsey, however, was helped back inside the ropes by the press and spectators around the ring, and then went on to win the fight.

WILDCAT—Larry Wilson [1938–] Football. H/F Wildcat Wilson, playing his entire thirteen year career (1960–1972) with the St. Louis Cardinals, received his intimidating nickname from a safety blitz employed by his team. The play, devised by Chuck Drulis, called for the safety to blaze through the offensive line and take down the quarterback. The code name for the blitz was "wildcat" and Wilson played it so well that the code name became his nickname. At the end of his career, Wildcat had made fifty-two interceptions for 800 yards. In 1966, he led the NFL in the number of interceptions (ten) and TDs scored on interceptions (two). He was elected to the Pro Football Hall of Fame in 1978.

WILD ELK OF THE WASATCH—Ed Heusser [1909–1956] Baseball. Heusser had grown up near the Wasatch Mountains in Utah. When he joined the GASHOUSE GANG in 1935, there was already a WILD HORSE OF THE OSAGE in Pepper Martin. As Heusser was 6 feet and 187 pounds to Martin's 5' 8" and 170 pounds, the local sports scribes put on their zoological caps and came up with Wild Elk of the Wasatch. In 1935, Heusser had a 1.80 ERA in relief. But his best year was in 1944 when he was 13–11 and had a league-leading 2.38 ERA.

WILD HORSE BOB—Robert Anderson Crosby [1897–19] Rodeo. He was such a great rodeo performer that he was awarded permanent possession of the Roosevelt Trophy, Rodeo's most coveted award. Until 1928 the Roosevelt Trophy was presented annually to the cowboy who scored the highest point total in all events at the Pendleton and Cheyenne rodeos. Crosby won it three times. His nickname was given to him because of the seeming recklessness that characterized many of his rides. Once, in fact, he won a steer-roping contest while he was temporarily blinded in one eye. Crosby was also called King of the Cowboys, but that sobriquet properly belongs to a non-athlete star, Roy Rogers.

WILD HORSE OF THE OSAGE [THE]—Johnny "Pepper" Martin [1904–1965] Baseball. Martin had two nicknames. He was called Pepper because of his spirited, peppery play. His more colorful nickname comes from playing halfback for a football team in Oklahoma sponsored by the Osage Indians. Apparently, he ran like a wild horse. Martin led the league in runs scored in 1933 (122) and stolen bases in 1933, 1934, and 1936. He was a fine-hitting shortstop with a .298 batting average for thirteen years and a .418 average in three World Series. See GASHOUSE GANG.

WILD THING—Mitchell Steven Williams [1964–] Baseball. This popular reliever for the Rangers, Cubs, and Phillies got tabbed The Wild Thing in reference to the popular song of the same title. Fans, in fact, frequently broke out into the opening lines of the song when he was brought in to pitch. And a Wild Thing Mitch Williams sometimes was (reminding fans of the old GASHOUSE GANG members), such as the time he used his head to block a line drive.

WILLIE THE WISP—Guglielmo Papelo [1922–] Boxing. H/F Willie Pep, as he was known, was the featherweight champion from 1942 to 1950. He received his nickname because he was so light on his feet and so swift at dancing all over the ring. He was to most opponents like a wisp of smoke. When he retired (to become a referee) he had won 229 fights, lost eleven, and drawn one. He was also called Old Master and Will o' the Wisp.

WIMPY—Melvin Leroy Harder [1909–] Baseball. On July 31, 1932, Cleveland Municipal Stadium hosted its first baseball game. On that day Lefty Grove of the Philadelphia Athletics outdueled Mel Harder of the Indians, 1–0. Wimpy Harder, sometimes called Chief, pitched his entire career for the Indians, winning 223 games against 186 losses. He struck out 1,160 batters and complied a 3.80 ERA. After retiring from pitching in 1946, Harder became a respected coach, finishing his major-league career with the Kansas City Royals in 1969, a span of forty-one years in the big leagues. He acquired his nickname for liking hamburgers with the relish of the Wimpy character in *Popeye*.

WINNY—Dave Winfield [1951–] Baseball. H/F This bigger-than-life outfielder won four Silver Bats, eight Gold Gloves, and a World Series ring in 1992. (Winny knocked in the winning run in the seventh game.) In 1993, he became the third player in major league history to post twenty or more home run seasons for five different teams.

WIZARD OF OZ [THE]—Ozzie Smith [1954–] Baseball. "I pride myself on defense. To me it's an art and like any other art you have to study all the time to make most of your skills, to be consistent, and to improve all you can," Ozzie Smith once said. "You can never stop learning, never let up and be satisfied with the way you're doing things." If any shortstop ever made the most of his skills, it was the shortstop known affectionately to his fans as "The Wizard of Oz" (a humorous allusion to the great fantasy by Frank Baum). Ozzie was a wizard at making spectacular and magical plays.

WOJIE—Alex Wojciechowicz [1915–1992] Football. H/F Wojciechowicz was once talked out of changing his name to Wojack. But no one talked others out of calling him by a simpler Wojie. Wojie was a two-time All-American center on Fordham's SEVEN BLOCKS OF GRANITE. From there he played on a poor Detroit Lion team from 1938 to 1946. Then he played linebacker for GREASY Neale and the Steelers, helping them win championships in 1948 and 1949.

WOOD—John Albert Elway [1960–] Football. He led the Broncos to victory in the 1986 AFC championships. He has played fifteen seasons of professional football and is one of the game's great quarterbacks. He topped 3,000 yards passing for every season from 1985–1991. Before every game Wood eats the same meal—French toast, eggs, and hash browns.

WRONG-WAY RIEGELS—Roy Riegels [active 1920s] Football. Reigels got his sobriquet by running the wrong way during the 1929 Rose Bowl game. After picking up a fumble and sprinting eighty yards to his own end zone, a teammate dragged him back out to the one-yard line. On the next play, California punted, but it was blocked and bounced out of the end zone for a safety. California lost to Georgia Tech, 8–7. Riegels later had this to say about his wrong-way play: "At least I was trying."

YANK—William James Yancey [1904–1971] Baseball [Negro Leagues], basketball. Yancey, whose nickname Yank is a shortened form of his name and an allusion to his northern origins, was an African American baseball star who played excellent shortstop for such teams as the Philadelphia Giants, the New York Black Yankees, and Philadelphia Stars. He was also a guard in professional basketball. In 1945, Yancey managed the Atlanta Black Crackers.

YANKEE CLIPPER—Joe DiMaggio [1914–   ] Baseball. H/F DiMaggio was as commanding in the lineup as the *Yankee Clipper* ship in days of yore. Before joining the New York Yankees, he had gone by the considerably less commanding epithet in the minors of "Dead Pan Joe." The biggest thrill for the Big Guy (6' 2", 195 pounds) was hitting safely in fifty-six games during the 1941 season. During game forty, Joe D questioned an umpire's decision—one of the few times he had ever done so. "It was a called strike that caused me to turn around and look back, but before I could say anything, the umpire blurted out, 'Honest to Gawd, Joe, it was right down the middle.' The idea of an umpire being apologetic for his decision appealed to me and helped ease the strain." During his thirteen-year career, DiMaggio batted .325 with 361 home runs and 1,535 RBIs. He was an All-Star every season and the American League's MVP three times. With DiMag in center field, the Yanks won the pennant ten times and the World Series nine times. As manager Casey Stengel said of Joe DiMaggio, "He was more than just a player—he was an institution." He was also called Big Guy, DiMag, Joe D, and JOLTIN' JOE.

YANKEE SULLIVAN—James Ambrose [active 1850s] Boxing. Ambrose was born in England, but he fled to America and claimed he was the American champion. One of Sullivan's big bouts was against Tom Hyatt on a deserted stretch of Maryland beach. Along with the spectators they had been chased from the original site by a boatload of police. (Boxing was illegal then.) Sullivan lost when his corner conceded the fight in the sixteenth round. The purse for the bout was a mighty $10,000.

YAT—Y.A. Tittle [1926–   ] Football. H/F A simple nickname—evolving from the player's initials—for a complex person. He came up to the Baltimore Colts of the AAFC in 1948, and, playing quarterback, completed 161 passes for 2,522 yards and sixteen touchdowns. Leading the New York Giants, he was the NFL's MVP in 1961, and the NFL Player of the Year in 1962, but his best season was probably in 1963, when, playing for the Giants, he completed thirty-six touchdown passes and tossed for 3,145 yards. In his career, he passed for a total of 33,070 yards and 242 TDs. He was elected to the Football Hall of Fame in 1971.

YATCHA—Johnny Logan [1927–   ] Baseball. Logan's first name in Ukrainian is Yatcha. This shortstop started with Boston and ended with Pittsburgh, but was primarily with the Milwaukee Braves as a shortstop in the fifties.

YAZ—Carl Yastrzemski [1939–   ] Baseball. H/F Yastrzemski is the kind of name to give fans and box-score writers fits. On the other hand, Yaz was also the kind of player to give opponents fits—the first major leaguer to achieve 3,000 hits and 400 or more home runs. Writing for *Life* magazine in August 20, 1971, CBS special correspondent Heywood Hale Broun observed, "At the end of the 1967 American League season Carl Yastrzemski brought Boston a last-day pennant by playing the two greatest games at bat and in the field I have ever seen."

YANKEE SULLIVAN—James Ambrose (active 1850s) Boxing.
He was born in England, but fled to the United States.

YIDDISH CURVER [THE]—Barney Pelty [1880–1939] Baseball. Pelty pitched for the St. Louis Browns from 1903 to 1912, and his best year was a 16–11 and a 1.59 ERA in 1906. Pelty's nickname stems from the fact that he was one of the first Jewish athletes to make his mark on professional baseball.

YOGI—Lawrence Peter Berra [1925–   ] Baseball. H/F Berra got his nickname during his youth back in the Italian section of St. Louis where he lived. After seeing a movie travelogue with some of his friends, Berra imitated the Hindu fakir. His friend Jack Maguire said Berra looked like a Yogi. Yogi was a hot prospect right off the bat. Working with Yankee catching great Bill Dickey, Berra developed into a catcher who once handled 950 chances without committing an error. A standout both behind the plate and at bat, Yogi achieved a lifetime batting average of .306. Capturing the American League MVP three times, Berra played on ten winning teams in fourteen World Series. He holds World Series records for most games (seventy-five), most at-bats (259), most hits (seventy-one) and most doubles (ten). As a manager, Berra has the distinction of winning pennants in both the American League (the Yankees in 1964) and the National League (the Mets in 1973). Yogi has provided almost as much linguistic baseball lore as Casey Stengel. Once having trouble seeing the ball at Yankee Stadium with the shadows of the autumn night approaching, he said: "It gets late early out there." He also noted that "You can see a lot by observing." "Baseball is 90 percent mental; the other half is physical," and "A nickel ain't worth a dime anymore." And more than a few people have said, "It's *deja vu* all over again" without knowing that Yogi had misspoken it first.

ZEKE FROM CABIN CREEK—Jerry West [1938–   ] Basketball. H/F Elgin Baylor first called West this because he thought West needed a nickname. Zeke was Baylor's name for a hillbilly. West hailed from Chelyan, West Virginia, a hamlet hard by Cabin Creek. At the University of West Virginia, West had been called The Tarantula because of the way he had his arms going every which way on defense. His junior year he was the NCAA tournament MVP as West Virginia lost 71–70 in the finals. His college coach, who also coached him on the Lakers, said of West: "He is the greatest clutch player I've ever seen." (A biography about him was titled *Mr. Clutch.*) West continued his clutch playing in the NBA, winning the East-West All-Star game in 1972 with a last second basket, scoring sixty-three points in one game. "I know there are good players in this league who don't want the ball in the tight situations. But I want the ball, I know I can do something with it." He was also called Mr. Clutch.

ZIMMY—A.A. ZIMMERMAN [1869–1936] Bicycle racing. Although modern athletes are known for endorsing clothing, shoes, and socks, and starting their own fashion lines, in the 1890s A.A. Zimmerman was so popular that there were Zimmy shoes, Zimmy toe clips, and an entire line of Zimmy clothing. He was an international sports star, and winner of hundreds of bicycle races, both amateur and professional. One paper in 1896 told its readers, "Mr. A.A. Zimmerman stands alone as the greatest racer the world has produced . . . the champion of the world in competitive contests where brain, brawn, and muscle combine for supremacy."

YOGI—Lawrence Peter Berra (b. May 12, 1925) Baseball.
Yogi appeared in more World Series games (75) than any other major league player.

ZONK—Larry Csonka [1946—] Football. H/F Csonka's nickname is the combination of his last name and the sound of helmets bonking off each other as the 6' 3", 235-pound Csonka plows straight ahead. Csonka's totals from 1968 to 1971 for Miami were 3,031 total yards for 4.5 yards per carry, and twenty-five touchdowns. He was also called LAWNMOWER; and with Jim Kiick (who was Cassidy) BUTCH CASSIDY AND THE SUNDANCE KID.

ZORRO—Zoilo Versalles [1939—] Baseball. Zoilo walked into a minor-league clubhouse where some teammates were watching *The Adventures of Zorro* on television. His appearance at that moment and his first name branded him as quickly as the sword blazing a Z in the opening credits. Playing twelve years for such teams as the Washington Senators, Minnesota Twins, and Los Angeles Dodgers, he compiled a lifetime .242 batting average, with 1, 246 hits in 5,141 at-bats.

TEAM NAMES

TEAM NAMES

The names of teams are often as captivating as the nicknames of the players and reflect a colorful aspect of American sports history. Part 2 lists the names of the teams in the National Hockey League (NHL), the National Basketball Association (NBA), baseball's American League (AL) and National League (NL), the National Football League (NFL), as well as the names of college teams and their conferences.

TEAMS OF THE NHL

AVALANCHE—Colorado [1995]
Western Conference/Northwest Division.
The Avalanche is not the first NHL hockey team in Colorado nor the first team to use this name. The Colorado Avalanche was once an indoor soccer team. Amazingly, the NHL Avalanche (or Avs) won the Stanley Cup in 1996, a year after entering the league.

BLACKHAWKS—Chicago [1926]
Western Conference/Central Division.
Major Frederick Mclaughlin named his team after the Black Hawk Division in World War I. In 1985, the nickname was changed from two words to one when it was discovered that the spelling in the charter is Blackhawk.

BLUES—St. Louis [1967]
Western Conference/Central Division.
The nickname Blues was a must for owner Sid Saloman, Jr. "The name of the team just has to be the Blues," Saloman said. "It's part of the city where W. C. Handy composed his famed song while thinking of his girl one morning."

BRUINS—Boston [1924]
Eastern Conference/Northeast Division.
Charles F. Adams, a wealthy owner of a grocery store chain, purchased the first NHL franchise for an American city and named it the Bruins.

CANADIENS—Montreal [1917]
Eastern Conference/Northeast Division.
In 1909, the French team in the National Hockey Association was known as *Les Canadiens* and *Les Habitants* (the inhabitants of the country). At the time only French-Canadians were allowed on the team. When Montreal became a part of the NHL, the team retained its use of Canadiens (the French spelling) as well as Habs (short for Habitants). That's why the letters *C* and *H* are found on their jerseys.

CANUCKS—Vancouver [1970]
Western Conference/Northwest Division.
There had been a Vancouver Canucks in the Western Hockey League, a team that folded when the NHL franchise moved in to take over not only their fans but their name as well. At one time Canucks referred to French-Canadians in particular; nowadays, it is commonly used to encompass all Canadians.

CAPITALS—Washington [1974]
Eastern Conference/Southeast Division.
In 1974, Abe Pollin was awarded a franchise in the NHL. A contest was held to suggest a nickname, and the most common suggestion from fans was Comet. Pollin, however, chose to call the team the Washington Capitals. It formed a tandem with his basketball franchise, the Washington Bullets; and both teams played in the Capital Center in Landover, Maryland.

COYOTES—Phoenix [1996]
Western Conference/Pacific Division.
Just as the Winnipeg Jets relocated to Phoenix on July 1, 1996, the coyote has in recent years been returning to Arizona.

DEVILS—New Jersey [1982]

Eastern Conference/Atlantic Division.
When the Colorado Rockies moved to the flatlands of New Jersey, a more appropriate name was needed. A contest was held and the most commonly suggested name was Devils. How come? There had once been a minor-league hockey team called the Devils, but the name reaches back longer than that. Over 250 years ago, or so the legend goes, there lived a Mrs. Leeds who gave birth to a demon. This Jersey Devil has been causing havoc in the area ever since.

FLAMES—Calgary [1980]

Western Conference/Northwest Division.
After moving from Atlanta, the franchise was originally called the Alberta Flames; however, the next year it switched from the name of the province to the city. Atlanta's nickname of Flames alluded to General Sherman's burning of Atlanta. Many had submitted this nickname in a contest, but the actual winner was a college student.

FLYERS—Philadelphia [1967]

Eastern Conference/Atlantic Division.
The Flyers nickname was the suggestion from fans that the owners liked the best.

HURRICANES—Carolina [1997]

Eastern Conference/Southeast Division.
The Hartford Whalers became the Carolina Hurricanes on May 6, 1997. The nickname of Hurricanes, or Canes for short, acknowledges the strong winds that buffet the North Carolina Coast each year.

ISLANDERS—New York [1972]

Eastern Conference/Atlantic Division.
Roy Boe, the owner, selected this nickname for his team because they are located in Nassau County on Long Island. The Islanders are also called the Isles (especially in the newspapers).

KINGS—Los Angeles [1967]

Western Conference/Pacific Division.
Owner Jack Kent Cooke gave his team this nickname when NHL hockey came to town in 1967.

LIGHTNING—Tampa Bay [1992]

Eastern Conference/Southeast Division.
Phil Esposito, originally a general partner of this expansion team, was eating in a Tampa restaurant when he looked outside the window and saw a bolt of lightning. Voilà!

MAPLE LEAFS—Toronto [1926]

Eastern Conference/Northeast Division.
In 1926, the Toronto St. Pats quickly became the Toronto Maple Leafs when Conn Smythe became head of the operation. Wanting a more secular name, he chose one of the symbols for the Canadian nation.

MIGHTY DUCKS—Anaheim [1993]

Western Conference/Pacific Division.
This team took its name from the popular Walt Disney movie about a young hockey team.

NORTH STARS—Minnesota [1967]

The team held a contest and this was the most frequently submitted name. Why? Minnesota's motto is *L'Etoile du Nord* (The Star of the North).

OILERS—Edmonton [1979]

Western Conference/Northwest Division.
The fans chose this name in a contest. There had already been an Oilers team in the WHA from 1972 to 1979. In 1979, the team was called the Alberta Oilers, but it was changed the next year to its present name.

PANTHERS—Florida [1993]

Eastern Conference/Southeast Division.
The Panther was once common in Florida, especially in the everglades, but is now so rare that it is practically a mythical beast.

PENGUINS—Pittsburgh [1967]

Eastern Conference/Atlantic Division.
Fans chose the nickname Penguins, and they play at an arena known as the Igloo.

PREDATORS—Nashville [1997]

Western Conference/Central Division.
The 1998-1999 season was the first season for this expansion team. Never a hotbed of ice hockey, this team had to prey on a few other teams for their roster.

RANGERS—New York [1926]

Eastern Conference/Atlantic Division.
This hockey team was nicknamed Tex's Rangers in honor of Tex Rickard, the man who had promoted prizefights and was president of Madison Square Garden. Over time, "Tex's" bit the dust, leaving just Rangers.

RED WINGS—Detroit [1933]

Western Conference/Central Division.
When owner James D. Norris was a youth, he had played on a team called the Winged Wheelers. (On their jerseys had been two red wings on a wheel.) The nickname and the symbol on their jerseys made sense for a hockey team in an auto town like Detroit.

SABRES—Buffalo [1970]

Eastern Conference/Northeast Division.
There were only a few nominees of Sabres in the thousands of suggestions for the team's nickname. Still, it was chosen because "a sabre is renowned as a clean, sharp, decisive, and penetrating weapon of offense, as well as a strong parrying weapon on defense."

SENATORS—Ottawa [1992]

Eastern Conference/Northeast Division.
The Ottawa Senators are a revival of one of the original NHL Teams, active from 1917 to 1934 when the franchise was relocated to St. Louis.

SHARKS—San Jose [1991]

Western Conference/Northwest Division.
Sharks was the second most popular name in a contest to name the team. The first choice? Blades. (It was thrown out because it sounded like the Knife and Gun Club on Saturday night.) According to a team official, Sharks fit the bill because they are plentiful in area waters, and like a good hockey team, they're "relentless, determined, swift, agile, bright, and fearless."

STARS—Dallas [1993]

Western Conference/Pacific Division.
When this franchise started out in Minnesota in 1967, a contest was held and this was the most frequently submitted name. Why? Minnesota's motto is _L'Etoile du Nord_ (The Star of the North). When the team moved to Big D, the name was shortened appropriately.

TEAMS OF THE NBA

BUCKS—Milwaukee [1968]

Eastern Conference/Central Division.
Fourteen thousand fans sent in their ideas for a nickname for Milwaukee's team in the NBA. The winning entry (there were forty-five in all who suggested Bucks) fulfilled the contest criteria: it fit the image of Wisconsin and basketball, it was good for promotional purposes and was different from the nicknames of the other teams in the NBA. Also, as winner R. D. Trebilcox from Whitefish Bay wrote: "Bucks are spirited, good jumpers, fast and agile. These are good qualities for basketball players."

BULLETS—Washington D.C. [1974]

Eastern Conference/Atlantic Division.
The first site of the franchise was outside of Baltimore near a WW II munitions dump. Also, the nickname referred to the team's "explosive

talent and speed in humbling the opposition." The Baltimore Bullets were originally in the ABL (1944–1947), then the BAA (1947–1949), and finally the NBA (1949–1955). The second NBA franchise, also called the Baltimore Bullets (1963-1973), had come from Chicago where it had been known as the Packers and the Zephyrs. For a short time in 1974, the team was known as the Capital Bullets because Washington is the nation's capital and the team played in the capital area. (From 1946 to 1970, there had also been three pro basketball teams called the Washington Capitols, and even one in 1946 mysteriously called the Washington Capitol's.) But later in 1974, the name finally became the Washington Bullets.

BULLS—Chicago (1966)
Eastern Conference/Central Division.
The franchise owners gave the team this name apparently for the city's longtime association with stockyards.

CAVALIERS—Cleveland (1970)
Eastern Conference/Central Division.
Fans chose this name in a contest. It was felt that the nickname "represents a group of daring, fearless men, whose life's pact was never surrender, no matter what the odds."

CELTICS—Boston (1949)
Eastern Conference/Atlantic Division.
Walter Brown, the team's owner, selected this name because of the large numbers of Irish in the Boston area. The name harks back to one of the first great teams—the New York Original Celtics. Before joining the NBA, the Boston Celtics were in the BAA from 1946 to 1949.

CLIPPERS—Los Angeles (1984)
Western Conference/Pacific Division.
The nickname originated when the team was in

San Diego from 1978 to 1984. The winning nickname in a contest, Clippers highlighted this coastal city's marine past when clipper ships sailed the high seas.

GOLDEN STATE WARRIORS—Oakland (1971)
Western Conference /Pacific Division.
When this franchise originated in 1926, it was called the Phillies. However, as there was already a Philadelphia baseball team with that name, Gordon Mackay of the Philadelphia *Inquirer* thought up a new one. "I saw a picture of Hannibal last night," recounted Mackay, "and the name popped right into my head. Warriors, that's the name for our bunch."

GRIZZLIES—Vancouver (1968)
Western Conference/Midwest Division.
The owners selected this name because it is powerful and represents British Columbia and Canada.

HAWKS—Atlanta (1968)
Eastern Conference/Central Division.
In 1946, the Erie County American Legion sponsored the Buffalo Bisons in the National Basketball League. That same year the team moved to the tri-cities area (Davenport, Iowa; Moline and Rock Island, Illinois) along the Mississippi River to become the Tri-Cities Blackhawks—a nickname in honor of Chief Blackhawk. In 1949, the Tri-Cities Blackhawks joined the NBA; and in 1951, the team moved to Milwaukee and shortened the nickname to Hawks. In 1955, the franchise was in St. Louis for the later great teams of Bob Petit, Cliff "LI'L ABNER" Hagen, and EASY ED Macauley; and in 1968, the team moved once again, this time to Atlanta, Georgia.

HEAT—Miami (1988)
Eastern Conference/Atlantic Division.

Out of the 20,000 entries in the contest to give the new franchise a nickname, the top three suggestions were Heat, Flamingoes, and Waves. A panel of sportswriters made the final selection, one that pleased one of the owners, Zev Bufman, because it "graphically can be turned into something very exciting, with colors like reds, yellows, and oranges."

HORNETS—Charlotte (1988)

Eastern Conference/Central Division.
The citizens of Charlotte are ever proud of their history. When the British troops were halted in Charlotte during the American Revolution, General Cornwallis had declared: "There's a rebel behind every bush. It's a veritable next of hornets." Surprisingly, the first nickname selected had been Spirit. However, the fans demanded an open contest, and Hornets won thumbs down.

JAZZ—Utah (1979)

Western Conference/Midwest Division.
This franchise was originally in New Orleans. When a contest was held in 1974 to name the team, the most often suggested name was Jazz. After all, New Orleans was the birthplace of this All-American art form. When the team moved in 1979 to a state more associated with Mormons than music it still retained its soulful nickname.

KINGS—Sacramento (1985)

Western Conference/Pacific Division.
In 1975, the Cincinnati Royals relocated to the Kansas City-Omaha area and needed a new nickname because there was already a Royals baseball team. Kings was selected in the fan balloting. When the team moved from Kansas City to Sacramento, the nickname was retained (though it seems to hold as little relevance in Sacramento as it had in K.C.).

KNICKERBOCKERS—New York (1949)

Eastern Conference/Atlantic Division.
In 1946, Ned Irish gave his New York team in the BAA this nickname because of the city's long association with Knickerbocker. (Washington Irving had cataloged the foibles and comic shortcomings of "the old burghers of the Manhattoes" in *Knickerbocker's History of New York*.) In 1949, the nickname was bestowed on the new New York team in the NBA—a nickname that is usually shortened to the more familiar Knicks.

LAKERS—Los Angeles (1960)

Western Conference/Pacific Division.
This nickname was started when the franchise was in Minneapolis because Minnesota is known as the Land of 10,000 Lakes. The Minneapolis Lakers were in the NBL (1947–1948), the BAA (1948–1949), and then the NBA (1949–1959) before moving to L.A.

MAGIC—Orlando (1989)

Eastern Conference/Atlantic Division.
The biggest number of suggestions from fans was for Magic and Juice. A panel of people mulled these two over and decided on Magic. After all, the Magic Kingdom is in the area.

MAVERICKS—Dallas (1980)

Western Conference/Midwest Division.
A local radio station had run a contest to name the team and a committee then recommended Mavericks (suggested by forty-six people) to owner Donald Carter.

NETS—New Jersey (1977)

Eastern Conference/Atlantic Division.
In 1968, the New Jersey team in the ABA needed a nickname and settled on Nets. (Perhaps if it had been in Ohio, it would have been Hoops.) When the team moved to Long Island, the team

kept the nickname. Hey, with the Jets and Mets, it was made to order. When the team became a part of the NBA in 1976 and went full circle to return to its birthplace the following year, it continued to call itself Nets.

NUGGETS—Denver (1976)

Western Conference/Midwest Division.
From 1967 to 1974, this team was in the ABA and nicknamed the Rockets because its owner ran the Rocket Truck Lines. The name was changed to the Nuggets in 1974 because of the impending merger with the NBA. One of the NBA teams was the Houston Rockets. Why the Nuggets? There had been an earlier NBA team called the Nuggets; also, it called to mind an earlier period in Colorado's history.

PACERS—Indiana (1976)

Eastern Conference/Central Division.
This NBA team took its nickname from the Indiana Pacers team that had played in the ABA from 1967 to 1976. One of the reasons that general manager Mike Storem had given in 1967 for choosing the nickname was the Indianapolis 500.

PISTONS—Detroit (1957)

Eastern Conference/Central Division.
Fort Wayne's team in the National Basketball League from 1941 to 1948 was the Zollner Pistons. (Fred Zollner was a sports enthusiast and the owner of a machine works that supplied pistons to Detroit.) Later, the team was simply known as the Pistons when it joined the BAA. In 1957, the team became the Detroit Pistons and a member of the NBA.

RAPTORS—Toronto (1995)

Eastern Conference/Central Division.
A contest was held and the public voted on ten choices. Raptors won the most votes.

ROCKETS—Houston (1971)

Western Conference/Midwest Division.
In 1967, the San Diego franchise held a contest to name the team and Rockets was the winner. When the San Diego Rockets relocated, Houston got both the team and the nickname. Rockets fell right in place with the space industry in the area.

76ers—Philadelphia (1963)

Eastern Conference/Atlantic Division. After the Syracuse Nationals were moved to Philadelphia, a contest was held to name the team. The winning entry evoked the spirit of liberty.

SPURS—San Antonio (1976)

Western Conference/Midwest Division.
When the Dallas Chaparrals (birds known as roadrunners) of the ABA were relocated to San Antonio in 1973, a contest was held to find a new nickname. The winner was the Spurs. The nickname stuck when the team joined the NBA three years later.

SUNS—Phoenix (1968)

Western Conference/Pacific Division.
The team held a contest and Suns was the most frequently submitted entry.

SUPERSONICS—Seattle (1976)

Western Conference/Pacific Division.
Surprisingly, 163 people sent in this nickname for the new Seattle basketball team in a fan contest. Supersonics is the official nickname, though only the Sonics appears on the uniform. (Perhaps if the official name were printed vertically on the jerseys, all the letters could fit.)

TIMBERWOLVES—Minnesota (1989)

Western Conference/Midwest Division.
A committee selected two nicknames from those submitted by fans to be voted on by all the

city councils in Minnesota. Second place was Polars.

TRAILBLAZERS—Portland [1970]

Western Conference/Pacific Division.
A committee chose this entry as the winner in a contest to name the team.

WIZARDS—Washington [1997]

Eastern Conference/Atlantic Division.
This team was originally called the Bullets because the first site of the franchise was outside of Baltimore near a World War II munitions dump. The Baltimore Bullets were in the ABL (1944–47), then the BAA (1947–49), and finally the NBA (1949–55). The second NBA franchise, also called the Baltimore Bullets (1963–73), had come from Chicago. For a short time in 1974 it was called the Capital Bullets, before being called the Washington Bullets again. In 1997, the owners felt it was time for a change. The fans were presented with five choices and Wizards won.

TEAMS OF THE AMERICAN LEAGUE AND NATIONAL LEAGUE

ANGELS—Anaheim [1966]

American League/West Division.
Originally from Los Angeles (1961–1965) the franchise took its nickname from the City of Angels. In 1966, the Los Angeles Angels moved to Anaheim and changed their name to the Anaheim Angels.

ASTROS—Houston [1965]

National League/Central Division.
In 1965, the Houston Colts began playing their games in the Astrodome. So, they changed their name to the Astros.

ATHLETICS—Oakland [1968]

American League/West Division.
This nickname originated in 1859. It was then that a group of well-to-do men who wanted to play baseball formed the Philadelphia Athletic Club. Since that time the team has passed through several stages. The Philadelphia Athletics have been in the National Association (1871–1975), the National League (1876), the American Association (1882–1991), and the American League (1901–1954). From 1955 to 1967, the team was known as the Kansas City Athletics. Today the franchise is at home in Oakland.

BLUE JAYS—Toronto [1977]

American League/East Division.
Thirty thousand fans sent in suggestions to give the new team a nickname. The most frequent entry received was Blues; however, the University of Toronto had a lock on that nickname. The selection committee then turned to one of the other ten finalists and chose Blue Jay.

BRAVES—Atlanta [1966]

National League/East Division.
James Gaffney, the owner of the ball club, was a member of Tammany Hall in New York City; and the members of this political machine were called braves. (There had once been a Native American chief by the name of Tammany.) The Boston Braves were in operation from 1912 to 1935, and from 1941 to 1952. In 1953, the franchise relocated to Milwaukee and became the Milwaukee Braves. In 1966, the Braves went to Atlanta.

BREWERS—Milwaukee [1970]

National League/Central Division.
There was a Brewers team in the American Association before the Seattle Pilots was transferred to Milwaukee in 1970. It seemed as natural as having a bratwurst and a beer to use the

nickname Brewers. The Brewers were an AL team, then switched to the NL in 1998.

CARDINALS—St. Louis (1900)
National League/Central Division.
In 1899, owner Frank Robinson bought new uniforms along with socks topped with a cardinal hue for the St. Louis team. Sportswriter William McHale first wrote the nickname in the *St. Louis Republic,* and soon others followed suit.

CUBS—Chicago (1900)
National League/Central Division.
After sportswriters and fans alike toyed with the names Colts and Orphans, the Cubs became the unofficial and then official name for the new team in town.

DEVIL RAYS—Tampa Bay (1998)
American League/ East Division.
For this 1998 expansion team, General Manager Chuck LeMar signed such quality players as Wade Boggs, Fred McGriff, Roberto Hernandez, Paul Sorrento, and Wilson Alverez.

DIAMONDBACKS—Arizona (1998)
National League/West Division.
This 1998 expansion team received its nickname as the result of a contest where fans submitted suggestions. The diamond back rattlesnake is associated with the desert regions of Arizona.

DODGERS—Los Angeles (1958)
National League/West Division.
The baseball team adopted this nickname when it was back in Brooklyn. Because of the many trolley tracks, the folks of Flatbush were referred to as Trolley Dodgers, and their team was known as the Brooklyn Dodgers. (1932–1957).

EXPOS—Montreal (1969)
National League/East Division.
In 1967, Montreal hosted the World's Fair.

Known far and wide as Expo '67, the baseball team merely adapted this for their nickname.

GIANTS—San Francisco (1958)
National League/West Division.
The team had a long history in New York (1885–1957). Although it had been called the Gothams, manager James Mutrie is often given credit for hastening the nickname change. It was widely quoted that he said about his team in the 1880s that they were "not only giants in stature but in baseball ability." The team and the nickname traveled to S.F. in 1958.

INDIANS—Cleveland (1915)
American League/Central Division.
In 1915, fans chose this nickname in a contest to honor the memory of Louis Sockalexis, a Native American who had played for Cleveland in the National League from 1897 to 1899.

MARINERS—Seattle (1977)
American League/West Division.
This nickname came from a contest for the fans. It was selected because it highlights the importance of the sea to life in Seattle.

MARLINS—Florida (1993)
National League/East Division.
This nickname was a natural for the youngest franchise ever to win the Word Series. Sadly, this superb team was dismantled after its splendid 1997 season and has since sunk to the bottom.

METS—New York (1962)
National League/East Division.
The Mets held a contest to name the team and the winner was Mets. (Skyliners was second.) The nickname Mets made sense because the official name of the team was the Metropolitan Baseball Club, Inc. Also, there is a tie to the

nineteenth-century New York Metropolitans of the American Association.

ORIOLES—Baltimore (1954)
American League/East Division.
In 1833, the nickname Orioles (for the state bird) was adopted for the Baltimore team in the AA.

PADRES—San Diego (1969)
National League/West Division.
The first Spanish mission was built in San Diego, and at one time the city had featured a minor-league team called the Padres. So, when San Diego won its franchise in the late sixties, the nickname came about without divine intervention.

PHILLIES—Philadelphia (1946)
National League/East Division.
It may have been owner A. J. Reach who bestowed this nickname on the team, or it may have come about as naturally as when a player from Texas gets the nickname Tex.

PIRATES—Pittsburgh (1891)
National League/Central Division.
The Pittsburgh Innocents signed a player that the Philadelphia Athletics maintained belonged to them. When Pittsburgh refused to release Louis Biebauer, the Athletics and the other teams in the American Association branded the Pittsburgh ball club "Pirates."

RANGERS—Texas (1972)
American League/West Division.
When the Washington Senators were transplanted to Texas, a contest was held to name the team. It was an easy selection process. Everybody has heard of the Texas Rangers.

REDS—Cincinnati (1946)
National League/Central Division.
The first professional baseball team was the

Cincinnati Red Stockings in 1869. The present team is the third one called the Cincinnati Reds (shortened from Red Stockings).

RED SOX—Boston (1907)
American League/East Division.
In 1907, John Irvin Taylor gave his team this name after his young daughter told him how much she liked the red stockings that many team members wore. (The reason they were in the habit of wearing red socks was because there had been a team called the Boston Red Stockings (1871–1975) that had patterned their uniforms after those of the Cincinnati Red Stockings.)

ROCKIES—Colorado (1993)
National League/West Division.
This team was named for the state's geological splendor.

ROYALS—Kansas City (1969)
American League/Central Division.
This nickname was the winning entry in a contest. However, the name was up in the air as it had been used by a Kansas City barnstorming baseball team during the 1940s.

TIGERS—Detroit (1901)
American League/Central Division.
The Detroit baseball team was at first called the Wolverines. But around 1896, it was changed to the Tigers because the players wore black and yellow striped stockings.

TWINS—Minnesota (1961)
American League/Central Division.
When Calvin Griffith moved the Washington Senators to Minneapolis/St. Paul, he wanted to call the team the Twin Cities. Soon, though, he changed in favor of a name that would be more inclusive. (However, the initials TC still appear on the uniforms.)

WHITE SOX—Chicago [1901]

American League/Central Division.
This nickname came from an earlier team in Chicago called the White Stockings. It was shortened to Sox for the benefit of newspapers.

YANKEES—New York [1913]

American League/East Division.
From 1903 to 1912, the New York Highlanders played in Hilltop Park in the Washington Heights section of New York City. When they moved to the Bronx to play closer to sea level at the Polo Grounds, the journalists also wanted them to come down to earth. Their new nickname became the Yankees because it was easier to squeeze into a headline.

TEAMS OF THE NFL

BEARS—Chicago [1922]

National Football Conference/Central Division (NFC C). In 1921, George Halas moved the Decatur Staleys to Chicago. That first year the Chicago Staleys played at Wrigley Field, the home of the Cubs. If baseball players were called Cubs, Cubs fan Halas reasoned, then the more ruggedly built football players should be known as Bears.

BENGALS—Cincinnati [1970]

American Football Conference/ Central Division (AFC C). Paul Brown chose this nickname because there had been three earlier football teams in Cincinnati called the Bengals (1937, 1940–1941, and 1968–1969).

BILLS—Buffalo [1970]

American Football Conference/ Eastern Division (AFC E). This is the nickname of an earlier football team, the Buffalo Bills of the AFL (1960–1969). There had also been a

Buffalo Bills team in the AAFC (1947–1949). The nickname refers to William F. Cody aka Buffalo Bill. (An earlier nickname of this team had been the Bisons.)

BRONCOS—Denver [1970]

American Football Conference/Western Division (AFC W). There had been a Denver Broncos team in the AFL (1960–1969). The nickname had been chosen in a contest: it referred to a baseball team of the 1920s and to Denver's Wild West heritage.

BUCCANEERS—Tampa Bay [1976]

National Football Conference/Central Division (NFC C). This was the winning entry in a fan contest. As the owner Hugh Culverhouse said, "We want our football team to be as aggressive, high-spirited, and colorful as were the old buccaneers."

CARDINALS—Phoenix [1988]

National Football Conference/Eastern Division (NFC E). The heritage of this team goes back to the Racine Cardinals. In 1899, a ragtag football team began playing at a field on Racine Avenue with some hand-me-down jerseys from the University of Chicago. The color may have been maroon, but it was close enough to cardinal for the nickname. By 1922 the name of this team had become the Chicago Cardinals, and they played in the NFL until 1959. In 1960, the franchise was moved to St. Louis; and in 1987, it was moved to Arizona.

CHARGERS—San Diego [1970]

NFL American Football Conference/Western Division (AFC W). In 1960, a contest was held to give a nickname to the new Los Angeles franchise in the AFL; and owner Baron Hilton chose the winner. Three reasons have sometimes been offered in explanation: the name sounded dynamic; the new club stationery featured a horse; and Hilton had recently instituted the Carte Blanche card. In 1970, the nickname made the trip along with the team to San Diego and the NFL.

CHIEFS—Kansas City (1970)

American Football Conference/Western Division (AFC W). The Kansas City Chiefs in the NFL were named after the Kansas City Chiefs of the AFL (1963–1969). The nickname Chiefs came about because H. L. Hunt (the owner of the relocated Dallas Texans) wanted to express his thanks to H. Roe "The Chief" Bartle, the mayor of Kansas City.

COLTS—Indianapolis (1984)

American Football Conference/Eastern Division (AFC E). The winning letter to name the Baltimore team in the AAFC (1947–1949) was submitted by Charles Evans who wrote, "Colts are the youngest entry in the league, Maryland is famous for its race-horses, and it is short, easily pronounced, and fits well in newspaper headlines." The nickname was carried over to two Baltimore football teams (1950; 1953-1983) and traveled with the franchise when it relocated to Indianapolis.

COWBOYS—Dallas (1960)

National Football Conference/ Eastern Division (NFC E). After rejecting the name Rangers because that might cause confusion with a local minor-league team, the owners in 1960 chose Cowboys for its association with the early days of Dallas.

DOLPHINS—Miami (1970)

American Football Conference/Eastern Division (AFC E). A contest was held to nickname the Miami team in the AFL (1966–1969) and the winner was Dolphins. When the franchise joined the NFL in 1970, the Dolphins made a splash as both the nickname and the mascot.

EAGLES—Philadelphia (1944)

National Football Conference/Eastern Division (NFC E). In 1944, one of the new co-owners named Bert Bell gave the team this nickname in honor of the eagle symbol used in the National Recovery Administration. It was certainly more regal than the previous nickname of Yellow Jackets.

FALCONS—Atlanta (1966)

National Football Conference/Western Division (NFC W). A high-school teacher named Julia Elliot submitted the nickname in a contest to name the team because "the Falcon is proud and dignified, with great courage and fight."

49ers—San Francisco (1950)

National Football Conference/Western Division (NFC W). In 1946, this nickname was suggested to owner Tony Marabito for his new team in the AAFC. He liked it because it harked back to San Francisco's colorful past during the Gold Rush. In the beginning, the nickname was spelled out; over time, it transmogrified into a combination of numbers and letters. In 1950, the nickname traveled to the new franchise in the NFL.

GIANTS—New York (1925)

National Football Conference/Eastern Division (NFC E). In 1925, Tim Mara named his football team the Giants because they would use the same Polo Grounds where the baseball Giants played. When the team crossed the Hudson River to take up residence in New Jersey, they kept the same nickname.

JAGUARS—Jacksonville (1995)

National Football Conference/Western Division (NFC W). In 1991, a contest for a nickname was held. Among the finalists of Stingrays, Panthers, and Sharks was Ray Potts' winning entry. Although Jaguars are usually associated with

South America, the local zoo boasted a twenty-four-year-old specimen.

JETS—New York [1970]
American Football Conference/Eastern Division (AFC E).When the New York Titans were bought in 1963, Sonny Werblin gave his team in the AFL the snappy nickname of Jets. (It sounded like the Mets baseball team, and there were more than a few jets flying over the area to nearby La Guardia Airport.) When the team entered the NFL in 1970, the team kept their nickname.

LIONS—Detroit [1934]
National Football Conference/Central Division (NFC C). In 1934, the owner G. A. Richards chose this name. There was already a Tiger baseball team in town, and there had once been a Panthers football team. The hope may have been that the Lions, the king of beasts, would lord it over the other cats.

OILERS—Tennessee [1997]
American Football Conference/Central Division (AFC C). The Oilers were originally a team in the AFL (1960–1969). In 1959, Kenneth BUD Adams gave them the name of Oilers for how he and Houston made money. The team became the Tennessee Oilers in 1997.

PACKERS—Green Bay [1922]
National Football Conference/Central Division (NFC C). In 1919, Earl CURLY Lambeau asked his employer for $500 to help with a football team he was forming. Frank Peck complied, and the team's jerseys read Indian Packing Co. The name was later shortened to Packers.

PANTHERS—Carolina [1995]
National Football Conference/Western Division (AFC W). The nickname for this new franchise was selected by one of the owner's sons. It was

a good choice because Mark Richardson is now the president.

PATRIOTS—New England [1970]
American Football Conference/Eastern Division (AFC E). In 1960, a group of sportswriters chose this name for its allusion to Patriot's Day (the anniversary of Paul Revere's ride). The nickname of the Boston Patriots of the AFL (1960–1969) was carried over to the Boston Patriots of the NFL.

RAIDERS—Oakland [1995]
American Football Conference/Western Division (AFC W). When Oakland received an AFL franchise in 1960, they held a contest to find a nickname. Ignoring the fans' choice of Senors, team officials instead called their team the Raiders. In 1970, the Oakland Raiders joined the NFL; and in 1982, Al Davis took the team to L.A.; in 1995 they returned home.

RAMS—St. Louis [1995]
National Football Conference/Western Division (NFC W). In 1936, the new Cleveland team in the AFL needing a nickname took theirs from one of the best college teams in the country, the Fordham Rams. The nickname remained when Cleveland joined the NFL the next year, and when the franchise journeyed to Los Angeles for the1946 season, and finally to St. Louis.

RAVENS—Baltimore [1996]
American Football Conference/Central Division (AFC C). After fifty years of the Browns in Cleveland, owner Art Modell moved the franchise to Baltimore. (The Browns' name and colors will remain in Cleveland.) Naturally there was sentiment in Baltimore for the Colts, but the final nod went to another bird for Baltimore. Why the Ravens? Edgar Allen Poe had lived and died in Baltimore.

REDSKINS—Washington [1937]

National Football Conference/Eastern Division (NFC E). In 1932, George Marshall received a NFL franchise for Boston. As the football team would be playing on the same field used by the baseball team the Boston Braves he gave his team the same nickname. When Marshall moved the football team to Fenway Park the following year, he continued the Native American feeling with the nickname Redskins (something many find offensive today). In 1937, the team found a new home in Washington, D. C.

SAINTS—New Orleans [1966]

National Football Conference/Western Division (NFC W). Team officials chose this nickname, but there are two pretty compelling reasons. The franchise was awarded on November 1, 1966—All Saints Day; and "When the Saints Go Marchin' In" is as closely associated with New Orleans as "I Left My Heart in San Francisco" is with the city on the bay.

SEAHAWKS—Seattle [1976]

American Football Conference/Western Division (AFC W). Of the 20,000 suggestions received in a contest to give the team a nickname, 151 were for Seahawks. Like the Mariners baseball team that later took up residence, it connotes the importance of the sea to Seattle.

STEELERS—Pittsburgh [1945]

American Football Conference/Central Division (AFC C). Needing a new nickname in 1939 for the Pittsburgh team in the NFL, a contest was held; however, Steelers was the idea of the wife of the ticket manager. (The first Steelers team was from 1939 to 1942; the second from 1945 to the present day.)

VIKINGS—Minnesota [1961]

National Football Conference/Central Division

(NFC C). Bert Rose, the general manager of the team in 1961, chose the nickname because there are many people of Scandinavian descent in the state and the nickname brings to mind a fierce band of tireless warriors.

NICKNAMES OF COLLEGE TEAMS

AGGIES—New Mexico State University (Las Cruces), North Carolina A & T (Greensboro), Texas A & M (College Station), Utah State University (Logan)

ANTEATERS—University of California at Irving

AZTECS—San Diego State University

BADGERS—University of Wisconsin (Madison)

BATTLING BISHOPS—Ohio Wesleyan University (Delaware, OH)

BEARCATS—University of Cincinnati (OH)

BEARKATS—Sam Houston State University (Huntsville, TX)

BEARS—Baylor University (Waco, TX), Brown (Providence, RI), Mercer University (Macon, GA), Morgan State University (Baltimore, MD), Southwest Missouri State University (Springfield)

BEAVERS—City College of New York (NY), Oregon State University (Corvallis)

BEES—University of Baltimore (MD)

BENGALS—Idaho State University (Pocatello), Louisiana State University (Baton Rouge; also called FIGHTING TIGERS, OLD LOU, OLE WAR SKULE)

BIG EIGHT—conference of University of Colorado, Iowa State University, University of

Kansas, Kansas State University, University of Missouri, University of Nebraska, University of Oklahoma, Oklahoma State University

BIG FIVE—La Salle College, University of Pennsylvania, St. Joseph's College, Temple University, Villanova University (basketball teams in Philadelphia area)

BIG GREEN—Dartmouth College (Hanover, NH)

BIG RED—Cornell University (Ithaca, NY)

BIG TEN—conference of University of Illinois, Indiana University, University of Iowa, University of Michigan, Michigan State University, University of Minnesota, Northwestern University, Ohio State University, Purdue University, University of Wisconsin

BIG THREE—Harvard, Princeton, Yale

BILLIKENS—St. Louis University (MO)

BISON—Bucknell University (Lewisburg, PA), Howard University (Washington, D.C.)

BLACK BEARS—University of Maine (Orono)

BLACK KNIGHTS—United States Military Academy (West Point, NY); also called CADETS

BLACKBIRDS—Long Island University (Brooklyn, NY)

BLAZERS—Alabama University (Birmingham)

BLUE DEMONS—DePaul University (Chicago, IL)

BLUE DEVILS—Central Connecticut State College (New Britain), Duke University (Durham, NC)

BLUE JAYS—Creighton University (Omaha, NE)

BLUE HENS—Delaware University (Newark)

BLUE RAIDERS—Middle Tennessee State University (Mufreesboro)

BLUE STREAKS—John Carroll University (Cleveland, OH)

BOBCATS—Montana State University (Bozeman), Ohio University (Athens), Southwest Texas State University (San Marcos)

BOILERMAKERS—Purdue University (Lafayette, IN)

BONNIES—St. Bonaventure University (NY)

BRAVES—Alcorn State University (Lorman, MS), Bradley University (Peoria, IL)

BRONCS—Rider College (Lawrenceville, NJ), Texas-Pan American (Edinburg)

BRONCOS—Boise State University (ID), Santa Clara University (CA), Western Michigan University (Kalamazoo)

BRUINS—Brown University (Providence, RI), University of California (Los Angeles)

BUCCANEERS—Charleston Southern (SC), Eastern Tennessee State University (Johnson City)

BUCKEYES—Ohio State University (Columbus)

BUFFALOES—University of Colorado (Boulder), West Texas State University (Canyon)

BULLS—Buffalo (NY), South Florida (Tampa)

BULLDOGS—Butler University (Indianapolis, IN), The Citadel (Charleston, SC), Drake University (Des Moines, IA), Fresno State (CA), Gonzaga University (Spokane, WA; also called ZAGS), Louisiana Tech University (Ruston), Mississippi State University (Starkville), Samford University (Birmingham, AL), South Carolina State College (Orangeburg), University of Georgia (Athens; also called 'DAWGS), University of North Carolina (Ashville), Yale University (New Haven, CT; also called ELIS)

CADETS—United States Coast Guard Academy (New London, CT), United States Military

Academy (West Point, NY; also called BLACK KNIGHTS)

CANTABS—Harvard University (Cambridge, MA; also called CRIMSON)

CARDINALS—Ball State University (Muncie, IN), Lamar University (Beaumont, TX), Stanford University (Stanford, CA), University of Louisville (KY), Wesleyan University (Middletown, CT)

CATAMOUNTS—University of Vermont (Burlington), Western Carolina University (Cullowhee, NC)

CAVALIERS—University of Virginia (Charlottesville)

CHANTICLEERS—Coastal Carolina (Conway, SC)

CHIPPEWAS—Central Michigan University (Mt. Pleasant)

COLONELS—Curry College (Milton, MA), Eastern Kentucky University (Richmond), Wilkes College (Wilkes-Barre, PA)

COLONIALS—George Washington University (Washington, D.C.)

COMMODORES—Vanderbilt University (Nashville, TN)

CORNHUSKERS—University of Nebraska (Lincoln)

COUGARS—Brigham Young University (Provo, UT), Chicago State University (IL), College of Charleston (SC), University of Houston (TX), Washington State University (Pullman)

COWBOYS—McNeese State University (Lake Charles, LA), Oklahoma State University (Stillwater), University of Wyoming (Laramie)

COYOTES—University of South Dakota (Vermillion)

CRIMSON—Harvard University (Cambridge, MA; also called CANTABS)

CRIMSON TIDE—University of Alabama (Montgomery; also called PLAINSMEN, TIGERS, WAR EAGLES)

CRUSADERS—College of the Holy Cross (Worcester, MA), Valparaiso University (IN)

CYCLONES—Iowa State University (Ames)

'DAWGS—University of Georgia (Athens; also called BULLDOGS)

DELTA DEVILS—Mississippi Valley State (Itta Bena)

DEMON DEACONS—Wake Forrest University (Winston-Salem, NC)

DEMONS—Northwestern State University (Natchitoches, LA)

DIABLOS—Los Angeles State University (CA)

DOLPHINS—Jacksonville University (FL)

DRAGONS—Drexel University (Philadelphia, PA), Moorhead State University (MN)

DUCKS—University of Oregon (Eugene)

DUKES—Duquesne University (Pittsburgh, PA), James Madison (Harrisonburg, VA)

EAGLES—American University (Washington, D.C.), Boston College (MA), Coppin Street College (Baltimore, MD), Eastern Michigan University (Ypsilanti), Eastern Washington State College (Cheney), Georgia Southern College (Statesboro), University of North Texas (Denton), Winthrop (Rock Hill, SC)

ELIS—Yale University (New Haven, CT; also called BULLDOGS)

ENGINEERS—Lehigh University (Bethlehem, PA)

EPHMAN—Williams College (Williamstown, MA)

EXPLORERS—La Salle College (Philadelphia, PA)

FALCONS—Bowling Green State University (Bowling Green, OH), United States Air Force Academy (Colorado Springs, CO)

FIGHTIN' BLUE HENS—University of Delaware (Newark)

FIGHTIN' HOOSIERS—Indiana University (Bloomington)

FIGHTING CAMELS—Campbell College (Buies Creek, NC)

FIGHTING GAMECOCKS—University of South Carolina (Columbia)

FIGHTING ILLINI—University of Illinois (Urbana)

FIGHTING IRISH—University of Notre Dame (Notre Dame, IN)

FIGHTING SCOTS—College of Wooster (OH)

FIGHTING TIGERS—Louisiana State University (Baton Rouge; also called Ole War Skule)

FLAMES—Illinois (Chicago), Liberty Baptist College (Lynchburg, VA)

FLYERS—University of Dayton (OH)

FLYING DUTCHMEN—Hofstra University (Hempstead, NY)

FORTY NINERS—Long Beach State University (CA)

FRIARS—Providence University (RI)

GAELS—Iona (New Rochelle, NY)

GAMECOCKS—Jacksonville State (FL)

GATORS—University of Florida (Gainesville)

GAUCHOS—University of California at Santa Barbara

GENERALS—Washington & Lee University (Lexington, VI)

GENTLEMEN—Centenary College (Shreveport, LA)

GOBBLERS—Virginia Polytechnic Institute & State University—VPI (Blacksburg; also called HOKIES)

GOLDEN BEARS—University of California (Berkeley)

GOLDEN EAGLES—Northeast Illinois University (Chicago), Tennessee Tech (Cookville), University of Southern Mississippi (Hattiesburg)

GOLDEN FLASHES—Kent State University (OH)

GOLDEN GOPHERS—University of Minnesota (Minneapolis)

GOLDEN GRIFFINS—Canisius College (Buffalo, NY)

GOLDEN HURRICANE—University of Tulsa (OK)

GOPHERS—University of Minnesota (Minneapolis)

GORILLAS—Pittsburgh State (PA)

GOVERNORS—Austin Peay State University (Clarkesville, TN)

GREEN KNIGHTS—St. Norbert College (De Pere, WI)

GREEN WAVE—Tulane University (New Orleans, LA)

GREYHOUNDS—Loyola College (Baltimore, MD)

GRIZZLIES—University of Montana (Missoula)

HATTERS—Stetson (De Land, FL)

HAWKS—Maryland—Eastern Shore University (Princess Anne), Monmouth College (Long

Branch, NJ), St. Joseph's College (Philadelphia, PA), University of Hartford (CT)

HAWKEYES—University of Iowa (Iowa City)

HIGHLANDERS—Radford College (VA)

HILLTOPPERS—Western Kentucky University (Bowling Green)

HOKIES—Virginia Polytechnic Institute & State University—VPI (Blacksburg; also called GOBBLERS)

HOOSIERS—Indiana University (Bloomington)

HORNED FROGS—Texas Christian University—TCU (Fort Worth)

HORNETS—Alabama State University (Montgomery), California State University (Sacramento), Delaware State College (Dover)

HOYAS—Georgetown University (Washington, D.C.)

HURONS—Eastern Michigan University (Ypsilanti)

HURRICANES—University of Miami (Coral Gables, FL)

HUSKIES—University of Connecticut (Storrs), Northern Illinois University (DeKalb), Northeastern University (Boston, MA), University of Washington (Seattle)

INDIANS—Arkansas State University (State University), College of William & Mary (Williamsburg, VA), Northeast Louisiana University (Monroe)

IVY LEAGUE—Brown University, Columbia University, Cornell University, Dartmouth College, Harvard University, Princeton University, University of Pennsylvania, Yale University

JACKRABBITS—South Dakota State University (Brookings)

JAGUARS—South Alabama (Mobile), Southern University (Baton Rouge, LA)

JASPERS—Manhattan College (Bronx, NY)

JAVELINAS—Texas A & I University (Kingsville)

JAYHAWKS—University of Kansas (Lawrence)

JUMBOS—Tufts University (Medford, MA)

KANGAROOS—University of Missouri (Kansas City)

KEYDETS—Virginia Military Institute—VMI (Lexington)

KOHAWKS—Coe College (Cedar Rapids, IA)

LEATHERNECKS—Western Illinois University (Macomb)

LEOPARDS—Lafayette College (Easton, PA)

LIONS—Columbia University (New York, NY), Southeast Louisiana (Hammond)

LITTLE QUAKERS—Swarthmore College (Swarthmore, PA)

LITTLE THREE—Amherst College, Wesleyan College, and Williams College; the basketball teams of Canisius College, Niagara University, and St. Bonaventure University

LOBOS—University of New Mexico (Albuquerque)

LOGGERS—University of Puget Sound (Tacoma, WA)

LONGHORNS—University of Texas (Austin)

LORD JEFFS—Amherst College (Amherst, MA; also called THE SABRINAS)

LORDS—Kenyon College (Gambier, OH)

LUMBERJACKS—Northern Arizona University (Flagstaff), S. F. Austin State (Nacogdoches, TX)

MATADORS—California State University (Northridge)

MAVERICKS—University of Texas (Arlington)

MEAN GREEN—North Texas State University (Denton)

MIDSHIPMEN—United States Naval Academy (Annapolis, MD; also, MIDDIES)

MINERS—University of Texas (El Paso)

MINUTEMEN—University of Massachusetts (Amherst)

MOCCASINS—University of Tennessee (Chattanooga)

MONARCHS—Old Dominion (Norfolk, VA)

MOUNTAINEERS—Appalachian State University (Boon, NC), Mount St. Mary's College (Emmitsburg, MD), West Virginia University (Morgantown)

MULES—Muhlenberg College (Allentown, PA)

MUSKETEERS—Xavier (Cincinnati, OH)

MUSTANGS—Southern Methodist University (Dallas, TX)

NITTANY LIONS—Pennsylvania State University (University Park)

OLE MISS—University of Mississippi (Oxford; also called REBELS)

OLES—St. Olaf College (Northfield, MN)

ORANGEMEN—Syracuse University (NY)

OWLS—Rice University (Houston, TX), Temple University (Philadelphia, PA)

PACIFIC TEN [PAC TEN]—Arizona State University, Oregon State University, Stanford University, University of Arizona, University of California (Berkeley), University of California at Los Angeles (UCLA), University of Oregon, University of Southern California, University of Washington, Washington State University,

PACKERS—Armour Institute of Technology (Chicago, IL; also called TECH HAWKS

PALADINS—Furman University (Greenville, SC)

PANTHERS—Eastern Illinois University (Charleston), Georgia State University (Atlanta), Middlebury College (Middlebury, VT), Northern Iowa University (Cedar Falls), Prairie View A&M University (TX), University of Pittsburgh (PA)

PATRIOTS—George Mason University (Fairfax, VA)

PEACOCKS—St. Peter's College (Jersey City, NJ)

PENGUINS—Youngstown State University (OH)

PILOTS—Portland University (OR)

PIRATES—East Carolina University (Greenville, NC), Seton Hall University (South Orange, NJ)

PLAINSMEN—Auburn University (Auburn, AL; also called CRIMSON TIDE, TIGERS, WAR EAGLES)

POLAR BEARS—Ohio Northern University (Ada)

PRESIDENTS—Washington & Jefferson College (Washington, PA)

PRIVATEERS—New Orleans University (LA)

PURPLE ACES—University of Evansville (IN)

PURPLE EAGLES—Niagara University (NY)

QUAKERS—University of Pennsylvania (Philadelphia)

RACERS—Murray State University (Murray, KY)

RAGIN' CAJUNS—University of Southwestern Louisiana (Lafayette)

RAIDERS—Wright State University (Dayton, OH)

RAINBOW WARRIORS—University of Hawaii (Honolulu)

RAMS—Colorado State University (Fort Collins), Fordham University (New York City), University of Rhode Island (Kingston)

RAMBLERS—Loyola University (Chicago, IL)

RATTLERS—Florida A & M University (Tallahassee)

RAZORBACKS—University of Arkansas (Fayetteville)

REBELS—University of Mississippi

RED FLASH—St. Francis College (Loretto, PA)

RED FOXES—Marist College (Poughkeepsie, NY)

RED RAIDERS—Colgate University (Hamilton, NY), Texas Tech University (Lubbock)

REDBIRDS—Illinois State University (Normal)

REDMEN—St. John's University (Jamaica, NY)

REDSKINS—Miami University (Oxford, OH)

RETRIEVERS—University of Maryland (Baltimore County)

ROADRUNNERS—University of Texas (San Antonio)

ROCKETS—University of Toledo (OH), Slippery Rock College (Slippery Rock, PA)

RUNNIN' REBELS—University of Nevada (Las Vegas)

SABRINAS [THE]—Amherst College (Amherst, MA)

SAINTS—St. Lawrence University (Canton, NY), Siena College (Loudonville, NY)

SALUKIS—Southern Illinois University (Carbondale)

SCARLET KNIGHTS—Rutgers—The State University (New Brunswick, NJ)

SCOTS—Alma College (Alma, MI)

SEAHAWKS—Wagner College (Staten Island, NY)

SEMINOLES—Florida State University (Tallahassee)

SEVEN SISTERS—Barnard, Bryn Mawr, Mount Holyoke, Radcliffe, Smith, Vassar, Wellesley

SHOCKERS—Wichita State University (KS)

SIOUX—University of North Dakota (Grand Forks)

SOONERS—University of Oklahoma (Norman)

SPARTANS—Michigan State University (East Lansing), San Jose State University (San Jose, CA), University of North Carolina (Greensboro),

SPIDERS—University of Richmond (VA)

STAGS—Fairfield University (CT)

SUN DEVILS—Arizona State University (Tempe)

SYCAMORES—Indiana State University (Terre Haute)

TAR HEALS—University of North Carolina (Chapel Hill)

TECH HAWKS—Armour Institute of Technology (Chicago, IL; also called PACKERS)

TERRAPINS—University of Maryland (College Park; also called Terps)

TERRIERS—Boston University (MA)

THUNDERBIRDS—Southern Utah State (Cedar City)

THUNDERING HERD—Marshall University (Huntington, WV)

TIGERS—Auburn University (AL; also called PLAINSMEN, WAR EAGLES), Clemens University (SC), Grambling University (LA), Jackson State University (Miss), Memphis State University (TN), Princeton University (NJ), Tennessee University (Nashville, TN), Texas Southern University (Houston, TX), Towson State (MD), University of Missouri (Columbia, MS), University of the Pacific (Stockton, CA)

TITANS—California State University (Fullerton), Detroit Mercy (MI)

TOMCATS—Thiel College (Greenville, PA)

TOREROS—University of San Diego (CA)

TRIBE—William & Mary College (Williamsburg, VA)

TROJANS—University of Arkansas (Little Rock), University of Southern California (Los Angeles)

UTES—University of Utah (Salt Lake City)

VANDALS—University of Idaho (Moscow)

VIKINGS—Cleveland State University (OH), Lawrence University (Appleton, WI), Upsala College (East Orange, NJ)

VOLUNTEERS—University of Tennessee (Knoxville)

WAR EAGLES—Auburn University (Auburn, AL; also called CRIMSON TIDE, PLAINSMEN, TIGERS)

WASPS—Emory & Henry College (Emory, VA)

WILDCATS—Bethune-Cookman College (Daytona Beach, FL), Davidson College (NC), Kansas State University (Manhattan), Northwestern University (Evanston, IL),

University of Arizona (Tucson), University of Kentucky (Lexington), University of New Hampshire (Durham), Villanova University (Villanova, PA), Weber State (Ogden, UT)

WOLFPACK—North Carolina State University (Raleigh)

WOLVERINES—University of Michigan (Ann Arbor)

YELLOW JACKETS—Georgia Institute of Technology—Georgia Tech (Atlanta), University of Rochester (NY)

ZAGS—Gonzaga College (Spokane, WA; also called BULLDOGS)

ZIPS—University of Akron (OH)

PART 3

NICKNAMES OF SPECIAL EVENTS, PLAYS, AND TEAMS

A LINE—The scoring line on the New York Rangers made up of Bill Cook, BUN Cook, and Frank Boucher.

AIN'TS—A derogatory nickname for the New Orleans Saints when they ain't winning.

ALEX'S BIGGEST STRIKEOUT—With the bases loaded and two men out, Grover Cleveland Alexander came in for the Cardinals during the seventh inning of the final game of the 1926 World Series with the Yankees. Alexander struck out Tony Lazzeri and then went on to preserve the 3–2 Cardinal victory.

ALI SHUFFLE—The fancy footwork often displayed by Muhammad Ali during a boxing match.

ALLEY-OOP—These were the desperation passes from Y. A. Tittle to R. C. Owens in the waning moments of San Francisco 49er football games during the 1950s.

AMAZIN' ONES [THE]—The 1969 New York Mets. After being the worst team in baseball, the Mets beat the Atlanta Braves in three straight for the National League title and then bested the Baltimore Orioles 4–1 for the World Series.

AMEN CORNER—The eleventh hole of the Augusta National course in Georgia where golf's Masters Tournament is held each year.

AMERICA'S TEAM—The Dallas Cowboys.

AMERKS—The nickname for the New York Americans hockey team.

ANNIE OAKLEY—An Annie Oakley was a punched free ticket; thus, in baseball it was a free pass to first base (base on balls).

APPLE TREE GANG [THE]—In 1888, five golfers founded the St. Andrews Golf Club in Yonkers, New York. They received their nickname because they laid out their six-hole golf course in an apple orchard.

ARNIE'S ARMY—The fans of golfer Arnold Palmer resembled a small army following him around the golf course. They were especially vocal during his many come-from-behind victories that were won on the green with a putter. Palmer even trademarked the name and made up buttons.

ATOMIC LINE [THE]—This was the Rangers' scoring line of Cal Garner, Church Russell, and Rene Trudell. Following the atomic ending of World War II, these three were brought up from the farm team of the Rovers.

BABY BIRDS—The 1960 Baltimore Orioles; they had many young players on the roster.

BABY SPLIT—A split of 2–7 or 3–10 in Bowling.

BATTLE OF ALBERTA—After moving from Atlanta to Calgary, The Calgary Flames outscored the Edmonton Oilers 92–74 during the first season (1980–1981) in which there were two NHL teams in the Canadian Province of Alberta. Since then, there have been other Battles of Alberta.

BATTLE OF NEW YORK—The series between the New York Islanders and the New York Rangers for hockey's Patrick Division championship. In 1988–1989, the Rangers won with only one goal deciding three of the five games.

BATTLE OF THE BILLS [THE]—The ongoing battle between LITTLE BILL Johnson and BIG BILL Tilden from 1915 to 1920.

BATTLE OF THE DECADE—In their 1986 meeting, Notre Dame chose to run out the clock with eighty-four seconds remaining after tying Michigan State 10–10.

BATTLE OF THE LONG COUNT [THE]—The return bout between Jack Dempsey and Gene Tunney on September 27, 1927. (Tunney had won a ten-round decision in the first fight of the championship.) In the seventh round, Dempsey floored Tunney. Stunned, Tunney sat on the canvas with a glove hanging onto the middle rope. Dempsey stood over him, so the referee did not begin the count until Dempsey had retreated to a neutral corner. Instead of only ten seconds, a total of seventeen seconds elapsed. Apparently, it was enough for Tunney to recover. The boxers, however, had very different perceptions about what was to become the number-one topic of boxing fans' discussions. Tunney maintained that he hadn't needed the extra time. And Dempsey later said, "It was the greatest break I ever got. It was probably time I stopped fighting." See THE MANASSA MAULER and THE FIGHTING MARINE.

BIG BAD BRUINS—The nickname of 1970–1971 Boston Bruins. The team scored a record 399 goals (Esposito had a record seventy-six) and a record 695 assists (Orr had a record 102) to win a record 57 games. However, they lost the East Division series to Montreal 4–3. See BOBBY AND PHIL AND THEM.

BIG FOUR [THE]—The four members of Philadelphia's Belmont Cricket Club—Louise Allderdice, Margarette Ballard, Ellen "Nellie" Hansell, and Bertha "Birdie" Townsend—who in 1886 began a tournament of women's singles, women's doubles, and mixed doubles. By the following year the tournament awarded a trophy to "the female champion of the United States," and would later develop into the women's national championship.

BIG RED MACHINE—The Cincinnati Reds in the early 1970s. Managed by Sparky Anderson, the team featured Pete Rose, Joe Morgan, Johnny Bench, Tony Perez, George Foster, Lee May, and Ken Griffey.

BIGSIDE—This was the nickname of football at Rugby because it was played on Old Bigside field.

BIRTHPLACE OF BASEBALL (THE)—According to one legend, Abner Doubleday invented the game in Cooperstown, New York. Most baseball historians, however, think the honor goes to Alexander J. Cartwright in Hoboken, New Jersey. Cooperstown, of course, is where the Baseball Hall of Fame is located.

BLACK-AND-BLUE DIVISION—The National Football Conference's Central Division in the NFL.

BLACK BETSY—The name SHOELESS JOE Jackson gave to his bat; it was also the name of the bat that BABE Ruth used for three years.

BLACK SOX SCANDAL (THE)—In the 1919 World Series, the Chicago White Sox besmirched their reputation when, favored to win, they dropped the Series five games to three. (To stay in step with the popularity of baseball, the series had been increased that year from seven to the best of nine.) It was feared that the reputation of baseball would be dragged down, too. The next year it was learned that gamblers had contacted players on the White Sox to "lay down." Even though SHOE-LESS JOE Jackson had batted .375 (and possesses the third-highest lifetime average at .356), he and seven others were banned from baseball for life by the new commissioner of baseball, Judge Landis. See CZAR OF BASEBALL.

BLEACHER BUMS—Fans of the Chicago Cubs.

BLEU, BLANC, ROUGE (BLUE, WHITE, RED)—A nickname of the Montreal Canadiens, acquired because of the colors of their uniform. They're also called THE FLYING FRENCHMEN and THE HABS.

BLITZ—In football, a defensive rush on the quarterback; also called a RED DOG.

BLOODY MONDAY—This is what football at Harvard was called three hundred years ago. The game was played between the freshmen and sophomores and the goal was, in the words of a contemporary Philip Stickles: "to dash him against the heart with their elbows, to butt him under the short ribs and peck him on his neck, with a hundred other such murthering devices."

BLOOPER BOWL—Baltimore over Dallas 16–13 in a mistake-riddled Super Bowl V.

BLUE-SHIRTED BOMBERS OF LESTER PATRICK (THE)—The 1940s New York Rangers team, and the last Rangers team to win the Stanley Cup.

BLUESHIRTS—The New York Rangers (for their jerseys).

BOBBY AND PHIL AND THEM—The 1970 Boston Bruins. Bobby Orr tapped in the Stanley Cup-winning goal in overtime. Phil Esposito was always in the thick of things in the slot (the ice from in front of the goal to the hashmark). The other Bruins were role players who followed their parts to a T. "They were hockey's GASHOUSE GANG," said coach Harry Sinden. "There was incredible confidence and togetherness on and off the ice." And most of the players had nicknames: Acer (Garnet Bailey), Buggsy (Don Awrey), Cash (Wayne Cashman), CHEESY (Gerry Cheevers), Chief (Johnny Bucyk), EJ (Eddie Johnston), ESPO (Phil Esposito), Half-ton (Dallas Smith), Hodgie (Ken Hodge), Johnny Pie (John McKenzie), Swoop (Wayne Carlton), and Turk (Derek Sanderson). The cohesion of this team was demonstrated at a reunion party held twenty years later. Every single player showed up for the four-day celebration. "I think we had more fun at the reunion," said Esposito, "than we had at the championship party."

BOLO—What welterweight champion Kid Gavilan called his best punch.

BOUNDING BILLY—This was the nickname for the golf ball developed by Coburn Haskell and Bertram Work. (Earlier, the ball had been the gutta percha—a solid ball of tree sap.) When Haskell and Work, an engineer at B. F. Goodrich, first wound rubber bands around a hard rubber core, the outside of the tree sap made the ball unpredictable in its flight—making it a Bounding Billy. However, when the pebbled surface was later added, it flew truer.

BOWERY AMERICANS [THE]—The *other* hockey team in New York. They contrasted sharply with the Rangers, also known as THE PARK AVENUE RANGERS for all their high-class fans.

BREAD LINE [THE]—This scoring line (center Neil Colville and brother Mac Colville at right wing, and left wing Alex Shibicky) for the Depression-era New York Rangers.

BRICKYARD [THE]—The Indianapolis Speedway where the Indy 500 is held.

BRIDEGROOMS—A Brooklyn baseball team in the 1890s. The nickname was because there were so many married men on the team.

BROAD STREET BULLIES—The hard-playing and hard-checking Philadelphia Flyers of the seventies won two straight Stanley Cups in 1974 and 1975. (Broad Street was a main thoroughfare in Philadelphia.) They were led by captain Bobby Clarke who once said, "All I ever wanted to do was play hockey and I just played it the way I thought it had to be played." They were also called Mad Squad and Freddie's Philistines.

BROADWAY BLUE SHIRTS—The New York Rangers.

BROADWAY BLUES—Another nickname for the New York Rangers. The name has to do with the location of where they played and their uniform and not the fact that they haven't won a Stanley Cup since 1940.

BRONCOMANIA—Refers to the intensity of feeling exhibited by Denver Broncos fans for their team; it is said that even lawbreakers stop what they're doing when the Broncos are playing.

BROOKLYN DODGER SYMPHONY [THE]—Dodger radio play-by-play man Red Barber nicknamed this group of musician-fans who played at Ebbets Field from 1937 to 1957. The specialty of this self-styled jazz group was to play a special song to razz a strikeout victim. When the visiting player would take his seat back in the dugout, the bass drummer would sound his defeat.

BROSSARD'S SWAMP—The infield playing area of the Chicago White Sox. Gene Broussard (1918–1998) was the groundskeeper at Comiskey Park and he kept the infield grass wet to slow down ground balls. It was also said of Broussard that he used loose dirt or tightly packed soil to help base runners, depending on whether the White Sox lineup had a speed advantage over the opposition.

BRUISE BROTHERS [THE]—Dave Corzine, Paul Griffin, Mark Olberding, and Kevin Restani formed a tough front line for the San Antonio Spurs in the early 1980s.

BULLDOG LINE [THE]—The New York Rangers line of Walter Tkaczuk, Steve Vickers, and Billy Fairbairn.

BULL RING [THE]—A place along the concourse of the Toronto's Maple Leaf Garden where bookies gathered to make bets on hockey games.

BUM OF THE MONTH CLUB—In 1941, Joe Louis defended his heavyweight title six times in six months. His opponents, who were all given this nickname, did not provide much of a contest.

BUMS—A vociferous fan sitting right behind home plate had the habit of shouting this epithet at his team, and the name stuck like a foul ball hit right back at the screen.

BUSBY'S BABES—Sir Matthew Busby was a Scottish footballer (soccer player) and president of the Manchester United Association Football team. His young team was known throughout Europe as Busby's Babes. In February 1958 when the plane in which the soccer team was traveling crashed on takeoff in Munich, Germany, eight of the starting players were killed.

BUTCH CASSIDY AND THE SUNDANCE KID—Running backs Jim Kiick and Larry Csonka were a one-two punch for the powerful Miami Dolphins teams that won the Super Bowls in 1972 and 1973. The name was from a popular movie of the day starring Paul Newman and Robert Redford.

CALAMITY JANE—Nickname given by Bobby Jones to his putter. Although it had been broken in two places, Calamity Jane helped Jones win both the British and American championships in 1920.

CALLED SHOT [THE]—Legend has it that with two strikes in a tie game of the 1932 World Series, Babe Ruth pointed toward the center field bleachers and hit the next pitch into that very spot.

CAMILLIA—The 485-yard number ten hole on the Augusta National Golf Club that runs through a corridor of pines and camellias.

CANVASBACKS—Football players were once called this because they wore sleeveless vests made from canvas.

CARDIAC CARDINALS—The 1975 and 1976 St. Louis Cardinals specialized in coming back in the closing seconds of football games. Quarterback Jim Hart would throw a bomb to the ever-elusive Mel Gray, or Terry Metcalf would break away for a long gain to give their fans one more heart-stopping ending.

CARDIAC KIDS (THE)—The 1968 University of Southern California football team that pulled several games out in the last few heart-stopping seconds.

CATCH (THE)—In the 1981 National Football Conference championship game, the Dallas Cowboys were leading the San Francisco 49ers, 27–21, with 4:51 left. Joe Montana moved his 49er team the length of the field with sweeps and short passes. Within striking distance of the goal line, the wide receiver Dwight Clark ran a hook pattern and drifted near the end zone as the secondary receiver. Montana threw a pass that was designed either to sail out of bounds or to be a high catch. Clark leaped high and pulled it down. San Francisco hung on to win, 28–27, and then went on to win the Super Bowl.

CAT'S TRAP—A small sand trap on the thirteenth hole of the Old Course at St. Andrews.

CHANG GANG—The Chang brothers of tennis—Michael and Carl. Michael is a tennis champion with a powerful serve that has been clocked at 120 mph, and Carl is Michael's coach. The term is a play on the familiar Chain Gang.

CHARLIE O—The mule that Charlie Finley would tie up beyond the outfield fence when the As were in Kansas City. Finley was always trying to think up something to stir up interest among fans whether it was fireworks after home-team home runs or coming up with the nickname Catfish for Hall of Fame pitcher Jim Hunter.

COBI—The cubist cartoon dog, official mascot of the 1992 Barcelona Summer Olympics. The name is derived from the Barcelona Olympic Organizing Committee (COOB). He was designed by Javier Mariscal, who said of his creation: "COBI is the first Olympic mascot to be sad, to be crying, to be depressed. They're usually congealed with a smile, but this guy has a sly grin. He's like a chameleon—he can be a baby, a poor little boy, a druggie, a guy who is cleaning your car windows, an athlete, an idealist carrying the Olympic flag, or a disillusioned youth."

COFFIN—Three sand traps on the thirteenth hole of the Old Course at St. Andrews.

CURSE OF MULDOON—In 1941, a sportswriter wrote that Pete Muldoon, the first coach of the Chicago Black Hawks, had said when he was fired that the team would never finish in first place. The "Curse" held true until 1966–1967.

CUTTY SARK—The nickname for Tug McGraw's fastball.

DAFFINESS BOYS—The 1926 Brooklyn Dodgers. Babe Herman, one of the daffiest of them all, once stole second when the bases were loaded.

DASHING DONS—Don Geyer and Don Heap of football.

DAZZLING DEANS [THE]—Brothers Paul "DAFFY" Dean and Jay Hanna "DIZZY" Dean who were pitchers for the St. Louis Cardinals' GASHOUSE GANG.

DEATH VALLEY—Left center field in Yankee Stadium is 457 feet to the outfield wall. Somewhere else it might be a hit, but in the HOUSE THAT RUTH BUILT it's a can of corn (a sure out).

DEM BUMS—The Brooklyn Dodgers.

DERRICK DOLLS—Cheerleaders for the old Houston Oilers.

DIAMOND GALS—The women of the All-American Girls Baseball League. Like Rosie the Riveter in the industrial sector, these players were a means to keeping up morale during World War II.

DIVE OF DEATH [THE]—A reverse three-and-a-half dive off the three-meter platform. Several divers have been killed attempting this difficult dive. Greg Louganis used it on his tenth dive to win the gold medal at the 1988 Olympic Games.

DOOMSDAY DEFENSE [THE]—The defensive unit of the Dallas Cowboys from the mid-1960s through the early 1970s featured Bob Lilly, George Andrie, Jethro Pugh, and Willie Townes in the line; Mel Renfro, Cornell Green, and Mike Gaechter in the backfield. In 1968, only two touchdowns were scored on the ground against the Dallas Doomsday Defense.

DOWNTOWN CONNECTORS—The Atlanta Flames' line made up of Eric Vail, Willi Plett, and Tom Lysiak.

DREAM GAME THAT FINALLY CAME [THE]—The 1983 Mideast finals between Kentucky and Louisville.

DREAM TEAM [THE]—The 1992 U.S. Olympic basketball team, featuring NBA professionals, Earvin "MAGIC" Johnson, Patrick Ewing, Larry Bird, Michael "AIR" Jordan, "SIR CHARLES" Barkley, Scottie Pippin, Karl "THE MAILMAN" Malone, Clyde "The Glide" Drexler, David Robinson, John Saxton, and Christian Laettner. To no one's surprise, they won the gold medal.

DUTCH 200—Alternating strikes and spares in bowling.

DYNAMITE LINE (THE)—The 1929 Boston Bruins scoring line of Dit Clapper, Cooney Weiland, and Dutch Gainor. The Dynamite Line led the Bruins to the 1929 Stanley Cup.

ELECTRIC COMPANY (THE)—The offensive linemen on the Buffalo Bills who blocked for THE JUICE (O. J. Simpson).

FAB FIVE—The five freshmen on the 1991–1992 Michigan State Wolverines who went all the way to the NCAA finals before losing to Duke University.

FABULOUS FORUM—Jack Kent Cooke's arena in Inglewood, California.

FAMILY (THE)—The 1979 Pittsburgh Pirates led by Willie "POP" Stargell. The team's theme song was "We Are Family" sung by Sister Sledge.

FANCY (THE)—This nickname for boxing was first used during England's golden era of boxing in the 1800s.

FASTNET (THE)—A 605-mile sailing race that goes from the Isle of Wright to Fastnet Rock off southwest Ireland. The return leg goes to Plymouth.

FEARSOME FOURSOME—The Detroit Lions' defensive line of the early 1960s made up of Roger Brown, Alex Karras, Darris McGord, and Sam Williams.

FEARSOME FOURSOME—The defensive line of the Los Angeles Rams from 1963 to 1969. This front four were fearsome for the other teams. Lamar Lundy was a 6' 7", 260-pound right end; Roosevelt Grier was a 6' 5", 300-pound right tackle (in 1967, the injured Rosey was replaced by Roger Brown); Merlin Olson a 275-pound left tackle; and Deacon Jones a 6' 5", 250-pound left end. As a unit they were superb. Grier (and later Brown) stopped up the middle; Lundy helped out the others; Olson and Jones took the chances. In 1967, the Fearsome Foursome helped the Rams to an 11–1–2 season. "The real game is in the pit," said Deacon Jones.

FERNANDOMANIA—A word to describe the excitement over Los Angeles Dodger pitcher Fernando Valenzuela as he won the Cy Young Award in 1981 at the age of twenty. Fernandomania continued in the 1980s as Fernando went on to win 141 major-league victories.

FIDDLIN' FIVE—The 1958 Kentucky basketball team made up of Ed Beck, Johnny Cox, John Crigler, Vernon Hatton, and Adrian Smith, and winners of the NCAA tournament. Coach Adolph (Baron) Rupp complained that his team too often fiddled around 'til the end of the game when they would finally get serious and win by only a point or two.

FIGHT OF THE CENTURY [THE]—Joe Frazier versus Muhammad Ali on March 8, 1971. The fifteenth round ended in a decision for Frazier and both fighters needing medical attention. (Many fights are billed as Fights of the Century; this fight, however, may have been.)

FIREWAGON HOCKEY—The brand of hockey played by the Montreal Canadiens. Also called THE FLYING FRENCHMEN, they were known for their fast skating, as if they were rushing to put out a fire.

FIRING SQUAD [THE]—The top scorers on the New York Rangers in 1955–1956: Andy Bathgate, Wally Hergesheimer, Danny Lewicki, and Dean Prentice.

FLYING FRENCHMEN [THE]—A nickname for the Montreal Canadiens. In the early years, only French-Canadians played for the Montreal team. In the early 1900s, there were Jack "SPEED MERCHANT" Laviolette and Didier "CANNONBALL" Pitre. And in the 1930s, the team had many fast skaters, such as Johnny "BLACK CAT" Gagnon, Aurel Joliet, Wildor Larochelle, Alfred "PIT" Lepine, and Howie "THE STRATFORD STREAK" Morenz.

FLYING KILOMETER or K.L. [Kilometro Lanciato]—A course for speed skiing located on the Plateau Rosa glacier between Cervinia, Italy, and Zermatt, Switzerland.

FLYING WEDGE [THE]—This V of linemen with the ball carrier behind was the invention of chess expert Lorin Deland. Harvard first used it in a game with Yale in 1892; in 1894, it was outlawed.

FOOTBALL CAPITAL OF THE SOUTH—Two places claim this title: Birmingham, Alabama and New Orleans, Louisiana.

FOOTBALL'S LONGEST DAY—The AFC playoff game between the Kansas City Chiefs and the Miami Dolphins on December 25, 1971. The game took eighty-two minutes and forty seconds (a NFL record) before Miami won 27–24.

FORT LANDRY—During his tenure as coach of the Dallas Cowboys, Tom Landry maintained a security conscious training camp at Thousand Oaks, California.

FOSBURY FLOP [THE]—This is the headfirst, faceup method that high jumpers use nowadays to clear the high jump bar. The high jumper seems to flop over the bar and collapse into the pit. Developed by Dick Fosbury, this technique has replaced the Western and Eastern rolls popular at one time and is now used by all world-class high jumpers. Fosbury originated the flop in 1963 during a high school meet his sophomore year in Grants Pass, Oregon. "As the bar got higher," remembered Fosbury, "I began to lean back further and further, making my back more parallel to the ground." By his sophomore year in college, Fosbury had set a record at Oregon State University of 6' 10". And at the Olympic trials the next year he jumped 7' 3" to qualify for the team. The stage was set for Mexico City. On October 20, 1968, Fosbury flopped his way to the gold medal at the Olympic Games. Few people in the audience had ever seen this headfirst, face-up way of high jumping. His jump of 7' 4¼" was both an American and Olympic record. But more importantly, it set the track world on its ear. High jumping has not been the same since. Now, all the world-class high jumpers use the Fosbury Flop.

FOUR MUSKETEERS—Four Frenchmen known as the Four Musketeers (Jean Bototra, Jacques Brugnon, Henri Cochet, and Rene Lacoste) kept the Davis Cup in France from 1927–1932.

FRENCH CONNECTION (THE)—The Buffalo Sabres' scoring line of Gil Perreault, Rick Martin, and Rene Robert from the early to mid-1970s. They helped lead the Sabres to the Stanley Cup in 1974–1975. (The Philadelphia Flyers defeated the Sabres in the first all-expansion team final.)

GAG LINE—In 1972, the New York Rangers featured a G-A-G (goal-a-game) Line with Rod Gilbert (forty-two goals), Jean Ratelle (forty-six goals), and Vic Hadfield (fifty goals).

GANG OF FOUR (THE)—The four defensive backs—Ronnie Lott, Eric Wright, Carlton Williamson, and Dwight Hicks—on the 1981 San Francisco 49ers were tough on offenses.

GARRISON FINISH—In 1882, Edward "Snapper" Garrison whipped his horse, Montana, down the stretch to come from behind and win the Suburban. It was Garrison's trademark finish, one he used over and over during his career. Nowadays, the expression a Garrison Finish can be used for any come-from-behind victory.

GASHOUSE GANG—The nickname was started by Leo Durocher who said the St. Louis Cardinals of the 1930s were just a bunch of gashouse players. They played with such verve and got their uniforms so dirty that it "appeared as if they worked in a gashouse and not a ballpark." Members of the Gashouse Gang were TEX Carleton, RIPPER Collins, SPUD Davis, DAFFY Dean, DIZZY Dean, LEO THE LIP Durocher, CHICK Fullis, WILD BILL Hallahan, WILD ELK OF THE WASATCH Heusser, PEPPER Martin, DUCKY Medwick, and DAZZY Vance. The team was managed by GABBY Street, who was replaced by Frankie Frisch, the FORDHAM FLASH, midway through the 1934 season.

GASHOUSE GANG ON ICE—The Toronto Maple Leafs of the 1930s were a hard-playing, happy-go-lucky team made up of the KID LINE, ACE Bailey, BALDY Cotton, HAP Day, and RED Horner.

GASOLINE ALLEY—The area where the garages are in which the crews of mechanics ply their magic to keep the racecars competitive.

GERELA'S GUERILLAS—Fans in the end zone who tried to catch the kicks of Pittsburgh's place kicker Ray Gerela.

GINGER BEER—The difficult sixth hole on The Old Course at St. Andrews got its name from a man called Old Daw who sold refreshments there.

GINTS—The New York Giants. Originally, this nickname referred to the baseball team that played at the Polo Grounds in the Bronx. (The word is a phonetic spelling for the Bronx pronunciation of Giants.) Now it is sometimes applied to the Giants football team that plays in New Jersey; occasionally, it is spelled Jints (for New Jersey).

GO-GO SOX—The 1959 White Sox won the pennant by ninety-four games, their first in forty years. Although as a team they batted only .250, they took the extra base, executed the hit-and-run to perfection, and did whatever it took to win. The team was paced by the swift Luis Aparicio who hit .332, stole fifty-six bases, and scored ninety-eight runs.

GODS [THE]—The peanut gallery at a boxing match in France.

GOLD DUST TWINS [THE]—Byron Nelson and Jug McSpaden. During the forties, it seemed that if Nelson didn't win the golf tournament, then McSpaden did. In 1949, for example, Nelson won nineteen tournaments, and McSpaden finished second to Nelson thirteen of those times. In a 1984 interview McSpaden said, "I can honestly say that I beat every great golfer of my time head to head—Hogan, Snead, Sarazen, Nelson, all of them."

GOLDEN AGE OF SPORTS [THE]—The 1920s boasted such athletic stars as Rogers Hornsby and BABE Ruth in baseball, Jack Dempsey and Gene Tunney in boxing, RED Grange and The Four Horsemen in football, Bobby Jones and Walter Hagen in golf, Bill Tilden and Helen Wills in tennis. It was a heady time indeed for the sports-minded.

GOLDEN ERA—The halcyon days of the 1960s for hockey goaltending when the NHL featured goalies Johnny Bower, Glenn Hall, Jacques Plante, Terry Sawchuck, and Gump Worsley.

GOLDEN OUTFIELD [THE]—The Boston Red Sox outfield made up of Duffy Lewis, Harry Hooper, and Tris Speaker from 1910–1915. Hooper and Speaker were later inducted into the Hall of Fame.

GOLDIE SHUFFLE [THE]—The victory dance that hockey's Bill Goldsworthy (1944–) went into whenever he scored a goal.

GRAND SLAM—This term is borrowed from contract bridge (and means winning all the tricks in one's hand). The Grand Slam in tennis is for winning the four major tennis championships in one calendar year: the Australian Open, the French Open, the U.S. Open, and Wimbleton. The Grand Slam of golf is for winning the four major golf championships consecutively: the U.S. Open, the Masters, the British Open, and the PGA Championship. (Originally the term was used in 1930 to honor Bobby Jones's achievement of winning the U.S. Amateur, the U.S. Open, the British Amateur, and the British Open.)

GREAT RACE [THE]—Detroit fell one game short of catching the Boston Red Sox in the pennant race of 1967.

GREAT TRIUMVIRATE [THE]—John Henry (J. H.) Taylor, Harry Vardon, and James Braid—three golfers who totally dominated the golfing scene from 1894–1914. Together they won the Open Championship sixteen times.

GREENBERG GARDENS—This was a section of Pittsburgh Pirates' ballpark where Hank Greenberg hit home runs during the twilight of his career.

GREEN UNIT—This was a crack group of Soviet hockey players that played for the Soviet national team. By 1989–1990, all were playing in the NHL: Sergei Makarov with Calgary, Viacheslav Fetisov and Alexei Kasatonov with New Jersey, and Vladimir Krutov and Igor Larionov with Vancouver.

GRETZKY—This name refers to shooting a ninety–nine on the golf course to break the magical 100 barrier because that is Wayne Gretzky's number on his jersey.

GREY CUP—This is both the trophy and the championship game of the Canadian Football League. The trophy was given by a Governor General of Canada, Albert Henry George Grey.

GRUESOME TWOSOME [THE]—After the L. A. Rams' FEARSOME FOURSOME of the 1960s, the defensive line in 1980 featured Fred Dryer and Jack Youngblood and they were given this title.

H BOYS—Hinkle, Herber, and Hutson of the Green Bay Packers. During the 1940s, Clarke Hinkle was one of the big linemen to provide protection, and Arnie Herber was the accurate quarterback who threw touchdowns to elusive super end Don Hutson.

HABS [THE]—This nickname for the Montreal Canadiens comes from *habitant,* French for "person of the land." (*Habitant* referred to the first settlers along the St. Lawrence River; so, sometimes the nickname is extended to the Habitants.) In the beginning, only French Canadians played for the Montreal hockey club. That's why the French spelling of *Canadiens* is used.

HAIL MARY—The fifty-yard touchdown pass from Roger Staubach to Drew Pearson in the closing seconds of the 1975 playoff game with the Minnesota Vikings that won the game for the Dallas Cowboys. Now the term applies to many a long, last-minute desperation pass. The name comes from the prayer that begins "Hail, Mary."

HALFWAY HOUSE [THE]—Seattle Mariners' manager Rene Lachemann used castoff players in the early 1980s who were trying to get their careers back on track.

HART MEMORIAL TROPHY—The MVP award to a player in the NHL was named for Cecil Hart, a one-time coach and manager of the Montreal Canadiens.

HARVEY'S WALLBANGERS—Manager Harvey Kuenn's Milwaukee Brewers' lineup of heavy hitters who won the 1982 pennant.

HEARTBREAK HILL—The hill that makes or breaks many a runner in the Boston Marathon.

HEAVENLY TWINS [THE]—Hugh Duffy (1866–1954) and Tommy McCarthy (1863–1922), two out-fielders for the Boston Braves in the 1890s.

HELL—A bunker on the fourteenth hole of the Old Course at St. Andrews.

HEM LINE—The scoring line of the Chicago Black Hawks: Bobby Hull, Phil Esposito, Chico Maki. The nickname came from the first letter of each of their last names.

HESITATION PITCH—SATCHEL Paige often used this pitch with a hitch to throw the timing of the batters off.

HESTON MASSACRE—In 1905, Billy Heston, a running back from the University of Michigan, suffered a severe break of his leg in only his second professional game, ending his career.

HILL [THE]—A bunker on the eleventh hole of the Old Course at St. Andrews. Among its victims was the defending champion in the 1933 British Open, Gene Sarazen. It took him three shots to escape.

HITLESS WONDERS—The 1906 Chicago White Sox, winners of the American League. Although they had only a .230 team batting average, their pitchers kept them on top with a total of thirty-two shutouts in their ninety-three wins. The Hitless Wonders also won the World Series, beating the hard-hitting Cubs, who set the major-league record for wins with 116. It's another example of good pitching beats good hitting.

HOLLY—The number eighteen hole of the Augusta National Golf Club.

HOLY GRAIL—The Stanley Cup of hockey.

HOT LINE [THE]—At one time this was the offensive line of the Detroit Lions.

HOT LINE [THE]—The scoring line for the Winnipeg Jets made up of Anders Hedberg, Bobby Hull, and Ulf Nilsson.

HOT STOVE LEAGUE [THE]—During the long winter, there are some baseball enthusiasts who field imaginary baseball teams to play imaginary baseball games around an imaginary potbellied stove.

HOUSE OF PAIN [THE]—What the Houston Oilers sometimes called their stadium.

HOUSE THAT RUTH BUILT [THE]—This is what sportswriter Fred Lieb called the $2.5 million three-tiered Yankee Stadium that opened on April 18, 1923 during the heyday of BABE Ruth.

ICE BOWL—The Green Bay Packers versus the Dallas Cowboys.

IGLOO [THE]—The Civic Arena in Pittsburgh where the hockey team plays has this nickname because of its shape. The nickname Igloo led to the team receiving its nickname Penguins.

IMPOSSIBLE DREAM [THE]—The 1967 pennant winning season for the Boston Red Sox. The year was christened the Impossible Dream (from the hit song from the musical about Don Quixote). The winning of a pennant by the Red Sox seemed to be impossible, since in 1966, the team had finished ninth with a 72–90 record, twenty-six games behind the Baltimore Orioles. When the 1967 season opened, the odds were 100–1 against the Sox taking the pennant. Led by Carl Yastremski, who won the Triple Crown, the Red Sox clinched the pennant on the final day of the season.

INDY—The Indianapolis 500.

INGO'S BINGO—Ingemar Johansson's knockout punch.

IRISH WHALES—Around the turn of the century, there was a tradition of New York City policemen participating in the weight events of track and field. The policemen, who were mostly Irish, bore the weight of being referred to as the Irish Whales.

IRON BYRON—The United States Golf Association's mechanical golfer used to standardize golf balls. A golf ball hit by this machine cannot travel farther than 280 yards.

ISLES [THE]—The New York Islanders.

JILLS—The Buffalo Bills' cheerleaders.

JINTS—The New York Giants in local parlance.

JUNIOR CIRCUIT [THE]—The American League.

JUNKYARD DOGS [THE]—This is what the Chicago Bears called their defense during their 1985-1986 Super Bowl season. It was after Jim Croce's song about Bad Leroy Brown.

JUNKYARD DOGS [THE]—The University of Georgia's football team.

KAMIKAZE KIDS [THE]—University of Oregon basketball teams in the early 1970s always seemed to be scrambling for loose balls.

KARDIAC KIDS—A nickname for the Cleveland Browns who staged several comebacks during the 1979 season.

KATZENJAMMER KIDS—Woody English, Augie Galan, and Bill Jurges of the Chicago Cubs received their nickname from the popular comic strip because of all the practical jokes and pranks these ballplayers pulled off in the 1930s.

KEYSTONE—A nickname for second base because like the keystone at the top of the arch that holds it together, much of the action swirls around the bag at second. The keystone combination is the second baseman and shortstop executing a double play.

KID LINE—The Edmonton Oilers' scoring line of Martin Gelinas, Adam Graves, and Joe Murphy in 1988–1989. The next year the Kid Line of Graves, Murphy, and Mark Lamb paced the Oilers to the Stanley Cup.

KID LINE (THE)—The Toronto Maple Leafs' scoring line consisting of center Joe Primeau and wings Charlie Conacher and Harvey "BUSHER" Jackson. In the 1931–1932 season, the kids were the first, second, and fourth highest scorers in the NHL.

KILLER B'S (THE)—The Miami Dolphins' defense (years of Super Bowl XVII and XIX) was made up of players whose names began with *B:* Baumhower, Betters, the Blackwood brothers, Bokamper, Bowser, and Brudzinski.

KILLER TOMATOES (THE)—The Santa Clara defense under football coach Ron DeMonner. The color of the uniforms was cardinal, and a cult film of the day was *Attack of the Killer Tomatoes.*

KINER'S KORNER—Outfield bleachers in Forbes Field where Ralph Kiner hit a lot of home runs.

KITTEN BALL—A nickname for softball.

KRAUT LINE (THE)—The Boston Bruins' scoring line of center Bobby Bauer and wings Milt Schmidt and Woody (or Porky) Dumart. They helped win the Stanley Cup in 1939 and 1941. In February 1942, all three were drafted into the Canadian military.

LADY TECHSTERS—Louisiana Tech, winner of the first NCAA title in women's basketball.

LAST GREAT RACE ON EARTH—The Iditarod Sled Dog Race run from Anchorage to Nome, Alaska. (The race has been held annually since 1973 in honor of the relay that rushed serum to Nome during a 1925 epidemic of diphtheria.) The winning musher of the 1993 race, Jeff King, set a new course record of ten days and fifteen hours for the 1,162-mile journey.

LAUNCHING PAD (THE)—Atlanta Fulton County Stadium. Many a home run is hit in this ballpark.

LAURA'S LEGIONS—Because of her beauty and skill, The "golden girl" of golf Laura Baugh (1955–) not only had fans following her around the golf course but also advertisers along Madison Avenue pursuing her for endorsements. Laura's Legions were legendary. Baugh began to play golf at the age of two. Winning her way up through Peewee golf to the Juniors, Baugh won the U. S. Women's Amateur at the age of sixteen—the youngest ever. Two years later when she turned pro, she was named Rookie Golfer of the Year.

LEE'S FLEAS—The fans of Lee "SUPERMEX" Travino.

LEICESTER HOAX [THE]—The bout in 1830 between Simon Byrne, the challenger, and Jem Ward, the champion. Ward was so easily beaten (and so much money exchanged hands) that he was dropped from bareknuckles boxing for a time. See THE BLACK DIAMOND.

LENG-LEN TRAIL A WINDING—The fans of Suzanne Lenglen who would form long lines to get into the stadiums to see her play. The nickname was a take-off of a popular song in the 1920s.

LEW ALCINDOR RULE—Before the 1967–1968 season, a rule was put into effect against dunking the ball in college basketball. (Alcindor had first noticed his ability to reach the rim during eighth grade. "One day in a game I jumped up and touched the rim," he once said. "I was amazed. I stayed around after the game was over and kept jumping up and touching it. I did it thirty times in a row just to prove to myself that I could do it.") The Lew Alcindor Rule was established to stop this dominating center who had led UCLA to a 30–0 season the year before while scoring 29.7 points a game.

LEW-CLA—A takeoff on Lew Alcindor's (now Kareem Abdul-Jabbar) alma mater of UCLA. During Lew's freshman year (they were not eligible for varsity sports then), Alcindor led the Bruin freshmen to a 75–60 victory over the varsity. As one sportswriter put it: "UCLA is number one in the country and number two on its own campus." His sophomore year, UCLA was 30–0 and winner of the NCAA championship. His junior year they were 47–0 when they lost to Houston 71–69. But when LEW-CLA later met Houston and the Big E (Elvin Hayes) in the NCAA playoffs, they won 101–69. UCLA won the final, too, beating North Carolina 78–55. "This is the best team of all time," said Dean Smith, the North Carolina coach. "And Alcindor is the best player who ever played college basketball." His senior year, Lew Alcindor changed his name to Kareem Abdul-Jabbar, but his winning ways continued.

LILY PAD SHOT [THE]—In the 1930 U.S. Open in Interlachen, Minnesota, Bobby Jones hit his second shot on the par five, 485-yard ninth hole right into the pond in front of the green. Onlookers said it caromed off a lily pad and came to rest near the hole. "It would have meant a six or a seven and would have cost me the tournament," said Jones later. "It was perhaps the luckiest shot I ever played in a championship." See THE KING OF THE LINKS.

LION'S MOUTH—A sand trap on the Old Course at St. Andrews.

LITTLE BEN—Ben Crenshaw's putter.

LITTLE MEN OF IRON—This was the nickname of the Montreal AAA led by Dickie Boon and Jimmy Gardner, the team that defeated the Winnipeg Victorias to win the Stanley Cup in 1902.

LOBOGATE—New Mexico Lobos' version of the Watergate scandal. The grades and credits of certain basketball players were found to be bogus.

LONG ISLAND LIGHTING COMPANY—The scoring line of Brian Trottier, Billy Harris, and Clark Gillies during The New York Islander's heyday in the 1980s. They were also called Trio Grande.

LOUIE AND BOUIE SHOW—Louis Orr and Roosevelt Bouie were basketball players at Louisville.

LUMBER COMPANY (THE)—The Pittsburgh Pirates of the 1980s with Willie "POP" Stargell, Dave "COBRA" Parker, et al.

LUNCH PAIL ATHLETIC CLUB—The Boston Bruins of the late 1970s. These "lunch pail" teams consisted of veterans who had knocked around from team to team rather than high-priced players.

M & M BOYS (THE)—Roger Maris & Mickey Mantle were mighty sweet to have in the Yankees' lineup. In 1961, The M & M Boys hit 115 home runs. Maris socked sixty-one homers to break Babe Ruth's one-season record established in 1927. Mantle who had been neck and neck most of the season knocked out fifty-four.

MACKMEN—Connie Mack's Philadelphia As. See THE OLD MAN and THE TALL TACTICIAN.

MARAMEN—The New York Giants when they were owned by Wellington Mara.

MARDI GRAS—The fake turf on the field of the Louisiana Superdome in New Orleans.

MARINO CORPS (THE)—The fans of Miami's quarterback Dan Marino.

MARKS BROTHERS (THE)—Mark Clayton and Mark Duper were two wide receivers on the Miami Dolphins in the 1980s. The name, of course, is a punning allusion to the great comedy team—The Marx Brothers.

MATCH OF THE CENTURY—Tennis match between Helen Wills (U.S.) and Suzanne Lenglen (France) in 1926. Lenglen won. Unfortunately, in a world of hype and overkill, almost every important tennis or boxing match today gets labeled as the "Match of the Century."

McHALE'S ARMY—The fans of Celtic forward Kevin McHale in the Boston Garden.

MECCA OF BOXING—Madison Square Garden in New York City.

MENDOZA LINE [THE]—Named for Mario Mendoza, a shortstop with the Pirates, whose batting average hovered around .200 during his five years in Pittsburgh. A major leaguer who sinks below the Mendoza Line may just wind up in the minors.

MILLION DOLLAR BABIES [THE]—Donny Anderson and Jim Grabowski. In 1966, the Green Bay Packers spent $1 million to sign this pair of NFL rookie running backs.

MILLION DOLLAR BACKFIELD [THE]—The 1947 Chicago Cardinals won a NFL championship with a backfield of quarterback Paul Christman, Pat Harder, Charlie Trippi, and Elmer Angsman.

MILLION DOLLAR BACKFIELD—The quartet in the backfield of the San Francisco 49ers in the early 1950s: Joe Arenas, Hugh KING McElhenny, YAT Tittle, and Joe "THE JET" Perry.

MILLION DOLLAR LINE—Chicago Black Hawks trio made up of center Red Hay and wings Murray Balfour and Bobby Hull in the early 1960s.

MIRACLE BRAVES [THE]—The 1914 Boston Braves won the National League pennant after being in last place by winning sixty-one of their last seventy-seven games. They then stunned a powerful Philadelphia As baseball team by winning four straight games in the World Series—the first team ever to perform this feat.

MIRACLE MADHOUSE ON MADISON STREET [THE]—The 1976 Chicago Bulls led by Norm Van Lier were a scrappy, madcap team that played in an arena on Madison Street. They qualified for the playoffs that year by winning twenty out of their last twenty-four games.

MIRACLE METS—In 1969, the New York Mets won 100 games and the World Series and earned this nickname.

MIRACLE OF COOGAN'S BLUFF [THE]—The miracle was the New York Giants overcoming a deficit of thirteen and a half games to take the pennant from the Brooklyn Dodgers with Bobby Thompson's home run in a playoff game on October 3, 1951. Coogan's Bluff was near the Polo Grounds. See THE SHOT HEARD AROUND THE WORLD.

MIRACLE ON MANCHESTER [THE]—In the third game of the semifinals between Los Angeles and Edmunton in 1981–1982, the Kings came back from 5–0 to tie the game at the end of regulation time and then to score a goal in overtime for the victory. The Kings play on West Manchester Boulevard in Inglewood, California.

MIRACLE TEAM [THE]—The 1914 Boston Braves. On July 19th, Boston was in last place. But not only did the Braves win the pennant (they are the only team to have won the pennant having been in last place on July 4), but they also won the World Series, sweeping the Athletics in four games.

MIRROR DEFENSE [THE]—Notre Dame patterned its defense after Texas, its opponent in the 1972 Cotton Bowl.

MISS HIGGINS—An elastic circle, developed by a Miss Higgins, that was used to hold a woman golfer's skirt in place when it was windy on the golf course. In the days before shorts and pants were worn on the links, a woman might find it hard to see the ball she was trying to hit.

MISTAKE ON THE LAKE [THE]—The nickname of the empty ballpark located on Lake Erie.

MR. FLING AND MR. CLING—Quarterback Terry Hanratty and end Jim Seymour of Notre Dame.

MONSTER [THE]—Hole number sixteen at the Firestone Country Club is 625 yards long.

MONSTERS OF THE MIDWAY [THE]—The Chicago Midway was built for the 1893 Colombian Exposition. The nickname of Monsters of the Midway was first used for Amos Alonzo Stagg's team at the University of Chicago; more recently it has been used for the Chicago Bears.

MOON SHOTS—Wally Moon's towering home runs.

MPH LINE [THE]—The line of Pit Martin, Jim Pappin, and Dennis Hull of the Chicago Blackhawks. The nickname came from the first letter of each of their last names. MPH also is the abbreviation for miles per hour.

MULLIGAN—When a golfer needs a second try at driving the ball off the first tee. A Mulligan is the second ball used. How the term came into being is disputed, but some trace it to a golfer named Mulligan.

MURDERERS' ROW—The New York Yankees' lineup in 1927. That year with Babe Ruth (60 home runs), Lou Gehrig (47 home runs), Earle Combs (231 hits), Tony Lazzeri (176 hits and 102 RBIs), and Bob Meusel (174 hits and 103 RBIs), the Yanks won 110 games and the pennant by 19 games. This bunch of "window breakers" then went on to win the World Series, beating the Pirates in four straight. "It was murder," said Babe Ruth about the 1927 Yanks. "We never even worried five or six runs behind."

MURPHY'S DEATH CAR—The car that racer Jimmy Murphy died in during a race in 1924. Wilbur Shaw used this rebuilt car, also known as the Jinx Special, to come in fourth at the 1927 Indianapolis 500.

NATIONAL PASTIME [THE]—Baseball.

NATS [THE]—The Washington Senators (1901–1960; 1961–1971)

NEW YORK SACK EXCHANGE [THE]—The front four of the New York Jets during a pass rush in the 1980s, featuring Marty Lyons, Joe Kleckoe, Mark Gastineau, and Abdul Salaam.

NIBLICK—The nine iron in golf.

NO-NAME DEFENSE—The defense of the Miami Dolphins from 1971 to 1974. Although no one seemed to remember any of their names, other teams couldn't forget them. Some of their hard-to-remember names were Nick Buoniconti (linebacker), Manny Fernandez (tackle), Dick Anderson (back), Jake Scott (back), Vern Den Herder (end), and Bob Matheson. The No-Name Defense was a major factor in Miami's ability to compile a 17–0 record in 1972–1973, including a 14–7 victory over the Washington Redskins in Super Bowl VII, as well as Miami's 1973–1974 season of 13–2 topped off with a 24–7 victory over the Minnesota Vikings in Super Bowl VIII.

NO-NO—A no-hitter. Ballplayers often do not mention a no-hitter while it is in progress. Call it a superstition, but it's a no-no.

OLD FOLKS' HOME [THE]—Punch Imlach's 1967 Toronto Maple Leafs. There were seven players on the team who were thirty-six years old or older.

ONE HUNDRED THOUSAND DOLLAR INFIELD—Connie Mack's Philadelphia Athletics starring John STUFFY McInnis at first base, Eddie COCKY Collins at second, Jack Barry at short, and Frank HOME RUN Baker at third. The Athletics won the World Series in 1910–1911 and 1913–1914.

ONE MILLION DOLLAR INFIELD—The 1948 Philadelphia As with Ferris "BURRHEAD" Fain at first base, Peter "PECKY" Suder at second base, Eddie "THE WALKING MAN" Yost at shortstop, Hank "HEENEY" Majeski at third base, and Buddy Rosar as catcher.

ORANGE CRUSH [THE]—At one time it was for the tough defense of the Cleveland Browns (who wore orange uniforms). In 1977, it referred to the Denver Broncos' crushing defense (and uniforms). The Broncos began using the 3–4–4 defense that the New England Patriots had developed. (Today, this is one of the main defensive alignments for every pro football team.) This put a nose tackle over the center and one more linebacker into the defense. The nose tackle for Denver was Rubin Carter; the linebackers were Randy Gradishar, Tom Jackson, Joe Rizzo, and Bob Swenson; two of the backs were Bill Thompson and Louis Wright; one of the linemen was Lyle Alzado. In 1977, the Orange Crush allowed only 148 points on the way to Denver's 12–2 record.

ORIGINAL NINE—Nine women (Jane "PEACHES" Bartkowicz, Rosie Casals, Judy Dalton, Julie Heldman, Billie Jean King, Kerry Melville, Kristy Pigeon, Nancy Richey, Valerie Ziegenfuss) who broke away from the USLTA in 1970 to begin the women's tour. This was the first step in ushering in more recognition for women's tennis and more prize money for women's tournaments.

ORIGINAL SIX—The six teams that made up the NHL from 1942 to 1967: Boston Bruins, Chicago Black Hawks, Detroit Red Wings, Montreal Canadiens, New York Rangers, and Toronto Maple Leafs.

OUTDOOR ROULETTE—Dog racing.

OVER-THE-HILL GANG [THE]—The 1972 Redskins were put together by George Allen by trading away future draft choices for aging players. These mastodons went all the way to Super Bowl VII where they lost to the unbeaten Miami Dolphins.

PADDY'S PIG—In the 1920s, the Chicago Cardinals had a mascot of a pig. Paddy Driscoll was one of the most important members of the team, so whenever the Cardinals scored a touchdown, Paddy's Pig was paraded up and down the sidelines.

PARK AVENUE RANGERS [THE]—Nickname of the New York Rangers in the 1920s and 1930s when there were many celebrity fans (Humphrey Bogart, Cab Calloway, Paul Muni, George Raft, Edward G. Robinson, the Duke and Dutchess of Windsor, and others).

PEGGY LEE [THE]—Tug McGraw's fastball was called this because it called to mind Lee's song, "Is That All There Is?"

PHANTOM PUNCH—On May 25, 1965, in less than a minute after the beginning of their return heavyweight title fight in Lewiston, Maine, Muhammad Ali (then Cassius Clay) KO'd Sonny Liston by a punch that no one seemed to see.

PHI SLAMMA JAMMA—The 1983–1984 University of Houston Cougars were a bunch of slam dunkers. Sportswriter Tommy Bonk gave them this nickname.

PLAY [THE]—In 1982, The university of California at Berkely came back to defeat Stanford, 25–20. The last play of the game was a fifty-seven-yard kickoff return, featuring five laterals and climaxed by U.C's Kevin Moran, who wove through the Stanford Band already on the field, bowling over a trombone player.

POP ANSON'S COLTS—The Chicago White Stockings (now the Cubs). Cap Anson managed the Chicago team from 1879 to 1897.

POSSUM BROTHERS [THE]—Danny Cox and Kurt Kepshire. These two Cardinal roommates slept all day and stayed up all night.

POWDER PUFF DERBY—International Women's Air Race.

PRINCIPAL'S NOSE [THE]—Bunkers on the near and far side of the green on the sixteenth hole of the Old Course at St. Andrews. In the 1978 British Open, Jack Nicklaus finessed his way onto the green for a birdie. In hot pursuit Simon Owen overshot the green and wound up with a five, putting him out of contention.

PRODUCTION LINE [THE]—Detroit Red Wings' scoring line in the late 1940s and early 1950s made up of Gordie "BLINKY" Howe, Ted "TERRIBLE TED" Lindsay, and Sid "BOOTNOSE" Abel. Alex Delvecchio later replaced Sid Abel. Like an assembly line in one of Detroit's automobile plants, the Production Line produced many points and seven straight league titles.

PROETTES—Nickname for women golf pros in the 1950s.

PUNCH LINE [THE]—The name given to the hockey trio of center Elmer Lach, left wing Hector "TOE" Blake, and right wing Maurice "ROCKET" Richard of the Montreal Canadiens. They juiced up the attack and punched in a lot of goals, capturing the league title four times from 1944 to 1947. During the 1943–1944 season, they scored eighty-two goals and led their team all the way (with only five losses) to the Stanley Cup. In 1946, the Punch Line paced the Canadiens to the cup again in 1946.

PURPLE PEOPLE EATERS—The Minnesota Vikings' defense from 1967 to the late 1970s. Outfitted in their purple uniforms—and named after a popular song of the time—were Carl Eller (6' 6", 246 pounds at left end), Gary Larsen (left tackle), Alan Page (right tackle), and Jim Marshall (right end). Their plan was to "meet at the quarterback." In 1971, Eller was the Most Valuable Defensive Player; Alan Page was the league's Most Valuable Player (the first time it was ever won by a player on defense). The Purple People Eaters were instrumental in the Minnesota Vikings making four trips to the Super Bowl. They were also called The Purple Gang.

QUARTERBACK U—The nickname of the University of Miami because the school has produced so many pro-style pocket passers, such as Jim Kelly, Vinny Testaverde, and Bernie Kosar.

RAZZLE DAZZLE LINE [THE]—The Montreal Canadiens' scoring line of Buddy O'Connor, Jerry Heffernan, and Pete Morin in the early 1940s. The three players originally came from the Montreal Royals.

RED DOG—A player on the defense, especially a linebacker, rushing the passer.

REDBANDS—The nickname of the Montreal Wanderers, because of the scarlet stripe on their jerseys. (They were also the first team in eastern Canada to wear numbered jerseys.) The Wanderers won the Stanley Cup four times between 1905 and 1910.

RENDEZ-VOUS 87—A two-game series between the Soviets and the NHL All-Stars played in Quebec in 1987. The NHL won the first 4–3; the Soviets the second 5–3.

RENS [THE]—Short for The Renaissance Big Five, The Rens was the nickname of this team from Harlem that traveled around the country playing all sorts of opponents from 1922 to 1948. During their best years from 1932 to 1936, the Renaissance Big Five won 473 games and lost forty-nine. This all African American team featured Charles "TARZAN" Cooper, John "CASEY" Holt, Clarence "FAT"

Jenkins, James "PAPPY" Ricks, Eyre "BRUISER" Saitch, Wee Willie Smith, and Bill Yancey. In 1963, the Rens were paid a great honor when the entire team was elected to the Hall of Fame.

RICHARD RIOT [THE]—On March 17–18, 1955, after striking a linesman, the Canadiens' Maurice "THE ROCKET" Richard was suspended by NHL president Clarence Campbell for the remainder of the 1954–1955 season. When Campbell later attended a critical game between Montreal and Detroit, the Forum exploded into a riot so severe that the game had to be forfeited to the Redwings. For hours afterward a mob of ten thousand roamed the streets of Montreal. By the raw light of morning, seventy people had been arrested and property damage had climbed to $100,000. It was also called The St. Patrick's Day Riot.

ROAD HOLE—The seventeenth hole on the Old Course at St. Andrews in Scotland. This famous 461-yard par-4 hole gets its name from the road that lies beyond the green. There is also a bunker before it called the "Sands of Nakajima" (for the Japanese golfer who got stuck in the bunker and wound up with a nine during the 1978 British Open).

ROPE-A-DOPE—What Muhammad Ali called resting against the ropes as his opponent threw punches and tired himself out.

RUMBLE IN THE JUNGLE [THE]—Muhammad Ali versus George Foreman in 1974.

RUPP'S RUNTS—In the mid-1960s Adolph Rupp's Kentucky team was short (for instance, Pat Riley at 6' 4" sometimes played center), but the Wildcats were ranked first nationally until losing to Texas Western in the NCAA finals.

SALLY—The South Atlantic championship started in 1926 at the Ormond Golf Club. (Today it has been renamed the Oceanside Country Club.) This women's tournament, first won by Dorothy Klotz, is known for its "Sally weather" (driving wind and rain).

SAVOY BIG 5—This was the original name of the basketball team that eventually became the Harlem Globetrotters.

SCHNOZZ'S SNOOZE—Before Reds catcher Ernie "Schnozz" Lombardi could get up after being bowled over by Charlie Keller racing in from third, Joe DiMaggio scored as well, and the Yankees went on to clinch the seventh game of the 1939 World Series.

SCOOTER LINE—Forwards Abe McDonald and Stan Mikita of Chicago formed one of the top scoring units in the NHL. (Another time the Scooter Line featured Makita, Doug Mohns, and Ken Wharram.) The scooter line led the Black Hawks to the Stanley Cup in 1961.

SENIOR CIRCUIT—Baseball's National League. The National League was founded in 1876, twenty-five years before the American League.

SEVEN BLOCKS OF GRANITE—The football line of Fordham University: Johnny Druze (right end), Al Babartsky (right tackle), Vince Lombardi (right guard), Alex Wojciechowicz (center), Nat Pierce (left guard), Ed Franco (left tackle), and Leo Pasquin (left end). Opponents scored only one touchdown against this defense in 1936. In the last game of the season, Fordham and Pitt played to a 0–0 tie before 55,000 at the Polo Grounds. It was the third year in a row that Fordham and Pitt had battled to a scoreless tie.

SEVEN MULES—The football line of Notre Dame in the 1920s. The Seven Mules blocked for The Four Horsemen. The Mules were: Joseph Bach (tackle), Chuck Collins (end), Ed Huntsinger (end), Noble Kizer (guard), Rip Miller (tackle), Adam Walsh (catcher), and John Weibel (guard).

SHOT HEARD AROUND THE WORLD (THE)—The home run that Bobby Thomson hit in the ninth inning of the final game of the 1951 season to win the National League pennant for the New York Giants over the Brooklyn Dodgers.

SIN-BINS—The boxes where penalized players sit during hockey games.

SIX-STAR FINAL (THE)—This sobriquet referred to the pitching staff of the 1923 New York Yankees.

SAD SAM Jones (21–8, 3.63)
Herb Pennock (19–6, 3.34)
Bullet Joe Bush (19–15, 3.42)
Wait Hoyt (17–9, 3.01)
Bob Shawkey (16–11, 3.51)
Carl Mays (5–2, X6.22)

SMURFS (THE)—The receiving team of the Washington Redskins from 1981 to 1984. Alvin Garrett and Virgil Seay, both wide receivers, were small at 5' 7", 179 pounds, and 5' 8", 175 pounds.

SNOW WHITE AND THE SEVEN DWARFS—In 1938, this referred to the New York Yankees and the rest of the American League.

SOLAR PLEXUS PUNCH—After losing seven rounds in their bout on March 17, 1897, Bob "RUBY ROBERT" Fitzsimmons hit GENTLEMAN Jim Corbett with a blow to the solar plexus. Corbett tried to get up before he was counted out, but he could not recover control of his lower body in time.

SPAGHETTI BOWL—In 1944, the U.S. armed forces held a football game in Rome, Italy.

STEEL CURTAIN (THE)—The defensive unit of the Pittsburgh Steelers from 1973 to 1976. It was as hard to drive through the Steeler's defense as through a steel curtain. The players on the line were MEAN Joe Green (left tackle), L.C. Greenwood (left end), Ernie "Fats" Holmes (right tackle), and Dwight White (right end). Backing them up were Jack Ham (left linebacker), Andy Russell (right linebacker), Jack Lambert (middle linebacker), and Mel Blout (defensive back). In 1975, all three linebackers and three of the four linemen (not including Holmes) were chosen All-Pro. That was the year the steel curtain held the Minnesota Vikings to only seventeen yards rushing in a 16–6 Super Bowl IX victory. In 1976, the Steelers defeated the Cowboys 21–17 in Super Bowl X.

STELLA—Dorothy Campbell's pet name for her putter. Campbell (1881–1963) won THE DOUBLE in 1909 and the British Ladies' Amateur in 1910 and 1911. See THOMAS.

STICK—A nickname for San Francisco's Candlestick Park.

SUBWAY SERIES [THE]—The first subway series was in 1921 between the New York Yankees and the New York Giants. (You could go by subway from Yankee stadium to the Polo Grounds.) These two teams also met in the 1922, 1923, 1936, and 1937 World Series. The Yankees and the Dodgers met in subway series in 1941, 1947, 1949, 1952, 1953, 1955, and 1956. (You could also go from Yankee stadium to Ebbets Field by subway.)

SUPER BOWL—The First Championship game after the merger of the American Football League and the National Football League was played on January 15, 1967. Officially, it was called the National Football League Championship Game. But story has it that during a meeting one of the owners had a super ball in his pocket that he had taken away from his child earlier in the day. He suggested the name Super Bowl. Someone in the press heard it and the name was printed. The public liked it and the name has stuck. To give the game a touch of class, Pete Rozelle added the Roman numerals.

SUPER SERIES—The 1972 series between the Soviets and team Canada. Canada won four games, the Soviets three, and there was one tie. Paul Henderson of the NHL scored the winning goal of the eighth and decisive game with only thirty-four seconds remaining. (In fact, he scored the winning goals in the last three games.) The match was also called The Summit Series.

SUPER SIX—The Ottawa Senators hockey team.

SWEET SCIENCE [THE]—This nickname for boxing was first used during England's Golden Era of Boxing in the early 1800s.

SWEET SPOT—The middle of the tennis racket.

TALL FIRS—The nickname was applied to four basketball stars (Slim Wintermute, Bobby Anet, Lauren Gale, and Wally Johansen), who formed the nucleus of the University of Oregon Basketball team.

TEENAGE BOWL—The 1944 Orange Bowl. So many men had gone off to war that sixteen and seventeen-year-olds were on the field. Louisiana State beat Texas A & M, 19–14.

TEX'S RANGERS—Sports promoter Tex Rickard put together what would become the New York Rangers.

$30,000 MUFF (THE)—In the final game of the 1912 World Series, Fred Snodgrass muffed a routine fly ball and the Boston Red Sox went on to defeat the New York Giants.

THOMAS—This is what Dorothy Campbell (1881–1963) called her five-iron. (It may have been named in honor of OLD TOM Morris who died shortly after the 1908 British Ladies' Championship.) A self-taught golfer, Campbell used it with great accuracy for a running approach to the green. She won THE DOUBLE in 1909 and the British Ladies' Amateur in 1910 and 1911. See also Stella.

THREE AMIGOS (THE)—Quarterback John Elway of the Denver Broncos gave this nickname to his three primary receivers: Mark Jackson, Vance Johnson, and Ricky Nattiel.

THRILLA IN MANILLA—The third great Muhammad Ali-Joe Frazier fight was held in the Philippines on September 30, 1975. Eddie Futch, Frazier's manager, threw in the towel before the start of the fifteenth round, giving Ali the victory by a TKO.

THOR'S HAMMER—Ingemar Johansson's right hand. Johansson was the World Heavyweight Champion from 1959 to 1960, and his right hand carried the knockout punch of the Norse god of thunder. It was also called Ingo's Bingo.

TOMATO CANS—So-so boxers.

TRIPLE CROWN LINE—Los Angeles Kings' line made up of Marcel Dionne, Dave Taylor, and Charlie Simmer. (Each player for the Kings has a crown on the front of his jersey.) The Triple Crown Line scored a record one goal or more in thirteen straight games and a total of 328 points during the 1979–1980 season. (Marcel Dionne and Wayne Gretzky of the Edmonton Oilers tied for the scoring lead with 137 points apiece.)

TRUSHINSKI BYLAW—This is the nickname of 12:6 in the rulebook that states a hockey player with only one eye cannot play hockey in the NHL. This rule was established when Frank "Snoozer" Trushinski lost his sight in one eye after a hockey injury, and then lost most of his sight in the other after another injury.

UNMATCHABLES—Cliff "L'IL ABNER" Hagan, Clyde "BIG WHITE WHALE" Lovellette, and Bob Petit formed the formidable nucleus of the St. Louis Hawks that won the NBA championship in 1958. The name gives a sly sidelong glance toward the Untouchables.

UKE LINE—Uke, short for Ukrainian, was the name of the Boston Bruins' line during the 1957–1958 season. It was made up of three Ukrainian players, Bronco Horvath, Vic Stasiuk, and John Paul Bucyk.

VARDON GRIP—The standard grip used by golfers and developed by Harry Vardon. Vardon (1870–1937) was a member of the GREAT TRIUMVIRATE. He won the British Open in 1896, 1898, 1899, 1903, 1911, and 1914. He also won the U.S. Open in 1900.

VOICE OF THE SIXTEENTH HOLE—Henry Longhurst (1909–1979). On telecasts of the Masters in the 1960s and 1970s, it was the hushed voice of Longhurst at the sixteenth that helped further the air of tension and excitement at the Augusta National Golf Club.

VENUS DE MILO OUTFIELD—Three outfielders without an arm among them.

VOW BOYS [THE]—After five straight losses to USC in the thirties, the freshmen footballers at Stanford took a vow that their teams would not lose to the University of Southern California.

WALL GAME [THE]—This was the nickname for football at Eton because it was played along a high wall. Because space was at a premium, there was only room for eleven players on a side. This remained true even when it was moved to a field and became The Field Game. A graduate of Eton later took the Field Game to Yale.

WALLY PIP—In baseball, this is akin to being given the pink slip. Wally Pipp was the Yankees' first baseman who took the day off because he was sick. Lou Gehrig, his replacement, filled in from June 1, 1925, to May 2, 1939.

WALTON GANG—Bill Walton and his UCLA teammates won seventy-five in a row and two NCAA championships in 1972 and 1973.

WAR PIGS [THE]—The offensive linemen of the Oklahoma State Cowboys in the late 1980s who blocked for Heisman Trophy winner Barry Sanders.

WHITE ELEPHANTS—Connie Mack's Philadelphia A's. John McGraw of the New York Giants once lambasted Mack with this epithet because Mack had lured many of his players from the National League with higher salaries. Mack originally used The White Elephant as a logo; and in 1988, the Oakland A's revived it.

WHIZ KIDS—The basketball team at Illinois (with Art Mathisen, Ken Menke, Andy Phillip, Jack Smiley, and Gene Vance) in the early 1940s. The name originated one night in 1942 when radio announcer Grayce Howlett said, "Gee, those kids really whiz down the floor."

WHIZ KIDS—The 1950 Philadelphia Phillies. The starting lineup was all under thirty years old, and to everyone's surprise (with players with names such as Mike Goliat, Russ Meyer, and Andy Seminick) they won the National League pennant. Their nickname was probably a take-off on the popular radio show of the time, "The Quiz Kids."

WILLIAMS' SHIFT [THE]—Lou Boudreau's strategy of placing three players on the first-base side of the infield. It was used to prevent Boston Red Sox slugger, Ted Williams, who batted from the left side of the plate, from getting a hit. It didn't work.

WONDER FIVE—St. John's basketball team from 1928 to 1931 with a record of 88–8.

WORLD SERIES OF SUDS—The 1982 World Series between the Milwaukee Brewers and the St. Louis Cardinals. This meeting of the two big beer towns saw the Cards go ahead 4–3.

YEAR OF THE PITCHER [THE]—In 1968, batting averages went down (American, .230; National, .234) along with the ERA (AL, 2.98; NL, 2.99). There were 335 shutouts and Denny McLain was 31–6.

YEAR OF THE QUARTERBACK [THE]—In 1970, the college ranks were filled with future pro quarterbacks: Lynn Dickey, Archie Manning, Dan Pastorini, Jim Plunkett, and Joe Theismann.

YEAR THE CELTICS LOST THE PENNANT [THE]—The Philadelphia Warriors defeated the defending champion Boston Celtics for the 1967 Eastern Division title in the fifth and final game by the score of 140–116.

PART 4

MORE SPORTS NICKNAMES

There have, of course, been thousands of nicknames invented by fans, writers, and players over the years, and new ones are being coined all the time. It's all part of the fun of sports, Here are hundreds more of the more colorful names that we've encountered. (Dates of birth and death for all players were not always available).

Abbreviations used:

1b-first baseman	g-goalie (hockey)	qb-quarterback
2b-second baseman	g-guard (basketball)	rw-right wing
3b-third baseman	hb-halfback	ss-shortstop
c-catcher (baseball)	h/f-hall of fame	t-tackle
c-center (basketball)	of-outfield	te-tight end
d-defenseman	p-pitcher	
fb-fullback	lw-left wing	

A-TRAIN—Artis Gilmore (1948–) Basketball.

AB—Albert George Demarco (1916–) Hockey.

AB—Alvin Brian McDonald (1936–) Hockey.

ABBA DABBA—Jim Tobin (1912–1969) Baseball.
What this pitcher said when he was performing one of his magic tricks in the clubhouse.

ABE—Abraham Attell (1884–1970) Boxing.
Attell was a featherweight champion, but he could defeat lightweights, almost beating BATTLING Nelson for the lightweight crown in 1908.

A.C.—Anthony Carr (1961–) Basketball.
Played for Atlanta and San Antonio.

ACCURATE ANGELO—Angelo B. Bertelli (1921–) Football.
Bertelli received his nickname because of his accurate passing. In 1943, Bertelli was the first player from Notre Dame to win the Heisman trophy. He was also known as the Springfield Rifle because he had a rifle for an arm and because he was born in Springfield, Ma.

ACE—Garnet Edward Bailey (1948–) Hockey.
This left winger played for the Boston Bruins when they won the Stanley Cup in 1970 and 1972.
Also called ACER

ACE—Irving Wallace Bailey (1903–1989) Hockey. **H/F**
Bailey, a right winger, was a member of the Toronto St. Pats 1926–1927, and then a member of the Toronto Maple Leafs' "Gashouse Gang on Ice" in the 1930s.

ACE—Robert Gruenig (1913–1958) Basketball. **H/F**
At 6' 8" and 220 pounds, Gruenig was one of the first big men in basketball. He was selected to the All- American AAU team ten times.

ACE—George Willis Hudlin (1906–) Baseball.
Hudlin won eighteen games and lost twelve his rookie season.

ACE—Ariel Maughan (1923–) Basketball.

ACE—Clarence Parker (1912–) Football. **H/F**

ACH—Bob Duliba (1935–) Baseball.

ACK ACK—Willie Aikens (1954–) Baseball.
Aikens received his nickname because he stuttered.

ACK-ACK—Tom Heinsohn (1930–) Basketball. **H/F**
Also known as Tommy Gun because of the frequency with which he took shots. (Ack Ack might be the sound a Tommie gun makes).

ADDIE—Glen Adams (1947–) Baseball.

ADDIE—Adrian Joss (1880–1911) Baseball. **H/F**
Addie won twenty or more games four years in a row.

ADMIRAL—Claude Berry (1880–1974) Baseball.

ADMIRAL [THE]—David Robinson (1965–) Basketball.
From 1989–1995, Robinson played 475 games for San Antonio and averaged 25.7 points per game. He received his nickname because, before becoming a pro, he had attended the Naval Academy in Annapolis.

ADONIS—William Terry (1864–1915) Baseball.
Terry pitched for Brooklyn when the team was known as the bridegrooms. In 1890, this handsome pitcher went 26–16 with a 2.94 ERA. He was a like matinee idol to the female baseball fans.

AGELESS—Johnny Bower (1924–) Hockey. **H/F**
See THE CHINA WALL.

AGGIE—Adolph Frank Kukulowicz (1933–) Hockey.

AGGIE—Forest Sale (1911–) Basketball. **H/F**
Sale studied agriculture at Kentucky, where he was a two-time All-American at forward.

AIRHEAD—Mark Littell (1953–) Baseball.

A. J.—Anthony Joseph Foyt (1935–) Auto racing. **H/F**
Foyt is the only person to have finished first four times at the Indy 500.

A. J.—Alfred Robertson (1891–1948) Basketball.
Robertson had a coaching record of 316–186 at Bradley.

AJAX—Bob Kaufmann (1946–) Basketball.
At 6′ 8″ 240 pounds, Kaufmann was a powerful player. In 1968, he was an All-American at Guilford, hitting 71.2 percent of his field goals. In his 1971 season in the NBA, he averaged over twenty points, four assists, and ten rebounds.

AL—Elbert Butler (1938–) Basketball.

AL—Alice Marie Haylett (active 1946–1949) Baseball (All-American Girls Baseball League). Al may have been short for Alice, but her nickname may also have had to do with the fact that she posted pitching stats that any man would have been proud of. In 1948, her ERA was a sizzling 0.77.

ALABAMA BLOSSOM [THE]—Guy Morton (1893–1934) Baseball. This pitcher for the Indians was from Alabama.

ALAMAZOO—Alfred Jennings (1851–1894) Baseball.
Jennings played catcher in Kalamazoo.

ALBA [EL] [THE DAWN]—Jose Gomez. Bullfighting.

ALBINO RHINO [THE]—Karl Mecklenburg (active 1980s–1990s) Football.

ALDERMAN—Charles Briody (1858–1903) Baseball.
Also called FATTY.

ALI BABA—Albert Babartsky (active 1930s) Football.
Ali Baba (his nickname is a contraction of his first and last names) was one of Fordham's SEVEN BLOCKS OF GRANITE.

ALL-AMERICAN MUSTANG—Doak Walker (1927–)
Football. Also, THE DOAKER, LITTLE MAN IN PRO FOOTBALL

ALL AMERICAN OUT [THE]—Leo Durocher (1905–1991) Baseball. Leo was not known for his hitting. See THE LIP.

ALL WORLD—Lloyd Free (1953–) Basketball.
The nickname Lloyd Free bestowed on himself (and later legalized). His "rainbow shot" sailed over taller NBA opponents.

ALLEY OOP—R. C. Owens (active 1957–1964) Football.
This nickname was for the far-flung passes from Y.A. Tittle that Owens, playing either end or flanker for the San Francisco 49ers during the 1950s, would gather in.

ALLIE—Alfred Heerdt (1881–1958) Basketball coach.
Founder of the Buffalo Germans, a team that was 792–86 around the turn of the twentieth century.

ALLIE—Alva Paine (1919–) Basketball.
In 1946, Allie was an All-American from Oklahoma.

ALPHABET—Craig Smajstrea (active 1988–) Baseball.
The nickname of this second baseman and the one below are for the unique combination of letters in their names.

ALPHABET MAN [THE]—Tom Abatemarco. Basketball.
This coach's last name contains A-B-C.

AMAZING EMU [THE]—Jim Kern (1949–) Baseball.

AMAZING GRACE—Mark Grace (1964–) Baseball.
Selected in the twenty-forth round of the 1985 draft, this first baseman was batting .314 for the Cubs in 1989. He turned out as sweet as the song.

AMERICAN ICE MASTER [THE]—Jackson Haines (1840-1876) Ice skating. Also called AMERICAN SKATING KING.

AMERICAN WONDER [THE]—George Seward (active 1840s) Track and field. In 1844 in England, professional runner George Seward ran the 100-yard dash in 9.25 seconds.

AMERICAN TOURISTER—James Donaldson (1957–)
Basketball.

AMERICA'S MOST PERFECTLY DEVELOPED MAN—Charles Atlas (1892–1972) Bodybuilding. His real name was Angelo Siciliano.

AMITYVILLE HORROR [THE]—Shelton Jones. Basketball.
This St. John's star was from Amityville, N.Y. His nickname alludes to the title of a popular horror film.

ANCIENT MARINER [THE]—Gaylord Perry (1938–)
Baseball. **H/F**

ANDRE—Joseph Armand Pronovost (1936–) Hockey.

ANDRE THE GIANT—Andre Roussimoff. Wrestling.

ANDRE TURNOVER—Andre Turner (1964–) Basketball.
Turnovers are not what basketball players wish to give up, and so his nickname (based upon his last name) is not exactly a compliment.

ANGEL SLEEVES—Ryerson Jones (active 1880s) Baseball.

ANGLEWORM—Ted Abernathy (1933–) Basketball.

A sidearm pitcher, Abernathy's pitches sometimes seemed to pop up out of the grass.

ANIMAL—Eddie Lopez. Boxing.

ANIMAL [THE]—Kenneth Bannister (1960–) Basketball. He played from 1981–1991 for New York and Los Angeles.

ANIMAL [THE]—Frank Fletcher. Boxing.

ANIMAL [THE]—Brad Lesley (1958–) Baseball.
This Cincinnati Reds relief pitcher received his nickname because of his size (6' 6" and 220 pounds) and because he sometimes seemed out of control on the pitcher's mound.

ANTELOPE [THE]—Keith Moreland (1954–) Baseball.

ANTMAN [THE]—Aubrey Stallworth. Basketball.

ANTS—Walter Atanas (1922–) Hockey.

APPLE CHEEKS—Harry Lumley (1926–) Hockey. **H/F**
Lumley, a goalie, won the Vezina Trophy in 1954 with a 1.86 goals-against average.

APPLES—Frank Kudelka (1925–) Basketball.

APPLES—Andy Lapihuska (1922–) Baseball.
This pitcher for the Phillies received his nickname because of his fondness for apples.

ARCH—Archie Griffin (1954–) Football.

ARGENTINA—Antonio Rocca. Wrestling.

ARKANSAS HUMMINGBIRD [THE]—Lonnie "Lou" Warneke (1909–1976) Baseball. The pitching motion of this pitcher from Arkansas was jerky and quick like a hummingbird moving back and forth among the blossoms.

ARKANSAS TRAVELER [THE]—Gene Bearden (1920–) Baseball.

ARM [THE]—Tom Hafey (1913–) Baseball.
Third baseman Hafey had a great arm for the long throw to first.

ARMY—George Armstrong (1930–) Hockey.
This Native American played twenty-one years for the Toronto Maple Leafs, scoring 292 goals and 476 assists. Also called CHIEF.

ARTFUL DODGER [THE]—Dave Needham. Boxing.

ARTHUR THE GREAT—Arthur Shires (1907–1967) Baseball, boxing. First baseman Shires took this ring name for his boxing career during the baseball off-season.

ASH—Donald Alan Ashby (1955–) Hockey.

ASSASSIN [THE]—Jack Tatum (1948–) Football.

ASTORIA ASSASSIN [THE]—Paul Berlenbach (1901–) Boxing. **H/F** This boxer was a light-heavyweight.

ASTRONAUT [THE]—DeWayne Scales (1958–) Boxing. Also called HOT MAN.

ATOM BOMB [THE]—Tom Tracey (1933–1978) Football. Also called TOM THE BOMB and THE BOMB.

ATOMIC PUNCHER [THE]—Rocky Graziano (1922–1990) Boxing. **H/F**

ATTACK—Takeo Harada. Boxing.
His nickname is a play upon his first name.

AUGIE—Eugene Freese (1934–) Baseball.
His Brooklyn teammates during his rookie year told the announcer that this third baseman's name was Augie, and that was the way Freese was introduced to the crowd.

AUSSIE JOE—Joseph Bugner. Boxing.
He was born in Hungary, but settled in Australia, after he had boxed in England.

AUSTRALIAN [THE]—Dan Quisenberry (1953–) Baseball. Quisenberry's submarine pitching motion came from down under.

AUSTRALIAN WIZARD [THE]—Walter Lindrum. Pool, billiards.

AUT—Autry Erickson (1938–) Hockey.

AUTOMATIC—Benjamin Agajanian (1919–) Football.
When Agajanian came on the field after a touchdown, the extra point was automatic. In 1947, he set a record fifteen field goals in a row in the AAFC. He also played in the AFL and NFL. Also called THE TOELESS WONDER.

AUTOMATIC—George Karamatic (1917–) Football.

AUTOMATIC JACK—Jack Manders (1909–) Football.

AUTOMATIC OTTO—Otto Graham (1921–) Football.

AVAILABLE—Sheldon Jones (1922–) Baseball.
When Jones was in the minors, he would always make sure the manager knew that he was available to pitch.

AWESOME AUSSIE [THE]—Greg Norman (1955–) Golf. See THE GREAT WHITE SHARK.

B. ROBBY—Brooks Robinson (1937–) Baseball.
Also called MR. THIRD BASE. See THE VACUUM CLEANER.

BABA—Nestor Jiminez (1947–) Boxing.

BABA—Dorothy Pim (active 1930s) Golf.
Pim was the Irish Ladies' Golf Champion in 1938.

BABA—Ivor Simmons (1959–) Boxing.

BABE—Thomas Barlow (1896–1983) Basketball. **H/F**

BABE—Herb Barna (1915–1972) Baseball.

BABE—Bill Borton (1884–1944) Baseball.

BABE—John H. Brown, Jr. (1891–1963) Football.
This Babe was president of National Football League Foundation and the Hall of Fame from 1954–1963.

BABE—Ellsworth Dahlgren (1912–) Baseball.
It was 2,210 games after Lou Gehrig replaced Wally Pip at first base that Dahlgren replaced Gehrig.

BABE—Cecil Henry Dye (1898–1962) Hockey. **H/F**
A defenseman with the Rangers and Maple Leafs, Dye led all scorers in 1922, 1923, and 1925.

BABE—Floyd Herman (1903–1987) Baseball.

BABE—Walt Kinderdine (1899–deceased) Football.
Played 1923–1925 for Dayton.

BABE—James McCarthy (1923–) Basketball coach.

BABE—Patrick Macdonald (1878–1954) Track and field.
This New York City policeman, hurling the fifty-six-pound weight, was the oldest person ever to win an Olympic title.

BABE—Vito Parilli (1930–) Football qb.

BABE—Ernest Gordon Phelps (1908–1992) Baseball.
Phelps weighed 225 to 250 pounds, so his nickname was ironic. This catcher also batted a hefty .310 from 1931 to 1942. Also called BLIMP.

BABE—Walter Pratt (1916–1988) Hockey. **H/F**
Pratt was a defenseman for the New York Rangers when they won the 1940 Stanley Cup.

BABE—Eddie Risko (1911–1957) Boxing (middleweight).

BABE—Jay Towne (1880–1938) Baseball.

BABE—Richard Tyselling (1910–) Basketball.
After a playing career at Central College in Iowa where he lettered sixteen times in four sports, Tyselling took over as coach and athletic director.

BABE RUTH OF BASKETBALL [THE]—John Beckman (1895–1968) Basketball. **H/F** Beckman was a member of the original Celtics.

BABE RUTH OF HOCKEY [THE]—Howie Morenz (1902–1937) Hockey. **H/F** Also called STRATFORD STREAK.

BABE RUTH OF HOCKEY [THE]—Maurice Richard (1921–) Hockey rw. **H/F** See ROCKET.

BABE RUTH OF HOCKEY [THE]—Eddie Shore (1902–1985) Hockey. **H/F** Shore made people aware of the game of hockey in the same manner as Ruth had drawn attention to the game of baseball. He won the Hart trophy four times. At the end of this defenseman's career, he had scored 105 goals and added 179 assists.

BABE RUTH OF POLO [THE]—Thomas Hitchcock, Jr. (1900–1944) Polo.

BABE RUTH'S LEGS—Sammy Byrd (1906–1981) Baseball.
In the twilight years of Ruth's career, Byrd replaced Babe on defense and the base paths.

BABY—Alberto Arizmendi (1914–) Boxing.

BABY—Ray Buford (active 1938–1948) Football.
Buford was a 6' 6", 250-pound tackle for the Green Bay Packers.

BABY BEAR—Jody Scheckter (1950–) Auto racing.
In 1973, Scheckter broke onto the Grand Prix racing circuit. He was a young, well-built Belgian who seemed to be on the verge of disaster at every turn.

BABY HUEY—Wayne Estes (1943–1965) Basketball.
Estes (6' 6", 225 pounds) was nicknamed after the popular cartoon and Harvey comic book character of an oversized baby goose. This Utah State player was electrocuted by a high voltage wire when he stopped to help at the scene of a car accident.

BABYCAKES—Jerry T. Smith (1943–) Football.
This tight end caught fifty-two TDs in the pros. Also called Shane.

BACH—William Bachrach (1879–1959) Swimming.
Bach was an Olympic swimming coach and the one who developed Johnny Weissmuller into a great swimmer.

BAD BILL—William Frederick Dahlen (1870–1950) Baseball. Dahlen got the thumb a lot for arguing with umps. This shortstop also committed 972 errors during his twenty-year career.

BAD NEWS—Jim Barnes (1941–) Basketball.

BAD NEWS—George Cafego (1915–) Football.
When Cafego was playing quarterback, it was bad news for his opponents.

BAD NEWS—Odell Hale (1908–1980) Baseball.
This second baseman was bad news to opposing pitchers. His career stats don't knock your socks off, but Hale had the knack for getting the big hit in a ball game.

BADGER [THE]—Bernard Hinault (1954–)Bicycle racing (French).

BAG LADY [THE]—JoAnne Carner (1939–) Golf.
Carner was known to use plastic bags as protection during rainy weather. See BIG MOMMA.

BAGS—John Edwin Bagley (1960–) Basketball.
He scored 5,802 points in his career, playing for

Cleveland, New Jersey, Boston, and Atlanta. His nickname is a play upon his last name, but it is also clear from the number of teams he played for that his bags were always packed.

BAGS—Jim Bakken (1940–) Football.
His nickname is a play upon his last name.

BAKE—Arnold Ray McBride (1949–) Baseball.
His dad, who had been a pitcher, also had the same nickname. The son, an outfielder, was the National League Rookie of the Year in 1974.

BAKER [THE]—George Millsom (active 1760s) Boxing.
Millsom was the English heavyweight bareknuckles champ from 1762 to 1765.

BAKER BOY—Joe Mandot. Boxing.

BALD BILLY—Billy Barnie (1853–1900) Baseball.
It will come as no surprise that this catcher was bald. His batting prowess was bald too. BALD BILLY appeared in only nineteen games in his two-year career for Baltimore of the American Association. He came to bat sixty-one times and got eleven hits, batting an ignominious .180.

BALD EAGLE [THE]—Y(elberton) A(braham) Tittle (1926–) Football. This baldheaded quarterback with the San Francisco 49ers and the New York Giants compiled a lifetime passing record of throwing for 28,339 yards (in 3,817 attempts) and 212 touchdowns. Also called Colonel Slick and Ya Ya.

BALDY—Brian Baldinger (1959–) Football.
His brothers Gary and Rich also played in the NFL. His nickname is a play upon his last name.

BALDY—Harry Cotton (1902–) Hockey.
Cotton played left wing for the Pittsburgh Yellow Jackets in the 1920s. He was also a member of the Toronto Maple Leafs' GASHOUSE GANG.

BALDY—Lawrence Northcott (1908–) Hockey.
This Montreal Maroon leftwinger scored an important goal in overtime of game two. Maroons went on to beat Toronto in the Stanley Cup.

BALDY—Richard Rudolph (1887–1949) Baseball.

BALKAN BANGER [THE]—Georgi Glouchkov (1960–) Basketball. This Bulgarian played forward for the Phoenix Suns.

BAM [THE]—Sam Cunningham (1950–) Football.
This fullback had a rhyming nickname that gave opponents some idea of how he ran the ball.

BAM-BAM—Dick Ambrose (active 1975–1984) Football.

BAM BAM—Richmond Webb (1967–) Football.
This tackle received his nickname at Texas A&M for the way he mowed down the opposition.

BAMA—Carvel William Rowell (1916–) Baseball. This member of the Boston Braves hailed from Alabama.

BAMBI—Lance Rentzel (1943–) Football.

BAMBINO [THE]—George Herman Ruth (1895–1948) Baseball. Bambino is Italian for Babe.

BAN—Byron Johnson (1864–1931) Baseball.
Johnson led the break away from the National League to start the Western League (renamed the American League in 1900). Johnson advertised better salaries for the players and clean baseball and more twenty-five-cent seats for the fans.

BANANAS—Joe Benes (1901–1975) Baseball.
This shortstop's nickname is a play on his last name.

BAND-AID—Derrick Chievous (1967–) Basketball.
This University of Missouri forward always wore a Band-Aid.

BANG BANG—Ken Bogner (1961–) Boxing.

BARBER [THE]—George Taylor (1718–1758) Boxing.
The Barber was the British bareknuckles heavyweight champion in 1735.

BARNACLE BILL—William J. Posedel (1906–1989) Baseball. This former coach with the Pittsburgh Pirates received his nickname because of his service in the Navy.

BARNEY—Norwood Ewell (1918–) Track and field.
Ewell won silver medals in 100- and 200-meter dashes and a gold medal in the 400-meter relay at the 1948 Olympics in London. His best times were a world record 10.2 in the 100 meters and 21.0 in the 200. The name Barney (as in Barney Oldfield, the racecar driver) is associated with pell-mell speed.

BARNEY—Walter Johnson (1887–1946) Baseball. **H/F**

BARNEY—Bernie E. Oldfield (1876–1946) Auto racing. **H/F**
Oldfield switched from bicycles to racing cars in two weeks to become Henry Ford's first racecar driver. In 1893, Barney raced old "999" to a new record of a mile in one minute. Some of baseball's hard-throwing pitchers were nicknamed Barney in honor of this speedster.

BARNEY—Russell Stanley (1893–1971) Hockey. **H/F**
Stanley played everywhere except in goal.

BARNUM—Larry MacPhail (1890–1975) Baseball.
Like P.T. Barnum of circus fame, MacPhail was an innovator. One of the things he introduced to baseball was the first night game. It was played on May 24, 1935.

BARNUM OF BASKETBALL—Abe Saperstein (1901–1966) Basketball. He was quite a showman.

BARON [THE]—Roy Face (1928–) Baseball p.

BARON [THE]—Pete Retzlaff (1931–) Football.
This receiver for the Philadelphia Eagles received his nickname because of his German heritage.

BARON OF BARLOW BEND [THE]—Frank Howard (1909–) Football. Howard coached at Clemson.

BASEBALL'S QUIET MAN—Bill Dickey (1907–1993) Baseball c. **H/F**

BASE BURGLER [THE]—Lou Brock (1939–) Baseball of. **H/F** See THE FRANCHISE.

BASQUE WOODCHOPPER [THE]—Paulino Uzcudun. Boxing.

BAT—Baskerville Holmes (active 1980s) Basketball.

BAT—Bernard E. Masterson (1911–1963) Football.

BAT—William Masterton (1938–) Hockey.
This center's nickname comes from the popular TV western hero Bat Masterson (sic). Bat Masterson, the U.S. marshal (1853–1921), was the pseudonym for William Barclay Masterson. Gene Barry portrayed the marshal on the 1950s TV series.

BAT 'EM BOB—Robert Kinney (1920–) Basketball.
This 6' 7", two-time All-American center and forward at Rice was known for his tip-ins, rebounding, and blocked shots.

BATMAN—Tony Ortega. Boxing.

BATMAN—Richard Wood (active 1975–1985) Football.

BATTLE HAWK—Kujoshi Kazama (active 1980s) Boxing. He was a junior lightweight.

BATTLESHIP—Bob Kelly (1946–) Hockey, lightweight boxer.

BATTLESHIP—Albert LeDuc (1902–) Hockey d.

BATTLING—Christopher Battalino (1908–1977) Boxing. Battalino was the featherweight champ from 1929 to 1932.

BATTLING BATTALINO—Bat Battalino (1908–1977) Boxing.

BATTLING BILLY—William Wells (1889–1967) Boxing.
You can see his arm hitting the gong in the opening to the old British-based J. Arthur Rank films.

BATTLING LEVINSKY—Barney Lebrowitz (1891–1949) Boxing. Lebrowitz was the light heavyweight champ

from 1916–1930. Also called King, The Furious Fishmonger, and The Mad Mackerel Merchant.

BATTLING NELSON—Oscar Matthew Nelson (1882–1954) Boxing. **H/F** Nelson lost to Joe Gans in 1906 by hitting him with a low blow in the forty-second round. Nelson was the lightweight champ from 1908 to 1910. Also called The Battler and The Durable Dane.

BAYONNE BLEEDER [THE]—Chuck Wepner. Boxing.

BAYONNE GLOBETROTTER [THE]—Jeff Smith (1891–1962) Boxing. **H/F**

BAZ—Aldege Bastien (1920–) Hockey.
The nickname for this goalie for the Toronto Maple Leafs (1945–1946) is a variation upon his last name.

BAZOOKA—Raphael Limon (1954–) Boxing.
On December 11, 1982, this junior lightweight boxer was defeated by Bobby Chacon for the World Boxing Council's 130-pound title.

BEAK—Danny Kravitz (1930–) Baseball.
Also called Dusty.

BEAN JACK—Sidney Walker. Boxing.

BEANO—Carroll Cook. Sports announcer.

BEANS—John E. Reardon. Baseball.
Umpire from 1926 to 1949. His nickname could be derived from the fact that he came from Boston or Beantown. Most likely, however, his nickname came from his flatulence problems, causing batters to taunt him with the colorful rhyme, "Beans, beans, the musical fruit, the more you eat, the more you toot."

BEAR—Fred Earl Gladding (1936–) Baseball.

BEAR—Frederick C. Glick (1937–) Football.

BEAR [THE]—Sonny Liston (1932–1970) Boxing.

BEAR TRACKS—Al Javery (1918–) Baseball.
Javery left tracks when he stomped around the mound to get it to his liking. He must have made a lot of tracks because he was 53–74.

BEAR TRACKS—Sam Mele (1923–) Baseball of.

BEAR TRACKS—John Schmitz (1920–) Baseball p.

BEASER [THE]—John Beasley (active 1967–1974) Football.

BEAST—George Trafton (1896–1971) Football.
When you play football, it is always a good idea to take on a nickname like "Beast" to intimidate your opponents. Trafton played twelve years as a center in the NFL.

BEAST [THE]—Jimmy Foxx (1907–1967) Baseball. **H/F** See DOUBLE X.

BEAST [THE]—John Mugabi (1951–) Boxing.

BEAU JACK—Sidney Walker (1921–) Boxing. **H/F**

BEAVER—Roland Bevan (active 1935) Football coach.

BEAVER—Russell Blinco (1908–) Hockey.

BEAVER [THE]—Kevin Houston. Basketball.

BEAVER PELT—Bruce Emmerson. Rodeo.

BECKY—Johnny Beckman (1895–1968) Basketball. **H/F**

BED—William Bedford (1963–) Basketball c.

BEDROCK—Steve Bedrosian (1957–) Baseball.
That's how steady and dependable Bedrock Bedrosian (alliteration too) was.

BEE CEE—Barry Clemens (1942–) Basketball.
Received his nickname from his initials.

BEEF—Arthur Wheeler (1872–1920) Football.
This guard was big (6' 1" 200 pounds) in his day.

BEETLE BAILEY—Bob Bailey (1942–) Baseball.
Third baseman Bailey was nicknamed after Beetle Bailey in the funny papers. Also called Beetles.

BELFAST SPIDER [THE]—Ike Welk. Boxing.

BELLICOSE BELGIAN—Earl Lambeau (1898–1965) Football.
H/F For his background and decibel level. See CURLY.

BELLS—Walt Bellamy (1939–) Basketball. **H/F**
This center's nickname is a word play upon his last name. Bells was the NBA's Rookie of the Year in 1962 when he averaged a whopping 31.6 points per game.

BELOVED BRUIN—William Henry Spaulding (1880–1966) Football coach.

BELTING EARL [THE]—John Colum (The Earl of Dumbries). Auto racing. In auto racing, to belt is to move at a very fast speed.

BENNY—Clint Benedict (1894–1976) Hockey.
Comes from this goalie's last name.

BEP—Armand Guidolin (1925–) Hockey.
When he joined the Boston Bruins as a forward in 1942, he was all of sixteen years old, and was thus, the youngest player ever to participate in a NHL game. Obviously, Bep had Pep.

BERLIN GUY—Guy Chamberlin (1894–1967) Football.

BERT—De Benneville Bell (1895–1959) Football.
Bert owned the Philadelphia Eagles from 1933 to 1941 and then became a part owner of the Steelers. In 1952, Bert was instrumental in starting the policy of blacking out the telecast of local games to hometown fans and of having the football commissioner negotiate a TV contract for the whole league.

BERT—Madison Pearson (active 1929–1937) Football.

BEST PLAYER IN HOCKEY—Gordie Howe (1928–) Hockey. See BLINKY.

BEVO—Robert Nordman (1939–) Basketball.

BEX—Hugo F. Bezdek (1884–1952) Football coach, baseball manager. Also called Hugo the Victor (a pun on the name of the great French writer Victor Hugo).

B.H.—Bertram Born (1932–) Basketball.
Every high school and college team he played for won or tied for the conference championship.

BID—John Alexander McPhee (1859–1943) Baseball 2b.

BIFF—Lawrence Jones (1895– 1954) Football.
Also called Captain of Excitement.

BIFF—Herman Schneidman (1913–) Football qb.

BIFFY—Langdon Lea (1874–1937) Football.

BIG A—Lewis Alcindor (Kareem Abdul-Jabbar) (1947–) Basketball c. **H/F** At fifteen and a student at Power Memorial in New York City, Alcindor was seven feet tall. Also called Mount Alcindor. See LEW-CLA.

BIG AL—Althea Gibson (1927–) Tennis. **H/F**
See SPIDER.

BIG BABOON [THE]—Babe Ruth (1895–1948) Baseball.
H/F This was a derogatory nickname applied to Ruth by opposing players. See BABE.

BIG BEAR [THE]—Mike Garcia (1923–1986) Baseball p.

BIG BEAR—Denny Hulme (active 1960s–1970s) Auto racing. This New Zealander and World Champion Formula One driver was big, balding, and brusque.

BIG BEAR [THE]—Charles "Sonny" Liston (1932–1970) Boxing. Ali called him The Big Ugly Bear.

BIG BERTHA—Louis Santop (1890–1942) Baseball (Negro Leagues). At 6' 4", 240 pounds, Santop (or Top as he was also known) was nicknamed after this big German Seige guns of World War I. Not only could this catcher poke the ball as far as 500 feet, he also sometimes called his shot a la Babe Ruth.

BIG BILL—William Bachrach (1879–1959) Swimming.
One of this 350-pound coach's star pupils was Johnny Weissmuller.

BIG BILL—Bill Dineen (1876–1955) Baseball umpire.

BIG BILL—Bill Henry (1937–) Basketball.
Henry was a 6' 9", 220- pound center. He made All-American twice for Rice as they won or shared the Southwest Conference three times.

BIG BILL—William Henry James (1887–1942) Baseball p.

BIG BILL—William Howard Taft (1857–1930) Wrestling. This U.S. President was quite an accomplished athlete. He received this nickname when he was the undergraduate wrestling champion at Yale.

BIG BILL—Bill Walton (1952–) Basketball c. **H/F**

BIG BILLY—Billy Gonsalves (1908–1977) Soccer. **H/F**

BIG BIRD—William Fitzgerald (active 1960s–1970s) Darts. By 1975 Fitzgerald had scored four perfect games of 301, and three times he has scored three darts in the double Bull's-eye.

BIG BIRD—Joel Garner (1952–) Cricket.

BIG BIRD—Joe Lavender (active 1973–1982) Football.

BIG BIRD—Larry Robinson (1951–) Hockey. This defenseman was 6' 3", 210 pounds.

BIG BIRD—Don Saleski (1949–) Hockey. This right winger for the Philadelphia Flyers stood 6' 3" and weighed 205 pounds.

BIG BOPPER—Muhammad Ali (1942–) Boxing. This was Ali's CB handle.

BIG BRAVE FROM MILWAUKEE—Gene Conley (1930–) Baseball p. Also called DADDY LONG ARMS.

BIG CAT—Andres Galarraga (1961–) Baseball 1b.

BIG CAT—Earl Lloyd (1928–) Basketball. Lloyd was 6' 6" and weighed 220 pounds. He scored 4,682 points during a career with four teams from 1950 to 1960.

BIG CAT—Ken Sears (1933–) Basketball. Sears was a 6' 9" forward and center who could lead the fast break and led the NBA in field goals two times. Playing for the Knicks and San Francisco, he averaged 13.9 points in 529 games.

BIG CAT—Rayfield Wright (1945–) Football. Defensive end for the Dallas Cowboys. Some call him the greatest pass blocker in NFL history.

BIG CAT [THE]—Johnny Mize (1913–) Baseball 1b. **H/F**

BIG COOP—Walker Cooper (1915–1991) Baseball. This 6' 3", 210 pound-catcher sometimes defiantly spit tobacco juice on the batters' shoes.

BIG D—Darrall Imhoff (1938–1928) Basketball. The Big D stood for this center's 6' 10" height and the way he played defense. In the 1959 NCAA final, Imhoff tipped in the ball in the closing seconds to edge West Virginia in California's 71–70 win. This two-time All-American played for six NBA teams.

BIG DADDY—Riddick Bowe (1967–) Boxing.

BIG DADDY—Shirley Crabtree (1936–) Wrestling.

BIG DADDY—Cecil Fielder (1963–) Baseball.

BIG DADDY—David Lattin (1943–) Basketball. At 6' 7" and 220 pounds, Lattin was an All-American forward at Texas University at El Paso.

BIG DADDY—Dan Wilkinson (1973–) Football. Defensive Lineman of Ohio State. In 1994, he became the highest-paid player in Cincinnati Bengals' history. Wilkinson, the first player taken in the April 24, 1994, NFL Draft, signed a six-year $14.4 million contract.

BIG DAN—Dennis Brouthers (1858–1932) Baseball. **H/F**

BIG DO—Reginald Frank Doherty (1874–1915) Tennis. His brother, Hugh Doherty, was known as Little Do.

BIG DOG—Peter L. Pihos (1923–) Football. This big two-way end scored sixty-one touchdowns for the Philadelphia Eagles during his nine-year career.

BIG DOG—Glenn Robinson. Basketball. A member of the 1996 Olympic Dream Team. In his 1994–1995 season with the Milwaukee Bucks, he averaged 21.9 points per game. He is a big dog, all right— 6' 7" and weighing 225 pounds. He was given his nickname by a custodian at Purdue University where Robinson attended college.

BIG E—Elden Jerome Campbell (1968–) Basketball. Played for the L.A. Lakers.

BIG ED—Edward Danowski (1911–) Football.

BIG ED—Edward Joseph Konetchy (1885–1947) Baseball 1b.

BIG ED—Ed McKeever (1910–) Football coach.

BIG ED—Edward Marvin Reulbach (1882–1961) Baseball. This pitcher tossed a one–hitter for the Cubs in 1906 and won 181 games during his career.

BIG ED—Ed Sadowski (1917–) Basketball c.

BIG ED—Edward Walsh (1881–1959) Baseball p. **H/F** Also called Big Moose.

BIG FEET—Earl H. Sande (1898–1968) Horse racing. **H/F** One of the best jockeys during the 1920s, THE GOLDEN AGE OF SPORTS, Sande had a habit of using his feet to push away other jockeys on their horses. In 1930, Sande rode Galant Fox to the Triple Crown.

BIG FOOT—Dave Johnson (1958–) Boxing.

BIG FOOT—Pete Ladd (1956–) Baseball. This pitcher got his nickname because of his appearance (he was a 6' 3", 240-pound bearded pitcher).

BIG FOOT—Derek Pringle (1958–) Cricket.

BIG FOOT—Bob Stanley (1954–) Baseball.

BIG G—John Gianelli (1950–) Basketball.
Big G was a 6' 11", 220-pound center.

BIG GAME—Leslie Hunter (1942–) Basketball.
Twice Hunter was the MVP during NCAA tournaments; his senior year this forward led Loyola to the 1963 national championship over Cincinnati.

BIG GAME—Monty Hunter (1959–) Football.
This safety plated for the Cowboys, Cardinals, and Redskins. His nickname is a pun on the phrase "Big Game Hunter" with double significance. An athlete with the last name of Hunter has a good chance of being tagged Big Game.

BIG GEORGE—George Foreman (1949–) Boxing.
Also called The Lightning Destroyer and Money.

BIG GREASY—William Betts. Baseball (Negro Leagues).

BIG GUY—Joe DiMaggio (1914) Baseball cf. **H/F**
Also called Joe D, JOLTIN' JOE, DIMAG, and YANKEE CLIPPER.

BIG HANDS—Gary Johnson (active 1975–1985) Football.

BIG HOUSE—Steve Moore (active 1983–1987) Football.

BIG JACK—John George McGill (1921–) Hockey.
McGill was a 6' 1", 180-pound center for the Boston Bruins.

BIG JEFF—Jim Jeffries (1875–1953) Boxing.
Also called Boilermaker and The California Hercules.

BIG JESS—Jess Willard (1883–1968) Boxing.
Also called Cowboy Jess, Kansas Giant, Pottawatomie Giant, Tall Pine of the Pottawatomie. See THE GREAT WHITE HOPE.

BIG JIM—Jim Thorpe (1888–1953) Football, track and field.

BIG KLU—Ted Kluzewski (1924–1988) Baseball 1b.
Also called Big K.

BIG LIS—Emil Liston (1890–1949) Basketball.
Coach Liston began the NAIA; 550 colleges now belong.

BIG LUKE—Luscious Luke Easter (1915–1979) Baseball.
Luscious was his given name. No wonder the big first baseman (6' 2", 240 pounds) preferred to be called Big Luke.

BIG MOMMA—Laura Davies (1964–) Golf.
Davies was the British and U.S. Open Golf champion in 1987. She weighed 161 pounds and stood 5'10". Not so big, actually.

BIG MOOSE—George Livingston Earnshaw (1900–1976)

Baseball. Earnshaw stood 6' 4" and tipped the scale at 210. In regular play he was 127–93 and 4–3 in three World Series. Also called Moose.

BIG O [THE]—Otto Velez (1950–) Baseball.

BIG PANCHO—Pancho Gonzalez (1928–) Tennis. **H/F**

BIG RED—Dave Cowens (1948–) Basketball cf. **H/F**

BIG RED—Frances Louise Janssen (active 1948–1952)
Baseball. She was a pitcher for the All-American Girls Baseball League. She had red hair.

BIG RED—Bill Walton (1950–) Basketball. **H/F**
This center was also called Beaver because his middle name of Theodore was like Theodore Cleaver on *Leave It to Beaver.*

BIG RED—Alex Webster (active 1955–1973) Football.

BIG SAM—Samuel Thompson (1860–1922) Baseball. **H/F**

BIG SHRIMP OF PRO FOOTBALL—Allie Sherman (1923–)
Football coach. Also called Pedantic Professor.

BIG SIX—Elton Leroy Auker (1910–) Baseball.
This pitcher reminded people of Christy Mathewson whose nickname was BIG SIX.

BIG SKY—Joe Montana (1956–) Football.
Montana chose this nickname for himself, but needless to say, it didn't catch on. What did catch on, however, was his success going from a national championship team at Notre Dame to winning four Super Bowls for San Francisco (1982, 1985, 1989, 1990). Montana also was the MVP of the NFL twice and of the Super Bowl three times.

BIG STASH—Stan Lopata. (1925–) Baseball.

BIG STEVE—Stephen Joseph Owen (1898–1964) Football.
H/F Owen was a 6', 240-pound, four-time All-Pro tackle. As head coach of the Giants, the team won the Division eight times and the NFL championship twice.

BIG T—Thirl Lee Bailey (1961–) Basketball.

BIG TOM—Tom Gorman (1916–1986) Baseball.
Gorman was a big umpire who also commanded and got respect.

BIG TRAIN—Lionel Billingy (1952–) Basketball.

BIG TRAIN—Lionel Pretoria Conacher (1901–) Hockey.
Conacher was voted Canada's Athlete of the Half-Century (1900–1950). After his retirement from playing left wing, he won a seat in Canada's Parliament. He stood 6' 1" and weighed 195 pounds; hence, the nickname.

BIG TRAIN—Al Johnson (1913–) Basketball.

BIG TRAIN—John Sisk (1906–) Football.

BIG TRAIN—Eric Douglas Vail (1953–) Hockey.

BIG TUBBY—Morris Raskin (1906–) Basketball coach.

BIG UGLY BEAR—Sonny Liston (1932–1971) Boxing. Cassius Clay's name for Liston. Clay later became Muhammed Ali.

BIG UN—Alfred Rose (1907–1988) Football.

BIG WHISTLE [THE]—William Chadwick (active 1940–1955) Hockey. **H/F** One night Chadwick, a player for the New York Rovers, was injured and the referee didn't show up. Chadwick refereed that night and for the next sixteen years. In spite of the little known fact that he was blind in his right eye, Chadwick went on to become a great NHL referee.

BIG WHITE WHALE—Clyde Lovellette (1929–) Basketball. **H/F** This 6' 9", 244-pound center got his nickname at the University of Kansas. Big Clyde helped the Jayhawkers win the NCAA championship and formed a dominating front line with Bob "FOOTHILLS" Kurland on the 1952 Olympic basketball team. See UNMATCHABLES.

BIG Z—Zenon Andrusyshyn (active 1978–1981) Football. Andrusyshyn was a kicker at UCLA and in the Canadian Football League and the USFL.

BIG Z—Zelmo Beatty (1941–) Basketball. Beatty was 6' 9" and 235 pounds. The center's biggest year was 1972 playing for the Utah Stars in the ABA. With an average of over twenty-three points for the year, he scored sixty-three points in one game against the Pittsburgh Condors.

BIGGIE—Marshall Goldberg (1917–) Football. Biggie Goldberg is a member of the National Football Foundation's College Hall of Fame.

BIGGLES—Ian Pearson. Soccer. Received his nickname from his love for flying. Biggles was the hero of a series of books about flying by W.E.F. Johnson.

BIKE [THE]—Mike Hailwood (active 1960s) Motorcycle racing. Hailwood was a top motorcyclist before he turned to Grand Prix racing.

BILL—Marquis Franklin Horr (1880–1955) Football.

BILL—Hubert George Quackenbush (1922–) Hockey. **H/F**

BILLY—Alfred Manuel Martin (1928–1989) Baseball. Billy Martin's first name started during the days when he was a bellisimo baby. After playing second base on four Yankee World Series teams, Martin managed the Yanks (five different times) to two pennants and one World Series.

BILLY BOO—Emerson Boozer (1943–) Football hb.

BILLY BUCKS—Billy Buckner (1949–) Baseball 1b.

BILLY THE KID—Willis S. Olson (1930–) Skiing. **H/F** Olson leaped onto the scene in 1950 with a ski jump of 297 feet at Stone Mountain. Over the next twenty-three years he remained one of the best American ski jumpers with a personal best of 393 feet.

BILLY THE KID—Billy Southworth (1893–1969) Baseball. Billy the Kid Southworth played in the big leagues from 1913-1929 and compiled a .297 lifetime average. In 1919 he and Rogers Hornsby tied for the National League leadership in triples (fourteen).

BILLY THE KID—William Taylor (1919–) Hockey.

BILLY THE QUID—William Walker (19__–) Boxing. Walker was the U.K. heavyweight champion. A pun on Billy the Kid, because Walker made money from his boxing ability.

BING—Winston Bryan Juckes (1926–) Hockey.

BING—John E. Miller (1903–1964) Football.

BINGO—Courtney Allen (1923–) Hockey.

BINGO—Ernie Banks (1931–) Baseball. See MR. CUB.

BINGO—Elwood DeMoss (1889–1965) Baseball (Negro Leagues). An outstanding second baseman, DeMoss was known for being able to hit the ball wherever he wanted.

BINGO—Arnold Charles Herber (1910–1969) Football.

BINGO—Rudolph Kampman (1914–) Hockey. When this defenseman bodychecked an opponent, a "bingo" resounded off the rafters.

BINGO—William McMahon (active 1929–1932) Football.

BINGO—Bobby Smith (1946–) Basketball.

BIRA B—Prince Birabongse Bhanuban (1914–) Auto racing. This Thai prince always remained calm under his blue helmet.

BIRD—William Rodney Averitt (1952–) Basketball. From 1973-1978, Bird appeared in 130 regular NBA games.

BIRD—Bobby Grich (1949–) Baseball.

BIRD CAGE—Lew Burdette (1926–) Baseball. In 1959, this pitcher was 21–15 and his record in two World Series was 4–2.

BIRD DOG—Bill Hopper (1890–1965) Baseball.

BIRD EYE—Harry Truby (1870–1953) Baseball 2b.

BIRD LEGS—Willie Jensen (active 1960s–1970s) Boxing. Jensen was the U.S. flyweight champ in 1970.

BIRD MAN—Mike Barrett (1943–) Basketball. This member of the 1968 U.S. Olympic basketball team received his nickname because of his flying stuff shots. This guard was All-Rookie in the ABA.

BIRDIE—William Franklin Cree (1882–1942) Baseball. Cree was once a jazz musician under the name of Burdee. As a major-league outfielder, he hit .292.

BIRDIE—George Tebbetts (1912–) Baseball. This American League catcher had a squeaky voice.

BIRMINGHAM BLACKSMITH [THE]—Joseph Burns (active late 1700s) Boxing. In 1777, a slave named Richmond defeated Burns when Burns was a sergeant with the British militia, a member of the occupying forces in Staten Island.

BISCUIT—Cornelius Bennett (active 1987–) Football.

BISCUIT PANTS—Lou Gehrig (1903–1941) Baseball. **H/F** Gehrig received this nickname because of the size of his buttocks, or as *Vanity Fair* said "due to certain architectural amplitudes." Also called IRON HORSE, Iron Man of Baseball, Larrupin' Lou, and PRIDE OF THE YANKEES.

BISHOP [THE]—Charles Kemp (1856–1933) Cricket.

BITSY—Bryan Grant (1910–) Tennis. Only 5' 5" and 120 pounds, Grant won the 1930, 1934, and 1935 National Clay Court Singles championships. Also called The Atlantic Atom and The Mighty Atom.

BLAB—Bill Schwartz (1884–1961) Baseball. Another player who enjoyed the gift of gab.

BLACK ANTELOPE [THE]—Jesse Owens (1913–1980) Track and field. **H/F** Also called Brown Bombshell and BUCKEYE BULLET.

BLACK BABE RUTH [THE]—Oscar Charleston (1896–1954) Baseball. **H/F** In fifty-three exhibition games against major-league pitching, Charleston of the Negro Leagues had sixty-two hits in 195 times at bat and eleven home runs.

BLACK BOMBER [THE]—Frank Brunn (1961–) Boxing.

BLACK CAT—Johnny Gagnon (1905–) Hockey. This goalie for the Montreal Canadiens received his nickname because of his dark complexion and jet black hair.

BLACK CLOUD—Larry Holmes (1949–) Boxing.

BLACK COBB [THE]—Spotswood Poles (1887–1962) Baseball (Negro Leagues). Poles was exceptionally fast on the base paths.

BLACK DEATH—Joseph Henry Blackburne (1841–1924) Chess.

BLACK DIAMOND [THE]—Jem Ward (1800–1884) Bareknuckles boxing. **H/F** Ward was a talented (white) champion in the 1800s, but he threw fights to win bets for himself and his friends. This became known as "playing for dark."

BLACK DICK BUTKUS [THE]—Isiah Robertson (active 1970s) Football. Robertson was an All-American in 1970.

BLACK GAZELLE [THE]—Wilma Rudolph (1940–1994) Track and field. **H/F** Also THE BLACK PEARL and SKEETER.

BLACK HERCULES—Mike Weaver (1952–) Boxing. Weaver had a sculpted physique and was the heavyweight champ from 1980–1982.

BLACK HOLE [THE]—Kevin McHale (1957–) Basketball. It was sometimes said that when you threw the ball into this player (who could play forward or center), you would not see it again.

BLACK JACK—Jack Brabham (active 1950s–1960s) Auto racing. An Australian World Champion driver of Formula One racing cars on the Grand Prix circuit.

BLACK JACK—John Lanza (1940–) Wrestling. Also called COWBOY JACK.

BLACK JACK—Jack McDowell (1966–) Baseball. Pitcher for the Chicago White Sox and the New York Yankees.

BLACK JACK—Jack Stewart (1917–1983) Hockey. **H/F**

BLACK LLOYD WANER [THE]—Jimmy Crutchfield. Baseball. Played outfield in the Negro Leagues for such teams as the Chicago American Giants, Homestead Grays, and Pittsburgh Crawfords.

BLACK MAGIC—Lewis Lloyd (1959–) Basketball.

BLACK MAMBA—Roger Mayweather (1961–) Boxing.

BLACK MIKE—Mickey Cochrane (1903–1962) Baseball. **H/F** Losing would throw Cochrane into a black funk. His lifetime .320 average is the best among catchers.

BLACK PEARL [THE]—Laurie Cunningham (1956–1989) Soccer.

BLACK PEARL [PEROLA NEGRA]—Pele (Edson Arantes de Nascimento) (1940–) Soccer. Perhaps the greatest soccer player of all-time, The Congress of Brazil has named him a national treasure. See PELE.

BLACK PEARL OF PHILADELPHIA—Jess Moulton (active late 1890s–early 1900s) Boxing.

BLACK PRINCE [THE]—Peter Jackson (active 1883–1899) Boxing. GENTLEMAN Jim Corbett once said, "Jackson could beat any heavyweight I ever saw."

BLACK RABBIT—Billy R. Smith (1935–) Boxing, football.

BLACK SAM OF RUTLAND, VT—Viro Small (1854–deceased) Boxing, wrestling. Born a slave near Buford, South Carolina, Viro Small fought in Vermont from 1870 to 1881. As the first African American professional wrestler, Small won sixty-three matches between 1882 and 1892.

BLACK SHADOW OF LEIPERVILLE [THE]—George Godfrey. Boxing.

BLACK UHLAN—Max Schmeling (1905–) Boxing. Schmeling was the heavyweight champ from 1930–1932. Also called Nazi Nailer.

BLACK WIDOW—Milton Owens. Boxing.

BLACK WONDER [MARAVILHA NEGRA]—Fausto Dos Santos (1905–1939) Soccer. This great Brazilian soccer player performed superbly in the 1930 World Cup.

BLACK WONDER [THE]—Bob Travers (active 1854–1864) Boxing. It was said that the boxing talents of Travers were second only to Molineau, THE MOOR.

BLACKIE—Alvin Dark (1923–) Baseball. Also Bright Star of the Boston Braves.

BLACKIE—Sam Joseph Dente (1922–) Baseball.

BLACKIE—Gus Mancuso (1905–) Baseball. This catcher, one of the best during the 1930s, had a swarthy complexion.

BLACKJACK—Harry E. Smith (1918–) Football.

BLACKY—Leo Allan Magnum (1900–) Baseball.

BLADE—Mike Belanger (1944–) Baseball. This pitcher was thin at 6' 1" and 170 pounds.

BLADE [THE]—Tom Hall (1947–) Baseball. This pitcher was 6 feet and weighed only 150 pounds.

BLAKE—Trevor Wesley (1959–) Hockey.

BLAZER [THE]—Don Blasingame (1932–) Baseball. Blasingame received his nickname because of his speed. This second baseman (also called The Corinth Comet as he hailed from Corinth, Mississippi) rarely hit into double plays.

BLAZING BEN—Ben Hogan (1912–) Golf. Also called BANTAM BEN, Golfdom's Mighty Mite, THE HAWK, and The Iceman.

BLIND BOMBER [THE]—George Glamack (1919–1987) Basketball. Glamack, who played center and forward, had bad eyesight and wore glasses on the court.

BLIND RYNE—Ryne Duren (1929–) Baseball. This relief pitcher threw a ninety-five-mph fastball, but with his poor eyesight and thick glasses, the batters were fearful of where he might throw it.

BLINK—William Bedford (active 1921) Football.

BLINKY—Fred Biletnikoff (1943–) Football. **H/F**

BLITZEN—Joe Benz (1886–1957) Baseball. Benz's pitching prowess shows in his ten wins over Walter Johnson. Also called Butcher Boy.

BLIX—Sylvester V. Donnelly (1914–1976) Baseball.

BLOBBO—Jack Nicklaus (1940–) Golf. See OHIO FATS and THE GOLDEN BEAR.

BLOND BLIZZARD [THE]—Robert Fenimore. Football.

BLOND BOMBER [THE]—William Walker. Boxing. Also called BILLY THE QUID.

BLOND BRUISER [THE]—Al Ettore. Boxing.

BLOND BULL—Ernie Nevers (1903–1976) Football. **H/F** See BIG DOG.

BLOND GUY—Guy Hecker (1856–1938) Baseball. On days when he wasn't pitching, Hecker would play first or in the outfield. In 1886, he did so well on these "off days" that he won the league batting crown with a .342.

BLONDIE—Al Owen (1913–) Football.

BLONDY—John Collins Ryan (1906–1959) Baseball. Ryan, who had blond hair, played shortstop in the 1933 and 1937 World Series for the New York Giants.

BLOOD—Johnny McNally (1903–1985) Football. **H/F**

BLOOP—Raymond Albert Bluth (1927–) Bowling. **H/F** In 1962, Bluth bowled the first 300 game ever at the ABC Masters.

BLOWER—Lew Brown (1858–1889) Baseball.

BLUE—Burgess Carey (1905–1961) Basketball. His nickname came from the fact that his school colors at Kentucky were blue and white.

BLUE DEVIL—Eric Tipton (1915–) Baseball. This outfielder had been an All-American football player at Duke University. Also called DUKIE.

BLUE GRIZZLY [THE]—Bill Tilden (1893–1953) Tennis. **H/F** Because of the bulky blue sweater he wore during warm-ups. Also called Court Jester. See BIG BILL.

BLUE MOON—Johnny Lee Odom (1945–) Baseball.

This pitcher was frequently down in the dumps; moon (a nickname left over from childhood) was because of his round face.

BLUEY—Arthur Bluenthal (1891–1918) Football.

BLUTO—Bob Babich (1947–) Football.
Played for San Diego and Cleveland. As comic strip fans know, Bluto was Popeye's rival.

BO—Robert Belinsky (1936–) Baseball.
Belinksy got into scrapes at school, so his chums nicknamed him after the fighter Bobo Olson. Bo was probably as well known for dating movie actress Mamie Van Doren as for pitching a no-hitter in 1962, the highpoint of his 28–51 pitching career.

BO—Douglass Bomeisler (1892–1953) Football.

BO—John R. Farrington (1936–1969) Football.

BO—Dwight Lamar (1951–) Basketball.
This two-time All-American guard at Southwestern Louisiana scored sixty-one points in a game in 1971.

BO—Al McMillan (1895–1952) Football qb/c.

BO—Glenn Schembechler (1929–) Football.
This football coaching legend compiled a 234–65–8 record with the Michigan Wolverines, taking them to the Rose Bowl twelve times.

BO—Norman Shephard (active 1924–1954) Basketball.
Shephard's record as a coach at North Carolina, Guilford, Randolph-Macon, Davidson, and Harvard was a combined 327–276.

BOARDS—Cornell Green (1940–) Football.
Received his nickname because of his tendency to hit the backboard when playing basketball. In football, however, he found his mark, setting the single season record for interception yards for the Dallas Cowboys.

BOBBY—Roderick John Wallace (1873–1960) Baseball.
H/F Playing every position except catcher, Wallace remained in baseball for sixty years as a manager, umpire, and scout. Also called Rhody.

BOBBY JOE—Robert J. Conrad (1935–) Football.

BOBIE—Norman Cahn (1892–1965) Football.

BOBO—Alva Holloman (1925–1987) Baseball p.

BOBO—Carl Olson (1928–) Boxing.
Olson was the middleweight champ from 1953 to 1955.

BOC—John Dominic Boccabella (1941–) Baseball.
The first baseman's last name shortened. (By the time you pronounced it, you would have forgotten what it was you wanted to say.)

BODIE—Morris Bodenger (1909–) Football.
His nickname is a play upon his last name.

BODY [THE]—John Brown (1922–) Football.
Brown played 1947–1949 for Los Angeles in the American Association. He received his nickname from the famous song "John Brown's Body."

BODY [THE]—Paul Hoffman (1925–) Basketball.

BODY [THE]—Gene Stanlee. Wrestling.

BOG TROTTER—Ron Delaney (active 1950s) Track and field. Delaney was from Dublin, Ireland.

BOILERYARD—William Jones Clarke (1868–1959) Baseball. Also called Nosy Bill.

BOILING BOILY—Burleigh Grimes (1893–1985) Baseball.
H/F Grimes was given this nickname because he always seemed to be mad when he pitched. His other nicknames were Ol' Stubble Beard and Wire Whiskers because he also never shaved on game day. It seemed to pay off as his record was 270–212.

BOLD BENDIGO—William Abednego Thompson (1811–1980) Boxing. **H/F** Thompson's nickname Bendigo was a variation of his middle name. Bendigo defeated James "Deaf" Burke in 1839 to become the champion of England.

BOLD MIKE—Mike McTigue (1892–1966) Boxing.

BOLEY—Frank Dancewicz (active 1944–1951) Football qb.

BOLLICKY—Billy Taylor (1855–1900) Baseball p.

BOMBER—Thomas George Bladon (1952–) Hockey.

BOMBER—Mark Bomback (1953–) Baseball p.

BOMBER [THE]—Charles William Conacher (1909–1967) Hockey rw. **H/F**

BOMBER—Maurice Van Robays (1914–1965) Baseball.

BONES—Frederick W. Ely (1863–1952) Baseball.
The player who replaced Ely at shortstop for Pittsburgh was Honus Wagner.

BONES—Horace McKinney (1919–) Basketball.
After playing for North Carolina and North Carolina State, McKinney was on the Washington and Boston teams in the NBA from 1947 to 1952.

BONES—Andy Nelson (active 1957–1964) Football.

BONES—Don Raleigh (1926–) Hockey.
New York Ranger center nicknamed for his skinny appearance. Raleigh scored winning goals for the Rangers in two overtime games in the 1950 Stanley Cup championships with the Detroit Red Wings.

BONECRUSHER—James Smith (1955–) Boxing.

For a short time Smith was the heavyweight champ.

BONECRUSHER BERNSTEIN—Joseph Bernstein (active 1920s) Football.

BONEY—Walter Grauman (1915–   ) Basketball.

BONNIE PRINCE CHARLIE—Claude Rayner (1920–   ) Hockey g. **H/F**

BOO—Donald Buse (1950–   ) Basketball.
Played for both the ABA and the NBA. Finished his career with Kansas City in 1984–1985. His nickname is a reference to his last name.

BOO—Steve Buechele (1961–   ) Baseball 3b.

BOO—Alex Ellis (1936–   ) Basketball.

BOO—Dave Ferris (1921–   ) Baseball.

BOO—Bruce Smith (active 1985–   ) Football.

BOOB—Byron Evard (1908–   ) Basketball.

BOOBIE—Charles Clark (1950–   ) Football.
This running back in the NFL received his nickname from his grandmother.

BOO BOO—Paul Palmer (active 1987–1989) Football.
In 1987, Palmer of the Kansas City Chiefs ran back thirty-eight kickoffs for 923 yards and two touchdowns.

BOO BOO—Curtis Rouse (active 1982–1987) Football.

BOOG—John Wesley Powell (1941–   ) Baseball.
Boog was a name from Powell's childhood. It seemed an odd moniker for a man who stood 6′ 4″ and weighed 230 pounds. During his career, this first baseman hit 339 home runs and played in four World Series.

BOOGER RED—Thomas Norbis, Jr. Football.

BOOM BOOM—Larry Cannon (active 1970s) Auto racing.

BOOM BOOM—Alain Luc Caron (1938–   ) Hockey.

BOOM BOOM—Willie Kirkland (1934–   ) Baseball.

BOOM-BOOM—Ray Mancini (1961–   ) Boxing.
Mancini beat Duk-Koo Kim senseless in their bout for the WBA middleweight title. After Kim died of his injuries, world title bouts were shortened from fifteen to twelve rounds.

BOOMER—Robert S. Brown. Football.

BOOMER—Donald D. Brumm (active 1963–1972) Football.

BOOTNOSE—Fred Hoffman (1894–1964) Baseball.
Played for the New York Yankees and the Boston Red Sox.

BOUNDING BASQUE [THE]—Jean-Robert Borota (1898–1994). Tennis. Borota, who was born in Arbonne, France, was one of Tennis' "Four

Musketeers"—Borota, Rene Lacoste, Jacques Brugnon, and Henri Cochet—who dominated amateur tennis in the 1920s and early 1930s. Borota received his nickname for his exuberance on the court. He was easily recognized because he wore a blue beret.

BRICKYARD—William Kennedy (1872–deceased). Baseball. Won 176 games for the Dodgers in the Nineteenth century. He received his nickname because he held a job as a bricklayer.

BRONK—Brian J. Brunkhorst (1945–   ) Basketball.
Played the 1968–1969 season for Los Angeles but appeared in only three games and scored twenty-five points. His nickname is a derivation of his last name.

BRUISER—Frank Kinard (1914–1985) Football.
Played from 1938 to 1942. One might think that football would be flooded with the nickname Bruiser but it is not as common in the NFL as it should be.

BUCKETS—Charles Goldenberg (1911–1986) Football.

BUCKEYE BULLET [THE]—Howie Kriss (1907–1992). Football. Kriss, as you might surmise from the nickname, played college ball for Ohio State. He turned pro and played one season for Cleveland in 1931.

BUDGE—Al Garrett (1893–1950) Football.

BUFFALO—Walter Napier (1936–   ) Football.

BUFFALO HEAD—Don Zimmer (1931–   ) Baseball.

BUG—James Wear Holliday (1867–1910) Baseball.

BUGGER—Frank Welch (1897–1957) Baseball.
Played nine years in the big leagues, mostly for the Philadelphia Athletics, and compiled a lifetime .274 batting average and hitting forty-one homers. He will be remembered, however, for bearing one of the more uncomplimentary nicknames.

BULL—Bill Johnson (1925–1978) Football.

BUM—A.R. Bright. Football. One of the owners of the Dallas Cowboys when he was among a group that purchased the team in 1984.

BUMPUS—Charlie Jones (1870–1938) Baseball.

BUSTER—James Douglas (1960–   ) Boxing.
On February 10, 1990, Buster Douglas shocked the boxing world by knocking out the undefeated Mike Tyson to win the heavyweight title.

BUTTER—Jack Fleishman (1982–   ) Football.
Played from 1925 to 1927. Fleishman is the name of a noted margarine.

BUZZ—Melwood Guy (1936–   ) Football.

CAB—Donald Martin Kolloway (1918–) Baseball. This second baseman was nicknamed after the song-and-dance man, Cab Calloway.

CAB—Jesse Renick (1917–) Basketball. This Native American was a two-time All-American at Oklahoma A & M, a two-time AAU All-American, and on the 1948 U.S. Olympic team.

CABBAGE PATCH—Wally Backman (1959–) Baseball. His nickname came into being when the cabbage patch dolls were all the fad.

CACHO—Angel Caro (1958–) Boxing. Argentine light heavyweight.

CACTUS—Gavvy Cravath (1881–1963) Baseball. This outfielder had a prickly personality.

CADDY—Leon Joseph Cadore (1891–1958) Baseball.

CADILLAC—Greg Anderson (1964–) Basketball.

CAESAR OF FOOTBALL—Louis Lawrence Little (1893–1979) Football coach. Little's original name was Luigi Piccolo. Also called Big Nose Louie.

CAKES—Jim Palmer (1945–) Baseball. This nickname came about because at the beginning of this Hall-of-Famer's career, he liked pancakes before pitching.

CAJUN CANNON—Bobby Hebert (active 1980s–1990s) Football. This quarterback for the New Orleans Saints received his nickname at Northwestern Louisiana.

CAL—Robert Hubbard (1900–1973) Football, baseball. **H/F**

CAL—Charles McCarthy, Jr. (1869–1895) Boxing.

CAL—Calvin Murphy (1948–) Basketball.

CAL—Carroll Schilling (1886–1950) Horse racing. **H/F** After a brilliant beginning, this jockey's career went down and down.

CALIFORNIA COMET [THE]—Maurice McLoughlin (1889–1956) Tennis.

CALIFORNIA GRIZZLY BEAR—James J. Jeffries (1875–1953) Boxing. Also called Big Jeff, The California Hercules, and BOILERMAKER.

CALIFORNIA TERROR—Joseph Choynski (1868–1943) Boxing. Choynski had a soft side as evidenced by his other nickname, Chrysanthemum Joe.

CALYPSO KID [THE]—Dory Dixon Wrestling.

CAMDEN BUZZSAW—Dwight Muhammad Qawi Boxing. A light-heavyweight boxer, Qawi's last name was originally Braxton.

CAMERA EYE—Max Bishop (1899–1962) Baseball. This second baseman had a good eye for balls and strikes. In 1929, he led the American League with 128 walks. Also called Tilly (for his high-pitched voice).

CAMPY—Roy Campanella (1921–) Baseball. **H/F** Campy was a three-time MVP on a Brooklyn Dodgers team that won the National League in 1949, 1952, 1953, and 1956, and the World Series in 1955.

CAMPY—Bert Camparneris (1942–) Baseball.

CANADIEN COMET—Howie Morenz (1902–1937) Hockey. Also called BABE RUTH OF HOCKEY, HURTLING HABITANT, MITCHELL METEOR, STRATFORD STREAK.

CANASTOTA ONION FARMER—Carmen Basilio (1927–) Boxing. Also called Uncrowned Champion.

CANDY—Tom Candiotti (1957–) Baseball.

CANDY—George LaChance (1870–1932) Baseball 1b.

CANDY MAN—John Candelaria (1953–) Baseball. This nickname comes from the pitcher's last name.

CANNONBALL—James Butler (1943–) Football. Played from 1965 to 1972 for Pittsburgh, Atlanta, and St. Louis. Shot through opponents like a cannonball.

CANNONBALL—Ed Crane (1862–1996) Baseball. This pitcher had a good fastball.

CANNONBALL—Eddie Martin (1903–) Boxing.

CANNONBALL [THE]—Dick Redding (1891–1940) Baseball (Negro Leagues) p.

CANNONBALL—Ledell Titcomb (1866–1950) Baseball.

CANNONBALL—Gus Weyhing (1866–1952) Baseball. Also called Rubber Winged Gus.

CAP—Fred Clarke (1872–1960) Baseball. **H/F** For many years, Clarke was the left fielder (with a lifetime .315 batting average), the captain, as well as the manager of Pittsburgh.

CAPPY—Franklin Cappan (1900–1961) Basketball.

CAPPY—Gino Cappelletti (1934–) Football.

CAPTAIN—Matthew Webb (1848–1883) Swimming. Webb was the first man to swim across the English Channel.

CAPTAIN AMERICA—Roger Staubach (1942–) Football. Also called THE ARTFUL DODGER and The Dodger.

CAPTAIN CRASH—Cliff Harris (1948–) Football. Harris was one of the hardest hitters in the NFL; hence, the nickname. Sounds as if he should be a superhero for Marvel Comics.

CAPTAIN CRAZY—Fulton Kuykendall (active 1975–1985) Football.

CAPTAIN CRUNCH—Barry Bec (1957–) Hockey.
Stood 6' 3" and weighed 215 pounds. Enough said?
Captain Crunch is also the name of a popular cereal.

CAPTAIN CRUNCH—Jean Gilles Marotte (1945–) Hockey.
The nickname comes from the way he used his body
on defense.

CAPTAIN EDDIE—Edward Henry Knipschield (1907–1964)
Aerialist.

CAPTAIN HOOK—George "Sparky" Anderson (1934–)
Baseball. Anderson received this nickname because
as a manager he went to the bullpen so often. (This
would be the equivalent of the stage manager in
vaudeville giving a bad act "the hook.") See SPARKY.

CAPTAIN HOOK—Mike Keenan. Hockey.
Keenan, the coach of the Chicago Blackhawks, would
take out the starting goalie in an attempt to motivate
his players during important games in 1988–1989.

CAPTAIN LATE—James Silas (1949–) Basketball.

CAPTAIN MIDNIGHT—Frank Johnson (1958–) Basketball.
This guard was the Washington Bullets' NBA Rookie of
the Year in 1981–1982.

CAPTAIN MIDNIGHT—Lee Walls (1933–) Baseball.
This nickname was for the outfielder's large glasses.
Captain Midnight was the name of a popular Saturday
Morning television show in the early 1950s.

CAPTAIN NICE—Mark Donohue (1937–1975) Auto racing.
Polite and popular with the fans, Donohue came out of
retirement to race a Formula One car he helped design.
While driving practice laps for the Austrian Grand Prix
in 1975, the car crashed and Mark Donohue was killed.

CAPTAIN OF EXCITEMENT—Lawrence McCeney (1895–)
Football. Also called Biff.

CAPTAIN SLICK—Y. A. Tittle (1926–) Football.
Tittle was a crafty quarterback. See YAY.

CAPTAIN VIDEO—Bill Fitch (1933–) Basketball.
When Fitch was coaching the Celtics, the players
noticed he was watching a lot of game film.

CARACOL [EL] [THE SNAIL]—Vincente Bernabe
Bullfighting.

CASABLANCA CLOUTER—Marcel Cerdan (1916–1949)
Boxing. **H/F** Many opponents of this fighter from
Algeria did not survive the early rounds.

CASEY—Charlie Jones (1876–1947) Baseball.
This outfielder's nickname was after the locomotive
engineer.

CASEY'S KID—Gilbert James McDougald (1928–)
Basketball.

CASH—Wayne Cashman (1945–) Hockey.
Cashman played forward for the Boston Bruins when
they won the Stanley Cup in 1970 and 1972.

CASH—Joseph "Bill" Taylor (1926–) Baseball.

CASPER THE FRIENDLY GHOST—Jerry Adair (1936–1987)
Baseball. This popular and unassuming second baseman was nicknamed after Casper the Friendly Ghost
was a popular cartoon and comic book character.

CASSIUS THE BRASHEST—Muhammad Ali (1942–)
Boxing. **H/F** Ali's original name was Cassius Marcellus
Clay. See THE GREATEST.

CAT—John Thompson (1906– deceased) Basketball. **H/F**
"That isn't a human being—that's a tree-cat," said
coach Romney at a Montana State Bobcat practice of
his guard, John Thompson. Thompson led the Bobcats
to two straight 36–2 records.

CAT—Gogen Yamaguchi. Karate.

CAT [THE]—Ernie Lad (1938–) Football.

CAT [THE]—Felix Mantilla (1934–) Baseball.

CATFISH—Jim Hunter (1946–) Baseball. **H/F**

CATFISH—Bill Klem (1874–1951) Baseball.
Some thought Klem bore a facial resemblance to a
catfish. If anyone dared to bring it up to this umpire
during a ballgame, he would automatically get the
thumb: "You're out-a here!"

CATFISH—George M. Metkovich (1921–) Baseball.
While fishing one day, he stepped on a catfish and cut
his foot, causing him to miss several days of play. He
is better remembered for what he did on another day,
however. On April 17, 1945, he made three errors at
first base.

CATFISH—Ralph Smith (active 1962–1964) Football.

CATFISH—Vernon Smith (active 1929–1931) Football.

CAV—Frank William Cavanaugh (1876–1932) Football
coach.

CECIL—Cecilia Leitch (1891–1977) Golf.
Cecil won the British Women's Championship four
times, the French Ladies' Open five times, and the
Canadian Ladies' Open once. She was the English
Women's Champion in 1914 and 1921.

CEECE—Cecil Graham Dillon (1908–) Hockey.

CEMENT HEAD—James Albert Hargreaves (1950–)
Hockey.

CHA CHA—Shirley Muldowney (1940–) Drag racing.
Beginning her drag strip racing career at thirty-five,
Muldowney was the first woman to speed through the
quarter mile in less than sixty seconds and the first to
break 240 mph. Also called Queen of the Drag Strip.

CHABOTSKY—Lorne Chabot (1900–) Hockey.
Press agent Johnny Bruno of the New York Rangers
gave goaltender Chabot (a French-Canadian) this
name in order to capture the attention of potential
Jewish fans in the New York area.

CHAD—Clyde Elias Kimsey (1905–1942) Baseball.

CHALKY—Albert Wright (1912–1957) Boxing.
Wright lost the featherweight title to Willie Pep in 1942.

CHAMP [THE]—Jack Dempsey (1895–1983) Boxing.
See THE MANASSA MAULER.

CHAMP—Anthony Dickerson (1957–) Football. In 1983,
this linebacker led the Dallas Cowboys in solo tackles.

CHAMP—Pete Mehringer (1910–1987). Football.

CHAMPAGNE PETER—Peter Revson. (d. 1974) Auto racing.
Revson came from a wealthy family, and when he won
he often sprayed those in the winners' circle with
champagne. In 1970, he teamed with actor Steve
McQueen to finish second in the Sebring 12 Hours.

CHAMPAGNE TONY—Tony Lema (1934–1966) Golf.
This 1964 British Open champion celebrated his victories with champagne parties for the press.

CHAMPION [THE]—William Gilbert Grace (1848–1915)
Cricket. Grace batted 54,896 runs during his career.

CHANGO—Erubey Carmona (1944–) Boxing.

CHAPPIE—George Johnson (1875–deceased) Baseball
(Negro Leagues).

CHAPPY—Ben Chapman (1908–) Baseball.
Chappy, an outfielder, was the American League's first
batter up in the first All-Star Game (1933).

CHARLES—Buster Chatham (1901–1975) Baseball.

CHARMER [THE]—George Zettlein (1884–1905) Baseball.

CHATTIE—Charles Reinage Cooper (1871–1966) Tennis.

CHAUCER—Edwin S. Elliott (1879–1913) Hockey. **H/F**

CHAUNCEY—Jean Dubec (1888–1958) Baseball.
This pitcher was banned from baseball by Judge
Landis after the Black Sox scandal of 1919.

CHEEKS—Leon Wagner (1934–) Baseball.
Also called Daddy Wags.

CHEESE—Al Schweitzer (1882–1969) Baseball of.
Cheese as in Swiss (Schweitzer) cheese.

CHEO—Pablo Cruz (1947–) Baseball.

CHEROKEE—Robert Johnson (1906–1982) Baseball.
Also called INDIAN BOB.

CHERRY—Gregg Bingham. Football.

CHESTY JOIE—Joie Ray (1894–1978) Track and field.
Ray's nickname began when he was called "a chesty
little guy with a great heart" in a sports article. In
1925, he ran the mile in an U.S. record of 4:12.

CHET—Chester Walker (1940–) Basketball.
Also called Chet the Jet.

CHEWING GUM—John O'Brien (1870–1913) Baseball.

CHICAGO SPIDER—Johnny Coulon (1889–1973) Boxing.
H/F This boxer who stood just five feet tall held the
bantamweight title in 1908.

CHICK—William Chalmers (1934–) Hockey.

CHICK—Tony Cuccinello (1907–) Baseball.

CHICK—Charles Evans (1890–1979) Golf.
Chick is often a nickname for Charles.

CHICK—Charles Fullis (1904–1946) Baseball.
Fullis had an eight-year career average of .295.
See GASHOUSE GANG.

CHICK—Charles Arnold Gandil (1887–1970) Baseball 1b.

CHICK—Charles Hafey (1903–1973) Baseball. **H/F**

CHICK—Francis Dayle Hearn. Basketball, broadcasting.
On Monday, January 19, 1998, Chick Hearn broadcast his
3,000th consecutive game for the Los Angeles Lakers.

CHICK—Herry Jagade (1928–1968) Football.

CHICK—John Francis Meehan (1893–1972) Football
coach.

CHICK—John Robert Webster (1921–) Hockey.

CHICKEN—Fred Stanley (1947–) Baseball.
This shortstop hailed from Farnhamville, Iowa.

CHICKEN—William Van Winkle Wolf (1862–1903) Baseball.
This outfielder once ate a chicken dinner immediately
before a game in which he committed many errors.
With his nickname and his batting average of .363 in
1890, he could just as easily have been called Rip.

CHICKEN PLUCKER [THE]—Bobby Riggs (1918–1948)
Tennis. Riggs lost the Battle of the Sexes tennis
match to Billie Jean King in 1973.

CHICO—Leo Cardenas (1938–) Baseball ss.
The meaning of *chico* in Spanish is "kid."

CHICO—Alfonso Colon Carrasquel (1928–) Baseball ss.
During his ten years in the majors, Carrasquel played
for the White Sox, the Indians, and the Orioles.

CHICO—Humberto Fernandez (1932–) Baseball.
This shortstop was from Havana.

CHICO—Ronald Patrick Maki (1939–) Hockey rw.

CHICO—Glenn Resch (1948–) Hockey g.

CHICO—Hiraldo Sablon Ruiz (1938–) Baseball.
This second baseman was from Santo Domingo, Cuba.

CHICO—Manny Ruiz (1951–) Baseball 3b.

CHICO—Ruthford Eduardo Salmon (1940–) Baseball.
This second baseman/outfielder was from Panama.

CHICO—Charles Vaughn (1940–) Basketball.

CHIEF—Jack Delane Aker (1940–) Baseball.
Aker was a Pottowatomie Indian. In 1966, he registered thirty-two saves, the most in the American League, and posted an ERA of 1.99.

CHIEF—Charles Bender (1883–1954) Baseball. **H/F**
This Hall of Fame pitcher was a Chippewa who pitched for Connie Mack's Philadelphia As. He had one no-hitter during the regular season and was 6–4 in five World Series for the MACKMEN. His record was 210–127 with a 2.46 ERA.

CHIEF—Clarence Boston (active 1930s) Football.

CHIEF—John Paul Bucyk (1935–) Hockey. **H/F**
His nickname was given to him by his Boston Bruin teammate Bronco Horvath because of Bucyk's "Indian-Chief" appearance. Chief played left wing for the Boston Bruins when they won the Stanley Cup in 1970 and 1972.

CHIEF—Arvel Hale (1908–1980) Baseball.
Also called Bad News.

CHIEF—Melvin Harder (1909–) Baseball.
See WIMPY.

CHIEF—Elon Chester Hogsett (1903–) Baseball.

CHIEF—Clyde James (1900–) Basketball.
James was a member of the Modoc tribe in Oklahoma. He set scoring records at Missouri Southwest State College in 1924–1925 and played AAU basketball in Tulsa from 1927 to 1947.

CHIEF—George Johnson (1886–1922) Baseball.
This pitcher was a member of the Winnebago tribe.

CHIEF—Phil King (active 1958–1966) Football hb/fb.

CHIEF—Ernie Koy (1909–) Baseball.

CHIEF—Harry Litwack (1907–) Basketball coach.
Litwack coached at Temple University from 1953 to 1973 and had a record of 373–193.

CHIEF—James Anthony Neilson (1941–) Hockey.

CHIEF—M. C. Reynolds (active 1958–1960) Football.

CHIEF—John Milton Warhop (1884–1960) Baseball.
Also called CRAB.

CHIEF—John Owen Wilson (1883–1954) Baseball.

CHIEF—Moses J. Yellowhorse (1900–1964) Baseball.

CHIEF [THE]—Reggie Leach (1950–) Hockey.
Leach's nickname was because of his Native American heritage. In 1976, Leach scored sixty-one goals during the regular season for the Flyers and nineteen during the playoffs. His eighty goals eclipsed Phil Esposito's record. Also called Rifle.

CHIEF [THE]—Jim Neilson (1940–) Hockey.
Neilson, a half-Cree Indian from Big River, Saskatchewan, was a defenseman on the New York Rangers for twelve seasons. He scored about five goals and made twenty assists a season in the late sixties and early seventies. In 1978, as a member of the Cleveland Barons, he played in his one thousandth game.

CHIEF [THE]—Robert Parish (1953–) Basketball.

CHIEF [THE]—Allie Reynolds (1915–) Baseball.
Also called WAHOO.

CHIEF TOKOHAMA—Charles Grant (?–1932) Baseball.
John McGraw once tried to have this second baseman from the Negro Leagues play for him by claiming Grant was Chief Tokohama. It didn't work.

CHILDE HAROLD—Hal Javrin (1892–1962) Baseball.
Having made the leap from public school to the Red Sox, Javrin was nicknamed after the knight in Lord George Byron's poem.

CHILI—Charles Davis (1960–) Baseball.
This outfielder's nickname was for chili bowl, the method used for giving him haircuts as a child.

CHILL—Willie Anderson (1967–) Basketball.
Appeared in 413 regular season games for the San Antonio Spurs and averaged 13.9 points per game.

CHING—Marcel Albert Dheere (1920–) Hockey.

CHING—Ivan Johnson (1897–1979) Hockey. **H/F**
Ching was a big defenseman for the New York Rangers for the first eleven years of their history. His nickname had to do with his facial features and his bald head that gave him the look of a Chinese warlord. Also called CHINAMAN, CHING-A-LING, and IVAN THE TERRIBLE.

CHINK—Arnett Pearson (active 1920s) Football.

CHINK—Ray Scott (1938–) Basketball.
Pulled down 7,154 rebounds in the NBA before becoming coach of the Detroit Pistons.

CHIPPER—Larry Wayne Jones (1973–) Baseball.
When this Atlanta Braves player was growing up his hero was Cal Ripken.

CHIPPIE—George Gaw (1892–1968) Baseball.

CHIPS—George Sobek (1920–) Basketball.

CHOCOLATE THUNDER—Daryl Dawkins (1957–) Basketball. Also Dr. Jam and Master Blaster.

CHOIRBOY—Walter Swinburn (1962–) Jockey.
This Englishman received his nickname from his youthful appearance.

CHOO-CHOO—Charles Boston. Boxing.

CHOO-CHOO—Charlie Brown (active 1980s) Boxing.

CHOO-CHOO—Clarence Coleman (1937–) Baseball.

CHOO CHOO—Irene May Hickson (active 1943–1951) Baseball (All-American Girl's Baseball League).

CHOO-CHOO—Charlie Justice (1924–) Football.
This legend at North Carolina (5,000 yards rushing, 42.6 yard punting average) even had a song named after him: "All the Way, Choo Choo."

CHOPPER—Dave Campbell (1951–) Baseball.

CHOPPY—James Adair (1907–1982) Baseball.

CHOPS—Siggy Broskie (1911–1975) Baseball c.
Broskie lasted only eleven games for the Boston Braves.

CHRIS—George W. Christensen (1909–1968) Football.

CHRYSANTHEMUM—Joe Choynski (1868–1943) Boxing. **H/F**

CHUB—Charles Feeney (1921–1994) Baseball.
He was president of the San Diego Padres in 1988 and once held the office of President of the National League, where he held the line against the use of the designated hitter. His grandfather was Charles Stoneham, who was the owner of the New York Giants.

CHUB—Endicott T. Peabody (1920–) Football.

CHUCK—Charles Hyatt (1908–1978) Basketball. **H/F**
Hyatt paced Pitt to national title in 1927–1928 with 266 points.

CHUCK—Charles Taylor (1901–1969) Basketball. **H/F**
Taylor introduced a basketball shoe in 1921 and later started the Converse Rubber Co. (This is the man whose signature is on the Converse.)

CHUCKIN' CHARLIE—Charlie O'Rouke (1917–) Football.
This quarterback was from Canada.

CHUCKLES—Rick MacLeish (1950–) Hockey c.

CINCINNATI COBRA—Ezzard Charles (1921–1975) Boxing. Also THE HAWK.

CIRCUS SOLLY—Arthur "Solly" Hofman (1882–1956) Baseball. Hofman pulled in many a circus catch in the outfield.

CITATION—Lloyd Archer Merriman (1924–) Baseball of.
Merriman's nickname was in honor of the horse that won the Triple Crown in 1948.

CITO—Clarence Gaston (1944–) Baseball.
When the Toronto Blue Jays won in 1992, Gaston became the first African American manager to win a World Series.

C. J.—Charlie Johnson (1949–) Basketball.

C. K.—Chuan-Kwang Yang (1935–) Track and field.
At the 1960 Olympic Games, Yang won seven of ten events in the decathlon but finished second to Rafer Johnson, his teammate and friend. With 8,334 points, Yang had also eclipsed the world record. (Johnson had 8,392.)

CLANCY—George Cutshaw (1887–1973) Baseball.

CLANK—Curtis LeRoy Blefary (1943–) Baseball.
His Baltimore Oriole teammates gave this outfielder this nickname because of his iron-gloved fielding.

CLARE—Clarence Drouillard (1914–) Hockey.

CLARENCE THE GREAT—Clarence DeMar (1888–1958) Running. Demar won the Boston Marathon seven times from 1911 to 1930.

CLARK KENT—Kurt Rambis (1958–) Basketball.
Rambis wore taped black tortoise shell glasses as he scrambled around the court, agile for a big forward.

CLASSY—Frederick Blassey. Wrestling.
This is a rhyming nickname.

CLASSY CLEO—Cleophus Littleton (1932–) Basketball.
Littleton was a high-scoring, two-time All-American forward at Wichita State.

CLAW [THE]—Otto Schnellbacher (1923–) Basketball.

CLEVELAND RUBBER MAN—Johnny Risko (1902–1953) Boxing. Also called Cleveland's Tireless Heavyweight and The Spoiler.

CLIMAX—Clarence Blethen (1893–1973) Baseball.
In 1923 for the Red Sox and 1929 for the Dodgers, Blethen posted the same pitching record of 0–0.

CLIPPER—John Smith. Football.
See LITTLE CLIPPER.

CLOG MAKER [THE]—Harry Gray (1740s) Boxing.

CLONES CYCLONE—Barry McGuigan. Boxing.

CLOUTING CLOWN—Max Baer (1909–1959) Boxing. See FISTIC HARLEQUIN.

CLOWN PRINCE OF BASEBALL [THE]—Al Schacht (1892–1984) Baseball. After a short career with the Washington Senators (1919–1921), Schacht toured the baseball diamonds of the country wearing long tails, top hat, and an oversized glove to highlight the funny side of baseball.

CLUTCH—Sammy Angott (1915–1980) Boxing. **H/F**

CLUTCH [THE]—Tommy Henrich (1913–   ) Baseball. See OLD RELIABLE.

CLYDE THE GLIDE—Clyde Drexler (1962–   ) Basketball. Whether playing guard or forward, Drexler was given this rhyming nickname for his ability to slide into the basket for a stuff shot.

COACH OF COACHES [THE]—Dave Tobey (1898–1988) Basketball. First Jewish athlete elected to the Naismith Basketball Hall of Fame. He was a great coach and was also known as "Pep."

COACHEE—Jack Holmes. Boxing
Holmes had once worked as a coachman. COACHMAN (THE)—George Stevenson (late 18th century) Boxing.

COASTER JOE—Joseph Connolly (1896–1960) Baseball.

COB—Jack Sharkey. Boxing.

COBBLES—Herbert Sturhahn (active 1920s) Football.

COBRA—Don Curry (1961–   ) Boxing.
This World Boxing Association champion received his nickname because of the speed of his punches.

COBRA [THE]—Dave Parker (1951–   ) Baseball.
Parker used a coiled batting stance.

COBRA—Gary Simmons (1944–   ) Hockey.
Simmons was very fast in goal with his glove to snare pucks hurtling toward the net.

COCA—Cesar Dario Gutierrez (1943–   ) Baseball.
This nickname was because he came from Venezuela.

COCKY—Edward Collins (1887–1951) Baseball. **H/F**
Bubbling over with self-confidence, Collins hit a cool .333 and stole 743 bases during a twenty-five-year career. This second baseman was a member of Connie Mack's $100,000 INFIELD.

COCKY OCCY—Mark Occhilupo. Surfing.

COCO—Jose Laboy (1939–   ) Baseball.

COCOA—Dan Woodman (1893–1962) Baseball.

COD—Albert Myers (1863–1927) Baseball.

COLBY JACK—John Coombs (1882–1957) Baseball.
Coombs had gone to Colby College in Maine. In 1910, his record was 31–9; in addition, he won three games for the Athletics in the World Series.

COLD WATER JIM—James Hughey (1869–1945) Baseball.
This pitcher was born and died in Cold Water, Michigan.

COLONEL—Earl H. Blaik (1897–1988) Football coach.
Also called RED and EARL OF HANOVER.

COLONEL JACK—John Albert Krohn (active 1908–1910) Long-distance walker.

COLUMBIA GEORGE—George Smith (1892–1965) Baseball.
This pitcher attended Columbia University. (One of Lou Gehrig's nicknames was Columbia Lou.)

COMET—Willie Davis (1940–   ) Baseball.

COMMY—Charles Comiskey (1859–1931) Baseball. **H/F**
See THE OLD ROMAN.

COMMUTER RALPH—Ralph Lumenti (1936–   ) Baseball.

CONNIE MACK OF PRO BASKETBALL—Frank Morganweck (1875–1941) Basketball. **H/F** Morganweck was a promoter and manager of basketball teams in the East for thirty-two years.

CONVERTIBLE CONN—Conn McCreary (1921–1979) Horse racing. **H/F** Won the 1951 Kentucky Derby aboard Conn Turf. Conn was aboard Conn.

COOCHIE—Gareth Chilcott. Rugby.
This nickname came from the baby talk of childhood (coochie-coochie-coo).

COOKIE—Carlton Gilchrist (1935–   ) Football.
Gilchrist didn't play college football; he went directly to Canadian football after high school. When he returned south of the border in 1962, Gilcrist led the AFL with 1,096 yards and thirteen touchdowns playing halfback for the Buffalo Bills.

COOKIE—Harry Lavagetto (1912–1990) Baseball.
Third baseman Cookie's claim to fame was his ability to pinch-hit.

COOKIE—Octavio Rojas (1939–   ) Baseball.

COOL HAND LUKE—John Lucas (1953–   ) Basketball.
His nickname makes allusion to the movie starring Paul Newman.

COONEY—Ralph Weiland (1904–1985) Hockey. **H/F**

COONSKIN—Curt Davis (1903–1965) Baseball.

This thirteen-year veteran liked the outdoors and hunting back home in Missouri.

COOT—Orville Veal (1932–) Baseball ss.

COOZ—Jerry Koosman (1943–) Baseball p.

CORDUROY—Michael Whelan (1870s) Wrestling.

CORK—Ted Wilks (1915–1989) Baseball p.

In both 1949 and 1951, Wilks led the league in saves. His nickname was for how he acted as a stopper, putting the cork in the bottle.

CORKY—David Calhoun (1950–) Basketball.

CORKY—Tommy Corcoran (1869–1960) Baseball.

Played in the major leagues for eighteen seasons, from 1890–1907, and finished with a lifetime BA of .257. His nickname comes naturally from his last name.

CORKY—Walter Devlin (1931–) Basketball.

CORKY—John Sullivan (1873–1924) Baseball.

This semi-pro catcher in Chicago lost a leg in a railroad accident when he was thirteen; however, he overcame his handicap to play ball with grace and courage.

CORNBREAD—Cedric Maxwell (1955–) Basketball.

That was this Boston Celtic forward's nickname when he was in college.

CORNBREAD RED—Bill Birge. Pool.

CORNCOB—Jerry Reichow. Football.

CORPORAL—Issy Schwartz (1902–) Boxing.

COS—Doug Cosby (1956–) Football.

COT—Ellis F. Deal (1923–) Baseball.

This nickname was short for cotton top.

COTNEY—John Leonard Hopp (1916–) Baseball of/1b.

He was a cotton top as a kid. Also called Hippity.

COTTON—Al Brazle (1913–1973) Baseball p.

COTTON—Francis Davidson (active 1954–1968) Football qb. Cotton was short for cotton top; it is the same as towhead.

COTTON—Lowell Fitzsimmons (1931–) Basketball coach.

COTTON—Charles Nash (1942–) Basketball. **H/F**

Called Cotton because of his light-colored hair, Nash was a three-time All-American at Kentucky.

COTTON—Charles Speyrer (1949–) Football.

Born with white hair, Speyrer was the hero of the 1969 Cotton Bowl.

COTTON—James Arthur Tierney (1894–1953) Baseball 2b.

COTTON—Irvine E. Warburton (1911–) Football qb.

COUGS—Gail R. Cogdill (1937–) Football.

COUNT—Asa Brainard (1841–1888) Baseball 2b.

COUNT—Donald Grosso (1915–) Hockey.

COUNT—John F. Orsi (active 1930s) Football.

COUNT OF LUXEMBOURG [THE]—Henry William Meine (1896–1968) Baseball. Also called HEINE.

COUNTRY—Keith Atherton (1959–) Baseball p.

COUNTRY—Todd Fowler (1962–) Football.

He received his nickname because he was born in Van, Texas—i.e. out in the country.

COUNTRY—Bonnie Graham (1914–) Basketball.

Graham pioneered the development of the hook shot.

COUNTRY—Jim King (1941–) Basketball.

From Tulsa, Oklahoma, King played guard for Tulsa and four teams in the NBA.

COUNTRY—Edward Meadows (1932–) Football.

From Oxford, North Carolina, Meadows was thrown out of the 1956 title game between the Bears and the Lions for hitting one of the Lions.

COUNTRY—Enos B. Slaughter (1916–) Baseball f. **H/F**

Slaughter was from North Carolina. He hit a sterling .300 over a nineteen-year career in the majors. His ability to hustle was shown in the seventh game of the 1946 World Series when he scored the winning run all the way from first base on a single.

COUNTRY—Lonnie Warnecke (1909–1976) Baseball.

Also called Arkansas Hummingbird, Dixie, and Ol' Arkansas.

COURT JOUSTER—Bill Tilden (1893–1953) Tennis. **H/F**

See BIG BILL.

COUSIN ED—Edward Barrow (1868–1953) Baseball. **H/F**

Barrow was the Yankees general manager from 1921 to 1945 when the team won fourteen pennants and ten World Series.

COWBOY—Tommy Anderson (1911–) Hockey.

This native of Edinburgh, Scotland, played left wing for the New York Americans.

COWBOY—Edward Convey (active 1930–1933) Hockey.

Convey played left wing for the New York Americans.

COWBOY—Leroy Edwards (1914–) Basketball.

COWBOY—William Meyer Flett (1943–) Hockey.

COWBOY—Wes Fry (1902–1970) Football.

COWBOY—Dick Hutton. Wrestling.

COWBOY—Jack Wills. Boxing.

COWBOY JACK—John Lanza (1940–) Wrestling.

Also called Black Jack.

COWBOY JESS—Jess Williard (1881–1968) Boxing. Williard, who was the heavyweight champion from 1915-19, once worked as a cowboy in Kansas. Also called THE GREAT WHITE HOPE.

COXIE—Danny Cox (1959–) Baseball.

COY—Lander M. Bacon. Football.

CRAB [THE]—Jesse Burkett (1868–1953) Baseball. **H/F** Although Burkett's natural disposition was crabby, he was also a natural hitter (.423 in 1895, .410 in 1896, and .402 in 1899).

CRAB—John Milton Warhop (1884–1960) Baseball. Also called Chief.

CRABAPPLE COMET [THE]—Johnny Rucker (1917–1985) Baseball. This speedy outfielder was from Crabapple, Georgia.

CRABBY—Estel Crabtree (1903–1967) Baseball. Crabtree, an outfielder, was from Crabtree, Ohio.

CRACKER [THE]—Ray Schalk (1892–1970) Baseball. **H/F** This catcher from Illinois threw the ball back to the pitcher so hard it made a cracking sound when it hit the glove.

CRAFTY TEXAN—Frank Childs (1867–deceased) Boxing.

CRANE—Frank Reberger (1944–) Baseball. This pitcher was 6' 5".

CRASH—Dick Allen (1942–) Baseball. Allen's autobiography is titled *Crash*.

CRASH—Jim Birr (1916–) Basketball.

CRASH—Ian Robertson Cushernan (1933–) Hockey. This big defenseman caused them on the ice.

CRASH—Vic Janowicz (1930–) Baseball. This catcher's nickname referred to his football days. At Ohio State, he had won the 1950 Heisman Trophy.

CRASH—John Mengelt (1949–) Basketball.

CRASHING DASHING KID [THE]—Ted Kid Lewis (1894–1970) Boxing. Lewis was one of the best boxers ever to come out of Great Britain.

CRAZY FATSO—Billy Casper (1931–) Golf.

CRAZY HORSE—Tim Foli (1950–) Baseball.

CREEPER [THE]—Ed Stroud (1939–) Baseball of. Stroud's walk made it appear as if he was sneaking around.

CREEPY—Frank Crespi (1918–1990) Baseball. When he played second base for the St. Louis Cardinals, he moved so slowly that he seemed to creep around the infield.

CRICKET—John Sidney Battle (1962–) Basketball. He was also called Pickle.

CRIP—Lou Polli (1901–) Baseball p.

CROCODILE [THE]—Rene Lacoste (1905–1996) Tennis. Lacoste, one of the FOUR MUSKETEERS, carried around a set of crocodile luggage. He won the Wimbledon singles championship in 1925 and 1928, the French in 1925 and 1927, and the U.S. men's in 1926 and 1927.

CROONING JOE—Joe Cascarella (1907–) Baseball. This pitcher also sang well enough to be on the radio.

CROSSFIRE—Earl Alonzo Moore (1878–1961) Baseball. Moore was not always in control of his fastball.

CROW—Warren Cromartie (1953–) Baseball of.

CROW—Frank Crosetti (1910–) Baseball ss/coach. When Crosetti of the New York Yankees talked, his raspy voice sounded something like a crow. That coupled with his name gave him this nickname.

CROW [THE]—Bob Hayes (1942–) Track and field. See THE FULLBACK.

CRUSHER—Steve Casey. Wrestling. Casey often administered the coup de grace to his opponents with his rowing machine hold.

CRUSHER—Steve Casey. Wrestling. Casey is shown using his famous "rowing machine" hold upon a hapless opponent.

CRUSHER—Reggie Lisowski. Wrestling.

CRYSTAL—Leo Klier (1923–) Basketball. Klier, who played forward and guard, was a two-time All-American at Notre Dame.

CUB—Howard Buck (active 1920s) Football. Buck was a big lineman and a place kicker for the Canton Bulldogs and the early Green Bay Packers.

CUBAN HAWK [THE]—Kid Gavilan (1926–) Boxing (welterweight).

CUBBIE—Mike Cubbage (1950–) Baseball c.

CUCKOO—Walter Christensen (1899–1984) Baseball. This unpredictable outfielder sometimes caught pop-ups in his pocket and did flips after a good catch.

CUDDLES—Clarence Marshall (1925–) Baseball. This pitcher was called cuddles because he was cute.

CUKE—Roland Barrows (1883–1955) Baseball.

CULLY—Carl Dahlstrom (1913–) Hockey. This Chicago Black Hawk center won a Calder Trophy for the 1937–1938 season.

CULLY—Carol Wilson (1893–deceased) Hockey.

CUPE—Clinton Rutherford Black, Jr. (1894–1963) Football.

CUPID—Clarence Childs (1886–1912) Baseball. Second baseman Childs may have been called cupid for the irony, for he acted more like a devil. However, he did look somewhat angelic.

CURLEY—Fern James Headley (1901–) Hockey.

CURLY—Harold C. Byrd (1889–1970) Football. In 1936, he became President of the University of Maryland.

CURRY—Charles Foley (1856–1898) Baseball p/of.

CURVELESS WONDER [THE]—Al Orth (1872–1948) Baseball. Orth was a rarity among pitchers. A success without being able to throw a curveball. In 1906, he posted a 27–17; for his fifteen year-career, he was 202–184.

CUSTODIAN OF THE LINKS—Old Tom Morris (1821–1908) Golf. Morris was a character and a fixture on the Old Course at St. Andrews for forty-four years. Also called OLD TOM.

CUY—Hazen Shirley Cuyler (1899–1950) Baseball. **H/F** Also called KIKI.

CY—Darrell Elijah Blanton (1909–1945) Baseball. Blanton had been called Cy back home in Oklahoma. Most pitchers nicknamed Cy reminded people of the great Cy Young.

CY—Frederick Peter Falkenberg (1880–1961) Baseball. Falkenberg had a hopping good fastball.

CY—William Wiley Moore (1896–1963) Baseball. Moore was one of the first relief pitchers.

CY—Harry Richard Morgan (1878–1962) Baseball.

CY—Charles H. Pfirman (1891–) Baseball umpire.

CY—Marvin Wentworth (1905–) Hockey.

CY—Fred Williams (1887–1974) Baseball. Although Williams may have looked like a rustic, he hit homers like a city slicker. He won the home-run crown of the National League in 1916 with twelve, in 1920 with fifteen, in 1923 with forty-one, and in 1927 with thirty.

CY THE SECOND—Irving Melrose Young (1876–1935) Baseball. Irving Young pitched from 1905 to 1911, at a time when the great Cy (Denton True) Young was on the mound, so Irving was called Cy the Second. However, Cy the Second's record of 62–94 was not as stellar as the original Cy's record.

CY THE THIRD—Harley E. Young (1883–1975) Baseball. In 1908, Harley Young pitched three games for the Boston Braves, losing all three. Still, he received his nickname the same year as the "real" Cy Young was 21–12.

CYCLONE—Daniel R. Ryan (1866–1917) Baseball. Just as there was a Cy Young, there was a Cy Ryan. Unfortunately, his nickname was a bit facetious, since Cy Ryan pitched in only three games over two seasons (1887 and 1891) and he won none and lost one. He recorded not one strikeout. After Cy Young made his mark, many a pitcher was nicknamed, appropriately or not, Cyclone.

CYCLONE—Fred Taylor (1883–1979) Hockey. **H/F** Taylor was famous for skating fast—like a cyclone—from one end of the ice rink to the other. As a center and rover, Cyclone scored 194 goals in 186 games. He helped both Ottawa and Vancouver win Stanley Cups. Also called The Ty Cobb of Hockey.

CYCLONE—Johnny Thompson (1876–1951) Boxing. It took twenty years for Thompson to win the middleweight championship; however, less than a year later he was too big to fight in that division.

CZAR OF BASEBALL—Ban Johnson (1863–1931) Baseball. During Johnson's tenure as commissioner from 1903 to 1920, the ballpark became a place where the family could comfortably go and baseball became the national pastime.

DAD—Arthur Hamilton Clarkson (1866–1911) Baseball. Usually players called Dad (or Pop) are older than their teammates. Clarkson was no exception.

DAD—Ray Luther Hale (1879–1946) Baseball.

DAD—Edward Benson Lytle (1862–1950) Baseball. Also called Pop.

DAD—Frank J. Meek (1922–) Baseball c.

DAD GUM—Bill Atwood (1911–) Baseball.
Atwood's nickname was also this catcher's favorite expression.

DADDY—Russell Ormond Christopher (1917–1954) Baseball. Daddy was for Daddy Long Legs because this pitcher was tall for his day (6' 3").

DADDY LONG ARMS—Gene Conley (1930–) Baseball. Conley, a pitcher, was very tall (6' 6") and a two-sport man (baseball for the Braves and basketball for the Celtics). He was also known for his drinking and carousing. Also called Big Brave from Milwaukee.

DADDY LONG ARMS—Don Contel (1933–) Basketball.

DADDY LONG LEGS—George Altman (1933–) Baseball. Altman was 6' 4".

DADDY HOOVES—Gus Gerrard (1953–) Basketball.

DADDY WAGS—Leon Wagner (1934–) Baseball. Also called Cheeks.

DAFF—John Ashley Gammons (1876–1963) Baseball. Outfielder Gammons acted daft.

DAISY—John A. Davis (1858–1902) Baseball.

DAN—Dominick Florio (1896–1965) Boxing. Florio was Jersey Joe Walcott's manager and Floyd Patterson's trainer.

DANCING MASTER—James John Corbett (1866–1933) Boxing. Corbett developed a "scientific" way of boxing. Instead of walking straight in, he would feint and dance away and hit when the moment was opportune. See GENTLEMAN JIM.

DANDELION—Fred Pfeffer (1860–1932) Baseball. A slick fielding second baseman, Pfeffer was good at grabbing the grounders bouncing no higher than a dandelion.

DANDY—Don Meredith (1938–) Football. Meredith, a quarterback at SMU and then for the Dallas Cowboys, was flamboyant in both dress and manner. After his retirement from playing football, he feuded for years on Monday Night Football with Howard "THE MOUTH" Cosell.

DANDY—George A. Wood (1858–1924) Baseball. A dandy on and off the field, Wood was popular with the damsels.

DANIEL BOONE WITH A DRIVER—Sam Snead (1912–) Golf. Slammin' Sammy holds the record for winning more PGA events than any other golfer (eighty-one).

(Jack Nicklaus is second with seventy PGA wins; Ben Hogan, with sixty-three victories, ranks third). But he never won the U.S. Open. Snead used to cut swamp maple to make his own golf clubs. See SWINGING SAM.

DANISH VIKING [THE]—George Pipgras (1899–1986). Baseball. He was the brother of Ed Pipgras (who pitched one season for the Brooklyn Dodgers). The Danish Viking pitched for the New York Yankees and the Boston Red Sox, winning 102 games and losing seventy-three. In 1928, he led American League pitchers with twenty-four wins and appeared in 300 innings of work. Pipgrass was Danish.

DANNY—Dan Roundfield (1953–) Basketball.

DANNY—Dan Schayes (1959–) Basketball.

DANNY D—Danny DiLiberto (1936–) Billiards.

DARK DESTROYER—Joe Louis (1914–1981) Boxing. See BROWN BOMBER.

DARKIE—Harlong Benton Clift (1912–1992) Baseball. Clift was called Darkie because this third baseman's first name was once mistaken for Harlem.

DARLING [THE]—Amos Booth (1853–1921) Baseball. Third baseman Booth was the darling of many a fan.

DASHER—John Joseph Troy (1856–1938) Baseball. Troy would dash from one side of the bag to the other in fielding his position at second.

DASHING DAN—Daniel Costello (1891–1936) Baseball. Dan Costello, an outfielder, was handsome.

DAUNTLESS DAN—Daniel Gardella (1920–) Baseball. Outfielder Gardella displayed plenty of spirit both on and off the field.

DAUNTLESS DAVE—David Danforth (1890–1970) Baseball. Danforth was always pitching himself in and out of trouble.

DAVE THE RAVE—Dave Stallworth (1941–) Basketball.

DAVE THE RAVE—Dave Winfield (1951–) Baseball. Winfield once bestowed this nickname on himself.

DEACON—Vernon Law (1930–) Baseball. Law, a pitcher, received his nickname from his work in the Mormon Church.

DEACON—Danny MacFayden (1905–1972) Baseball.

DEACON—James Thomas McGuire (1863–1936) Baseball. McGuire acted like a gentleman. During his twenty-six-year career, he caught 1,611 games, most of them barehanded. Later, he managed.

DEACON—Bill McKechnie (1886–1965) Baseball. **H/F**
After his eleven-year playing career at third base was over, this deacon in the Methodist Church managed for twenty-five years. McKechnie's teams finished first four times and won the World Series twice.

DEACON—Ray Murray (1917–) Baseball.
This catcher for the Indians once imitated a preacher.

DEACON—Clyde Passeau (1909–) Baseball.
The nickname Deacon was bestowed on Passeau because the 162–150 pitcher acted like a gentleman.

DEACON—Charles Phillippe (1872–1952) Baseball.
In the 1903 World Series, Phillippe calmly won three and lost two games. He walked only five batters during those fifty innings.

DEACON—L. Everett Scott (1892–1960) Baseball.
Proper acting on the field at shortstop and off, Scott played in five World Series from 1915 to 1923.

DEACON—Walt Stankey (1911–) Basketball f-c.

DEACON—James White (1847–1939) Baseball.
White, a Sunday school superintendent and third baseman, batted .387 for the Boston Braves in 1877.

DEACON DAN—Dan Towler (1928–) Football.
Towler became an ordained minister while playing for the L.A. Rams.

DEACON DANNY—Daniel MacFayden (1905–1972)
Baseball. MacFayden, a pitcher, was very religious.

DEADEYE—Jack Thorpe (1899–d.) Football.
Played for two years in the pros, 1921–1923.

DEAF 'UN [THE]—James Burke (1809–1845) Boxing.
In 1832, Englishman Burke fought Irishman Simon Byrne in the longest bare-fisted heavyweight fight ever. It lasted ninety-nine rounds and took over three hours. Byrne later died from his injuries. Burke reigned as the heavyweight champ from 1833 to 1839.

DEAN [THE]—Dean Cromwell (1879–1962) Track and field coach. During Cromwell's thirty-nine-year rein as track coach at USC, the Trojans won twelve NCAA championships and set seventeen world records. He also coached ten gold medal winners in the Olympics. Also called THE MAKER OF CHAMPIONS.

DEAN—Edward Kennedy (1963–) Hockey d.

DEAN OF AMERICAN TRAINERS—James Edward Fitzgerald (1874–1966) Horse racing.

DEAN OF BOXING WRITERS—Pat Fleischer (1888–1972)
Sportswriter. Also called MR. BOXING

DEAN THE DREAM—Dean Meminger (1948–) Basketball.
Meminger played like a dream for Marquette, spearheading them to a 78–9 record. Later he helped the Knicks in their 1973 championship season.

DEAR OLD ROGER—Roger Connor (1857–1931) Baseball 1b. **H/F** Connor was called Dear Old Roger because he was such a cherished member of the seven ball teams he played for during his eighteen-year career. Rapping out 136 homers and 233 triples, Dear Old Roger was the outstanding long ball hitter before the Babe Ruth era.

DEATH—Stephen Oliver Boxing.

DEATH TO FLYING THINGS—John Curtis Chapman (1843–1916) Baseball. Sportswriters gave him this nickname because Chapman barehanded so many fly balls hit his way in the outfield.

DEATH TO FLYING THINGS—Bob Ferguson (1845–1994)
Baseball. Ferguson was a sure fielding second baseman. Also called Fighting Bob for his feisty nature, he later became an umpire.

DEATH VALLEY JIM—James Scott (1888–1957) Baseball.
Born in Deadwood, South Dakota, Scott was nicknamed for Death Valley Scotty, a famous inhabitant of the desert. In 1914, Scott pitched a no-hitter for the White Sox for nine full innings before losing the game in the tenth. Scott died in Palm Springs, California.

DECKHAND CHAMPION OF AMERICA [THE]—Mike McCoole (active mid-1800s) Bareknuckles fighter. McCoole worked on riverboats out of Cincinnati. In 1863, he lost to Joe Coburn after sixty-seven rounds. In 1868, he "won" a return bout with an out-of-shape Coburn who staged his own "arrest" by a federal agent as he entered the ring (so he wouldn't have to fight).

DEDE—James Lloyd Klein (1910–) Hockey lw.

DEE—Wilson Daniel Miles (1909–1976) Baseball of.
(active 1935–1943) Miles was called by the initial of his middle name.

DEERFOOT—George Barclay (1876–1909) Baseball.
This outfielder stole thirty bases his rookie season.

DEERFOOT—Harry Bay (1878–1952) Baseball.
In 1903 and 1904, outfielder Bay led the American League with forty-five and thirty-eight stolen bases.

DEERFOOT—Jesse Clyde Milan (1887–1953) Baseball of/mgr. In 1912, Milan stole eighty-eight bases en route to a career total of 495 stolen bases.

DEFORMED ONE [THE] [O TORTO]—Manuel Francisco dos Santos. Soccer. Portuguese soccer star whose legs were slightly deformed when he suffered polio as a child. Also called The Fool.

DELAWARE PEACH [THE]—John Townsend (1879–1963) Baseball. A pitcher from Delaware, Townsend sometimes had a peach of an outing. When he had an off day, he was called The Delaware Lemon. He was also called Happy.

DELAWARE PEACH [THE]—Vic Willis (1876–1947) Baseball p.

DER BOMBER—Gerhard Muller (1945–) Soccer. This center from West Germany was one of the highest scorers in the history of the game, second only to Pele.

DER PAPIERENE—Matthias Sindelar (1903–1939) Soccer. See MAN OF PAPER.

DERBY DICK—Herbert John Thompson (1881–deceased) Horse racing. **H/F** Thompson earned his nickname by training four winners of the Kentucky Derby.

DESERT FOX—Fred Snowden (1936–) Basketball coach.

DESPERATE—Desmond Beatty (1893–1969) Baseball. Desperate was a modification of his name of Desmond, but it could also refer to the fact that this shortstop appeared in only two games during his career.

DESTROYER [THE]—Al Attles (1936–) Basketball g.

DESTROYER—Bill Russel hot blocking, Russell rendered many opposing players ineffective. See NUMBER SIX.

DEVIL MAY KAER—Morton A. Kaer (active 1931) Football.

DEWEY—Dwight Evans (1951–) Baseball. Evans was an eight-time Gold Glover in right field who could hit with power.

DIAMOND JIM—James Brady (1936–) Baseball. Nicknamed for New York City's notorious wheeler-dealer, this Diamond Jim Brady was a bonus baby with Detroit. Brady was shelled in the six innings he pitched, fleeing the majors with a hefty 28.4 ERA.

DIAMOND MAN [THE]—Calvin Peete (1943–) Golf. Peete at one time sold jewelry and even had diamonds inlaid into his front teeth. He became a pro at forty-six and then let his golf game speak for himself.

DICK—Dixon Henric (1933–) Basketball. Henric averaged twenty-four points and seventeen rebounds at Wake Forest, before playing two years with the Boston Celtics.

DICK—E. L. Romney (1895–1969) Basketball, football coach. Romney coached at Utah State from 1920 to 1941 and had a 225–159 record in basketball. His record as the football coach was 128–92–15.

DICK THE BRUISER—Richard Afflis (1943–) Wrestling. Also called RICHARD THE RUFFIAN.

DIESEL—Douglas Allen Mohns (1933–) Hockey. This defenseman received his nickname because of his speed on the ice.

DIGGER—Alfred Nichols Cervi (1917–) Basketball. Played from 1937–1953 for such teams as Buffalo, Rochester, and Syracuse.

DIGGER—William O'Dell (1933–) Baseball. William O'Dell's name and voice made some think of Digger O'Dell, the undertaker on "Life of Riley," a popular television show in the 1950s.

DIGGER—Richard Phelps. Basketball. Longtime basketball coach at Notre Dame.

DIGGER—George Stanley (1883–deceased) Boxing (bantamweight).

DIGITAL—Vitalis Takawira. Soccer. He plays for the Kansas City Wizards. He received his nickname because of the quick decisions he makes on the field.

DIM DOM—Dom Dallassandro (1913–1988) Baseball of. Dim referred to Dallassandro's diminutive 5' 6" build.

DIMAG—Joe DiMaggio (1914–) Baseball. **H/F** Also called Big Guy, Joe D, JOLTIN' JOE, and YANKEE CLIPPER.

DIMPLES—Clayton Dalrymple (1936–) Baseball c. Dalrymple's nickname was a play on his last name. He played nine years for the Phillies.

DIMPLES—Frederick Iott (1876–1941) Played in 1903 for Cleveland and appeared in only three games in his career. Also known as Happy Iott.

DIMPLES—Edward "Pop" Tate (1861–1932) Baseball.

DING—Jack Ingoldsby (1924–) Hockey rw.

DING—Winthrop H. Palmer (1906–1970) Hockey. In 1927, this Yale player scored seven goals in a game against New Hampshire.

DING DONG—Bill Bell (1933–1962) Baseball p. This nickname stems from his last name.

DING-A-LING—Dain Clay (1919–1994) Baseball of.

DINGER—Erling Doane (1897–1949) Football b.

DINGER—Homer J. Sanders II (1967–) Motorcycle racing.

DINGLE—Frank Croucher (1914–1980) Baseball ss.

DINGO—Dino Restelli (1924–) Baseball.
Played for the Pirates in 1949 and 1951.

DINK—Robert Templeton (1897–1962) Track and field.
Templeton was fourth in the long jump (22' 9⅜") at
the 1920 Antwerp Olympics. Later at Stanford, he
became one of the most successful track coaches.
Nineteen of his athletes became NCAA champions.

DINNY—Chuck Dinsmore (1903–) Hockey f.

DINTY—Walter Barbare (1891–1965) Baseball 3b.

DIPPY—Fred Evans (active 1940s) Football. In 1948,
Evans of the Chicago Bears recovered a record two
fumbles in a game with the Washington Redskins.

DIPPY—Don Simmons (1931–) Hockey g.

DIPSY DOODLE DANDY FROM DELISLE—Max Bentley
(1920–) Hockey **H/F**

DIRT—Dick Tidrow (1947–) Baseball.
Tidrow, a pitcher, could even get his uniform dirty in
pregame practice.

DIRT—Dennis Winston (active 1977–1986) Football lb.

DIRTY—Kurt Bevacqua (1947–) Baseball.
Because of his hard-playing style, this third baseman's
uniform always seemed to be covered with dirt.
Bevacqua's specialty was pinch hitting.

DIRTY AL—Alan Gallagher (1945–) Baseball.
This nickname does not refer to the style of play but
the sanitation. This third baseman also had an
infield's worth of given names: He was Alan Mitchell
Edward George Patrick Henry Gallagher.

DIRTY JACK—Jack Doyle (1869–1958) Baseball 1b.

DISCO DAN—Darnell Glenn Ford (1952–) Baseball of.

DIT—Aubrey Victor Clapper (1907–1978) Hockey. **H/F**
When he was a kid, his folks called him Vic; however,
when Vic tried to say his own name, it sounded more
like Dit. The nickname stayed with him through the right
winger's twenty-year career with the Boston Bruins.

DIXIE—Frank Talmadge Davis (1890–1944) Baseball.
Davis, a pitcher, was from North Carolina.

DIXIE—William Dean (1907–1980) Soccer.
England's great goal-scoring center forward. In
1927–1928, he booted home sixty goals.

DIXIE—Homer Elliott Howell (1919–1990) Baseball.
Howell, a catcher, was from Louisville, Kentucky.

DIXIE—Millard Howell (1913–) Football b/coach.

DIXIE—Fred Walker (1910–) Baseball coach.

Walker's father, Edward Walker, was also a major-
leaguer, and also nicknamed Dixie. Fred Walker was
later given another nickname, THE PEOPLE'S
CHERCE, by the faithful of Ebbetts Field.

DIXIE—Lonnie Warnecke (1909–1976) Baseball p/umpire.
Also called ARKANSAS HUMMINGBIRD, and Country
Ol' Arkansas.

DIXIE KID—Aaron L. Brown (1883–1934) Boxing (welterweight). **H/F**

DIXIE THRUSH [THE]—Sammy Strang (1876–1932)
Baseball. Third baseman Strang hailed from
Chattanooga, Tennessee.

DIZ—Howard Dean Reed (1936–1984) Baseball.
This pitcher was tagged with the nickname Diz
because he made many people think of the one and
only Dizzy Dean.

DIZZY—Jay Hanna Dean (1911–1974) Baseball p. **H/F**

DIZZY—William Dismukes (1890–1961) Baseball
(Negro Leagues). Dizzy was a corruption of this submarine pitcher's last name.

DIZZY—Clyde Kirkendall (d. 1957) Softball. **H/F**
Nicknamed after Dizzy Dean, Kirkendall once struck
out sixty-seven batters during a thirty-three-inning
fast-pitch softball game.

DIZZY—Paul Howard Trout (1915–1972) Baseball.
Pitcher Trout sometimes acted like a fish out of water.

DJ—Dennis Johnson (1954–) Basketball g.

DO IT—Ron Pruitt (1951–) Baseball of.
Pruitt was usually up for a dare; he would just do it.

DO-LITTLE—Jack Hardy (1879–1921) Baseball.
Although this was not exactly a complimentary nickname, Doolittle was his middle name. Parents, be
careful what you name your children!

DOAKER [THE]—Doak Walker (1927–) Football.
This is what the SMU fans called their star tailback
(operating out of the single-wing formation) who ran,
threw, and caught touchdowns. Also called All-
American Mustang, DAUNTLESS DOAK, Little Man in
Pro Football, .

DOC—Yancey Wyatt Ayers (1890–1968) Baseball.
Ayers had once studied medicine before becoming a
major-league pitcher.

DOC—Frank Bagley. Boxing.

DOC—Felix Blanchard (1924–) Football. Fullback
Blanchard's father was a doctor. See MR. INSIDE.

DOC—Bobby Brown (1924–) Baseball.
In 1954, this third baseman retired from baseball to practice medicine; and in 1984, Dr. Brown retired from medicine to become president of the American League.

DOC—Albert John Bushong (1856–1908) Baseball.
This Doc had a dental practice while he was a major-league catcher.

DOC—Henry Carlson (1894–1964) Football, basketball coach. Also called Red.

DOC—Edward Casey (1894–1966) Football, boxing.
After his playing days were over, Casey trained BATTLING Battalino and Max Schmelling.

DOC—James Peter Casey (1870–1936) Baseball.
Casey was a dentist and third baseman.

DOC—Roger Maxwell Cramer (1905–1990) Baseball of/coach. As a boy, Cramer had worked for a doctor. He was also called Flit because he was as effective against fly balls as insect repellent is against fleas.

DOC—James Otis Crandall (1887–1951) Baseball.
As one of baseball's first relievers, he would come to the aid of the Giants' other pitchers. Damon Runyon wrote that Cramer was "The Doctor of Ball Games."

DOC—Howard Rodney Edwards (1937–) Baseball.
Edwards had been a medic in the Marine Corps before becoming a major-league catcher.

DOC—Edward Farrell (1902–1966) Baseball.
This second baseman drilled teeth during the offseason.

DOC—Harvey Homer Gessler (1880–1924) Baseball.
Outfielder Gessler later graduated from medical school. Also called Brownie.

DOC—E. O. Hayes (1906–1973) Basketball.
Hayes coached at SMU from 1948 to 1967 and had a 299–192 record.

DOC—Wheeler Rogers Johnston (1887–1961) Baseball 1b.

DOC—Jack Kearns (1862–1963) Boxing manager.
Kearns is the one who discovered Jack Dempsey in 1917. He also handled Abe Attell and Archie THE OLD MONGOOSE Moore. Also called Perfume Jack.

DOC—John Leonard Lavan (1890–1952) Baseball.
Shortstop Lavan practiced medicine during the off season.

DOC—William Riddle Marshall (1875–1959) Baseball.
Marshall was a doctor and a catcher.

DOC—James McCutcher McJames (1873–1901) Baseball.
McJames pitched his way through medical school. His best year on the mound was the twenty-seven games he won in 1898.

DOC—Walter E. Meanwell (1884–1953) Basketball coach. Also Little Doctor.

DOC—George Medich (1948–) Baseball.
This pitcher was studying medicine while pitching for the Yankees. On more than one occasion he went into the stands to aid a stricken fan. After his pitching days were over, Medich practiced sports medicine.

DOC—Roy Oscar Miller (1883–1938) Baseball.
Miller was a doctor-outfielder.

DOC—Eustace James Newton (1877–1931) Baseball.
Newton was a pitcher and doctor. On August 4, 1905, his catcher was Mike Powers, also a doctor.

DOC—Harley Parker (1872–1941). Baseball. On June 21, 1901 Parker could have used a doctor. Toiling for Cincinnati, he hurled the worst pitched game in major league history. Pitching against the Brooklyn Dodgers, he gave up twenty-six hits and twenty-one runs. The Reds released Doc Parker the next day.

DOC—Mike Powers (1870–1909) Baseball.
In addition to being a catcher, Powers was a doctor. In 1905, Doc Powers caught Doc Newton.

DOC—James Thompson Prothro (1893–1971) Baseball.
Prothro was a dentist, a third baseman, and later a coach.

DOC—Glenn Rivers (1961–) Basketball g.

DOC—Elwin Romnes (1909–) Hockey f.

DOC—Warren Schrage (1920–) Basketball f.

DOC—Clarence Wiley Spears (1894–1964) Football coach.

DOC—Ernie Vandeweghe (1928–) Basketball fg.

DOC—Charles John Watson (1885–1949) Baseball.
Pitcher Watson was nicknamed after Arthur Conan Doyle's Doctor John Watson.

DOC TWINK—Howard Earle Twinning (1894–1973) Baseball. Twinning's nickname was for having gone to medical school and his last name. After racking up an ERA of 13.5 in a single game, Twining wound up in medicine full time.

DR. CYCLOPS—Max Manning (1918–) Baseball. In 1946, Dr. Cyclops (Manning wore thick glasses) compiled an awesome 15–1 record pitching for the Newark Eagles in the Negro League. Also known as Mr. Magic.

DR. DEATH—Skip Thomas (active 1972–1977) Football. This Oakland defensive back was a deadly tackler.

DOCTOR DIRT—Tim Wilkison (1959–) Tennis. Wilkison played with intensity, throwing himself around the court even in exhibitions and dirtying his outfit. He might also have been called Fiddlesticks—something he was sometimes heard to exclaim when others might curse.

DR. DUNK—Darnell Hillman (1949–) Basketball f-c.

DOCTOR DUNKENSTEIN—Darrell Griffith (1958–) Basketball. Griffith, a guard, received his nickname while playing for Louisville.

DOCTOR J—Julius Erving (1950–) Basketball. **H/F**

DR. J—Julius Erving [b. February 22, 1950) Basketball. The above photo shows the DR. being guarded by THE BIG E (Elvin Hayes).

DR. JUNK—Wilbur Holland (1951–) Basketball g.

DOCTOR STRANGEGLOVE—Dick Stuart (1932–) Baseball. This nickname was a pun on Stanley Kubrick's movie *Dr. Strangelove*. Stuart was at best a mediocre fielder at first base.

DODE—Joe Birmingham (1884–1946) Baseball of.

DODE—Joseph Francis Cicero (1910–1983) Baseball. Dode stood for Doughty, the name this outfielder used when he played professional baseball in high school.

DODGER [THE]—Roger Staubach (1942–) Football qb. See THE ARTFUL DODGER.

DODO BIRD—Frank Bird (1869–1958) Baseball. This unflattering nickname was in reaction to his last name. Also, after catching seventeen games in the bigs, Bird became extinct.

DOG—Dave Manders (1941–) Football. This center received this nickname because of the way he worked—he worked like a dog during practice and during games.

DOG [THE]—Clyde Douglas Turner (1919–) Football c/coach. Also called Bulldog and The Kid from Sweetwater.

DOGGIE—Alvin Julian (1901–1967) Basketball coach. **H/F** After coaching at Holy Cross, Julian went to the Boston Celtics in 1948. Bob Cousey, his star player, also went from Holy Cross to the Celtics.

DOGGIE—George Miller (1853–1929) Baseball c. Also called Calliope and Foghorn.

DOGPATCH—Dan Swartz (1934–) Basketball. Swartz was from Owingsville, Kentucky. He was an All-American forward at Morgan State where he scored over twenty-eight points a game in 1956.

DOLLY—Dolores B. Brumfield (active 1947–1953) Baseball (All-American Girls Baseball League). Brumfield got her nickname because she had been only fourteen when she began playing second base in the pros.

DOLLY—Sam Gray (1897–1953) Baseball. Gray, a pitcher, was nicknamed after William Denton Gray.

DOLLY—William Denton Gray (1878–1956) Baseball. This pitcher got his nickname from a popular song in the early 1900s.

DOLPH—Adolph Schayes (1928–) Basketball.

DOLLAR BILL—Bill Bradley (1943–) Basketball f. **H/F**

DOME—Houston Hoover (1965–) This big tackle (6' 2", 290 pounds) with the first name Houston was called Dome (for the Houston Astrodome) by his Atlanta Falcon teammates.

DONIE—Owen Joseph Bush (1888–1972) Baseball. After striking out, this shortstop returned to the bench and asked a teammate what the pitch had been. "Donieball" was the reply.

DONK—Dean White (1923–) Basketball f.

DONNA—John J. Fox (1897–1956) Bobsledding.

DONORA GREYHOUND [THE]—Stan Musial (1920–) Baseball. **H/F** He was lean as a greyhound and was born in Donora, Pennsylvania. Also called STAN THE MAN and Stash.

DOOLEY—Frank David Adams (active 1944–1955) Horse racing. **H/F** Adams was the leading American steeplechase rider of his day.

DOONESBURY—Mike Dunleavy (1954–) Basketball g. After the comic strip by Garry Trudeau.

DORNY—Gary Dornhoefer (1943–) Hockey rw.

DOT—Rich Dotson (1959–) Baseball p.

DOTS—John Barney Miller (1886–1923) Baseball.

A sportswriter once asked the Cardinal great Honus Wagner who their new second baseman was. "Dot's Miller," replied Wagner in his heavy German accent. While playing for the Pirates and Cardinals from 1909 to 1921, Dots had a .263 batting average.

DOUBLE CHEESEBURGER—Reggie Cleveland (1948–) Baseball p. Also called Snacks.

DOUBLE D—Dwight Davis (1949–) Basketball.

This forward's nickname was for his initials.

DOUBLE NO HIT—Johnny Vander Meer (1914–1997) Baseball. Vander Meer received his nickname because he pitched two consecutive no-hit games. On June 11, 1938, he hurled a no-hit game against Boston; four days later, he held Brooklyn hitless. Also called THE DUTCH MASTER.

DOUBLE 0—Alvin O'Neal McBean (1938–) Baseball p. McBean was nicknamed after James Bond, 007 agent.

DOUGHNUT—Bill Carrick (1873–1932) Baseball.

Carrick was fond of—you guessed it—doughnuts. In 1899, he also led the National League in hits allowed (485).

DOUR DENNY—Denny Shute (1904–1974) Golf. **H/F**

DOUR SCOT—John Bain Sutherland (1889–1948) Football coach. Also called JOCK, OVERLAND MAN, SCOTSMAN.

DOWNTOWN—Charlie Brown (active 1982-87) Football rw.

DOWNTOWN—Fred Brown (1948–) Basketball g.

DOWNTOWN—Ollie Brown (1944–) Baseball of.

In 1964, Brown hit forty home runs for Fresno in the Pacific League. He hit the ball into downtown Fresno.

DRACULA—Pecho Borbon (1946–) Baseball p.

Borbon once bit an opponent during a melee.

DREAM [THE]—Dean Meminger (1948–) Basketball.

Meminger, a guard, starred for Marquette from 1969 to 1971 and then played for the Knicks, helping them win their championship in 1973.

DREAM [THE]—Akeem Olajuwun (1963–) Basketball.

Since 1990, this seven-foot center has been called Hakeem.

DRISK—Peter John Driscoll (1954–) Hockey lw.

DROOPY—Charles Leonard Estrada (1938–) Baseball p.

This was a childhood nickname.

DUBBIE—Russell Bowie (1880–1959) Hockey. **H/F**

Bowie played in the pre-NHL days as a rover and cen-

ter for the Montreal Victorias. During his amateur career in hockey, he scored 234 goals.

DUCK—Don Chaney (1946–) Basketball.

For seven years Chaney, a guard, was the swingman or sixth man on the Boston Celtics.

DUCK—Robert Dowell (1912–) Basketball. c-f.

DUCK—Garland Shifflet (1935–) Baseball p.

DUCK [THE]—Dick Snyder (1944–) Basketball g-f.

DUCK—James White (active 1976–1983) Football dt.

DUCK—James Williams (active 1991–1992) Football de.

DUCKY—James William Holmes (1869–1932) Baseball of.

Only 5' 6" and 170 pounds, Holmes reportedly waddled when he walked.

DUCKY—Dick Schofield (1935–) Baseball.

Schofield had this nickname because his father had been called Ducky. Dick Schofield, a shortstop, had a son, also named Dick Schofield, who also played shortstop in the major leagues, but who didn't carry on the nickname.

DUCKY—Raymond Pond. Football coach.

When Former President Gerald Ford heard his pep talk before the 1935 Harvard game, Ford recalled that "Ducky wasn't a fiery speaker, but he spoke very movingly. He talked about the Yale alumni, his experiences, and what The Game meant to him. In a quiet way, it was very emotional." (Al Young in *USA Today*). Yale went on to win that game 14–7.

DUCKY—Harry Swan (1887–1946) Baseball p.

DUDE—Thomas John Esterbrooke (1860–1901) Baseball.

Third baseman Esterbrooke was a snappy dresser.

DUDE—Rudy May (1944–) Baseball.

This nickname was ironic because May, a pitcher, was a sloppy dresser.

DUDE, THE—Lenny Dykstra (1963–) Baseball.

"Europe might not be ready for Lenny Dykstra, but The Dude jetted out of New York's Kennedy International Airport Thursday prepared to preach the gospel of major league baseball to folks in such places as Paris; Dusseldorf; and Amsterdam." (Hal Bodley in *USA Today* November 19, 1993).

DUDS—Rick Dudley (1949–) Hockey lw.

DUFFMEIER—Hugh Duffy (1886–1954) Baseball. **H/F**

In 1894, Duffy played outfield and batted .438, the highest average ever in the major leagues. After his playing days were over, he was a manager.

DUFFY—on Robert Dyer (1945–) Baseball.
The favorite radio show of this catcher's mother was *Duffy's Tavern*.

DUFFY—George Edward Lewis (1888–1979) Baseball.
Duffy was this outfielder's mother's maiden name.

DUGIE—Slater Martin (1925–) Basketball. **H/F**
Martin was nicknamed after a character in the cartoon "Mutt and Jeff." After playing college ball for Texas, Martin was a guard on five NBA championship teams (four with Minneapolis, one with St. Louis).

DUKE—Louis J. Abbruzzi (1921–) Football.

DUKE—Gino Cappelletti (1934–) Football. When he kicked a thirty-eight-yard field goal, he scored the first three points in the American Football League. In 1964 he was the AFL Player of the Year. See CAPPY.

DUKE—Leon James Carmell (1937–) Baseball.
Carmell nicknamed himself as a boy for his favorite ball player, Duke Snider. He also was an outfielder.

DUKE—Paul Derringer (1906–1988) Baseball.
This pitcher dressed royally.

DUKE—Laudas Joseph Dutkowski (1902–) Hockey d.

DUKE—Charles Andrew Farrell (1866–1925) Baseball.
Farrell had once been introduced to the ballpark crowd not only as the catcher but also as The Duke of Marlborough. Farrell hailed from Marlborough, Mass.

DUKE—George Francis Harris (1942–) Hockey rw.

DUKE—Paul Hogue (1940–) Basketball.
Two-time All-American at Cincinnati when the won NCAA championships in 1961–1962. He played guard with New York and Baltimore in the NBA.

DUKE—Gordon Keats (1895–1972) Hockey. **H/F** Keats, a center who played for the Bruins, the Red Wings, and the Black Hawks, was one of hockey's first superstars.

DUKE—Duane Frederick Maas (1929–1976) Baseball p.
Maas started calling himself Duke because he did not like the name Duane.

DUKE—Harry Markell (1923–1984) Baseball.
Markell, a pitcher, was called Duke because his middle name was Duquesne.

DUKE—Hugh Mulcahy (1913–) Baseball.
Mulcahy was also called LOSING PITCHER because he lost twice as many as he won. (His record was 45–89.)

DUKE—Duane Sims (1941–) Baseball c.
Sims had a manager who called him Duke because he did not think Duane was a good name for his catcher.

DUKE—Fred Slater (1898–1966) Football.

DUKE—John David Wathan (1949–) Baseball.
Wathan was called Duke because some thought this catcher looked like actor John "Duke" Wayne.

DUKE OF DULUTH—Herbie Lewis (1907–) Hockey. **H/F**
This title was bestowed upon left winger Lewis for four high-scoring seasons with the Duluth Hornets in the AHL. During eleven seasons playing for the Detroit Red Wings, Lewis served as captain, played in the NFL's first All-Star Game in 1934, and spurred the Red Wings on to two consecutive Stanley Cup championships.

DUKE OF PADUCAH—Joseph Francis Klukay (1922–) Hockey lw.

DUKIE—Eric Gordon Tipton (1915–) Baseball.
Tipton, an outfielder, had gone to Duke University. Also called BLUE DEVIL.

DUM DUM—Jose Luis Pacheco (1949–) Boxing (welterweight).

DUMB DAN—Dan Morgan (1873–1955) Boxing manager.

DUMMY—Edward Joseph Dundon (1859–1893) Baseball.
Dundon, a pitcher, was called Dummy because he was deaf and dumb.

DUMMY—George Michael Leitner (1871–1960) Baseball.
Leitner was a deaf-mute and a pitcher.

DUMMY—Matthew Daniel Lynch (1927–1970) Baseball.
Lynch, an outfielder, was also a deaf-mute.

DUMMY—Luther Taylor (1875–1958) Baseball.
Taylor, a deaf-mute, won 115 games during his nine-year career. Most of Taylor's Giant teammates learned the hand alphabet, and manager John McGraw used it to give his signs.

DUNC—Duncan Robert Fisher (1927–) Hockey rw.

DUPEE—Frederick Shaw (1859–1938) Baseball.
Shaw bragged about how he duped batters into striking out.

DURABLE DANE—Oscar Nelson (1882–1954) Boxing. **H/F**
Born in Copenhagen, Denmark, Nielson was the lightweight champion from 1908 to 1910. Also called The Battler and BATTLING NELSON.

DURANGO KID—Johnny Ray Seale (1938–) Baseball.
Seale was a pitcher from Durango, Colorado. The reference is to a famous series of western movies featuring a masked man on a white horse—The Durango Kid—starring Charles Starrett.

DUSKY METEOR—Kenny Washington (active 1940s) Football hb.

DUSTER—Walter Mails (1895–1974) Baseball.
Mails was given this nickname after beaning a batter. See THE GREAT.

DUSTY—Tyton Boggess (1904–1968) Baseball.
As a child, this National League umpire had always returned home dusty.

DUSTY—Allen Lindsey Cooke (1907–1987) Baseball.
Cooke, an outfielder, was so fast that the dust flew when he galloped around the bases.

DUSTY—Melvin Lloyd Parnell (1922–) Baseball.
Parnell often threw the ball into the dirt. However, in 1949, Parnell found his control and registered twenty-five wins, tops in the American League that year.

DUSTY—Gordon Rhodes (1907–1960) Baseball.
Players with last names of Rhodes inevitably have Dusty nicknames. Rhodes was also a pitcher.

DUSTY—James Rhodes (1927–) Baseball.
This nickname was because of the outfielder's last name. With two homers and seven RBI's, Rhodes was a hero of the 1954 World Series. See THE COLOSSUS OF RHODES.

DUTCH—Jim Bolger (1932–) Baseball.
This outfielder's nickname was for his German heritage. (This is true of almost everyone with the nickname Dutch.)

DUTCH—Ken Campbell (1926–) Basketball f.

DUTCH—Henry Dehnert (1898–1979) Basketball. **H/F**
This member of the Original Celtics and the Cleveland Rosenblums developed basketball's pivot play. He had the skill and luck to be on the winning team 1,900 times.

DUTCH—Armond Romeo Delmonte (1925–) Hockey c.

DUTCH—Henry John Dotterer (1931–) Baseball.
Dotterer, a catcher, was nicknamed for his father.

DUTCH—Herm Fuetsch (1918–) Basketball g.

DUTCH—Norman Gainor (1904–) Hockey c.

DUTCH—Jack Garfinkel (1918–) Basketball g.

DUTCH—Ernest Joe Harrison (1910–1982) Golf.

DUTCH—Frank Hiller (1920–1987) Baseball p.

DUTCH—Wilbert Hiller (1915–) Hockey.
Swift-skating left wing for the New York Rangers who helped in 1940 to win the Rangers last Stanley Cup.

DUTCH—Hubert Benjamin Leonard (1892–1952) Baseball p.

DUTCH—Emil John Leonard (1909–1983) Baseball.
Nicknamed for Hubert Benjamin Leonard, Emil is the only pitcher to have led both the National and American leagues for losses in a given season.

DUTCH—Arthur Lonborg (1899–1985) Basketball coach.
H/F Lonborg's twenty-three-year record at Northwestern was 237–198.

DUTCH—Russell McIntosh (active 1921) Football.

DUTCH—Charles Mason (1912–) Hockey f.

DUTCH—Lambert Dalton Meyer (1915–) Baseball.
Meyer, a second baseman, was nicknamed for his uncle, Leo Robert Meyer.

DUTCH—Leo Robert Meyer (1898–1982) Football coach.
Meyer spent his career at Texas Christian University, starting out as a player and winding up as the athletic director. Also called OLD IRON PANTS and SATURDAY FOX.

DUTCH—Frank Nighbor (1893–1966) Hockey. **H/F**
Nighbor, a center, was the first NHL player to receive the Hart trophy (awarded to the league's most valuable player).

DUTCH—Hubert Peck (1898–) Basketball.
Peck was a two-time All-American guard at Pennsylvania. To show how low scoring the games were at the time, Penn won the decisive championship game with Chicago in 1920 by the score of 23–21.

DUTCH—Earl Reibel (1930–) Hockey.
Reibel, a center, was on a line for Detroit with Gordie Howe and Ted Lindsay.

DUTCH—Walter Henry Ruether (1893–1970) Baseball p/manager.

DUTCH—Frank John Schwab (1895–1965) Football.

DUTCH—Ed Sternamen (active 1920–1927) Football player/owner.

DUTCH—Norm Van Brocklin (1926–1983) football qb. **H/F**
Also called THE DUTCHMAN.

DUTCH—Emil Verban (1915–) Baseball 2b.
Verban has the odd distinction of hitting only one homer in 2,911 at-bats. Also called THE ANTELOPE.

DUTCH—Art Wilson (1885–1960) Baseball c.

DUTCH—Edward Zwilling (1888–1978) Baseball.
This outfielder played for all three teams in Chicago—the Cubs, the White Sox, and the Federal League's Chicago Whales.

DUTCH DEMON—Fred Taral (1867–1925) Horse racing **H/F**
This jockey earned his nickname by whipping his
mounts to spur them on to the finish line. He also had
another nickname because he palled around with
John L. Sullivan at night. The two of them were known
as Big Casino and Little Casino.

DUTCH MASTER [THE]—Johnny Vander Meer (1914–)
Baseball. Vander Meer was a master pitcher. In 1938,
he threw two consecutive no-hitters.
See DOUBLE NO-HIT.

DUTCH SAM—(1775–deceased) Boxing.
Dutch Sam was one of the first to use the uppercut in
boxing.

DUTZ—Julius Cohn (1886–1954) Football.

DX—Dana Xenophon Bible (1891–) Football coach.
Also called THE FOOTBALL CLASSICIST.

DYBBER—Jerry Dybzinski (1955–) Baseball ss.

DYNAMITE—Michael Dokes (1958–) Boxing
(heavyweight).

DYNAMITE—Seraphim Post (active 1920s) Football.

DYNAMITE JOE—Joe Bellino (1938–) Football hb.
Also called JOE THE JET, THE NAVY'S DESTROYER,
THE PLAYER WHO IS NEVER CAUGHT FROM BEHIND.

DYNAMO—Dino Chiozza (1912–1972) Baseball.
Dino did not exactly have a dynamic career, playing his
position of shortstop in only two major-league games.

E—Elaine Marjorie Roth (active 1948–1951) Baseball
(All-American Girls Baseball League). Outfielder Roth
had been nicknamed *E* as a child; her ball-playing sister, Eilaine, was called *I*.

EAGLE EYE—John Clement Schulte (1896–1978)
Baseball. An Eagle Eye, like this catcher, has a good
eye for balls and strikes.

EAGLE EYE—Jake Beckley (1867–1918) Baseball. **H/F**
Beckley, a first baseman, received his nickname
because he so rarely struck out. While collecting 2,931
hits over the course of twenty seasons, Eagle Eye
fanned only 270 times.

EARACHE—Benny Meyer (1888–1974) Baseball.
Meyer, an outfielder, kept up a constant stream of
chatter.

EARL OF HANOVER [THE]—Earl Blaik (1897–1989)
Football coach. Also called RED and COLONEL.

EARL OF SNOHOMISH [THE]—Earl Averill (1902–1983)
Baseball. **H/F** Averill, an outfielder, hailed from

Snohomish, Washington. Also called ROCK and
TORGY.

EARL THE PEARL—Earl Monroe (1944–) Basketball.
This rhyming nickname stood for this guard's value
and smooth moves.

EARTHQUAKE—Daryl Dawkins (1954–) Basketball.
Also called CHOCOLATE THUNDER.

EARTHQUAKE—Bill Enyart (active 1969–1972) Football.

EARTHQUAKE—Jim Hunt (1938–) Football.
Defensive tackle for the Boston Patriots, Hunt was a
mover and shaker.

EASTON ASSASSIN [THE]—Larry Holmes (1949–)
Boxing. The heavyweight champion from 1978 to 1985,
Holmes was born and raised in Easton, PA.

EBBIE—Ebenezer Goodfellow (1907–) Hockey c. **H/F**
In 1939–1940, Ebbie was the MVP in the NHL.

EBONY ANTELOPE [THE]—Jesse Owens (1913–) Track
and field. Also called The Ebony Express, The Brown
Bombshell, THE BUCKEYE BULLET.

EBONY EEL [THE]—Aze Simmons. Football.

ECLIPSE—Benny Ayala (1951–) Baseball.
Ayala explained that he was an eclipse ballplayer—i.e.
you don't see him very often.

EDDIE—Joseph Alain Godin (1957–) Hockey.

EDDIE MATTRESS—Eddie Mathews (1931–) Baseball
3b. **H/F**

EDMONTON EXPRESS [THE]—Eddie Shore (1902–)
Hockey. **H/F** Shore was a speedy defenseman from
Edmonton.

EEL [THE]—Camile Henry (1933–) Hockey.
Because of his tall slender appearance, the second
syllable of his first name, and his slick playing ways,
Henry was nicknamed The Eel. During the 1983–1984
season this center scored twenty-four goals for the
New York Rangers and was voted Rookie of the Year.

EFFREN—Alacran Torres (1943–) Boxing (flyweight).

EGGIE—James Edgar Lennox (1885–1939) Baseball.
This third baseman's nickname of Eggie was a corruption of Edgar.

EGYPTIAN—John J. Healy (1866–1899) Baseball.
Healy, a pitcher, hailed from Cairo, i.e., Cairo
(pronounced *Karo*), Illinois.

EJ—Eddie Johnston (1935–) Hockey.
Johnston played goalie for the Boston Bruins when
they won the Stanley Cup in 1970 and 1972.

EL ALBA [THE DAWN]—Jose Gomez Bullfighting.

EL DIABLO [THE DEVIL]—Willie Wells (1905–1989) Baseball (Negro Leagues). Willie Wells played short-stop—well—like The Devil. In a career that lasted from 1925 to 1949, Wells batted .332. Against major-league pitching he fared even better (.392).

EL DIMANTE NEGRO—Jose de la Caridad Menchez Mendez (1888–1928) Baseball (Negro Leagues) p.

EL DIVINO CALVO—Raphael Gomez Ortega. Bullfighting. This matador was known as The Divine Baldy for his superb passes and bald pate.

EL DIVINO LOCO—Ruben Colon Gomez (1927–) Baseball. Gomez, a pitcher, was called The Divine Crazy for his inspired antics.

EL GATO [THE CAT]—Antonio Francesco Pena (1957–) Baseball. Tony Pena won his nickname in his native Dominican Republic before moving on to the major leagues. This big catcher was known for his quick and accurate throws.

EL MAESTRO—Adolfo Pedernera (1918–) Soccer. One of the greatest, if not the greatest Argentine forward of all time.

ELBOWS—Donald William Awrey (1943–) Hockey. Elbows were what this defenseman was known for using against his opponents.

ELBOWS—George McFadden (1872–1951) Boxing (lightweight).

ELBOWS—Eric Nesterenko (1933–) Hockey rw.

ELECTRIC EYE [THE]—Flynn Robinson (1941–) Basketball.

ELEPHANT DRAWERS—Mark Aquirre (1959–) Basketball. Aquirre wore droopy drawers when he played forward and guard for the Dallas Mavericks. Also called FAT DADDY and MUFFIN MAN.

ELEVATOR MAN [THE]—Bob Staak Basketball.

ELK—Lawrence C. Elkins (1943–) Football e.

ELMER—Dave Conception (1948–) Baseball. The shortstop Conception was called Elmer because one day when *E* was listed after his last name (for error), a player asked if it stood for Elmer.

ELMER THE GREAT—Walter William Beck (1904–1987) Baseball. The overconfident Beck made some think of the character in Ring Lardner's short story, "Elmer the Great." However, it didn't seem to help this pitcher's underachiever's record of 38–69. See BOOM BOOM.

EMERGENCY—Jeff Ward Football.

EMLIN THE GREMLIN—Em Tunnell (1925–1975) Football db/hb.

EMMO—Emerson Fittipaldi (active 1970s) Auto racing. In 1973, Brazilian Emerson (he was named for Ralph Waldo Emerson) Fittipaldi was World Champion on the Grand Prix circuit at the age of twenty-three.

EMU—James Kern (1949–) Baseball p. Two teammates were filling out a crossword puzzle when Kern walked by making an odd birdlike sound. They were up to a three-letter word for a large bird that can't fly—the emu.

END ZONE—Keith Jones (active 1989–) Football.

ENFANT TERRIBLE—Ilie Nastase (1946–) Tennis. See NASTY.

ENTERTAINER [THE]—Eddie Shack (1937–) Hockey.

EPPA JEPTHA—Eppa Rixey (1891–1963) Baseball p. **H/F** A sportswriter came up with this unusual rhyming nickname.

EPPIE—Charlotte Epstein (1885–1938) Swimming coach. Eppie was an affectionate nickname for Epstein. Also called THE MOTHER OF AMERICAN WOMEN'S SWIMMING.

EPPIE—Edward Robert Miller (1916–) Baseball. This shortstop's nickname Eppie was a corruption of Eddie.

ERASER [THE]—Marvin Barnes (1952–) Basketball. The defensive prowess of Barnes, who played forward and center, erased many an attempted shot. Also called GOOD NEWS and THE MAGNIFICENT.

E. T.—Marcus Allen (1960–) Football. Allen was called this by his U.S.C. teammates for his out-of-this-world play.

E. T.—Kevin Moley (active 1980s) Boxing (junior middleweight).

EUGENE—Mercury Morris (active 1969–1976) Football hb.

EURO MAGIC—Toni Kukoc. Basketball. Kukoc was a 6' 10" player from Croatia.

EVIL DOCTOR BLACKHEART—Pat Smith. Basketball.

EXPRESS—Nolan Ryan (1947–) Baseball. He was also called America's Flamethrower.

EYE OF THE HURRICANE—Michael Irving (1966–) Football. He played football for the University of Miami Hurricanes and his last name begins with *I*—hence the punning nickname. In three years with the hurricanes he caught 143 passes and made twenty-six touchdown receptions.

EYECHART—Doug Gwosdz (1960–) Baseball.
This catcher's last name could hang on the wall in an optometrist's office.

FAMOUS AMOS—Amos Lawrence (active 1981–1984) Football. Reference to the cookie maker.

FANCY [THE]—Bobby Chacon (1951–) Boxing.
In 1974, Chacon won the WBC featherweight title.

FANNY—Frank Niehaus (1902–1985) Football.

FARGO EXPRESS [THE]—Billy Petrolle (1905–) Boxing.

FAST EDDIE—Ed Giacomin (1939–) Hockey. **H/F**
Giacomin was not only a fast goaltender around the net, he also intimidated any opposing player in the area.

FAST EDDIE—Eddie Johnson (1955–) Basketball.

FAST EDDIE—Eddie Jorday (1955–) Basketball.

FAST EDDIE—Eddie Sachs. Auto racing.

FAT—Freddie Fitzsimmons (1901–1979) Baseball.
This hefty Giants' pitcher was 217–146.

FAT—Bob Fothergill (1879–1938) Baseball.
This outfielder, who weighed 230 and stood 5' 10", hit .359 in 1927 for the Detroit Tigers.

FAT—Ernie Holmes (active 1972–1978) Football.
Holmes was a stout member of Pittsburgh's STEEL CURTAIN.

FAT—George Latham (active 1921–1923) Football.

FAT—Lafayette Lever (1960–) Basketball.
Portland's first-round draft choice in 1982 was only a 6' 3" and 175-pound guard, but he was called Fat because of a mispronunciation of his first name.

FAT FREDDIE—Freddie Scolari (1922–) Basketball.
Scolari weighed 180 pounds and stood 5' 10½".

FAT JACK—Jack Fisher (1939–) Baseball.

FAT MAN [THE]—George Steinbrenner (1930–)
Baseball owner. This unflattering epithet was bestowed on the off-again, on-again majority owner of the Yankees by Richard "Goose" Gossage, a one-time ace relief hurler on the Yankees. At Yankee Stadium, the game's not over until the Fat Man sings.

FATHER OF AMERICAN LAWN TENNIS [THE]—Dr. James Wright (1852–1917) Tennis. A doubles champion with R. D. Sears in 1882, 1883, 1884, 1886 and 1887, Wright was president of the United States National Lawn Tennis Association (USNLTA) from 1882 to 1884 and from 1894 to 1911.

FATHER FLANAGAN OF THE NBA [THE]—Gene Shue (1931–) Basketball coach. Shue received his nickname because he recruited players who were unwanted by other teams.

FATHER—John Kelley (1859–1908) Baseball.

FATHER OF AMATEUR TRAPSHOOTING—George S. McCarty (1868–1945) Trapshooting.

FATHER OF AMERICAN YACHT REPORTING—William P. Stephens (1855–1946) Sports journalist.

FATHER OF BASKETBALL—Dr. James Naismith (1861–1939) Basketball. **H/F**

FATHER OF BASKETBALL TACTICS—Harry Baum (1882–deceased) Basketball coach.

FATHER OF BOXING—Jack Broughton (1704–1789) Boxing. **H/F**

FATHER OF HOT RODDING—Ed Winfield (1901–) Auto racing.

FATHER OF INSIDE BASEBALL—John Joseph McGraw (1873–1934) Baseball 3b/manager. Also called LITTLE NAPOLEON.

FATHER OF INTERNATIONAL FOOTBALL—Charles William Alcock (1842–1907) Soccer. He received this sobriquet because he initiated the international soccer matches between Scotland and England.

FATHER OF MODERN TENPIN BOWLING—Mark Roth (1951–) Bowling. He was the second bowler in history (after Earl Anthony) to earn $1,000,000 bowling.

FATHER OF MODERN VOLLEYBALL—A. Provost Idell (1889–1965) Volleyball player/coach/official.

FATHER OF NIGHT BASEBALL—E. Lee Keyser (1886–1950) Baseball official.

FATHER OF THE BROOKLYN DODGERS—Charles H. Ebbets (1859–1925) Baseball entrepreneur.

FATHER OF THE CATCHER'S CHEST PROTECTOR—William J. Sullivan, Sr. (1875–1965) Baseball c/manager.

FATHER OF THE CURVE BALL—William Arthur Cummings (1848–1924) Baseball p/of. **H/F** See CANDY.

FATHER OF THE DAVIS CUP—Dwight F. Davis (1879–1945) Tennis.

FATHER OF THE FORWARD PASS—Edward B. Cochems (1876–1953) Football.

FATHER OF THE INDIANAPOLIS MOTOR SPEEDWAY—Carl Graham Fisher (1874–1939) Auto racing.

FATHER OF THE OUTBOARD—Ole Evinrude (1877–1934) Inventor.

FATHER OF THE RING—James Figg (1695–1720) Boxing. Figg was not only the first English champion of the ring (it was actually fighting with the cudgel or stick) but also the first manager and promoter.

FATHER TIME—Phil Niekro (1939–) Baseball. Niekro was still throwing his knuckler well into his forties. Also called KNUCKSIE.

FATS—Verne Clemons (1892–1959) Baseball c.

FATS—Alex Delvecchio (1931–) Hockey. Delvecchio played twenty-three seasons with the Detroit Red Wings. In 1,549 games, he scored 456 goals and 1,281 points. Three times he won the Lady Byng Trophy.

FATS—Wilbur F. Henry (1897–1952) Football. **H/F** "Bouncing around like a rubber ball" is how Grantland Rice once described this 5' 10", 240-pound lineman. But Henry was graceful as a slinky when it came to kicking: booting a NFL-record ninety-four-yard punt, a fifty-yard dropkicked field goal, and forty-nine drop-kicked conversions in a row.

FATS—Ernie Holmes (active 1972–1978) Football. This defensive right tackle who played for Pittsburgh's STEEL CURTAIN had a ravenous appetite.

FATS—Clarence Jenkins (1898–1968) Baseball (Negro Leagues). This outfielder was given this nickname because it was what an older brother had been called.

FATSO—Bruce Sloan (1914–1973) Baseball. This outfielder was only 5' 9" and tipped the scales at 195 pounds.

FATTY—Charles Briody (1858–1903) Baseball. This catcher was shorter than 5' 9" and weighed 190 pounds. Also called ALDERMAN.

FATTY—William J. Foulke (1900s) Soccer. At 6' 3" and 311 pounds, Foulke must have been one of the biggest people ever to play soccer. And what position did he play? Why goalie, of course.

FEARLESS [THE]—Owen Moran. Boxing.

FEETS—Nathaniel Broudy (active 1960s–1986) Basketball official. Broudy ran the clock at Madison Square Garden.

FERGIE—John Bowie Ferguson (1938–) Hockey lw.

FERGIE—Lorne Robert Ferguson (1930–) Hockey lw.

FERGIE—Ferguson Jenkins (1943–) Baseball p. **H/F**

FERNIE—Ferdinand Charles Flamin (1927–) Hockey. **H/F** After a seventeen-year career as a defenseman

capped by the Stanley Cup in 1951, Fernie coached teams to championships in the AHL, CHL, and WHL.

FIDDLER—Eddie Basinski (1922–) Baseball. During the winter, this infielder played violin with a symphony orchestra.

FIDDLER—Frank J. Corridon (1880–1941) Baseball. This Phillies pitcher was forever fiddling with the baseball before pitching.

FIDDLER—William Henry McGee (1909–1987) Baseball. This pitcher played the fiddle.

FIDGETY—Phil Collins (1900–1948) Baseball. Collins was a mass of minute motions on the pitcher's mound. From 1923 to 1935, he was 80–85.

FIDO—Marcus Elmore Baldwin (1865–1929) Baseball. Baldwin, a pitcher, never seemed to get along with CAP Anson, the manager of the Chicago White Stockings. Baldwin was in the doghouse so often he was called Fido.

FIDO—Herbert Kempton Football.

FIDO—Clifford Purpur (1916–) Hockey. This Black Hawk forward had all the characteristics of a terrific dog. He could be ferocious when needed and friendly at other times, willingly signing his autograph until the lights were turned out.

FIFTEEN-YARD DADDY—Gene Lipscomb (1931–1963) Football, wrestling. Lipscomb also had this nickname because he was frequently called for roughness penalties. See BIG DADDY.

FIGGY—Ed Figueroa (1948–) Baseball p. Also called EDUARDITO.

FIGHTING—Masahiko Boxing.

FIGHTING—Harada (1943–) Boxing. Harada was the featherweight champion from 1962 to 1963 and the bantamweight champion from 1965 to 1968.

FIGHTING FOOL [THE]—Jack Sharkey (1902–) Boxing.

FIGHTING IRISHMAN FROM TROY [THE]—John J. Evers (1883–1947) Baseball 2b. **H/F** Evers was part of the famous double-play combination of Tinkers to Evers to Chance. Also called THE CRAB and THE TROJAN.

FIGHTING PREACHER [THE]—Trevor Berbick (1952–) Boxing (heavyweight). Fight promoter Don King gave Berbick this nickname.

FINGER—Calvin Pearly Gardner (1924–) Hockey c.

FINN—Laurie Niemi (1925–1968) Football.

FIRE—Virgil Trucks (1919–) Baseball.
This nickname was given to Trucks because of his fastball and last name. Also called Fireball.

FIREBALL—Warren Gerber (1921–) Softball. **H/F**
Gerber won 500 games, including fifty no-hitters and four perfect games.

FIREBALL—Glenn Roberts (1929–1964) Auto racing.
True to his nickname, Roberts died in a fiery crash in 1964.

FIREMAN—Joe Beggs (1910–1983) Baseball.
Beggs was a reliever who was known for coming in and putting out the fire. He had a record of twenty-nine wins in relief and twenty-nine saves.

FIREMAN—Jim Flynn (active 1910s) Boxing.
Police stopped his heavyweight fight with Jack Johnson on September 14, 1912.

FIREMAN—William Juzda (1920–) Hockey d.
Also called BEAST.

FIREMAN—Joe Page (1917–1980) Baseball.
In 1949, this reliever had thirteen wins and twenty-seven saves. Because he liked to party, he was also called THE GAY RELIEVER.

FIRP—Waldo Greene (active 1927) Football.

FIRST GREAT RACER [THE]—George Hepburn Robertson (1885–1955) Auto racing.

FIRST INDY FOUR-HOUR WINNER [THE]—Lee Wallard (1910–1963) Auto racing.

FIRST LADY OF AMERICAN TENNIS [THE]—Hazel Hotchkiss Wightman (1866–1974) Tennis. This winner of forty-five national titles was not only an active tennis player in later life, but she even won a national title when she was sixty-eight.

FIRST LADY OF BASEBALL [THE]—Laraine Day (1920–) Baseball. Wife of Leo "THE LIP" Durocher.

FIRST LADY OF BLACK BASEBALL [THE]—Effa Manley (1897–1981) Baseball. Manley owned the Neward Eagles. In 1946, they won the Black World Series with players such as Larry Doby, Monte Irvin, and Don Newcombe.

FIRST SUPER END—Don Hutson (1913– 1997) Football. See ALABAMA ANTELOPE.

FISH—Benny Bass (1904–1975) Boxing.
Fish, who had 213 bouts, won the world junior lightweight title in 1929.

FISH—Roy Fisher (1968–) Basketball.

This University of California forward's nickname was from his first name.

FISH—Len Grant (1906–1938) Football.

FISH HOOK—Allyn Stout (1904–1974) Baseball.
This pitcher hooked himself on a fishing expedition.

FISHIN' MAGICIAN [THE]—Mark Pavelich (1927–) Hockey lw.

FISHY—Phil Rabinowitz Basketball.

FIST [THE]—Dennis Fykes Boxing.

FISTIC HARLEQUIN—Max Baer (1909–1959) Boxing.
Also called CLOUTING CLOWN, LARRUPING LOTHARIO OF PUGILISM, LIVERMORE BUTCHER BOY, LIVERMORE LARRUPER, MADCAP MAXIE, MAGNIFICENT SCREWBALL, PLAYBOY OF PUGILISM, PUGILISTIC POSEUR.

FIVE YARDS—Eddie Novak (1897–1984) Football.
From 1920–1926, this fine halfback could be counted on to gain at least five yards per carry.

FLACO—Jose Arcia (1943–) Baseball.
At 6' 3" and 170 pounds, this shortstop was thin (the meaning of his nickname in Spanish).

FLACO—Alvaro Teheran (1967–) Basketball.
At 7' 1", 245 pounds, this University of Houston center was thin.

FLAKEY—John G. Brandt, Jr. (1934–) baseball 3b/of.

FLAME—Lee Delhi (1890–1966) Baseball.
This pitcher may have had a good fastball, but he flamed out after only three innings with an ERA of 9.00.

FLAME—Eddie Mustafa Muhammad (1952–) Boxing.
This boxer, whose original name was Eddie Gregory, won the WBA light heavyweight title in 1981.

FLAME THROWER [THE]—Harry Fanok (1940–) Baseball p.

FLAPPING EAGLE—Lionel Harney. Boxing.

FLASH—Frankie Brian (1923–) Basketball.
Brian went from playing guard at Louisiana State to the NBA.

FLASH—Gabriel Elorde (1935–) Boxing.
This fighter won the Oriental bantamweight and the Filipino lightweight titles.

FLASH—Joe Gordon (1915–) Baseball.
Gordon's nickname was after Flash Gordon, the sci-fi film hero. In 1942, Flash Gordon hit .322 and was named the American League MVP. After playing second base eleven years for the Yankees and the Indians, he became a manager for four years.

FLASH—William Hollet (1912–) Hockey d.

FLASH—John Suther (active 1930s) Football.

FLAT—James Patrick Walsh (1897–) Hockey g.

FLEA [THE]—Eric Allen (active 1988–) Football db.

FLEA—Herman E. Clifton (1910–) Football.

FLEA [THE]—Freddie Patek (1944–) Baseball.
This shortstop was only 5' 5" and 145 pounds.
Also called MOOCHIE.

FLEA [THE]—Walter Roberts (active 1964–1966) Football.
This wide receiver was only 5' 10" and 167 pounds.

FLICK—Alex English (1954–) Basketball f.

FLIGHT 45—Dave Smith (1955–) Baseball p.

FLINTSTONE—Fred Gladding (1936–) Baseball.
Some say this pitcher resembled the cartoon
character.

FLIP—Frank Bernard Lafferty (1854–1910) Basketball.

FLIP—Al Rosen (1925–) Baseball 3b.

FLIP—Phillip Saunders. Basketball.
Because that's how his first name sounds when said fast.

FLIP FLAP—Oscar Jones (1879–1946) Baseball p.

FLIPPER—Willie Anderson (active 1988–1992)
Football rw.

FLIPPER—Robert James Dorey (1947–) Hockey.
At one time this defenseman held the record for the
most penalty minutes in a single game (forty-eight
minutes in the penalty box).

FLOAT—Don Zimmermann (1949–) Football.
Played from 1973–1976.

FLOP—Paul Gorrill (1900–deceased) Football.
Played one season (1926) for Colorado.

FLORENCE NIGHTINGALE—Clara Donahue. Baseball
(All-American Girls Baseball League). Donahue was
asked to bunt to advance the runner so often that she
was nicknamed for this selfless nurse.

FLY—Steve Mingori (1944–) Baseball p.

FLY [THE]—Richard Rozelle. Boxing.

FLY—James Williams. Basketball.
Williams, a legend on the playgrounds of Brooklyn,
played at Jacksonville.

FLYING DUTCHMAN [THE]—Herman C. Long (1866–1909)
Baseball ss. Also called GERMANY.

FLYING DUTCHMAN [THE]—Norm Van Brocklin
(1926–1983) Football. **H/F**

FLYING NORSEMAN [THE]—Torger D. Tokle (1920–1945)
Ski jumping.

FLYING PARSON [THE]—Gil Dodds (1918–1977) Track and
field. Dodds was a miler and a minister; later he
became a track coach.

FLYING SCOT [THE]—Eric Liddel (1902–1945) Track and
field. Liddel won a gold medal at the 1924 Summer
Olympics.

FLYING SCOT [THE]—Bobby Thomson (1923–) Baseball
of. Thomson was born in Glasgow, Scotland. Also
called THE STATEN ISLAND SCOT.

FLYING TEXAN (THE)—A. J. Foyt (1935–) Auto racing.
Foyt has raced in thirty-five and won four Indianapolis
500 races.

FLYING YANKEE—Arthur A. Zimmerman (1869–1936)
Cycling. **H/F** Zimmie set a world record at the half-
mile. Also called KING OF THE WHEEL.

FOG [THE]—Fred Shero (1925–1990) Hockey.
Coach Shero got his nickname when he locked himself out of the arena where his Philadelphia Flyers
were playing. He stood in the hallway and called out
like a foghorn, until someone let him back in.
Also called FREDDIE THE FOG.

FOGGY—Joe Altobelli (1932–) Baseball 1b/mgr.

FOGHORN—Forrest Claire Allen (1885–1974) Basketball,
baseball coach. Also called Dr. Foghorn and PHOG.

FOGHORN—George Miller (1853–1929) Baseball c.
Also called CALLIOPE and DOGGIE.

FOGHORN—George Myatt (1914–) Baseball 2b.
Also called MERCURY and STUD.

FONZIE—Edgardo Alfonzo (1973–) Baseball 3b.
Anyone who watched the television show *Happy Days*,
a sitcom that ran from 1974–1984, remembers Henry
Winkler as Arthur Fonzarelli a.k.a. the Fonz. Alfonzo's
nickname is a reminder of that character. When
Fonzie started for the Mets on May 5, 1995, he became
the 100th third baseman in the history of the Mets'
franchise.

FOOT—Bob Locker (1938–) Baseball p.

FOOTBALL CLASSICIST—Dana Xenophon Bible
(1891–1980) Football coach. Also called DX.

FOOTBALL DOCTOR—Edward Anderson (1900–1976)
Football e/coach.

FOOTBALL SCHOLAR—Carl Grey Snavely (1894–1975)
Football coach.

FOOTBALL STATESMAN [THE]—Fritz Crisler (1899–)
Football coach.

FOOTBALL'S GREATEST COACH—Robert Reese Neyland, Jr. (1892–1962) Football.

FOOTBALL'S OLD MAN RIVER—Amos Alonzo Stagg (1862–1965) Football coach. Also called GRAND OLD MAN OF FOOTBALL.

FOOTS—Bill La Fitte (1926–) Football.
Since his last name is pronounced La Feet, it is natural that he be nicknamed Foots.

FOOTS—Clarence Walker (1951–) Basketball.
Clarence wore a size eleven shoe when he was in the first grade. In high school, Walker broke Carl Yastrzemski's scoring records in high school, and then went on to play guard for Cleveland and New Jersey in the NBA.

FOOTSIE—Wayne Belardi (1930–) Baseball.
People with this nickname (including this first baseman) often are clumsy or have big feet or both.

FOOTSIE—Donald E. Lenhardt (1922–) Baseball of.

FOOTSIE—Johnny Marcum (1908–1984) Baseball p.

FORDDY—Forrest Anderson (1919–) Basketball.
His record in college coaching from 1947–1971 was 369–234.

FOUR SACK—Ervin Dusak (1920–1994) Baseball.
This outfielder won his nickname for clouting a four-bagger in one of his first plate appearances in the minors. In the majors, however, it was another story; he only hit twenty-four in nine years.

FOXY GRANDPA—Jimmy Bannon (1871–1948) Baseball.

FRAN THE MAN—Frantisek Musil (1964–) Hockey.

FRECK—Marv Owen (1906–1989) Baseball 3b.

FRECKLED BOB—Bob Fitzsimmons (1863–1917) Boxing. **H/F**

FRED—Fernando Valenzuela (1960–) Baseball.
This is a nickname that reflected the Americanization of Fernando, who hails from Sonora, Mexico.

FREDDIE THE FOOT—Fred Cox (active 1963–1977) Football. Cox was a field goal kicker for Minnesota.

FRENCHY—Albert Belanger (1906–) Boxing.
This French Canadian won the NBA flyweight title in 1927.

FRENCHY—Stanley Bordagaray (1912–) Baseball.
Bordagaray's French heritage was bolstered by the goatee and mustache this outfielder wore. His most stellar performance came in 1938 when he pinch-hit safely twenty times in forty-three times at bat.

FRENCHY—John DeMoisey (1912–) Basketball.

FRENCHY—Joseph Julien (1907–) Lacrosse. **H/F**

FRENCHY—Jim Lefebvre (1943–) Baseball.

FRENCHY—Joseph LeFleur (1896–1973) Football.

FRESHEST MAN ON EARTH [THE]—Walter "Arlie" Latham (1860–1952) Baseball. Latham kept up a steady stream of chatter directed toward the other team. Whether he was sitting on the bench, playing third base, or later as a third-base coach, Latham had a "fresh" mouth. As a coach, he even developed a comedy routine for the coach's box to keep the crowd in stitches.

FRITZ—Harry Dorish (1921–) Baseball.

FRITZ—Wilfred Edgar Knothe (1904–1963) Baseball 3b.
Fritz often referred to a Germanic background.

FRITZ—Fred Lewis (1944–) Basketball.
After college basketball at Arizona State, Lewis played guard for the Royals in the NBA and the Pacers in the ABA.

FRITZ—Frederick Raymond Ostermueller (1907–1957) Baseball.

FRITZ—Ron Williams (1944–) Basketball.
His childhood nickname of Frisky was transmogrified into Fritz. An All-American at West Virginia, Williams was the number one draft pick of the San Francisco Warriors. In 1971–1972, he led the team in assists.

FROG—Dan Reeves (1944–) Football. In 1970, Frog Reeves was chosen to be Tom Landry's assistant coach. Reeves was then the youngest coach in the NFL.

FROGGY—Joseph Paul DeMaestri (1928–) Baseball. Also called OATS.

FROGGY—James Williams (1928–) Football.
This end kicked the winning field goal with eight seconds remaining for the 17–15 victory of Rice over Texas.

FROSTY—Len Bias (19__–1986) Basketball.
His nickname came from his coolness on the court. Tragically, this number one draft pick of the Celtics died of a drug overdose in 1986.

FROSTY—Forrest Cox (1907–1962) Basketball.
Cox coached Colorado to a 147–89 record, including the 1940 NIT championship.

FROSTY BILL—Bill Duggleby (1874–1944) Baseball.
This pitcher had a barnburner of a beginning by hitting a grand slam in his first major league at-bat. His attitude toward his teammates, however, was less than warm. And in the dog days of summer, he appeared downright cold by wearing dark suits after the game.

FUDD—Milt May (1950–) Baseball.
This catcher reminded some of the noted cartoon character, Bugs Bunny's nemesis—Elmer Fudd.

FUDGEHAMMER—Frank Nunley (1945–) Football.
Played 1967–1976 for San Francisco.

FUNGO—Joe Hesketh (1959–) Baseball.
Long and lean, this pitcher was nicknamed after the bat.

FURNACE FACE—Billy Kilmer (active 1961–1978) Football qb.

FUZZ—Albert White (1918–) Baseball of.

FUZZY—Aaron Harry Kallet (1887–1965) Football.

FUZZY—Andrew Levane (1920–) Basketball.
After the guard led St. John's to the 1943 NIT title, he was a player and a coach in the NBA. When Levane was a coach for the Knicks, Red Holzman was his scout.

FUZZY—Al Smith (1928–) Baseball.
This outfielder, who had a quick-growing beard, led the American League in runs scored with 123 in 1955.

FUZZY—Fred Thurston (active 1958–1967) Football g.

FUZZY—Robert Vandivier. Basketball. **H/F**

G—Gary Waites (1969–) Basketball.

GABBER—Joseph Charles Glenn (1908–1985) Baseball.
This catcher liked to gab behind the plate.

GABBY—Lloyd Gilford Gronsdahl (1921–) Hockey.

GABBY—Neil Johnston (1929–) Basketball c.

GABBY—Dave Jolly (1924–1963) Baseball p.

GABBY—John H. Roseboro (1933–) Baseball c.

GABBY—Glen Weldon Stewart (1912–) Baseball ss.

GABBY—Alma Kathryn Ziegler (active 1944–1954)
All-American Girls Baseball League p/2b.

GABE—Roman Gabriel (1940–) Football qb.

GABY—Jose Canizales (active 1980s) Boxing (bantamweight).

GALLATIN SQUASH [THE]—Herbert Rodney Perdue (1882–1968) Baseball. Perdue was a stout pitcher (5' 10", 192 pounds) who was born in Gallatin, Tennessee.

GALLOPING MAJOR OF HUNGARY—Ferenc Puskas (1927–) Soccer. Puskas was the Hungarian scoring leader in soccer for the years 1948, 1949, 1950, and 1953.

GALLOPING SPRAFKA—Joseph Sprafka (active 1916) Football.

GALVESTON GIANT [THE]—Jack Johnson (1878–1946) Boxing. This dominant heavyweight of his day was 6' 1",

221 pounds, and from Galveston, Texas. Also called BIG SMOKE and LI'L ARTHUR.

GAME CHICKEN [THE]—Henry "Hen" Pearce (1777–1809) Boxing (heavyweight). England's Pearce, an unbeaten barefisted champion from 1803 to 1806, was always game, and "hen" didn't seem to fit.

GANDER—Monty Stratton (1912–1982) Baseball p.

GARBAGE MAN [THE]—Steve Shutt (1952–) Hockey.
Shutt, a left wing, specialized in getting pucks on the rebound.

GARBAGE MAN [THE]—Sly Williams (1958–) Basketball f-g.

GARFIELD GUNNER—Tippy Larkin (1917–) Boxing (welterweight).

GARO—Garabed Yepremian (1944–) Football k. **H/F**

GASEOUS CASSIUS—Muhammad Ali (1942–) Boxing (heavyweight). See THE GREATEST.

GATES—William Brown (1939–) Baseball.
Before becoming an outfielder, a pinch hitter (he led the league in 1968 and 1974), and a designated hitter for the Detroit Tigers, Brown had done time in prison.

GATES—Gaetano Orlando (1962–) Hockey c.

GATESHEAD CLIPPER [THE]—Jack White (active mid-1800s) Running. In 1862, Englishman Jack White beat Native American Louis "Deerfoot" Bennett at six miles in less than thirty minutes. See DEERFOOT.

GATOR—Ron Guidry (1950–) Baseball p.
Also called LOUISIANA LIGHTNING.

GAUSE GHOST [THE]—Joe Gregg Moore (1908–) Baseball.
This fast outfielder, who was from Gause, Texas, collected two hits in one inning of the 1933 World Series.

GAVVY—Clifford Carlton Cravath (1881–1963) Baseball.
In 1915, this big outfielder smashed twenty-four home runs. From 1912 to 1920, he led the National League in home runs six times.

GAY—Gabriel Bromberg (active 1930s) Football.

GAY CASTILLION [THE]—Vernon "Lefty" Gomez (1909–1989) Baseball p. **H/F** See GOOFY.

GAZELLE [THE]—Joseph Gerard Gravelle (1925–) Hockey. Some say Gravelle was the fastest skater in the history of the NHL (hence his nickname). Unfortunately, this right wing was not much good at scoring. Also called LEO.

GEE—Walter Ancker (1894–1954) Baseball p.
Also called LIVER.

GEE—Gerald Walker (1908–) Baseball.
This outfielder's nickname is the pronunciation of the letter of his first name. He hit .294 during his fifteen years in the majors.

GEE GEE—Gus Getz (1899–1969) Baseball.
This third baseman's nickname stood for his initials.

GEE GEE—James Joseph Gleeson (1912–1996) Baseball.
The nickname of this outfielder resulted after a slight liberty was taken with his initials.

GEEZER—Howard Porter (1948–) Basketball f-c.

GENERAL—Alvin Floyd Crowder (1899–1972) Baseball.
Crowder was nicknamed for General Crowder who had declared that baseball players would not be exempt from WW I. (Alvin Crowder became a sergeant.) Crowder was a workhorse of a pitcher in the American League from 1926–1936. His three best years were 21–5, 26–13, and 24–15.

GENERAL [THE]—John Reed Kilpatrick Hockey.
Kilpatrick was a military hero and the president of the New York Rangers for twenty-five years.

GENERAL [THE]—Ivan Putski. Wrestling.
Hailing from Kralow, Poland, The General (as his fans call him) stands for Polish Power in the ring. His fans are known as "The Polish Army." Twice he has won tag-team titles in Texas.

GENTLEMAN—Joe Primeau (1906–1989) Hockey.
This center on the Toronto Maple Leafs' KID LINE had a kind disposition.

GENTLEMAN DAVE—David J. Mararcher (1894–1982) Baseball (Negro Leagues). This third baseman graduated from New Orleans University, thus his nickname.

GENTLEMAN FIGHTER [THE]—Dick Humphries.
Bareknuckles Boxing. Humphries and Daniel Mendoza fought several fierce fights.

GENTLEMAN GERRY—Gerry Cooney (1956–) Boxing (heavyweight).

GENTLEMAN JAKE—Jacob Daubert (1884–1924) Baseball.
This first baseman was not gentle with his bat. In 1913, he hit .350; he knocked out 2,326 hits during his fifteen-year career.

GENTLEMAN JIM—James Lonborg (1942–) Baseball p.

GENTLEMAN JOE—Joseph Black (1924–) Baseball.
Black always gave credit to others for whatever pitching success he had. He was most complimentary in 1952 when he achieved a record of 15–4.

GENTLEMAN JOHN—John Enzmann (1890–1984) Baseball p.

GENTLEMAN JOHN—Johnny Parsons. Auto racing.

GENTLEMANLY BOBBY—Bobby Clack (1851–1933) Baseball of.

GEORGIA DEACON [THE]—Theodore "Tiger" Flowers (1895–1927) Boxing. Tiger was the middleweight champ from 1926 to 1931.

GEORGIA FIREBALL—Frank Sinkwich (1920–) Football.
In 1943, Sinkwich scored a TD in Georgia's 9–0 victory in the Rose Bowl.

GEORGIE—Georgiana Bishop (active 1900s) Golf.
Georgie won the 1904 U.S. Women's Amateur Championship.

GERM—Gerald Leeman (1922–) Wrestling. Leeman's style was to be all over his opponent like a cold germ.

GERMANY—Herman C. Long (1866–1909) Baseball ss.
Also called FLYING DUTCHMAN.

GERMANY—Herman A. Schaefer (1877–1919) Baseball.
Schaefer's historical roots were German, but his hysterical roots were zany. This second baseman liked to steal first base (from second). The rulebook now precludes this practice.

GERMANY—Adolph George Schultz (1883–1951) Football.
This 6' 4", 245-pound center was the first to use the spiral snap and the first to stand behind the scrimmage line to rove around on defense like today's linebacker.

GERMANY—George J. Smith (1863–1927) Baseball ss.

GERMANY—Harry Smith (19–) Football.

GERTIE—George Gravel (active 1940s) Football.
This NFL official got his nickname from Gravel Gertie, a character in the Dick Tracy comic strip.

GETTYSBURG EDDIE—Edward Plank (1875–1926) Baseball p. **H/F**

GHETTO WIZARD—Benny Leonard (1896–1947) Boxing **H/F** In 1917, Benny won the World Lightweight Championship, and in 1918 he appeared in the Broadway show *Yip-Yip Yak, Yank.*

GHOST—Dave Casper (active 1974–1984) Football.
Casper received his nickname because this end sometimes seemed as elusive as the cartoon character.

GHOST OF THE GHETTO—Sid Terris (1904–) Boxing (bantamweight).

GIANT—Jack Conroy (active 1930s) Football.

GIANT KILLER—Virgil Cheeves (1901–1979) Baseball. This pitcher was so successful against the New York Giants. Also called CHIEF.

GIANT KILLER [THE]—Harry Coveleski (1886–1950). Baseball. In 1908, as a pitcher for the Phillies, he earned his nickname by beating the Giants three times in the late season. His brother is Hall-of-Famer Stanley Covelski. Also called THE SILENT POLE.

GIFFER [THE]—Frank Gifford (1930–) Football hb. **H/F** Also called THE GOLDEN BOY.

GILPATRICK—Gilbert Patrick (active 1836–1955) Horse racing. **H/F** His nickname was a shortening and combining of his two names.

GIMPY—Lloyd Brown (1904–1974) Baseball p.

GIMPY—Milt Pappas (1939–) Baseball. This was a high-school nickname for this pitcher with a 209–164 record in the majors.

GINGER—Clarence Beaumont (1876–1956) Baseball. This first batter-up in the 1903 World Series had reddish hair.

GINGER—Cal Gardner (1924–) Hockey. This center had red hair.

GINK—Harvey Hendrick (1897–1941) Baseball of.

GITZ—Warren Miller (1885–1956) Baseball.

GIPPER [THE]—Roland A. Locke (1903–1952) Track and field. In 1926, Locke set world records at 220 yards and 200 meters while at the University of Nebraska.

GIZ—Paul Nowak (1914–) Basketball c. Also called BUTCH.

GIZMO—Henry Williams (active 1989) Football rw.

GIZZY—Wilfred Harold Hart (1903–) Hockey lw.

GLACIER [THE]—Dave Pezzuoli Football. This lineman was difficult to move.

GLASGOW GOBBLER [THE]—Andy Aitkenhead (1904–) Hockey. Aitkenhead was born in Glasgow.

GLASS ARM EDDIE—Eddie Brown (1891–1956) Baseball. As a glass jaw is to a boxer, a glass arm is to an outfielder. Brown's throws from the outfield were weak and erratic. However, he made up for it at the plate with four straight .300 seasons.

GLIDE [THE]—Benny Clyde (1951–) Basketball. Clyde played forward for Florida State and the Boston Celtics.

GLIDE [THE]—Clyde Drexler (1962–) Basketball. At guard or forward, this rhyming nickname captures Drexler's ability to slide toward the bucket with a stuff shot.

GLIDER [THE]—Ed Charles (1933–) Baseball. Charles glided around the bases. For his ability to versify, this third baseman was also called THE POET.

GLOBE TROTTER [THE]—Jeff Smith (1891–1962) Boxing (middleweight). **H/F**

GLOOMY GUS—August Williams (1888–1964) Baseball.

GNAT—Larry Bowa (1945–) Baseball. He was a pesky batter.

GO—Hisami Numata. Boxing.

GOAT—Edward John Anderson (1880–1923) Baseball. Anderson made a lot of errors in the outfield.

GOAT [THE]—Earl Manigault (c.1940–) Basketball. Once a legend on the basketball courts of Harlem, the Goat has been slowed in recent years by drug addiction and physical ailments.

GOB—Garland Buckeye (1897–1975) Baseball, football. A navy veteran (gob referred to the old practice of putting tar on the collar to hold the hair in place), the 260-pound Buckeye played both pro baseball (primarily as a pitcher for Cleveland) and pro football (for the Bulls, Cardinals, and Tigers in Chicago.) Also known as Ponderosa because of his large size.

GOD—Doug Harvey (1930–) Baseball. Harvey was a highly regarded National League umpire.

GODFATHER [THE]—Tommy Lasorda (1927–) Baseball. With Dodger blue in his veins, Lasorda runs the ball club as if it were his own big family.

GOINGS—Ronald Anderson (1945–) Hockey. Anderson received this nickname because he played right wing with so many different teams.

GOLD DOG—Melvin Cheatum (1968–) Basketball f.

GOLD ELA—Elzbieta Krzesinska (1934–) Track and field. She received her nickname because of her blonde hair and her many victories. She won a gold medal in the 1956 Melbourne Olympics when she tied the world long jump record of 20' 10". At the 1960 Rome Olympics, she won a silver medal.

GOLDEN ARM—Masanichi Kaneda (1930–) Baseball. This Japanese pitcher won over 400 games.

GOLDEN BOY—Arthur Anthony Aragon. Boxing. In 109 bouts, he scored 61 knockouts and 26 decisions, with 4 draws and 18 losses.

GOLDEN BOY—Robert W. Brown (1924–) Baseball. This third baseman received a $50,000 bonus for signing with the New York Yankees.

GOLDEN BOY [THE]—Frank Gifford (1930–) Football. Led the Giants to three NFL title games and was the NFL's MVP in 1956. He started a second career as a sports broadcaster in 1958. Also called Giff.

GOLDEN BOY [THE]—Bobby Hull (1939–) Hockey. **H/F** See THE GOLDEN JET.

GOLDEN BOY OF ENGLISH SOCCER [THE]—Bobby Moore (1942–) Soccer. This defender played in over 1,000 games over a period of twenty years. But the highlight of his career was in 1966 when he was the captain of the English team that defeated West Germany 4–2 in the World Cup championship.

GOLDEN GIRL—Donna Hartley (19__–) Track and field. Hartley was a blonde sprinter from Great Britain.

GOLDEN GOLDEN—Bobby Orr (1948–) Hockey. **H/F** Defenseman Bobby Orr was always conspicuously minus a nickname; however, television announcer Bill Mazur once loaded this one on him. See BOBBY HOCKEY.

GOLDEN GREEK [THE]—Harry Agganis (1930–1955) Baseball 1b.

GOLDEN GREEK [THE]—Bob Chakales (1927–) Baseball p. Also called CHICO.

GOLDEN GREEK [THE]—George Kaftan (1928–) Basketball f.

GOLDEN HAWK—Bobby Hull (1939–) Hockey. **H/F** Blond Bobby Hull made a lot of money playing left wing for the Chicago Black Hawks. Later, he was known as the Golden Jet when he signed a big contract to play for the Winnipeg Jets. See THE GOLDEN JET.

GOLDEN WHEELS—Elbert Dubenion (active 1960–1968) Football. The speedy Dubenion was one of quarterback Jack Kemp's favorite targets on the Buffalo Bills.

GOLDFINGER—Maureen Flowers (19__–) Dart throwing. Great Britain's Flowers had blonde hair and was the women's world champion at darts.

GOLDIE—Gordon Frederick Goldsberry (1927–deceased) Baseball 1b.

GOLDIE—George Prodgers (1892–deceased) Hockey f.

GOLFBALL—Dolphus Hull (19–) Golfing caddie.

GOLFDOM'S MIGHTY MITE—Ben Hogan (1912–) Golf. Hogan stood 5' 9" and weighed 160 pounds. During his career, he won four U.S. Opens, two Masters, and the British Open. Also called BANTAM BEN, THE HAWK, The Iceman. See HOGAN'S ALLEY.

GOMER—Claude Wilson Osteen (1939–) Baseball p.

GOOBER—Bill Zuber (1913–1982) Baseball. This pitcher (43–42) had a rhyming nickname.

GOOCH—Ed Lewinski (1920–) Basketball f.

GOOD KID—George Susce (1908–1986) Baseball. This is what this catcher called other players, for he couldn't remember their monikers.

GOOD NEWS—Marvin Barnes (1952–) Basketball c/f. Also called THE ERASER & THE MAGNIFICENT.

GOOD TIME BILL—William Lamar (1897–1970) Baseball of.

GOO-GOO—Augie Galan (1912–1993) Baseball of.

GOOGS—Tom Gugliotta (1969–) Basketball. Plays for the Washington T-Wolves. A headline in *USA Today* for January 13, 1998 read: "T-Wolves' Googs an Unsung Hero Among Superstars."

GOOSE—Mel Counts (1941–) Basketball c-f.

GOOSE—Wayne Embry (1937–) Basketball c-f.

GOOSE—Jack Givens (1956–) Basketball f-g.

GOOSE—Austin Gonsoulin (1938–) Football b.

GOOSE—Rich Gossage (1951–) Baseball. Gossage began as a reliever with Pittsburgh. In those days he kept a goose, and thus gained his nickname. With the Yankees in 1980, Gossage pitched ninety-nine innings and had thirty-three saves. Gossage ranks second in total saves.

GOOSE—Benoit Gosselin (1957–) Hockey. Gosselin, a left wing, was nicknamed Goose because of his last name.

GOOSE—Johnny McCormick (1925–) Hockey. McCormick, a center, had a long neck.

GORDIE—Gordon Bell (1925–) Hockey. Gordie was the goalie for the Toronto Maple Leafs 1945–1946 and for the New York Rangers in 1956.

GORDIE—Gordon Roberts (1957–) Hockey d.

GORDY—Gordon Howe (1928–) Hockey rw. **H/F**

GORGEOUS—George Davis (1870–1940) Baseball ss. **H/F**

GORGEOUS DAN—Daniel Gable (1949–) Wrestling.

GORGEOUS GEORGE—George Sisler (1893–1973) Baseball. **H/F** Sisler played first base for the St. Louis Browns from 1915 to 1929 and had the gorgeous career batting average of .340. Also called THE BROWN BLASTER and THE PERFECT BALLPLAYER.

GORGEOUS GEORGE—George Raymond Wagner (1915–1963) Wrestling. Wagner was a wrestler in the 1950s with bleached blond hair. The name George came from Georges Carpentier, the French boxer who was known for his style (unlike Gorgeous George).

GORGEOUS GEORGES—Georges Carpentier (1894–1975) Boxing. **H/F** See THE ORCHID MAN.

GORGO—Richard Alonzo Gonzales (1928–) Tennis. **H/F** See PANCHO.

GORGO—John Niland (1944–) Football.
Niland received his nickname because of his ability to gorge himself at meals. Also a reference to the Japanese movie monster.

GOSHEN SCHOOLMASTER [THE]—Sam Leever (1871–1953) Baseball. Before pitching for Pittsburgh (his record was 193–101), Leever had been a school-teacher in Goshen, Ohio.

GOVERNOR—Frank Ellerbe (1895–1988) Baseball.
This shortstop's father was William Ellerbe, the governor of South Carolina from 1897 to 1899.

GOYO—Gregorio Peralta. Boxing.

GRABO—Austin Grabowski (1944–) Basketball.

GRABBO—Joe Grabowski (1930–) Basketball.

GRABBY—Bill Grabarkewitz (1946–) Baseball 3b.
Also called BULLDOG.

GRAN GATO [BIG CAT]—Andres Galarraga (1961–)
Baseball. This first baseman received this nickname playing for the Expos in French-speaking Montreal.

GRAND OLD MAN—Cornelius Mack (1862–1956) Baseball.
H/F Mack was a catcher for eleven years and manager for over fifty. He was called the GOM because he didn't retire from the game until he was seventy-four. See TALL TACTICIAN.

GRAND OLD MAN OF RACING—James Edward Fitzsimmons (1874–1966) Racehorse trainer. Also called DEAN OF AMERICAN TRAINERS, MR. FITZ, and SUNNY JIM.

GRANDE ORANGE [LE]—Daniel Joseph "Rusty" Staub (1944–) Baseball. Staub was nicknamed Rusty for his red hair when an infant, but he received the nickname of Le Grand Orange when he was playing right field for the Montreal Expos.

GRAND VETERAN [THE]—Walter Perry Johnson (1887–1946) Baseball p/manager. Also called BARNEY, Best Pitcher in Baseball, and SWEDE. See BIG TRAIN.

GRANDMA—John Joseph Murphy (1908–1970) Baseball pitcher for the New York Yankees. Played in six World Series where he won two games and lost none. Also known as Fireman and Fordham Johnny.

GRAND OLD MAN OF SOCCER—Jack Rottenberg Soccer.

GRAPE JUICE—Greg Johnson (1950–) Track and field, Football. Perhaps because he drank a lot of grape juice?

GRASSHOPPER—Charles Dudley (1950–) Basketball g.

GRAVY—Adam Graves (1968–) Hockey lw.
Also called TRAIN.

GRAY FLAMINGO [THE]—Tom Brennan (1952–)
Baseball. Brennan's hair had turned gray and his pitching style looked like a flamingo balancing on one leg.

GRAY FOX [THE]—Jim Northrup (1939–) Baseball of.

GREASEBALL—Tom Maloney (19–) Boxing (heavyweight).

GREAT [THE]—Terous McDuffie (1910–) Baseball (Negro Leagues) p.

GREAT [THE]—Nate Thurmond (1941–) Basketball.
This 6' 11" center had a rhyming nickname that told about his defensive play. After starring at Bowling Green, he was an often hurt All-Star for the San Francisco Warriors.

GREAT ALL-AMERICAN [THE]—Fish Hamilton (1888–?)
Football. Fish was also from a great family of politicians.

GREAT GABBO [THE]—Frank Gabler (1911–1967)
Baseball. Gabler was a boaster and a brawler.

GREAT GUN OF WINDSOR [THE]—Tom Cannon (1790–1858) English bareknuckles boxing. Cannon, whose nickname was for his birthplace and his punching ability, shot himself when he was sixty-nine.

GREAT GUNDY [THE]—JoAnne Gunderson (Carner) (1939–) Golf. Gunderson was called Gundy by the other golfers. After winning the Women's Amateur five times she was called The Great Gundy. See BAG LADY and BIG MAMA.

GREAT JOCKEY OF THE GOLDEN AGE OF SPORTS [THE]—Earl H. Sande (1898–1968) Horse racing.

GREAT JOHN L. [THE]—John Lawrence Sullivan (1858–1918) Heavyweight boxing. Also called JOHN L., THE STRONG BOY OF BOSTON. See THE BOSTON STRONG BOY.

GREAT MAILS [THE]—Walter Mails (1895–1974) Baseball press agent. See DUSTER.

GREAT MAN [THE]—Jay Hanna Dean (1911–1974) Baseball p/announcer. SEE DIZZY.

GREAT MICK [THE]—Mickey Mantle (1931–) Baseball cf. **H/F** See THE COMMERCE COMET.

GREAT ONE [THE]—Roberto Clemente (1934–1972) Baseball of. **H/F** See ARRIBA.

GREAT STONE FACE [THE]—Fred Hutchison (1919–1964) Baseball. After his playing days as a pitcher were over, Hutchison became a widely respected manager. His nickname was for his stern exterior that belied his warmth and sense of fairness.

GREAT WHITE DOPE [THE]—Gerry Cooney (1956–) Boxing (heavyweight). This was the nickname that Larry Holmes gave his challenger.

GREATEST BOWLER IN HISTORY [THE]—Don Carter (1926–) Bowling. Also called BOSCO.

GREATEST PLAYER OF HOCKEY [THE]—Bobby Orr (1948–) Hockey. **H/F** See BOBBY HOCKEY.

GREEK [THE]—Bobby DelGreco (1933–) Baseball. DelGreco was actually Italian, not Greek.

GREEK [THE]—Charlie George (1912–) Baseball c.

GREEK—Gus Niarhos (1920–) Baseball c.

GREEK [THE]—Jimmy Snyder (19–) Gambler and odds-maker.

GREEK PEAK [THE]—Rony Seikaly (19–) Basketball. This Syracuse center stood 6' 10".

GREY EAGLE [THE]—Tristram Speaker (1888–1958) Baseball of. **H/F** Speaker played a very shallow center field for the Boston Red Sox and later the Cleveland Indians. When a long ball was hit, the gray-haired Speaker swooped back like an eagle in flight to snare the ball; thus, his nickname the Grey Eagle. Not only could he field, he could also hit. From 1907 to 1927 Speaker had an average of .344. Also called Tris and SPOKE.

GREY GHOST OF GONZAGA [THE]—Anthony Robert Canadeo (1919–) Football. **H/F**

GREYHOUND [THE]—Walter Davis (1954–) Basketball. After playing on the 1976 Olympic team, Davis played for Phoenix, Denver, and Portland.

GREYHOUND—Eddie Milner (1955–) Baseball. This Cincinnati outfielder was fast.

GRIN—George Washington Bradley (1852–1931) Baseball. Bradley grinned his way through a 138–127 pitching career.

GROOVE—Don Baylor (1949–) Baseball. Known for being a hitter in the groove, Baylor's best year was with Oakland in 1979 when he scored 120 runs and had 139 RBIs. Baylor later became a desig-nated hitter, a leader in the clubhouse, and the first manager of the Colorado Rockies.

GROS BILL [LE]—Jean Beliveau (1931–) Hockey. **H/F** This center scored a league high forty-seven goals in 1955–1956, and in 1965, he won the first Conn Smythe Trophy (for being the post-season MVP) as his team, The Montreal Canadiens, won the Stanley Cup. All told, Big Bill played on ten Stanley Cup championship for THE HABS, scoring 507 goals during the regular season and seventy-nine during the playoffs. Also called BIG JEAN.

GROTESQUE [THE]—Sambo Sutton (active 1839–1848) Boxing. This boxer taught Charles Kingsley, the great novelist, how to box.

GRUMP—Harold Irelan (1890–1944) Baseball. Grump (nickname referred to his general disposi-tion) played one season, 1914, for Philadelphia NL and appeared in sixty-seven games.

GRUMPS—Mike Bragg (active 1968–1980) Football k.

GRUNTING JIM—Jim Shaw (1893–1962) Baseball. Shaw grunted when he delivered his pitch.

GULLIVER—Paul Lehner (1920–1967) Baseball. In 1951, this outfielder played for four different teams. The nickname is a reference to Jonathan Swift's *Gulliver's Travels;* Gulliver also traveled a lot.

GUMBY—Jim Gantner (1953–) Baseball. This second baseman tended to get everything twisted up like the Gumby doll.

GUMP—Otis Clymer (1880–1926) Baseball of.

GUMP—Lorne Worsley (1929–) Hockey g. **H/F**

GUNBOAT—Walter Hudson (1898–) Baseball sportswriter.

GUNBOAT SMITH—Edward J. Smyth (1887–1974) Boxing (heavyweight) and referee. Also called THE GUNNER.

GUNNER—James Moir (1879–deceased) Boxing (heavyweight). Moir was the European champion from 1906 to 1909.

GUNNER—Bobby Reeves (1904–1993) Baseball. This third baseman had a great arm.

GUPPY—John Troup (19__–) Bowling. As a youngster, Troup bowled for a group called The Guppies.

GUS—August Bodnar (1925–) Hockey c.

GUS—Roy Giesebrecht (1918–) Hockey c.

GUS—Walter Lawrence Kyle (1923–) Hockey d.

GUS—Felix Mancuso (1914–) Hockey f.

GUS—Gustavus Welch (1892–1970) Football.
A star at Carlisle Institute during Jim Thorpe's day, Welch went on to play pro football. Later, he became the head coach at Washington State University.

GUS—Early Wynn (1920–) Baseball. **H/F**
This pitcher was said to look like he should have been named Gus. With a twenty-three-year record of 300–244, he could also have been named Great. Also called THE OLD INDIAN.

GUS THE GOAT—Gus Sonnenberg (1898–1944) Wrestling.
This navy veteran and former football player employed a flying tackle against his opponents in the ring.

GUTS—Ishimatsu Suzuki (1949–) Boxing (lightweight).
Guts was champ from 1974–1976.

GUY—Guyle Abner Fielder (1930–) Hockey c.

GYP—Cliff Battles (1910–1991) Football.
Starred for the Boston Redskins and then the Washington Redskins from 1932–1937. In his career, he rushed for 3,403 yards in 832 attempts. Battles ended his career as a coach for the 1947 Brooklyn Dodgers.

GYPSY—Joe Harris (1948–1988) Boxing.
This junior middleweight had a talent for boxing but a dislike of training. He came from the streets of North Philadelphia, which probably accounts for his nickname. His career was over after only four years when it was discovered he was blind in one eye.

GYPSY [THE]—Jem Mace (1831–1910) Boxing (heavyweight). **H/F** Mace was a champion from 1866 to 1873.

HAC MAN—Jeff Leonard (1955–) Baseball.
One year when Leonard was playing outfield in the minors and feeling estranged from his teammates at Phoenix, he announced he would swing at the first pitch every time. And like the predictable Pac-Man of computer fame, he did just that for the rest of the season.

HACK—Lafayette Abbott (1895–1965) Football.

HACK—Lawrence H. Miller (1894–1971) Baseball.
This outfielder, who could uproot trees and twist iron, might have been nicknamed for Hercules rather than the powerful wrestler Hackenschmidt.

HACKSAW—Jack Reynolds (active 1970–1984) Football.
Reynolds once sawed an old car in half after his University of Tennessee team lost to Mississippi, 38–0. He later played linebacker for the 49ers and Rams.

HAILEYBURY HURRICANE [THE]—Leo Labine (1931–)
Hockey. The fast-skating Labine was from Haileybury.

HAIRBREADTH HARRY—Jack Hamilton (1938–) Baseball.
Hamilton would often pitch himself into jams and then have to rescue himself at the last minute. In 1962, for instance, he led the National League in bases on balls with 107. Then he would have to bear down in order to get the Phillies out of trouble. Hairbreadth Harry was also the name of an old comic strip.

HAKKI—Matti Risto Hagman (1955–) Hockey.

HALF PINT RYE—Gene Rye (1906–1980) Baseball.
Outfielder Rye was only 5' 6". He also only lasted thirty-nine at-bats in the majors for the 1931 Red Sox. If had played with Granny Hammer we could have had Ham on Rye.

HALF-TON—Dallas Smith (1941–) Hockey.
Smith played for the Boston Bruins when they won the Stanley Cup in 1970 and 1972.

HAL-LELUJAH—Hal Johnston (1949–) Basketball.
Hal was the savior to the Roanoke basketball team, this slick-playing guard leading them to the NCAA division championship in 1972. For his efforts, Johnston was recognized as the MVP of the tournament, an All-American, and his shirt ascended to the rafters of the gym.

HAM—Tom Hamilton (1935–) Baseball.

HAM—Granny Hammer (1927–) Baseball.
His nickname is an obvious play upon his last name.

HAMBONE—Art Williams (1939–) Basketball.

HAMBY—Sam Hamilton Shore (1886–deceased) Hockey lw.

HAMMER [THE]—Mike Ditka (1939–) Football.
Achieved fame as both a player and as a coach of the Chicago Bears. Ironically, he received his nickname because of the way he played basketball in college. As a player, Ditka scored forty-three touchdowns in his career.

HAMMER—Bob Hamelin (1967–) Baseball.
Kansas City Royals. His nickname is a play upon his last name.

HAMMER [THE]—Stanley Kostka (active 1930s) Football.

HAMMER—John Milner (1949–) Baseball.
As a youngster, this first baseman had revered HAMMERIN' HANK Aaron.

HAMMER [THE]—Dave Schultz (1950–) Hockey.

HAMMER [THE]—Fred Williamson (active 1960–1964)
Football. Williamson was a Kansas City Chiefs'
defensive back who prided himself on hitting
receivers hard. He once threatened to use his "hammer" against the Packers in the Super Bowl; however,
he was the one knocked out. He became a 1970s
film star.

HAMMER OF THE NORTH [THE]—Bernard William
Bierman (1894–1977) Football coach. Also called THE
SILVER FOX OF THE NORTHLAND.

HAMMOND HUMMER—Robert Carl Anderson (1935–)
Baseball. Anderson was a pitcher from Hammond,
Indiana.

HANDS—Johnny Bench (1947–) Baseball. **H/F**
Catcher Johnny Bench had such large hands he could
hold seven baseballs in only one hand.

HANDS OF STONE (MANOS DE PIEDRA)—Roberto Duran
(1951–) Boxing. Duran scored sixty KOs during a
career that saw him hold world titles as a lightweight,
welterweight, junior middleweight, and middleweight.
Unfortunately for this Panamanian, he may be most
remembered for uttering "No Mas" before the start
of the eighth round of his title bout with Sugar Ray
Leonard in 1980.

HANDSOME JOHNNY—John Barend (1945–) Wrestling.
Also called HANDSOME ONE, PRINCE OF DARKNESS,
THE PSYCHO.

HANDSOME HARRY—Harry Howell (1876–1956) Baseball.
Howell looked good on the mound, hurling thirty-five
complete games in 1905, and capping a thirteen-year
career with twenty shutouts and a 2.74 ERA.

HANDSOME RANSOM—Ransom (Randy) Jackson (1926–)
Baseball. This third baseman had a rhyming nickname.

HANDY ANDY—Andy High (1897–1981) Baseball.
High could play third, second, and short. He played
from 1922–1934 in the NL. Because he was only 5' 6",
he was also called KNEE HIGH.

HANDY GUY NAMED SANDE [A]—Earl Sande (active
1920s) Jockey. **H/F**

HANK—Harry Finkel (1942–) Basketball c.

HANK—Alan Hangsleben (1953–) Hockey d.

HANK—Henry P. Iba (1904–1993) Basketball. **H/F**
His team at Oklahoma A&M played slow but steady;
during his career he compiled a record of 767–338. He
also coached the U.S. team to victory in the 1964 and

1968 Olympics before losing in a hotly contested final
to the Soviet Union in 1972.

HANK—Harry Stram (active 1960–1977) Football coach.

HANK—Henry Whitney (1939–) Basketball.

HANS—John Bernard Lobert (1881–1968) Baseball
3b/coach. He was called Hans because of his German
background. (It's German for John.) He was also
called Honus because some said he played like Honus
Wagner.

HANS—John Peter Wagner (1874–1955) Baseball ss.
See THE FLYING DUTCHMAN and HONUS.

HAP—Clarence Henry Day (1901–) Hockey.
This Toronto Maple Leafs defenseman was a member
of the Toronto Maple Leafs' GASHOUSE GANG ON ICE.
Also called HAPPY.

HAP—Leighton Emms (1905–) Hockey.
Emms played left wing for the Maroons in the 1920s.

HAP—Harry Holmes (1889–1941) Hockey. **H/F**
Holmes played in goal on four Stanley Cup championship teams.

HAPPY—Albert B. Chandler (1907–1991) Baseball commissioner. **H/F**

HAPPY—Clarence Day (1901–) Hockey lw. **H/F**
Day did it all: player, coach, general manager, referee.

HAPPY—James Patrick Feller (active 1970s) Football k.

HAPPY—Oscar Felsch (1881–1964) Baseball. This happy-
go-lucky outfielder was banned from baseball for his
involvement in the Black Sox scandal of 1919.

HAPPY—Harold Hairston (1942–) Basketball.
This happy-go-lucky shooter hit 51.8 percent of his
shots in his career at NYU (1962–1964). He averaged
thirteen points and thirteen rebounds for the Los
Angeles Lakers, the 1972 NBA champions.

HAPPY—Walter Herbert Harnott (1909–) Hockey f.

HAPPY—Burt Hooton (1950–) Baseball.
This pitcher had an opposite nickname: he always
looked unhappy. His best year was 19–10 for the
Dodgers.

HAPPY BOY—Nkosana Mgxaji (active 1969–1980s) Boxing.
This fighter is from South Africa.

HAPPY HUMPHREY—William J. Cobb Wrestling.
Humphrey weighed over 800 pounds.

HAPPY JACK—Jack Chesbro (1874–1931) Baseball. **H/F**
Chesbro was a great spitball pitcher in the days
before the pitch was outlawed. His nickname was

given him by a patient at the mental institution where Chesbro once worked as an attendant.

HAPPY RABBIT—Stan Rojek (1920–) Baseball.
Joined the Brooklyn Dodgers at the end of the 1942 season. He played for eight seasons in the big leagues, mostly at shortstop. He batted .266 in 522 games.

HARD GUY—Harvey Guy Bedwell (1876–1950) Horse racing. **H/F** Bedwell was a demanding trainer of thoroughbreds.

HARD LUCK BRUDER—Henry Bruder (1907–1970) Football qb.

HARD ROCK FROM DOWN UNDER [THE]—Tom Heeney (1898–) Boxing. This tough fighter was from Australia.

HARDROCK—Gary Allenson (1955–) Baseball c.

HARDY—Otis Bates (active 1980s) Boxing (heavyweight).

HARLEM COFFEE COOLER [THE]—Frank Craig (1870–deceased) Boxing.

HARLEM SPIDER [THE]—Tommy Kelly (1867–deceased) Boxing. In 1887, Kelly was the first bantamweight champion. Also called Harlem Tommy. See SPIDER.

HARPO—Bob Gladieux (active 1969–1972) Football.

HARRISBURG HOUDINI [THE]—Bob Davies (1920–) Basketball g-f. **H/F**

HARRY THE HORSE—Harry Danning (1911–) Baseball. Danning's horsey face led to the nickname of Harry the Horse, the name of a character from Damon Runyan's *Guys and Dolls.* A catcher for the New York Giants, Danning batted .285 over ten years.

HAT [THE]—Harry Walker (1918–) Baseball.
As an outfielder and manager, Walker had the habit of constantly adjusting his ballcap. At bat, he invariably took his hat off three times before every pitch. In 1947, it apparently paid off for he pulled off a .363 average. His career average was a more mortal .292.

HAUGHTON OF HARVARD—Percy Duncan (1876–1924) Football coach. Also called PD.

HAVANA BON BON—Kid Chocolate (1910–) Boxing. **H/F** Kid Chocolate was the ring name of Eligio Sardinias, a fighter from Cuba.

HAWK—Willie Adams (1941–) Football.

HAWK [THE]—Ezzard Charles (1921–1975) Boxing. **H/F**

HAWK—Clay Carroll (1941–) Baseball p.

HAWK—Andre Dawson (1954–) Baseball.
Dawson received this nickname when he was snaring line drives in the outfield for the Montreal Expos.

Also called AWESOME.

HAWK—Tony Dorsett (1954–) Football.
Dorsett was called Hawk when he went to Pittsburgh. See T. D.

HAWK [THE]—Kid Gavilan (1926–) Boxing. **H/F** Kid Gavilan was the welterweight champ from 1951–1954. His real name was Geraldo Gonzalez.

HAWK [THE]—Larry McNeil (1951–) Basketball f-c.

HAWK—Ken Silvestri (1916–) Baseball c.
Silvestri had a good arm behind the plate and could nip a runner trying to steal.

HAWK—Robert Dale Taylor (1939–) Baseball c.

HAWKEYE—Charles Whitney (1957–) Basketball g-f.

HEADY EDDY—Eddie Arcaro (1916–) Horse racing.

HEAT [THE]—James Kinchen Boxing (middleweight).

HEATHCLIFF—Cliff Johnson (1947–) Baseball.
Johnson (6' 4", 215 pounds), nicknamed for the big character in Charlotte Bronte's *Wuthering Heights,* had a record twenty pinch-hit home runs.

HEENEY—Henry Majeski (1916–1991) Baseball 3b.
Heeney was a nickname for Henry.

HEINIE—Henry Knight Groh (1889–1968) Baseball.
The nickname of Heine is for a Germanic heritage. (This is true for the following players nicknamed Heine.) Groh, a third baseman, appeared in five World Series. In the 1922 Series, he batted .474 for the Giants.

HEINIE—Henry Emmett Manush (1901–1971) Baseball of. **H/F** Twice Heinie batted .378. For his seventeen-year career, his batting average was .330 and his fielding average was .980.

HEINIE—Henry William Meine (1896–1968) Baseball p.
Also called THE COUNT OF LUXEMBOURG.

HEINIE—Clarence Franklin Mueller (1899–1975) Baseball of.

HEINIE—Henry Clement Peitz (1872–1943) Baseball c.

HEINIE—Henry William Scheer (1900–1976) Baseball 2b.

HEINIE—Henry George Schuble, Jr. (1906–1990) Baseball ss/3b.

HEINIE—Henry Zimmerman (1887–1969) Baseball 2b/3b.

HEITY—Hector Cruz (1953–) Baseball of.

HELICOPTER—Charlie Hentz (1947–) basketball f.

HELICOPTER [THE]—Herman Knowings (19__–)
Basketball. Knowings was one of the legends who played in Harlem's Rucker League. He could stay in the air so long he seemed to be in flight.

HEN—Henry Pearce (1777–1809) Boxing.
Hen was short for Henry. In 1805 Pearce beat James "Jem" Belcher and became The Game Chicken.

HERC—Harold Wolfe (1931–) Basketball.
Herc hit twenty-five field goals in one game and scored sixty-two points in another in NAIA action.

HERCULES—Mary Promitis (active 1920s) Dancing.
Promitis was a champion marathon dancer. (In marathon dancing, contestants danced for one hour and then rested for fifteen minutes before dancing again.) One of Promitis' secrets was to soak her feet in vinegar and brine for weeks before a contest.

HERCULES—Mike Weaver (1952–) Boxing.
Weaver had a sculpted, Herculean build. Also called BLACK HERCULES.

HERGIE—Wally Hergesheimer (1927–) Hockey rw.

HERK—Herschel Davis Baltimore (1921–1968) Basketball.
He played fifty-eight games for St. Louis (1946–1947). His nickname is a play upon his first name.

HERKIMER HURRICANE—Lou Ambers (1913–) Boxing (Lightweight). Lou Ambers was the ring name of Louis D'Ambrosio.

HERKY JERKY—Elmer Horton (1869–1920) Baseball.
Horton's pitching motion was the opposite of smooth.

HI—Arthur Ladd (1870–1948) Baseball.
Ladd was .000 in four games. It was hi and goodbye.

HIB—Herbert Milks (1902–) Hockey lw.

HICK—Forrest Leroy Cady (1886–1946) Baseball.
Cady was a catcher from a dot on the map of Illinois.

HICKIE—George Wilson (?–1914) Baseball.
Wilson had skin problems. He also had problems hitting the ball, so this outfielder only lasted twenty-four games.

HICKORY—Walt Dickson (1878–1918) Baseball p.

HIGHBALL—Howard Wilson (1878–1934) Baseball p.

HIGH HENRY—Henry Finkle (1942–) Basketball.
Finkle stood 7-feet tall and weighed 240. His senior year at Dayton, the team was 23–6. High Henry played center in the NBA for Los Angeles, San Diego, and Boston.

HIGHWAY 63—Gene Upshaw (1945–) Football.
This lineman for the Raiders wore number sixty-three. He was such an effective blocker that backs were told to follow Highway 63.

HIKER—William P. Joy (active 1930s) Football coach.

HIKER—Albert Moran (1912–) Baseball.
When he was growing up in Rochester, N.Y., this pitcher liked to go on hikes.

HILL [THE]—Bill McGill (1939–) Basketball.
When he played for Seton Hall, McGill received his nickname for his size (6' 9" and 225 pounds) and the rhyme. His senior year at Seton Hall, he averaged over thirty-eight points per game. He played for several NBA teams in three years, averaging ten points a game for 159 games.

HILLBILLY BILDILLI—Emil Bildilli (1912–1946) Baseball.
Not only was this pitcher from a wide spot in the road somewhere in Indiana, but also his last name completed the rhyme.

HINKEY—William Edward Harris (1952–) Hockey rw.

HINKY—Bill Harris (1935–) Hockey c.

HIPPITY [or HIPPETTY HOPP]—Johnny Hopp (1916–) Baseball. Johnny's nickname was in response to his last name. This outfielder also hopped around from the Cards to the Braves to the Pirates to the Yankees, and appeared in five World Series.

HIPPO—Jim Vaughn (1888–1966) Baseball.
By the end of Vaughn's career he was close to 300 pounds. In 1918, he led the National League in strikeouts (148); in 1919, he had an ERA of 1.74 for the Cubs.

HIT MAN—Mike Easler (1950–) Baseball of.

HIT MAN [THE]—Thomas Hearns (1958–) Boxing.
Hearns held five different world titles.
Also called THE MOTOR CITY COBRA.

HITLER OF CHESS [THE]—Bobby Fischer (1943–) Chess.

HITTING MACHINE [THE]—Eugene Lockhart (active 1984–) Football lb.

HJALLIS—Hjalmar Andersen (1923–) Speed skating. Andersen, a Norwegian, won three gold medals at the 1952 Winter Games in Oslo. He set an Olympic record in the 5000 meters of 8 minutes 10.6 seconds to break the Olympic record by nine seconds.

HOAGY—Albert R. Carmichael (active 1953–1961) Football.
This halfback's nickname was after the singer.

HOCKEY BOB—Bob Lamey (1934–) Sportscaster.

HOD—William Stewart (1894–1964) Hockey d. **H/F**

HODGIE—Ken Hodge (1944–) Hockey.
Hodge played right wing for the Boston Bruins when they won the Stanley Cup in 1970 and 1972.

HOGMEAT—Chuck Howley (1936–) Football.
One of the members of the Doomsday Defense for the Dallas Cowboys. His nickname, not altogether flattering, is a reference to his size.

HOJO—Howard Johnson (1960–) Baseball.
This was an automatic. This ball player who has played in both the infield and outfield received his nickname after the nickname of the restaurant.

HOLLYWOOD—Thomas Henderson (1953–) Football.
Noted for his flash and his penchant for talking trash, Hollywood Henderson was a linebacker for the Dallas Cowboys in the 1970s. Here is how he once explained his actions on and off the field: "I don't like to be dull, or just an old, ugly linebacker." His story is chronicled in his 1987 autobiography—*Out of Control: Confessions of a NFL Casualty* (with Peter Knobler).

HOMBRE—Alan E. Atkinson (active 1965–1975) Football.

HOME RUN—Grant Johnson (1874–deceased) Baseball (Negro Leagues) ss.

HOME RUN—Jerry Smith (active 1965–1977) Football.
Smith was the first professional athlete to die from AIDS.

HOME RUN JOE—Joe Marshall (1875–1934) Baseball.
This first baseman earned his nickname by never hitting one.

HONDO—Frank Howard (1929–1980) Baseball.
The meaning of hondo in Spanish is "big." Howard was 6' 7" and weighed 255 pounds. He also hit some big home runs for the Washington Senators, leading the league in 1968 and 1970 with forty-four homers each year. Also called THE CAPITAL PUNISHER.

HONDO HURRICANE [THE]—Clint Hartung (1922–) Baseball. From Hondo, Texas, Hartung batted .309 in his first year with the New York Giants—not bad for a pitcher. But 1947 was his one and only banner year. Six years later he departed with a 29–29 record and a .238 batting average.

HONEST JACK—Jack Boyle (1866–1913) Baseball.

HONEST JOHN—John Anderson (1873–1949) Baseball.
After being awarded first base for being hit by a pitch, this outfielder refused to go, insisting to the umpire that the ball had not touched him.

HONEST JOHN—John Kelly (1856–1926) Baseball.
A farmer once loaned his horse and carriage to Kelly so he could get home. Unfortunately, the horse died

during the night, so when Kelly returned the carriage the next day he paid the farmer twenty dollars. The farmer told Kelly he was an honest man. He was to become an umpire.

HONEST JOE—Joseph Kelly (1857–1894) Baseball rf. **H/F**
See KING.

HONEY—John Barnes (1900–1981) Baseball.

HONEY—Billy Mellody (1884–1919) Boxing.
Mellody was the welterweight champion from 1906–1907.

HONEY—John Russell (1903–1973) Basketball. **H/F**
Russell played in 3,200 professional games (player-coach for twenty of his twenty-eight years), and once held the scoring record for one game with twenty-two points. Later, Honey coached at Seton Hall and had a 294–129 record. He also coached two years with the Boston Celtics.

HONEYCOMB—Gus Johnson (1938–) Basketball.
Johnson was a five-time All-Star on the Baltimore Bullets.

HONOLULU—Henry (Hank) Hughes (1907–deceased).
Played in 1932 for Boston.

HONUS—Hans Lobert (1881–1968) Baseball.
This Phillies' third baseman was given the name Honus in honor of Honus Wagner because Lobert was a good fielder in his own right.

HONUS—John Peter Wagner (1874–1955) Baseball ss. **H/F**
Also called HANS. See THE FLYING DUTCHMAN.

HOOKS—Raymond Dandridge (1913–1994) Baseball (Negro Leagues). **H/F** Dandridge could hook most any ball hit in his direction. As Monte Irving once put it: "I saw all the greats—Brooks, Nettles—but I've never seen a better third baseman than Ray Dandridge. He had the best hands. In a season he seldom made more than one or two errors. If the ball took a bad hop, his glove took a bad hop."

HOOKS—George August Dauss (1899–1963) Baseball.
This pitcher had a wicked curveball. He played fifteen seasons with the Detroit Tigers (1912–1926).

HOOKS—John Dillon (1924–) Basketball.

HOOKS—Edward Mylin (1895–1975) Football coach.

HOOKS—George L. Wiltse (1880–1959) Baseball.
This pitcher had the knack of hooking balls hit back toward the mound.

HOOKS—Hank Wyse (1918–) Baseball p.

HOOLEY—Reginald Smith (1905–1963) Hockey. **H/F**
Smith, a defenseman, scored 200 goals during his
career from 1924 to 1941 with the New York
Americans, the Ottawa Senators, and the Montreal
Maroons. On the Maroons, Hooley played on the S
LINE with two other Hall of Famers, Nels Stewart and
BABE Siebert.

HOOLIE—Julian Javier (1936–) Baseball.
From the Dominican Republic, this nickname for the
All-Star second baseman's first name.

HOOSIER COMET—Oscar Charleston (1896–1954)
Baseball (Negro Leagues) of/mgr.

HOOSIER HAMMERER [THE]—Chuck Klein (1904–1958)
Baseball. **H/F** Klein's batting average for his
seventeen-year career was .320. He also set the
National League record for most extra base hits in a
season with 107. In addition, this outfielder led the
league six times in fielding.

HOOSIER SCHOOLMASTER—Vic Aldridge (1893–1973) Baseball. This pitcher had once taught school in Indiana.

HOOSIER THUNDERBOLT [THE]—Amos Wilson Rusie
(1871–1942) Baseball p. **H/F**

HOOT—Walter Arthur Evers (1921–1991) Baseball.

HOOT—Bob Gibson (1935–) Baseball. **H/F**
Nicknamed after the movie cowboy, Gibson was a
twenty-game winner five times. Overall, he won 251
games and was 7–2 in World Series play.

HOOT—Samuel Gibson (1900–1962) Baseball.

HOOT—Ward Gibson (1921–) Basketball.

HOOTIE—Burt Hooton (1950–) Baseball.
Also called HAPPY (because he always looked sad).

HOPALONG—Bill Howerton (1921–) Baseball.
This outfielder had once been a cowboy.

HORIZONTAL HARRY—Harry Thomas. Boxing.
The nickname indicates he was knocked down a lot.

HORSE—Harold Akins (1945–) Football.

HORSE [THE]—Harry Gallatin (1928–) Basketball.
Galloping in from Northwest Missouri State in 1948,
this 6' 6", 210-pound center played in 682 consecutive
games for the New York Knicks. In the 1953–1954 season, he grabbed 1,098 rebounds for an average of over
fifteen per game.

HORSE [THE]—Dan Issel (1948–) Basketball.
At 6' 9" and 240 pounds, Issel pulled down 1,327
rebounds at Kentucky. In the ABA he was the

co-Rookie of the Year with a 29.9 average.

HORSE [THE]—Alberto Juantorena (1951–) Track and
field. Juantorena of Cuba ran in long graceful strides
and was as strong as a horse as he took firsts in both
the 400- and 800-meter races at the 1976 Olympic
Games in Montreal. Juantorena is the only person
ever to win this Olympic double.

HORSE [THE]—Harry Wright (d. 1993) Football qb.
He quarterbacked Notre Dame to an undefeated season in 1941.

HORSE BELLY—Joe Sargent (1893–195) Baseball 2b.

HORSEFACE—Togie Pittinger (1871–1909) Baseball.
We guess Pittinger, who played for the Phillies, wasn't
known for his good looks.

HOSS—Horace Clarke (1940–) Baseball 2b.

HOSS—Jeff Hostetler (1962–) Football qb.

HOT—Louis Lipps (1962–) Football.
At Southern Mississippi Louis had been called Sweet,
but when he joined the Pittsburgh Steelers as a wide
receiver he became Hot.

HOT MAN—DeWayne Scales (1958–) Basketball.

HOT POTATO—Luke Hamlin (1906–1978) Baseball.
Hamlin had the habit of tossing the ball up and down
in his hand as if it were a hot potato. When he finally
threw it, he was 73–76. His best year was 1939 when
he was 20–13.

HOT POTATO—Larry Jackson (1931–) Baseball p.

HOT ROD—Rod (rique) Gilbert (1941–) Hockey.
Also called MR. RANGER and ROCKY.

HOT ROD—Rodney Hundley (1934–) Basketball.
Three-time All-American Rod Hundley grabbed his
nickname with his flashy style of playing guard and by
tossing in 2,236 points at West Virginia. Then he spent
six seasons with the L.A. Lakers.

HOT ROD—John Williams (1961–) Basketball f-c.

HOT SAUCE—Kevin Saucier (1956–) Baseball. This
pitcher's nickname came from his culinary last name.

HOT SHOT—Eddie Mayo (1910–) Baseball 2b.

HOTHOUSE CHAMPION—Irving B. Jaffe (1906–) Ice
skating.

HOUDINI OF THE HARDWOOD—John Townsend (1916–)
Basketball. Townsend was an All-American guard at
Michigan who was known for his pinpoint passing.

HOUND—Bob Kelley (1950–) Hockey.
Left winger Kelly hounded opponents of the

Philadelphia Flyers during the early 1970s (along with Andre Dupont and Dave Schultz).

HOUNDOG—Ted McLain (1947–) Basketball. McClain was from the country music capital ("You ain't nothin' but a hound dog"), Nashville, Tennessee, and was a three-time All-American guard at Tennessee State.

HOUSE—Rich Jones (1946–) Basketball f-c.

HOUSE—Cliff Levingston (1961–) Basketball.
Levingston had once carried bricks for a living.

HOUSE—Robert Newhouse (1950–) Football.
His nickname is a shortened form of his last name.

HOUSTON HURRICANE [THE]—A. J. Foyt (1935–) Auto racing. Also called SUPER TEX. See HARD-NOSED DEMON OF THE OVALS.

HOWDY—Howard Wilcox II (1899–1924) Auto racing. Wilcox raced in the first eleven Indy 500s and died after a crash in a race in Altoona, PA.

HOWIE—Howard Carl (1938–) Basketball.
In high school Howard's nickname was Hersh because he was so fond of the candy bar.

HOWL—Harold Edward Darragh (1902–) Hockey f.

HOWLING HILDA—Hilda Chester (deceased) Baseball. Chester got her nickname for being an extremely noisy fan at Ebbets Field during the 1940s and 1950s. Also called Queen of the Bleachers.

HOYT—James Wilhelm (1923–) Baseball p. **H/F**
Wilhelm was the first fulltime reliever to enter the Hall of Fame. His rookie year he won fifteen games in relief; he won 123 games in relief during his twenty-one-year career. Six times he had a 2.0 ERA. Also called OLD SARGE.

HUB—Hubert Reed (1936–) Basketball.
A two-time All-American at Oklahoma City, Reed played 479 games in the NBA for four different teams.

HUCK—Walter M. Betts (1897–1987) Baseball p.
Also called Huckleberry.

HUEVO—Vincente Romo (1943–) Baseball p.

HUFF THE MAGIC DRAGON—Gary Huff (active 1973–1985) Football qb.

HUG—Miller James Huggins (1879–1929) Baseball 2b/manager. **H/F** Also called Flea and Mighty Mite.

HUGO THE VICTOR—Hugo Bezdek (1884–1952) Football coach/baseball manager. Also called BEX.

HULK HOGAN—Terry Bollea (19–) Wrestling.
Hogan was once called Sterling Golden.

HUMAN BOWLING BALL [THE]—Don Nottingham (active 1971–1978) Football. Nottingham was a short, round running back for the Baltimore Colts.

HUMAN CHAINSAW [THE]—Jerry Sloan (1942–) Basketball. Sloan won his nickname for his ferocity in fighting for a loose ball.

HUMAN DEER [THE]—Herb Elliot (1938–) Track and field. Australian runner.

HUMAN ERASER [THE]—Marvin Webster (1952–) Basketball. At Morgan State Webster knocked away many of the shots taken around the basket.

HUMAN EYEBALL [THE]—Bristol Lord (1883–1964) Baseball. Received his nickname because of his eagle-sharp eyesight.

HUMAN FLY [THE]—George Willig (1950–) Climbing. Willig scaled one of the towers of the World Trade Center. The City of New York considered hitting him with a stiff penalty, but he became such a folk hero they settled for a slight fine.

HUMAN FREIGHT CAR [THE]—Ed Dunkhorst. Boxing.

HUMAN HIGHLIGHT FILM [THE]—Dominique Wilkins (1960–) Basketball. Wilkins received his nickname when he played guard for the Atlanta Falcons because he had so many moves.

HUMAN HOWITZER [THE]—Millard "Dixie" Howell (1913–1971) Football. Grantland Rice gave tailback Howell this nickname for his passing ability. In the 1935 Rose Bowl, Howell passed for 160 yards (and rushed for 111) as Alabama beat Stamford, 29–13.

HUMAN MOSQUITO [THE]—Jimmy Slagle (1873–1956) Baseball. Slagle got his nickname for his size (5' 7", 150 pounds.) and his quickness. In 1907, this outfielder stole six bases in one World Series. Also called SHORTY and RABBIT.

HUMAN PENCIL IN SNEAKERS [THE]—Manute Bol (1962–) Basketball. At 7' 7", Bol is the tallest player in the history of the NBA. When Bol left the University of Bridgeport in 1986 for the Washington Bullets, he weighed only 190 pounds. Twice Bol has led the league in blocked shots.

HUMAN PRESS [THE]—Tyrone Bogues (1965–) Basketball. Bogues was a demon on defense for the Wake Forest Deacons. Also called Muggsy.

HUMAN PUNCHING BAG [THE]—Joe Grim. Boxing.

HUMAN RAIN DELAY [THE]—Mike Hargrove (1949–)

Baseball. This first baseman took a lot of time between pitches when he was batting.

HUMAN SCISSORS [THE]—Harry Harris (1880–1959) Boxing. Harris was 5' 7" and very skinny.

HUMAN SKYSCRAPER [THE]—Henry Johnson Boxing.

HUMMER—Dick Drott (1936–1985) Baseball. This pitcher threw a humming fastball.

HUMP—Bruce Campbell (1909–) Baseball of.

HUMPHREY—Steve Bilko (1928–1978) Baseball. Bilko (6' 1", 230 pounds.) was nicknamed after the cartoon character Humphrey Pennyworth, the big guy who was Joe Palooka's manager.

HUNCHY—Bob Hoernschemeyer (active 1940s–1950s) Football. Hunchy helped the Detroit Lions win two NFL titles in the 1950s.

HUNK—Heartley Anderson (1899–1978) Football g/coach.

HUNT THE SHUNT—James Hunt (1947–1993) Grand Prix racing. In 1973, this inexperienced Englishman was given the rhyming nickname of Shunt (British slang for *accident*).

HURRICANE—Rubin Carter (1938–) Boxing (middleweight).

HURRICANE—Bob Hazle (1930–) Baseball. South Carolinian Hazle joined the Milwaukee Braves as an outfielder in June 1957, and had a hard-hitting month when people still had Hurricane Hazel on their minds.

HURRICANE—Tommy Jackson (1933–) Boxing (light heavyweight).

HURRYIN' HUGH—Hugh McElhenny (1928–) Football hb. **H/F** See KING.

HURRYING HARRY—Harry Harkness (active 1900s) Auto racing. Harkness captured the first driving championship in 1902.

HURT [THE]—Stan Williams (1936–) Baseball. This 6' 5", 230-pound Williams could put the hurt on people with his strength.

HURTLING HABITANT—Howie Morenz (1902–1937) Hockey. *Hurtling* was Morenz's skating style; *habitant* was for being a French Canadian. Also called BABE RUTH OF HOCKEY, CANADIEN COMET, MITCHELL METEOR, and STRATFORD STREAK.

HUSK—Frank LeRoy Chance (1877–1924) Baseball 1b/manager. Also called PEERLESS LEADER.

HUSK—Christy Mathewson (1880–1925) Baseball p. **H/F** Also called MATTY THE GREAT. See BIG SIX.

HUSKY—Ed Walczak (1915–) Baseball. Although at 5' 11", 180 pounds, this second baseman doesn't seem big by today's standards, he was considered husky during his time.

HUSLIA HUSTLER—George Attla (active 1958–1973) Dog-sled racing. Hailing from an Indian village called Huslia, using his own dogs as well as other people's dogs, Attla has won scores of races, including the World Championship Sled Dog Race at Anchorage four times.

HYPE—Herbert A. Igoe (1877–1945) Sportswriter.

ICE—Cedric Z. Ceballos (1969–) Basketball. Played for Phoenix.

ICE BOX—Elton P. Chamberlain (1867–1929) Baseball. Chamberlain, a pitcher from 1886 to 1896, always seemed to stay calm on the mound. The last pitcher in the major leagues to pitch both left-handed and right-handed in the same game (1888).

ICE MAN—Bob Coolidge. Boxing.

ICED TEA—Howard Johnson (1960–) Baseball if/of. Also called HOJO.

ICEMAN—Michael Dunne (1962–) Baseball p.

ICEMAN [THE]—Ben Hogan (1912–) Golf. **H/F** This was the nickname that the English used for Hogan. (The Scots called him Wee Ice Mon.) Hogan was known for shunning publicity and seeming cold and aloof. Also, called BANTAM BEN, GOLFDOM'S MIGHTY MITE, and THE HAWK.

ICEMAN [THE]—George Woolf (1915–1946) Horse racing. **H/F**

ICICLE—Weston Diockson Fisler (1841–1922) Baseball. Played in 1876 for Philadelphia in the National League and compiled a .288 batting average that season. He finished with a lifetime .310 average in 273 games. He probably wasn't known for the warmth of his personality.

ICICLE—James Reeder (1859–deceased) Baseball of.

IDI AMIN—Ron Springs (1956–) Football. This running back received his nickname from the time he took a pistol on a fishing trip with the intention of shooting fish instead of catching them.

IDOL OF BASEBALL FANDOM [THE]—Ty Cobb (1886–1961) Baseball. **H/F** Considering how disliked Cobb was by many players and fans, this is a strange sobriquet, to say the least. See the movie *Cobb*.

Also called GEORGIA PEACH.

IDOL OF THE AMERICAN BOY [THE]—Babe Ruth (1895–1948) Baseball p/of. **H/F** This was the nickname that Babe Ruth fancied. For other nicknames, see BABE.

IKE—Murray Mendenhall (1899–) Basketball.

ILLINOIS THUNDERBOLT [THE]—Ken Overlin (1910–) Boxing. Overlin was the middleweight champion in the Navy.

ILLINOIS THUNDERBOLT [THE]—Billy Papke (1868–1930) Boxing.

IMMORTAL [THE]—Jose Azue (1939–) Baseball. This catcher caught his nickname for a batting streak he enjoyed in 1963.

IMP—Jim Begley (1902–1957) Baseball 2b.

INCH—Frank Gleich (1894–1949) Baseball of.

INCREDIBLE HULK—Brian Downing (1950–) Baseball. After a disappointing 1978, Downing spent the winter lifting weights and increased not only his chest measurement but his batting average from .255 to .324.

INDIAN [THE]—Roman Gabriel (1940–) Football qb. Also called GABE.

INDIAN—Jack Jacobs (1921–1974) Football.

INDIAN BOB—Robert Lee Johnson (1906–1978) Baseball of. Part Cherokee, this seven time All-Star was a lifetime .296 hitter with 288 home runs. Also called CHEROKEE.

INDOMITABLE BRONK—Bronislau Nagurski (1908–1990) Football, wrestling. Also called BIG UKRAINIAN and THE BRONK. See BRONKO.

INFANT PRODIGY—Mickey Mantle (1931–) Baseball cf. **H/F** Also called THE GREAT MICK, THE M & M BOYS, MILLION DOLLAR INVALID, WOUNDED HERO.

INKY—Pete Incaviglia (1964–) Baseball of. A play on his last name.

INKY—Edward Lake (1916–1995) Baseball.

INSTANT CHAMPION—George Foreman (1949–) Boxing. This described Foreman the first time around. After he was lured out of retirement by the vacuum at the top, he was known more for his eating prowess (a real heavyweight) and his humor.

IRASCIBLE EASTERNER—James Valiant (1940–) Wrestling.

IRISH—Emil Frederick Meusel (1893–1963) Baseball of.

IRISH JACK—Louis Murphy Boxing.

IRON BATTER [THE]—Lipman Pike (1845–1893) Baseball. Lip played for five years (between 1875 and 1882) and compiled a lifetime batting average of .304 in 163 games. He has earned immortality in baseball lore because some historians of the game regard him to be the first Jewish professional baseball player. Some claim he was the first professional ballplayer (along with Jimmy Creighton, Lipman was paid to play ball) to hit a home run. He received the sobriquet The Iron Batter because he hit the baseball with iron-like power and because he refused to show pain when hit with a pitch. Also called Lip.

IRON HANDS—Chuck Hiller (1934–) Baseball. This second baseman made a lot of errors.

IRON HORSE [THE]—Lou Gehrig (1903–1941) Baseball 1b. **H/F**

IRON JOE—Joe Procita. Pool.

IRON MAJOR [THE]—Frank W. Cavanaugh (1876–1933) Football.

IRON MAN—Larry Brown (1902–1972) Baseball (Negro Leagues). Brown loved to catch. In 1930, he was behind the plate for 234 games.

IRON MAN—Ralph W. Hutton (1948–) Swimming.

IRON MAN—Kasuhisa Inao (1938–) Baseball. This Japanese ballplayer was an incredible workhorse. One year he pitched 404 innings. Inao had an ERA of 1.98 while compiling a career record of 276 wins and 137 losses.

IRON MAN—Murray Murdoch (1904–) Hockey lw.

IRON MAN—Garry Unger (1947–) Hockey. Unger played in 914 consecutive games over eleven seasons. He had also scored thirty or more goals in eight straight seasons.

IRON MAN—John Edward Wilson (1929–) Hockey lw.

IRON MAN [THE]—Joe Grim (1881–1939) Boxing. Joe Grim was the ring name; his real name was Saverio Giannone.

IRON MAN [THE]—Joe McGinnity (1871–1929) Baseball. **H/F**

IRON MAN [THE]—Ray Starr (1906–1963) Baseball. When he was in the minors, Starr routinely pitched both games of doubleheaders. In the majors, Starr was a more routine 37–35.

IRON MAN [THE]—Damon Wetzel (active 1935–1936) Football.

IRON MIKE—Frank Bowerman (1868–1948) Baseball. Bowerman was a tough catcher, able to play even when hurt.

IRON MIKE—Mike Caldwell (1949–) Baseball. Coming off elbow surgery, Caldwell was the Comeback Player of the Year in 1978 with a record of 22–9 and twenty-three complete games. Also called MR. WARMTH.

IRON MIKE—Mike Ditka (1939–) Football e. **H/F**
In a variation on a theme by Lombardi, Ditka, the former head coach of the Chicago Bears once said: "Winning isn't everything. But it beats the heck out of losing." Ditka's won-loss record with the Bears was 112–67.

IRON PONY—Santos Conde "Sandy" Alomar (1943–) Baseball. This second baseman won his nickname by playing in 648 games in a row (far short of Lou IRON HORSE Gehrig's 2,130 straight games).

IRONHEAD—Craig Heyward (active 1988–) Football fb.

IRONMAN—John T. Meyers (1880–1971) Baseball. Meyers caught almost every game of Christy Mathewson and the other New York Giant pitchers from 1908 to 1915. In 1912, he batted .358; and his lifetime average was .291. A member of the Cahuilla tribe in California, he was also called Chief Meyers.

IRONWOMAN—Constance Rose Wisniewski (active 1944–1952) Baseball (All-American Girls Baseball League). Wisniewski earned her nickname in 1945 when she pitched both games of a doubleheader. However, this was in the days when they played softball. It was not until 1948 that it became overhand baseball.

IRREPRESSIBLE EGOIST [THE]—Richard Lee Stuart (1932–) Baseball 1b.
Also called OLD STONEFINGERS.

ITALIAN STALLION [THE]—Rick Cerone (1954–) Baseball c.

ITALIAN STALLION [THE]—Lee Mazzilli (1955–) Baseball of.

ITALIAN STALLION—Johnny Musso (active 1975–1978) Football hb.

IVAN THE TERRIBLE—Ivan Calderon (1962–) Baseball of. He owns a farm in Puerto Rico where he raises fighting roosters with Ruben Sierra.

IVAN THE TERRIBLE—Evan Duane Irwin (1927–) Hockey d.

IVAN THE TERRIBLE—Ivan Willard Johnson (1897–1979) Hockey. **H/F** Johnson, a defenseman on the New York

Rangers, was on the NHL All-Star team from 1930 to 1934. See CHING.

IVORY TOWER [THE]—Jim Petersen (1962–) Basketball. Peterson was called this when he used to substitute for the Houston Rockets' Twin Towers, Akeem Olajuwon and Ralph Sampson.

IVY—Ivan Massie Olson (1885–1965) Baseball ss.

JABBO—George Jablonski (1919–) Basketball c.

JABO—Raymond Leo Jablonski (1926–1985) Baseball 3b. The nickname of this third baseman was a contraction of his last name.

JACK—Robert Robinson (1927–) Basketball. In 1948, Robinson was an All-American at Baylor and on the U.S. Olympic team.

JACK THE GIANT KILLER—Jack Dempsey (1895–1983) Boxing. Also called THE CHAMP, KID BLACKIE, MIGHTY JACK, and THE THOR OF THE RING. See THE MANASSA MAULER.

JACK THE GIANT KILLER—Jack Dillon (1891–1942) Boxing. The real name of this light-heavyweight boxer (Jack Dillon was his ring name) was Earnest Cutler Price. Although he weighed only 158 pounds, he was able to outbox fighters in heavier divisions.

JACK THE RIPPER—Jack Clark (1955–) Baseball. This outfielder/first baseman has taken some big rips at the plate. (The allusion is to the notorious Jack the Ripper, who once put fear in the hearts of Londoners.)

JACK ROOT—Janos Ruthaly (active 1900s) Boxing. Jack Root became the first light heavyweight champion in 1903.

JACKIE—John Gordon (1928–) Hockey.

JACKLING—Thomas Johnson (eighteenth century) Boxing. Thomas Johnson used the ring name Thomas Jackling.

JACKRABBIT—Jim Abbitt (1916–) Football hb.

JACKRABBIT—J. R. Smith (19–) Football.

JAGUAR JON—Jon Arnett (19–) Football.

JAKE—Howard G. Cann (1895–1992) Basketball coach.

JAKE—D'Arcy Flowers (1902–1962) Baseball. Flowers' friends in school called him Jake because people named D'Arcy didn't play baseball. During his ten-year career, this second baseman hit .256.

JAKE—Jerry Dean Gibbs (1938–) Baseball.

JAKE—Jack Kramer (1921–) Tennis. See BIG JAKE.

JAKE—Jacob LaMotta (1921–) Boxing. LaMotta was the

middleweight champion from 1949–1951. Also called THE BRONX BULL. See THE RAGING BULL.

JAMMY—Harry Moskowitz (1904–) Basketball coach.

JAP—Forrest Douds (1905–1979) Football.

JAPANESE LOU GEHRIG [THE]—Shigeo Nagashima. Baseball. This third baseman batted behind Sadaharu Oh (The Japanese Babe Ruth) for Yomiuri.

JARRIN' JAWN—John Kimbrough (1918–) Football. With ten flat speed in the 100, the 6' 3", 220 pounds, Kimbrough was a Texas A & M fullback with straight-ahead power.

JASPER—Harry Davis (1873–1947) Baseball.

JAWS—Ron Jaworski (active 1970s) Football. This quarterback received this nickname when a Ram (1974–1977) as a play on his last name. For his arm and his heritage, he was also called THE POLISH RIFLE.

JAWS—Skip Lockwood (1946–) Baseball. This pitcher was nicknamed after the movie Jaws for the way he went after batters.

JAWS—Osvaldo (Ossie) Ocasio (1955–) Boxing. In 1982, Ocasio won the WBA junior heavyweight title.

JAY—Jesus Alou (1942–) Baseball. In 1963, Alou played with his brothers Matty and Felipe in an all-Alou San Francisco Giant outfield. Jesus was nicknamed Jay be-cause many felt funny calling him by such a Biblical name.

JAY—Gordon Wells (1959–) Hockey.

JAZBO—Ralph Clayburn Fulkerson (1905–1949) Rodeo clown.

JB—Jim Barr (1948–) Baseball p.

JEDGE—George Herman Ruth (1895–1948) Baseball. **H/F** This is what Babe Ruth's Yankee teammates called him because catcher Benny Bengough pronounced George as Jedge. Also called BAMBINO, IDOL OF THE AMERICAN BOY, KING OF SWAT, SULTAN OF SWAT. See BABE RUTH.

JEEP—Lee Handley (1913–1970) Baseball. The style of this third baseman was rough.

JEEP—Don Heffner (1911–1989) Baseball.

JEEP—Hernell Jackson (1965–) Basketball. Jackson used to ride a tricycle around the campus at the University of Texas at El Paso.

JEFF—Charles Monroe Tesreau (1889–1946) Baseball.

JELLY—Floyd Gardner (1895–) Baseball (Negro Leagues).

JELLY—Frank Anthony Jelincich (1919–) Baseball. His nickname is a play on his last name. Jelly Jelincich played in only four major league games (for the Chicago Cubs in 1941) and managed one hit in eight at bats.

JELLYBEAN—Joe Bryant (1954–) Basketball.

JEM—James Belcher (1781–1811) Boxing.

JERSEY—Willis Jones (active 1920s) Hockey press agent. Jersey Jones worked for the early New York Rangers.

JERSEY BOBCAT [THE]—Young Joe Shugrue (1894–) Boxing.

JERSEY JOE—Joseph Valentine Stripp (1903–1989) Baseball. This third baseman was from New Jersey.

JERSEY JOE—Joe Walcott (1914–1994) Boxing. His real name was Arnold Raymond Cream, and he was the heavyweight champion from 1951–1952.

JESSE—Jeff James (1941–) Baseball. This pitcher was nicknamed after the gangster.

JET—Sam Jethroe (1922–) Baseball. This outfielder was fast, leading the major leagues in stolen bases in 1950 and 1951 (thirty-five).

JET [THE]—Chet Walker (1940–) Basketball. This two-time All-American at Bradley who later played for the Philadelphia Warriors and the Chicago Bulls, was fast.

JETSTREAM—James Smith (1932–) Football.

JEWEL [THE]—Julius Adams (1948–) Football. Adams played tackle and end for the New England Patriots. His nickname is a variation of his first name.

JEWEL OF THE GHETTO [THE]—Ruby Goldstein (1907–) Boxing. Goldstein was the winner of twenty-three straight lightweight and welterweight bouts. Later, he became a referee.

JIGGER—Arnold Statz (1897– 1988) Baseball. This nickname was a corruption of chigger, the small insect. It was for Statz's small size (5' 7" and 150 pounds.)

JIGGS—Andy Cvercko (1937–) Football.

JIM—Floyd Crow (active 1910–1960) Football player/scout.

JIM BLUEJACKET—James Smith (1895–1974) Baseball.

JIM THORPE OF HASKELL [THE]—John Levi (1896–1946) Football, basketball, baseball, track and field.

JIMBO—Jim Covert (active 1983–) Football.

JIMBO—Jim Eagins (1946–) Basketball.

JITTERBUG—Bobby Kellogg (active 1940s) Football.

JITTERY JOE—Jonas Berry (1904–1958) Baseball. Berry had a lot of nervous mannerisms between pitches. In 1944 (a rookie at the age of thirty-nine) and 1945, he led the American League in relief with 10–8 and 8–7 records.

J. J.—John Johnson (1949–   ) Basketball.

J. J.—John Jefferson (active 1978–1985) Football.

J. J.—Jim Johnson (1942–   ) Hockey.

J. J.—John Johnson (1947–   ) Basketball.

J. K.—John McKay (active 1976–1978) Football.

JOCK—John Bain Sutherland (1889–1948) Football. A player at Pittsburgh under POP Warner, Sutherland later coached Pittsburgh to a record of 111–20–12. Also called DOUR SCOT, OVERLAND MAN, and SCOTSMAN.

JOCKEY—Bibb Falk (1899–1989) Baseball. Falk spent much of his career riding the bench. However, in 1930, this outfielder led the American League in pinch-hitting with thirteen hits in thirty-four at-bats.

JOCKEY—Raymond Carl Kolp (1894–1967) Baseball. This pitcher kept up a steady stream of chatter when on the bench.

JOCKO—John Bertrand Conlan (1898–1988) Baseball umpire. **H/F**

JODY—Joseph Gage (1959–   ) Hockey.

JOE D—Joe DiMaggio (1914–   ) Baseball cf. **H/F** Also called BIG GUY, DIMAG, and JOLTIN' JOE. See YANKEE CLIPPER.

JOE E—Thurmon Tucker (1863–1935) Baseball. This outfielder received his nickname because of his resemblance to comedian Joe E. Brown.

JOE THE JET—Joseph Bellino (1938–   ) Football. Also called DYNAMITE JOE, NAVY'S DESTROYER, PLAYER WHO IS NEVER CAUGHT FROM BEHIND.

JOE WILLIE—Joseph Namath (1943–   ) Football. See BROADWAY JOE.

JOEY MAXIM—Joseph Berardinelli Boxing.

JOHN L.—John Lawrence Sullivan (1858–1918) Boxing. Also called THE GREAT JOHN L., THE STRONG BOY OF BOSTON. See THE BOSTON STRONG BOY.

JOHNNY O—John Olszewski (active 1955–1962) Football.

JOHNNIE PIE—John McKenzie (1937–   ) Hockey. McKenzie played right wing for the Boston Bruins when they won the Stanley Cup in 1970 and 1972.

JOHNNY BUFF—John Lesky (1888–1955) Boxing.

JOHNNY ONE DOZEN—Craig Baynham (1944–   ) Football. This running back received this nickname because he signed footballs quickly.

JOHNNY U—Johnny Unitas (1933–   ) Football qb. **H/F**

JOHNNY-WON'T-HIT-TODAY—John William Henry Tyler Douglas (1882–1930) Cricket.

JO JO—Alice Starbuck. Figure skating.

JO JO—Joseph White (1946–   ) Basketball. White was a two-time All-American guard at Kansas, who starred on the 1968 U.S. Olympic team, and later for the Boston Celtics.

JO-JO—Joe Moore (1908–   ) Baseball. Also called The Gause Ghost.

JO-JO—Joyner Clifford White (1909–1986) Baseball.

J. P.—Jean-Paul LeBlanc (1946–   ) Hockey.

J. P.—Jewan Paul Parise (1941–   ) Hockey lw.

JR—Bart Starr (1934–   ) Football. Packer players gave their quarterback this nickname. He seemed as cold as the Dwayne Hickman character of JR on the TV show *Dallas*.

JR SUPERSTAR—Johnny Rodgers (1951–   ) Football. This is what Canadians called the former Heisman Trophy winner when he played in the Canadian Football League.

J. T.—John Neidert (active 1968–1970) Football.

JT—John Turner (1967–   ) Basketball.

JUDGE—Glen Carberry (1896–1976). Football.

JUDGE—Kenesaw Mountain Landis (1866–1944). Baseball commissioner. Also called CZAR OF AMERICAN BASE-BALL, CZAR OF BASEBALL, and CZAR OF THE NATIONAL PASTIME.

JUDGE—Ralph Works (1881–1941) Baseball. This pitcher was called Judge because he looked like one.

JUDY—Robert Gans (active 1910s) Baseball. In 1914, Gans played infield for the American Giants in the Negro Leagues.

JUG—Francis Earpe (1896–1969) Football.

JUG—Harold McSpaden (1908–1995) Golf. He was a top golfer who as known for coming in second in many tournaments. He and Byron Nelson finished 1–2 in so many tournaments that they became known as the Gold Dust Twins.

JUGHANDLE JOHNNY—Johnny Morrison (1895–1966)

Baseball. The overhand curve ball of this Pirate pitcher broke down like the handle of a jug.

JUICE—Julio Cruz (1954–) Baseball. Seattle Mariners teammate Juan Bernhardt called Cruz, their second baseman, Juice because he couldn't pronounce Julio.

JUMBO—Walter George Brown (1907–1966) Baseball. This pitcher (33–31 over twelve years) stood 6' 4" and weighed in at 295 pounds.

JUMBO—Floyd Cummings. Boxing.

JUMBO—James Thomas Elliott (1900–1970) Baseball. This pitcher stood 6' 3" and weighed 230 pounds.

JUMBO—John Elliott (active 1988–) Football.

JUMBO—Jim Nash (1945–) Baseball. This pitcher was 6' 5" and weighed 215 pounds.

JUMBO—Tommy Tsuruta (active 1970s–1980s) Wrestling. Jumbo Tsuruta represented Japan in the 1972 Olympic Games in Munich, Germany. He won the American Wrestling Association (AWA) title on February 23, 1984, when he defeated Nick Brockwinkel after thirty-two minutes.

JUMBO JOE—Joe Stydahar (1912–1977) Football. **H/F** This 6' 4", 230-pound two-way tackle started for the Chicago Bears his rookie season. During his day he was all-Pro four straight years and helped the Bears win three NFL championships. Stydahar wouldn't don a helmet until the rules required he do so.

JUMP STEADY—Garry Templeton (1956–) Baseball. When a youngster, this shortstop jumped around when he danced.

JUMPING—Joe Williams (active 1971–1972) Football.

JUMPING G-MAN—Horace Ashenfelter III. (1923–) Track and field. He was a member of the FBI when he won the 1952 Olympics 3000-meter steeplechase. Also known as NIP.

JUMPIN' JACK—Jack D. McCracken (1911–1958) Basketball. **H/F** McCracken was the center on the Maryville Bearcats during their forty-three-game winning streak. In 1939, he was called the AAU's greatest player of all time.

JUMPING JACK—Barney Spinella (1893–deceased) Bowling. **H/F** Spinella received his nickname for the way he jumped around after releasing the bowling ball.

JUMPING JOE—Joe Dugan (1897–1982) Baseball. Though he was a member of the famed Yankees'

MURDERER'S ROW, Dugan's nickname comes from a more wimpish side of his career. When a rookie, he ran away from the Philadelphia A's.

JUMPING JOE—Paul Joseph Perrault (active 1950s) Skiing. **H/F** Jumping Joe broke the North American distance ski jumping record twice on February 26, 1949.

JUMPING JOE—Joseph Savoldi (1909–1974) Football, wrestling.

JUMPIN' JOHNNY—John Green (1933–) Basketball.

JUMPY—James Geathers (1960–) Football.

JUNE—Salmon Hamilton (1893–1962) Basketball. Hamilton was an All-American at Princeton in 1913.

JUNE BUG—Vernon Perry (active 1979–1983) Football.

JUNGLE JIM—James Loscutoff (1930–) Basketball. After Oregon, the 6' 5" Loscutoff played for the Boston Celtics from 1956 to 1964. Jungle Jim was a popular comic strip and film character.

JUNIE—Ernie Andres (1918–) Basketball g-f.

JUNIE—James McMahon, Jr. (1912–1974) Bowling. **H/F** McMahon bowled eight perfect 300 games during competition.

JUNIOR—Cloyd Boyer (1927–) Baseball. This pitcher had an opposite nickname. Actually, he was the older brother of Ken and Clete Boyer.

JUNIOR—Angel Cordero, Jr. (1942–) Horse racing **H/F** Cordero won the Belmont once, the Preakness twice, and the Kentucky Derby three times.

JUNIOR—Glenn W. Davis (1924–) Football. See MR. OUTSIDE.

JUNIOR—Jim Gilliam (1928–1978) Baseball. Gilliam was called Junior because at twenty he was the youngest player on the Baltimore Elite Giants in the Negro National League. In 1953, as a member of the Brooklyn Dodgers, Gilliam was the Rookie of the Year. After his playing days were over, he was a coach for the BUMS until his untimely death. The L. A. Dodgers retired this infielder/outfielder's number—nineteen.

JUNIOR—Robert G. Johnson. Auto racing.

JUNIOR—Walt Kirk (1924–) Basketball.

JUNIOR—George Robert Kline (1909–) Baseball. Also called KING KONG.

JUNIOR—Albert Langlois (1934–) Hockey.

JUNIOR—John McEnroe (1958–) Tennis. See THE BRAT.

JUNIOR—Jack Stephens (1933–) Basketball g-f.

JUNIOR—Vern Stephens (1920–1968) Baseball ss. Also called THE LITTLE SLUG OF THE BOSTON RED SOX.

JUNIOR—Kirk Walton (1924–) Basketball. Walton was an All-American guard at Illinois in 1945. He later played pro ball for Fort Wayne and Tri-Cities—Milwaukee.

JUNK MAN [THE]—Stu Miller (1927–) Baseball. Miller also threw junk, or offspeed pitches. His record was 105–103 from 1952 to 1968.

K-MART—Kelvin Martin (1965–) Football. A clever play on his name, referring to the popular chain of stores.

KAK—Jon Francis Koncak (1963–) Basketball.

KANGAROO—Donald A. Smith (1946–) Basketball. Smith played forward and changed his name to Zaid Abdul-Aziz.

KANGAROO KID [THE]—Billy Cunningham (1943–) Basketball. Cunningham, who played forward and center, had great jumping ability.

KANGAROO KID [THE]—Jim Pollard (1922–) Basketball f. **H/F**

KANSAS COMET [THE]—Gayle Sayers (1943–) Football hb. **H/F** See MAGIC.

KANSAS CYCLONE [THE]—Dwight D. Eisenhower (1890–1969) Football. From Abilene, Kansas, the general was a whirlwind when he played for West Point.

KANSAS GIANT [THE]—Jess Willard (1883–1968) Boxing (heavyweight). Also called BIG JESS, COWBOY JESS, POTTAWATOMIE GIANT, and TALL PINE OF THE POTTAWATOMIE. See THE GREAT WHITE HOPE.

KANSAS RUBE [THE]—Rube Ferns (1874–1952) Boxing (welterweight). His real name was James Rube.

KARATE POET—Joseph Reid (1954–) Karate. Reid's interests were karate and poetry.

KAVA—Carl F. Karilivacz (1930–1969) Football. Along with Jack Christiansen, Jim David, and Yale Lary, Kava was a member of Detroit's outstanding defensive backfield.

KAYO—George Chaney (1892–1958) Boxing (lightweight). **H/F** Chaney won his nickname the same way he won most of his bouts. He won at least eighty-six of his fights by knockout.

K. C.—Kevin Clark (active 1987–) Football db.

KEMO—Filomeno (Phil) Coronado Ortega (1939–) Baseball. This Native American was nicknamed after Kemo Sabe on *The Lone Ranger.* Ortega's record was 46–62 over ten years.

KENTUCKY LION—Jackson Whipps Showalter (1860–1935) Chess.

KENTUCKY RIFLE [THE]—Glen Combs (1946–) Basketball g.

KENTUCKY ROSEBUD [THE]—Howie Camnitz (1881–1960) Baseball. Camnitz had twenty wins in three different seasons. Also called RED.

KENTUCKY ROSEBUD [THE]—Walter Edgerton (1868–1923) Boxing.

KETTLE—Elwood Wirtz (1897–1968) Baseball c.

KEWPIE—Dick Barrett (1906–1966) Baseball p.

KEWPIE—Percival Rollo Dahl (1919–) Football. The Kewpie doll was popular back when Dahl was playing.

KEWPIE—Johnny Ertle (1896–1976) Boxing (bantamweight). At 4' 11" and 112 pounds, Ertle had a passing resemblance to one of those popular plastic dolls.

KI—Charles Aldrich (1938–) Football c.

KICK—John Kelly (1859–1908) Baseball c. Also called FATHER.

KICKAPOO CHIEF—Ed Summers (1884–1953) Baseball. Summers was a member of the Fox tribe, and one of their languages was called Kickapoo. As a member of the Detroit Tigers, his pitching record was 68–45.

KID [THE]—Kenny Anderson (1970–) Basketball. In his first 273 games with the New Jersey Nets, he averaged 15.3 points per game.

KID—Hogan Bassey (1932–1998) Boxing (featherweight). Kid was a pet nickname for a young boxer. Bassey's real name is Okon Bassey Asuque. This featherweight lost and won fights with Davy Moore for the world title.

KID—Jack Berg (1909–) Boxing (junior lightweight). Berg's real name was Judah Bergman. Also called WHITECHAPEL WHIRLWIND.

KID—Kirk Blair (1960–) Boxing (Australian lightweight).

KID [THE]—Gary Carter (1954–) Baseball. This catcher was filled with boyish enthusiasm even when he became long in the tooth.

KID [THE]—Steve Cauthen (1960–) Horse racing.

KID—Mal Eason (1879–1970) Baseball p.

KID—Normal Arthur Elberfeld (1875–1944) Baseball c.

KID—Eddie Foster (1888–1937) Baseball 3b.

KID—William Gleason (1866–1933) Baseball.
This pitcher turned second baseman was nicknamed Kid because he was short and he loved to play the game. His spirits were later dampened when he was the manager of the White Sox when they threw the World Series in 1919. See THE BLACK SOX SCANDAL.

KID—Perry Ivia Graves (1892–) Boxing (welterweight).
In 1914, Graves claimed the world welterweight title.

KID—Louis Kaplan (1902–1970) Boxing (featherweight).
Also called LITTLE NAPOLEON.

KID—George Lavigne (1869–1928) Boxing.

KID—Ted Lewis (1894–1970) Boxing. **H/F**
Lewis was the ring name. (His real name was Gershon Mendeloff.) Lewis fought Jack Britton twenty times over a six-year period.

KID—Harry Matthews (active 1950s) Boxing (heavyweight). A young leading contender, Matthews was beaten by Rocky Marciano on July 28, 1952. Marciano's victory earned him the title shot with Jersey Joe Walcott.

KID—Charles McCoy (1873–1940) Boxing lc.
See THE REAL McCOY.

KID—William Lawrence McPartland (1878–1953) Boxing (lightweight)/referee.

KID—Juan Meza (1956–) Boxing.
Mexican junior featherweight

KID—Benny Paret (1937–1962) Boxing.
Paret won the welterweight title at twenty-three; he lost the title and his life two years later in the ring at the hands of Emile Griffith.

KID [THE]—George Ratterman (1926–) Football qb.

KID [THE]—Phil Rizzuto (1917–) Baseball ss.
Also called LITTLE MONKEY and SCOOTER.

KID—Leo Roy (1906–1955) Boxing (featherweight and lightweight). Leo Roy was also known as Leo Paradis.

KID—Steve Sullivan (1897–) Boxing (lightweight).
Sullivan (the ring name of Stephen J. Tricamo) beat Johnny Dundee for the world junior lightweight title in 1924.

KID—Jack Wolfe (1895–) Boxing (junior featherweight).

KID BLACKIE—Jack Dempsey (1895–1983) Boxing (heavyweight). **H/F** Also called THE CHAMP, JACK THE GIANT KILLER, MIGHTY JACK, and THE THOR OF THE RING. See THE MANASSA MAULER.

KID CHOCOLATE—Seligio Sardinias. Boxing (featherweight). Kid Chocolate was the featherweight

champion in 1933. Also called THE CUBAN BON-BON.

KID DIXIE—Aaron L. Brown. Boxing.

KID DYNAMITE—Jorge Morales (active 1976–1980s) Boxing.

KID FROM SWEETWATER—Clyde Douglas Turner (1919–)
Football c/coach.

KID GAVILAN—Gerardo Gonzalez (1926–) Boxing. **H/F**
Gavilan had a windmill boxing style topped off with his famous BOLO PUNCH.

KID McCOY—Charles McCoy (1873–1940) Boxing (welterweight). Fights fans can see Kid McCoy box in D. W. Griffith's classic silent film, *Broken Blossoms.* Also, called CORKSCREW KID and REAL MCCOY.

KID McCOY—Norman Selby (1873–1940) Boxing (welterweight).

KID MURPHY—Peter Frascella. Boxing.

KID NORFOLK—Willie Ward (1898–deceased) Boxing.

KID SAGINAW—Kid Lavigne (1869–1928) Boxing.
Lavigne was from Saginaw and at 5' 3" looked like a kid. In the 1890s, he stopped England's Dick Burge in the seventeenth round to become the lightweight champion.

KID SNOWBALL—Ted Broadribb. Boxing.
In 1910, Broadribb defeated the sixteen-year-old Georges Carpentier in Paris.

KID WILLIAMS—Johnny Gutenko. Boxing.

KIDDO—George Willis Davis (1902–1983) Baseball.
In the 1933 World Series, Davis (playing outfield for the New York Giants) batted .368 against the Washington Senators.

KIF—Cliff Aberson (1921–1973) Football.

KIKI—Hazen Shirley Cuyler (1899–1950) Baseball. **H/F**
Cuyler's nickname began when sportswriters heard his fellow fielders call him off a fly ball with "Cuy, Cuy." The Pirates outfielder was a lifetime .321 hitter.

KIKO—Alfonso Garcia (1953–) Baseball.
This infielder for Baltimore and Houston received his nickname from his grandparents.

KILLER—Carl Banks (active 1984–) Football lb.

KILLER—Mel Davis (1950–) Basketball f.

KILLER—Alexander Kaleta (1919–) Hockey.
This nickname was ironic. Left winger Kaleta was everything but a vicious player.

KILLER KOWALSKI—Wladek Kowalski. Wrestling.

KING—Larry LaJoie (1874–1959) Baseball 2b/mgr. **H/F**
Also called NAP.

KING—Pierre Larouche (1955–) Hockey.

KING—Hal Lear (1935–) Basketball.

The nickname of this Temple University guard plays on an association with his prowess on the court and Shakespeare. In 1956, King Lear beat out Bill Russell and K.C. Jones to win the MVP of the NCAA tournament.

KING—Bill Linderman. Rodeo.

KING [THE]—Dick Lundy (1899–1965) Baseball (Negro Leagues) ss.

KING—Bid McPhee (1859–1943) Baseball.

Bid was the best second baseman during his day.

KING OF AMATEUR SWIMMING—Mark Spitz (1950–) Swimming. **H/F**

KING COBRA—Lloyd Kelsey. Wrestling.

KING COLE—Leonard Cole (1886–1916) Baseball p.

KING KONG—Eddie Kahn (1911–1945) Football.

KING KONG—Charlie Keller (1916–1990) Baseball.

Charlie Keller was not all that big (5' 10", 185 pounds), but it was reported that this outfielder was one of the strongest men in baseball. That's why he was compared to the movie ape.

KING KONG—Robert George Kline (1909–1987) Baseball p. Also called JUNIOR

KING KONG—Jerry Korab (1948–) Hockey.

KING KONG—Caifas Masondo. Boxing.

KING KONG—Charles Philyaw (active 1976–1984) Football.

This defensive end was 6' 9" and 276 pounds.

KING KONG KAHN—Eddie Kahn (1911–1945) Football.

KING LEAR—Charles Lear (1891–1976) Baseball.

In nicknaming this pitcher, it can't be said that ballplayers didn't know from Shakespeare.

KING LEAR—Fred Lear (1894–1955) Baseball.

The Bard again. Not only was this third baseman known as King Lear, but also Phil Regan was known as The Vulture. Maybe someone had read the play.

KING LEVINSKY—Barney Williams (1891–1949) Boxing. Also called BATTLING LEVINSKY.

KING OF THE CANEBRAKES—Young Stribling. Boxing.

KING OF THE COURTS—Billie Jean King (1943–) Tennis. **H/F** Also called OLD LADY and TENNIS TYCOON.

KING OF THE DERBIES—Georges Stern (1882–1928) Horse racing. In one year he won the French, Austrian, and German Derbies, and finished second in the Belgian Derby. Also called KING OF THE JOCKEYS.

KING OF THE FAIRS—Carlos Figueroa. Trainer of harness-horses.

KING OF THE HILL—Grant Hill (1972–) Basketball. Named Co-Rookie of the Year (with Jason Kidd) for the 1994–1995 season. Hill's mother Janet was Hillary Rodman Clinton's roommate at Wellesly.

KING OF SNOWBOARDING—Terje Haakonsen (1974–) Snowboarding. Haakonsen won the world halfpipe championship in 1997, his third world title in four years.

KING OF SOFTBALL PITCHERS—Bob Fesler. Softball.

KING OF SWAT—George Herman (Babe) Ruth (1895–1948) Baseball p/of. **H/F** Also, BAMBINO, IDOL OF THE AMERICAN BOY, and SULTAN OF SWAT. See BABE RUTH.

KING OF THE NETS—Bill Tilden (1893–1951) Tennis. Tilden won over seventy tennis championships with his big serve and quick feet. See BIG BILL.

KING OF THE STAKES RIDERS—Eddie Arcaro (1916–) Horse racing. **H/F** Arcaro won 554 stakes winners, a record in 1961. Willie Shoemaker later broke and surpassed this total. See BANANA NOSE, BIG A, THE MASTER, and SHOE.

KING OF THE UMPIRES—Thomas J. Lynch (1859–1924) Baseball.

KING RICHARD—Richard Brodeur (1952–) Hockey g.

KING TUT—Guy Tutwiler (1889–1930) Baseball.

Like Tutankhamen himself, this first baseman played a minor role.

KINGFISH—Alexander Levinsky (1910–) Hockey. Levinsky came by his nicknames of Kingfish and MINE BOY because of his ability to dig in the corners and come up with the gold in the form of a puck.

KIP—Kipchoge Keino (1940–) Track and field. This Kenyan runner won gold medals at the 1968 Olympics in the 1,500 meters and at the 1972 Games in the steeplechase.

KIT—Rosario Joanette (1919–) Hockey.

KITCHEN [THE]—Nate Newton (1961–) Football. Newton stood 6' 3" and weighed well over 300 pounds. He received his nickname because of his weight. He could eat anything and everything in the kitchen. Newton weighed 332 pounds at his first Cowboys' training camp. Thus, his nickname is a good companion for William Perry's The Refrigerator.

KITE—Keith Thomas (1924–) Baseball of.

KITTY—William Edward Bransfield (1875–1946) Baseball 1b.

KITTY—Jim Kaat (1938–) Baseball.

This pitcher turned announcer pitched during four different decades, won sixteen straight Golden Gloves, and racked up a 283–237 record. His nickname was a natural.

KLEGGIE—Clarence Hermsen (1923–) Basketball.

This 6' 9" standout went to the Celtics in 1948.

KLONDIKE—Bill Douglass (1872–1953) Baseball 1b.

KLONDIKE—Harry Kane (1883–1932) Baseball p.

KNIGHT OF THE CLEAVER [THE]—Jack Slack (d. 1778) British bareknuckles champion. Slack beat the only Frenchman to fight during the bareknuckles era, Monsieur Petit (who stood six-six and weighed 220 pounds) in a fight that lasted twenty-five minutes.

KNIGHT OF THE WHISTLE [THE]—Patrick Joseph Lally (1868–1956) Lacrosse.

KNOBBY—Grant David Warwick (1921–) Hockey.

Warwick at right wing was the top scorer for the Bruins in the 1948–1949 season and the winner of the Calder Trophy.

KNOCKOUT BROWN—Valentine Braun (1891–1948) Boxing (lightweight).

KNUCKSIE—Phil Niekro (1939–) Baseball.

The knuckleball kept Niekro on the pitcher's mound until he was forty-eight. His career record was 318–274. His longevity led to his other nickname, FATHER TIME.

KO—Meyer Christner. Boxing (heavyweight).

KONG—Dave Kingman (1948–) Baseball of/1b.

KOOFOO—Sandy Koufax (1935–) Baseball p. **H/F**

Also THE MAN WITH THE GOLDEN ARM.

K. T.—Ken Landreaux (1954–) Baseball.

Outfielder Landreaux gave this nickname to himself.

L. A.—Albert Bell (active 1988) Football rw.

Also called LITTLE AL.

LADDIE—Lauren Gale (1916–deceased) Basketball f. **H/F**

LADY—Charles Baldwin (1859–1937) Baseball.

Baldwin acted like a perfect la—er, gentleman. He neither drank, nor smoked, nor chewed, nor cussed. In 1886, Lady won forty-two games.

LADY OF THE LANES—Marion Ladewig (1914–) Bowling.

LADY LINDY—Amelia Earhart (1898–1937) Aviation.

LAM JONES—Johnny Jones (active 1980–1987) Football rw.

LARRUPING LOTHARIO OF PUGILISM—Max Baer (1909–1959) Boxing (heavyweight). Also called CLOUTING CLOWN, FISTIC HARLEQUIN, LIVERMORE BUTCHER BOY, LIVERMORE LARRUPER, MADCAP MAXIE, MAGNIFICENT SCREWBALL, PLAYBOY OF PUGILISM, PUGILISTIC POSEUR.

LARRUPIN' LOU—Lou Gehrig (1903–1941) Baseball 1b. **H/F**

Also called BISCUIT PANTS, IRON MAN OF BASEBALL, and PRIDE OF THE YANKEES. See IRON HORSE.

LARRY—Napoleon Lajoie (1875–1959) Baseball 2b/mgr.

LARRY—Leland Stanford McPhail (1890–1975) Baseball (club president). Also called WIZARD OF BASEBALL.

LAST AMERICAN HERO [THE]—Junior Johnson (19__–) Auto racing. Stock car racer Junior Johnson received his nickname from the writer Tom Wolfe.

LAST OF THE SIXTY-MINUTE MEN [THE]—Charlie Bednarik (1925–) Football c/lb.

LAST OF THE SPITBALL PITCHERS—Burleigh Arland Grimes (1893–1985) Baseball p. **H/F**

Also called OLD STUBBLEBEARD and SENATOR.

LATERAL PASS—Bill Stern. Sports announcer.

Stern once reported during an Army football game that Blanchard was running with the ball. Glenn Davis, however, was the one with the ball. When he realized his mistake, he amended it to "Lateral to Davis."

LAVE—Lafayette Cross (1866–1927) Baseball 3b.

LAVVIE—Lavern R. Dillweb (1903–1968) Football.

LAWYER—Vic Sorrell (1901–1972) Baseball p.

Also called ACE, BABY DOLL, THE PHILOSOPHER.

LEAKY—Bob Fausett (1908–1994) Baseball p.

LEAPER [THE]—Louie Fontinato (1932–) Hockey d.

LEAPING—Mike Menosky (1894–1983) Baseball.

This outfielder for the Senators and Red Sox was nicknamed for the way he leaped for fly balls about to sail over the fence.

LEE—Lido John Fogolin (1926–) Hockey g.

LEFTY—Al Aber (1927–) Baseball p.

LEFTY—Bobby Burke (1907–1971) Baseball p.

LEFTY—George Brunet (1935–) Baseball p.

LEFTY—Steve Carlton (1944–) Baseball.

This left hander won twenty or more games six times and the Cy Young Award four times. A fitness enthusiast, Carlton practiced the martial arts and plunged his arms into tubs of rice to increase his strength. Also called PHILLY JILLY.

LEFTY—Cliff Chambliss (1922–) Baseball p.

LEFTY—Charles Driesell (1931–) Basketball coach.

LEFTY—William Frizzell (active 1984–) Football db.

LEFTY—Vernon Louis Gomez (1908–) Baseball p. **H/F**
Also called GOOFY. He once attributed his success to "clean living and a fast outfield."

LEFTY—Felix Leach (active 1930s) Football.

LEFTY—George James (active 1920s–1930s) Football coach.

LEFTY—Frank Joseph O'Doul (1897–1969) Baseball p/of.

LEFTY—Harold Ross Phillips (1919–1972) Baseball manager.

LEFTY—Joseph Benjamin Shaute (1899–1970) Baseball p.

LEFTY—Ralph Sproull (1893–) Basketball.
An All-American at Kansas University, Sproull scored forty points, a record that lasted until Clyde "BIG WHITE WHALE" Lovellette broke it thirty-nine years later. (Sproull's Sunday school teacher was Dr. James Naismith, THE FATHER OF BASKETBALL.)

LEFTY—George Albert Tyler (1889–1953) Baseball p.

LEFTY—Claude Preston Williams (1893–1959) Baseball p.

LEFTY—Ross Ingram Wilson (1919–) Hockey g.

LEGS—Roy M. Hawley (1901–1954) Athletic director (college).

LEM—Bob Lemon (1920–) Baseball p/manager. **H/F**
Lem's fifteen-year record as a pitcher was 207–128; his eight-year record as manager, 432–401.

LEMONS—Julius Joseph Solters (1906–1975) Baseball of. Also called MOOSE.

LENA—Russell Blackburne (1886–1968) Baseball coach. Also called SLATS.

LENNY—Leonard Wilkens (1937–) Basketball. **H/F**
After a playing career that landed him as a guard on eight All-Star teams, Wilkins has been a successful coach in the NBA, most recently with Cleveland.

LES—Lester Steers (1917–) Track and field.
In 1941, Steers held the world high jump mark at 6' 11".

LICK—Archibald Malloy (1886–1961) Baseball p. Also called ALEX.

LIEF—Dick Errickson (1914–) Baseball.
This pitcher's nickname was a tip of the cap to the Scandinavian explorer.

LIGHT OF ISRAEL [THE]—Daniel Mendoza (1764–1836) Boxing (heavyweight). **H/F**

LIGHTHORSE HARRY—Harry E. Wilson (1902–) Football, basketball. Wilson was an All-American in both sports and played at Penn State and West Point.

LIGHTNING DESTROYER—George Foreman (1949–) Boxing (heavyweight).

LI'L ABNER—Paul Erickson (1915–) Baseball. Erickson was a big pitcher from a small town in Illinois.

LI'L ARTHUR—Jack Johnson (1878–1946) Boxing **H/F**
Johnson was the first black heavyweight champion. Also called THE GALVESTON GIANT. See BIG SMOKE.

LINCOLN LOCOMOTIVE [THE]—Leo Lewis (active 1955–1965) Football. This halfback, who played for Lincoln University in Jefferson City, Missouri, later scored 450 points for the Blue Bombers in the Canadian Football League. (Burnham Holmes fondly recalls playing catch and running windsprints with Lewis toward the end of both of their football careers.)

LINDY—James Hood (1907–) Basketball.
In 1930, Hood was an All-American center, leading Alabama to a 20–0 season.

LINE DRIVE—Lynn Nelson (1905–1955) Baseball.
Nelson gave up a lot of stinging line drives on his way to a lifetime ERA of 5.25.

LINK—Bobby Lowe (1868–1951) Baseball 2b.

LION [THE]—Leo Nomellini (1924–) Football. **H/F**
The nickname of this 6' 3", 264-pound defensive tackle from Italy came from his first name, his strength, and his style of play. Nomellini starred for the San Francisco 49ers from 1950–1963, playing in 174 straight games.

LITHUANIAN [THE]—Jack Sharkey (1902–) Boxing.
Also called BAY STATER, BOSTON GOB, BOSTON SAILOR, and GABBY LITHUANIAN.

LITTLE AL—Albert Bell. Football. Also called L.A.

LITTLE ALL RIGHT—Claude Cassius Ritchey (1873–1951) Baseball.

LITTLE BEAVER—Marcel Dionne (1951–) Hockey f.

LITTLE BEAVER—Frank Rowe. Rodeo.

LITTLE BIG MAN—Nate Archibald (1948–) Basketball. Also called NATE THE SKATE. See TINY.

LITTLE BO PETE—Dwight Lamar (1951–) Basketball.

LITTLE BOX OF TRICKS—Thomas Palmer (1876–1949)

Boxing (Bantamweight). Palmer stood only 5' 3".
Also called PEDDLAR.

LITTLE BOY BLUE—Albie Booth (1908–1959) Football,
basketball, baseball. This 5' 7", 144-pound sophomore
halfback was a substitute in the second quarter of a
game between Yale and Army with the Eli behind
13–0. By game's end, Booth had accounted for 233
yards rushing, a seventy-yard punt return, twenty-one
points, the victory, and the beginning of a legend. Also
called LITTLE ALBIE, MIGHTY ATOM, MIGHTY MITE.

LITTLE CLIPPER—John Philip Smith (1904–1973)
Football coach/athletic director.

LITTLE COLONEL [THE]—Harold "Pee Wee" Reese
(1919–) Baseball. **H/F** Reese, the shortstop for the
Dodgers from 1940 to 1958, was from Elkon, Kentucky.
Although he was 5' 10", he was still associated with
being short. See PEE WEE.

LITTLE DAVID—Robert David O'Brien (1917–) Football.
O'Brien took over at quarterback at TCU after Sammy
Baugh left. Also called SLINGSHOT.

LITTLE DOCTOR—Walter E. Meanwell (1884–1953)
Basketball coach and doctor. Also called DOC.

LITTLE FOOT—Chris Bahr (active 1976–1989) Football.

LITTLE GENERAL [THE]—Eddie LeBaron (1930–)
Football qb.

LITTLE GIANT—Aurel Emile Joliat (1901– 1986) Hockey.
H/F Also called MIGHTY ATOM.

LITTLE GLOBE TROTTER [THE]—Billy Earle (1867–1946)
Baseball. This catcher received his nickname because
he played for three different teams within three
years. He had a reputation for being able to hypnotize
his teammates.

LITTLE HEBREW [THE]—Abe Attell (1884–1970) Boxing.
Attell once said he had become a boxer because
"I either had to hold my own with those tough Irish
lads or be chased off the block." This boxer reigned
as the featherweight champion from 1901 to 1912.

LITTLE INDIAN—Wilbur Moore (1916–1965) Football b.

LITTLE ITALIAN [THE]—Al Gionfrido (1922–) Baseball.
Gionfrido was an outfielder for the Pirates and
Dodgers.

LITTLE JACK—John McGill (1910–) Hockey g.
McGill stood 5' 10" and weighed 158 pounds.
See BIG JACK.

LITTLE LOUIE—Luis Aparicio (1934–) Baseball.

This shortstop was only 5' 9" and weighed 160 pounds.

LITTLE MAJOR—Bill Corum (1894–1958) Sports
journalist.

LITTLE MAN IN PRO FOOTBALL—Doak Walker (1927–)
Football. **H/F** Also called ALL-AMERICAN MUSTANG.
See THE DOAKER.

LITTLE MISS COOL—Chris Evert (1954–) Tennis.
See ICE MAIDEN.

LITTLE MISS SURE SHOT—Annie Oakley (1860–1926)
Sharpshooter.

LITTLE MO—Maureen Catherine Connolly (1934–1969)
Tennis. **H/F**

LITTLE MO—Dick Modzelweski (1931–) Football.
Little Mo may have been short for a tackle, but he
made All-American at Maryland in 1952.

LITTLE MONKEY—Phil Rizzuto (1917–) Baseball ss.
Also called THE KID and SCOOTER.

LITTLE NEMO—James Stephens (1883–1965) Baseball c.

LITTLE O—Obert Logan (1941–) Football.
He was 5' 10" and weighed about 180 pounds in a
world of bruisers.

LITTLE PANCHO—Pancho Segura (1921–) Tennis. **H/F**
See BIG PANCHO and PANCHO.

LITTLE POISON—Lloyd James Waner (1906–1982) Baseball
of.

LITTLE POTATO—Camilo Pascual (1934–) Baseball.
Even though Camilo was younger, he was bigger
(and 170 games more successful) than his brother,
Carlos "Potato" Pascual, who was also a pitcher.

LITTLE RED—Danny Lopez (1952–) Boxing (middleweight). Won the WBC featherweight title in 1976.

LITTLE ROUND MAN—Wally Butts (1907–73) Football
coach.

LITTLE SHEPHERD OF COOGAN'S BLUFF—Leo Durocher
(1905–1991) Baseball ss/manager.

LITTLE SKEE—George Levi (1899–) Football,
basketball, track and field. George Levi was the
younger brother of BIG SKEE, John Levi. Little
Skee's football team at Haskell Institute was the
highest scoring team in the nation in 1926.

LITTLE SLUG OF THE BOSTON RED SOX—Vern Stephens
(1920–1968) Baseball ss. Also called JUNIOR.

LITTLE STEAM ENGINE [THE]—James Galvin (1855–1902)
Baseball p. **H/F** Also called PUD. See GENTLE JEEMS.

LITTLE STEW—Jimmy Stewart (1939–) Baseball of/2b.

LITTLE TRAIN—Lionel James (active 1984–1988) Football. The nickname of this wide receiver came from his small stature of 5' 6½" (the shortest in the NFL in 1985) and his first name.

LITTLE TUBBY—Julius Raskin (1906–) Basketball coach.

LIVER—Walter Ancker (1894–1954) Baseball p. Also called GEE.

LIVERMORE BUTCHER BOY—Max Baer (1909–1959) Boxing (heavyweight).

LIVERMORE LARRUPER—Max Baer (1909–1959) Boxing (heavyweight).

LOCO—Jose Herrera (1942–) Baseball. Played from 1967–1970 for the Houston Astros.

LOCO LOCO—Ricardo Bennett (1958–) Boxing (featherweight).

LOLLYPOP—Wade Killefer (1884–1958) Baseball. This outfielder was the brother of Reindeer Bill (William Killefer). Also called RED.

LOLO—Rosie Couture (1905–) Hockey rw.

LOMBO—Thomas A. Lombardo (1922–1950) Football b/qb.

LONE STAR—William H. Dietz (1886–1964) Football. Dietz captained the Carlisle Indians in 1911 and coached the Boston Redskins in 1933–1934.

LONG BOB—Bob Meusel (1896–1977) Baseball. Meusel was 6' 3" and an outfielder on the Yankees that won six pennants during the 1920s. He was a member of the famed MURDERER'S ROW.

LONG GONE—L. G. Dupre (active 1955–1961) Football hb.

LONG JIM—James Barnes (1887–1966) Golf. Barnes was tall for his day (6' 3"), but his nickname also described the way he drove the ball off the tee. He won the first PGA in 1916.

LONG-HAIRED WONDER—Steve Clarke (1943–) Swimming.

LONG JOHN—John Duncan (1933–) Hockey g.

LONNIE—Amos Alonzo Stagg (1862–1965) Football coach. Also called FOOTBALL'S OLD MAN RIVER and THE UNRECONSTRUCTED AMATEUR. See THE GRAND OLD MAN OF FOOTBALL.

LOONEY TUNES—Bill Faul (1940–) Baseball. In *A Pitcher's Story*, Juan Marichal (with Charles Einstein) tells us about this pitcher for the Chicago Cubs: "Faul had a reputation of his own. They say he did yoga exercises and hypnotized himself before going in to pitch. Some of the players in the league called him 'Looney Tunes.'"

LORD—Jan Bleers (19__–) Wrestling.

LORD [THE]—Fritz Crisler (1899–1982) Football coach. Also called FOOTBALL STATESMAN.

LORD BYRON—William J. Byron (1872–1954) Baseball. See SINGING UMPIRE.

LOSING PITCHER—Hugh Mulcahy (1913–) Baseball. Mulcahy registered several league-leading records: ninety-seven bases on balls in 1937, twenty games lost in 1938, and twenty-two lost in 1940 along with 283 hits given up. Losing Pitcher Mulcahy's career record was 45–89.

LOU COSTELLO—Henry John Damore (1919–) Hockey c.

LOUD LARRY—Leland Stanford McPhail (1890–1975) Baseball (president of baseball club). Also called WIZARD OF BASEBALL.

LOUISVILLE LIP—Muhammad Ali (1942–) Boxing (heavyweight). **H/F** Back in the days when he was still in Louisville, the then Cassius Clay was quite a talker. Later, Muhammad Ali was the heavyweight champion 1964–1970, 1974–1978, and 1978–1979. See THE GREATEST.

LOWELL KID [THE]—Andrew St. Jean. Pool.

LU—Luzerne Atwell Blue (1897–1958) Baseball 1b.

LUCKIEST FOOL ALIVE—Alvin Anthony Kelly (1885–1952) Flagpole sitting. Also called SAILOR. See SHIPWRECK KELLY.

LUCKY—Jack Lohrke (1924–) Baseball. This third baseman escaped WW II's Battle of the Bulge without a scratch, missed catching a plane that crashed, and was traded during a minor-league bus trip. Shortly after he got off the bus, nine players were killed in a traffic accident.

LUCKY PIERRE—Pierre Larouch (1955–) Hockey. Larouch had a fifty-goal season with Pittsburgh, so he was as skillful as he was lucky.

LULU—Louis Bender (1910–) Basketball.

LULU—Louis Gilbert Denis (1928–) Hockey rw.

LUKE—Maurice Lucas (1952–) Basketball f-c.

LUKE—James Luther Sewell (1901–1987) Baseball. Luke managed the St. Louis Browns when they won their one and only pennant.

LUMBER—Joe Price (1897–1961) Baseball. This outfielder swung the lumber in only one game for an average of .000.

LURCH—John Dutton (1951–) Football. This 6' 7", 248 pound tackle could lurch from side to side very fast.

LUVI—Victor Callejas (1960–) Boxing (junior featherweight) from Puerto Rico.

MA—Marshall Newell (1871–1997) Football. Newell was an All-American tackle at Harvard from 1890 to 1893, and the first salaried football coach at Cornell from 1893 to 1894.

MAC THE SACK—Tony McGee (active 1971–1984) Football. McGee was a Washington Redskins lineman in the 1980s who enjoyed sacking the quarterback.

MAC THE TRUCK—MacArthur Lane (active 1968–1978) Football rb.

MACARONI PONY [THE]—Bob Coluccio (1951–) Baseball. This outfielder was too small in the stirrups to be labeled an Italian Stallion.

MACFAT—Paul MacLean. Football. MacLean was overweight when he reported to the Winnipeg Jets training camp.

MACHINE GUN—Charles Carter (active 1980s) Boxing (middleweight).

MACHO—Hector Camacho (1962–) Boxing. From Puerto Rico, Camacho was the lightweight champion in 1985.

MACHO MAN—Randy Savage. Wrestling. Randy Poffo (his real name) had been a baseball player.

MACK THE KNIFE—Mack Jones (1938–) Baseball of. Jones' nickname came from the famous song from *The Three Penny Opera.*

MAD BOMBER—Richard Fulqua (active 1970s) Basketball. In 1972, he scored 1,006 points to become the nation's highest major college scorer.

MAD BOMBER—Daryle Lamonica (1941–) Football. Raiders' quarterback Daryle Lamonica liked to heave long passes to Warren Wells and Fred Biletnikoff.

MAD BOMBER [THE]—Clint Longley (1952–) Football. He received this nickname from his teammates because of his wild passes (bombs) made during practice games with the Cowboys.

MAD CANADIAN—Ken Carter (19–) Stunt driver.

MAD DAWG—Bob Golic (active 1979–) Football. Golic was part of The Dawgs, the 1984 Cleveland Browns secondary, who barked at their linemen to fire them up.

MAD DOG—Fred Carter. Basketball. Carter was the coach for the Philadelphia 76ers. About his nickname, Carter once said, "The name came to me because of defensiveness and tenaciousness and hopefully that's what we're going to see. That's my personality. I'm not a finesse guy."

MAD DOG—Mike Curtis (1943–) Football. This Baltimore Colts linebacker was so intense and aggressive that he once got in a fight in practice with Bill Curry, his roommate. Mike Curtis' autobiography was titled *Stay Off My Turf.* Also called THE ANIMAL.

MAD DOG—Bill Madlock (1951–) Baseball 3b. His nickname came from a run-in he once had with an umpire. Madlock won the National League batting title four times and ended his fourteen-year career with a .305 average.

MAD DOG—Jock O'Billovich (19–) Football.

MAD DOG—Danny Paul. Boxing.

MAD DUCK [THE]—Alex Karras (1935–) Football t. Also called TIPPY TOES.

MAD MACKEREL MERCHANT [THE]—Barney Lebrowitz (1891–1949) Boxing (light heavyweight). Also called BATTLING LEVINSKY and THE FURIOUS FISHMONGER.

MAD MATT—Matt Zunic (1919–) Basketball g-f.

MAD MAX—Max Baer (1909–1959) Boxing. Baer was the heavyweight champ in 1934.

MAD RUSSIAN [THE]—Lou Novikoff (1915–1970) Baseball of.

MAD SCIENTIST [THE]—Bart Buetow (1950–) Football. Buetow played only nine games in the NFL. Too bad he didn't last longer because he had a great nickname.

MAD STORK [THE]—Ted Hendricks (1947–) Football. A three-time All-American at end from the University of Miami, this nonconformist was an intense 6' 7", 220-pound linebacker for the Colts and the Raiders. His size made it difficult for quarterbacks to pass over him and backs to run around him.

MADCAP MAXIE—Max Baer (1909–1959) Boxing (heavyweight). In seventy-nine bouts, Baer registered fifty knockouts and fifteen decisions with thirteen losses and one non-decision. When Baer fought Joe Lewis, he said: "I looked across the ring and realized I wanted-ed to go home early." He did. Also called CALIFORNIA MUSCLEMAN and BUTCHER BOY.

MADDY—Clarence James Maddern (1921–1986) Baseball of.

MADGE—Florence Madeline-Syers (active 1900s) Figure skating. She was a great skater from Britain at the turn of the twentieth century.

MADMAN FROM MISSISSIPPI [THE]—Gerald Walker (1908–1981) Baseball of. Also called GEE.

MAGIC—Rafael Santana (1958–) Baseball. ss.

MAGIC DRAGAN [THE]—Dragan Dzajic (1946–) Soccer.

MAGIC MAN—Don Majkowski (1964–) Football qb.

MAGIC MAN [THE]—Kent Nilsson (1956–) Hockey.
Nilsson, a center, was known for his ability to wield a hockey stick. This Swedish export played for Atlanta, Calgary, Minnesota, and Edmonton.

MAGICIAN—Marlin Briscoe (1945–) Football.
In 1968, Briscoe became the first African American to play quarterback on a regular basis for a pro team (the Denver Broncos).

MAGNIFICENT [THE]—Marvin Barnes (1952–)
Basketball. Also called THE ERASER and GOOD NEWS.

MAGNIFICENT MONGOOSE [THE]—Archie Moore (1916–)
Boxing. Moore was the light heavyweight champion. Also called AGELESS ARCHIE, OLD MAN RIVER, and THE OLD MONGOOSE. See THE MONGOOSE.

MAGNIFICENT RUBE [THE]—Tex Rickard (1870–1929)
Promoter. Also called DINK and NAPOLEON OF PRO-MOTERS. See KING OF THE SPORTS PROMOTERS.

MAGNIFICENT SCREWBALL—Max Baer (1909–1959)
Boxing (heavyweight).

MAGNIFICENT SKEPTIC—Gil Dobie (1879–1948) Football coach. Also called GLOOMY.

MAILMAN [THE]—Karl Malone (1963–) Basketball.
One of the top power forwards in the NBA (twenty-eight points per game), Malone was a member of the 1992 DREAM TEAM.

MAJOR—Ralph Houk (1919–) Baseball.
Houk, who managed the Yankees, the Tigers, and the Red Sox, had been a major during WW II.

MAJOR—George Magerkurth (1888–1966) Baseball.
This umpire was the special target of Leo Durocher. But if called "Meathead," Magerkurth would as often as not eject the assailant.

MAJOR—Marshall W. Taylor (1878–1932) Cycling.
This popular African American won the 1899 world championship bicycle races at .5, 1, and 2 miles.

MAIL CARRIER [THE]—Earle Combs (1899–1976)
Baseball **H/F** See THE KENTUCKY COLONEL.

MALTZY—Gordon Malzberger (1912–1974) Baseball p.

MAN [STAN THE]—Stan Musial (1920–) Baseball of/1b. **H/F**

MAN FROM TEXAS [THE]—A. J. Foyt (1935–) Auto racing.

MAN IN THE BROWN SUIT—Adolph Rupp (1901–1977)
Basketball coach. See BARON.

MAN IN THE IRON MASK [THE]—Charles Leo Hartnett (1900–1972) Baseball c. **H/F** Also called GABBY.

MAN IN THE MIDDLE [THE]—Sam Huff (1934–) Football linebacker.

MAN MOUNTAIN—Fred Toney (1888–1953) Baseball.
At 6' 6", 245 pounds, Toney was a mighty imposing pitcher in his day (or any day). His record was 137–102.

MAN MOUNTAIN DEAN—Frank S. Levitt (1890–1953)
Wrestling.

MAN OF A THOUSAND CURVES—Johnny Sain (1917–)
Baseball. Sain did not just have a curve ball; he had several kinds of curve balls that behaved differently to fluster batters even more.

MAN OF A THOUSAND MOVES [THE]—Elgin Baylor (1934–) Basketball f. **H/F**

MAN OF PAPER [THE]—Matthias Sindelar (1903–1939)
Soccer. The greatest soccer player in Austria's history received his nickname because he was so thin and because his movements on the field resembled a piece of paper floating through the air.

MAN WITH THE GOLDEN ARM [THE]—Sandy Koufax (1935–) Baseball p. **H/F** Also called KOO.

MAN WITH THE MUSTACHE [THE]—Mauri Rose (1906–1981) Auto racing. Also called TOP WHEEL AT THE BRICKYARD.

MANDO—Armando Ramos (1948–) Boxing. From 1968 to 1972 Ramos won and lost lightweight title fights.

MANDRAKE THE MAGICIAN—Don Mueller (1927–)
Baseball. Mueller, who played in the outfield for the New York Giants from 1948 to 1959, had excellent bat control and was able to drive the ball to any part of the ballpark. Mandrake the Magician was a famous comic strip character.

MANITO—Juan Marichal (1938–) Baseball **H/F**
In 1966, Marichal had a record of 25–6. Six times he

won over twenty games and he had fifty-two shutouts. Over his career of sixteen years, Marichal's record was 243–142 with an ERA of 2.89. Also called THE DOMINICAN DANDY.

MANOLETE—Manuel Rodriguez Sanchez . Bullfighting.

MANSTER—Randy White (1953–) Football.
A Dallas Cowboy teammate once said that White was equal parts man and monster.

MANTEQUILLA—Jose Napoles (1940–) Boxing. Napoles won seventy-two of seventy-eight bouts and defended his world welterweight championship nine times.

MARINE [THE]—George LaBlanche (active 1880s) Boxing (middleweight). George Blais (his real name) was the middleweight champion in 1889.

MAROOSH—John Mariucci (1916–) Hockey.
His nickname is a play upon his last name.

MARTI—Martin Liquori (1949–) Track and field.
In 1971, Liquori ran the mile in 3:54.6, and the 1500 meters in 3:36.0.

MARV—Marvel Harshman (1918–) Basketball.
Harshman's coaching record was 155–181 at Washington State from 1959 to 1971.

MARVELOUS—Marvin Hagler (1954–) Boxing (middleweight).

MARVELOUS MARV—Marvin Eugene Throneberry (1933–) Baseball. Marv Throneberry, better known as Marvelous Marv, was a klutzy first baseman for the hapless new New York Mets.

MASTER OF THE AERIAL CIRCUS—Ray Morrison (active 1915–1951) Football coach.

MASTER STRATEGIST [THE]—Joe Jeannette (1879–deceased) Boxing. Jeannette fought eight times with the great Jack Johnson. The Master Strategist won two, lost one, and the rest were either draws or no decisions.

MASTER TEACHER [THE]—Bobby Dobbs (1858–1930) Boxing. Dobbs, who had been born a slave in Knoxville, Tennessee, fought in England.

MATADOR [THE]—Severiano Ballesteros (1957–) Golf. This two-time winner of the Masters and three-time winner of the British Open is from Spain.

MATCHES—Matt Kilroy (1866–1940) Baseball.
As a rookie for Baltimore in the American Association in 1884, Kilroy burned 513 batters with strikeouts. Kilroy also threw four no-hitters in the 1880s. (At that

time, the distance to home plate was only fifty feet. It wasn't changed to 60' 6" until 1893.)

MATTY—William R. Matthews (1873–1948) Boxing (welterweight). Matty won the welterweight title in 1900 by defeating Jim "Rube" Ferns; a title he lost to Ferns the following year.

MATTY THE GREAT—Christy Mathewson (1880–1925) Baseball p. **H/F** Also called HUSK. See BIG SIX.

MAXIE THE TAXI—Max McGee (1932–) Football.
This tight end and pass catcher for the Green Bay Packers was known for staying out late with Paul Hornung. He'd try to make curfew by catching a cab.

MAYOR DALEY—Johnny Rice (1920–) Baseball.
This American League umpire bore a striking resemblance to Chicago's Mayor Daley.

M. C.—Mike McCoy (active 1976–1984) Football db.

McMAHON—Arnold Horween. Football.

MEAL TICKET [THE]—Carl Hubbell (1903–1988) Baseball p. **H/F**

MEAN JOE GREEN—Joe Green (1946–) Football dt. **H/F**

MEAT—Jim Brosnan (1929–) Baseball p.
Also called PROFESSOR.

MEAT CLEAVER—Eddie Weaver (19–) Football.
Weaver played a wicked defense for Georgia.

MECHANICAL MAN—Byron Nelson (1912–) Golf.
Nelson's golf game was as smooth and flawless as if he were made of something more substantial than flesh and blood. See LORD.

MED—Medford Park (1933–) Basketball.

MEIN BOY—Alexander Levinsky (1912–) Hockey.

MEMO—Guillermo Romero Luna (1930–) Baseball.
This nickname was a combination of letters in his first and middle names. With a record of 0–1 for the Cards in 1954, he turned out to be a small note.

MEMPHIS BILL—William Neely Mallory (1901–1945) Football. Also called BULL.

MEMPHIS BILL—Bill Terry (1898–1989) Baseball. **H/F**
This first baseman was from Memphis, Tennessee.

MEMPHIS PAL—Thomas Wilson Moore (1894–1953) Boxing.

MENDY—Marvin Rudolph (1938–1979) Basketball referee.

MEOW—Len Gilmore (1917–) Baseball.
In 1944, Gilmore was 0–1 in his only game for the Pirates.

MERCURY—Eugene Morris (1947–) Football rb.

MESS-OVER—Leon Spinks Boxing.
For a short time Spinks was the heavyweight champion. Also called NEON LEON.

METROPOLIS MAULER—Betty Colleen Weaver (active 1950–1954) Baseball (All-American Girls Baseball League). From Metropolis, Illinois, Weaver mauled the ball at the plate. In 1950, she hit .346; the next year she hit .368.

MEX—Keith Hernandez (1953–) Baseball.
This first baseman's father was actually from Spain. In 1987, Hernandez was the captain of the New York Mets, prized for his intensity and clutch hitting.

MICHE—Robert Perreault (1931–) Hockey g.

MICHIGAN WILDCAT [THE]—Ad Wolgast (1888–1955) Boxing. Wolgast was the lightweight champion from 1910 to 1912.

MICK [THE]—Mickey Mantle (1931–) Baseball cf. **H/F**
Also called THE GREAT MICK, INFANT PRODIGY, MILLION DOLLAR INVALID, and WOUNDED HERO. See THE COMMERCE COMET.

MICK THE QUICK—John Milton Rivers (1948–) Baseball. Called "Mickey," this center fielder was quick on the base paths. Also called THE AMBASSADOR.

MICK [THE]—Mickey Mantle (1931–) Baseball cf. **H/F**
Also called THE GREAT MICK, INFANT PRODIGY, MILLION DOLLAR INVALID, and WOUNDED HERO. See THE COMMERCE COMET.

MICKEY—Neal Francis Finn (1903–1933) Baseball 2b.

MICKEY—Newton Michael Grasso (1920–1975) Baseball. This catcher resembled catcher Mickey Cochrane.

MICKEY—Fred J. Ion (active 1930s–1940s) Hockey. **H/F**

MICKEY—Duncan MacKay (1894–1940) Hockey c. **H/F**

MICKEY—Arthur McBride (1887–1972) Football manager and founder.

MICKEY—Maurice Joseph McDermott (1928–) Baseball p.

MICKEY—Joe Medwick (1911–1975) Baseball of. **H/F**
Also called DUCKIE WUCKIE and MUSCLES. See DUCKIE.

MICKEY—Arnold Malcolm Owen (1916–) Baseball c.

MICKEY—Marvin Rottner. Basketball.

MICKEY—Lee Thompson (1928–) Auto racer.

MICKEY FINN—Cornelius Francis Neal (1904–1933) Baseball. This second baseman's nickname was for his willingness to fight at the drop of a bat.

MICKEY MANTLE'S CADDY—Ross Moschitto (1945–) Baseball. Moschitto was an outfielder who substituted for Mantle in the late innings when the game was on ice. Another player who also figuratively carried Mick's clubs was Jack Reed (1933–).

MICKEY MOUSE—Clifford George Melton (1912–) Baseball p. Also called COUNTRY MUSIC and MOUNTAIN MUSIC.

MIDGET—Don Ferrarese (1929–) Baseball.
This Orioles' pitcher was small (5' 9" and 170 pounds).

MIDGET MAGICIAN [THE]—Eddie LaBaron (1930–) Football. This NFL quarterback stood only 5' 7".

MIDGET SMITH—William J. Smith. Boxing.

MIGHTY ATOM [THE]—Albie Booth (1908–1959) Football, basketball, baseball. Also called LITTLE ALBIE, LITTLE BOY BLUE, and THE MIGHTY MITE.

MIGHTY ATOM [THE]—Joseph L. Greenstein (1883–1977) Wrestler.

MIGHTY ATOM [THE]—Jimmy Wilde (1892–1969) Flyweight boxing. **H/F**

MIGHTY JACK—Jack Dempsey (1895–1983) Boxing (heavyweight). **H/F** Also called THE CHAMP, JACK THE GIANT KILLER, KID BLACKIE, and THE THOR OF THE RING. See THE MANASSA MAULER.

MIGHTY MITE—Donna Adamek (1957–) Bowling. From 1978 through 1981, Mighty Mite was voted the Woman Bowler of the Year. During the 1981–1982 season, she rolled three (count 'em-three) 300 games.

MIGHTY MITE [THE]—Albie Booth (1908–1959) Football, basketball, baseball. Also called LITTLE ALBIE, LITTLE BOY BLUE, MIGHTY ATOM.

MIGHTY MITE [THE]—Miller Huggins (1879–1929) Baseball 2b/mgr. **H/F** At 5' 6", and 140 pounds, Huggins was a small but steady force for thirteen years at second base on the Reds and Cardinals, and for seventeen years as a manager of the Cardinals and Yankees. He took the Yankees to the World Series in 1921, 1922, 1923, 1926, 1927, and 1928. Also called HUG and FLEA.

MIGHTY MITE—Calvin Murphy (1948–) Basketball. At 5' 9", this guard was one of the smallest players in the NBA but one of the mightiest at the free-throw line. In 1981, Murphy hit seventy-eight straight en route to a .958 free-throw shooting percentage.

MIGHTY MITE [THE]—Mel Ott (1909–1958) Baseball of.

MIGHTY MO—Ed Modzelewski (active 1950s) Football. Mo was a mighty lineman for Maryland and the star of the Terps' 28–13 win over Tennessee in the 1952 Sugar Bowl.

MIGHTY MOUSE—Chuck Fenenbock (1918–) Football.

MIGHTY MOUSE—Elaine Tanner (1951–) Swimming. This Canadian star was only 5' 2".

MIGHTY MOUSE—Don Thompson (active 1960s) Race walking. Great Britain's small but strong Don Thompson won the fifty-kilometer race-walk at the 1960 Olympics in Rome.

MIKE—Miles W. Casteel (active 1910–1920) Football coach.

MILE-A-MINUTE MURPHY—Charles M. Murphy (1870–1950) Bike Racing. On June 30, 1899, Murphy became the first person to break the one-minute barrier on a bicycle. Riding behind a Long Island Railroad train he completed the mile in 57.8 seconds a record that stood until 1941.

MILES—Milan Komenick (1920–1977) Basketball. Komenick played from 1946–1950 for Fort Wayne and Anderson. His nickname is a play upon his first name.

MILKMAN JIM—James Riley Turner (1903–) Baseball. During the off season this pitcher pitched in on his family's dairy farm.

MILLION DOLLAR INVALID [THE]—Mickey Mantle (1931–) Baseball cf. **H/F** Also called THE GREAT MICK, INFANT PRODIGY, and WOUNDED HERO. See THE COMMERCE COMET.

MINER—Mordecai Brown (1876–1948) Baseball p. **H/F** See THREE FINGER BROWN.

MINI TANK—Leroy Hughes. Football.

MINISTER OF DEFENSE [THE]—Reggie White (1961–) Football de.

MINNESOTA GOPHER [THE]—Bert Blyleven (1951–) Baseball. Blyleven, a native of Holland not Minnesota, tossed enough gopher balls for the Minnesota Twins to set a major-league record of forty-nine home runs in 1986.

MINNIE—Saturnino Orestes Arrieta Minoso (1922–) Baseball of.

MIRACLE MAN [THE]—George Stallings (1867–1929) Baseball. In 1914, Stallings was the manager of The Miracle Braves, the team that went from last place to win the World Series. See THE MIRACLE BRAVES and THE MIRACLE TEAM.

MISS CHOP AND DROP—Elizabeth Ryan (1892–1979) Tennis. **H/F** Ryan's chop shot was a forehand with so much spin on it that it squirted low and away; her drop shot died over the net. Elizabeth Ryan and French champion Suzanne Lenglen formed a doubles team that went without losing a match for seven years.

MISSISSIPPI MUDCAT [THE]—Guy Bush (1901–1985) Baseball. From Aberdeen, Mississippi—catfish country—Bush not only started 308 games, but he also relieved 234. During his seventeen-year career, he was 176–136. One of the 177 hits The Mississippi Mudcat gave up in 1927 was Babe Ruth's 714th home run.

MISTER—Reynaldo Snipes (1956–) Heavyweight boxing. In 1981, Snipes lost to Larry Holmes in his bid for the WBC heavyweight title.

MR. AUGUST—Robert Lavette (active 1985–1987) Football. Lavette was only great in preseason play for the Dallas Cowboys.

MR. AUTOMATIC—Leo Cardenas (1938–) Baseball. This 1978 Gold Glover at shortstop was so smooth he made it seem automatic. Also called CHICO.

MR. AUTOMATIC—Dennis Eckersley (1954–) Baseball. He is one of the all-timer great relief pitchers. When he comes into a game, victory is nearly automatic.

MR. BASEBALL—Connie Mack (1862–1956) Baseball. Connie Mack, whose real name was Cornelius McGillicuddy, was a player for eleven years and a manager for fifty-three years! Also called THE TALL TACTICIAN. See CONNIE MACK.

MR. BASKETBALL—Kent Benson (1954–) Basketball. This guard got his nickname playing college ball at Indiana University.

MR. BASKETBALL—George Mikan (1924–) Basketball c. **H/F** Also called BIG GEORGE. See BIG NUMBER 99.

MR. BASKETBALL—Dean Smith (1931–) Basketball. **H/F** Smith has been coaching at North Carolina for over thirty years.

MR. BILL—James William Cartwright (1957–) Basketball. Played for New York and Chicago, and scored 12,644 points in his lifetime.

MR. BOXING—Nat Fleischer (1888–1972) Boxing. **H/F** Fleischer was the founder of *Ring Magazine*. Also called THE DEAN OF BOXING WRITERS.

MR. BUZZER-BEATER—Rory Sparrow (1958–)
Basketball. Sparrow, a guard, received his nickname
for his last second scoring at Villanova.

MR. CHIPS—Bob Chipman (1918–1971) Baseball.
Goodbye, Mr. Chips by James Hilton was a popular
novel in the 1930s and 1940s. Perhaps he was also fond
of potato chips?

MR. CLEAN—Steve Garvey (1948–) Baseball.
This first baseman with a .294 average gave the
appearance of being squeaky clean for most of his
nineteen-year career.

MR. CLUTCH—Joe Cronin (1906–1984) Baseball ss/mgr.
H/F

MR. CLUTCH—Jerry West (1938–) Basketball g. **H/F**
See ZEKE FROM CABIN CREEK.

MR. CONSISTENT—David Greenwood (1957–)
Basketball. Greenwood started every game for three
straight years while playing forward for the Chicago
Bulls in the early 1980s.

MR. DIRT—Dick Tidrow (1947–) Baseball p.

MR. EVERYTHING—George Follmer (1934–) Auto racing.
Follmer achieved success in both road racing and oval
track racing.

MR. FITZ—James Edward Fitzsimmons (1874–1966)
Horse racing. Also called DEAN OF AMERICAN TRAIN-
ERS, GRAND OLD MAN OF RACING, SUNNY JIM.

MR. HOCKEY—Gordie Howe (1928–) Hockey rw. **H/F**
See BLINKY.

MR. HOCKEY—Bobby Orr (1948–) Hockey d. **H/F**
See BOBBY HOCKEY.

MR. HO-MAH—Bob Horner (1957–) Baseball.
This was the nickname that the Japanese bestowed on
Horner in 1987 when he clouted eleven ho-mahs in
twenty-nine games for the Yakult Swallows.

MR. HOME RUN—Ralph Kiner (1922–) Baseball. **H/F**
This Pirate outfielder led the National League for
seven straight years in home runs and home run
percentage. Kiner hit 369 home runs during his ten-
year career. See KINER'S CORNER.

MR. HOW-ABOUT-THAT—Mel Allen (1913–) Sports
announcer.

MR. IMPOSSIBLE—Brooks Robinson (1937–) Baseball
3b. **H/F** Also called THE HOOVER and THE HUMAN
VACUUM CLEANER.

MR. INSIDE—Felix "Doc" Blanchard (1924–) Football fb.

MR. KNICKERS—Gene Sarazen (1902–) Golf. **H/F**
Many old photos of Sarazen show him wearing
knickers.

MR. LU—Liang Huan Lu (1936–) Golf.
This favorite of the galleries was active in the 1970s.

MR. MAY—George Steinbrenner's disparaging sobriquet
for Dave Winfield when both were with the Yankees.
The nickname was meant as a cruel allusion to Reggie
Jackson's Mr. October. However, still playing superb
baseball at the age of forty-one, Winnie vindicated
himself by knocking in two runs with a double in the
top of the eleventh inning in the seventh game of the
1992 World Series to win it all for the Toronto Blue
Jays over the Atlanta Braves.

MR. MEAN—Larry Smith (1958–) Basketball f-c.

MR. MOIST—Gaylord Perry (1938–) Baseball.
This pitcher received this nickname in reference to
his spitball.

MR. MOVES—Campy Russell (1952–) Basketball f.

MR. MURDER, INC.—Montford (Monte) Irving (1919–)
Baseball. This nickname was given to the outfielder by
teammate Bob Klinger.

MR. MUSTACHE—Roland "Rollie" Fingers (1946–)
Baseball. **H/F** Sporting a Salvador Dali-like
mustachio, Fingers was one of the first premier relief
pitchers. In addition to his total of 341 career saves,
Fingers also owned seven saves in World Series play.
Rollie Fingers was only the second reliever (Hoyt
Wilhelm was the first) to be inducted into the Hall of
Fame.

MR. PERSEVERANCE—Charlie Tickner (1953–) Figure
skating.

MR. QUARTERBACK—Sid Luckman (1916–1998) Football.
H/F Luckman received his nickname while playing for
Columbia University. He continued as Mr. Quarterback
for the Chicago Bears from 1939 to 1950.

MR. QUARTERBACK—Johnny Unitas (1933–) Football.
H/F Also called JOHNNY U.

MR. RANGER—Rod Gilbert (1941–) Hockey. In 1972, the
Rangers featured a G-A-G Line with Gilbert (forty-two
goals), Ratelle (forty-six goals) and Hadfield (fifty
goals). Also called HOT ROD and ROCKY.

MR. ROBINSON—David Robinson (1965–) Basketball.
This 7' 1" center was the NBA's 1992 Defensive Player
of the Year. That year he was also a member of the

DREAM TEAM; he was a member of the 1988 Olympic team, too. His nickname is a humorous reference to the hit song "Mrs. Robinson."

MISTER ROGERS—Mike Rogers (1954–) Hockey.
The nickname alludes to a popular host of a television show for children.

MR. ROLLER DERBY—Charlie O'Connell (active 1940s and 1950s) Roller skating. O'Connell was a star of the Roller Derby for twenty years and one of its highest paid players.

MR. SCOOP—Al Oliver (1946–) Baseball.
Oliver seemed able to scoop up everything that came his way in the outfield.

MR. STONEFACE—Bud Grant (1927–) Football coach.

MR. SUNSET—Jeff Hakman (1948–) Surfing.
Hakman was a world champion surfer by the time he was seventeen. His life is chronicled in the book—*Mr. Sunset* by Phil Jarratt.

MR. SUNSHINE—Ernie Banks (1931–) Baseball ss. **H/F** Also called MR. CUB.

MR. TENNIS—Perry Jones (1888–1970) Tennis.
Jones set up many junior programs and tennis clinics for young players on the West Coast.

MR. TIGER—Al Kaline (1934–) Baseball. **H/F**
He spent his entire career with the Detroit Tigers.

MR. ZIG ZAG—Jim Zorn (active 1976–1987) Football.
This quarterback for the Seattle Seahawks was unpredictable. Sometimes when he was stopped, he would run every which way attempting to break away.

MITCH THE STITCH—Mike Mitchell (1956–) Basketball.
This San Antonio Spurs forward sewed his own clothes.

MITCHELL METEOR—Howie Morenz (1902–1937) Hockey.
Also called THE BABE RUTH OF HOCKEY, THE CANADIEN COMET, THE HURTLING HABITANT, and THE STRATFORD STREAK.

MITE MANAGER—Miller Huggins (1879–1929) Baseball 2b/mgr. **H/F** Also called HUG.

M L—Michael Leon Carr (1951–) Basketball f-g.

MO—Lonzell Hill (active 1987–1990) Football rw.

MO—Dennis Layton (1948–) Basketball.
After his playing days with the USC Trojans were over, this guard was the first pick of the Phoenix Suns.

MO—Francis Mahoney (1927–) Basketball.

MO—Maurice Martin (1964–) Basketball f-g.

MOANIN' MATTY—Madison Bell (19__–) Football coach.
Moanin' Matty would make predictions of disaster each week in order to get his team psyched up.

MODEL [THE]—Rick Martel (19–) Wrestling.
Not only is The Model a wrestler, but his two brothers, Pierre and Maurice, were also wrestlers who sometimes teamed up for tag-team matches. Maurice, unfortunately, lost his life in a wrestling accident.

MOE—Edward Frank Burtschy (1922–) Baseball.
Moe was short for Molasses Foot—a nickname given to this pitcher because he was so slow.

MOE—Myron Walter Drabowsky (1935–) Baseball p.

MOE—Morris Roberts (1907–) Hockey.
Morris played in goal for the Boston Bruins, the New York Americans, and the Washington Lions of the Eastern League.

MOE—Morris Udall (1922–) Basketball f.

MOGUL [THE]—Eddie Gottlieb (1898–1979) Basketball.
H/F Gottlieb organized the overseas tours of the Harlem Globetrotters before taking charge of the Philadelphia Warriors as a coach and owner.

MOLESTER [THE]—Lester Hayes (1955–) Football.
Played 1977–1986 for Oakland and the Los Angeles Raiders.

MONEY—Eddie Murray (active 1981–) Football.
This kicker was right on the money in forty of forty-two field goals from 1988 to 1989.

MONEY BAGS—Tom Qualters (1935–) Baseball.
This nickname referred to Qualters signing as a bonus baby. He came up empty though. In 1953, he registered an ERA of 162.0. During his three years in the majors, he neither won nor lost a game.

MONGO—Steve McMichael (1980–1991) Football rw.

MONGOOSE—Eddie Lukon (1920–) Baseball of.

MONK—Walter John Dubiel (1919–1969) Baseball.
Some thought Dubiel looked more like a cowled monk than a capped ballplayer. In 1951, he was the pitcher of record for four games and four games in relief, but he was 2–2 with a 2.30 ERA in both.

MONK—Don Meineke (1930–) Basketball.
Meineke was a two-time All-American for Dayton, and in 1953 the first Rookie of the Year for the Fort Wayne Pistons.

MONKEY—Pete Hotaling (1856–1928) Baseball of.

MONSTER [THE]—Dick Radatz (1937–) Baseball.

At 6' 6" and 230 pounds, reliever Radatz cut an imposing figure on the mound.

MONTANA RED—Don Tate Rodeo.

MONTE—Monford Irvin (1919–) Baseball of. **H/F**

MONTE—John Montgomery Ward (1860–1925) Baseball.
H/F Ward threw shutouts in his first two games and also hurled a perfect game on his way to a record of 39–24 before switching to shortstop because of a sore arm. So, after setting twenty-six records as a pitcher, he went on to establish twenty-nine as a shortstop and eighteen as a batter. Ward also became the president of the first baseball players' association.

MOOCHIE—Freddie Patek (1944–) Baseball.
This shortstop was only 5' 5" and weighed 148. Also called THE FLEA.

MOOKIE—Willie Wilson (1956–) Baseball.
When Wilson was a youngster back in South Carolina, mookie was the way he pronounced milk. Mookie's love for the game was total. In 1978, this outfielder was married at home plate.

MOON—Ralph Baker (active 1964–1974) Football lb.

MOON—William Wilbur Evans (1907–deceased) Lacrosse.
H/F Moon was one of the best lacrosse players in the late 1920s.

MOON—Lawrence A. Mullins (1908–1968) Football.
This coach was named after Moon Mullins in the funny papers.

MOON MAN—Jay Johnstone (1945–) Baseball.
On a 1984 Fleer baseball card, Moon Man Johnstone is shown wearing an umbrella hat. Received his nickname from his way-out sense of humor. Moon Man Johnstone, in fact, is the author of several humorous baseball books, including *Over the Edge.*

MOON MAN [THE]—Greg Minton (1951–) Baseball.
On his day off, this pitcher got a sunburned bum.

MOONIE—Lowell Miller (1899–1962) Baseball.
This catcher had a round face.

MOONLIGHT—Archibald Graham (1879–1965) Baseball.
This outfielder who briefly appeared in only one game for the Giants was the basis for the character in the novel *Shoeless Joe* and the movie *Field of Dreams.*

MOONLIGHT ACE—Fred Fussell (1895–1966) Baseball.
In 1933, Fussell pitched a minor-league no-hitter as darkness fell.

MOONMAN—Mike Shannon (1939–) Baseball.
His Cardinal teammates sometimes thought Shannon acted like he was from outer space.

MOOSE—Dale Alexander (1903–1978) Baseball.
In 1932, this big first baseman batted .367.

MOOSE—Tom Boerwinkle (1945–) Basketball.
This 7 foot, 270-pound center got his nickname from "Bullwinkle the Moose" of cartoon fame.

MOOSE—Vine Boryla (1927–) Basketball f.

MOOSE—Walter Dropo (1923–) Baseball.
This first baseman's nickname had to do with his size (6' 5", 220 pounds) and his birthplace (Moosup, Connecticut).

MOOSE—Andre Dupont (1949–) Hockey.
Along with Dave Schultz and Bob Kelly, this big defenseman was an intimidator on the Philadelphia Flyers in the early 1970s.

MOOSE—George Earnshaw (1900–1976) Baseball.
Called Moose for his size (6' 4", 210 pounds), this pitcher had a career record of 127–93.

MOOSE—Carl Eller (1942–) Football.
At 6' 6" and 265 pounds, Ellers was a mainstay on the PURPLE PEOPLE EATERS.

MOOSE—F. X. Goheen (1894–1979) Hockey. **H/F**
Goheen was a defenseman on the U.S. team in the 1920 Winter Olympics.

MOOSE—Bryan Haas (1956–) Baseball p.

MOOSE—Ernie Johnson (active 1900s) Hockey. **H/F**
Johnson was a defenseman on the Montreal Wanderers.

MOOSE—Bob Lee (1937–) Baseball.
At 6' 3", 225 pounds, Lee was an imposing figure on the mound. Also called HORSE.

MOOSE—Amos Marsh (1939–) Football.
His nickname refers not only to his size, but is also a sly variation on his first name.

MOOSE—Harry Elwood McCormick (1881–1962) Baseball.
This outfielder was the first dependable pinch-hitter in the major leagues. A newspaper called McCormick Moose because of his eight-foot stride when he ran.

MOOSE—Gordon Ephraim Sherritt (1922–) Hockey.

MOOSE—Bill Skowron (1930–) Baseball.
Apparently this first baseman was not named for his size, but after Mussolini (because it was said Moose bore a resemblance to IL Duce when he was a child).

MOOSE—Wilbur Thompson (1921–) Track and field. This 6 foot, 195 pound shot-putter set a world record of 56' 2" in taking the gold medal at the 1948 Olympic Games.

MOOSE—Elmer Vasko (1935–) Hockey d.

MOOSE—Harry Percival Watson (1923–1957) Hockey lw. **H/F** Also called WHIPPER.

MOOSE—Earl Wilson (1934–) Baseball p.

MORNING GLORY—Alonzo Mourning (1970–) Basketball. This 6' 9" player from Georgetown was chosen second in the 1992 NBA draft by the Charlotte Hornets.

MORRIS—Eugene Lukowich (1956–) Hockey lw.

MORTIMER SNERD—Dick Selma (1943–) Baseball. Selma's nickname came about because he made some of teammates think of the Charlie Bergen dummy.

MOSES—Joe Shipley (1935–) Baseball. Shipley was 0–1 after a four-year career.

MOSEY—Moses King (1884–1956) Boxing coach.

MOTHER—Walter Watson (1865–1898) Baseball. Watson pitched long enough to lose one game and get a nickname. Mother meant he neither smoked, drank, swore, brawled, lied, nor cheated—things every self-respecting ballplayer did in those days.

MOTHER OF AMERICAN WOMEN'S SWIMMING [THE]—Charlotte Epstein (1885–1938) Swimming coach.

MOTOR CITY COBRA [THE]—Thomas Hearns (1958–) Boxing. See HITMAN.

MOTOR MOUTH—Paul Blair (1944–) Baseball. Blair was an outfielder who loved to talk.

MOTSY—Phil Handler (1908–1968) Football. This coach's nickname was short for Motzoh. His record was 7–34.

MOUNT—Jack Morris (1956–) Baseball. On the pitching mound, Morris has been known to blow his stack at umpires.

MOUNT ALCINDOR—Lewis Alcindor (Kareem Abdul-Jabbar) (1947–) Basketball. At fifteen, Alcindor was 7 feet tall; in the NBA, he was 7' 1⅜". Also, called BIG A. See LEW-CLA.

MOUNTAIN MAN—John Kruk (1961–) Baseball. Standing 5' 10" and sometimes weighing 220 pounds, this first baseman is a throwback to junk food and not staying in shape. Health habits aside, however, he batted over .300 in his first two years in the majors.

MOUNTAIN MAN—Bill Walton (1952–1986) Basketball. **H/F** In 1977, a shaggy-headed Walton played center for the Portland Trailblazers. It was publicized that he ate nuts and berries, went for long walks in the woods, and meditated in the mountains.

MOUNTAIN MUSIC—Cliff Melton (1912–1986) Baseball. This pitcher liked to accompany himself on guitar as he sang country music from back home in the mountains of Tennessee. Also called COUNTRY MUSIC and MICKEY MOUSE.

MOUNTAIN STAG—Ben Hart (active mid1800s) Track and field. Hart got his nickname because of his name. The best long jump of this English professional athlete was 23' 6".

MOUSE—Darrel Davis (active 1990–) Football de.

MOUSE—Pat Fischer (active 1961–1977) Football. This defensive back was only 5' 7" and 170 pounds.

MOUSE—Ken McFadden (19__–) Basketball.

MOUSE—Mel Riebe (1916–) Basketball g-f.

MOUSE [THE]—Bruce Strauss (1952–) Boxing. In December of 1997, the film —*The Mouse*—opened. It is about the life of Bruce Strauss who made a living in boxing by being a professional opponent. He allegedly once changed weight classes by fighting with fifteen pounds of lead in his pants. He is sometimes referred to as Boxing's greatest loser. A mouse in slang parlance is a black eye, and Strauss received many of them.

MOUSEY—Roy T. Hartsfield (1925–) Baseball 2b.

MOUSEY—Maury Wills (1932–) Baseball. This shortstop may have been small, but he was big on the base paths. In 1962, Wills stole 104 bases to shatter Ty Cobb's single season record of ninety-six.

MOUSIE—Walter Blum. Horse racing. **H/F** Blum was small even by jockey standards.

MOUTH [THE]—Howard Cosell (1920–1995) Sports announcer.

MOVE UP JOE—Joe Gerhardt (1855–1922) Baseball. This second baseman tried to take the extra base.

MOXIE—Edwin G. Divis (active 1917) Baseball. He was a Cleveland sandlot star who unsuccessfully tried out for the Athletics.

MOXIE—Emory Hengle (1857–1924) Baseball 2b. Moxie had a meaning similar to gumption.

MUD—Modere Bruneteau (1914–) Hockey rw.

MUDCAT—Jim Grant (1935–) Baseball. As a kid growing up in Lacoochie, Florida, Grant could usually be found fishing. On the mound from

1958–1971, he was 145–119.

MUDD—Modere Bruneteau (1914–) Hockey.
Bruneteau, a right wing for the Detroit Red Wings (1935–1946), scored the winning goal in the longest game ever played in the NHL. This game between the Red Wings and Montreal Maroons on March 24, 1936, lasted 116 minutes and 30 seconds.

MUDDY—Harold Ruel (1896–1963) Baseball.
This catcher for the Washington Senators fell into a mud puddle as a child.

MUFFIN—Helen Spencer-Devlin. Golf.
Spencer-Devlin bore the mark on her forehead of the forceps used during her difficult delivery. This mark was in the shape of a muffin.

MUGSY—Tyrone Bogues (1965–) Basketball g.
He stands on 5' 3" and is the shortest player ever to play in the NBA.

MUGGSY—Eddie Stanky (1916–) Baseball.
The nickname of this second baseman and manager was for his tendency to act like a tough guy. See THE BRAT.

MUGS—Max J. Lorber (active 1923–1924) Football.

MULDOON'S CYCLONE—Fred Morris (1872–1911) Boxing.
Morris was managed by a William Muldoon who toured the country with a troupe of boxers and wrestlers.

MULE—Gary Bolden (active 1987–) Football dt.

MULE—Dick Dietz (1941–) Baseball c.

MULE—Ray Fosse (1947–) Baseball c.

MULE—George Haas (1903–1974) Baseball.
Haas, an outfielder, had a workhorse-like .292 batting average for twelve years.

MULE [THE]—Merlin Olsen (1940–) Football.
Olsen (6' 5", 270 pounds), a perennial Pro Bowl tackle, was a key member of the L. A. Rams. See FEARSOME FOURSOME.

MULE—John Reeves Watson (1896–1949) Baseball.
This pitcher had the work ethic of a pack horse; Watson hurled three complete doubleheaders during his career.

MUMBLES—Bill Tremel (1929–) Baseball.
This pitcher actually murmured more than he mumbled.

MURDER—Don Murdoch (1956–) Hockey rw.

MURPH—Erwin Groves Chamberlain (1915–) Hockey c.

MURPH THE SURF—Jack Murphy (19–) Surfing.
The real Murph the Surf won several national surfing championships before a life of crime that crested with twenty-one years in prison.

MURPH THE SURF—William Murphy (1944–) Baseball.
This New York Giants outfielder's nickname was after the famous New York City jewel thief.

MUSCLES—Joe Medwick (1911–1975) Baseball of. **H/F**
Medwick was a fanatic about keeping fit. Also called DUCKIE WUCKIE and MICKEY. See DUCKY.

MUSCLES—Ken Rosewall (1934–) Tennis. **H/F**

MUSCLES—Thomas Upton (1926–) Baseball ss.

MUSCLES—Lloyd James Waner (1906–) Baseball of.
Also called (with Paul Waner) POISON TWINS. See LITTLE POISON.

MUSH—Maurice Dubofsky (active 1929–1931) Football g.

MUSH—Harold March (1908–) Hockey.
March was a high scoring right wing for the Chicago Black Hawks from 1928 to 1945.

MUSH—Donald Muller (active 1930s) Football.

MUSHY CALLAHAN—Vincent Morris Scheer (active 1920s) Boxing. Scheer was the junior welterweight champion from 1926 to 1930.

MUSICIANLY BOXER—Rory Calhoun (1934–) Boxing.
Rory—his real name was Herman—Calhoun was also a musician.

MUSKRAT—Bill Shipke (1882–1940) Baseball.
The real name of Shipke, a third baseman, was Shipkrethaver. Also called SKIPPER.

MUTE ROCKNE—Bob Pulford (1936–) Hockey.
Pulford may have been an inspiring coach, but he was a man of few words.

MUTT—Jewel Ens (1889–1950) Baseball coach.

MUTT—Johnny Riddle (1905–) Baseball c.

MUTT—David Carter Williams (1891–1962) Baseball.
This nickname was an allusion to the character in "Mutt and Jeff," for Williams was a tall pitcher.

MUZZ—Frederick Murray Patrick (1915–1998) Hockey d.

MX—Darrell Green (active 1983–) Football.
Noted for his speed, this defensive back of the Washington Redskins was nicknamed for a missile.

MYSTERIOUS BILLY—Amos Smith (1871–1937) Boxing.
Smith held the American welterweight title from 1892 to 1894.

NACHO—Ignacio Jiminez Boxing.

NAKINA—Dalton J. Smith (1915–) Hockey c.

NASHVILLE NARCISSUS [THE]—Red Lucas (1902–1986) Baseball p.

NAUGATUCK NUGGET [THE]—Frank Joseph (Spec) Shea (1920–) Baseball. Shea was from Naugatuck, Connecticut. His best year was his rookie year when he was 14–5 and picked up the win at the All-Star Game. He was also called SPEC for his freckles.

NAILER [THE]—Billy Stevens (1936–1981) Boxing. A bareknuckles heavyweight champion of England who nailed his opponents.

NAP—George Napoleon Rucker (1884–1970) Baseball p.

NAPOLEON OF THE PRIZE RING [THE]—Tom Sayers. Boxing. A bareknuckles champion in the 1800s.

NAPOLEON OF PROMOTERS—Tex Rickard (1870–1929) Promoter. Also called DINK and MAGNIFICENT RUBE. See KING OF SPORTS PROMOTERS.

NAPOLEON OF THE RING [THE]—Jem Belcher (1781–1811) Boxing (English bareknuckles).

NASHVILLE NARCISSUS [THE]—Charles Fred (Red) Lucas (1902–) Baseball p.

NASTY—Ilie Nastase (1946–) Tennis.

NAT—Ignatius Volpe (1919–) Basketball. After starring at Manhattan, Volpe became a college and high-school basketball coach.

NATE THE GREAT—Nate Thurmond (1941–) Basketball c. Also called DR. DEFENSE.

NATE THE SKATE—Nate Archibald (1948–) Basketball. See TINY.

NATURAL [THE]—James Murphy (?–1924) Auto racing.

NAVY BILL—William Ingram (1897–1943) Football coach.

NAVY'S DESTROYER—Joe Bellino (1938–) Football. Also called DYNAMITE JOE, JOE THE JET, and THE PLAYER WHO IS NEVER CAUGHT FROM BEHIND.

NEBRASKA WILDCAT [THE]—Ace Hudkins (1905–1973) Boxing.

NED—Edward Simmons Irish (1905–1982) Basketball. **H/F** Irish introduced the basketball doubleheader to help make Madison Square Garden the MECCA OF BAS-KETBALL. In 1946, Irish founded the New York Knicks.

NEEDLE—Frank Gates (1921–) Basketball g.

NELS—Nelson Stewart (1902–1957) Hockey. **H/F**

NELSON—Frederick Pyatt (1953–) Hockey c.

NEMO—Harry Liebold (1892–1977) Baseball. At 5' 6" and 157 pounds, Liebold was nicknamed for the roly-poly Little Nemo cartoon character. In a career that spanned from 1913 to 1925, this outfielder played in four World Series.

NEON DEION—Deion Sanders (active 1989–) Football, baseball. Also called PRIME TIME.

NEON LEON—Leon Spinks (1953–) Boxing (heavyweight).

NERVOUS GREEK [THE]—Lou Skizas (1932–) Baseball 3b/of.

NEVADA—Jack Rose Rodeo.

NEVER NERVOUS—Pervis Ellison (1967–) Basketball. Ellison, a center, helped Louisville win the NCAA championship in 1986.

NEW ORLEANS MULATTO—Andy Bowen (1867–1894) Boxing. Nat Fleischer once said of Bowen that "a braver fighter in American ring history cannot be found."

NEW SULTAN OF SWAT—Henry Aaron (1934–) Baseball of. **H/F** See HAMMERIN' HANK.

NEW YORK FATS—Rudolf Walter Wanderone, Jr. (1903–) Pool. See MINNESOTA FATS.

NEWK—Don Newcombe (1926–) Baseball p.

NEWT—Fred Hunter (1880–1963) Baseball 1b.

NIBS—Thomas Neil Phillips (1880–1923) Hockey. **H/F** Phillips was a forward for the Kenora Thistles before the days of the NFL.

NIBS—Clarence Price (1889–1968) Basketball. Price was one of the most successful college coaches ever with a 463–298 record at California from 1925 to 1954.

NICK—Norman Andrew Cullop (1887–1961) Baseball p.

NIGHT RIDER—Don Larsen (1929–) Baseball p.

NIP—Horace Ashenfelter (1923–) Track. Ashenfelter won a gold medal in the steeplechase at the 1952 Helsinki Olympic Games, passing Kazontsev in the last stage of the race.

NIP—Fred Felber (1909–) Football. Played for only one pro season, in 1932.

NIPPER—Don O'Hearn (1928–) Hockey g.

NO D—Ernie DiGregorio (1951–) Basketball.

NO KID—Fredrick Glover (1928–) Hockey. Glover's pro career began at twenty-one and ended at twenty-five.

NO-NECK—Walter Williams (1943–) Baseball. This outfielder's head seemed to be set squarely on his shoulders. His best year was in 1961 when he hit .304 for the White Sox. His ten-year average was .270.

NO-NONSENSE—Leo W. Williams (active 1980s) Track and field. Williams was all business around the high-jumping pit. In 1981, he set a NCAA record of 7' 5¼".

NOODLES—Frank Zupo (1939–) Baseball c.

NORDY—Frank Hoffman (active 1930s) Football.

NORT—Darrel Chaney (1948–) Baseball. Channey, who played in the infield for Cincinnati and Atlanta, had the word *Nort* on the back of his Braves' uniform. Nort is short for Ed Norton of *The Honeymooners*.

NORWEGIAN DOLL—Sonja Henie (1912–1969) Figure skating. See GOLDEN GIRL.

NUMBER ONE—Bill McGowen (1896–1954) Baseball umpire. **H/F**

NUMBER SIX—Bill Russell (1934–) Basketball c. **H/F**

OATS—Joe DeMaestri (1928–) Baseball.

OBS—Orville Russell Heximer (1910–) Hockey.

OCTOBULL—Moses Malone (1955–) Basketball.

OCTOPUS [THE]—Martin (Marty) Marion (1917–) Baseball. Marion won this nickname because of his great reach at shortstop. See SLATS.

ODIE—Ogilvie Cleghorn (1891–1956) Hockey.

ODIE—Norman E. Lowe (1928–) Hockey.

ODIE—Adrian Smith (1936–) Basketball. Smith's nickname was from a character on the *Grand Ole Opry*. Odie played guard on Kentucky's 1958 NCAA championship team, the 1960 Olympic team, and in the NBA on the Cincinnati Royals, San Francisco Warriors, and Virginia Squires.

OH! OH!—Orlando Woolridge (1959–) Basketball.

OIL—Earl Smith (1897–1963) Baseball.

OIL CAN—Dennis Boyd (1959–) Baseball. Back where he comes from in, Meridian, Mississippi, people refer to beer as oil.

O. J.—Otis Anderson (1957–) Football.

OKLAHOMA KID [THE]—Alvan Adams (1964–) Basketball. This center for the Phoenix Suns had three times been the Big Eight conference's Player of the Year while at the University of Oklahoma.

OL' ARKANSAS—Lonnie Warnecke (1909–1976) Baseball p/umpire. Also, called ARKANSAS HUMMINGBIRD, COUNTRY, and DIXIE.

OL' DIZ—Jay Hannah Dean (1911–1974) Baseball. This Card pitcher went by the name of Jerome Herman Dean as well. Also called THE GREAT MAN. See DIZZY DEAN.

OL PERFESSER [THE]—Charles Dillon Stengel (1890–1975) Baseball of/mgr. **H/F** See CASEY.

OL' REDHEAD [THE]—Walter "Red" Barber (1908–1992) Sportscaster. See RED.

OL' STUBBLEBEARD—Burleigh Grimes (1893–1985) Baseball. **H/F** Also called BOILING BOILY and WIRE WHISKERS.

OLD ALEX—William Anderson Alexander (1899–1950) Football coach. Also called ALEX and OLD MAN.

OLD BONES—Joe Brown (1926–) Boxing. Brown won the championship at the advanced age of thirty. From 1956 to 1961, he defended his lightweight crown eleven times.

OLD BONES—Harrison Dillard (1923–) Track and field. **H/F**

OLD BONES—Horace McKinney (1919–) Basketball. McKinney 's last season was 1951–1952 with the Boston Celtics.

OLD BONES—Earl Morrall (1934–) Football. Morral certainly did have old bones. He sported a twenty-one-year NFL career as a backup quarterback to no less than three Hall-of-Famers.

OLD CHOCOLATE—George Godfrey (1853–deceased) Boxing. This African American had his first bout at the age of twenty-nine.

OLD DOG—MacArthur Lane (1942–) Football. Lane was still playing for the Kansas City Chiefs at the age of thirty-four. He also has a liking for old things. "I hate to see anything of the past destroyed," Old Dog once said.

OLD DOG—Louis Ritter (1875–1952) Baseball.

OLD FAITHFUL—Gene Woodling (1922–) Baseball. With an average of .318, Woodling was as dependable a hard-hitting left fielder for the Yankees in their five straight World Series (1949–1953) as the geyser in Yellowstone.

OLD 5-4-1—Von Hayes (1958–) Baseball. The Philadelphia Phillies traded five players (Jay Baller, Julio Franco, Manny Trillo, George Vukovich, and Gerry [Rats] Willard) to the Cleveland Indians for this outfielder.

OLD FOLKS—Ellis Kinder (1914–1968) Baseball. This pitcher began his major-league career at thirty-two. His best year was 1949 when he was 23–6, but he was still pitching at the age of forty-three.

OLD FOLKS—Herman Pillette (1895–1960) Baseball.

OLD FOX [THE]—Tommy Prothro. Football coach.

OLD FRITZ—Ferdinand Henry John Zivic (1913–) Boxing. Also called FRITZIE.

OLD GRAY FOX—Everett Case (1900–1966) Basketball.

OLD HUSTLER [THE]—Joe Mathes (1891–1978) Baseball. During a career that lasted almost seventy years (as a second baseman and a scout), Mathes called everyone Hustler.

OLD INDIAN [THE]—Early Wynn (1920–) Baseball. **H/F** Also called GUS.

OLD IRON PANTS—Leo Robert Meyer (1898–) Football coach. Also called DUTCH and SATURDAY FOX.

OLD MAN—William Anderson Alexander (1899–1950) Football coach. Also called ALEX and OLD ALEX.

OLD MAN—Gil Johnson (active late 1940s) Football. A balding Johnson also played tailback during Doak (DOAKER) Walker's years at SMU.

OLD MAN OF THE GRIDIRON—George V. Kenneally (1902–) Football coach.

OLD MAN RIVER—Julius Boros (1920–) Golf. See THE MOOSE.

OLD MASTER—Joseph Sarfuss Butts (1874–1910) Boxing. Butts' other name was Joe Gans. (Actually, his real name was Gaines.) Joe Gans fought Battling Nelson in 1906 for a purse of $35,000 put up by Tex Rickard, the sports promoter. In the forty-second round, Gans won because of a low blow by Nelson.

OLD MASTER—Bob Gibson (1935–) Baseball. Also called HOOT.

OLD MASTER—Willie Pep (1922–) Boxing. Pep's real name was William Gugliermo Papaleo. Also called WILL-O'-THE MASTER.

OLD MASTER [THE]—Willie Hoppe (1887–1959) Billiards. Also called Boy Wonder.

OLD 98—Tom Harmon (1919–1990) Football. This halfback gained 2,338 yards during his career at the University of Michigan. Amos Alonzo Stagg, THE GRAND OLD MAN OF FOOTBALL, once said: "I'll take Harmon on my team and you can have all the rest."

OLD PARD—Win Ballou (1897–1963) Baseball. Ballou may have been called this because the pitcher was from horse-racing country in Kentucky.

OLD RELIABLE—Jules Carlson (1904–) Football coach.

OLD RELIABLE—Tommy Henrich (1913–) Baseball of.

Also called THE CLUTCH.

OLD RELIABLE—Joe Start (1842–1927) Baseball 1b.

OLD ROMAN [THE]—Charles Comiskey (1859–1931) Baseball. Comiskey received his nickname because with his noble demeanor, his white hair and profile the owner of the Chicago White Sox had the appearance of someone who could be on an old Roman coin.

OLD SARGE—Jim Bagby, Sr. (1889–1954) Baseball. This pitcher's nickname comes from a character in a Broadway play, Sargent Jimmy Bagby.

OLD SARGE—Charles Evard Street (1882–1951) Baseball c. See GABBY.

OLD SCRAP IRON—Clint Courtney (1927–1965) Baseball c.

OLD SCOTSMAN—Gordon McLendon (active 1920s and 1930s) Sports announcer.

OLD SECOND INNING—Tim McCarver (1941–) Baseball. McCarver, a catcher for the Cards and the Phillies usually disappeared into the dugout for a pitstop between the first and second inning.

OLD STARLIGHT—Edward C. Rollins (active 1885–1905) Boxing. This fighter began his career when he was thirty-four and was still at it when he was fifty-six.

OLD STONEFINGERS—Richard Lee Stuart (1932–) Baseball 1b. Also called IRREPRESSIBLE EGOIST.

OLD STUBBLEBEARD—Burleigh Arland Grimes (1893–1985) Baseball p. **H/F** Also called LAST OF THE SPITBALL PITCHERS and SENATOR.

OLD TOM—Tom Morris, Sr. (1821–1908) Golf. Morris was runner-up in the first British Open in 1860, but then went on to win in 1861, 1862, 1864, and 1867. Along with his son, YOUNG TOM, the Morrises won the British Open eight times.

OLD TREETOP—Cliff Robinson (1960–) Basketball. TV announcer Al McGuire kept calling him by this nickname during a game when he couldn't remember the center's name.

OLD TRUE BLUE—Abram Harding Richardson (1855–1931) Baseball 2b/of. Also called HARDY.

OLD WOMAN IN THE RED CAP [THE]—Charles Pabor (active player in the 1870s) Baseball. Received his nickname because of his constant complaining.

OLDEST ROOKIE [THE]—William Alsup (1939–) Auto racing.

OLE—Harold Olson (1895–1953) Basketball.

Olson was 259–197 as the coach at Ohio State from 1923 to 1946.

OLLIE—Elmer Oliphant (1892–1975) Football, basketball. An All-American in both sports, Oliphant went to Purdue and West Point.

OLLIE ROCCO—Oliver Reinikka (1901–) Hockey. Press agent Johnny Bruno of the New York Rangers gave Finnish player Oliver Reinikka this name to attract the attention of the many Italians in the New York area. Ollie went scoreless in the sixteen games he played.

ON THE GAS—Danny Ongais. Auto racing.

ONE ARM—Hugh Daily (1857–deceased) Baseball. This pitcher, whose real name was Harry Criss, had lost his left hand in a hunting accident. This didn't stop him from compiling a league-leading strike-out total of 483 in 1884. His six-year career won-loss record was 73–89.

ONE-ARMED SCOUT—Henry Crisp (1896–1970) Football scout.

ONE GRAND—Ernest J. Schmidt Basketball. **H/F**

ONE-PLAY McAFEE—George McAfee (1918–) Football. **H/F** This halfback gained his nickname by breaking games open—scoring thirty-nine touchdowns during his career, almost all on long runs from scrimmage. McAfee also averaged 12.8 yards per punt return.

ONIONHEAD—Gilberto Reyes (1963–) Baseball. The shape of this catcher's head was like one.

ONLY [THE]—Edward Nolan (1857–1913) Baseball p.

ONWARD CHRISTIAN CAGLE—Christian Keener Cagle (1905–1942) Football b. Also called RED.

OOM PAUL—Otto Krueger (1876–1961) Baseball. This shortstop was given the same nickname as that of a South African leader.

ORANGE CRUSH—Steve Atwater (1966–) Football. Plays for the Denver Broncos and wears a bright orange jersey as part of the Bronco's uniform. Orange crush is also the name of a popular soft drink. Atwater earned his nickname because he is one of the hardest hitting safeties in the NFL.

ORANGE JUICE—O. J. Simpson (1947–) Football hb. **H/F** Contrary to what some fans thought, Simpson's real name was Orenthal James. See THE JUICE.

ORIGINAL WHITE HOPE [THE]—Carl Morris (1887–1951) Boxing (heavyweight). Also called SADULPA GIANT.

ORVILLE MOODY—Terry Kennedy (1956–) Baseball.

This catcher was known to be moody.

OTT—Ehrhardt Henry Heller (1910–) Hockey d.

OTTAWA FIREMAN [THE]—Alex Connell (1902–1958) Hockey. **H/F** Connell, a goalie for the Ottawa Senators, once held the opposition scoreless for six straight games.

OTTO THE SWATTO—Otto Velez (1950–) Baseball of/dh.

OUR 'ENERY—Henry Cooper Boxing. Cooper was popular in that part of London where they swallow their h(s).

OVERLAND MAN—John Bain Sutherland (1889–1948) Football coach. Also called DOUR SCOT, JOCK, and SCOTSMAN.

OWATONNA THUNDERBOLT [THE]—Herb Joesting (1905–1963) Football. He played professional football 1929–1932. He hailed from Minnesota.

OWL WITHOUT A VOWEL [THE]—Bill Mlkvy (1931–) Basketball. Mlkvy, who played for the Temple Owls, once scored seventy-three points in a game. That same year, 1951, the All-American averaged 29.2 points per game.

OWNIE—Owen T. Carroll (1903–1975) Baseball p.

OYSTER—Thomas P. Burns (1864–1928) Baseball if/of.

OYSTER—Joe Martina (1889–1962) Baseball p.

OX—Oscar George Eckhardt (1901–1950) Baseball. This outfielder was 6' 1" and 185 pounds, hardly ox-like by today's standards.

OX—Grover Emerson (active 1931–1938) Football. 6 feet and 190 pounds, this guard played for the Portsmouth Spartans, the Detroit Lions, and the Brooklyn Dodgers.

OX—John Da Grosa (1902–1953) Football coach.

OX—Frank Pennie. Football.

OYSTER JOE—Joe Martina. Baseball (Minor leagues). In 1921, this pitching star was traded from Dallas to New Orleans for two barrels of oysters. After that he was known as Oyster Joe.

OZARK IKE—Terry Bradshaw (1946–) Football qb. **H/F**

OZARK IKE—Gus Zernial (1923–) Baseball. Zernial was actually from Texas, but a minor-league manager thought the outfielder looked like the character from the Ozark Ike comic strip.

OZZIE—Osborne Cowles (1899–) Basketball.

PA—William H. Corbin (1864–1943) Football.

PACKY—Patrick McFarland (1888–1936) Boxing.

PADDY—Pat De Marco (1928–) Boxing.

PADDY—Patrick Joseph Moran (active 1902–1913) Hockey.
   H/F Moran was the goalie for the Quebec Bulldogs when they won the Stanley Cup in 1912 and 1913.

PADDY—George F. Patterson (1906–) Hockey.

PADDY—A. P. Smithwick (1927–1973) Horse racing.

PAGS—Mike Pagliarulo (1960–) Baseball.
   Manager Yogi Berra may have started this nickname. At least this is what he called the third baseman.

PANAMA—Al Brown (1902–1951) Boxing.
   Al Brown was born in Panama.

PANCAKE—Broderick Perkins (1954–) Baseball 1b.
   Perkins hit .240 for San Diego in 1978.

PANCHO—Frank J. Snyder (1893–1962) Baseball.

PANCHO VILLA—Juan Berenguer (1954–) Baseball.
   From Panama, this pitcher sometimes had a mean look about him.

PANQUE—Felipe Rojas Alou (1935–) Baseball.
   This outfielder was born on the Feast Day of San Pancracio.

PANTS—Clarence H. Rowland (1879–1969) Baseball mgr/umpire.

PAPA—James Thomas Bell (1903–) Baseball. **H/F**
   Also called BLACK TY COBB. See COOL PAPA.

PAPA—Jim Brewer (1951–) Basketball.

PAPPY—Charlie Joachim (1920–) Basketball.

PAPPY—Art Lewis (1911–1962) Football player/coach.

PAPPY—Lynn O. Waldorf (1902–1981) Football coach.

PARAKEET—Tito Fuentes (1944–) Baseball.
   This second baseman chattered away indiscriminately to anyone within earshot.

PARISIAN BOB—Bob Caruthers (1864–1911) Baseball.
   Caruthers, who journeyed to Paris in 1875, was a pitcher with the distinction of hitting two homers in one game.

PARTRIDGE—George Adams (active 1879) Baseball.

PARTY—Stan Partenheimer (1891–1971) Baseball.

PAT—Clifford Rankin Crawford (1902–1994) Baseball.

PAT—Martin Joseph Egan (1918–) Hockey.

PAT—Marlin Harder (active 1946–1953) Football.
   Harder was a 5' 11", 205-pound fullback for the Chicago Cardinals and the Detroit Lions.

PAT—Percy Lay Malone (1902–1943) Baseball.

PAT—Harlan Page (1887–1965) Basketball. **H/F**
   Page led the University of Chicago to the national title

in 1908, and coached there from 1911 to 1920, establishing a 200–127 record.

PAT—Joe Patanelli (1919–) Basketball.

PATSY—Francis Charles Winslow Callighen (1906–) Hockey.

PATSY—Patrick Joseph Flaherty (1876–1968) Baseball.

PATSY—Oliver Wendell Tebeau (1864–1918) Baseball.

PD—Percy Duncan Haughton (1876–1924) Football coach.
   Also called HAUGHTON OF HARVARD.

PEA RIDGE—Clyde Day (1899–1934) Baseball.
   Hailing from Pea Ridge, Arkansas, Day would sometimes emit a hog call when he struck out a batter.

PEA SOUP—George Dumont (1895–1956) Baseball.

PEACEFUL VALLEY—Roger Denzer (1871–1949) Baseball.
   This pitcher came from the valley in Minnesota known for its LeSeur peas.

PEACH—Chauncey Fisher (1872–1939) Baseball.

PEACH PIE—Jack O'Connor (1869–1937) Baseball.
   Also called ROWDY JACK.

PEACHES—Jane Bartkowicz (active 1970s) Tennis.
   In 1970, Bartkowicz spoiled Evonne Goolagong's debut on Wimbledon's Centre Court with a 6–4, 6–0 drubbing. See ORIGINAL NINE.

PEACHES—Ray Davis (1905–1995) Baseball p.

PEACHES—Lou Saban (1921–) Football.
   Coach of the Buffalo Bills from 1972 to 1976 and now a high school football coach where his players call him Peaches.

PEACHES—John Charles Werhas (1938–) Baseball.

PEACHTREE BART—Steve Bartkowski (active 1975–1985) Football. Bartkowski got his nickname because he was the quarterback for the Atlanta Falcons.

PEAHEAD—Douglas C. Walker (1899–1970) Football.
   The nickname was because this coach had a slightly smaller head. Walker didn't get a swelled head though he had a winning career record (77–51–6) at Wake Forest from 1936 to 1950.

PEANUT—Jim Davenport (1933–) Baseball.
   This third baseman (not so small at 5' 11", 180 pounds) was also called GOLDEN GLOVE. (He won it in 1962.)

PEANUTS—Marnie Johnson. Baseball (Negro Leagues).
   He received his nickname because of his small size.

PEANUTS—Harry Lee Lowry (1918–1986) Baseball.
   Upon seeing this future outfielder soon after birth, an uncle exclaimed: "He's no bigger than a peanut."

PEANUTS—John Benedict O'Flaherty (1918–) Hockey. This right winger stood 5' 7" and weighed 154 pounds.

PEARL—Dwayne Washington (1964–) Basketball. A high school standout in Brooklyn, then a star at Syracuse, then a guard with the New Jersey Nets.

PEBBLES—Walter Rock (active 1963–1973) Football.

PEBBLY JACK—John W. Glasscock (1859–1947) Baseball. This shortstop received his nickname for the way he groomed the area around his position of pebbles. For five seasons Pebbly Jack led all shortstops in assists, and in one game he was 6 for 6—all singles.

PECK—Bernard Hickman (1911–) Basketball. Hickman's Louisville teams had a 443–183 record from 1945 to 1967.

PECK—Charles Pieculewicz (active 1929–1932) Football.

PECKY—Peter Suder (1916–) Baseball. This second baseman was part of the 1948 Philadelphia As $1,000,000 infield.

PEDLAR—Thomas Palmer (1876–1949) Boxing.

PEE MAN—Daryl Jones. Boxing.

PEE WEE—Thomas Butts (1919–1973) Baseball (Negro Leagues). Only 5' 9" and 145 pounds, Butts was one of the outstanding shortstops in the 1940s. Also called COOL BREEZE.

PEE WEE—Ernie Dunbar. Boxing.

PEE WEE—Melvin Dean Read (1922–) Hockey. This center was only 5' 6" and 165 pounds.

PEE WEE—Harold Henry Reese (1919–) Baseball. This shortstop, who was not short (he was 5' 10"), had been a marbles champion as a youngster back in Louisville. "I didn't use an immie," said Reese, recalling those days. "I used a pee wee." See THE LITTLE COLONEL.

PEE WEE—Robert Rucker (1960–) Boxing.

PEE WEE—Arcadio Suarez. Boxing.

PEE WEE—William Arthur Summerhill (1915–) Hockey. This right winger was 5' 9" and 170 pounds.

PEEK-A-BOO—William Veach (1862–1937) Baseball. This first baseman had to fill in at pitcher one day, so he peeked over to his coach to see if he should throw to first to keep the runner close. He played for Kansas City in 1884 and for Louisville in 1887, then in 1890 he played for Cleveland in the National League and for Pittsburgh.

PEERLESS PAAVO—Paavo Nurmi (1897–1973) Track and field. See THE FLYING FINN and THE PHANTOM FINN.

PEET—Petrus Bothma (1955–) Boxing.

PEGGY—James Beaton O'Neill (1913–) Hockey.

PEGGY—George Parratt (active 1906) Football. On October 27, 1906, quarterback Parratt threw the first forward pass in a football game.

PELLE—Per-Erik Eklund (1963–) Hockey.

PELUSA [HAIR]—Diego Maradona (1960–) Soccer. Maradona, who has a full head of pelusa, led Argentina to the 1986 World Cup championship and to the 1990 final in the World Cup.

PEMBROKE PEACH [THE]—Frank Nighbor (1893–) Hockey. Nighbor, a peach of a player, received his nickname from his hometown of Pembroke, Ontario. Also called DUTCH.

PENGUIN [THE]—Ron Cey (1948–) Baseball. Cey's short legs caused him to waddle somewhat like a penguin. He played third base for seventeen years, appearing in four World Series for the Los Angeles Dodgers.

PENITENTIARY FACE—Jeffrey Leonard (1955–) Baseball.

PENNY—Fred Bailey (1895–1972) Baseball.

PENNY—Pentti Alexander Lund (1925–) Hockey.

PEOPLE'S CHOICE [or, CHERCE] [THE]—Fred Walker (1910–) Baseball. The fans at Ebbets Field had a special place in their hats for this .306 lifetime outfielder from Villa Rica, Georgia. Also called DIXIE.

PEP—Regis J. Kelly (1914–) Hockey.

PEP—John Panelli (1926–). Football.

PEP—Frank Saul (1924–) Basketball.

PEP—David Tobey (1898–) Basketball.

PEP—Lemuel Floyd Young (1907–1962) Baseball. Also called WHITEY.

PEP—Ross Youngs (1897–1927) Baseball. **H/F** In his ten-year career for the New York Giants, Youngs hit .322. He also set the record for most errors and assists for a right fielder in World Series play.

PEPE—Jesus Maria Frias (1948–) Baseball.

PEPI—Joe Pepitone (1940–) Baseball. This first baseman's confessional best-seller was called *Joe, You Coulda Made Us Proud*.

PEPPER—James Philip Austin (1879–1965) Baseball 3b/coach.

PEPPER—Johnny Leonard Roosevelt Martin (1904–1965) Baseball. This outfielder was nicknamed Pepper because of his peppery, spirited play. See WILD HOSS OF THE OSAGE and GASHOUSE GANG.

PEPPER BOX—Richard Bartell (1907–) Baseball. Also called ROWDY DICK and ROWDY RICHARD.

PEPPERMINT—Alfonso Frazer (1948–) Boxing. Frazer was the junior welterweight champion in 1972.

PEPSODENT—Amanda Borden (active l990s) Gymnastics. Her nickname was bestowed upon her at the 1990 Junior Olympics because of her sparkling smile. Pepsodent is the name of a popular toothpaste.

PERK—Percival Galbraith (1899–) Hockey.

PERK—Don Perkins (active 1961–1968) Football.

PERPETUAL MOTION—Henry Armstrong (1912–) Boxing. In 1938, Armstrong held three titles at the same time (featherweight, welterweight, and lightweight).

PET OF THE FANCY—Dick Curtis (active 1820–1928) Boxing. This fan favorite held the lightweight championship.

PETE—Grover Cleveland Alexander (1887–1950) Baseball. **H/F** See OLD PETE.

PETE—Ervin Fox (1909–1966) Baseball.

PETE—Clyde Jennings Manion (1896–1967) Baseball.

PETE—Alvin Rozelle (1926–1996) Football. **H/F** Rozelle was the football commissioner for twenty-nine years.

PETER PUCK—Peter Pocklington Hockey. Former owner of The Edmonton Oilers.

PHAINTING PHIL—Phil Scott. Boxing. Scott lost to Jack Sharkey in 1930.

PHANTOM [THE]—Monte Jackson (active 1975–1983) Football.

PHANTOM [THE]—Julian Javier (1936–) Baseball.

PHANTOM—Joe Malone (1890–1969) Hockey. **H/F** Malone scored seven goals for the Canadiens in a game against the Toronto St. Pats on January 31, 1920. This NHL record has never been broken.

PHANTOM FINN [THE]—Paavo Nurmi (1897–1973) Track and field.

PHAT—Gordon Wilson (1895–1970) Hockey. **H/F**

PHENOMENAL—John Smith (1864–1952) Baseball. The pitcher's real last name was Gammon.

PHIL THE THRILL—Phil Sellers (1953–) Basketball.

PHILADELPHIA JACK—Jack O'Brien (1878–1942) Boxing.

PHILLY DOG—Mike Gale (1950–) Basketball.

PHILOSOPHER [THE]—Vic Sorrell (1901–1972) Baseball. Also called ACE, BABY DOLL, and LAWYER.

PHONEY—Alphonse Martin (1845–1933) Baseball.

PIANO [THE]—Jaime Cardriche Football. Cardriche weighed 395 pounds when he was at Oklahoma State.

PIANO LEGS—George Gore (1857–1933) Baseball. This outfielder's nickname referred to his build; but he also liked bar stools and piano bars. In 1880, he hit a hefty .360 to lead the National League.

PIANO LEGS—Charles Hickman (1876–1934) Baseball. Stocky-legged Hickman played every position except catcher. His adaptability may help to explain his other nickname Cheerful Charlie. He switched from third to first base so fewer balls would roll between his piano legs.

PIANO MOVER—Frank Smith (1879–1952) Baseball. The pitcher's real last name was Schmidt. Also called NIG.

PICK—Lou Dehner (1914–) Basketball. Setting up a pick is a very important play in basketball.

PICK—John Quinn (1885–1956) Baseball. Quinn may have caught only one game in the major leagues in 1911 (Philadelphia), but he was around long enough to pick up a nickname.

PICKLES—Bill Kennedy (1938–) Basketball. In 1960, Kennedy was an All-American guard at Temple.

PIDGE—George Browning (1899–) Basketball. Along with brother Arthur, the Brownings played together in 1921 for the University of Missouri.

PIE—John Albert McKenzie (1937–) Hockey. McKenzie, who played right wing for the Bruins, had a round face that led to his nickname of Pieface, or Pie for short.

PIG—Robert Goff (active 1988–1992) Football.

PIG—Frank House (1930–) Baseball. This catcher, a bonus baby for the Tigers, received his nickname when he really was a baby. Upon hearing his family say he was as "big as a house," Frank repeated it as "pig."

PIG—Gordon Lambert (active 1968–1969) Football.

PIGSKIN—Thomas O'Brien (1918–1978) Baseball. O'Brien, a Pittsburgh Pirates outfielder and third baseman in 1943, received his nickname because he also played football. Also called OBIE.

PIGTAIL BILLY—William Riley (1857–1887) Baseball.

PILLS—Byron Gentry (1913–1992) Football.

PILLSBURY DOUGHBOY [THE]—Mark Aguirre (1959–)
Basketball. Aguirre was overweight as an NBA rookie
guard.

PINBALL—Dave Twardzik (1950–) Basketball.

PINCH—George McBride (1880–1973) Baseball.
This shortstop was always good in a pinch.

PINCHES—Earl Kunz (1899–1963) Baseball.
In 1923, Kunz was 1–2 for Pittsburgh.

PING—Frank Stephen Bodie (1887–1961) Baseball.
Bodie's given name was Francesco Stephano Pezzolo.
This outfielder changed his name to Bodie which was
the California town where his father used to work.
Ping was the nickname of someone the family knew.

PINK—Harlan F. Baker (active 1920s) Football.

PINK—Emerson Hawley (1872–1938) Baseball.

PINK ELEPHANT [THE]—John Madden (1936–) Football.
This was the nickname that the Raiders used for their
overweight football coach.

PINKEY—William McKinley Hargrave (1896–1942) Baseball.

PINKEY—Match Pincus (1904–1944) Basketball.

PINKIE—Robert Howard Davie (1912–) Hockey.

PINOCCHIO—Max Bentley (1920–) Hockey.
Bentley, a center, had a long nose.

PIPER—Lorenzo Davis (1917–1997) Baseball (Negro
Leagues) 1b. He received his nickname because he
came from Piper, Alabama. In 1943, Piper Davis hit .386.

PIPINO—Jose Cuevas (1957–) Boxing.
Cuevas held the WBA welterweight title from 1976 to
1980, when he lost to Thomas "HIT MAN" Hearnes on
August 2.

PISTOL PETE—Pete Reiser (1919–1981) Baseball.
Whether in the outfield or at the plate, Reiser was a
pistol. His best year was 1941 when he led the
National League with a .343 for the Dodgers. He
played outfield for the Brooklyn Dodgers in the 1940s.

PISTOL PETE—Henry Wisniewski (active 1929–1932)
Football.

PIT—Napoleon Bourque (1885–1963) Auto racing.

PIT—Alfred Lepine (1901–1955) Hockey.

PIT—Hubert Jacques Martin (1943–) Hockey.

PIT BULL—Livingstone Bramble (1960–) Boxing.

PITCHIN' MORTICIAN [THE]—Waite Hoyt (1899–1984)
Baseball. **H/F** Hoyt, who pitched for twenty-one years

and had a record of 237–182, sometimes helped out
his father, who was an undertaker.

PITCHIN' PAUL—Paul Governali (1921–1978) Football.

PITCHING POET [THE]—Edward Benninghaus Kenna
(1877–1972) Baseball. Kenna's poetry was more pro-
lific than his pitching: his volume of verse was called
"Lyrics of the Hills"; his record was 1–1 with the 1902
Philadelphia As.

PITCHING PROFESSOR [THE]—Ted Lewis (1872–1936)
Baseball. A graduate of Williams College, this pitcher
(ninety-four wins, sixty-four losses) taught at Harvard
and Princeton before going on to become the
President of the University of New Hampshire.

PITTSBURGH HURRICANE [THE]—Bobby Hunt.
Wrestling.

PITTSBURGH KID [THE]—Billy Conn (1917–1993) Boxing.
H/F Conn, the light heavyweight champion from 1939
to 1941, fought a losing battle with Joe Louis for the
heavyweight championship in 1941.

PITTSBURGH WINDMILL [THE]—Edward Henry Greb
(1894–1926) Boxing. Also called THE HUMAN
WINDMILL.

PLAYER WHO IS NEVER CAUGHT FROM BEHIND [THE]—
Joe Bellino (1938–) Football. Also called DYNAMITE
JOE, JOE THE JET, and NAVY'S DESTROYER.

PLAYBOY OF PUGILISM [THE]—Max Baer (1909–1959)
Boxing. Also called CLOUTING CLOWN, FISTIC
HARLEQUIN, LARRUPING LOTHARIO OF PUGILISM,
LIVERMORE BUTCHER BOY, LIVERMORE LARRUPER,
MADCAP MAXIE, MAGNIFICENT SCREWBALL, and
PUGILISTIC POSEUR.

PLINKY—Elizabeth Topperwein (?–1945) Trapshooting.
In 1904, Topperwein was the first to break 100 traps in
a row—a feat she accomplished more than 200 times.
Even Annie Oakley thought she was the greatest
woman shooter.

PLOWBOY—Tom Morgan (1930–1987) Baseball. Morgan
was branded with this epithet because it took him so
long to return to the pitcher's mound that it seemed
he was reluctantly returning to the fields after lunch.

POCKET HERCULES—Naim Suleymanoglu (1967–)
Weightlifting. Although only 5 foot and 132 pounds,
Suleymanoglu lifted 336 pounds in the snatch compe-
tition (lifting in an unbroken motion) at the 1988
Olympic Games.

POCKET HERCULES OF AMERICAN GOLF—Gene Sarazen. Golf. **H/F** Also known as the Cheshire Cat because of his broad smile. Elected to the PGA/World Golf Hall of Fame in 1974.

POET [THE]—Edwin Douglas Charles (1933–) Baseball. Charles, a third baseman, liked to recite poetry in the clubhouse. Also called THE GLIDER.

POGO—Joe Caldwell (1941–) Basketball. Caldwell, who played forward and guard, was given this nickname because he could jump so high.

POINT-A-MINUTE—Fielding Harris Yost (1871–1946) Football. **H/F** The University of Michigan's football teams coached by Fielding Yost from 1901 to 1905 consistently scored a point a minute. See HURRY-UP.

POISON—Joe Brennan Basketball. **H/F**

POISON—David Kotey (1951–) Boxing. Kotey was the featherweight champion in 1975.

POISON IVIE—Mike Ivie (1952–) Baseball. This infielder's nickname was inevitable.

POISON IVY—Ivy Paul Andrews (1907–1970) Baseball.

POISON JOE—Joseph R. Brennan (1900–) Basketball. **H/F** One of the great players in the days before the NBA.

POKEY—Eldon Reddick (1964–) Hockey.

POLISH MESSIAH [THE]—Chester Marcol (1949–) Football. This Green Bay Packer place kicker's first name was really Czelslaw, and he was a reconverted soccer player.

POLISH PRINCE [THE]—Pete Stemkowski (1943–) Hockey. Also called STEMMER.

POLISH RIFLE [THE]—Ron Jaworski (active 1974–1989) Football qb.

POLLY—Paul Birch (1911–) Basketball.

POLLY—Emile Paul Drouin (1916–) Hockey.

POLO—Stan Andrews (1917–1995) Baseball. This catcher's real name was Andruskewicz.

POLYPHEMUS—Andrew Wyant (1873–1964) Football. Nicknamed for the one-eyed giant in Homer's *The Odyssey,* Wyant played center for Alonzo Stagg at the University of Chicago.

POMPADOUR JIM—Jim Corbett (1866–1933) Boxing. **H/F** Corbett's hair was always brushed as if he'd just slipped off a barber's chair rather than a boxing stool. See GENTLEMAN JIM.

PONGO—Joe Cantillon (1861–1930) Baseball. Charlie Dryden claimed in jest that Cantillon's real name was Pelipe Pongo Cantillon. Fans went along with the joke.

POOCH—Clyde Barnhart (1895–1980) Baseball.

POODLES—Joe Hutcheson (1905–1993) Baseball. Hutcheson played in fifty-five games for Brooklyn— long enough for the outfielder to acquire a .255 batting average and another nickname of Slug.

POODLES—Bill Willoughby (1957–) Basketball.

POP—John Corkhill (1858–1921) Baseball. Corkhill was thirty-two when he broke into the major leagues as an outfielder. In fifty-one games for Brooklyn, he batted .225.

POP—Frank Dillon (1873–1931) Baseball 1b.

POP—William Fuller (active 1920s–1930s) Tennis. Fuller was the coach of both Helen Jacobs and Helen Wills Moody. These two players met frequently in tennis finals in the 1930s, Moody usually coming out on top.

POP—William Gates (1917–) Basketball. **H/F**

POP—Jesse Haines (1893–1978) Baseball. **H/F** Haines pitched for the St. Louis Cardinals from 1920 to 1937. Pop was 210–158.

POP—A. Provost Idell (1889–1967) Volleyball. Idell spent his life in volleyball, as a player, a coach, an official. Also called THE FATHER OF MODERN VOLLEYBALL.

POP—Frank Ivy (active 1940–1964) Football. Ivy was the Houston Oilers' coach from 1962 to 1964.

POP—Oscar Bane Keeler (1882–1950) Golf journalist.

POP—Ernie Lewis. Basketball. This former college player for Providence had siblings nicknamed Snap and Crackle.

POP—John Henry Lloyd (1884–1965) Baseball ss/mgr. Babe Ruth once said that Lloyd was the best player of all time. He played for twenty-six years and compiled a .340 batting average. See THE BLACK HONUS WAGNER.

POP—Theodore Meyers (1874–1954) Auto racing. Meyers worked his way up from ticket sales to vicepresident at the Indianapolis Motor Speedway.

POP—George Steers (1820–1956) Yachting. Steers designed a fast-racing boat called America; the America's Cup is named after it.

POP—Charles Smith (1856–1927) Baseball. Smith bounced back and forth between the major leagues and AA ball. He was still playing the infield in AA baseball at the age of thirty-five.

POP—Edward "Dimples" Tate (1860–1932) Baseball.

POP-BOY—Clarence Smith (1892–1924) Baseball.

POP-EYE—Leroy Mehaffey (1904–) Baseball.

POPEYE—Jose Bronzone (1960–) Boxing.
This junior welterweight was from Argentina.

POPEYE—Steve Garvey (1948–) Baseball.
Played most of his career with the Dodgers. Jay Johnstone said of Garvey, "Steve Garvey is the kind of guy who for laughs does impersonations of Tom Landry."

POPEYE—Roy Mahaffey (1903–1969) Baseball.

POPCORN—Kirby Walters. Rodeo.

POPS—Wilver "Willie" Stargell (1940–) Baseball. **H/F**

PORK CHOP—John Hoffman (1943–) Baseball.

PORK CHOP—Jeff Mullins (1942–) Basketball.
Mullins was a 6' 4", 200 pound All-American guard at Duke who later led scoring for the San Francisco Warriors from 1969 to 1972.

PORKY—Woody Dumart (1916–) Hockey. **H/F**

PORKY—Edward S. Oliver (1916–1961) Golf.
Oliver, who was 5' 9" and weighed 225 pounds, won the 1941 Wester Open and came close in several other tournaments.

PORKY—Hal Reniff (1938–) Baseball.

PORTERILLO—Sandalio Consuegra (1920–) Baseball.
This pitcher hailed from Potrerillo, Cuba.

POSSUM—Stan Powell (1890–deceased) Football.
Played in 1923 for the Oorang Indians.
Also known as WRINKLE MEAT.

POSSUM—George Bostic Whitted (1890–1942) Baseball.
From North Carolina, this outfielder was an ol' possum hunter.

POSTAGE—Sylvester Stamps (active 1984–1989) Football.
This nickname stems from his last name.

POT—Ernest Graves (1880–1953) Football.

POT—Frank LaPorte (1880–1939) Baseball.
LaPorte's nickname was a shortening of the second baseman's last name.

POTATO—Carlos Pascual (1950–) Baseball.
This pitcher's nickname was for his height, only 5' 6".

POTSY—George Clark (1896–1972) Football coach.

POTTAWATOMIE GIANT—Jess Willard (1883–1968) Boxing.
Also called BIG JESS, COWBOY JESS, KANSAS GIANT,

TALL PINE OF THE POTTAWATOMIE. See THE GREAT WHITE HOPE.

POZ—Phil Pozderac (1959–) Football.

PREACHER—Elwin Charles Roe (1915–) Baseball.
Roe had once thought about being a minister before becoming a major-league pitcher.

PRETTY BOY—Jim Floyd (1950–) Pool.
Nicknamed by the legendary MINNESOTA FATS, Floyd bags about $15,000 a year in sanctioned tournaments. The rest of his considerable income he makes hustling in pool halls.

PRETZEL—David Banks (1901–1952) Basketball.

PRETZELS—Charlie Getzein (1864–1932) Baseball.
This pitcher, whose background was German, was 30–1 in 1886.

PRETZELS—John Pezzullo (1910–1990) Baseball.
Pezzullo's windup or his name or both gave him his nickname.

PRIEST—Simon Nxawe. Boxing.

PRIDE OF FLATBUSH—Floyd Caves "Babe" Herman (1903– 1987) Baseball.

PRIDE OF THE GHETTO [THE]—Joseph Bernstein (1877–1931) Boxing.

PRIDE OF THE GHETTO [THE]—Barney Ross (1909–1967) Boxing. Ross' real name was Beryl David Rosofsky. In seventy-eight fights, this fighter from New York City's Lower East Side was never knocked down.

PRIDE OF HAVANA [THE]—Dolf Luque (1890–1957) Baseball. Luque, who hailed from Havana, pitched for twenty years in the majors, compiling a 193–179 record. In 1923, he led the National League with a 1.93 ERA.

PRINCE—Henry Oana (1908–1976) Baseball. Oana was from Waipahu, Hawaii. He broke in with the Phillies as an outfielder when he was twenty-six. He was next seen in the majors at thirty-five with the Tigers.

PRINCE HAL—Harold Chase (1883–1946) Baseball.
Chase fielded his first base position royally. Unfortunately, he fell into the moat and was banned from baseball for life for his involvement in the Black Sox scandal of 1919.

PRINCE HAL—Hal Schumacher (1910–1993) Baseball.
In addition to Shakespeare's Prince Hal, Schumacher was nicknamed the prince because he was the second best pitcher on the Giants pitching staff. The best was

Carl "KING" Hubbell. The two pitched the Giants into the World Series in 1934, 1936, and 1937.

PRINCE VALIANT—Phil Simms (1957–) Football qb.

PRINCESS [THE]—Helen Wills Moody (1906–1998) Tennis. **H/F** Also called THE PRINCESS. See LITTLE MISS POKER FACE and QUEEN HELEN.

PRINCETON CHARLIE—Charlie Reilly (1855–1937) Baseball. This third baseman, who had once attended Princeton University, was in 1892 the first pinch hitter.

PRODIGY—Al Barlick (1915–) Baseball. Barlick began his career as a National League umpire when he was only twenty-five. This ump was selected for a record seven All-Star Games.

PROF—Monte Weaver (1906–1994) Baseball. This pitcher held more than just a rosin bag; he held two college degrees.

PROFESSOR—Jim Brosnan (1929–) Baseball. Brosnan, a pitcher, was one of the most scholarly players in baseball. He not only read books but even wrote two: *Long Season* (1960) and *Pennant Race* (1964).

PROFESSOR—Mike Donovan (1847–1918) Boxing. English middleweight champion. Donovan, who received an honorary degree for his style of scientific boxing, worked at the New York Athletic Club for thirty years teaching members how to box.

PRUNE JUICE—Rocky Bleir (active 1968–1980) Football. Bleir's Steeler teammates gave the halfback this nickname.

PRUSSIAN LEPRECHAUN—Francis William Leahy (1908–1973) Football. Coach at North Dakota.

PSYCHO—Steve Lyons (1960–) Baseball. Lyons, an outfielder, was very unpredictable when running the bases.

PSYCHO [THE]—John Barend (1945–) Wrestling. Also called HANDSOME JOHNNY, HANDSOME ONE, and PRINCE OF DARKNESS.

PTERODACTYL—Charlie Kerfeld (1963–) Baseball p.

PUD—James Galvin (1855–1902) Baseball. **H/F** Also called THE LITTLE STEAM ENGINE. See GENTLE JEEMS.

PUDDIN'—Walt Garrison (1944–) Football. In nine seasons with the Dallas Cowboys, Puddin' Garrison ran for 3,886 yards.

PUDDIN' HEAD—Willie Jones (1925–) Baseball. This third baseman's nickname came from a song ("Wooden head, puddin' head Jones") that was popular when Jones was a young man.

PUDGE—Thurman Munson (1947–1979) Baseball c. Also called SQUATTY, ROUND MAN, and BAD BODY.

PUDGE—Paul Pardonner (1910–1989) Football.

PUEBLO FIREMAN [THE]—Jim Flynn. Boxing.

PUFF—Graig Nettles (1944–) Baseball. This six-time All Star, who won two Golden Gloves for his sparkling fielding, also hit 390 homers (and a record 319 for American League third basemen).

PUG—Horace Allen (1899–1981) Baseball. Allen, a would-be outfielder, lasted only four games for the Brooklyn Dodgers.

PUGILISTIC POSEUR—Max Baer (1909–1959) Boxing (heavyweight). Also called CLOUTING CLOWN, FISTIC HARLEQUIN, LARRUPING LOTHARIO OF PUGILISM, LIVERMORE BUTCHER BOY, LIVERMORE LARRUPER, MADCAP MAXIE, and MAGNIFICENT SCREWBALL.

PUKER [THE]—Paul Pryor (active 1960s) Baseball. This major league umpire once threw up on catcher Johnny Roseboro at Dodger Stadium.

PULLMAN—Andrew Porter (active 1932–1950) Baseball (Negro Leagues). At one time, the natural word association with this pitcher's last name was railroad rolling stock.

PULPWOOD—Andre Smith. Football. The father of this former running back at Georgia operated a lumber mill.

PULVERIZING POLE [THE]—Jadwiga Jedryejowska. Tennis.

PUNCH—Lyle Judy (1913–) Baseball. Second baseman Judy lacked punch, batting .000 in eight games for the Cards in 1935.

PUNJAB—Jim Yarbrough (active 1969–1977) Football. Yarbrough, who played tackle for the Detroit Lions, was nicknamed after Punjab in *Little Orphan Annie.*

PUNK—Robert L. Barrymore (1893–1988) Football coach.

PUP—Al Graham (1908–1966) Football.

PUP—Brent Sutter (1962–) Hockey.

PURPLE STREAK [THE]—Ben Boynton (1898–1963) Football. Boynton played quarterback at Williams College.

PUTSY—Ralph Joseph Cabellero (1927–) Baseball. The nickname of this second baseman is from childhood.

Q—Quintin Dailey (1961–) Basketball. The 1982–83 NBA rookie from the University of San Francisco started his pro career with the Chicago Bulls.

Q-TIP—Brad Lohaus (1964–) Basketball.

QUICK—James Tillis. Boxing (heavyweight).

QUICK [THE]—Nick Werkman (1942–) Basketball. Werkman was able to sneak inside quickly for underhanded layups. The Quick averaged thirty-two points a game for Seton Hall from 1962–1964.

QUIET AVENGER [THE]—Aaron Wallace (1967–) Football. This soft-spoken linebacker set a record of forty-two sacks of the quarterback at Texas A&M.

QUIG—Ernest C. Quigley (1880–1968). Baseball, basketball, and football referee. Quig was the man in blue or black and white for 5,400 baseball games and 1,500 basketball games (he used his voice instead of a whistle), and 400 football games.

RABBI OF SWAT [THE]—Moses Solomon (1900–1966) Baseball. Though Moses batted a heavenly three-for-eight, he only lasted two games for the N.Y. Giants.

RABBIT—Jim Bradshaw (active 1963–1967) Football.

RABBIT—Thomas Glantano Glaviano (1923–) Baseball. In 1946 at Fresno, Glaviano played shortstop and stole sixty-four bases to earn his nickname.

RABBIT—Charles McVeigh (1898–) Hockey.

RABBIT—Keith F. Molesworth (1906–1966) Football qb.

RABBIT [THE]—Floyd Patterson (1935–) Boxing. This was a pejorative nickname given to Patterson by Muhammad Ali (then Cassius Clay).

RACEHORSE—Charles Robertson (1897–1984) Baseball. Robertson, a pitcher, was once described as having a face like a racehorse.

RACING LEGEND—Ted Horn (1910–1948) Auto racing.

RAGS—Clarence Eldon Raglan (1927–) Hockey.

RAGS—Raymond Matthews (1905–) Football.

RAGS—Dave Righetti (1958–) Baseball.

RAINBOW—Willie Sojourner (1948–) Basketball.

RAINBOW—Steve Trout (1957–) Baseball. This pitcher's nickname came from his last name. His father was Paul Howard (Dizzy) Trout, a major-league pitcher from 1939–1957.

RAINMAN—Andrew Charles Benes (active 1989–) Baseball. There were rain delays during many of the games that Benes was slated to pitch.

RAMBO—Mike Diaz (1960–) Baseball.

RAMBO—Tim Wilkison (1959–) Tennis. Also called DR. DIRT.

RAMROD—Emmett Nelson (1905–1967) Baseball.

This pitcher was tall and thin (6' 3", 180 pounds).

RANDY—Randel Matson (1945–) Track and field. Matson was the first to hurl the shot put over seventy feet. He put the shot 70' 7¼" on May 8, 1965, to break the world record by almost three feet.

RAT [THE]—Jamie Easterly (1953–) Baseball p.

RAT [THE]—Ken Linseman (1958–) Hockey. This member of the 1970s Broad Street Bullies had a rat tattooed on his leg.

RAT—Ira E. Rodgers (1895–1963) Football. One of the first successful passers, Rodgers threw a fifty-one-yard strike in 1917.

RAT—Frank William Thomas (1898–1959) Football coach.

RAT—Harry Westwick (1876–1957) Hockey. **H/F** Small and shifty was the reason that Westwick was stuck with the nickname Rat. Playing as a rover for the Ottawa Senators, the Rat scurried about to help them win three Stanley Cup championships from 1903–1905.

RATON—Rafael Alonso (active 1980s) Boxing. (Mexican flyweight).

RATON—Raul Macias (1934–) Boxing (bantamweight).

RATTLE SNAKE—Thomas Calvin Baker (1913–1991) Baseball. Baker, a pitcher, liked to tell his teammates stories about the rattlers back in Texas.

RAVE [THE]—Dave Stallworth (1941–) Basketball. Stallworth was a two-time All-American forward and record setter at Wichita State. After one year with the New York Knicks, he had a heart seizure and did not play again until two years later when he played all eighty-two games.

RAY—Raymondo Giuseppi Giovanni Baptiste Malavase (1930–) Football. We know Ray isn't much of a nickname, but we use it here because we wanted to share his full name with you.

RAZOR—Anthony Shines (1956–) Baseball. Shines hit sharp line drives, but he lost his place on the Expos to Tim Raines.

RAZOR—Ralph Ledbetter (1894–1969) Baseball p.

RAZOR [THE]—Jerry Richardson (active 1959–1969) Football fl/hb.

RAZZLE DAZZLE—Cornelius (Con) Murphy (1863–1914) Baseball. Murphy's pitching style was more spectacular than his record of 12–28.

READING RIFLE [THE]—Carl Furillo (1922–) Baseball. Hailing from a place near Reading, Pennsylvania,

Furillo had a powerful arm. His ability to rifle the ball from deep right field of Brooklyn's Ebbetts Field to home plate kept many a baserunner honest. See SKOONJ.

READY—Bill Cash Baseball (Negro Leagues).

REAL DEAL [THE]—Shaquille O'Neal (1972–) Basketball. The number one draft pick in the NBA in 1992, this center who may turn out to be as great or greater than Russell, Chamberlain, and Jabaar, went to the Orlando Magic. See THE SHACK.

REAL McCOY [THE]—Charles McCoy (1873–1940) Boxing (welterweight). Also called THE CORKSCREW KID and KID McCOY.

REBEL—Thomas Nobel Oliver (1903–1988) Baseball. This outfielder was born south of the Mason-Dixon Line.

RED—Ralph Clayton Almas (1924–) Hockey g.

RED—Leon Kessling Ames (1882–1936) Baseball. Ames was a pitcher and his nickname Red is the second most common nickname (after Lefty). The reason is just as obvious as for a left-hander—the color of a person's hair. This is true for the all the following Reds.

RED—Arnold Auerbach (1917–) Basketball. **H/F** Shaper of the dynasty in Boston, Auerbach's career record as coach was 1,037–548—the most coaching wins ever. Red was famous for lighting a cigar when (in his estimation) the game was out of reach by the other team.

RED—Morris Badgro (active 1930–1936) Football e. **H/F**

RED [THE]—Gordon Berenson (1939–) Hockey. Also called THE RED BARON.

RED—Earl Blaik (1897–1989) Football coach. Also called COLONEL and EARL OF HANOVER.

RED—Christian Keener Cagle (1905–1942) Football. Also called ONWARD CHRISTIAN CAGLE.

RED—Henry C. Carlson (1894–1964) Football e/basketball coach. Also called DOC.

RED—Freddie Cochrane (1915–) Boxing. Cochrane held the world welterweight title during the World War II years until he lost it to Rocky Graziano in 1945.

RED—Bill Consright (active 1937–1942) Football c/lb.

RED—William Conway (active 1930s) Football.

RED—Sam Crane (1894–1955) Baseball ss.

RED—Gene Desautels (1907–1994) Baseball c.

RED—Francis Donahue (1873–1913) Baseball p.

RED—Charles Dooin (1879–1952) Baseball c/mgr.

RED—John Michael Doran (1911–) Hockey c.

RED—Lloyd George Doran (1921–) Hockey c.

RED—Mervyn Dutton (1898–1987) Hockey. **H/F** Dutton, a defenseman, played for the Maroons in the 1920s. He later became a coach and the second president of the NHL (1943–1946).

RED—Charles Embree (1917–1996) Baseball p.

RED—Urban Charles Faber (1888–1976) Baseball **H/F** Red Faber's best year was in 1921 when he was 25–15 with a 2.48 ERA. He also won three games in the 1917 World Series. Overall, he won twenty or more games four times and had thirty shutouts. In his twenty-year career for the Chicago White Sox, Faber was 254–212.

RED—Ray Flaherty (active 1920s–1930s) Football coach.

RED—Dudley Garrett (1924–) Hockey d.

RED—Wayne Garrett (1947–) Baseball 3b.

RED—Harold E. Grange (1903–1991) Football hb. Also called WHEATON ICEMAN. See GALLOPING GHOST.

RED—Clifford Goupille (1915–) Hockey d.

RED—Robert George Hamill (1917–) Hockey lw.

RED—Bill Hay (1898–) Hockey lw.

RED—Myron Claude Hayworth (1915–) Baseball c.

RED—George David Henry (1926–) Hockey g.

RED—Robert Geatrex Heron (1917–) Hockey c.

RED—Arthur L. Herring (1907–) Baseball p. Also called SANDY.

RED—Howard Hickey (active 1940s) Football e/coach.

RED—Dale Gordon Hoganson (1949–) Hockey d.

RED—Reginald Horner (1909–) Hockey. Horner was a defenseman on the Toronto Maple Leafs' GASHOUSE GANG ON ICE, and later an interim president of the NHL.

RED—Walter Jackson (1908–) Hockey f.

RED—John Thomas Keating (1916–) Hockey lw.

RED—Leonard Patrick Kelly (1927–) Hockey. Kelly won the first Norris Trophy (awarded to the top defenseman). In addition, he not only won the Lady Byng Trophy four times (for sportsmanship) but was on no less than eight Stanley Cup championship teams.

RED—Johnny Kerr (1932–) Basketball. After starring at Illinois, Kerr played for Syracuse-

Philadelphia and Baltimore in the NBA, starting in 844 consecutive games. He also coached at Chicago and Phoenix.

RED—Louis Klotz (1920–) Basketball.
Klotz was only 5' 7", one of the shortest players ever in the NBA. He later became the player-manager for the Washington Generals, the team that lost 180 games a year to the Harlem Globetrotters.

RED—Benjamin Kramer (1913–) Basketball.

RED—Ralph Kress (1907–1962) Baseball ss.

RED—Charles Lucas (1902–) Baseball p.
Also called THE NASHVILLE NARCISSUS.

RED—Tony Matal (active 1930s) Football.

RED—John Joseph Murray (1884–1958) Baseball of.

RED—Phil Murrell (1933–) Basketball.
Murrell scored 51, 45, and 41 points for Drake, and 1,657 points during his career from 1956 to 1958.

RED—Thomas Llewellyn Owens (1874–1952) Baseball 2b.

RED—Sidney Quarrier (active 1920s) Football.

RED—Bob Richardson (active 1966) Football db.

RED—Austin Robbins (1944–) Basketball.
Robbins was also called "a walking one iron" because of his physique. He played for New Orleans and Utah in the ABA.

RED—Ephraim Rocha (1923–) Basketball c/coach.

RED—Robert A. Rolfe (1908–1969) Baseball 3b/mgr.

RED—James Smith (1890–1966) Baseball 3b.

RED—Louis J. Salmon (1880–1965) Football.

RED—Henry Russell Sanders (1905–1958) Football coach.

RED—Albert Fred Schoendienst (1923–) Baseball 2b. **H/F**

RED—Christopher Schlachter (active c. 1915) Football.

RED—Emil M. Sitko (1923–1973) Football b.
Also called SIX YARDS.

RED—Richard Paul Smith (1904–1978) Baseball c/football b/coach. Also called TOLEDO'S RED SMITH.

RED—Roy Storey (active 1951–1959) Hockey umpire. **H/F**

RED—Norman Strader (1902–1956) Football qb/coach.

RED—William Stuart (1899–) Hockey d.

RED—George James Sullivan (1929–) Hockey c/coach.

RED—Charles Thomas (1918–) Basketball.
After starring at Northwestern State in Arkansas, he coached there.

RED—George Wolfe (1908–) Basketball.

RED—Al Worthington (1930–) Baseball p.

RED CROSS MIKE—Michael Riley Powers (1870–1909) Baseball. He was the catcher as well as the physician for the old Philadelphia As.

RED DEVIL—James Robert Horner (1957–) Baseball. Bob Horner earned this nickname while he was playing baseball in Japan because of his reddish blonde hair. When he hit eleven home runs in his first twenty-nine games in Japan, fans called him "MR. HO-MAH."

RED EYE—James Hay (1931–) Hockey d.

RED ROOSTER—Rick Burleson (1951–) Baseball.
Johnny Pesky, a Boston Red Sox coach, bestowed shortstop Burleson with this nickname for his cockiness. Also called ROOSTER.

RED ROOSTER—Doug Rader (1944–) Baseball.
When Rader played third base for the Astros, his long red hair spilled down his neck like a coxcomb. Also called ROOSTER and ROJO.

REDS—Francis Bagnell Football.

REDSKIN—Raleigh Leonidas Aitchison (1887–1958) Baseball. Aitchison, a pitcher, was a Native American from South Dakota.

REGGIE—Reginald Fleming (1936–) Hockey lw.

REINDEER BILL—William Lavier Killefer (1888–1960) Baseball. The nickname of this catcher (and later manager) was probably one of opposites as Killefer was slow.

RENE—Ireneo Barrientos (1942–) Boxing (junior lightweight).

REV—Walter Canaday. Baseball (Negro Leagues) 2b.

REVEREND [THE]—Tommie Agee (1964–) Football.
As a running back for the Dallas Cowboys, Agee received his nickname because of his positive influence during team meetings.

REVEREND T. L. [THE]—Tom Landry (1924–) Football. **H/F** Coach of two Dallas Cowboy Super Bowl winners, Landry was a pious person, and was active in the Methodist Church.

REVVIE—Peter Revson (?–1974) Auto racing.
Also called CHAMPAGNE PETER.

REX—Warren Cawley (1940–) Track and field.
In 1964, Cawley set a world record of 49.1 in the 400-meter hurdles in the Olympic trials. At the 1964 Tokyo Olympic Games, Cawley came from behind to win the gold medal in the 400-meter hurdles in 49.6.

RHINO—Homer Jones (active 1964–1970) Football rw.

RHODY—Roderick Wallace (1873–1960) Baseball ss/mgr.
H/F In twenty-five years of playing ball, Rhody won twelve awards for fielding and collected 2,314 hits.

RIBS—Frank Raney (1923–) Baseball.
Born Frank Robert Donald Raniszewski. He was eventually given the nickname Ribs because he was so skinny his ribs poked out. Ribs Raney only played for two seasons in the big leagues, 1949 and 1950, as a pitcher for the St. Louis Browns. He appeared in four games, won one and lost three, striking out seven batters and walking fourteen.

RICHARD THE RUFFIAN—Richard Afflis (1943–) Wrestling. Also called DICK THE BRUISER.

RICO—Americo Peter Petrocelli (1943–) Baseball 3b.

RIFLE—Rudy Bukvich (active 1953–1968) Football.
In 1965, he led the NFL with twenty touchdowns.

RIFLE [THE]—Sam Etchevary (active 1961–1962) Football qb.

RIFLE [THE]—Roger Strickland (1940–) Basketball.
An All-American at Jacksonville University, this forward set a scoring record his junior year of 32.6 points per game. RILEY—William Milton Hern (1880–1929) Hockey. **H/F** Hern was a goalie for the Montreal Wanderers when they took the Stanley Cup championship in 1907, 1908, and 1910.

RILES—Pat Riley (1945–) Basketball.
Ultra successful, slicked-back head coach of the L.A. Lakers, N.Y. Knicks, and now the Miami Heat.

RILEY—Arlene Kotil (active 1949–1951) Baseball (All-American Girls Baseball League). Kotil, an infielder, got her nickname from the old William Bendix show on television, *The Life of Riley,* because her grandmother relieved her of any housework so there would be more time for baseball.

RING GORILLA—Phil Boom (1894–) Boxing.
Of his 172 fights, ninety-six ended in a draw.

RINGO—Oscar Bonavena. Boxing (heavyweight).

RINTY—John Joseph Monaghan (active 1940s) Boxing.
In 1948, Irishman Monaghan knocked out Scotsman Jackie Paterson in the seventh round of their flyweight championship fight.

RIP—Walter Coleman (1931–) Baseball p.

RIP—Harry Warren Collins (1896–1968) Baseball.
In the 1921 World Series this pitcher had an ERA of 54.00 in 2/3rds of an inning. Pitchers are sometimes nicknamed Rip for letting the ball rip; however, this pitcher was called Rip because he liked to drink. Collins' eleven-year record was 108–82.

RIP—James Anthony Collins (1905–1970) Baseball 1b.

RIP—Charles A. Engle. Football. Engle compiled a 194–48–4 record as the Penn State football coach.

RIP—Raymond A. Radcliff (1906–1962) Baseball.
This outfielder could let it rip when it came to hitting. He hit .311 during ten years in the majors. During his last year, he pinch-hit 11-for-44.

RIP—Howard Joseph Riopelle (1922–) Hockey lw.

RIP—Elmer Ripley (active 1911–1960) Basketball.
Ripley played pro ball for twenty years with many teams and coached for many colleges during a twenty-four-year career.

RIP—Truett Sewell (1908– 1989) Baseball p.

RIPPER—Jimmy Collins (1904–1970) Baseball.
Collins, a hard-hitting first baseman, once knocked the cover off the ball. In 1934, he led the National League in thirty-five home runs. Ripper's nine-year batting average was .296. See GASHOUSE GANG.

RIVERBOAT—Robert Smith (1928–) Baseball.
A sportswriter once described this pitcher as being like a riverboat gambler with pitches up his sleeve.

RIVERTON RIFLE [THE]—Reggie Leach (1950–) Hockey.
Leach grew up playing hockey in Riverton, Manitoba. In 1974 and 1975, the Riverton Rifle scored 106 goals from his right wing position for the Philadelphia Flyers.

ROAD RUNNER—Ralph Garr (1945–) Baseball of.

ROADBLOCK—Sherman Jones (1935–) Baseball.
Jones was 2–6 in three years of pitching for three teams (the Giants, the Reds, and the Mets). But in the minors he earned his nickname when he won both games of a doubleheader as a reliever.

ROADRUNNER—Gene Clines (1946–) Baseball.
Clines was a fast-moving outfielder.

ROARING—Bill Kennedy (1867–1915) Baseball.
This pitcher (who won 184 games and lost 160) talked loud, no matter the situation.

ROBBIE—Lawson Robertson (1883–1951) Track and field.
Robertson was the coach at Penn and the 1924 Olympic track coach.

ROBIN—Robert Roberts (1926–) Baseball.
Robin Roberts was a six-time twenty-game winner. He

had forty-five shutouts, 2,357 strikeouts, and an ERA of 3.41. His career record was 286–245.

ROBOCOP—Jim Thornton (active 1988–) Football te.

ROCCO—Fernando Castro (1954–) Boxing. Peruvian welterweight.

ROCCO—Oliver Mathias Reinikka (1901–) Hockey f.

ROCHDALE THUNDERBOLT [THE]—Jock McAvoy (active 1930s–1940s) Boxing (middleweight). McAvoy held the British middleweight crown from 1933 to 1944. One fascinating aspect of this fighter was that he regularly fought boxers who were much heavier.

ROCK—Earl Averill (1902–1983) Baseball. **H/F** In 1936, Averill batted .378. For his thirteen-year career he had a .318 average. An outfielder, he also won fielding awards five times. Hailing from Snohomish, Washington, he was also called THE EARL OF SNOHOMISH.

ROCK [THE]—Rocky Colavito (1933–) Baseball. In 1959, Colavito led the league with forty-two home runs (he hit four in one game); in 1965, this outfielder was the leader in ribbies with 108.

ROCK [THE]—Larry Zeidel (1928–) Hockey. He was a rock solid defenseman.

ROCKET—Roger Clemens (1962–) Baseball. This two-time Cy Young Award winner with a ninety-five-mph fastball struck out a major-league record twenty batters on April 29, 1986.

ROCKET [THE]—Rod Foster (1960–) Basketball g.

ROCKET—Raghib Ismail (active 1980s–1990s) Football.

ROCKET [THE]—Rod Laver (1938–) Tennis. **H/F**

ROCKING CHAIR CATCHER—Lloyd Basset (active 1935–1950) Baseball (Negro Leagues). When Bassett was with the Indianapolis Clowns, part of his act was to catch while sitting in a rocker.

ROCKY—Rosendo Alsonso (active 1978–1980s) Boxing (Mexican flyweight).

ROCKY—Robert Bleir (active 1968–1980) Football. When this halfback was born, his grandfather said he looked like a rock.

ROCKY—Rocco Domenico Colavito (1933–) Baseball of.

ROCKY—Jim Colven (1937–) Football.

ROCKY—Rod Gilbert (1941–) Hockey. Also called HOT ROD and MR. RANGER.

ROCKY—Warren Godfrey (1931–) Hockey d.

ROCKY—Ricky Lockridge (1959–) Boxing.

In 1984, Lockridge won the junior lightweight title.

ROCKY—Glenn Richard Nelson (1924–) Baseball 1b.

ROCKY—John Vernon Stone (1918–1986) Baseball p.

ROCKY—Ron Swoboda (1944–) Baseball of.

ROCKY KANSAS—Rocco Tozzo (1895–1952) Boxing (lightweight).

RODGER THE DODGER—Rodger Ward. Auto racing. **H/F**

ROGIE—Rogatien Vachon (1945–) Hockey g.

ROJO—Doug Rader (1944–) Baseball 3b/mgr.

ROLIE—Bengt Roland Eriksson (1954–) Hockey c.

ROSCOMMON GIANT [THE]—Jim Coffey Boxing.

ROSY—Herschel Caldwell (active 1920s) Football.

ROSY—Emmett O'Donnell, Jr. (1906–1971) Football.

ROSEY—Roosevelt Grier (1932–) Football.

ROSEY—Albert K. Rowswell (1883–1955) Sports announcer.

ROTTEN—Ralph Neely (1943–) Football. "He's so good," said Cowboys' defensive tackle Bob Lilly. "That he's the only player I ever knew who was never a rookie." Hence, his nickname is the opposite of Neely's actual abilities.

ROUGH CARRIGAN—William Francis Carrigan (1883–1969) Baseball c/mgr.

ROUND MOUND OF REBOUND [THE]—Charles Barkley (1963–) Basketball f. Also called SIR CHARLES.

ROUNDS—Danny Thomas (1953–) Basketball. Rounds would be an even better nickname for a boxer!

ROWDY—Russ Meyer (1923–) Baseball. See THE MAD MONK.

ROWDY JACK—Jack O'Connor (1869–1937) Baseball. Also called PEACH PIE.

ROWDY RICHARD—Dick Bartell (1907–1995) Baseball. Bartell got his nickname for being a touch, hard-playing shortstop. Also called ROWDY DICK.

ROXEY—Jack Albert Crouch (1905–) Baseball c.

RUBBER—Gene Krapp (1888–1923) Baseball. Krapp's record on the mound was 39–47 from 1911–1915.

RUBBER ARM—George Walter Connally (1898–1978) Baseball p. Also called RIP, SARGE, and SNORTER.

RUBBERLEGS—Lee Guttero (1912–) Basketball. Guttero was an All-American center for USC in 1934–35. Although he was only 6' 2", Rubberlegs could really jump and seldom lost out on a jump ball.

RUBBERLEGS—Roscoe Miller (1876–1913) Baseball. Miller was 39–46 from 1901–1904.

RUBE—John Cleveland Benton (1890–1937) Baseball. Benton was nicknamed after Rube Waddell. Both were pitchers from the sticks who liked to drink.

RUBE—Raymond Bloom Bressler (1894–1966) Baseball. Bressler was 26–31 from 1914–1920.

RUBE—Raymond Benjamin Caldwell (1888–1967) Baseball. Caldwell was 134–120 from 1910–1921. Also called SLIM.

RUBE—Bill Chambers (active 1920s) Baseball (Negro Leagues) p.

RUBE—George Foster (1949–) Baseball of.

RUBE—Richard William Marquard (1889–1980) Baseball. He got his nickname by being compared to Rube Waddell. But he was a legend in his own right. His banner year was 1912 when he was 27–11 for the New York Giants and won two games in the World Series. Marquard was 205–177 for his career.

RUBE—George Edward Waddell (1876–1914) Baseball. **H/F** Waddell set a one season strike-out record of 349 in 1904. It stood until 1973 when Nolan Ryan struck out 383 batters.

RUBE—George Elvin Walberg (1896–1978) Baseball. Walberg was 156–142 from 1923–1937.

RUBE—Albert Bluford Walker (1926–) Baseball c.

RUBY—Ralph Zunich (1910–) Hockey d.

RUNAWAY TRAIN—Preben Elkjaer Soccer.

RUSTY—Russell Callow (1890–1961) Rowing. Callow coached at Pennsylvania from 1927 to 1950 and at Navy from 1951 to 1959. His crews at Navy won thirty-one consecutive races.

RUSTY—Russ Critchfield (1946–) Basketball g.

RUSTY—Daniel Joseph Staub (1944–) Baseball of/1b. See LE GRAND ORANGE.

RYNO—Ryne Sandberg (1959–) Baseball 2b.

SABLE SNIPER [THE]—Leroy Haynes. Boxing. Also called HOWITZER HAYNES.

SAD SAM—Samuel Jones (1925–) Baseball. Jones was nicknamed after Samuel Pond Jones (SAD SAM). Both seemed sad when they were on the mound. Also called TOOTHPICK.

SADULPA GIANT [THE]—Carl Morris (1887–1951) Boxing. Also called THE ORIGINAL WHITE HOPE.

SAGINAW KID—George Kid Lavigne (1869–1928) Boxing. Born in Saginaw, Michigan, Lavigne was undefeated as a lightweight from 1885 through 1896.

SAILOR—Jack Sharkey (1902–) Boxing.

Sharkey was the heavyweight champion in 1932. Also called THE BOSTON GOB.

ST. PAUL CYCLONE [THE]—Mike O'Dowd (1895–1957) Boxing.

ST. PAUL PHANTOM [THE]—Mike Gibbons (1887–1956) Boxing. **H/F**

SALT—David Walther (1948–) Auto racing.

SALTY—Francis James Parker (1913–1992) Baseball. This shortstop who later became a manager liked salted peanuts.

SAM—Sylvio Bettio (1928–) Hockey.

SAM—Robert Lee Huff (1934–) Football.

SAM—Sabath Anthony Mele (1923–) Baseball. This outfielder's nickname was formed by his initials.

SAMMY—Hogomer Gabriel Godin (1909–) Hockey.

SAMSON—Harlin Pool (1908–1963) Baseball. Pool was strong. He also started out strong. His first year for Cincinnati he hit .327; his second year .147.

SAMSON OF PRINCETON—Lawson Fiscus (active 1900s) Football. Fiscus was a tough lineman for Greensburg in one of the early pro games.

SANDMAN—Clayman Parker. Boxing.

SANDY—Alex Herd (1868–1944) Golf. Herd won the 1902 British Open Championship using a new Haskell ball. The gutty would not be used again.

SANDY—Arthur L. Herring (1907–) Baseball. Herring had light-brown hair. Herring was 34–38 in his eleven years. Also called RED.

SANDY—Donald Alexander McGregor (1939–) Hockey.

SANDY—Joseph Saddler (1926–) Boxing. **H/F** Sandy could have been The Sandman for he KO'd 103 opponents in 143 bouts.

SANDY—William Alexander Snow (1946–) Hockey.

SANDY—Alexander Fitzgerald Stewart (1944–) Hockey.

SANDY—Joseph Albert Vance (1905–) Baseball. This pitcher's hair, naturally.

SARGE—James Charles Jacob Bagby, Sr. (1889–1954) Baseball. Bagby, a pitcher, was called Sarge after Sergeant Jimmy Bagby, a character in a Broadway play.

SARGE—George Walter Connally (1898–1978) Baseball. A winner of the Congressional Medal of Honor, Connally was a sergeant in the Marines in WW I. His pitching record was 49–60 for the White Sox and the Indians.

SARGE—Bob Kuzava (1923–) Baseball. That was this pitcher's rank during WW II.

SARGE—Gary Matthews (1950–) Baseball.

SARGE [THE]—Moody Orville (1934–) Golf. Also called UNKNOWN SOLDIER.

SASHA—Alexander Volkov (1958–) Basketball f.

SASSAFRAS—George L. Winter (1878–1951) Baseball. Winter was 82–102 for the Red Sox.

SATCH—Lawrence William Sacharuk (1952–) Hockey. This defenseman's nickname is probably a play on his last name.

SATCH—Thomas Sanders (1938–) Basketball f.

SAUSAGE NOSE—Ernie Lombardi (1908–1977) Baseball. **H/F** See SCHNOZZ.

SAVAGE—Ed Turner Boxing.

SAY NO—Otto Moore (1946–) Basketball c-f.

SCHNOZZ—Ernesto (Ernie) Natali Lombardi (1908–1977) Baseball. **H/F** Lombardi, a catcher, had a Cyrano de Bergerac of a nose. Also called BOCCI.

SCHOOLBOY—Alta Albert Cohen (1910–) Baseball of.

SCHOOLBOY—John Knight (1885–1965) Baseball. This shortstop went from high school to the starting lineup of the Philadelphia Athletics.

SCHOOLBOY—Lynwood Thomas Rowe (1912–1961) Baseball. When he was pitching as a teenager, a fan yelled encouragement to the batter about not being struck out by a mere schoolboy.

SCISSORS—Erskine John Mayer (1891–1957) Baseball p.

SCOOP—Arthur Otto Scharein (1905–1969) Baseball. Scharein could easily handle ground balls in the infield.

SCOOPS—Max George Carey (1890–1976) Baseball of. **H/F** Carey was a smooth fielding outfielder.

SCOOPS—Jimmy Cooney (1894–1991) Baseball. Cooney was a slick fielding shortstop.

SCOOTER—Ray McLean (1915–1964) Football b/coach.

SCOOTER—Merlin Patrick (1932–) Auto racing.

SCOOTER—Philip Francis Rizzuto (1918–) Baseball ss/announcer. Scooter fielded his position well.

SCOTCH WOP [THE]—Johnny Dundee (1893–1965) Boxing (featherweight). His ring name (Johnny Dundee) was Scottish, but he originally hailed from Sicily. SCOTS-MAN (THE)—John Bain Sutherland (1889–1948) Football coach. Also called DOUR SCOT, JOCK, and OVERLAND MAN.

SCOTT—Donald Howson (1960–) Hockey c.

SCOTTY—William Bowman (1933–) Hockey. This coach, who guided Montreal to five Stanley Cups and Pittsburgh to one, has won more games than any other coach in NHL history.

SCOTTY—Allan M. Davidson (1890–1915) Hockey. **H/F**

SCOTTY—Floyd Hamilton (1921–) Basketball. In 1942, Hamilton became the first All-American at West Virginia.

SCOTTY—Ian Morrison. Hockey. In 1987, this former referee was appointed the first president of the Hockey Hall of Fame.

SCOW—Fay Thomas (1904–1990) Baseball p.

SCRAP IRON—Clint Courtney (1927–) Baseball. This catcher for the St. Louis Browns earned his nickname for his ability to play when hurt. He was also called the Toy Bull Dog because he got into fights.

SCRAP IRON—Phil Garner (1949–) Baseball. This second baseman made up for talent with determination.

SCRAP IRON—Fred James Hatfield (1925–) Baseball 3b.

SCRAPPY—Bill Joyce (1865–1941) Baseball. This third baseman was always ready to mix it up.

SCREENO—Howard H. Bailey (1913–) Football t.

SEACAP—Walter Christensen (1899–) Baseball. This outfielder batted .315 in two years for Cincinnati. See CUCKOO.

SEA LION—Charlie Hall (Carlos Clolo) (1885–1943) Baseball. This pitcher could bark like a seal.

SEATTLE SEAL [THE]—Jack Medica. Swimming.

SEATTLE BILL—William Jones (1892–1971) Baseball. Jones was born in—yes, you guessed it—Florida. So go figure.

SECRETARY OF DEFENSE [THE]—Garry Maddox (1949–) Baseball. Also called BUGGY WHIP.

SEED—Robert Thomas Goring (1949–) Hockey. Also called BUTCH.

SEN-SEN—John P. J. Sensenderfer (active 1871–1874) Baseball. It was easier to say "Sen-Sen" than this outfielder's real name. Also called COUNT.

SENOR [EL]—Al Lopez (1908–) Baseball c. **H/F**

SEPP—Josef Maler (1944–) Soccer. Some say Sepp was the world's greatest goalkeeper of the 1970s.

SEVE—Severiano Ballesteros (1957–) Golf.

SHAD—John C. Barry (1876–1936) Baseball of.

SHAD—Charles Flint Rhem (1901–1969) Baseball p.

SHAD—Clay Roe (1901–1956) Baseball. This pitcher's nickname flows from his last name.

SHAG—Frank J. Shaughnessy (1883–1969) Baseball, football coach.

SHAKEY—Michael Robert Walton (1945–) Hockey c.

SHANO—John Francis Collins (1885–1955) Baseball of/mgr.

SHERIFF—David Stanley Harris (1900– 1973) Baseball of.

SHERIFF—Hal Burnham Lee (1907–) Baseball of.

SHERIFF—Tal Maples (1911–1975) Football.

SHERRY—Sherwood Magee (1884–1924) Baseball of.

SHERRY—Sherrad Smith (1891–1949) Baseball p.

SHIPWRECK—John Simms Kelly (active 1930s) Football b.

SHIPWRECK KELLY—Alvin Anthony Kelly (1885–1952) Flagpole sitting.

SHOES—Billy Johnson (1952–) Football.

One of only three players in NFL history to gain 3,000 yards in punt returns. (The other two were Val Sikahema of the Philadelphia Eagles and Rick Upchurch.) Also called WHITE SHOES.

SHON—Alex Klein (active 1922–1926) Football.

SHOOK—Elmer Brown (1883–1955) Baseball p.

SHORTY—Gordon Carpenter (1919–) Basketball.

SHORTY—Wilfred Green (1896–1960) Hockey. **H/F**

This right wing played for the New York Americans.

SHORTY—Clair Long (active 1916) Football.

SHOT [THE]—Jack Foley (1940–) Basketball.

Foley, a 6' 5" forward, had a great jump shot. An All-American at Holy Cross, he averaged 28.4 points for a career total of 2,185 points.

SHOTGUN—Mike Chartak (1916–1967) Baseball p.

SHOTGUN—John Hargis (1920–) Basketball g-f.

SHOTGUN—George Shuba (1924–) Baseball.

Baseball outfielders were frequently called Shotgun if they had a "rifle" for an arm.

SHOULDERS—Tom Acker (1930–) Baseball p.

SHOULDERS—Arnold Barry Latman (1936–) Baseball p.

SHOWBOAT—Arnold Boykin. Football.

On December 1, 1951, Showboat Boykin of Mississippi scored seven (yes, count them—seven) touchdowns against Mississippi State. The final score was 49–7.

SHOWBOAT—Bob Hall (active 1949–1970s) Basketball.

Hall was a slick ballhandler (a showboat among showboats) on the Harlem Globetrotters.

SHOWDOWN MAN—Homer Hill Norton (1895–1965) Football coach.

SHRIMP—Jim Foly (1903–deceased) Football.

SHRIMP—Roy Worters (1900–1957) Hockey. **H/F**

Worters may have been a small goalie (5' 3" and 130 pounds) but in 1929 and 1931 he had a goals-against average of 1.21 and 1.68.

SHUG—Ralph Jordan. Football coach (Auburn).

SHUNT HUNT—James Hunt (1947–1993) Auto racing.

Englishman Hunt was accident prone at the beginning of his career, and shunt is British slang for *accident.*

SI—Sihugo Green (1934–) Basketball. This two-time All-American guard scored thirty-three points to lead Duquesne to the championship of the NIT.

SIBBY—Sebastian Daniel Sisti (1920–) Baseball if/of.

SIGGY—Larry Siegfried (1939–) Basketball.

SIKI—J. V. Sikes (active 1920s) Football.

SILENT CAL—Ray Adelphia Benge (1902–) Baseball.

Both he and President Coolidge were known for their silent approach toward life.

SILENT GEORGE—George Hendrick (1949–) Baseball.

This four-time All Star played right field and first base, knocked in 1,111 runs and homered 267 times. He did everything except talk to newspaper reporters.

SILENT JIM—James Tatum (1919–1967) Football coach.

SILENT POLE [THE]—Harry Coveleski (1886–1950) Baseball p. See THE GIANT KILLER.

SILENT TOM—Thomas Smith (1878–1957) Horse trainer.

SILK—Jean Derouillere (1968–) Basketball g.

SILK—Len Wilkes (1937–) Baseball.

SILK STOCKING—Harry Schafer (1846–1935) Baseball 3b.

SILKY—Peter Gerald Sullivan (1951–) Hockey c.

SILVER FOX [THE]—David Pearson. Auto racing.

SILVER FOX [THE]—Lawrence Timothy Shaw (1899–1977) Football coach. Also called BUCK.

SILVER FOX OF THE NORTHLAND [THE]—Bernard William Bierman (1894–) Football coach. Also called THE HAMMER OF THE NORTH.

SILVER JET [THE]—Dennis Hull (1944–) Hockey.

Dennis was the younger brother of Bobby Hull, THE GOLDEN JET. When Bobby Hull left the Black Hawks in 1972 for Winnipeg, Dennis took his place on the line with Pit Martin and Jim Pappin.

SILVER KING—Charles Frederick Koenig (1868–1938) Baseball. Koenig had silver streaks in his hair and his last name means king. Throwing sidearm without a windup (even without men on base), the Silver King compiled a record of 206–152.

SILVER SCOTT [THE]—Tommy Armour (1895–1968) Golf. **H/F** See THE SILVER FOX.

SIR—Charles Barkeley (1963–) Basketball. Known for demanding and earning respect on the court, this forward netted his 15,000th point in 1993.

SIR—Fran Tarkenton (1940–) Football qb. **H/F** In his purple uniform, the ever-confident Tarkenton seemed royal. He was definitely in charge of his offense. Sir Tarkenton sometimes even drew up new plays for his teammates while in the huddle. See THE SCRAMBLER.

SIR RICHARD—Duff Cooley (1873–1937) Baseball. This outfielder carried himself like a gentleman.

SIS—John Winton Hopkins (1883–1929) Baseball of.

SIX FINGERS—Antonio Alfonseca. Baseball. This pitcher for the Florida Marlins really has six fingers on each hand. "I think God gave me more fingers and toes because He wanted to show that I'm special and that I will be special someday," he said. Also known as "The Octopus."

SIX-MILLION DOLLAR MAN—John Elway (1960–) Football. In 1983, this quarterback signed a five-year contract worth $6 million.

SIX YARDS—Emil M. Sitko (1923–1973) Football. This Notre Dame running back earned his nickname by averaging that many yards per carry. Also called RED.

SIXTH MAN [THE]—Frank Ramsey (1931–) Basketball. The first man off the bench, Ramsey was considered the "sixth starter" for the Boston Celtics. He averaged 13.4 points over 623 games. See THE KENTUCKY COLONEL.

SKEETER—Carson Lee Bigbee (1895–1964) Baseball. This outfielder earned the nickname Skeeter because he was 5' 9" and 157 pounds.

SKEETER—Larmar Ashby Newsome (1910–1989) Baseball. At 5' 9" and 155 pounds, this shortstop was slightly smaller than the Skeeter above.

SKEETER—Clyde Wright (1941–) Baseball. This pitcher was given his nickname so he wouldn't have to be called Clyde.

SKEETER—Victor Teal (1949–) Hockey rw.

SKI—Oscar Donald Melillo (1899–1963) Baseball 2b.

SKIDS—John J. Lipton (1922–) Baseball ss.

SKIM—Gordon F. Brown (1880–1911) Football. One of three men to make All-American four times (Frank Hinkey and Truxton Hare were the other two).

He also earned a Phi Beta Kappa key and was a successful banker with J. P. Morgan & Company, before his death at thirty-one.

SKINNY—Bill Johnson (1911–1980) Basketball. **H/F**

SKINNY—Wally Shaner (1900–1992) Baseball. This outfielder was 6' 2" and 195 pounds. He was nicknamed after a character called Shinny Shaner in *Us Boys*, a comic strip.

SKINS—John Jones (1901–1956) Baseball of.

SKIP—Nicholas Buoniconti (1940–) Football.

SKIP—Jules Harlicka (1940–) Basketball.

SKIP—Philip Gordon Krake (1943–) Hockey c.

SKIP—Gene Maunch (1925–) Baseball. Maunch won Manager of the Year three times, but he never won a World Series.

SKIP—Allen Leslie Teal (1933–) Hockey c.

SKIP—Alonzo Thomas. Football db.

SKIP—Duane Thoren (1943–) Basketball c.

SKIPPY—S. R. Shapoff (1919–) Horse trainer.

SKIPPY—Lucian Whittaker (active 1954–1955) Basketball.

SKOONJ—Carl Furillo (1922–1989) Baseball. A Skoonj is an Italian snail; his nickname referred to this right fielder's liking for Italian cuisine. Also called THE READING RIFLE.

SKUNK—Daryl Sanders (active 1963–1964) Football t.

SKY—Ralph Siewert (1923–) Basketball. This was a 7' 1" center from Dakota Wesleyan.

SKY—Kenny Walker (1964–) Basketball f-g.

SKY KING—Dave Kingman (1948–) Baseball. Kingman hit tremendous home runs. Sky King was a radio and television character of the early 50's. Also called BIG BIRD. See KING KONG.

SKYROCKET—Samuel Smith (1868–1916) Baseball. This first baseman hit a total of one home run for Louisville.

SLAM BAM—Sam Cunningham (active 1973–1981) Football fb.

SLAPPER—Steve Wilson (1964–) Baseball. This pitcher's nickname refers to his days back in British Columbia when he played hockey.

SLASH—Kordell Stewart (1972–) Football. Quarterback for the Pittsburgh Steelers. In a 1997 game against the Patriots, Slash threw for 266 yards and ran for fifty-seven, giving the Steelers a 24–21 victory.

SLASHER—Ted Atkinson (active 1950s) Jockey.

SLATS—Raymond H. Baxter (active 1910–1920) Football.

SLATS—Amory Gill (1901–1966) Basketball.
Gill had a 599–392 record in a thirty-six year coaching career at Oregon State.

SLATS—Marty Marion (1917–) Baseball.
At 6' 2" and 170 pounds, Marion was a very slender shortstop. He and the Cards played in the 1942, 1943, 1944, and 1946 World Series. See THE OCTOPUS and GASHOUSE GANG.

SLATS—Cornelius Alexander McGillicuddy (active 1886–1896) Baseball. Slats was the first talking catcher. He crouched close to the batter and chattered away the whole time while the batsman was attempting to hit.

SLATS—Glen Cameron Sather (1943–) Hockey lw.

SLATS—Bill Sattler (1916–) Basketball c.

SLEEPY—Eric Floyd (1960–) Basketball.
This guard played for Georgetown, Houston, and New Jersey.

SLEUTH—Tom Fleming (1873–1957) Baseball of.

SLEWFOOT—Cecil Butler (1937–) Baseball p.

SLICK—Bob Leonard (1932–) Basketball.
Two-time All-American guard at Indiana, Leonard later played for the Lakers and the Bulls from 1957 to 1963.

SLIDING BILLY—William Robert Hamilton (1866–1940) Baseball of. **H/F** Sliding Billy was baseball's first great base stealer. (And with 2,158 hits and 1,187 bases on balls, he was on base a lot.) His total of stolen bases is 937.

SLIM—Raymond Benjamin Caldwell (1888–1967) Baseball p. Also called RUBE.

SLIM—Harold Halderson (1900–) Hockey d.

SLIM—Ed Haughton (1890–1942) Baseball p.

SLIM—Grover Lowdermilk (1885–1968) Baseball p.

SLIM—Harry Franklin Sallee (1885–1950) Baseball.
Slim at 6' 3" and 180 pounds, Sallee's pitching stats were 172–143 from 1908 to 1921.

SLIM—Urgel Wintermute (1917–) Basketball.
Wintermute got his nickname early because he was 6' 7" in high school. He played for Oregon and later pro ball for the Detroit Eagles and the Portland Boilermakers.

SLINGSHOT—David O'Brien (active 1930s) Football.
Also called LITTLE DAVID.

SLIP—Edward P. Madigan (1896–1965) Football.

SLOPPY—Hollis Thurston (1899–1973) Baseball p.
Thurston inherited the nickname from his father, who ran a high-class restaurant in Tombstone, Arizona, that became known as Sloppy Thurston's place because of the proprietor's habit of feeding soup to tramps. See HOT STOVE LEAGUE.

SLOW JOE—Joe Doyle (1881–1947) Baseball.
It was a long game the days Doyle pitched.

SLUGGER—Jack Burns (1907–1975) Baseball.
Burns had the unenviable job of replacing Gorgeous George Sisler at first base.

SMACK—Lawrence Reisor (active 1920s) Football.

SMACKOVER—Clyde Scott (1924–) Football.

SMALL MONTANA—Benjamin Gan (1913–) Boxing.
His name meant "little mountain." This flyweight was 79–31 during his career and once held the world title.

SMASHER—Bob Asher (active 1970–1975) Football.
This hard-hitting tackle was 6' 5" and 254 pounds.

SMILEY—Dale Hall (1924) Basketball.
Hall was an All-American guard at West Point in 1944 and 1945.

SMILEY—Howard W. Johnson (1910–1945) Football.

SMILEY—Bob Keegan (1920–) Baseball.
This pitcher with a 40–36 record had an omnipresent smile on his face.

SMILEY—William Meronek (1917–) Hockey.

SMILING—Stan Hack (1909–1979) Baseball.
This third baseman was as warm and friendly as his smile. Hack hit .301 during his sixteen-year career.

SMILING MICKEY—Michael Francis Welch (1859–1941) Baseball p. **H/F**

SMILING TIMOTHY—Timothy John Keefe (1857–1933) Baseball p. **H/F**

SMITTY—Jean Guy Gendron (1934–) Hockey.

SMOKE HERRING—Bill Herring (1893–1962) Baseball.

SMOKY—Forrest Burgess (1927–) Baseball.
This six-time All Star catcher, who caught his nickname from his father, batted .295 during his seventeen-year career.

SMOKY JOE—Joe Wood (1889–1985) Baseball.
In 1912, this fastball pitcher was 34–5 (sixteen wins in a row), along with two wins and a save in the World Series. After hurting his thumb, he finished his career as an outfielder.

SMOKEY STOVER—William Stover McIlwain (1939–1966)

Baseball. This pitcher was named for a cartoon character.

SMOOTH AS SILK—Jamaal Wilkes (1953–) Basketball. This forward with a rhyming nickname displayed his silky style at UCLA before moving on to the Golden State Warriors.

SMURF—David M. Smith. Cricket.

SNACKS—Reggie Cleveland (1948–) Baseball. This pitcher liked to eat. Also called DOUBLE CHEESEBURGER.

SNAKE—Knowlton Ames (1868–1931) Football. He was tricky as a snake in that he used a fake kick.

SNAKE [THE]—Ruby Ortiz. Boxing.

SNAKE [THE]—Jacques Plante (1929–1986) Hockey. **H/F** Jake the Snake is rhyming slang.

SNAKE [THE]—Don Prudhomme. Auto racing.

SNAKE MAN [THE]—Moe Drabowsky (1935–) Baseball. Drabo, a pitcher, liked to stick snakes in teammates' lockers.

SNAKEHIPS—William Tucker (active 1967–1971) Football.

SNAKEHEAD—Charles Sheppard. Rodeo.

SNAPPER—Edward Garrison (1868–1930) Horse racing. This jockey gave to the language the phrase— "Garrison Finish"—a come-from-behind victory.

SNAPPER—Ford Garrison (1915–) Baseball. Also called ROCKY.

SNIPE—Roy Emil Hansen (1907–1978) Baseball.

SNOOKER—Morrie Arnovich (1910–1959) Baseball.

SNOOKS—John Kelley (1907–) Hockey. Kelley was the longtime hockey coach at Boston College.

SNOOP—Artie Wilson (1920–) Baseball. "Artie was one of the greatest shortstops anybody ever saw," said Monte Irvin, "in the old Negro League we named him Octopus because it seemed as though he had eight arms."

SNOOZER—Frank Trushinski. Hockey. After losing the sight in one eye following a hockey injury, Trushinski who played for the Kitchener Greenshirts was injured in his other eye. This led to a rule change in hockey. See TRUSHINSKI BY LAW.

SNOW-SHOE—John Albert Thompson (1827–1876) Skiing. **H/F** For thirteen years Thompson delivered the mail to northern California on skis.

SNOWY—Reginald Baker (active 1908) Boxing (middleweight). The Australian Baker lost the 1908

Games title to J.W.H.T. Douglas.

SNUFFY—Clinton James Smith (1913–) Hockey. **H/F** Smith, a winner of the Lady Byng Trophy twice, had very few penalties during his twelve-year career.

SNUFFY—George Henry Stirnweiss (1918–1958) Baseball 2b/3b/ss.

SNUFFY SMITH—Clint Smith (1913–) Hockey. Named for the cartoon character, this center was only 5' 7" but an important part of the 1940 New York Ranger team that was unbeaten for nineteen games on the way to the Stanley Cup championship.

SOBIE—Ron Sobieszczyk (1934–) Basketball.

SOCKS—Harry Seibold (1896–1965) Baseball.

SOFT DOE [THE]—Peggy Fleming (1948–) Figure skating. This was the nickname given to Fleming in Europe for her soft facial features and delicate manner. Fleming won the world championship three times and a gold medal in the 1968 Olympics.

SOLDIER BOY—George Curry (1888–1963) Baseball p.

SONAR—Joe Hassett (1955–) Basketball. This guard's nickname came from his penchant for shooting long field goals for the Golden State Warriors.

SONNY—John Dixon (1924–) Baseball p.

SONNY—Edward Gluck (1902–1973) Basketball.

SONNY—Sidney Hertzberg (1922–) Basketball. Hertzberg played guard for CCNY and in the NBA.

SONNY—Christian Jurgensen (1934–) Football. **H/F** Jurgensen played quarterback for the Philadelphia Eagles from 1957 to 1963 and for the Washington Redskins from 1964 to 1974.

SONNY—Charles Liston (1932–1970) Boxing (heavyweight). Cassius Clay called him The Big Ugly Bear.

SONNY—Alphonse Moyse (1898–1973) Bridge.

SONNY—David Werblin (1912–1993) Football.

SONNY—Raymond Workman (1909–1966) Horse racing. **H/F** A jockey for the Whitneys and the Vanderbilts, Workman collected 1,169 wins, 870 seconds, and 785 third places.

SOUP—Clarence Campbell (1915–) Baseball of.

SOUP—Clark Daniel Shaughnessy (1892–1970) Football coach.

SOUR MASH—Harold Jack Daniels (1927–) Baseball. This outfielder was nicknamed after Jack Daniels whisky.

SOX—Silas Seth Griffis (1880–1950) Hockey d. **H/F** Also called SI.

SPARKPLUG—Jim Keenan (1898–1926) Baseball p.

SPARKY—Albert Lyle (1944–) Baseball.
This Cy Young Award-winning pitcher threw 1,265 innings in relief for the Red Sox and the Yankees.

SPARKY—Wilbur Stalcup (1910–1972) Basketball.
Stalcup coached at the University of Missouri where he had a 195–179 record.

SPARKY—Melville Vail (1906–) Hockey d.

SPARKY—Malcolm Wade (1914–) Basketball.
Wade played guard for Louisiana State University where he often sparked the offense with displays of his dribbling ability.

SPARROW—William Morton (deceased) Baseball p.

SPARROW—Charles Young (1865–1951) Trapshooting.
H/F When Young began his successful shooting career, sparrows were used instead of clay pigeons.

SPATS—Lenny Moore (active 1956–1963) Football hb.
H/F Also called SPUTNIK.

SPEC—Orban Sanders (active 1950s) Football qb.

SPEC—Frank Joseph Shea (1920–) Baseball.
Shea had freckles. His other nickname was The Naugatuck Nugget because he was from Naugatuck, Connecticut. He was most like a nugget his first year when he was 14–5.

SPECIAL DELIVERY—Edgar Jones. Football.

SPECIAL K—Clark Kellogg (1961–) Basketball. Kellogg received his nickname for his last name and the cereal when he played forward at Ohio State. He went on to become the NBA Rookie of the Year for 1982–83.

SPECIAL K—Larry Kenon (1952–) Basketball f.

SPECIAL K—Kermit Washington (1951–) Basketball f-c.

SPECS—Robert H. Crawford (active 1918–1928) Horse racing. **H/F** This jockey had freckles.

SPECS—Carmen Hill (1895–1990) Baseball.
In 1915, this pitcher was one of the first to wear glasses. Also called BUNKER.

SPECS—Henry Lee Meadows (1894–1963) Baseball.
Meadows wore glasses. He was 189–180 during his fifteen-year pitching career.

SPECS—Bill Rigney (1919–) Baseball 2b/mgr.
Rigney was wearing glasses in 1946 when few ballplayers did so. His other nickname Cricket was for the way he moved around the bag.

SPECS—George Torporcer (1899–1989) Baseball.
Playing shortstop with the Cardinals in 1921, Torporcer became the first player in major-league history to wear spectacles.

SPEED DEMON—Pasquale Agati. Auto racing.

SPEED MERCHANT—Jack Laviolette (1879–1980) Hockey.
Laviolette, a defenseman, and Didier CANNONBALL Pitre were members of the Montreal Canadiens in the early 1900s. Their skating ability led their team to be known as THE FLYING FRENCHMEN.

SPEEDY—Louis W. Babbs (1908–1976) Motorcycle racing.

SPEEDY—Achille Mitchell. Boxing (middleweight).

SPEEDY GONZALEZ—Jose Gonzalez. Boxing (lightweight).
Gonzalez was nicknamed after the cartoon character.

SPEEDY GONZALEZ—Zeferino Gonzalez. Boxing (junior middleweight).

SPIDER—Willis Bennett (1943–)
Spider Bennett played one season (1968–69) with Dallas-Houston, and scored 440 points in fifty-nine games.

SPIDER—John Jorgensen (1919–) Baseball.
Third baseman Jorgensen's nickname stems from his high school days when he turned out for basketball wearing black.

SPIDER—Tommy Kelly (1867–deceased) Boxing.

SPIDER—Carl Lockart (active 1965–1975) Football db.

SPIDER—Edward Joseph Mazur (1929–) Hockey.
The appearance of this left winger was tall and gangly.

SPIDER—Johnny Newman (1963–) Basketball f-g.

SPIDER—Emile Pladner (1906–1980) Boxing (flyweight).

SPIDER—Vladimir Sabich (1946–1976) Skiing.

SPIDER—Jerry Sloan (1942–) Basketball g-f.

SPIDER—Travis Webb. Auto racing.

SPIDERMAN—Jimmy Allen (active 1974–1981) Football db.

SPIDER BILL—Bill Cissell (1904–1949) Baseball 2b.

SPIKE—William Eckert (1909–1971) Baseball commissioner.

SPIN—Isadore Solario (active 1960s) Basketball coach.

SPINACH—Oscar Melillo (1899–1963) Baseball.
Third base coach when Lou Boudreau managed the Cleveland Indians in 1942. As a player for the St. Louis Browns and the Boston Red Sox, he compiled a .260 batting average over twelve seasons. When this outfielder came down with Bright's Disease, Melillo went on a diet that kept him eating spinach, spinach, and

more spinach. (At one time it was thought to be a cure.) Also called SKI and THE LITTLE WOP.

SPIRIT [THE]—Mickey Davis (1950–) Basketball f-g.

SPITTIN' BILL—Bill Doak (1891–1954) Baseball p.

SPLENDID SPLINTER [THE]—Jim Rayl (1941–) Basketball. Rayl was a 6' 2", 155-pound guard for Indiana. Twice he scored fifty-six points in a game and once made thirty-two free throws in a row.

SPOILER [THE]—Johnny Risko (1902–1953) Boxing.

SPOKE—Mark Devlen (1894–1973) Football. Quarterback for Cleveland (1920) and New York (1924).

SPOKE—Tris Speaker (1888–1958) Baseball of. **H/F** Spoke is the past tense of speak. See THE GREY EAGLE.

SPONGE—Howard Edward Storie (1911–1968) Baseball c.

SPOOK—Forrest Jacobs (1925–) Baseball. Many of second baseman Jacobs' hits fell just out of reach of the outstretched arms of the fielders.

SPOOK—Carmen Salvino (1933–) Bowling. Salvino's nickname, a professional bowler for forty years, meant that he was jumpy.

SPOOK—Bob Speake (1930–) Baseball. Speake, an outfielder, was skinny and kind of spooky. His nickname is a play on his last name.

SPOOK—Isadore Spector (active 1939–1941) Football.

SPOOKS—Walter Gerber (1891–1951) Baseball. It was spooky how the ball seemed to find its way into Gerber's glove. Gerber was one of the best short-stops at executing the double play.

SPOT—Chet Falk (1905–) Baseball p.

SPRATT—Jack Cobb (1905–1966) Basketball. This player of the year in 1926 received his nickname from Jack Spratt of nursery rhyme fame.

SPRINGFIELD RIFLE [THE]—Vic Raschi (1919–1988) Baseball. Raschi was born in West Springfield, Massachusetts. In 1951, this pitcher led the American League in strikeouts with 164.

SPUD—Spurgeon Chandler (1907– 1990) Baseball. This pitcher's nickname was a shortening of Spurgeon.

SPUD—Virgil Lawrence Davis (1904–1984) Baseball. Davis liked potatoes and ate them three times a day. He also liked to hit: this catcher's sixteen-year average was .308. See GASHOUSE GANG.

SPUD—Howie Krist (1916–1989) Baseball p.

SPUD—Anthony Webb (1963–) Basketball. Although Webb was less than 5' 6" tall, that was not the reason for his nickname. A friend of the family had thought his head at birth looked like Russia's Sputnik. Spud was a shortened version of his family nickname of Sputnikhead.

SPUR—Danny Spradlin (1957–) Football.

SQUARE JAW—Bill Ramsey (1921–) Baseball. Though his features were chiseled in stone, this out-fielder's career lasted less than a year.

SQUAREHEAD—Frank Finley Rodeo.

SQUASH—Carl Cardarelli (1895–1969) Football.

SQUASH—Frank Wilson (1901–1974) Baseball.

SQUATTY—Thurman Munson (1947–1979) Baseball c. Also called PUDGE, ROUND MAN, and BAD BODY.

SQUEAKY—Otto Adam Bluege (1909–1977) Baseball ss.

SQUEAKY—Eugene Melchiorre (1927–) Basketball. This guard's nickname came from his high-school days when his voice was changing. He later played college ball at Bradley where he scored 1,576 points. His career was ended by his involvement in the basketball scandals of the 1950s.

SQUEEKY—Jeff Medlen. Golf. He is Nick Price's caddy.

SQUID—Sidney Moncrief (1957–) Basketball g.

SQUIDLY—Sid Fernandez (1962–) Baseball p. Also called EL SID (a pun on the Spanish hero El Cid).

SQUIRE OF KENNET SQUARE [THE]—Herb Pennock (1894–1948) Baseball p. **H/F**

SQUIRREL—Roy Sievers (1926–) Baseball of./3b.

STAN THE MAN UNUSUAL—Don Stanhouse (1951–) Baseball p.

STARVIN' MARVIN—Marvin Freeman (1963–) Baseball p.

STASH—Stan Mikita (1940–) Hockey c. Also called STOSH. See MIKITA MOUSE.

STATEN ISLAND SCOT [THE]—Bobby Thomson (1923–) Baseball of. Thomson was born in Glasgow, Scotland, and grew up on Staten Island. Also called THE FLYING SCOT. See THE SHOT HEARD AROUND THE WORLD.

STEADY EDDIE—Eddie Lopat (1918–1992) Baseball.

STEAMBOAT—Clem Dreisewerd (1916–) Baseball. Dreisewerd worked around steamboats before he became a baseball pitcher.

STEAMBOAT—Rees Williams (1892–1979) Baseball p.

STEAMER—Fred G. Maxwell (1890–1975) Hockey. **H/F**
Maxwell, who played rover on several teams, earned
his nickname for his ability to skate.

STEMMER—Peter David Stemkowski (1943–) Hockey.
This center's nickname was a shortening of his last
name.

STEWART—Robert Gavin (1960–) Hockey lw/rw.

STICK—Gene Michael (1938–) Baseball.
This nickname came from the shortstop's sticklike
appearance (6' 2" and 183 pounds).

STILT [THE]—Wilt Chamberlain (1936–) Basketball.
Wilt the Stilt was a nickname given to Chamberlain by
sportswriters. The nickname that this first player in
NBA history to score 30,000 points preferred was THE
BIG DIPPER.

STINKY—Harry Albert Davis (1910–) Baseball.
This first baseman was said to look like the character
of the same name in a comic strip.

STIX—Leroy Morley (1906–) Basketball.
Morley's coaching record was 367–213 in twenty-two
years at Western Illinois.

STOCKS—Wally Stocking. Boxing (lightweight).

STONE HANDS—Roberto Duran (1951–) Boxing.
Duran was the lightweight champion from 1972 to 1978
and the welterweight champion in 1980.

STONEFINGERS—Dick Stuart (1932–) Baseball.
Stuart had an inability to field simple ground balls at
first base. He was also known as the Boston Strangler.
See DR. STRANGEGLOVE.

STONEY—George E. McLinn (1884–1953) Sportscaster.

STOOPING—Jack Gorman (1859–1889) Baseball 1b.

STORK [THE]—Jim Ryan (1947–) Track and field. **H/F**
Ryan, one of the premier distance runners of his age,
lost to Kip Keino in the 1972 Olympics.

STORM—George Davis (1961–) Baseball p.

STORMIN'—Norm Cash (1934–) Baseball 1b.

STORMIN' GORMAN—Gorman Thomas (1950–) Baseball.
This rhyming nickname was for a big outfielder who
swung big as well as struck out big. Also called BIG
SPIKE.

STORMIN' NORMAN—Norman Van Lier, III (1947–)
Basketball. Also called THE STORM.

STORMY—Roy Weatherly (1915–1991) Baseball.
This outfielder's nickname was hooked up with his
last name.

STORMY—Charles Wolfner, Jr. Football owner.

STOSH—Stanley Mikita (1940–) Hockey c.

STRATFORD STREAK [THE]—Howie Morenz (1902–1937)
Hockey f. **H/F**

STRAW MAN [The]—Darryl Strawberry (1962–) Baseball
of.

STRAWBERRY BILL—William Bernhard (1871–1949)
Baseball p. (active 1899–1907) Bernhard was a strawberry blond.

STRETCH—Leon Brown (1919–) Basketball f.

STRETCH—Willie Lee McCovey (1938–) Baseball. **H/F**
The 6' 4" McCovey was able to field most errant
throws to first base. He was also terrific at bat. He was
the home-run leader three times and finished his
career with 521 homers.

STRETCH—Francis Meehan (1898–1968) Basketball.
Meehan was 6' 7", a big player for his day. During his
four seasons, Seaton Hall was 50–10. He played for
several pro teams, often receiving $100 per game.

STRETCH—Jack Dorn Phillips (1921–) Baseball.
Phillips had a long reach for difficult throws to him at
first base.

STRETCH—Howie Schultz (1922–) Basketball c-f.

STROLL—Lemuel Barney (1945–) Football. In his rookie
season with the Detroit Lions, Barney made three
touchdown interceptions, tying an NFL mark.

STRONG BOY OF BOSTON [THE]—John Lawrence Sullivan
(1858–1918) Boxing (heavyweight). **H/F**
Also called THE GREAT JOHN L. and JOHN L.
See BOSTON STRONG BOY.

STRONGEST MAN IN THE WORLD [THE]—Louis Cyr
(1863–1912) Weight lifting. Cyr once picked up over
550 pounds with one finger; another time he lifted a
platform with eighteen men standing on it.

STRUTTIN' JIM—James Leroy Bottomley (1900–1959)
Baseball 1b. See SUNNY JIM.

STUB—Leonard B. Allison (active 1920s–1940s) Football
coach.

STUB—Joseph Michael Erautt (1921–) Baseball.
This Chicago White Sox catcher was 5' 7" and 175
pounds. He had also been chubby in school.

STUBBY—Harold Kruger (1897–1965) Swimming.

STUBBY—Frank Overmire (1919–1977) Baseball.
Stubby was 5' 7", 170 pounds, and 58–67 for his
pitching career.

STUBBY—Charles M. Pearson (1920–1944) Football.

STUD—George "Foghorn" Myatt (1914–) Baseball. Second baseman Myatt was a loud-mouthed womanizer, who was fast on the base paths. Also called MERCURY.

STUDENT [THE]—George F. Slosson (1854–1949) Billiards.

STUFFY—John Phalen McInnis (1890–1960) Baseball. As a player, McInnis had the right stuff. In 1921, this first baseman handled 1,300 chances without an error. He also batted .308 and played in three World Series.

STUMPY—Gail Goodrich (1943–) Basketball. Although only 6' 1", Stumpy helped UCLA win two NCAA titles in 1964 and 1965. In 1965, he was also All-American and averaged 24.8 points a game. Later he starred for the Los Angeles Lakers. In 1972, he was the team's high scorer with a 25.9 average.

STUTZ—Stan Modzelewski (1920–) Basketball. Stutz, a simplification of his last name, starred at Rhode Island from 1939–1942. This two-time All-American was twice the nation's scoring leader.

SUDDEN SAM—Sam McDowell (1942–) Baseball. His nickname described his quick pitching delivery.

SUDS—Gene Fodge (1931–) Baseball. After a shellacking in the minors, this pitcher was sent to the showers early.

SUDS—Bill Sudakis (1946–) Baseball. This third baseman's nickname is short for Sudakis.

SUGAR—Bob Cain (1907–1975) Baseball. This pitcher's nickname is a play on his last name. Ditto for the next four Sugars.

SUGAR—John Cain (active 1930s) Football.

SUGAR—Merritt Patrick Cain (1907–1975) Baseball p.

SUGAR—Frank Kane (1895–1962) Baseball of.

SUGAR—Tom Kane (1906–1973) Baseball 2b.

SUGAR—Ultiminio Ramos (1941–) Boxing. Ramos was the world featherweight champion from 1963 to 1964.

SUGAR—Michael Ray Richardson (1955–) Basketball g.

SUGAR—Ray Robinson (1920–) Boxing. **H/F**

SUGAR—Ray Seales. Boxing (middleweight).

SUGARBEAR—Randy Crowder (active 1972–1982) Football t.

SUGAR JIM—Samuel James Henry (1920–) Hockey g.

SUGAR SHACK—Eddie Shack (1937–) Hockey. This right wing's nickname came from the 1960s pop

song, "Sugar Shack." Fast Eddie (another nickname) was a crowd favorite—a player who played fast and loose and also tallied twenty or more goals for five different teams.

SUGARBEAR—Larvell Blanks (1950–) Baseball. Shortstop Larvell was as eager as a hungry bear at the plate; a song called "Sugar, Sugar" was in the air at the time.

SUICIDE—Ted Elder. Rodeo.

SUITCASE—Harry Leon Simpson (1925–) Baseball. Simpson played first base and in the outfield for seventeen teams in eleven years.

SUITCASE—Gary Smith (1944–) Hockey. Smith played for ten teams in as many years.

SUITCASE BOB—Robert Ira Seeds (1907–) Baseball. Seeds played nine years in the big leagues and compiled a respectful .277 lifetime batting average. He received his nickname because he played for a number of different teams in his career and was frequently packing his suitcase.

SUN GOD [THE]—Paul Westphal (1950–) Basketball. Westphal, a guard, got this nickname while performing for the Phoenix Suns in the late 1970s and early 1980s.

SUNDAY PITCHER [THE]—Ted Lyons (1900–1986) Baseball p. **H/F**

SUNNY JIM—Jim Bottomley (1900–1959) Baseball 1b. **H/F** Bottomley had a sunny disposition. He was also a slick fielding first baseman who collected 2,313 hits and a .310 batting average during his sixteen-year career.

SUNNY JIM—James W. Coffroth (1874–1943) Promoter.

SUNNY JIM—Jimmy Dygert (1884–1936) Baseball p.

SUNNY JIM—James Edward Fitzsimmons (1874–1966) Horse trainer. **H/F** Two of Sunny Jim's horses won the Triple Crown—Gallant Fox (1930) and Omaha (1935). In all, his horses won 2,275 races. Also called DEAN OF AMERICAN TRAINERS, GRAND OLD MAN OF RACING, and MR. FITZ.

SUPER GNAT—Noland Smith (active 1967–1969) Football rw.

SUPER JOHN—John Williamson (1952–1996) Basketball g.

SUPER KID—Steve Cruz (1963–) Boxing (junior featherweight).

SUPER TEX—A. J. Foyt (1935–) Auto racing. **H/F**

SUPERBRAT—John McEnroe (1959–) Tennis.

SUPERCHIEF—Allie Reynolds (1915–) Baseball.

Native Americans are oftentimes called Chief. Reynolds was a half-blood Cherokee from Oklahoma. And with his two no-hitters, his thirteen-year record of 182–107, and his 7–2 record in six World Series, Reynolds was a super pitcher for the Yankees.

SUPERFOOT—Bill Wallace (1945–) High-kick karate.

SUPERJEW—Mike Epstein (1943–) Baseball. Epstein was 6' 4", weighed 230 pounds, and was Jewish. Manager Rocky Bridges gave Epstein this nickname after the first baseman was voted *The Sporting News'* Minor League Player of 1966.

SUPERMAN [LE]—Jean-Claude Killy (1943–) Skiing. Killy earned his nickname along with three gold medals at the 1968 Winter Olympics.

SUPERMAN OF THE LONDON OLYMPICS [THE]— Bob Mathias (1930–) Track and field. **H/F**

SUPERSUB—Phil Linz (1939–) Baseball. Linz could play anywhere in the infield and outfield.

SUPERSWEDE—Ronnie Peterson (active 1970s) Auto racing. In 1973, Peterson won four Grand Prix and set the fastest practice laps at nine others.

SURE SHOT—Fred Dunlop (1859–1902) Baseball. Dunlop earned his nickname by being the best fielding second baseman in the National League from 1880 to 1891.

SWAFFHAM GYPSY [THE]—Jem Mace (1831–1910) Boxing. **H/F**

SWAMP BABY--Charlie Wilson (1905–1970) Baseball. From Clinton, South Carolina, Wilson played shortstop for the Braves in 1931 and the Cards from 1932 to1935.

SWAMP RAT—Don Garlitz (1933–) Auto racing. Also called BIG DADDY.

SWAMPY—Atley Donald (1910–1992) Baseball. This pitcher grew up in the Louisiana bayou.

SWAMPY—Herschel R. Thompson. Baseball (minor leagues) if.

SWEATSHIRT KID—Bobby Fischer (1943–) Chess. Also called BOY ROBOT and CORDUROY KILLER.

SWEDE—Adolph D. Carlson (1897–1967) Bowling.

SWEDE—Rudolf Hagberg (1907–1960) Football c.

SWEDE—Wade Halbrook (1933–) Basketball. At 7' 3", Halbrook was the tallest player of his time. An All-American center in 1955, he had thirty-six rebounds in one game. As a pro, he had thirty-three rebounds in a game in the NIBL and played for Syracuse in the NBA.

SWEDE—Andrew Viggo Hansen (1924–) Baseball. This pitcher was from Scandinavia.

SWEDE—Mally Johnson (1909–) Basketball f-g.

SWEDE—Walter Perry Johnson (1887–1946) Baseball p/mgr. **H/F** Johnson's background was Swedish. Also called BARNEY and Best Pitcher in Baseball. See BIG TRAIN.

SWEDE—Emergy Ellswoth Larson (1899–1945) Football coach.

SWEDE—Andrew J. Oberlander (1905–1968) Football.

SWEDE—Charles August Risberg (1894–1975) Baseball. Risberg's heritage was Swedish. Risberg, a shortstop, was one of the eight players that Judge Landis banned from baseball for life for his role in the 1919 Black Sox scandal.

SWEDE—David Savage (1947–1973) Auto racing.

SWEDE—Rip Terjesen (1915–) Basketball f-c.

SWEDE—Arnold William Umbach (1903–) Wrestling coach.

SWEDISH EXPRESS [THE]—Anders Hedberg (1951–) Hockey. Hedberg, a right wing, was the first Swedish player on the New York Rangers.

SWEENY—David Schriner (1911–1990) Hockey. **H/F** Schriner led the league in scoring twice as a member of the New York Americans, once with forty-six points (twenty-one goals and twenty-five assists).

SWEET—Reggie Hanson (1968–) Basketball f.

SWEET LOU—Lou Hudson (1944–) Basketball f-g.

SWEET LOU—Lou Piniella (1943–) Baseball. This outfielder had a near-perfect swing. In recent years he has been the manager of the Reds and the Mariners.

SWEET PEA—Roy Jefferson (active 1965–1976) Football rw.

SWEET PETE—Pete Sampras (1971–) Tennis. Sweet Pete (because of his calm personality) certainly ranks as one of the greatest tennis players of all time. In 1990, he won the Men's singles title at the United States Open, the youngest player ever to accomplish that feat. In 1993, he became the first professional tennis player to record more than 1,000 service aces.

SWEET SWINGIN'—Billy Williams (1938–) Baseball. Obviously, this outfielder had a sweet swing.

SWEETBREADS—Abraham Lincoln Bailey (1895–1939) Baseball. This pitcher liked sweetbreads.

SWEET PETE—Pete Sampras (b. August 12, 1971) Tennis. He dominated men's tennis in the 1990s and had a most pleasant personality (in contrast to the "nasty" boys who played in the previous two decades).

SWEETWATER—Nat Clifton (1925–1990) Basketball. One of the first black players in the NBA, and a star forward with the New York Knicks. He was inducted into the Black Athletes Hall of Fame in 1976.

SWEETNESS—Walter Payton (1954–) Football **H/F** Not only did this halfback score 109 touchdowns, but he also rushed for 16,726 yards.

SWEETWATER—Nathaniel Clifton (1922–) Basketball c-f.

SWEETWATER SWATTER—Lew Jenkins (1916–) Boxing. **H/F** Jenkins was born Verlin Jenks in Milburn, Texas.

SWIMMING NUN [THE]—Stella Taylor. Swimming.

SWISH—Bill Nicholson (1914–) Baseball. This outfielder received his nickname for the healthy cuts he took at the plate. In 5,546 at-bats, Swish struck out 884 times. Swish Nicholson also connected, leading the National League in home runs in 1943 with twenty-nine and in 1944 with thirty-three.

SWOOP—Wayne Carleton (1946–) Hockey. Carleton played left wing for the Boston Bruins when they won the Stanley Cup in 1970 and 1972.

SYMPHONY—Larry Ciaffone (1924–) Baseball. The nickname for this one-time Cardinal outfielder came from the symphonic sound of his last name. Ciaffone was hitless in all of his eight major-league at-bats.

T-BONE—Artimus Parker (1952–) Football. Perhaps he was fond of steak?

TABASCO KID [THE]—Norman Elberfeld (1875–1944) Baseball. This hot-tempered shortstop often dared baserunners to spike him.

TAFFY—Taft Wright (1911–1981) Baseball.

Taffy was a diminutive for his first name. This outfielder batted .311 during his nine-year career.

TAIHO [GREAT BIRD]—Koki Naya. Sumo wrestling.

TAKAMIYAMAE—Jesse Kuhaulua. Sumo wrestling.

TAL THE TERRIBLE—Mikhail Tal (1937–1992) Chess. Tal was a cutthroat champion chess player.

TALL PINE OF THE POTTAWATOMIE—Jess Willard (1883–1968) Boxing. Also called BIG JESS, COWBOY JESS, KANSAS GIANT, and POTTAWATOMIE GIANT. See THE GREAT WHITE HOPE.

TANK [THE]—Bob Brannum (1925–) Basketball.

TANK—George McLaren (d. 1967) Football.

TANK—Sherman Eugene Plunkett (1934–1989) Football. He played in the NFL from 1958–1967. His nickname is an allusion to the Sherman Tank and to his size (6' 4", 290 pounds).

TANK—Mike Williams. Boxing.

TANK—Paul Younger (1928–) Football. George Halas once told this L.A. Rams fullback that he was "the greatest, dirtiest, best football player in the league."

TAP—Art Harris Boxing.

TAP TAP—Elijah Makhatini. Boxing.

TAPS—John Gallagher (1904–) Basketball. Gallagher's coaching record at Niagara was 465–264.

TAR BABY [THE]—Sam Langford (1886–deceased) Boxing.

TARZAN—Charles Cooper (1927–) Basketball. **H/F** This strong center (6' 4", 225 pounds) helped the New York Rens compile a 1,303–203 record.

TARZAN—Dave Lemanczyk (1950–) Baseball.

TARZAN—Homer Thompson (1916–) Basketball.

TASMANIAN DEVEL [THE]—Dean Hamel (active 1985–1990) Football.

T.D.—Tony Dorsett (1954–) Football. **H/F**. These initials carried a double meaning for this halfback: Tony Dorsett and touchdown. As a youngster, Dorsett had been called HAWK EYES, or simply HAWK, for his wide-eyed look.

TED—James Meredith (1892–1957) Track and field. Meredith set world records at 800 meters (1:51.9) and 880 yards (1:52.5) at the 1912 Stockholm Olympics and at 400 meters and 440 yards (47.4) in 1916 at Cambridge, Massachusetts.

TEDDY BALLGAME—Theodore Samuel Williams. Baseball. See also SPLENDID SPLINTER and THE KID.

TEE—Clarence Carptenter Boxing (light heavyweight).

TEEDER—Ted Kennedy (1925–ᅠ) Hockey c. **H/F**
Kennedy, the captain, led the Toronto Maple Leafs to
five Stanley Cup championships.

$10,000 BEAUTY [THE]—Michael Joseph Kelley
(1857–1894) Baseball. **H/F** See KING.

TENNESSEE TIGRESS [THE]—Wilma Rudolph (1940–ᅠ)
Track and field. See SKEETER.

TENNIS BALL HEAD—Steve Hovley (1944–ᅠ) Baseball of.

TERRIBLE—Terry McGovern (1880–1955) Boxing
(featherweight). **H/F** McGovern defeated Peddler
Palmer for the world bantamweight title in 1899 and
George Dixon for the world featherweight title in 1900.

TERRIBLE [THE]—Ivan Duane Irwin (1927–ᅠ) Hockey d.
Also called IVAN THE TERRIBLE.

TERRIBLE TED—Ted Turner (1938–ᅠ) Baseball.
This owner of the Atlanta Braves is also called THE
MOUTH OF THE SOUTH.

TERRIBLE TEDDY—Ted Williams (1918–ᅠ) Baseball lf.
H/F Also called TEDDY BALLGAME. See THE KID and
THE SPLENDID SPLINTER.

TEX—James Otto Carleton (1906–1977) Baseball.
Carleton was a pitcher from Comanche, Texas. On
April 30, 1940, he threw a no-hitter for Brooklyn
against Cincinnati. See GASHOUSE GANG.

TEX—Frank Carswell (1919–ᅠ) Baseball.
Carswell was an outfielder from Palestine, Texas.
Also called WHEELS.

TEX—Randy Cobb (1954–ᅠ) Boxing (heavyweight).
One of the many events that turned Howard Cosell
against boxing was reporting the pathetic fight
between Larry Holmes and Randy Cobb. At one point,
Cosell even suggested that his viewers not watch.

TEX—Dewitt Coulter (active 1946–1952) Football.
This tackle played for the New York Giants and the
Montreal Alouettes.

TEX—Jack Evans (1938–ᅠ) Hockey.
Evans was a defenseman who was just that. In fourteen years he scored only twenty-one goals.

TEX—George Lewis Rickard (1870–1928) Sports promoter.
When Tex was the chief officer of Madison Square
Garden, the hockey team became known as Tex's
Rangers, and then the New York Rangers.

TEX—Wilfred Belmont White (1901–deceased) Hockey f.

TEX—Fred Winter (1922–ᅠ) Basketball.

Winter was from Wellington, Texas. He coached at
Marquette, Kansas State, and Washington from 1952
to 1971, compiling a record of 333–176. He also
coached the Houston Rockets for a year.

TEXAS JACK—Jack Kraus (1918–1976) Baseball.
Kraus, a pitcher, hailed from San Antonio.

TEXAS TORNADO [THE]—Jim Kern (1949–ᅠ) Baseball.
Although he was born in Michigan, he received his
nickname from his pitching in the Texas League. See
EMU.

THIN MAN [THE] [EL FLACO]—Johan Cruyff. Soccer.
The nickname of this soccer star.

THIN MAN [THE]—Red Rocha (1923–ᅠ) Basketball c-f.
The nickname is not merely a physical description of
an athlete, but it is also a sly allusion to the mystery
novel by Dashiell Hammett.

THIRTEEN-INCH SHELL—Hugo F. Bezdek (1884–1952)
Football. Bezdek coached both major college football
and managed major-league baseball teams. Also
called BEX and HUGO THE VICTOR.

3 DOG—Willie Davis (1940–ᅠ) Baseball of.
Three was the number on his shirt. He was also fond
of dog racing.

THRILL—Tony Hill (1956–ᅠ) Football.
Hill caught 479 passes during his career with the
Dallas Cowboys, with many of his catches providing
last-minute thrills for Cowboy fans.

THOMINATOR—James Howard Thome (1970–ᅠ) Baseball.
The nickname of this Cleveland Indians' star plays
with the film title *The Terminator*.

THRILL [THE]—Will Clark (1964–ᅠ) Baseball lb.
Also called THE NATURAL.

THROWIN' SAMOAN [THE]—Jack Thompson
(active 1979–1984) Football qb.

THUMPER—Hardy Brown (1924–1991) Football.
Thumper is also the name of the rabbit in Walt
Disney's film version of Bambi.

THUMPER [THE]—Ted Williams (1918–ᅠ) Baseball.
Williams hit 521 career home runs as a Boston Red
Sox left fielder. Also called TEDDY BALLGAME.
See THE KID and THE SPLENDID SPLINTER.

THUNDER—Andre Thorton (1949–ᅠ) Baseball lb.

THUNDER MAKER—Howard Jones (1886–1941) Football
coach.

THUNDER PUP—Shawon Dunston (1963–ᅠ) Baseball ss.

TICKEY—Luther Burden (1953–) Basketball.
After a great year in the ABA, this guard fizzled with the Knicks.

TIDO—Tom Daly (1866–1939) Baseball 2b.

TIE—Tahir Domi (1969–) Hockey rw.

TIGER—Theo Flowers (1895–1927) Boxing (middleweight). **H/F** Flowers was the middleweight champion from 1926 to 1931. Also called GEORGIA DEACON.

TIGER—George Greene (active 1985–1990) Football db.

TIGER—Don Hoak (1928–) Baseball.
Hoak was a one-time fighter before he became a third baseman. But even after joining the Brooklyn Dodgers, he still liked to fight. Hoak's shining moment was for Pittsburgh in the 1960 World Series.

TIGER—Bob Lilly (1939–) Football.
This tackle did not miss a single game in fourteen years with the Dallas Cowboys. His nickname is a play upon the flower Tiger Lily.

TIGER—Frank Walton (1911–1953) Football.

TIGER—Dave Williams (1954–) Hockey.

TIGHT PANTS—John Titus (1876–1943) Baseball.
His nickname is a play upon his last name plus an accurate description of his clothing. Also called Silent John, since he rarely spoke.

TIM—Miles Gilbert Horton (1930–) Hockey d.

TIM BUG—Tim Hardaway (1966–) Basketball.
Guard for the Golden State Warriors. In the 1994–1995 season Tim Bug set a team record by scoring 168 three-pointers.

TIMARU TERROR—Tom Baines. Boxing.
Eighteen-year-old Bob "RUBY" ROBERT Fitzsimmons beat Tom Baines in 1882. See RUBY ROBERT.

TINY—John Andrews (1951–) Football.
Since Andrews stood 6' 6" and weighed 251 pounds Tiny was a joking nickname.

TINY—Ernest Edward Bonham (1913–1949) Baseball.
This pitcher was 6' 2" and 215 pounds, so his nickname was ironic. His best year was 1942 when he posted a 21–5 record for the Yankees.

TINY—Elvin Feather (1903–) Football.
He weighed nearly 200 pounds and stood six feet. Yet another example of nickname reversal.

TINY—Cecil Thompson (1905–1981) Hockey.
Thompson was a small goalie (5' 5", 160 pounds) for the Boston Bruins, but he won four Vezina Trophies.

In 1938, his goals-against record was eighty-nine goals in forty-eight games.

TINY—Claude E. Thornhill (1893–1956) Football.
This longtime coach got his nickname playing tackle because he looked like a giant on the gridiron.

TIP—Elizabeth Lawrence (active 1880s) Tennis.
After tennis was introduced at Smith College in 1881, Lawrence was one of the first women tennis players.

TIPTON SLASHER [THE]—William Perry (1819–1918) Boxing (heavyweight). One of the last of the British bareknuckles champions. In 1857, Perry was defeated by a much smaller Tom Sayers whose specialty was punching an opponent around the eyes.

TITO—John Patsy Francona (1933–) Baseball 1b.

TITO—Terry Landrum (1954–) Baseball.
This outfielder's nickname means *little* in Italian.

TOAST—Elvis Patterson Football.
Patterson was a cornerback who was often burned by receivers who got behind him.

TOBACCO CHEWIN' JOHNNY—Johnny Lanning (1910–1989) Baseball. This pitcher always had a chaw in his cheek.

TOD—Thomas Oscar Davis (1924–) Baseball.
This shortstop's nickname was his initials.

TOD—James F. Sloan (1874–1933) Horse racing. **H/F**
As a youngster Sloan had been called Toad. When he became a jockey, he shortened his nickname to Tod. Sloan was the first to use the "monkey crouch" (sometimes called the "monkey-on-a-stick") that all jockeys use nowadays to reduce air resistance.

TOE—Hector Blake (1912– 1995) Hockey. **H/F**
Blake played left wing on the Montreal Canadiens' Punch Line. As a coach of the Canadiens, his team won eight Stanley Cups. Also called THE OLD LAMP-LIGHTER. See THE PUNCH LINE.

TOELESS WONDER [THE]—Ben "Automatic" Agajanian (1919–) Football. As the first kick specialist in the NFL (he played for the Eagles and the Steelers in 1945).

TOM TERRIFIC—Tom Seaver (1944–) Baseball p.
See THE FRANCHISE.

TOM THE BOMB—Tom Tracey (active 1956–1964) Football hb/fb.

TOMATO FACE—Nick Cullop (1900–1978) Baseball of.
Cullop received his nickname because his face would turn bright red when he was upset.

TOMATO FACE—Jack Lamabe (1936–) Baseball p.

TOMATOES—Frank "Jake" Kafora (1888–1928) Baseball c.

TOMBSTONE—Albert Bemiller (active 1961–1969) Football. Bemiller, who played center and guard with the Buffalo Bills, got his nickname because he was planning to be a mortician.

TOMBSTONE—Rich Jackson (1941–) Football de.

TONTO—John L. Brewer (active 1961–1970) Football. This Cleveland Brown lineman was of Indian ancestry.

TONY—Melvin E. Bettenhausen (1916–1961) Auto racing. **H/F**

TONY—Elmer Charles Hemmerling (1913–) Hockey lw.

TONY—Paul Hinkle (active 1927–1970) Baseball, basketball, football coach. Hinkle coached all three sports at Butler. In his forty-one-year career, he won over 1,000 games.

TONY—Angelo Musi (1918–) Basketball g.

TONY—Tolia Solaita (1947–) Baseball. Born in Samoa, this first baseman hit three home runs in one game in 1974.

TONY C—Tony Conigliaro (1945–1990) Baseball. Tony had a brother named Billy also on the Red Sox, and C was easier to say than Conigliaro. Tony C, an outfielder, hit a league-leading thirty-two home runs in 1965, but his career went downhill after he was hit in the head by a pitch in 1967.

TOO-HARD-TO-HANDLE—Randall Cunningham (1963–) Football qb.

TOO MEAN—Harvey Martin (1950–) Football. When Martin paired up with Too Tall Jones, sportswriters tried to give the duo matching nicknames. Too Tall worked better and was more appropriate. Too Mean didn't quite catch on.

TOOKIE—Harold Joseph Gilbert (1929–1967) Baseball. When this first baseman was a small child, he called a cookie a tookie.

TOOL [THE]—Stanley Morgan (active 1977–1990) Football rw.

TOOL BOX—Ed West (active 1984–) Football te.

TOOTHPICK—Samuel Jones (1925–) Baseball. Whenever Jones was at bat, he had a toothpick in his mouth. In 1950, Jones struck out the side in the ninth inning to preserve his no-hitter for the Chicago Cubs. See SAD SAM.

TOOTHPICK—Maurice McHartley (1942–) Basketball g-f.

TOOTS—Albert Robert Holway (1902–) Hockey d.

TOPPER—Emory Rigney (1897–1972) Baseball ss.

TOPPER—Zellio Topazzini (1931–) Hockey. Zellio, a right wing, was Jerry's older brother.

TOPSY MAGGIE—George Mason (1875–1943) Baseball ss.

TORNADO FATS—Arvind Savur. Pool.

TORO [EL] [THE BULL]—Fernando Valenzuela (1961–) Baseball. What they called Valenzuela back in Etchohuaquila, Mexico. After playing for the Los Angeles Dodgers and winning 141 games, he was released and ended up back in Mexico playing ball.

TORPEDO MURPHY—Billy Murphy (1863–1939) Boxing (featherweight).

TOT—Forest Pressnell (1906–) Baseball. Pressnell was the youngest of eight children. Ironically, this pitcher made his major-league debut at the ripe age of thirty-two.

TOUCH—Greg Coleman (active 1977–1988) Football k.

TOUCH [THE]—Max Zaslofsky (1925–) Basketball. Zaslofsky, a guard, had the scoring touch as he led the Chicago Stags to the finals with Philadelphia in 1946.

TOUCHDOWN MAKER [THE]—Stephen Baker (1964–) Football. Played six years for the New York Giants. "Stephen Baker, The Touchdown Maker"—nice example of a rhyming nickname.

TOUCHDOWN TOMMY—Tom Wilson (active 1956–1963) Football hb/fb.

TOUCHDOWN TONY—Anthony Adams (active 1975–1968) Football. Adams was responsible for sixty-two touchdowns during his college career.

TOUGH—Tony Canzoneri (1908–1959) Boxing. **H/F** Tough Tony held world bantamweight, featherweight, junior welterweight, and lightweight titles.

TOUGH TONY—Anthony Joseph Leswick (1923–) Hockey lw.

TOUGHEY—Earl Abell (1892–deceased) Football. This tackle was also the captain of the Colgate team.

TOUGHIE—Midge Brashun (active 1950s) Roller skating. The hair-pulling, elbow-throwing Brashun was one of the Roller Derby's roughest players.

TOWERING CLIFF OF BLACK MOUNTAIN [THE]—Cliff Melton (1912–1986) Baseball. Also called MOUNTAIN MUSIC.

TOY CANNON [THE]—Jimmy Wynn (1942–) Baseball. This small (5' 9") Houston Astro outfielder had a great arm and exploded for 291 home runs during his career.

TRACTOR—Bill Lesuk (1946–) Hockey lw.

TRADER [THE]—Frank Lane (1896–deceased) Baseball general manager.

TRADER—Jack McKeon (1930–) Baseball.
This general manager of the San Diego Padres likes to make deals.

TRADER PHIL—Phil Esposito (1942–) Hockey. **H/F**
In 1986–1987, Phil Esposito became the general manager of the New York Rangers. Before the year was up, he had made nineteen trades and he was his own coach behind the bench. See BOBBY AND PHIL AND THEM and ESPO.

TRAINWRECK—Tom Novack. Football.
Novack was an All-American at Nebraska.

TRAPPER—Arthur Edmund Coulter (1909–) Hockey.
H/F Coulter, a defenseman, was a fishing and hunting enthusiast.

TRASH—Greg Garrity (active 1983–1989) Football rw.

TRAVELIN'—Travis Tidwell (active 1950–1951) Football qb.

TREE—John W. Adams (1921–1969) Football rb.

TREE—Wayne Rollins (1955–) Basketball.
At 7' 1", this center towered above others when he played for the Atlanta Hawks.

TREES—Terry Foster (1952–) Baseball p.

TREES—Mark LaForest. Hockey.

TRICKY DICK—Dick Donovan (1927–) Baseball p.

TROJAN [THE]—John Evers (1881–1947) Baseball.
Evers, a second baseman, hailed from Troy, New York. See THE CRAB.

TROJAN GIANT [THE]—Paddy Ryan (1853–1900) Boxing.
H/F The 6' 1", 210-pound Ryan spent his youth in Troy, New York. In 1880, he won the American championship in only his second professional fight when he stunned the champion Joe Goss, then hurled him to the ground. In his third fight, Ryan lost the championship to Yankee Sullivan.

TROLLEY LINE—Johnny Butler (1894–1967) Baseball.
Butler played shortstop for Brooklyn, the Trolly Dodgers.

TROOPER—Tom Washington (1944–) Basketball f-c.

TROTS—Bryan Trottier (1956–) Hockey c.

TRUCK—Charles Egan. Baseball.
Egan was the home-run king of the Pacific Coast League in the early part of the century.

TRUE GUN—Bill Hart (1913–1968) Baseball.
William S. Hart made a movie called *True Gun*, and third baseman Bill Hart had a true gun for an arm.

TRUTH [THE]—Carl Williams (active 1982–1990s) Boxing.

TUBBY—Kenneth Leslie McAuley (1921–) Hockey g.

TUG—Frank Edwin McGraw, Jr. (1944–) Baseball.
McGraw earned his nickname as a child tugging at things. Later, he became a fiery relief pitcher from 1965 to1984 for the Mets ("Ya gotta believe") and the Phillies.

TURK—Dick Farrell (1934–1977) Baseball p.

TURK—Omar Lown (1925–) Baseball.
The pitcher liked to eat turkey.

TURK—Derek Sanderson (1946–) Hockey.
Rookie of the Year in 1967, Sanderson was known for killing penalties and bar hopping. He played center for the Boston Bruins when they won the Stanley Cup in 1970 and 1972.

TURK—Steven John Wendell (1986–) Baseball.
This pitcher was selected by the Atlanta Braves in the fifth round of the June 1988 free agent draft.

TURKEY—Joe Jones (active 1970–1980) Football de.

TURKEYFOOT—Frank Brower (1893–1960) Baseball.
This first baseman's nickname was misunderstood to be turkey; he later became turkeyfoot because he was fast on the base paths.

TWEET—Joe Walsh (1917–) Baseball.
Walsh, a shortstop, was nicknamed for an old-time minor leaguer. He was hitless in eight tries.

TWICKENHAM TERRIER—Melbourne Inman. Pool.

TWIG—Willard Wayne Terwilliger (1925–) Baseball.
This second baseman, whose nickname was an off-shoot of his last name, hit .240 over his nine-year stint in the majors.

TWIGGY—Wayne Rasmussen (1942–) Football.
Played 1964–1972 for Detroit.

TWILIGHT—Ed Killian (1876–1928) Baseball.
Killian pitched in a lot of games that went into extra innings. In the days before lights, he was pitching in the twilight.

TWIN—Jack Sullivan (1878–1947) Boxing (welterweight and middleweight).

TWIN—Michael Sullivan (1878–1937) Boxing (welterweight and middleweight).

TWINE—Houston Antwine (active 1961–1972) Football.

This tackle's nickname was from the last five letters of his last name.

TWINKLETOES—George Selkirk (1908–1987) Baseball. Selkirk took Babe Ruth's place in the Yankee outfield.

TWIRL [THE]—Earl Williams (1951–) Basketball c-f.

TWISTER—Paul Steinberg (1880–deceased) Basketball coach.

TWITCH—Marv Rickert (1921–) Baseball. Twitch played in the outfield for the Boston Braves in the 1948 World Series.

TWITCHES—Dick Porter (1901–1974) Baseball. Porter was always shifting around, adjusting something, moving in the outfield. He also hit .308 during his six years in the majors. Also called WIGGLES.

TWOGIE—Forrest Twogood (1907–1972) Basketball. Twogood was the USC coach from 1951 to 1966 with a record of 225–180.

TY COBB OF HOCKEY [THE]—Fred Taylor (1883–1979) Hockey. **H/F** The *New York Times* first called Taylor the Ty Cobb of Hockey. Taylor was better know as Cyclone. See CYCLONE.

TY TY—Johnny Tyler (1906–1972) Baseball. Ty was for Tyler. This outfielder hit .321 in two years for the Boston Braves.

UBBO UBBO—Michael Hornung (1857–1931) Baseball.

ULI—Ullrich Hiemer (1962–) Hockey.

UNCLE CHARLIE—Charles Moran (1879–1949) Baseball, football. Moran pitched and caught for St. Louis, umpired major-league baseball for twenty-four years, and coached football at Centre College, Texas A&M, and Bucknell.

UNCLE TOM—Thomas Bannon (1869–1950) Baseball.

UNCLE YOOLUS—Julius P. Blegen (active 1911–1924) Skiing. **H/F** Originally from Norway, Blegen won the U.S. cross-country championship in 1911 and 1912, and was on the Olympic team in 1924.

UNCROWNED CHAMPION—Carmen Basilio (1927–) Boxing. **H/F** Basilio held the world welterweight and middleweight titles in the 1950s. Sometimes it seemed he was fighting on television every Friday night. Also called CANASTOTA ONION FARMER.

UNION MAN—Walter Holke (1892–1954) Baseball. Holke could be counted on to be ready and on time as if he were the best card-carrying member of a union imaginable. This first baseman's batting average over

eleven years was .287.

UNKNOWN—Edward Winston (active 1930s) Boxing (heavyweight).

VENETIAN GONDOLIER [THE]—Tito Alberto di Carni (active early 1700s) Bareknuckles boxing. After James Figg came out of retirement to defeat him in 1733, di Carni returned to his native Venice.

VERN—Arild Verner Agerskov Mikkelsen (1928–) Basketball. This center switched to forward because he played on the Minneapolis Lakers with George (BIG 99) Mikan. Vern scored an average of 14.4 points in 700 NBA games, fouling out a record 127.

VERTICAL HYPHEN [THE]—Johnny Horan (1934–) Basketball c-f.

VICTORY—Charles Victor Faust (1880–1915) Baseball. This pitcher's nickname came from his middle name and how he helped the Giants win the National League championship in 1911.

VINEGAR BEND—Wilmer Mizel (1930–) Baseball. From Vinegar Bend, Alabama, Mizel was 90–88 during his nine-year pitching career.

VITAMIN—Verda Smith (active 1949–1953) Football fb.

VOICE OF RUNNING—Kurt Steiner (1922–1993) Track and field. An announcer for years in the New York City area, he was famous for declaring: "If you are within the sound of my voice, you can break four hours."

VOICELESS—Tim O'Rourke (1864–1938) Baseball if. O'Rourke compiled a .291 batting average in 387 games.

VOLGA BATMAN [THE]—Mike Chartrak (1916–1967) Baseball. His sobriquet is a punning reference to the Volga Boatman. He was better known, because of his throwing arm as Shotgun.

WAGON TONGUE—Bill Keister (1874–1924) Baseball. This infielder used a big bat. He also hit over .300 five straight seasons, capped by a .320 in 1903.

WAH WAH—Wallace Jones (1926–) Basketball. Jones' nickname came from the way his baby sister pronounced *Wallace*. Jones was a member of the FABULOUS FIVE at Kentucky.

WAHOO—Edward McDaniels (active 1960s) Football. McDaniel was the son of a Choctaw. He played linebacker for the Raiders and the Jets; in the off season, he wrestled under the name Chief Wahoo.

WAHOO—Thomas Yarr (1908–1941) Football.

Yarr was a member of the Snohomish tribe in Washington. Playing center on Knute Rockne's Notre Dame national champions in 1930, Yarr was the captain in 1931.

WALES—Jim Walewander (1962–) Baseball 2b.

WALKING MAN [THE]—Eddy Yost (1926–) Baseball. Third baseman Yost drew 1,614 walks during his career—over one per ball game.

WALLY WORLD—Wally Joyner (1962–) Baseball.

WALRUS [THE]—Craig Stadler (1953–) Golf. At 5' 10" and 200 pounds and sporting a mustache, Stadler sometimes gave the appearance of a walrus.

WAMBY—Bill Wambsganss (1894–) Baseball. This second baseman's name was shortened so that it would fit into a box score.

WANDERING—Eric Brook. Soccer. Brook played in Great Britain.

WARRIOR—Bob Friend (1930–) Baseball. This pitcher had to battle for Pittsburgh, a perennial loser.

WARRIOR—Fumika Hanada. Boxing.

WASHER WOMAN [THE]—George Chuvalo. Boxing (heavyweight). Muhammad Ali gave Chuvalo this derogatory nickname for his boxing style.

WATCH-CHARM GUARD [THE]—Bert Metzger (active 1928–1930) Football. Metzger was a 5' 9", 145-pound guard for Notre Dame. His senior year he made All-American and helped Notre Dame win the unofficial national championship.

WATTY—James Arthur Watson (1943–) Hockey.

WAYNE—Leonard Merrick (1952–) Hockey.

WAYNE THE WALL—Wayne Embry (1937–) Basketball. At 6' 7" and 250 pounds, Embry was a tough man for his taller opponents to get around. Embry, a center, played in five All-Star Games and had a 12.5 point average in 831 NBA games.

WEASEL [THE]—Don Bessent (1931–) Baseball.

WEE BLUE DEVIL [THE]—Alan Morton (1896–1971) Soccer. Morton was the best loved player of Scottish soccer.

WEE WILLIE—William Henry Keeler (1872–1923) Baseball. **H/F** Although Wee Willie was only a shade over 5' 4", he had the uncanny ability to "Hit 'Em Where They Ain't." And that was his other nickname. (So successful was Keeler in spraying his hits around

the field he hit .341 over a nineteen-year career.)

WEE WILLIE—Willie Smith (1911–) Basketball.

WEE WILLIE—Wilbur Wilkin (1973–) Football. As this tackle for the Redskins was 6' 6" and weighed 280 pounds, this was an opposite nickname.

WEED—Alex Groza (1926–) Basketball. Groza had shot up to become a 6' 7", 220-pound center of Kentucky's FABULOUS FIVE. All-American from 1947 to 1949, he and his teammates won gold medals at the 1950 Olympics. Later, admitted that he and a teammate had conspired to fix a game at Kentucky.

WEENIE BERNIE—Bill Staton. Pool.

WEEPING—Willie Willoughby (1898–1973) Baseball. Willoughby lost some heartbreakers and was 38–58.

WELSH WIZARD—Freddie Welsh (1886–1927) Boxing (lightweight). **H/F**

WEST INDIAN GIANT—Peter Felix (1866–1926) Boxing. In his biggest fight, Felix lost to Jack Johnson in the first round of their bout on February 19, 1917, in Sydney, Australia.

WEST VIRGINIA HILLBILLY [THE]—Sammy Snead (1912–) Golf. **H/F** See SLAMMIN' SAMMY.

WHACK—John Hyder (1912–) Basketball. Coach of Georgia Tech Yellow Jackets (1952–1973) with a 293–270 record.

WHALE—Fred Walters (1912–1980) Baseball.

WHAMMY—Charles Douglas (1935–) Baseball. Douglas' glass eye led to his nickname. Somebody came up with the idea that the eye was putting a hex or whammy on the batters. Be that as it may, Douglas was only 3–3 for the Pirates in 1957.

WHATAMAN—Charles Arthur Shires (1907–1967) Baseball. Shires chose this nickname for himself along with Art the Great. They also doubled as ring names as he fought during the off season. In his four years wearing a baseball uniform, this first baseman batted .291.

WHAT'S THE USE—Pearce Chiles (1867–deceased) Baseball. This outfielder wasn't talking about himself but rather he was speaking to the opposing batters as they came up to the plate.

WHEAT PICKER—J. D. Smith (active 1959–1966) Football.

WHEELS—Frank Carswell (1919–) Baseball. Carswell was fast and from Palestine, Texas. This outfielder was also out of major-league baseball after sixteen games. Also called TEX.

WHIP [THE]—Ewell Blackwell (1922–) Baseball. Blackwell received his nickname in 1947. His 6' 6" height and sidearm pitching motion somewhat resembled a buggy whip being cracked. In 1947, his best year, he was 22–8 with 193 strikeouts.

WHIPLASH—Julio Navarro (1936–) Baseball. This nickname was used to describe his pitching motion.

WHIPPER—Billy Watson. Wrestling.

WHISKEY—Billy Kilmer (active 1961–1978) Football qb.

WHISPERING BILL—Bill Barrett (1900–1951) Baseball. An ironic nickname because the outfielder actually spoke quite loudly.

WHISPERING JOE—Joe Wilson (active 1950s) Sports announcing. Wilson's hushed voice commented on the action during television's *Championship Bowling* in the 1950s.

WHISTLING BOB—Robert A. Smith (1870–1943) Horse racing. **H/F** This good-natured trainer was always whistling around the stables.

WHITE RAT—Dorrel "Whitey" Herzog (1931–) Baseball. Herzog was nicknamed Whitey for his white hair. The White Rat, however, was a misnomer. Someone thought he looked like Bob Kuzava, who carried that nickname. Herzog played outfield for four teams in eight years. As a manager he stayed put with the Cards.

WHITE LIGHTNING—Charlie Brown (active 1980s) Boxing (lightweight).

WHITE SHOES—Billy Johnson (active 1974–1981) Football. This wide receiver for the Houston Oilers always wore white shoes.

WHITECHAPEL WHIRLWIND—Jack "Kid" Berg (1909–) Boxing (junior welterweight).

WHITEY—William H. Bell (1932–) Basketball. The nickname Whitey is usually given to someone with white hair.

WHITEY—Morris Bimstein (1897–1969) Boxing. After a career as a featherweight, Whitey became a trainer for Ray Arcel and helped develop Max Baer, Jim Braddock, Primo Carnera, Rocky Graziano, Barney Ross, and Gene Tunney.

WHITEY—Walter Leslie Farrant (1912–) Hockey.

WHITEY—Edward Charles Ford (1926–) Baseball p. **H/F** His hair was white. Also called CHAIRMAN OF THE BOARD. See SLICK.

WHITEY—Carroll Lockman (1926–) Baseball. Lockman was a solid performer at first base for the New York Giants and appeared in two World Series.

WHITEY—Johnny MacKnowski (1923–) Basketball.

WHITEY—Louie Sauer (1915–) Basketball.

WHITEY—Ben Scharnus (1918–) Basketball.

WHITEY—Meyer Skoog (1926–) Basketball. This guard's nickname was for his hair color, but he was known for his jump shot. An All-American at Minnesota, Skoog played six years for the Minneapolis Lakers before becoming the head coach at Gustavus Adolphus in St. Paul.

WHITEY—Pat Stapleton (1940–) Hockey.

WHITEY—Juha Markku Widing (1947–) Hockey.

WHIZ—Johnny Gee (1915–) Baseball. This pitcher had a reverse nickname.

WHOOPS—Pat Creeden (1906–1992) Baseball. This second baseman had an iron glove.

WHOPPER [THE]—Billy Paultz (1948–) Basketball. Paultz played center for the San Antonio Spurs and the Houston Rockets.

WIBS—Wilbur Kautz (1915–) Basketball. In 1939, this All-American guard scored 341 points to lead Loyola to an undefeated season.

WICKED WORM—Bobby Warmack. Football.

WIDOW—William Conroy (1877–1959) Baseball. This third baseman went out of his way to help the boys around the neighborhood.

WIG—Ralph Weigel (1921–) Baseball. Wig is this catcher's shortened last name.

WIGGIE—William Vance Wylie (1928–) Hockey.

WILD BILL—Bill Donovan (1876–1923) Baseball. This pitcher was wild, leading the National League in walks in 1901 with 152.

WILD BILL—William Ezinicki (1924–) Hockey.

WILD BILL—Burnis Wright (1914–1996) Baseball. Wild Bill was a star in the old Negro Leagues. Also known as The Bunsen Burner, a nice play on his last name.

WILD GIRAFFE [THE]—Kresimir Cosic (1948–) Basketball. From Yugoslavia, Cosic was 6' 11" and played center at Brigham Young.

WILD HELICOPTER [THE]—Edgar Jones (1956–) Basketball.

WILD HORSE—Neill Sheridan (1921–) Baseball.

If Sheridan ever played like one, his .000 batting average didn't get out of the stable.

WILD THING—Al Iafrate (1966–) Hockey.

WILDFIRE—Frank Schulte (1882–1975) Baseball.
A big fan of Lillian Russell's, Schulte was nicknamed for a play she was starring in. (He even named his horse Wildfire.) Schulte also played like a wildfire, hitting .270 during his fifteen-year career, mostly for the Chicago Cubs, and .309 in four World Series.

WILDMAN—Tommy Byrne (1919–) Baseball.
The Yankees' Byrne lost the final game of the 1955 World Series 2–0 to the Dodgers' Johnny Podres. During his thirteen-year career Byrne was 85–69.

WILLIE—Bo Morgan Linstrom (1951–) Hockey.

WILLIE THE PHILLIE—Willie Montanez (1948–) Baseball. One of the best examples of a rhyming nickname. Unfortunately it was good for only part of Montanez's career since he was with the Phillies for only five seasons.

WILT THE STILT—Wilt Chamberlain (1936–) Basketball. Given to him by a sportswriter, this was a nickname that the 7 foot Chamberlain did not like. He preferred THE BIG DIPPER.

WIMPY—Mary Louise Baumgartner (active 1949–1954) Baseball (All-American Girls Baseball League). Baumgartner, a catcher, acquired her nickname as a child for liking hamburgers with the relish of the Wimpy character in *Popeye.*

WIMPY—Jerry Halstead. Boxing.

WIMPY—Luther Lassiter. Pool.

WIMPY—Tom Paciorek (1946–) Baseball.
Tommy Lasorda gave the outfielder this nickname after the character in the Popeye comic strip because Paciorek ate hamburgers.

WINDY—John McCall (1925–) Baseball.
McCall got his nickname from Ted Williams. McCall was always asking him questions. Perhaps he should have asked him more because he wound up 11–15.

WINDY—Ward Miller (1884–1958) Baseball.
Miller, an outfielder, jawed a lot. In 1910, Miller led the National League in pinch hitting with 11–40.

WINDY—Thomas O'Neill (1923–) Hockey.

WINGY—George Joseph Johnston (1920–) Hockey.

WINGY—Hawthorne Wingo (1948–) Basketball.

WINO—Bobby Wine (1934–) Baseball.

His nickname is an obvious play upon his last name.

WIZ—Ray Kremer (1893–1965) Baseball p.

WIZARD [THE] [EL BRUJO]—Juan Cabello Bullfighting.

WIZARD [THE]—Gus Williams (1953–) Basketball g.

WIZARD OF OZ [THE]—Ozzie Smith (1954–) Baseball ss.

WIZARD OF WESTWOOD [THE]—John Wooden (1910–) Basketball. **H/F** Wooden was the longtime coach of UCLA, located in Westwood, California. Wooden coached UCLA to ten NCAA titles, and has the distinction of being the only person in the Basketball Hall of Fame as both a player and a coach.

WOCHY—Stephen Wojciechowski (1922–) Hockey.

WOCKY—Nelson Rupp (1891–deceased) Football.
Played in 1921 for Dayton.

WOLFIE—Jim Wohlford (1951–) Baseball.

WONDER DOG—Rex Hudler (1960–) Baseball.
Hudler made his major-league debut with the New York Yankees in 1984. He received his nickname because Rex is a popular name for a dog.

WONDERFUL WILLIE—Willie Smith (1939–) Baseball.
At Syracuse in 1963, Willie had been just that. He was 14–2 on the mound and .380 at the plate. In the majors he was 2–4 and played mostly in the outfield.

WOODY—Woodrow Dumart (1916–) Hockey. **H/F** This 6' 1", 200-pound left winger was also called PORKY.

WOODY—Wayne Hayes (1913–) Football.
Coach Hayes once said: "Statistics always remind me of the fellow who drowned in the river whose average depth was three feet."

WOODY—Forrest Main (1922–) Baseball p.
His nickname is an allusion to his first name.

WOODY—Elwood Romney (1911–1970) Basketball.

WORLD—Kevin Mitchell (1962–) Baseball of.

WORLD B.—Lloyd Free (1953–) Basketball.
Free, a guard, had his nickname legally changed in 1980 to be his name.

WORLD CLASS—Gerald Glass (1967–) Basketball f-g.

WORLD'S FASTEST HUMAN [THE]—Bob Hayes (1942–) Track and field. Hayes ran the 100-yard dash in 9.1 seconds and the 200-meter dash in 20.6. He was once clocked at 26.9 mph during a race. See THE FULLBACK.

WORLD'S GREATEST ATHLETE—Bob Mathias (1930–) Track and field. Mathias won gold medals in the decathlon at the 1948 Olympic Games (with a score of

7,139 points) and the 1952 Olympics (7,887 points).

WORLD'S GREATEST DRIBBLER—Marques Haynes (1926–) Basketball. Haynes could dribble the basketball three times a second, and playing in a game for the Harlem Globetrotters he once dribbled the ball for eight straight minutes. After seven years with the Globetrotters, he left in 1953 to form his own touring team called the "Fabulous Magicians."

WORM [THE]—Willie McCarter (1946–) Basketball. McCarter paced Drake to a 26–5 season in 1969.

WORM [THE]—Willie Monroe (active 1970s–1980s) Boxing (middleweight). Monroe was the only fighter to beat Marvelous Marvin Hagler between 1976 and 1986.

WORM—Dennis Rodman (1961–) Basketball. He received this unappealing nickname because of his ability to "worm" around players on his way to the basket.

WOUNDED WONDER—Eugene Criqui (1893–1977) Boxing. After holding French and European flyweight and featherweight titles, Criqui won the world featherweight championship in 1923. However, he lost his world title the following month to Johnny Dundee.

WRONG FOOT—Lou Campi (active 1950s–1960s) Bowling. Campi was a righthander who delivered the bowling ball off his right foot. (Bowlers usually use the opposite foot in order to maintain proper balance.)

WYLIE'S WORLD—Joe Wylie (1968–) Basketball f.

X-FACTOR—Xavier McDaniels. Basketball.

YAK [THE]—Alexander Yakushev (active 1966–1980) Hockey. This left winger was first seen by North American fans when the Soviet National team played the Canadian NHL team in 1972.

YALE—James J. Hogan (1876–1910) Football. This Bulldog footballer was called Yale because he was so enthusiastic about his alma mater.

YAM—Clarence Yaryan (1892–1964) Baseball. This catcher had big yam-like feet.

YANK—Yancey Durham (1921–1973) Boxing manager.

YANKEE KILLER [THE]—Frank Lary (1930–) Baseball. This Detroit pitcher always seemed to have a good outing against the Yanks. In 1956, Lary was 5–1 against New York; in 1958, he was 7–0. Lifetime, Lary's record was 27–13 versus the Bronx Bombers. Also called MULE.

YANQUI MATADOR—John Fulton (1932–) Bullfighting.

Fulton was a gringo in a difficult sport for Yankees to learn.

YATCHA—Johnny Logan (1927–) Baseball ss.

YIDDISH YANKEE [THE]—Ron Blomberg (1948–) Baseball. As a first baseman he played from 1969 to 1978 for the New York Yankees and the Chicago White Sox. His claim to fame, however, was that The Yiddish Yankee was the first major leaguer to come to bat as a designated hitter. He compiled a .293 lifetime batting average in 461 games.

YIP—Harry Foster (1907–) Hockey d.

YIP—Harry John Radley (1910–) Hockey.

YOUNG—Victor Perez (1911–1942) Boxing (flyweight). This boxer began his career at seventeen and died young at thirty-one in a German concentration camp.

YOUNG BARNEY—Barney Aaron (1836–1907) Boxing. Aaron won the American lightweight championship when he was twenty-one. After losing it the next year, he came out of retirement in 1976 to defeat Sam Collyer for the title in sixty-seven rounds.

YOUNG CASANOVA—Hector Medina. Boxing.

YOUNG CORBETT II—William H. Rothwell. Boxing. Rothwell's nickname was in reference to Jim Corbett, the first scientific fighter. Rothwell himself was the featherweight champion in 1901.

YOUNG CORBETT III—Ralph C. Giordano. Boxing. Again, the nickname went back to Gentleman Jim Corbett. Giordano was the welterweight champion in 1933.

YOUNG GRIFFO—Albert Griffiths (1871–1927) Boxing. Griffiths won the world featherweight title at nineteen. He was a natural boxer, seldom bothering to train. Three times he climbed into the ring with George Dixon, and each bout ended in a draw.

YOUNG JACK THOMPSON—Cecil L. Thompson (1904–1946) Boxing. Thompson was the welterweight champion in 1930. Thirty-one of his forty-six bouts were KOs.

YOUNG MONTREAL—Morris Billingkoff (1898–) Boxing (flyweight).

YOUNG NORLEY—George Hall. Bareknuckles boxing. Hall once fought a 160 rounder—110 of them with a broken arm.

YOUNG TOM—Tom Morris, Jr. (1851–1875) Golf. Young Tom won the British Open at the age of seventeen; he went on to win the title in 1869, 1970, and 1971. With his father OLD TOM, the Morrises won the British Open eight times.

YOUNG ZULU KID—Joe de Melfi (active 1916) Boxer (flyweight).

YO-YO—Pompeyo Davalillo (1931–) Baseball. Davalillo played shortstop in only nineteen games for the Washington Senators.

YUSSEL THE MUSCLE—Joe Jacobs (1906–) Boxing manager.

ZACK—James Wren Taylor (1898–1974) Baseball. Taylor, a catcher and later a manager, thought he was related to President Zachary Taylor, so he was given the nickname Zack.

ZAINER—Rodney Carl Zaine (1946–) Hockey.

ZEKE—Virgil Barnes (1897–1958) Baseball.

ZEKE—Henry John Bonura (1908–1987) Baseball. Well-built, Bonura's nickname was short for physique. During his seven-year career, the first baseman batted .307 and hit 119 home runs.

ZEKE—Edmund Bratowski (active 1954–1971) Football. Bratowski received his nickname as a youngster because he wore a baseball uniform bearing the name of Zeke Bonura.

ZEKE—Allen Lee Zarilla (1919–) Baseball. A St. Louis Brown teammate thought Zarilla was sneaky fast in the outfield. Zarilla and sneaky combined to make Zeke.

ZEKE—Robert Zawoluk (1930–) Basketball. Zawoluk scored sixty-five points in one game and 1,799 points from 1950–1952 under Frank McGuire at St. John's University.

ZIG ZAG—Jim Zorn (1953–) Football. Zorn played QB for Seattle, Green Bay, and Tampa Bay from 1976 to 1987.

ZIP—Prisciliano Castillo. Boxing.

ZIP—Joseph Jaeger (1895–1963) Baseball. Jaeger pitched in 1920 for the Cubs. He had an ERA of 12.00, so his fastball could have used more zip.

ZIP—George W. Zabel (1891–1970) Baseball. Zabel was a reliever who had zip in his pitch. On June 17, 1915, Zabel hurled 18 1/3 innings to win in relief.

INDEX

Since the individuals in this book are listed under their nicknames, the following index of real names is provided to help the reader find a favorite player by his given name. As an index of the hundreds of names in this volume would ultimately run as long as the book itself, the index includes only those names found in Part 1.

ABOUT THE AUTHORS

Louis Phillips, a widely published poet, playwright, and short story writer, has written over thirty books for children and adults. Among his recent works are, *A Dream of Countries Where No One Dare Live,* a collection of his short stories; *Hot Corner,* a collection of his baseball writings; and *Envoi Messages,* a full-length play. Phillips teaches creative writing at the School of Visual Arts in New York City. He lives in Manhattan with his wife, Pat, and his two sons, Ian and Matthew.

Burnham Holmes is a writer, teacher, and editor. His previous books include an award-wining biography of George Eastman for young adult readers, and *The TV Almanac* (with Louis Phillips). In addition, Holmes has authored children's books about the first baseball game, Queen Nefertiti, Cesar Chavez, Seeing Eye dogs, and Army basic training. For the American Heritage series on the Bill of Rights, Holmes wrote books about the first and third Amendments. Holmes lives in Vermont with his son Ken.